CONSTITUTIONS AND DOCUMENTS

ILLUSTRATIVE OF THE

HISTORY OF FRANCE, 1789-1907

THE CONSTITUTIONS

AND OTHER

SELECT DOCUMENTS

ILLUSTRATIVE OF THE

HISTORY OF FRANCE

1789-1907

BY

FRANK MALOY ANDERSON

PROFESSOR OF HISTORY IN THE UNIVERSITY OF MINNESOTA

SECOND EDITION,
REVISED AND ENLARGED

NEW YORK / RUSSELL & RUSSELL

FIRST PUBLISHED IN 1904
SECOND EDITION REVISED, 1908
REPRINTED FROM THE SECOND EDITION AND
REISSUED, 1967, BY RUSSELL & RUSSELL
A DIVISION OF ATHENEUM HOUSE INC.
L. C. CATALOG CARD NO: 66–24665

PRINTED IN THE UNITED STATES OF AMERICA

PREFACE

The practice of studying documents in connection with the history courses given in American universities, colleges, and high schools has now become so general, and the results attained so satisfactory, that the method no longer requires any defence. With the introduction of the system has come a new kind of manual, the document book. So many excellent books of this description have already appeared that the editor of still another may be reasonably expected to offer an adequate explanation for its publication.

Three considerations have induced me to prepare this volume. The first of these is personal and local. For several years past I have made a practice of dividing my class in modern European history into small sections which I could meet once each week around the seminary table. At these meetings we have studied together a considerable part of the documents here included, but the work has been hampered by the lack of a convenient collection of the documents. Fidelity to the interest of my pupils seemed to impose upon me the obligation to remove this difficulty. The second consideration lies in the attractiveness of the documents. After considerable experience in the use of various classes of documents upon European history I have reached the conclusion that students find the modern French documents more attractive than any others. Doubtless the chief reasons for this preference are that modern documents are more easily comprehended than those of more remote periods and that the style of the French is superior to that of English and German documents. Since documentary study must usually be confined to a small part of the field traversed by a class, I believe that for classes in modern European history the preference of the students may well be allowed to control the selection of the period to be studied. The third consideration is the importance of the field covered. The history of France since the beginning of the revolution surely deserves a volume in English presenting as large a proportion as possible of the important documents.

The task of selecting the documents for a book of this description is a difficult one. It may be safely asserted that no two persons would make the same selections, however well agreed they might be upon the general principles of choice. My first and foremost aim has been to pick out those documents likely to be serviceable to teachers. I have especially striven to avoid the error of a too rigid application of some definition of the term document or of some classification. The special reason for the inclusion of most of the documents will be found at least hinted at in the introductions. The more general principles which I have applied require some explanation. There appear to be at least five important ways in which a document-book may be profitably used in the teaching of history. (1) Much historical data can be acquired through such study. It must be admitted, however, that the same amount of time spent upon a good text-book will in this particular usually produce better results, for the reason that the documents studied are so few in number and so disconnected that no adequate idea of any considerable period is obtained. The defect can be remedied in large measure by using a single class of documents running through a considerable period. In modern French history the constitutions serve the purpose admirably. For this reason all of these are included and no elisions have been made, excepting two or three tabular lists of territorial divisions. (2) Documents may be used as the basis for oral or written reports; usually the work should be done in connection with secondary accounts, but the proofs for the principal statements should be drawn from the documents. Many of the groups, with their accompanying references, are inserted for this purpose. It should be observed that these groups usually contain the materials out of which the student should be able to deduce some quite definite result, such as the evolution of a policy or of an institution or the manner in which an institution operated. (3) In the opinion of many teachers the greatest value to be derived from the study of documents is a certain familiarity with the methods of historical investigation. I believe that a large number of the documents here given present unusually good opportunities for exercises designed with that intent. (4) The meaning of technical terms and the significance of constantly recurring allusions can often be more satisfactorily explained in connection with a document than by any other method. None of the selections have been made principally for this reason, but with quite a number it has been an important factor. (5) With many instructors the use of original sources in the teaching of history is valued chiefly for its vitalizing effect. For this purpose documents are perhaps less effective than contemporary narratives. Yet there are many exceptions. Several of the documents not otherwise of the highest worth have been included for their value in this particular.

Most of the documents in this collection will serve several of these purposes, but the superior value of a document for but one of these is often the decisive reason for its inclusion.

The brevity of the introductions has made it necessary that I should confine myself to pointing out only a very few of the ways in which the documents are of interest. In some cases I regret that the plan has not made possible more extended comment, but in general I believe that as much has been furnished the student as he can profitably receive. He needs to be started, but he should not be told all of the things to be obtained from the document. In the furnishing of data I have tried to supply such information as is indispensable for the understanding of the document, provided it is not to be found in the document itself. The references have been purposely confined to a limited number of well known works, all of which are in English or in French. By this method I believe that all students who use the book may be induced to become quite familiar with nearly all of the works in English and, if they read any French, with the few French works cited. To have given more, I fear, would have defeated this purpose.

I am greatly indebted to Mrs. Helen Dresser Fling, to the editors of the *Annals of the American Academy of Political and Social Science,* and to the editors of that admirable series issued by the history department of the University of Pennsylvania, *Translation and Reprints from the Original Sources of European History,* for permission to employ their excellent translation wherever I have had occasion to use a document that has already appeared in their publications. In using these translations, as well as a number of others from noncopyrighted sources, I have made separate acknowledgment in every instance and have reproduced them exactly as printed, excepting some slight typographical errors and a few changes kindly supplied by Mrs. Fling. In my own translations I have striven to be as literal as possible, having a decent regard for the idioms of the English language. Probably I have been more literal than was absolutely requisite, but I have believed that the translator of documents should err upon the side of literary form rather than meaning. In the matter of paragraphing I have invariably followed the form of the document as originally printed in French, even when a single sentence is made to run into a dozen paragraphs. As to other features of form, such as punctuation and capitals, I have been guided by two canons—to treat each document separately so as to produce the best result for that particular document, and to follow the originals as closely as English usage would allow.

It is a pleasure to acknowledge help received from several friends in addition to those already mentioned. Professor Willis Mason West, my colleague and chief, has generously responded to my frequent appeals for advice. Profesor Fred Morrow Fling of the University of Nebraska kindly looked over the list of materials and made several helpful suggestions. I am under great obligation to my publishers for permission to make the volume considerably larger than stipulated in our agreement. Most of all I am indebted to my wife, Mary Steele Anderson. To her constant encouragement, literary criticisms, and assistance with the manuscript and proofs, I owe a large part of whatever value the volume may possess.

Frank Maloy Anderson.

University of Minnesota.

April 30, 1904.

Both the material and the arrangement of this edition correspond closely to the original publication. Several documents of a later date than 1902 have been added and a few changes have been made in a number of the groups of documents relating to some single topic. The principal difference between this and the original edition is in details. All of the translations have been gone over carefully and numerous changes made, especially in the second half of the book. Quite a number of additional references have been inserted. As several widely-used text-books have inserted references to documents contained in the collection I have endeavored to preserve the original pagination as far as possible. Almost invariably a reference to the first edition will be found on the corresponding or the next page of this edition.

September 2, 1908.   F. M. A.

CONTENTS

TITLES AND EDITIONS CITED

Actes du gouvernment revolutionnaire de Paris. 18 Mars-21 Mai, 1871. Revue de France supplement. Paris. n. d.

Adams, Henry. History of the United States during the administrations of Jefferson and Madison. Nine vols. New York, 1889-1891.

from the Congress of Vienna to the present time. Two vols. New York, 1896-1898.

American catholic quarterly review. Vol. 1—. Philadelphia, 1876.

American Historical Association. Annual report for the year 1894. Washington, 1895.

American historical review. Vol. 1—. New York, 1895—.

American state papers, foreign relations. Six vols. Washington, 1832-1859.

Andrews, Charles M. The political history of modern Europe

[Angeberg, Comte]. Recueil des traités, conventions et actes diplomatiques concernant l'Autriche et l'Italie. Paris, 1859.

Annals of the American academy of political and social science. Vol. 1—. Philadelphia, 1890—.

Archives diplomatiques. Vol. 1—. Paris, 1861—.

Aulard, A. Histoire politique de la révolution française. Paris, 1901.

—La société des Jacobins. Recueil de documents pour l'histoire du club des Jacobins de Paris. Six vols. Paris, 1889-1897.

Bismarck, Prince. Bismarck, the man and statesman, being the reflections and reminiscences of Otto, Prince von Bismarck. Two vols. New York, 1899.

Bodley, John Edward Courtenay. France. Two vols. New York, 1898.

Boutmy, Emile. Études politique. Paris, 1907.

British and foreign state papers, compiled by the librarian and keeper of the papers, foreign office. Vol. 1—. London, 1812—.

Browning, Oscar. The flight to Varennes and other historical essays. London, 1892.

Buchez, P. J. B., and Roux-Lavergne, P. C. Histoire parlementaire de la révolution française. Forty vols. Paris, 1834-1838.

Cambridge modern history; planned by Lord Acton, ed. by A. W. Ward, et al. Vol. 1—. New York, 1903—.

Clapham, J. H. The causes of the war of 1792. Cambridge, 1899.

Coubertin, Pierre de. The evolution of France under the third republic. New York, 1897.

Debidour, A. Histoire des rapports de l'église et de l'état en France de 1789 à 1870. Paris, 1898.

Clercq, [A. J. H.] de and Jules de. Recueil des traités de la France publié sous les auspices du Ministère des affaires étrangères. Vol. 1—. Paris, 1880-1904.

Delbruck, Hans, et al. Preussiche jahrbücher. Vol. 1—. Berlin, 1861—.

Dickinson, G. Lowes. Revolution and reaction in modern France. London, 1892.

Droysen, G. Allegemeiner historischer handatlas. Leipsic. 1886.

Duvergier, J. B., et al. Collection complète des lois, decrets, ordonnances, reglements, avis du Conseil d'État. Second ed. of vols. 1-31 inclusive. First ed., 32—. Paris 1834-.

Ensor, R. C. K. (editor.) Modern Socialism. New York, 1904.

Feuillet de Conches, F. Louis XVI, Marie Antoinette, et Madame Elizabeth. Four vols. Paris, 1856.

Fisher, H. A. L. Studies in the Napoleonic statesmanship: Germany. Oxford, 1903.

Fling, Fred M. and Helene Dresser. Source studies on the French revolution. Second ed. Lincoln, 1907

Fournier, August. Napoleon I. Eine biographie. Three vols. Leipsic, 1886-1889.

—Napoleon the first; a biography. (Translation ed. by Edward Gaylord Bourne.) New York, 1903.

Fyffe, C. A. A history of modern Europe. Three vols. (Vol. I, second ed.) New York, 1890-1891. Popular ed. New York, 1896.

Gardiner, Bertha Meriton. The French revolution. London, 1897.

Gerard, John. The French associations law, its motives and
    methods. London, 1902.
Hanotaux, Gabriel. Contemporary France. Three vols. New
    York, 1903-1907.
Hansard, T. Curson. Parliamentary history of England,
    1066-1803. Thirty-six vols. London, 1806-1820.
Headlam, James Wycliffe. Bismarck and the foundation of
    the German empire. New York, 1901.
Hélie, Faustin-Adolphe. Les constitutions de la France. Paris,
    1880.
Hertslet, Edward. The map of Europe by treaty showing
    the various political and territorial changes which have
    taken place since the general peace of 1814. Four
    vols. London, 1875-1891.
Hume, Martin A. S. Modern Spain. New York, 1900.
Jaurès, Jean (editor). Histoire socialiste (1789-1900). Twelve
    vols. Paris, 1901-1908.
Jellinek, Georg. The declaration of the rights of man and
    citizen. A contribution to modern constitutional his-
    tory. (Translated by Max Ferrard.) New York, 1901.
Journal des economistes. Six series, vol. 1—. Paris, 1842—
Journal officiel de la republique Française. Vol. 1—. Paris,
    1870—.
King, Bolton. A history of Italian unity. Two vols. New
    York, 1899.
L'internationale ouvriére et socialiste. Rapports soumis au
    congrès socialiste internationale de Stuttgart (18-24
    août 1907). Three vols. Brussels, 1907.
La Gorce, Pierre de. Histoire de la seconde republique fran-
    çaise. Fourth ed. Paris, 1904.
—Histoire du second empire. Seven vols. Paris, 1904-1906.
Lanfrey, P. The history of Napoleon the first. Four vols.
    Second ed. London, 1886.
Larousse, Pierre. Grand dictionnaire universel. Seventeen
    vols. Paris, 1866-1890.
Lavisse, Ernest, and Rambaud, Alfred (editors). Histoire
    générale du IVe siècle à nos jours. Twelve vols.
    Paris, 1896-1901.
Lecky, William Edward Hartpole. A history of England in
    the eighteenth century. Eight vols. London, 1878-
    1890.
—French revolution (edited by H. E. Bourne). New York,
    1904.

Lowell, A. Lawrence. Governments and parties in continental Europe. Two vols. Boston, 1897.

McCarthy, Justin. Pope Leo XIII. New York, 1896.

Mahan, A. T. The influence of sea power upon the French
revolution and empire, 1793-1812. Two vols. Eighth
ed. Boston, 1897.

Martens, R. Recueil des traités et conventions conclus par
la Russie avec les puissances étrangères. Vol. 1—. St.
Petersburg, 1874—.

Martinengo-Cesaresco, Evelyn Lilian. Cavour. London,
1898.

Mavidal, J., and Laurent, E. Archives parlementaires de
1787 à 1860. Première série (1787 à 1799). Fifty-two
vols. Paris, 1867-1897.

Mathews, Shailer. The French revolution. A sketch. New
York, 1901.

Messages and documents, department of state. Washington,
1870.

Moniteur. Réimpression de l'ancien moniteur. Thirty-one
vols. Paris 1858-1870.

—Le moniteur universel. One hundred seventy vols. Paris,
1789-1870.

Napoleon I. Correspondance de Napoleon Ier. Thirty-two
vols. Paris, 1858-1870.

Peixotto, Jessica. The French revolution and modern French
socialism. New York, 1901.

Phillips, W. Alison. Modern Europe, 1815-1899. Second ed.
London, 1902.

Political science quarterly. Vol. 1—. New York. 1866—.

Poole, Reginald Lane, et al. Historical atlas of modern
Europe from the decline of the Roman empire. Oxford, 1902.

Putzger, F. W. Historischer Schul-Atlas zur alten, mittleren
und neuen Geschichte. Twenty-seventh ed. Leipsic,
1903.

Rambaud, Alfred. Histoire de la civilisation contemporaine en
France. Sixth ed. Paris, 1901.

Robinson, James Harvey, and Beard, Charles A. The development of modern Europe. Two vols. New York.
1907-1908.

Rose, John Holland. The life of Napoleon I. Two vols.
New York, 1901.
—The development of the European nations 1870-1900. Two
vols. New York, 1905.
Sabatier, Paul. Disestablishment in France. New York, 1906.
Schrader, F., et al. Atlas de géographie historique. Paris,
1896.
Seignobos, Charles. A political history of Europe since 1814.
Edited by S. M. MacVane. New York, 1899.
Simon, Jules. The government of M. Thiers, from 8th Feb-
ruary, 1871, to 24th May, 1873. Two vols. New York,
1879.
Sloane, William Milligan. The French revolution and re-
ligious reform. New York, 1901.
—Life of Napoleon Bonaparte. Four vols. New York, 1896.
Sorel, Albert. Histoire diplomatiquue de la guerre franco-
allemande. Two vols. Paris, 1875.
—L'Europe et la révolution française. Eight vols. Paris,
1897-1904.
Stephens, H. Morse. A history of the French revolution.
Two vols. New York, 1886-1891.
Stillman, W. J. The union of Italy, 1815-1895. Cambridge,
1899.
Sybel, Heinrich von. The founding of the German empire
by William I. Seven vols. New York, 1890-1898.
—History of the French revolution. Four vols. London,
1867-1869.
Times, The. London, 1809—.
Tocqueville, Alexis de. The recollections of Alexis de Toc-
queville. New York, 1866.
University of Pennsylvania, department of history. Trans-
lations and reprints from the original sources of Eu-
ropean history. Seven vols. Philadelphia, 1892-1900.
Vidal-Lablache, Paul. Histoire et géographie; atlas generale.
Paris, 1894.
Vivenot, Alfred. De politik des oesterr. staatskanzlers für-
sten Kaunitz-Rietberg unter Leopold II bis zur fran-
zösischen Kriegserklärung. Five vols. Vienna, 1873-
1890.
Yale review, The. Vol. 1—. New York, 1892—.

Constitutions and Documents

Illustrative of the

History of France

1. Decree upon the National Assembly.

June 17, 1789. Duvergier, *Lois*, I, 23.

The States-General met May 5, 1789. It contained approximately twelve hundred members—three hundred nobles, three hundred clergy, six hundred deputies of the Third Estate. As Louis XVI had failed to provide regulations respecting its organization and method of voting, a controversy immediately developed over these questions. The nobles and clergy desired separate organization and vote by order; the Third Estate demanded a single organization and vote by head. This decree was finally adopted by the Third Estate alone, after an invitation to the other two orders had met with no general response. The document indicates the method by which the Third Estate proposed to proceed, the arguments by which the method was justified, and the general temper which characterized the proceedings.

REFERENCES. Mathews, *French Revolution*, 119-120; Gardiner, *French Revolution*, 37-39; Stephens, *French Revolution*, I, 58-62; Von Sybel, *French Revolution*, I, 54-65; *Cambridge Modern History*, VIII, 153-154; Aulard, *Révolution française*, 32-34; Lavisse and Rambaud, *Histoire générale*, VIII, 56-59; Jaurès, *Histoire socialiste*, I, 244.

The Assembly, deliberating after the verification of its credentials, recognizes that this assembly is already composed of the representatives sent directly by at least ninety-six per cent of the nation.

Such a body of deputies cannot remain inactive owing to the absence of the deputies of some bailliages and some classes of citizens; for the absentees, who have been summoned, cannot prevent those present from exercising the full extent of their rights, especially when the exercise of these rights is an imperious and pressing duty.

Furthermore, since it belongs only to the verified representatives to participate in the formation of the national opinion,
and since all the verified representatives ought to be in this assembly, it is still more indispensable to conclude that the interpretation and presentation of the general will of the nation
belong to it, and belong to it alone, and that there cannot exist
between the throne and this assembly any *veto,* any negative
power.—The assembly declares then that the common task of
the national restoration can and ought to be commenced without delay by the deputies present and that they ought to pursue it without interruption as well as without hindrance.—The
denomination of NATIONAL ASSEMBLY is the only one which is
suitable for the Assembly in the present condition of things;
because the members who compose it are the only representatives lawfully and publicly known and verified; because they
are sent directly by almost the totality of the nation; because,
lastly, the representation being one and indivisible, none of the
deputies, in whatever class or order he may be chosen, has the
right to exercise his functions apart from the present assembly.—The Assembly will never lose the hope of uniting within
its own body all the deputies absent today; it will not cease to
summon them to fulfil the obligation laid upon them to participate in the holding of the States-General.   At any moment
when the absent deputies present themselves in the course of
the session which is about to open, it declares in advance that
it will hasten to receive them and to share with them, after
the verification of their credentials, the remainder of the great
labors which are bound to effect the regeneration of France.—
The National Assembly orders that the motives of the present
decision be immediately drawn up in order to be presented to
the king and the nation.

2. The Tennis Court Oath.

June 20, 1789. Duvergier, *Lois,* I, 24.

When the deputies of the Third Estate went to their hall on
June 20, 1789, they found it closed to them and placards posted
announcing a royal session two days later.   Fearing that this
foreshadowed a command from the king for separate organization
and vote by order, they met in a neighboring tennis court and
with practical unanimity formulated the resolution embodied in
this document.

REFERENCES. James Harvey Robinson, *Political Science Quarterly*, X, 460-474; Von Sybel, *French Revolution*, I, 65-66; *Cambridge Modern History*, VIII, 155-156; Jaurès, *Histoire socialiste*, I, 246.

The National Assembly, considering that it has been summoned to determine the constitution of the kingdom, to effect the regeneration of public order, and to maintain the true principles of the monarchy; that nothing can prevent it from continuing its deliberations in whatever place it may be forced to establish itself, and lastly, that wherever its members meet together, there is the National Assembly.

Decrees that all the members of this assembly shall immediately take a solemn oath never to separate, and to reassemble wherever circumstances shall require, until the constitution of the kingdom shall be established and consolidated upon firm foundations; and that, the said oath being taken, all the members and each of them individually shall ratify by their signatures this steadfast resolution.

3.　Documents upon the Royal Session of June 23, 1789.

These documents show the parts played by the King and the Third Estate at the royal session of June 23, 1789. Document A is a command, although expressed as a wish. Document B has a special interest since it indicates approximately how far Louis XVI was ready to go in the way of reform. Mirabeau's famous defiance of the royal usher was an important factor in nerving the Third Estate to take the action embodied in document C.

REFERENCES. Fling's *Source Studies, The Royal Session* contains other interesting documents, bearing upon this event. See also Mathews, *French Revolution*, 121-124; Stephens, *French Revolution*, I, 62-63; Von Sybel, *French Revolution*, I, 66-69; *Cambridge Modern History*, VIII, 156-159; Jaurès, *Histoire socialiste*, I, 247-253.

A. Declaration of the King upon the States-General. June 23, 1789. Duvergier, *Lois*, I, 24-25. Translation. Mrs. Fred M. Fling, Fling's *Source Studies, The Royal Session*, 33-36.

1. The King wishes that the ancient distinction of the three orders of the state be preserved in its entirety, as essentially linked to the constitution of his kingdom; that the deputies, freely elected by each of the three orders, forming

three chambers, deliberating by order, and being able, with
the approval of the sovereign, to agree to deliberate in common, can alone be considered as forming the body of the
representatives of the nation. As a result, the king has declared null the resolutions passed by the deputies of the order
of the Third Estate, the 17th of this month, as well as those
which have followed them, as illegal and unconstitutional.

2. His Majesty declares valid all the credentials verified
or to be verified in each chamber, upon which there has not
been raised nor will be raised any contest; His Majesty orders that these shall be communicated by each order respectively to the other two orders.

As for the credentials which might be contested in each
order, and upon which the parties interested would appeal,
it will be enacted, for the present session only of the States-
General, as will be hereafter ordered.

[Articles three to six set aside the instructions given to
members in regard to their action upon the organization of
the States-General and announced that imperative instructions
would not be permitted in the future.]

7. His Majesty having exhorted the three orders, for the
safety of the state, to unite themselves during this session of
estates only, to deliberate in common upon the affairs of general utility, wishes to make his intentions known upon the
manner of procedure.

8. There shall be particularly excepted from the affairs
which can be treated in common, those that concern the ancient and constitutional rights of the three orders, the form of
constitution to be given to the next States-General, the feudal
and seignioral rights, the useful rights and honorary prerogatives of the first two orders.

9. The especial consent of the clergy will be necessary for
all provisions which could interest religion, eccelsiastical discipline, the régime of the orders and secular and regular bodies.

.   .   .   .

11 . If, with the view of facilitating the union of the
three orders, they desire that the propositions that shall have
been considered in common, should pass only by a majority of
two-thirds of the votes, His Majesty is disposed to authorise
this form.

12. Matters which shall have been decided in the assembly

of the three orders united shall be taken up again the next day for deliberation, if one hundred members of the assembly unite to ask for it.

. . . .

15. Good order, decency, and liberty of the ballot even, require that His Majesty prohibit, as he expressly does, that any person, other than the members of the three orders comprising the States-General, should be present at their deliberations, whether they deliberate in common or separately.

B. Declaration of the Intentions of the King. June 23, 1789. Duvergier, *Lois*, I, 26-28. Translation, Mrs. Fred M. Fling, Fling's *Source Studies, The Royal Session*, 36-44.

1. No new tax shall be established, no old one shall be continued beyond the term fixed by the laws, without the consent of the representatives of the nation.

2. The new taxes which will be established, or the old ones which will be continued, shall hold only for the interval which will elapse until the time of the following session of the States-General.

3. As the borrowing of money might lead to an increase of taxes, no money shall be borrowed without the consent of the States-General, under the condition, however, that in case of war, or other national danger, the sovereign shall have the right to borrow without delay, to the amount of one hundred millions: for it is the formal intention of the king never to make the safety of his realm dependent upon any person.

4. The States-General shall examine with care the situation of the finances, and they shall demand all the information necessary to enlighten them perfectly.

5. The statement of receipts and expenses shall be made public each year, in a form proposed by the States-General and approved by His Majesty.

6. The sums attributed to each department, shall be determined in a fixed and invariable manner, and the king submits to this general rule even the funds that are destined for the maintenance of his household.

7. The king wishes, in order to assure this fixity of the different expenses of the state, that provisions suitable to accomplish this object be suggested to him by the States-General; and His Majesty will adopt them, if they are in accord-

ance with the royal dignity and the indispensable celerity of the public service.

8. The representatives of a nation faithful to the laws of honor and probity, will make no attack upon the public credit, and the king expects from them that the confidence of the creditors of the state will be assured and secured in the most authentic manner.

9. When the formal dispositions announced by the clergy and the nobility, to renounce their pecuniary privileges, shall have became a reality by their deliberations, it is the intention of the king to sanction them, and there will no longer exist any kind of privileges or distinctions in the payment of taxes.

10. The king wishes that to consecrate a disposition so important, the name of *taille* be abolished in the kingdom, and that this tax be joined either to the *vingtièmes,* or to any other land tax, or finally that it be replaced in some way, but always in just and equal proportions and without distinction of estate, rank and birth.

11. The king wishes that the tax of *franc-fief* be abolished from the time when the revenues and fixed expenses of the state exactly balance.

12. All property rights, without exception, shall be constantly respected, and His Majesty expressly understands under the name of property rights, tithes, rents, annuities, feudal and seignorial rights and duties, and, in general, all the rights and prerogatives useful or honorary, attached to lands and fiefs or pertaining to persons.

13. The first two orders of the state shall continue to enjoy exemptions from personal charges, but the king would be pleased to have the States-General consider means of converting this kind of charges into pecuniary contributions and that then all the orders of the state may be equally subjected to them.

14. It is the intention of His Majesty to determine, in accord with the States-General, what the employments and duties shall be which will preserve in the future the privilege of giving and transmitting nobility. His Majesty, nevertheless, according to the inherent right of his crown, will grant titles of nobility to those of his subjects who by services rendered to the king or to the state shall show themselves worthy of this recompense.

15. The king, desiring to assure the personal liberty of all citizens in the most solid and durable manner, invites the States-General to seek for and to propose to him the means that may be the most fitting to conciliate the orders known under the name of *lettres de cachet,* with the maintenance of public security and with the precautions necessary in some cases to guard the honor of families, to repress with celerity the beginning of sedition or to guarantee the state from the effects of criminal negotiations with foreign powers.

16. The States-General shall examine and make known to His Majesty, the means most fitting to reconcile the liberty of the press with respect due to religion, custom, and the honor of the citizens.

17. There shall be established in the different provinces or generalities of the kingdom, provincial-estates composed thus: two-tenths of the members of the clergy, a part of whom will necessarily be chosen in the episcopal order; three-tenths of members of the nobility, and five-tenths of members of the Third Estate.

18. The members of these provincial-estates shall be freely elected by the respective orders, and a certain amount of property shall be necessary to be an elector or eligible.

19. The deputies to these provincial-estates shall deliberate in common upon all affairs, following the usage observed in the provincial assemblies, which these estates shall replace.

20. An intermediary commission, chosen by these estates, shall administer the affairs of the province, during the interval from one session to another, and these intermediary commissions becoming alone responsible for their conduct, shall have for delegates persons chosen wholly by them or the provincial-estates.

21. The States-General shall propose to the king their views upon all the other parts of interior organization of the provincial-estates, and upon the choice of forms applicable to the election of the members of this assembly.

22. Independently of the objects of administration with which the provincial assemblies are charged, the king will confide to the provincial-estates the administration of the hospitals, prisons, charity stations, foundling homes, the inspection of the expenses of the cities, the surveillance over the maintenance of the forests, the protection and sale of the wood, and

over other objects which could be more usefully administered by the provinces.

23. The disputes occurring in the provinces where ancient estates exist, and the protests that have arisen against the constitution of the assemblies, ought to claim the attention of the States-General; they will make known to His Majesty the dispositions of justice and wisdom that it is suitable to adopt to establish a fixed order in the administration of these same provinces.

24. The king invites the States-General to occupy themselves in the quest of the proper means to turn to account the most advantageously the domains which are in his hands, and to propose to him equally their views upon what can be done the most conveniently with the domains that have been leased.

25. The States-General shall consider the project conceived a long time ago by His Majesty of transferring the collection of tariffs to the frontiers of the kingdom, in order that the most perfect liberty may reign in the internal circulation of national or foreign merchandise.

26. His Majesty desires that the unfortunate effects of the impost upon salt and the importance of this revenue be carefully discussed, and that in all the substitutions, means of lightening the collection may at least be proposed.

27. His Majesty wishes also that the advantages and inconveniences of the internal revenue tax on liquors and other taxes be examined attentively, but without losing sight of the absolute necessity of assuring an exact balance between the revenues and expenses of the state.

28. According to the wish that the king manifested by his declaration of the 23rd of last September, His Majesty will examine with serious attention the plans which may be presented to him, relative to the administration of justice, and to the means of perfecting the civil and criminal laws.

29. The king wishes that the laws that he will have promulgated during the session and after the advice or according to the wish of the States-General, may experience in their registration and execution no delay nor any obstacle in all the extent of his kingdom.

30. His Majesty wishes that the use of the *corvée* for

the making and maintenance of the roads, be entirely and forever abolished in his kingdom.

31. The king desires that the abolition of the right of *main-morte,* of which His Majesty has given the example in his domains, be extended to all France, and that means be proposed to him for providing the indemnity which would be due the lords in possession of this right.

32. His Majesty will make known at once to the States-General the regulations with which he occupies himself for the purpose of restricting the *capitaineries,* to give, furthermore, in this connection, which touches the most nearly his own pleasures, a new proof of his love for his people.

33. The king invites the States-General to consider the drawing for the militia in all its aspects and to study the means of reconciling what is due to the defence of the state, with the extenuations that His Majesty desires to procure for his subjects.

34. The king wishes that all the dispositions of public order and kindness toward his people, that His Majesty will have sanctioned by his authority, during the present session of the States-General, those among others, relative to personal liberty, the equality of contributions, the establishment of the provincial-estates, may never be changed without the consent of the three orders, given separately. His Majesty places them in the same rank with the national properties, that like all other property, he wishes to place under the most assured protection.

35. His Majesty, after having called the States-General to study, together with him, great matters of public utility and everything which can contribute to the happiness of his people, declares, in the most express manner, that he wishes to preserve in its entirety and without the least impairment, the constitution of the army, as well as every authority, both police authority and military power over the militia, such as the French monarchs have constantly enjoyed.

Discourse of the King.

You have, gentlemen, heard the substance of my dispositions and of my wishes; they are conformable to the earnest desire that I have for the public welfare; and, if, by a fatality far from my thoughts, you should abandon me in so fine an enterprise, alone I will assure the well being of my people, alone I will consider myself as their true representative; and knowing your *cahiers*, knowing the perfect accord which exists between the most general wish of the nation and my kindly intentions, I will have all the confidence which so rare a harmony ought to inspire and I will advance towards the goal that I wish to attain with all the courage and firmness that it ought to inspire in me.

Reflect, gentlemen, that none of your projects, none of your dispositions can have the force of a law without my special approbation. So I am the natural guarantee of your respective rights, and all the orders of the state can depend upon my equitable impartiality. All distrust upon your part would be a great injustice. It is I, at present, who am doing everything for the happiness of my people, and it is rare, perhaps, that the only ambition of a sovereign is to come to an understanding with his subjects that they may accept his kindnesses.

I order you, gentlemen, to separate immediately, and to go tomorrow morning, each to the chamber allotted to your order, in order to take up again your sessions. I order, therefore, the grand master of ceremonies to have the halls prepared.

C. Decree of the Assembly, June 23, 1879. *Procès-verbal de l'assemblée nationale*, 1789. No. 5, 3. Translation, Mrs. Fred M. Fling, in Fling's *Source Studies, Royal Session*, 31.

The National Assembly unanimously declares that it persists in its previous resolutions.

The National Assembly declares that the person of each of the deputies is inviolable; that any individuals, any corporations, tribunal, court or commission that shall dare, during or after the present session, to pursue, to seek for, to arrest or have arrested, detain or have detained, a deputy, by reason of any propositions, advice, opinions, or discourse made by him in the States-General: as well as all persons who shall lend their aid to any of the said attempts by whomsoever they may be ordered, are infamous and traitors to the nation, and guilty of capital crime. The National Assembly decrees that, in the aforesaid cases, it will take all the necessary measures-ures to have sought out, pursued and punished those who may be its authors, instigators or executors.

4. The Fourth of August Decrees.

August 4-11, 1789. Duvergier. *Lois*, I, 33-35. Translation, James Harvey Robinson, *University of Pennsylvania Translations and Reprints.*

The overthrow of the Bastile on July 14, 1789, was followed by a revolution in the provinces. Directed principally at the destruction of those feudal arrangements which bore most harshly upon the peasantry, this revolution was marked by much violence and misery. A report upon the condition of the provinces read in the Constituent Assembly on the night of August 4 led to the adoption of this decree. It was passed in a burst of enthusiasm for the regeneration of France. This haste made necessary some slight modifications a week later.

REFERENCES. Gardiner, *French Revolution*, 49-51; Mathews. *French Revolution*, 138-141; Stephens, *French Revolution*, I. 165-168; Von Sybel, *French Revolution*, I, 82-86; *Cambridge Modern History*, VIII, 179-180, 715-717; Lavisse and Rambaud, *Histoire générale*, VIII, 70-72; Jaurès, *Histoire socialiste*, I, 277-299, 306-308.

1. The National Assembly completely abolishes the feudal regime. It decrees that, among the rights and dues, both feudal and *censuel*, all those originating in real or personal serfdom, personal servitude, and those which represent them, are abolished without indemnification; all others are declared redeemable, and that the price and mode of the redemption shall be fixed by the National Assembly. Those of the said dues which are not extinguished by this decree shall, nevertheless, continue to be collected until indemnification takes place.

2. The exclusive right to maintain pigeon-houses and dove-cotes is abolished; the pigeons shall be confined during the seasons fixed by the communities; and during that time. they shall be regarded as game, and every one shall have the right to kill them upon his own land.

3. The exclusive right to hunt and to maintain unenclosed warrens is likewise abolished; and every land-owner shall have the right to kill or to have destroyed upon his own land only, all kinds of game, observing, however, such police regulations as may be established with a view to the safety of the public.

All *capitaineries*, royal included, and all hunting reserves, under whatever denominations, are likewise abolished, and provision shall be made, in a manner compatible with the respect due to property and liberty, for maintaining the personal pleasures of the king.

The president of the assembly shall be commissioned to ask of the king the recall of those sent to the galleys or exiled simply for violations of the hunting regulations, as well as for the release of those at present imprisoned for offences of this kind, and the dismissal of such cases as are now pending.

4. All manorial courts are suppressed without indemnification; nevertheless the magistrates of these courts shall continue to perform their functions until such time as the National Assembly shall provide for the establishment of a new judicial system.   .

5. Tithes of every description and the dues which have been substituted for them, under whatever denomination they are known or collected, even when compounded for, possessed by secular or regular congregations, by holders of benefices, members of corporations, including the Order of Malta and other religious and military orders, as well as those impropriated to lay persons and those substituted for the *portion congruë,* are abolished, on condition, however, that some other method be devised to provide for the expenses of divine worship, the support of the officiating clergy, the relief of the poor, repairs and rebuilding of churches and parsonages, and for all establishments, seminaries, schools, academies, asylums, communities and other institutions, for the maintenance of which they are actually devoted. And moreover, until such provision shall be made and the former possessors shall enter upon the enjoyment of an income on the new system, the National Assembly decrees that the said tithes shall continue to be collected according to law and in the customary manner. Other tithes of whatever nature they may be, shall be redeemable in such manner as the Assembly shall determine. Until such regulation shall be issued, the National Assembly decrees that these, too, shall continue to be collected.

6. All perpetual ground rents, payable either in money or in kind, of whatever nature they may be, whatever their origin, and to whomsoever they may be due, as to members of corporations, domanial apanagists, or to the Order of Malta, shall be redeemable; *champarts,* of every kind and un-

der every denomination, shall likewise be redeemable at a rate fixed by the assembly. No due shall in the future be created which is not redeemable.

7. The sale of judicial and municipal offices shall be suppressed forthwith. Justice shall be dispensed gratis; nevertheless, the magistrates at present holding such offices shall continue to exercise their functions and to receive their emoluments until the assembly shall have made provision for indemnifying them.

8. The fees of the country *curés* are abolished, and shall be discontinued as soon as provision shall be made for increasing the minimum salary (*portion congruë*) for priests and for the payment to the curates; and there shall be a regulation drawn up to determine the status of the priests in the towns.

9. Pecuniary privileges, personal or real, in the payment of taxes are abolished forever. The assessment shall be made upon all the citizens and upon all property, in the same manner and in the same form; and plans shall be considered by which the taxes shall be paid proportionally by all, even for the last six months of the current year.

10. Inasmuch as a national constitution and public liberty are of more advantage to the provinces than the privileges which some of these enjoy, and inasmuch as the surrender of such privileges is essential to the intimate union of all parts of the realm, it is declared that all the peculiar privileges, pecuniary or otherwise, of the provinces, principalities, districts, cantons, cities and communes, are once for all abolished and are absorbed into the law common to all Frenchmen.

11. All citizens, without distinction of birth, are eligible to any office or dignity, whether ecclesiastical, civil or military; and no profession shall imply any derogation.

12. Hereafter no remittances shall be made for annates or for any other purpose to the court of Rome, the vice-legation at Avignon, or to the nunciature at Lucerne; but the clergy of the diocese shall apply to their bishops for all provisions in regard to benefices and dispensations, which shall be granted gratis, without regard to reservations, expectancies, and monthly divisions, all the churches of France enjoying the same freedom.

13. The rights of *deport,* of *côte-morte, dépouilles, vacat, censaux,* Peter's pence, and other dues of the same kind, under

whatever denomination, established in favor of bishops, archdeacons, archpresbyters, chapters, *curés primitifs* and all others, are abolished, but appropriate provision shall be made for
those benefices of archdeacons and archpresbyters which are
not sufficiently endowed.

14. Pluralities shall not be permitted hereafter in cases
where the revenue from the benefice or benefices held shall
exceed the sum of three thousand livres. Nor shall any individual be allowed to enjoy several pensions from benefices,
or a pension and a benefice, if the revenue which he already
enjoys from such sources exceeds the same sum of three
thousand livres.

15. The National Assembly shall consider, in conjunction
with the king, the report which is to be submitted to it relating to pensions, favors and salaries, with a view to suppressing all such as are not deserved and reducing those which
shall prove excessive; and the amount shall be fixed which
the king may in the future disburse for this purpose.

16. The National Assembly decrees that a medal shall be
struck in memory of the recent grave and important deliberations for the welfare of France, and that a *Te Deum* shall be
chanted in gratitude in all the parishes and the churches of
France.

17. The National Assembly solemnly proclaims the king,
Louis XVI, the *Restorer of French Liberty*.

18. The National Assembly shall present itself in a body
before the king, in order to submit to His Majesty the decree
which has just been passed, to tender to him the tokens of its
most respectful gratitude, and to pray him to permit the *Te
Deum* to be chanted in his chapel, and to be present himself
at this service.

19. The National Assembly shall consider, immediately
after the constitution, the drawing up of the laws necessary
for the development of the principles which it has laid down
in the present decree which shall be transmitted without delay
by the deputies to all the provinces, together with the decree
of the tenth of this month, in order that both may be printed,
published, announced from the parish pulpits, and posted up
wherever it shall be deemed necessary.

5.   Declaration of the Rights of Man and Citizen.

August 26, 1789. Duvergier, *Lois,* I, 38.

This is the most famous document connected with the early stages of the revolution. Until recently it has been regarded as an outgrowth of the doctrinaire ideas of the pre-revolutionary thinkers, especially of Rousseau. It should be studied, however, in the light of recent investigations into its origin and character. These investigations show (1) that the idea of formulating such a declaration was taken from the bills of rights attached to American state constitutions and (2) that in general each of its provisions is aimed at some great existing abuse.

REFERENCES.   Jellinek, *Declaration of the Rights of Man and Citizen;* James Harvey Robinson, *Political Science Quarterly,* XIV, 653-662; *Cambridge Modern History,* VIII, 178-179, 727-728; Aulard, *Révolution française,* 39-48; Jaurès, *Histoire socialiste,* 1, 156-174, 299-308, 342-347; Boutmy, *Études politiques,* 117-182.

[This was subsequently incorporated in the constitution of 1791. See No. 15.]

6.   Documents upon the Constituent Assembly and the Church.

These documents show both the general attitude of the Constituent Assembly towards religion and the revolution which it sought to effect in the position of the Gallican Church. Careful attention to the phraseology of the documents will reveal much concerning the ideas upon which the assembly proceeded.

REFERENCES.   Mathews, *French Revolution,* 161-163; Sloane, *French Revolution and Religious Reform,* Chs. v-viii; Gardiner, *French Revolution,* 67-69; Stephens, *French Revolution,* I, Ch. x; *Cambridge Modern History,* VIII, 194-198; Debidour, *L'Église et L'État,* Part I, Chs. i and ii; Jaurès, *Histoire socialiste,* I, 521-548.

A. Decree upon the Church Lands. November 2, 1789, Duvergier, *Lois,* I, 54-55.

The National Assembly decrees, 1st, that all the ecclesiastical estates are at the disposal of the nation, on condition of providing in a suitable manner for the expense of worship, the maintenance of its ministers, and the relief of the poor, under the supervision and following the directions of the provinces; 2d, that in the provisions to be made, in order to provide for the maintenance of the ministers of religion, there can be assured for the endowment of each curé *not less than twelve hundred livres per annum,* not including the dwelling and the gardens attached.

B. Decree upon Monastic Vows. February 13, 1790. Duvergier, *Lois,* I, 100.

1. The constitutional law of the kingdom shall no longer recognize solemn monastic vows of persons of either sex; in consequence, the orders and congregations living according to rule in which such vows have been made are and shall remain suppressed in France, without there being any similar ones allowed in the future.

2. All persons of either sex living in the monasteries and religious houses may leave them by making their declarations before the municipality of the place, and there shall immediately be provision made for their existence by a suitable pension. There shall also be houses set aside to which the religious who do not wish to profit by the provision of the present [article] shall be required to retire. Moreover, there shall be no change for the present in respect to the houses charged with public education and the establishments of charity and any that have until now taken part in these matters.

3. The religious may remain in the houses in which they are at present, excepting those described in the article which requires the religious to unite several houses into one.

C. The Civil Constitution of the Clergy. July 12, 1790. Duvergier, *Lois,* I, 242-248. Translation based upon that of James Harvey Robinson, *University of Pennsylvania Translations and Reprints.*

The National Assembly, after having heard the report of the Ecclesiastical Committee, has decreed and does decree the following as constitutional articles:—

Title I. Of the Ecclesiastical Offices.

1. Each department shall form a single diocese, and each diocese shall have the same extent and the same limits as the department.

2. The seats of the bishoprics of the eighty-three departments of the kingdom shall be established as follows:

That of the department of the Lower Seine at Rouen; that of the department of Calvados at Bayeux . . . . [The names of the remaining episcopal sees are here omitted.]

All other bishoprics in the eighty-three departments of the kingdom, which are not included by name in the present article, are and forever shall be abolished.

The kingdom shall be divided into ten metropolitan districts, of which the sees shall be situated at Rouen, Rheims, Besançon, Rennes, Paris, Bourges, Bordeaux, Toulouse, Aix and Lyons. . . .

3. [This article enumerates the departments included in each archbishopric.]

4. No church or parish of France nor any French citizen may acknowledge upon any occasion or upon any pretext whatsoever, the authority of an ordinary bishop or of an archbishop whose see shall be under the supremacy of a foreign power, nor that of their representatives residing in France or elsewhere; without prejudice, however, to the unity of the faith and the intercourse which shall be maintained with the visible head of the universal church, as hereinafter provided.

5. After the bishop of a diocese shall have rendered his decision in his synod upon the matters lying within his competence an appeal may be carried to the archbishop, who shall give his decision in the metropolitan synod.

6. A new arrangement and division of all the parishes of the kingdom shall be undertaken immediately in concert with the bishop and the district administration. The number and extent of the parishes shall be determined according to rules which shall be laid down.

7. The cathedral church of each diocese shall be restored to its primitive condition, and be hereafter at once the church of the parish and of the diocese, by the suppression of parishes and by the redistribution of dwellings which it may be deemed necessary to include in the new parish.

[Articles 8 to 13, here omitted, regulate the organization of the cathedral church and provide for one seminary in each diocese.]

14. The vicars of the cathedral churches, the superior vicar and directing vicars of the seminary, shall form the regular and permanent council of the bishop, who shall perform no official act which concerns the government of the dio-

cese or of the seminary until he has consulted them; the bishop may, however, in the course of his visits issue such provisional ordinances as may be necessary.

15. There shall be but a single parish in all cities and towns having not more than 6,000 inhabitants; the other parishes shall be abolished or absorbed into that of the episcopal church.

16. In cities having a population of more than 6,000 inhabitants a parish may include a greater number of parishioners, and as many parishes shall be perpetuated as the needs of the people and localities shall require.

17. The administrative assemblies, in concert with the bishop of the diocese, shall indicate to the next legislative assembly, the country and subordinate urban parishes which ought to be contracted or enlarged, established or abolished; and they shall lay out these districts according to what the needs of the people, the dignity of religion, and the different localities shall require.

.   .   .   .

20. All titles and offices other than those mentioned in the present constitution, *dignités,* canonries, prebends, half-prebends, chapels, chaplainships, both in cathedral and collegiate churches, all regular and secular chapters for either sex, abbacies and priorships, both regular and *in commendam,* for either sex. as well as all other benefices and prestimonies in general, of whatever kind or denomination, are from the day of this decree extinguished and abolished and shall never be re-established in any form.

.   .   .   .

Title II. Appointments to Benefices.

1. Beginning with the day of publication of the present decree there shall be but one mode of choosing bishops and *curés,* namely that of election.

.   .   .   .

2. All elections shall be by ballot and shall be decided by the majority of the votes.

3. The election of bishops shall take place according to the forms and by the electoral body designated in the decree of December 22. 1789, for the election of members of the departmental assembly.

6. The election of a bishop can only take place or be undertaken upon Sunday, in the principal church of the chief town of the department, at the close of the parish mass, at which all the electors are required to be present.

7. In order to be eligible to a bishopric, one must have fulfilled for fifteen years at least the duties of the church ministry in the diocese as a parish priest, officiating minister or curate, or as superior, or as directing vicar of the seminary.

17. The archbishop or senior bishop of the province shall have the right to examine the bishop-elect in the presence of his council upon his belief and his character. If he deems him fit for the position he shall give him the canonical institution. If he believes it his duty to refuse this, the reasons for his refusal shall be recorded in writing and signed by the archbishop and his council, reserving to the parties concerned the right to appeal on the ground of an abuse of power as hereinafter provided.

18. The bishop applied to for institution may not exact of the person elected any form of oath except that he makes profession of the Roman Catholic and Apostolic religion.

19. The new bishop shall not apply to the Pope for any form of confirmation, but shall write to him as the Visible Head of the Universal Church, as a testimony to the unity of faith and communion maintained with him.

21. Before the ceremony of consecration begins, the bishop-elect shall take a solemn oath in the presence of the municipal officers, the people and the clergy, to guard with care the faithful of his diocese who are confided to him, to be loyal to the nation, the law and the king, and to support with all his power the constitution decreed by the National Assembly and accepted by the king.

25. The election of the parish priests shall take place according to the forms and by the electors designated in the decree of December 22, 1789, for the election of members of the administrative assembly of the district.

29. Each elector, before depositing his ballot in the ballot

box, shall take oath to vote for that person whom he has conscientiously selected in his heart as the most worthy, without having been influenced by any gift, promise, solicitation or threat. The same oath shall be required at the election of the bishops as in the case of the parish priests.

. . . .

38. The *curés* elected and installed shall take the same oath as the bishops on a Sunday in their church, in the presence of the municipal officers, the people and the clergy of the place. Until then they shall not perform any priestly function.

40. Bishoprics and *curés* shall be looked upon as vacant until those elected to fill them shall have taken the oath above mentioned.

. . . .

Title III. Salaries of the Ministers of Religion.

1. The ministers of religion, performing as they do the first and most important functions of society, and forced to live continuously in the place where they discharge the offices to which they have been called by the confidence of the people, shall be supported by the nation.

2. Every bishop, priest and officiating clergyman in a chapel of ease, shall be furnished with a suitable dwelling, on condition, however, that the occupant shall make all the necessary current repairs. This shall not affect, at present, in any way, those parishes where the priest now receives a money equivalent instead of his dwelling. The departments shall, moreover, have cognizance of suits arising in this connection, brought by the parishes and by the priests. Salaries shall be assigned to each, as indicated below.

3. The bishop of Paris shall receive 50,000 livres; the bishops of cities having a population of 50,000 or more, 20,000 livres; other bishops, 12,000 livres.

4. [Article 4 fixes the salaries of the vicars of cathedral churches. These ranged from 6000-3000 livres].

5. The salaries of the *curés* shall be as follows: In Paris, 6000 livres.

In cities having a population of 50,000 or over, 4000 livres.

In those having a population of less than 50,000 and more than 10,000, 3,000 livres.

In cities and towns of which the population is below 10,000 and more than 3,000, 2,400 livres.

In all other cities, towns and villages where the parish shall have a population between 3000 and 2500, 2000 livres; in those between 2500 and 2000, 1800 livres; in those having a population of less than 2000, and more than 1000, the salary shall be 1500 livres; in those having 1000 inhabitants and under, 1200 livres.

6. [The salaries of the curates, fixed by article 6, ranged from 2400 livres at Paris to 700 in the small places.]

7. The salaries *in money* of the ministers of religion shall be paid every three months, in advance, by the treasurer of the district.

.   .   .   .

11. The schedule fixed above for the payment of the ministers of religion shall go into effect upon the day of publication of this decree, but only in the case of those who shall be afterward provided with ecclesiastical offices. The remuneration of the present holders, both those whose offices or functions are abolished and those whose titles are retained, shall be fixed by a special decree.

12. In view of the salary which is assured to them by the present constitution, the bishops, *curés,* and curates shall perform the episcopal and priestly functions gratis.

Title IV. Of the Law of Residence.

1. The law of residence shall be strictly observed, and all vested with an ecclesiastical office or function shall be subject thereto without any distinction or exception.

2. No bishop shall absent himself from his diocese more than fifteen days consecutively during the year, except in case of real necessity, and with the consent of the directory of the department in which his see is situated.

3. In the same manner the *curés* and the curates may not absent themselves from the place of their duties beyond the term fixed above, except for weighty reasons, and even in such cases the *curés* must obtain the permission both of their bishop and of the directory of their district, and the curates that of their *curés*.

4. In case a bishop or a *curé* shall violate this law requiring residence, the municipal government of the place

shall inform the *procureur-general-syndic* of the department,
who shall issue a summons to him to return to his duties, and,
after a second warning, shall take steps to have his salary declared forfeited for the whole period of his absence.

.   .   .   .

6. Bishops, *cures* and curates may, as active citizens, be
present at the primary and electoral assemblies, they may
be chosen electors or as deputies to the legislative body, or as
members of the general council of the communes or of the
administrative councils of their districts or departments; but
their duties are declared incompatible with those of mayor and
other municipal offices and those of the members of the directories of the district and of the department; and if elected
to one of these last mentioned offices they must make a
choice between it and their ecclesiastical position.

7. The incompatibility of office mentioned in article 6 shall
only to be observed in the future; and if any bishops, *cures*, or
curates have been called by the wish of their fellow-citizens
to the offices of mayor or to other municipal offices, or have
been elected members of the directory of the district or of
the department they may continue to exercise their functions.

D. Decree upon the Clerical Oath. November 27, 1790.
Duvergier, *Lois,* II, 59-60.

1. The bishops and former archbishops and the *cures* kept
in their positions shall be required, if they have not already
done so, to take the oath for which they are liable . . .
concerning the civil constitution of the clergy. In consequence they shall swear . . . to look with care after the faithful of their diocese or the parish which is intrusted to them,
to be faithful to the nation, to the law and to the king, and to
maintain with all their power the constitution decreed by the
National Assembly and accepted by the king; to wit those who
are actually in their diocese or their parish within a week;
those who are absent therefrom but are in France, within a
month; and those who are abroad within two months. All
to date from the publication of the present decree.

2. [The same requirement, except the first clause, is made
of "all other ecclesiastical public functionaries."]

.   .   .   .

5. Those of the said bishops, former archbishops, *curés,* and other ecclesiastical public functionaries, who shall not have taken . . . the oath which is prescribed for them respectively, shall be reputed to have renounced their office and there shall be provision made for their replacement, as in case of vacancy by resignation. . . .

. . . .

E. Decree upon the Publication of Papal Documents, June 9, 1791. Duvergier, *Lois,* III, 10.

The National Assembly, after having heard its united constitutional and ecclesiastical committees, considering that it is of importance for the national sovereignty and the maintenance of public order within the kingdom, to determine constitutionally the conservative forms of the ancient and salutary maxims by which the French nation has always kept clear of the encroachments of the court of Rome, without lacking in the respect due to the head of the catholic church, declares as follows:

1. No briefs, bulls, rescripts, constitutions, decrees, or other documents of the court of Rome, under any denomination whatsoever, shall be recognized as such, received, published, printed, posted, or otherwise put into execution within the kingdom, but they shall here be null and of no effect, unless they have been presented to the legislative body, seen and verified by it, and unless their publication and execution have been authorised by a decree sanctioned by the king and promulgated in the forms established for the notification of the laws.

2. The bishops, *curés,* and other public functionaries, whether ecclesiastical or lay, who in contravention of the preceding article, shall read, distribute, cause to be read, distributed, printed, posted, or shall otherwise give publicity or execution to the briefs, bulls, rescripts, constitutions, decrees, or other documents of the court of Rome, not authorised by a decree of the legislative body sanctioned by the king, shall be prosecuted criminally as disturbers of the public order and punished with the penalty of civic degradation, without prejudice to the execution of article 2 of the decree of May 7 last.

7. Decrees for Reorganizing the Local Government System.

These documents exhibit the general outline of the scheme for local government devised by the Constituent Assembly in order to replace that of the old régime, which largely disappeared during the revolution in the provinces following the overthrow of the Bastile. The extent of the revolution in local affairs may be seen by comparing this scheme of government with that which it replaced. Some parts of the scheme here outlined have been permanent, others have been seriously modified or discarded; the permanent features should be particularly noted.

REFERENCES. Stephens. *French Revolution*, I. 278-284 ; *Cambridge Modern History*, VIII, 190-191, 204-206 ; Lavisse and Rambaud. *Histoire générale*, VIII, 79-84 ; Jaurès, *Histoire socialiste*, I, 399-400, 403-412.

A. Decree upon the Municipalities. December 14, 1789. Duvergier, *Lois*, I, 63-67.

1. The actually existing municipalities in each city, borough, parish, or community, under the titles of *hôtels-de-ville*, mayoralities, aldermanates, consulates, and generally under any title or qualification whatsoever, are suppressed and abolished; the municipal officers actually in service, however, shall continue their functions until they may be replaced.

2. The offices and members of the existing municipalities shall be replaced by means of election.

3. The rights of presentation, appointment, or confirmation, and the rights of presidency or of presence in the municipal assemblies, claimed or exercised as being attached to the possession of certain lands, to the functions of province or city commandant, bishoprics, or archbishoprics, and in general by any other title whatsoever, are abolished.

4. The head of every municipal body shall bear the title of mayor.

5. All the active citizens of each city, borough, parish or community, may participate in the election of the members of the municipal body.

6. The active citizens shall meet in a single assembly in the communities where there are less than four thousand inhabitants; in two assemblies in the communities of four to eight thousand inhabitants; in three assemblies in the communities of eight to twelve thousand inhabitants, and so on.

7. The assemblies shall not form themselves by crafts, professions, or corporations, but by quarters or districts.

.   .   .   .

12. The conditions of eligibility for the municipal administrations shall be the same as for the department and district administrations; nevertheless, the kinsmen and relatives by marriage in the degrees of father and son, father-in-law and son-in-law, brother and brother-in-law, uncle and nephew, cannot be at the same time members of the same municipal body.

13. The municipal officers and the notables who shall be spoken of hereinafter can be chosen only from among the eligible citizens of the commune.

.   .   .   .   .

24. After the elections, the active citizens of the community shall not remain assembled, or assemble again in communal body, without an express convocation ordered by the general council of the commune, which shall be spoken of hereinafter. This council shall not refuse it, if it is requested by one-sixth of the active citizens in the communities below 4,000 souls and by 150 active citizens in any of the other communities.

25. The members of the municipal bodies of the cities, boroughs, parishes, or communities, shall be three in number, including the mayor, when the population shall be less than 500 souls; six, including the mayor, from 500 souls to 3,000; nine from 3,000 souls to 10,000; twelve from 10,000 to 25,000; fifteen from 25,000 to 50,000; eighteen from 50,000 to 100,000; twenty-one above 100,000 souls. As to the city of Paris, in consequence of its enormous population, it shall be governed by a special regulation which shall be given by the National Assembly upon the same basis and after the same principles as 'the general regulation for all the municipalities of the kingdom.

26. There shall be in each municipality a communal *procureur* without deliberative voice; he shall be charged to defend the interests and to prosecute the suits of the community.

.   .   .   .   .   .

30. The active citizens of each community shall select, by a single *scrutin de liste* and plurality of the votes, a number

of notables double that of the members of the municipal body.

31. These notables shall form, with the members of the municipal body, the great council of the commune, and they shall be summoned only for important matters, as hereinafter provided.

· · · · · · · · · ·

34. Each municipal body composed of more than three members shall be divided into a council and a bureau.

35. The bureau shall be composed of a third of the municipal officers, including the mayor, who shall always make up part of it; the other two-thirds shall form the council.

36. The members of the bureau shall be chosen by the municipal body every year and cannot be re-elected for a second year.

37. The bureau shall be charged with all executive tasks and confined to simple administration. In the municipalities reduced to three members the executive function shall be entrusted to the mayor alone.

38. The municipal council shall assemble at least once per month; it shall begin by agreeing upon the accounts of the bureau, when there is occasion; and after that operation is completed, the members of the bureau shall have sitting and deliberative voice with those of the council.

39. All the deliberations necessary for the discharge of the functions of the municipal body shall be taken in the united assembly of the members of the council and of the bureau, with the exception of deliberations relative to the closing of the accounts, which, as has been provided, shall be taken by the council alone.

· · · · · · · ·

42. The municipal officers and the notables shall be elected for two years and renewed each year by half. · · · ·

43. The mayor shall remain in service for two years; he may be re-elected for two years; but following that it shall not be permissible to elect him again until after an interval of two years.

· · · · · · · ·

45. The election assemblies for the annual renewals shall be held in all the kingdom the Sunday following Martinmasday, upon the call of the municipal officers.

· · · · · · ·

49. The municipal bodies shall have two kinds of functions to fulfill; one appertaining to the municipal authority; the other appertaining to the general administration of the state and delegated by it to the municipalities.

50. The functions appertaining to the municipal authority, under the surveillance and supervision of the administrative assemblies, are: to manage the common possessions and revenues of the cities, boroughs, parishes, and communities; to control and to pay those local expenses which ought to be paid out of the common funds; to direct and to cause to be executed the public works which are under the charge of the community; to administer the establishments which belong to the community and are maintained out of its funds or which are especially intended for the use of the citizens of whom it is composed; to cause the inhabitants to enjoy the advantages of a good police, especially for property, health, security, and tranquility in the streets, public places and buildings.

51. The functions appertaining to the general administration which can be delegated to the municipal bodies in order to be discharged under the authority of the administrative assemblies are: the apportionment of the direct taxes among the citizens of whom the community is composed; the collection of these taxes; the deposit of these taxes in the coffers of the district or department; the immediate direction of the public works within the jurisdiction of the municipality; the immediate management of the public establishments intended for general utility; the surveillance and the agency necessary for the preservation of the public properties; the direct oversight of the works of repair and reconstruction of the churches, parsonages, and other things related to the service of religious worship.

52. For the exercise of the functions belonging to or delegated to the municipal bodies, they shall have the right to make requisition for the necessary assistance of the national guards and other public forces as shall be more fully set forth.

.   .   .   .   .   .

54. The general council of the commune, composed as well of the municipal body as of the notables, shall be convoked whenever the municipal administration shall think proper. It cannot dispense with convoking it when there are measures to be taken upon the acquisition or alienation of

real estate, extraordinary taxes for local expenses, loans, public works, the employment of the proceeds of sales, reimbursements or recoveries, suits to be instituted, even upon suits to be defended, in case the basis of the rights shall be contested.

55. The municipal bodies shall be entirely subordinate to the department and district administrations for every thing which concerns the functions which they have to discharge by delegation of the general administration.

56. As to the exercise of the functions appertaining to the municipal authority, none of the decisions for which the convocation of the general council of the commune is necessary, according to article 54 above, can be executed except with the approval of the department administration or directory, which shall be given, if there is occasion, upon the notification of the district administration or directory.

57. All the accounts of the management of the municipal bureaus, after they have been received by the municipal council, shall be verified by the district administration or directory, and agreed to definitively by the department administration or directory, upon the notification of that of the district or of its directory.

.   .   .   .

60. If a citizen believes himself to be personally injured by any act of the municipal body, he may set forth his matters of complaint to the department administration or directory, which shall do right therein, upon the notification of the district administration, which shall be charged with the verification of the facts.

61. Every active citizen may subscribe to and present against the municipal officers a denunciation of the administrative offences of which he claims that they have rendered themselves guilty; but prior to carrying this denunciation before the tribunals, he shall be required to submit it to the department administration or directory, which after having taken the opinion of the district administration or its directory, shall send the denunciation, if there be need, before the judges who must take jurisdiction of it.

62. The active citizens have the right to meet peaceably and without arms in special assemblies, in order to draw up addresses and petitions to the municipal body, or to the de-

partment and district administrations, or to the legislative body, or to the king, under the condition of giving notice to the municipal officers of the time and the place of these assemblies, and that not over ten citizens be deputed to bring and present these petitions and addresses.

B. Decree upon the Departments and Districts. December 22, 1789. Duvergier, *Lois,* I, 73-78.

1. There shall be made a new division of the kingdom into *departments,* both for representation and administration. These departments shall be from seventy-five to eighty-five in number.

2. Each department shall be divided · into *districts,* of which the number, which shall not be less than three nor more than nine, shall be determined by the National Assembly, according to the need and convenience of the department, after having heard the deputies of the provinces.

3. Each district shall be divided into divisions called *cantons,* of about four square leagues (common leagues of France).

.   .   .   .

5. There shall be established at the head-town of each department a higher administrative assembly, under the title of *department administration.*

6. There shall likewise be established at the head-town of each district a subordinate administrative assembly, under the title of *district administration.*

7. There shall be a municipality in each city, borough, parish or rural community.

.   .   .   .

Section II. Of the formation and organization of the administrative assemblies.

1. There shall be only one degree of election intermediate between the primary assemblies and the administrative assemblies.

2. After having selected the representatives to the National Assembly, the same electors in each department shall elect the members, to the number of twenty-six, who shall compose the *department administration.*

3. The electors of each district shall meet afterwards at the head-town of their district and shall there select the members, to the number of twelve, who shall compose the *district administration*.

4. The members of the department administration shall be chosen from among the eligible citizens of all the cantons of the department, in such a manner, however, that there shall always be in that administration at least two members from each district.

5. The members of the district administrations shall be chosen from among the eligible citizens of all the cantons of the district.

6. In order to be eligible to the district and department administrations it shall be necessary to unite to the conditions requisite for active citizenship that of paying a larger direct tax and which amounts to at least the local value of ten days of labor.

.   .   .   .

12. Each administration, whether department or district, shall be permanent and the members shall be renewed by half every two years; the first time by lot, after the first two years of service, and afterwards by order of seniority.

13. The members of the administrations shall thus be in office for four years, with the exception of those who shall go out by lot at the first renewal after the first two years.

.   .   .   .

20. Each department administration shall be divided into two sections, one under the title of *department council,* the other under that of *department directory*.

21. The department council shall hold annually one session in order to determine the regulations for each part of the administration, to order the public works and the general expenses of the department, and to receive an account of the administration of the directory. The first session may be of six weeks, and that of the following years of a month at most.

.   .   .   .

23. The members of each department administration shall elect, at the end of their first session, eight from among themselves to compose the directory; they shall renew these every year by a half. The president of the department administration may be present and shall have the right to preside at all

the sittings of the directory, which may, nevertheless, choose a vice-president.

24. At the opening of each annual session, the department council shall begin by hearing, receiving, and agreeing to the account of the administration of the directory; afterwards the members of the directory shall take their seats and shall have deliberative voice with those of the council.

. . . .

27. Everything which is prescribed by articles 22, 23, and 24 above, for the functions, the form of election and of renewal, the right of sitting and of deliberative voice of the members of the department directory, shall likewise apply to those of the district directories.

28. The district administrations and directories shall be entirely subordinate to the department administrations and directories.

29. The district councils may hold their annual session for only fifteen days at most and the opening of this session shall precede by a month that of the department council.

30. The district councils shall attend only to the preparation of the requests to be made and the matters to be submitted to the department administration in the interest of the district, arrange for methods of execution, and receive the accounts of the administration of their directory.

31. The district directories shall be charged with the executive function within the extent of the jurisdiction of their district, under the direction and authority of the department administration and of its directory, and they cannot cause the execution of any orders of the district council in matters of general administration, unless approved by the department administration.

SECTION III. Of the functions of the administrative assemblies.

1. The department administrations are charged, under the supervision of the legislative body and in virtue of its decrees; 1st, with the apportionment of all the direct taxes imposed upon each department; this apportionment shall be made by the department administrations among the districts of their jurisdiction and by the district administrations among the municipalities; 2d, to order and to cause to be made up,

according to the forms which shall be established, the assessment rolls of the taxpayers of each municipality; 3d, to regulate and to supervise everything which relates to both the collection and deposit of the product of these taxes and the service and functions of the agents who shall have charge of them; 4th, to order and to cause to be executed the payment of the expenses which shall be allowed in each department out of the product of the same taxes.

2. The department administrations shall be further charged, under the authority and supervision of the king, as supreme head of the nation and of the general administration of the kingdom, with all the parts of that administration, especially with those which relate to: 1st, the relief of paupers and the police regulation of mendicants and vagabonds; 2d, the supervision and improvement of the management of hospitals, *hôtels-dieu,* charitable establishments and workshops, prisons, jails, and houses of correction; 3d, the supervision of public education and political and moral instruction; 4th, the custody and employment of the funds set aside in each department for the encouragement of agriculture, industry, and every form of public beneficence; 5th, the preservation of public property; 6th, forests, rivers, roads, and other public property; 7th, the direction and execution of work for the making of highways, canals and other public works authorised in the department; 8th, the maintenance, repair, and reconstruction of the churches, parsonages, and other things necessary for the service of religious worship; 9th, the maintenance of the public health, security, and tranquility; 10th, lastly, the disposal and employment of the national guards, as shall be regulated by special decrees.

3. The district administrations shall participate in these functions, within the extent of the jurisdiction of each district only, under the interposed authority of the department administrations.

4. The department and district administrations shall be always required to conform, in the exercise of all these functions, to the regulations established by the constitution and to the legislative decrees sanctioned by the king.

5. The decisions of the department administrative assemblies upon all the matters which shall concern the régime of the general administration of the kingdom or upon new un-

dertakings and extraordinary works shall be executed only after having received the approval of the king. The special authorisation of the king shall not be necessary with respect to the despatch of local matters and anything which is carried out in virtue of decisions already approved.

6. The department and district administrations shall not establish any tax, for any purpose or under any denomination whatsoever, by assessing anyone in excess of the sums and the time fixed by the legislative body; nor make any loan, unless authorised by it, except to provide for the establishment of suitable means to procure for themselves the necessary funds for the payment of the local debts and expenses and for imperative and urgent needs.

7. They cannot be disturbed in the exercise of their administrative functions by any act of the judicial power.

8. From the day when the department and district administrations shall be formed, the provincial-estates, the provincial assemblies, and the inferior assemblies which exist at present, shall be suppressed and shall entirely cease their functions.

9. There shall not be any intermediary between the department administrations and the supreme executive powers. The abolished commissioners, and the intendants and their sub-delegates, shall cease all functions as soon as the department administrations shall have entered into service.

10. In the provinces which have had up to the present a common administration and which are divided among several departments, each department administration shall appoint two commissioners who shall meet together in order to effect the liquidation of the debts contracted under the preceding régime, to establish the apportionment of these debts among the different parts of the province and to finish up old business. The account thereof shall be rendered to an assembly formed of four other commissioners appointed by each department administration.

8. Decree for Abolishing the Nobility.

June 19, 1790. Duvergier, *Lois,* I, 217-218.

The French revolution was a social even more than a political revolution. On its social side it was marked by a passionate desire for equality, i.e., the removal of inequalities created or sanctioned by the law. This decree is typical of many passed by the Constituent Assembly for the purpose of removing legal sanction for social inequalities.

REFERENCE. Von Sybel, *French Revolution,* I, 238-241.

1. Hereditary nobility is forever abolished; in consequence the titles of prince, duke, count, marquis, viscount, vidame, baron, knight, *messire, écuyer, noble,* and all other similar titles, shall neither be taken by anyone whomsoever nor given to anybody.

2. A citizen may take only the true name of his family; no one may wear liveries nor cause them to be worn, nor have armorial bearings; incense shall not be burned in the temples, except in order to honor the divinity, and shall not be offered for any one whomsoever.

3. The titles of *monseigneur* and *messeigneurs* shall not be given to any society nor to any person, likewise the titles of excellency, highness, eminence, grace, etc.; nevertheless, no citizen, under pretext of the present decree, shall be permitted to make an attack on the monuments placed in the temples, the charters, titles and other tokens of interest to families or properties, nor the decorations of any public or private place; nevertheless, the execution of the provisions relative to the liveries and the arms placed upon carriages shall not be carried out nor demanded by any one whomsoever before the 14th of July for the citizens living in Paris and before three months for those who inhabit the country.

4. No foreigners are included in the provision of the present decree; they may preserve in France their liveries and their armorial bearings.

9. Decree for Reorganizing the Judicial System.

August 16, 1790. Duvergier, *Lois,* I, 310-333.

One of the worst features of the old régime was its system for administering justice. This document, better than any other one, exhibits the work of the Constituent Assembly in the field of judicial reform. Other important decrees are those of October 8 and 9, 1789, and of September 16 and 25, 1791, unfortunately too long to be included here.

REFERENCES. Stephens, *French Revolution*, I, 284-288 ; *Cambridge Modern History*, VIII, 206-207, 745-746 ; Lavisse and Rambaud, *Histoire générale*, VIII, 84-85 , 491-497 ; Rambaud, *Civilisation contemporaine*, 73-77.

Title I. Of the Arbiters.

1. Arbitration being the most reasonable means for the termination of disputes between citizens, the legislature shall not make any provision which may tend to diminish either the popularity or the efficiency of the compromise.

.   .   .   .

Title II. Of the Judges in General.

1. Justice shall be rendered in the name of the king.

2. The sale of judicial offices is abolished forever; the judges shall render justice gratuitously and shall be salaried by the state.

3. The judges shall be elected by the justiciable.

4. They shall be elected for six years; at the expiration of this term a new election shall take place, in which the same judges may be re-elected.

.   .   .   .

12. They shall not make regulations, but they shall have recourse to the legislative body, whenever they think necessary, either to interpret a law or to make a new one.

13. The judicial functions are distinct and shall always remain separate from the administrative functions. The judges, under penalty of forfeiture, shall not disturb in any manner whatsoever the operations of the administrative bodies, nor cite before them the administrators on account of their functions.

14. In every civil or criminal matter, the pleadings, testimony, and decisions shall be public, and every citizen shall have the right to defend his own case, either verbally or in writing.

15. Trial by jury shall occur in criminal matters; the examination shall be made publicly and shall have the publicity which shall be determined.

16. All privilege in matters of jurisdiction is abolished; all citizens, without distinction, shall plead in the same form and before the same judges in the same cases.

17. The constitutional order of the jurisdictions shall not

be disturbed, nor the justiciable removed from their natural judges, by any commission, nor by other attributions or evocations than those which are determined by the law.

18. All citizens being equal before the law, and every preference for rank and the turn to be tried being an injustice, all suits, according to their nature, shall be tried when they have been examined in the order in which their trial shall have been applied for by the parties.

19. The civil laws shall be reviewed and reformed by the legislatures; and there shall be made a general code of laws that are simple, clear, and in harmony with the constitution.

20. The code of civil procedure shall be reformed forthwith in such a manner that it may be rendered more simple, more expeditious, and less expensive.

21. The penal code shall be reformed forthwith in such a manner that the penalties may be proportionate to the offences; taking good care that they be moderate and not losing sight of that maxim of the declaration of the rights of man that *the law can establish only penalties which are strictly and evidently necessary.*

Title III.   Of the Justices of the Peace.

1. There shall be in each canton a justice of the peace and *prud'hommes* assessors of the justice of the peace.

．　　．　　．　　．　　．　　．　　．　　．

3. The justices of the peace may be chosen only from among the citizens eligible to the department and district administrations, fully thirty years of age, without any other condition of eligibility.

4. The justices of the peace shall be elected, with individual ballot and majority of the votes, by the active citizens met in primary assemblies. . . .

．　　．　　．　　．　　．　　．　　．　　．

6. The same electors shall select from among the active citizens of each muncipality, by *scrutin de liste* and plurality, four notables to perform the duties of assessors of the justice of the peace. This justice shall call upon those who shall be selected in the municipality of the place where there is need for their assistance.

．　　．　　．　　．　　．　　．　　．

8. The justices of the peace and the *prud'hommes* shall be selected for two years and may be continued by re-election.

9. The justice of the peace, assisted by two assessors, shall have jurisdiction by themselves over all cases dealing solely with persons and personal property, without appeal up to the value of fifty livres and subject to appeal up to the value of a hundred livres. . . . The legislature shall not raise the amount of this competency.

10. He has jurisdiction, likewise, without appeal up to the value of fifty livres and subject to appeal at whatever value the complainant can prove.

. . . [Here follow six classes of additional civil actions.]

.   .   .   .

12. The appeal from the judgments of the justice of the peace, when they are subject to appeal, shall be carried before the judges of the district and tried by them in the last resort in audience and summarily upon the simple writ of appeal.

.   .   .   .

Title IV. Of the Judges of First Instance.

1. There shall be established in each district a tribunal composed of five judges, with whom there shall be an officer charged with the functions of the public ministry. The substitutes for them shall be four in number, of whom two at least shall be taken from within the city of the establishment or required to reside in it.

.   .   .   .

4. The district judges shall have jurisdiction in the first instance over all personal, real estate, and mixed suits of every kind, except only those which have been declared above to be within the jurisdiction of the justices of the peace, commercial suits in the districts where there are no commercial tribunals established, and the litigious affairs of the municipal police.

5. The district judges have jurisdiction in first and last resort over all suits involving persons and personal property, up to the value of a thousand livres of principal, and over real estate suits of which the chief item shall be of fifty livres of fixed income, either in rent or in lease price.

.   .   .   .

Title V. Of the Judges of Appeal.

1. The district judges shall be judges of appeal with respect to each other, according to the relations which shall be established in the following articles.

.   .   .   .

Title X. Of the Peace Bureaux and the Family Tribunal.

1. In all matters which shall exceed the competency of the justice of the peace, this justice and his assessors shall form a bureau of peace and conciliation.

2. No principal action in civil matters shall be received before the district judges between parties who shall all be domiciled in the jurisdiction of the same justice of the peace, whether in the city or in the country, unless the plaintiff gives at the head of his writ a copy of the certificate of the peace bureau attesting that his opponent has been summoned to no purpose before this bureau or that it has employed its mediation without result.

.   .   .   .   .   .

12. If any dispute arises between husband and wife, father and son, grand-father and grand-son, brothers and sisters, nephews and uncles, or between kinsmen of the above degrees, as also between pupils and their tutors in matters relative to their tutelage, the parties shall be required to appoint kinsmen or, in their default, friends or neighbors, as arbiters before whom they shall explain their difference and who, after having heard them and having obtained the necessary knowledge, shall render a decision which includes a statement of the reasons for it.

13. Each of the parties shall select two arbiters; and if one of them refuses, the other may apply to the judge, who, after having authenticated the refusal, shall appoint official arbiters for the refusing party. When the four arbiters find themselves divided in opinion they shall choose an umpire to remove the division.

14. The party who believes himself injured by the arbitral decision may appeal to the district tribunal, which shall pronounce in the last resort.

.   .   .   .

Title XI. Of the Judges in Matters of Police.

1. The municipal bodies within the precincts of each municipality shall look to and supervise the execution of the police laws and regulations, and shall have jurisdiction over the litigation to which this execution may give rise.

.   .   .   .   .   .

5. Contraventions of the police regulations shall be punished only by one of these two penalties, either by condemnation to a pecuniary penalty or imprisonment by way of correction for a time which in the most serious cases shall not exceed three days in the country and eight days in the cities.

6. Appeals from the judgments in police matters shall be carried to the tribunal of the district and these judgments shall be executed provisionally, notwithstanding the appeal and without prejudice to it.

.   .   .   .

Title XII. Of the Judges in Matters of Commerce.

1. There shall be established a commercial tribunal in the cities where the department administration, deeming these establishments necessary, shall frame a request for them.

2. This tribunal shall have jurisdiction of all commercial suits, both by land and sea, without distinction.

.   .   .   .   .   .

7. The commercial judges shall be elected in the assembly of the merchants, bankers, traders, manufacturers, ship-owners and ship-captains of the city where the tribunal is established.

.   .   .   .   .   .

10. Circular Letter of Louis XVI to Foreign Courts.

April 23, 1791. *Archives parlementaires*, XXV, 312-313.

On April 18, 1791, Louis XVI was prevented from going to St. Cloud by the Paris crowds, who feared that he was trying to escape from the capital. This document, communicated to the Constituent Assembly as well as to the foreign courts, was obviously intended to quiet these fears and to conceal the king's preparations for flight. In connection with No. 12 A it did much to establish a firm belief in the king's insincerity. The views expressed, though certainly not the real views of the king, are of interest, as substantially those of Frenchmen loyal to the king and the revolution alike.

REFERENCE. Aulard, *Révolution française*, 116-117.

The king charges me to inform you that it is his most express wish that you should make known his sentiments upon the French revolution and constitution at the court where you reside. The ambassadors and ministers of France at all the courts of Europe are receiving the same directions, in order that there may not remain any doubt about the intentions of His Majesty, or about the free acceptance which he has given to the new form of government, or about his irrevocable oath to maintain it.

His Majesty convoked the States-General of the kingdom and determined in his council that the commons should have in it a number of deputies equal to that of the other two orders which then existed. This act of provisional legislation, which the obstacles of the moment did not permit to be made more favorable, announced sufficiently the desire of His Majesty to re-establish the nation in all of its rights.

The States-General met and took the title of *National Assembly;* soon a constitution, qualified to secure the welfare of France and of the monarch, replaced the former order of things, in which the apparent power of the kingship only concealed the actual power of certain aristocratic bodies.

The National Assembly adopted the form of representative government in conjunction with hereditary kingship. The legislative body was declared permanent; the election of clergymen, administrators, and judges was made over to the people; the executive power was conferred upon the king, the formation of the law upon the legislative body, and the sanction upon the monarch. The public force, both internal and external, was organized upon the same principles and in accordance with the fundamental basis of the distinction of the powers; such is the new constitution of the kingdom.

What is called the revolution is only the abolition of a multitude of abuses accumulated in the course of centuries through the error of the people or the authority of the ministers, which has never been the authority of the king. These abuses were not less disastrous to the monarch than to the nation; under wise reigns authority had not ceased to attack these abuses, but was not able to destroy them. They no longer exist; the sovereign nation has no longer any but citizens equal in right, no despot but the law, no organs except the public functionaries, and the king is the first of these functionaries: such is the French revolution.

It was bound to have as enemies all those who in the first moment of horror, on account of personal advantage, mourned for the abuses of the former government. From this comes the apparent division which has manifested itself within the kingdom, but which is enfeebled each day; from this, also, perhaps, come some severe and exceptional laws which time will correct; but the king, whose real power is inseparable from that of the nation, who has no other ambition than the welfare of the people, nor any real authority other than that which is delegated to him; the king was bound to agree without hesitation to a happy constitution which would regenerate at one and the same time his authority, the nation, and the monarchy. He has retained all his authority, except the redoubtable power to make the laws; he remains in charge of the negotiations with foreign powers, the task of defending the kingdom and of repulsing its enemies; but the French nation henceforth will not have any enemies abroad except its aggressors. It no longer has internal enemies except those who, still nourishing foolish hopes, believe that the will of 24,000,000 men entered again upon their natural rights, after having organized the kingdom in such a manner that only the memory of the old forms and former abuses remains, is not an immovable and irrevocable constitution.

The most dangerous of these enemies are those who seek to spread doubts as to the intentions of the monarch; these men are indeed culpable or blind; they believe themselves the friends of the king; they are the only enemies of the monarchy; they would have deprived the monarch of the love and confidence of a great nation, if his principles and probity had been less known. Ah! what has the king not done to show that he counts both the French revolution and the constitution among his titles to glory. After having accepted and sanctioned all the laws, he has not neglected any means to cause them to be executed. Even in the month of February last in the midst of the National Assembly, he promised to maintain them; he took an oath thereto in the presence of the general federation of the kingdom. Honored with the title of Restorer of French Liberty, he will transmit more than a crown to his son; he will transmit to him a constitutional monarchy.

The enemies of the constitution do not cease to repeat that the king is not happy, as if there could be for the king any other happiness than that of the people! They say that his authority is dishonored; as if authority founded upon force was not less powerful and more uncertain than the authority of the law! In fine, that the king is not free: an atrocious calumny, if it is supposed that his will could be forced; an absurd one, if they take as lack of liberty the consent that His Majesty has several times expressed to remain in the midst of the citizens of Paris, a consent which he was bound to concede to their patriotism, even to their fears, and especially to their love.

These calumnies, however, have penetrated even into foreign courts; they have been repeated there by Frenchmen who have voluntarily exiled themselves from their fatherland, instead of sharing its glory, and who, if they are not its enemies, have at least abandoned their posts as citizens. The king charges you, sir, to defeat their intrigues and their plans. These same calumnies, in spreading false ideas about the French revolution, have caused the intentions of French travelers to be suspected among several neighboring nations; and the king especially recommends that you protect and defend them. Give, sir, the idea of the French constitution which the king himself has formed; do not allow there to be any doubt about the intention of His Majesty to maintain it with all his power. In assuring the liberty and equality of the citizens, that constitution founds the national prosperity upon the most enduring basis; it consolidates the royal authority through the laws; it forestalls by a glorious revolution the revolution which the abuses of the former government would have soon caused to break forth, thus causing perhaps the dissolution of the kingdom. Finally, it will be the happiness of the king. The task of justifying it, defending it, and of taking it for the rule of your conduct, must be your first duty.

I have already expressed several times the sentiments of His Majesty in this matter; but after what has been reported to him of the opinion which is sought to be established in for-

eign countries upon what has taken place in France, he has
ordered me to charge you to communicate the contents of this
letter to the court at which you are; and in order to give it
the utmost publicity, His Majesty has just ordered the printing of it.

Signed,   MONTMORIN.

Paris, April 23, 1791.

11. Decree upon the Organization of Trades and Professions.

June 14, 1791. Duvergier, *Lois*, III, 22.

By a decree of March 2, 1791, the Constituent Assembly abolished all of the vocation monopolies of the old régime and laid
down the principle that "every person shall be free to engage in
such business or to practice such profession, art or craft as he
shall find profitable." This document is the complement of that
decree. In it may be seen the intense feeling against the old vocation monopolies and the determination to secure an absolutely
free field for individual activity.

REFERENCE. Jaurès, *Histoire socialiste*, I, 605-630.

1. The suppression of all sorts of corporations of the citizens of the same calling and profession being one of the fundamental bases of the French constitution, the re-establishment of them under any pretext or any form whatsoever is
forbidden.

2. Citizens of a like calling or profession, employers, shop-
keepers, workers and journeymen of a certain trade, shall
not, when they shall meet together, name a president, or secretaries, or syndics, nor keep registers, nor pass resolutions
or make decisions, nor form regulations for their so-called
common interests.

3. All the administrative or municipal bodies are forbidden to receive any address or petition under the denomination
of a calling or profession or to make any response to such;
and they are enjoined to declare void the deliberations which
may have been taken in that manner and to see to it, carefully that no effect or execution be given to them.

4. If, contrary to the principles of liberty and the constitution, citizens engaged in the same professions, arts and
crafts, should hold deliberations or should make among them-

selves agreements which aim at refusing in concert or granting only at a settled price the assistance of their skill or their labors, the said decisions and agreements, whether accompanied by an oath or not, are declared unconstitutional, attacks upon liberty and the declaration of the rights of man, and of no effect; the administrative and municipal bodies shall be required to declare them such. The authors, leaders and instigators who shall have provoked, drafted, or presided over them, shall be cited before the police tribunal, at the request of the *procureur* of the commune, condemned to a fine of five hundred livres each and suspended from all the rights of active citizenship and of entrance into the primary assemblies.

5. All administrative and municipal bodies are forbidden, on penalty of their members responding for it in their own names, to employ, to admit or suffer to be admitted to the labors of their professions in any public works those of the employers, workers, and journeymen who shall have suggested or signed the said deliberations or agreements, except in case they have of their own motion presented themselves at the clerk's office of the police tribunal in order to retract or disavow them.

6. If the said deliberations or summons, posted placards or circular letters, contain any threats against the employers, artisans, workers, or foreign journeymen who shall come to work in the place, or against those who shall content themselves with a lower compensation, all authors, instigators, and signatories of the documents or writings shall be punished by a fine of a thousand livres each and three months in prison.

7. Those who shall use threats or violence against workers who use the liberty granted by the constitutional laws to labor and skill shall be prosecuted in a criminal way and punished according to the severity of the laws as disturbers of the public peace.

8. All mobs composed of artisans, workers, journeymen, day laborers, or those incited by them against the free exercise of skill and labor, appertaining to every sort of person and under every kind of condition, arranged by mutual agreement, or against the action of the police and the execution of the judgments rendered in this matter, as well as against public sales and auctions of various sorts, shall be deemed

seditious mobs and as such shall be dispersed by the depositories of the public force, upon the legal requisition which shall be made upon them, and punished according to all the severity of the laws upon the authors, instigators and leaders of the said mobs, and all those who shall have committed the real acts and deeds of violence.

12. Documents upon the King's Flight.

The flight of Louis XVI to Varennes was one of the most decisive events of the revolution. Historical interest in it lies mainly along two lines. (1) It inspired a widespread distrust of the king which none of his subsequent professions or actions could remove. A careful perusal of. document A, especially if taken in conjunction with No. 10 and the reply of the assembly to the king's manifesto (See Legg's *Select Documents*, II, 62-68) will reveal the reason for this distrust. (2) The absence of the king forced upon the Constituent Assembly the task of devising a temporary government : the régime then established had a large influence in determining the form of government after the deposition of the king in 1792. Documents B to I, selected from a large number of decrees, show the attitude of the assembly during the crisis and exhibit the character of the temporary government.

REFERENCES. Stephens, *French Revolution*, I, Ch. xv ; *Cambridge Modern History*, VIII, 198-201 ; Aulard, *Révolution française*, Part I, Ch. v.

A. The King's Declaration. June 20, 1791. *Procès-verbal de l'Assemblée Nationale*, June 21, 1791, I *suite*, 5-23.

As long as the king could hope to see order and the welfare of the kingdom rise again through the means employed by the National Assembly, and by his residence near that assembly in the capital of the kingdom, no personal sacrifice was too expensive; he would not even have asserted the nullity with which all proceedings since the month of October, 1789, are involved, owing to his complete lack of liberty, if that hope had been fulfilled; but today when the only recompense for so many sacrifices is to see the destruction of the monarchy, all authority held in contempt, property violated, the security of person everywhere placed in danger, crimes remaining unpunished, and a complete anarchy established above the laws, without even the prospect that the authority which the new constitution gives him will be sufficient to repair even one of the evils which afflict the kingdom; the king, after having solemnly protested against all the acts emanating from him during his captivity, believes that he ought to put before the eyes of the French and all the world a picture of his conduct and that of the government which is established in the kingdom.

. . . [In the omitted passage the king reviews the events of July and October, 1789, and complains of the condition of the Tuileries and of the replacement of his old body guard by a detachment of the Parisian national guards, declaring that he was thereby virtually made a prisoner.]

But the more the king made sacrifices for the welfare of his people, the more the factious labored to depreciate the value thereof, and to represent the monarchy under the most false and odious colors.

The calling of the States-General, the doubling of the deputies of Third Estate, the efforts which the king made to clear up the difficulties which might delay the meeting of the States-General, and those which arose after its opening, all the retrenchments which the king made in his personal expenditure, all the sacrifices which he made for his people in the session of June 23, finally the union of the orders, brought about by the expression of the king's desire, a measure which His Majesty then judged indispensable for the inauguration of the States-General: all his anxiety, all his efforts, all his generosity, all his devotion to his people, all have been disparaged, all have been misconstrued.

The time when the States-General, assuming the name of the National Assembly, began to busy itself with the constitution of the kingdom, calls to mind the memoirs which the factious were cunning enough to cause to be sent from several provinces and the movements of Paris to cause the deputies to disregard one of the principal clauses contained in all their *cahiers,* which provided that *the making of the laws should be done in concert with the king.* In defiance of that clause, the assembly put the king entirely outside the constitution, in refusing to him the right to grant or to withhold his sanction to the articles which it regarded as constitutional, while reserving to itself the right to reckon in that class those which it thought belonged there, and by restraining for those regarded as purely legislative the royal prerogative to a right of suspension until the third legislature; a purely illusory right, as so many examples prove only too fully.

What remains to the king, beyond the vain similitude of royal power? . . .

Let the different parts of the government be examined in turn.

Justice. The king has no share in the making of the laws; he has only the right to put a stop to those whose purpose is not regarded as constitutional until the third legislature, and that of praying the National Assembly to busy itself with such and such matters, without having the right to make a formal proposition thereon. Justice is rendered in the name of the king, . . . but it is only a matter of form, . . . One of the latest decrees of the assembly has deprived the king of one of the fairest prerogatives everywhere attached to royal power, that of pardoning and commuting penalties. . . . How much, moreover, that diminishes the royal majesty in the eyes of the people so long accustomed to have recourse to the king in their needs and in their difficulties, and to see in him the common father who can relieve their afflictions!

Internal administration. It is entirely in the hands of the departments, districts, and municipalities, too many authorities, who clog the movement of the machine and often thwart each other. All these bodies are elected by the people, and have no relations with the government, according to the decrees, except for their execution and for those special orders which are issued in consequence thereof. . . .

Finances. The king had declared, even before the meeting of the States-General, that he recognized in the assemblies of the nation the right to grant subsidies, and that he no longer desired to tax the people without their consent. All the *cahiers* of the deputies to the States-General were agreed in placing the re-establishment of the finances in the first rank among the matters with which that assembly must busy itself; some imposed restrictions in favor of articles to be previously acted upon. The king removed the difficulties which these restrictions might have occasioned by going forward himself and granting, in the session of June 23, everything which had been desired. . . .

This form of government, so vicious in itself, becomes still more so for these reasons. 1st. The assembly, by means of its committees, constantly exceeds the limits which it prescribes for itself; it busies itself with matters which deal only

with the internal administration of the kingdom, and with that
of justice, and thus gathers up all authority; it also exercises, through its investigating committee, a veritable despotism, more barbarous and insufferable than any of those of
which history has ever made mention. 2d. There are established in almost all of the cities, and even in many towns
and villages, associations known under the name of Friends
of the Constitution: contrary to the tenor of the decrees,
they do not suffer any others to exist which are not affiliated
with them; thus they form an immense corporation, more
dangerous than any of those which formerly existed. Without being authorised thereto, but even in defiance of the decrees, they deliberate upon all questions of government, correspond among themselves upon all matters, make and receive complaints, post decrees, and have acquired such a preponderance that all the administrative and judicial bodies,
not even excepting the National Assembly itself, almost always obey their orders.

The king does not think that it would be possible to govern a kingdom of so great extent and importance as France
through the means established by the National Assembly, as
they exist at present. His Majesty, in granting to all the decrees without distinction the sanction, which he well knew
could not be refused, was induced thereto by the desire to
avoid all discussion, which experience had shown to be at
least useless; he feared, moreover, that it would be thought
he desired to retard or to bring about the failure of the labors of the National Assembly, to whose success the nation
attached so great an interest; he put his confidence in the
wise men of that assembly. . . .

But the nearer we see the assembly approach the end of
its labors, the more we see the wise men lose their credit,
the more we see increased measures which make difficult or
even impossible the carrying on of the government and create
for it lack of confidence and disfavor; other regulations, instead of applying balm to the wounds which still bleed in
many provinces only increase the uneasiness and provoke dis-
content. The spirit of the clubs dominates and invades everything; thousands of calumniating and incendiary newspapers
and pamphlets, which increase daily, are only their echoes
and prepare men to become what they wish them to be. The

National Assembly has never dared to remedy that license, so far removed from true liberty; it has lost its credit, and even the force of which it would have need in order to turn upon its steps and to change that which would seem to it well to correct. We see by the spirit which reigns in the clubs, and the manner in which they make themselves masters of the new primary assemblies, what must be expected from them; and if they allow to become perceptible any inclinations to turn back upon any matter, it is in order to destroy the remainder of the monarchy and establish a metaphysical and philosophic government impossible to put into operation.

Frenchmen, is that what you intended in sending your representatives to the National Assembly? do you desire that the anarchy and despotism of the clubs should replace the monarchical government under which the nation has prospered for fourteen hundred years? do you desire to see your king covered with injuries, and deprived of his liberty, while he is occupied only with the establishment of yours?

Love for their kings is one of the virtues of the French, and His Majesty has received personally too many proofs thereof to be able ever to forget them. The factious know well that as long as this love abides, their work can never achieve success; they know, likewise, that in order to enfeeble that it is necessary, if it be possible, to destroy the respect which has always accompanied it; and that is the source of the outrages which the king has received during the past two years, and of all the evils which he has suffered. His Majesty would not trace here the distressing picture of them, if he did not desire to make known to his faithful subjects the spirit of these factions who rend the bosom of the fatherland, while feigning to wish its regeneration. . . .

In view of all these reasons and the impossibility for the king, from the position in which he is placed, effecting the good and preventing the evil which is perpetrated, is it astonishing that the king has sought to recover his liberty and to put himself and his family in safety?

Frenchmen, and especially Parisians, you inhabitants of a city which the ancestors of His Majesty were pleased to call the good city of Paris, distrust the suggestions and lies of your false friends; return to your king; he will always be your father, your best friend: what pleasure will he not take in forgetting all his personal injuries, and in beholding himself again in the midst of you, when a constitution, which he shall have freely accepted, shall cause your religion to be respected, the government to be established upon a firm footing and made useful by its operation, the property and status of each person no longer disturbed, the laws no longer violated with impunity, and, finally, liberty founded upon firm and immovable foundations.

Signed,   LOUIS.

Paris, June 20 1791.

The king forbids his ministers signing any order in his name, until they receive further orders; he commands the keeper of the seal of the state to send it to him, as soon as may be required on his part.

Signed,   LOUIS.

Paris, June 20, 1791.

B. Decree for the Arrest of the King. June 21, 1791. Duvergier, *Lois,* III, 53.

The National Assembly orders that the minister of the interior shall immediately send couriers into all the departments, with orders to all the public functionaries and the national guards or troops of the line of the kingdom, to arrest or cause the arrest of all persons whomsoever leaving the realm, as well as to prevent all removal of goods, arms, munitions of war, and every species of gold, silver, horses, vehicles and munitions of war; and, in case the said couriers should encounter any persons of the royal family and those who may have assisted in their removal, the said public functionaries or national guards and troops of the line shall be required to take all the necessary measures to stop the said removal, to prevent them from continuing their route, and to render account of everything to the legislative body.

C. Decree for the Maintenance of Public Order. June 21, 1791. Duvergier, *Lois,* III, 52.

The National Assembly declares to the citizens of Paris and to all the inhabitants of the kingdom, that the same firmness which it has exhibited in the midst of all the difficulties that have attended its labors will control its deliberations upon the occasion of carrying away the king and the royal family. It notifies all citizens that the maintenance of the constitution and the safety of the empire have never more imperatively demanded good order and public tranquility; that the National Assembly has taken the most energetic measures to follow the traces of those who have made themselves guilty of carrying away the king and the royal family; that, without interrupting its sittings, it will employ every means in order that the public interest may not suffer from that event; that all citizens ought to rely entirely upon it for the arrangements which the safety of the kingdom may demand; and that everything which may excite trouble, alarm individuals, or menace property, would be all the more culpable since thereby liberty and the constitution might be compromised.

It orders that the citizens of Paris hold themselves in readiness to act for the maintenance of public order and the defence of the fatherland, in accordance with the orders which will be given them in conformity with the decrees of the National Assembly.

It orders the department administrators and the municipal officers to cause the present decree to be promulgated immediately and to look with care to the public tranquility.

D. Decree for Giving Effect to the Measures of the Assembly. June 21, 1791. Duvergier, *Lois*, III, 53.

The National Assembly decrees as follows:

1. The decrees of the National Assembly already rendered which may not have been sanctioned or accepted by the king, as well as the decrees to be rendered which cannot be sanctioned or accepted, by reason of the absence of the king, shall nevertheless bear the name and have within the entire extent of the kingdom the force of laws, and the customary formula shall continue to be employed for them.

2. The minister of justice is commanded to affix the seal of the state, without any need of the sanction or the acceptance of the king, and to sign the drafts of the decrees which must be deposited in the national archives and in those of the chancellery, as well as the copies of the laws which must be sent to the tribunals and administrative bodies.

3. The ministers are authorised to meet in order to for-

mulate and sign collectively proclamations and other acts of
the same nature.

E. Decree in regard to Foreign Affairs. June 21, 1791.
Duvergier, *Lois,* III, 52.

The National Assembly, the king absent, orders that the
minister of foreign affairs shall make known to the ambassadors and ministers of foreign powers residing at present in
Paris, as well as the ambassadors of France in foreign states
and kingdoms, the desire of the French nation to continue
with the said states and kingdoms the relation of friendship
and good understanding which has existed up to the present
and shall inform the said ambassadors and residents for the
powers, that they ought to remit to M. Montmorin the official notes with which they are charged on the part of the
respective princes and states.

F. Decree for calling out the National Guards. June 21,
1791. Duvergier, *Lois,* III, 52-53.

1. The national guards of the kingdom shall be called
into service, according to the arrangements set forth in the following articles.

2-3. [Provided for calling out two to three thousand or
more from each department.]

4. In consequence, all citizens and sons of citizens in condition to bear arms, and those who wish to take them for the
defence of the state and the maintenance of the constitution,
shall cause themselves to be enrolled immediately after the
publication of the present decree, each in his municipality,
which shall send at once the list of the enrolled to the commissioners whom the directory of the department shall appoint, either from among the members of the general council
or the other citizens, in order to proceed to the formation.

.   .   .   .

G. Decree upon the Oath of Allegiance. June 22, 1791.
Duvergier, *Lois,* III, 55.

The National Assembly decrees as follows:

1. That the oath ordered on June 11 and 13, the present month, shall be taken in the following form:

"I swear to employ the arms placed in my hands for the defence of the fatherland and to maintain against all its enemies within and without the constitution decreed by the National Assembly; to perish rather than to suffer the invasion of French territory by foreign troops, and to obey only the orders which shall be given in consequence of the decrees of the National Assembly."

2. That commissioners, taken from within the body of the assembly, shall be sent into the frontier departments in order to receive there the above-mentioned oath, a record of which shall be drawn up, and to concert there with the administrative bodies and the commanders of the troops the measures which they think suitable for the maintenance of public order and the security of the state, and to make for that purpose all the necessary requisitions.

.   .   .   .

H. Decree upon the Commissioners from the Assembly. June 24, 1791. Duvergier, *Lois*, III, 63.

The National Assembly decrees as follows:

1. The civil commissioners whom it has sent into the frontier provinces, if circumstances demand it, shall make all necessary requisitions to the administrative and municipal bodies for the purpose of procuring for the generals of the army the national guards of whom they may have need for co-operation with the military service.

.   .   .   .

I. Decree concerning the King. June 24, 1791. Duvergier, *Lois*, III, 64.

1. As soon as the king shall have arrived at the chateau of the Tuileries he shall temporarily be given a guard, which, under the orders of the commanding general of the Parisian national guard, shall look after his security and shall be responsible for his person.

.   .   .   .

5. Until it shall have been otherwise ordered, the decree rendered on the 21st of this month, which ordered the min-

ister of justice to affix the seal of the state to the decrees of the National Assembly, without needing the sanction or the acceptance of the king, shall continue to be carried out in all of its provisions.

6. The ministers, the director of the public treasury, until the entrance into office of the commissioners of the national treasury, the commissioner of the king for the extraordinary and liquidation fund, are likewise authorised provisionally to continue to perform each in his own department and under his responsibility, the functions of the executive power.

J. The Protest of the Right. June 29, 1791. Buchez and Roux, *Histoire parlementaire*, X, 433-437.

.   .   .   .

The decrees of the National Assembly have united in it the whole royal power: the seal of the state has been deposited upon its table; its decrees are rendered executory without having need of sanction; it gives direct orders to all the agents of the executive power; it causes to be taken in its name oaths in which Frenchmen do not even find the name of their king; commissioners who have received their commission from it alone travel over the provinces in order to receive the oaths which it requires and to give orders to the army; thus at the moment in which the inviolability of the sacred person of the monarch has been annihilated, the monarchy has been destroyed and even the semblance of royalty no longer exists: a republican interim is substituted for it.

.   .   .   .   .   .

K. Decree concerning the King. July 16, 1791. Duvergier, *Lois*, III, 111-112.

1. If the king, after having taken his oath to the constitution, retracts it, he shall be considered to have abdicated.

2. If the king puts himself at the head of an army in order to direct its forces against the nation, or, if he orders his generals to carry into effect such a project, or finally, if he does not by a formal act put himself in opposition to any action of that sort which may be conducted in his name, he shall be considered to have abdicated.

3. A king who shall have abdicated, or who shall be considered to have done so, shall become a simple citizen and he shall be accusable, according to the customary forms, for all offences subsequent to his abdication.

4. The effect of the decree of the 24th of last month, which suspends the exercise of the royal functions and the functions of the executive power in the hands of the king, shall continue only until the moment when, the constitution being completed, the entire constitutional act shall have been presented to the king.

.   .   .   .

13. The Padua Circular.

July 5 or 6, 1791. Vivenot, *Kaiserpolitik Oesterreichs*, I, 185-186.

This circular letter to the principal sovereigns of Europe was sent by the Emperor, Leopold II, as soon as he learned of the failure of the king's flight. It was only the amplification of ideas which he had already broached in less formal communications. In France there was suspicion that efforts were being made to form such a concert as the circular suggests, but this document was kept a profound secret. None of the powers responded favorably, except Prussia.

REFERENCES. Clapham, *Causes of the War of 1792*, 48-57; Sorel, *L'Europe et la révolution française*, II, 228-230.

I am persuaded that Your Majesty will have learned of the unprecedented outrage of the arrest of the King of France, of my sister the queen, and of the royal family, with as much surprise and indignation as I have, and that your sentiments cannot differ from mine upon an event which, causing fear of the most horrible results yet to come and implanting the seal of illegality upon the excesses which have previously taken place in France, compromises directly the honor of all the sovereigns and the safety of all the governments.

Determined to carry into effect what I owe to these considerations, and as head of the Germanic body by its selection, and as sovereign of the Austrian states, I propose to the kings of Spain, England, Prussia, Naples, and Sardinia, as well as to the Empress of Russia, to determine to unite among themselves and with me for counsel, co-operation and meas-

ures, in order to restore the liberty and honor of the Most
Christian King and of his family and to put limits to the dangerous extremities of the French revolution.

The most pressing [measure] seems to be that we should
all unite in order to cause to be delivered by our ministers in
France a common declaration, or similar and simultaneous
declarations, which may cause the leaders of the violent party
to come to themselves and may prevent desperate resolutions,
still leaving open to them ways for an honest repentance and
the pacific establishment of a state of things in France which
preserves at least the dignity of the crown and the essential
considerations of the general tranquility, and I propose for
that purpose to Your Majesty the draft which you will find
annexed and which appears to me to accomplish these aims.

But as the success of such a declaration may be problem-
atical, and as one can promise complete success only on condition of being ready to sustain it by sufficiently respectable
means, my minister to Your Majesty will receive immediately
the necessary instructions to enter with your minister upon
such concert of vigorous measures as the circumstances may
demand, reserving to myself to cause him to communicate
also the replies which I shall receive from the other powers,
as soon as they shall have reached me.

I regard as an infinitely precious advantage that the dispositions which they all manifest for the re-establishment of
repose and harmony promise to remove the obstacles which
might be injurious to a unanimity of views and sentiments
about an occurrence which involves closely the well being of
all Europe.

Signed,   LEOPOLD.

Project of the Common Declaration.

Padua, July 5 or 6, 1791.

The undersigned are charged to make known what follows
on the part of their respective sovereigns:

That, notwithstanding the notorious deeds of constraint
and violence which have preceded and followed the acts of
consent granted by the King of France to the decrees of the
National Assembly, they had nevertheless still wished to suspend their opinion upon the degree to which that consent
represented or did not represent the conviction and free will

of His Most Christian Majesty; but the effort undertaken by that prince to set himself at liberty, being a most manifest proof of the state of confinement in which he formerly found himself, no longer left any doubt that he had been made to do violence to his religion in several respects, at the same time that the last attack in his actual arrest and that of the queen, the dauphin and Madame Elizabeth, inspires just alarms about the ultimate projects of the dominant party;

That the said sovereigns cannot delay any longer to manifest the sentiments and resolutions which in this state of things the honor of their crowns, the ties of blood, and the maintenance of the public order and tranquility of Europe require of them: they have ordered their undersigned ministers to declare:

That they ask that this prince and his family may be immediately put at liberty and they claim for all these royal persons the inviolability and respect which the law of nature and men imposes upon subjects toward their princes;

That they will unite in order to avenge in a striking manner subsequent attacks which may be committed or may be allowed to be committed against the security, the person and honor of the king, queen, and royal family;

That, finally, they will recognize as law and constitution legally established in France only those which they shall find provided with the voluntary consent of the king, in enjoyment of a perfect liberty; but that in the contrary case, they will employ in concert all the means placed in their power to cause to cease the scandal of a usurpation of power which bears the character of an open revolt, and of which it is important for all governments to check the disastrous example.

14. The Declaration of Pilnitz.

August 27, 1791. Vivenot, *Kaiserpolitik Oesterreichs,* I, 234. Translation, James Harvey Robinson, *University of Pennsylvania Translations and Reprints.*

This document was a direct result of No. 13. It seems certain that the signatories, the sovereigns of Austria and Prussia, attached but little importance to it. For them the qualifying words were the emphatic ones. This, however, was not thoroughly understood in France, and a little later the declaration was an important factor in persuading the French people that they must fight Europe in order to prevent interference with the course of the revolution in France.

REFERENCES. Clapham, *Causes of the War of 1792*, 76-82; Lecky, *England in the Eighteenth Century*, V, 556-558 (*French Revolution*, 326-328, 569); Von Sybel, *French Revolution*, 361-368; *Cambridge Modern History*, VIII, 398-399; Sorel, *L'Europe et la révolution française*, II, 252-264.

His Majesty, the Emperor, and his Majesty, the King of Prussia, having given attention to the wishes and representations of *Monsieur* (the brother of the King of France), and of M. le Comte d'Artois, jointly declare that they regard the present situation of His Majesty the King of France, as a matter of common interest to all the sovereigns of Europe. They trust that this interest will not fail to be recognized by the powers, whose aid is solicited, and that in consequence they will not refuse to employ, in conjunction with their said majesties, the most efficient means in proportion to their resources to place the King of France in a position to establish, with the most absolute freedom, the foundations of a monarchical form of government, which shall at once be in harmony with the rights of sovereigns and promote the welfare of the French nation. In that case [*Alors et dans ce cas*] their said majesties the Emperor and the King of Prussia are resolved to act promptly and in common accord with the forces necessary to obtain the desired common end.

In the meantime they will give such orders to their troops as are necessary in order that these may be in a position to be called into active service.

LEOPOLD. FREDERICK WILLIAM.

Pilnitz, August 27, 1791.

15. Constitution of 1791.

September 3, 1791. Duvergier, *Lois*, III, 239-255.

This constitution represents a large part of the labors of the Constituent Assembly. Many of its provisions had already been put into operation by separate decrees. It was given its final shape during the ten weeks following the return of the king to Paris and shows many traces of the conservative reaction of that period. A careful study of it will throw light upon many features of the revolution.

REFERENCES. Lavisse and Rambaud, *Histoire générale*, VIII, 73-79; *Cambridge Modern History* VIII, 176-183, 186-189, 200-210. Of contemporary estimates the most famous are Burke's *Reflections on the Revolution in France* (a strongly adverse view), and Mackintosh's reply, *Vindiciae Gallicae*, or *Defence of the French Revolution*.

Declaration of the Rights of Man and Citizen.

The representatives of the French people, organized in National Assembly, considering that ignorance, forgetfulness or contempt of the rights of man, are the sole causes of the public miseries and of the corruption of governments, have resolved to set forth in a solemn declaration the natural, inalienable, and sacred rights of man, in order that this declaration, being ever present to all the members of the social body, may unceasingly remind them of their rights and their duties; in order that the acts of the legislative power and those of the executive power may be each moment compared with the aim of every political institution and thereby may be more respected; and in order that the demands of the citizens, grounded henceforth upon simple and incontestable principles, may always take the direction of maintaining the constitution and the welfare of all.

In consequence, the National Assembly recognizes and declares, in the presence and under the auspices of the Supreme Being, the following rights of man and citizen.

1. Men are born and remain free and equal in rights. Social distinctions can be based only upon public utility.

2. The aim of every political association is the preservation of the natural and imprescriptible rights of man. These rights are liberty, property, security, and resistance to oppression.

3. The source of all sovereignty is essentially in the nation; no body, no individual can exercise authority that does not proceed from it in plain terms.

4. Liberty consists in the power to do anything that does not injure others; accordingly, the exercise of the natural rights of each man has no limits except those that secure to the other members of society the enjoyment of these same rights. These limits can be determined only by law.

5. The law has the right to forbid only such actions as are injurious to society. Nothing can be forbidden that is not interdicted by the law, and no one can be constrained to do that which it does not order.

6. Law is the expression of the general will. All citizens have the right to take part personally, or by their representatives, in its formation. It must be the same for all,

whether it protects or punishes. All citizens being equal in its eyes, are equally eligible to all public dignities, places, and employments, according to their capacities, and without other distinction than that of their virtues and their talents.

7. No man can be accused, arrested, or detained, except in the cases determined by the law and according to the forms that it has prescribed. Those who procure, expedite, execute, or cause to be executed arbitrary orders ought to be punished: but every citizen summoned or seized in virtue of the law ought to render instant obedience; he makes himself guilty by resistance.

8. The law ought to establish only penalties that are strictly and obviously necessary, and no one can be punished except in virtue of a law established and promulgated prior to the offence and legally applied.

9. Every man being presumed innocent until he has been pronounced guilty, if it is thought indispensable to arrest him, all severity that may not be necessary to secure his person ought to be strictly suppressed by law.

10. No one should be disturbed on account of his opinions, even religious, provided their manifestation does not derange the public order established by law.

11. The free communication of ideas and opinions is one of the most precious of the rights of man; every citizen then can freely speak, write, and print, subject to responsibility for the abuse of this freedom in the cases determined by law.

12. The guarantee of the rights of man and citizen requires a public force; this force then is instituted for the advantage of all and not for the personal benefit of those to whom it is entrusted.

13. For the maintenance of the public force and for the expenses of administration a general tax is indispensable; it ought to be equally apportioned among all the citizens according to their means.

14. All the citizens have the right to ascertain, by themselves or by their representatives. the necessity of the public tax. to consent to it freely, to follow the employment of it, and to determine the quota, the assessment, the collection, and the duration of it.

15. Society has the right to call for an account of his administration from every public agent.

16. Any society in which the guarantee of the rights is not secured, or the separation of powers not determined, has no constitution at all.

17. Property being a sacred and inviolable right, no one can be deprived of it, unless a legally established public necessity evidently demands it, under the condition of a just and prior indemnity.

French Constitution.

The National Assembly, wishing to establish the French constitution upon the principles which it has just recognized and declared, abolishes irrevocably the institutions that have injured liberty and the equality of rights.

There is no longer nobility, nor peerage, nor hereditary distinctions, nor distinctions of orders, nor feudal régime, nor patrimonial jurisdictions, nor any titles, denominations, or prerogatives derived therefrom, nor any order of chivalry, nor any corporations or decorations which demanded proofs of nobility or that were grounded upon distinctions of birth, nor any superiority other than that of public officials in the exercise of their functions.

There is no longer either sale or inheritance of any public office.

There is no longer for any part of the nation nor for any individual any privilege or exception to the law that is common to all Frenchmen.

There are no longer *jurandes*, nor corporations of professions, arts, and crafts.

The law no longer recognizes religious vows, nor any other obligation which may be contrary to natural rights or to the constitution.

Title I. Fundamental Provisions Recognized by the Constitution.

The constitution guarantees as natural and civil rights:

1. That all the citizens are eligible to offices and employments, without any other distinction than that of virtue and talent;

2. That all the taxes shall be equally apportioned among all the citizens in proportion to their means;

3. That like offences shall be punished by like penalties, without any distinction of persons.

The constitution likewise guarantees as natural and civil rights:

Liberty to every man to move about, to remain, and to depart without liability to arrest or detention, except according to the forms determined by the constitution;

Liberty to every man to speak, to write, to print and publish his ideas without having his writings subjected to any censorship or inspection before their publication, and to follow the religous worship to which he is attached;

Liberty to the citizens to meet peaceably and without arms, in obedience to the police laws;

Liberty to address individually signed petitions to the constituted authorities.

The legislative power cannot make any law that attacks and impedes the exercise of the natural and civil rights contained in the present title and guaranteed by the constitution; but as liberty consists only in the power to do anything that is not injurious to the rights of others or to the public security, the law can establish penalties against acts which, in attacking the public security or the rights of others, may be injurious to society.

The constitution guarantees the inviolability of property or a just and prior indemnity for that of which a legally established public necessity may demand the sacrifice.

Property intended for the expenses of worship and for all services of public utility belongs to the nation and is at all times at its disposal.

The constitution guarantees the alienations that have been or that shall be made under the forms established by law.

The citizens have the right to elect or choose the ministers of their religious sects.

There shall be created and organized a general establishment of *public relief* in order to bring up abandoned children, relieve infirm paupers, and provide work for the able-bodied poor who may not have been able to obtain it for themselves.

There shall be created and organized a *system of public instruction,* common to all citizens, gratuitous as regards the parts of education indispensable for all men, and whose establishments shall be gradually distributed in accordance with the division of the kingdom.

There shall be established national fêtes to preserve the memory of the French revolution, to maintain fraternity among the citizens, and to attach them to the constitution, the fatherland, and the laws.

A code of civil laws common to all the kingdom shall be made.

Title II. Of the Division of the Kingdom and of the Condition of the Citizens.

1. The kingdom is one and indivisible; its territory is divided into eighty-three departments, each department into districts, each district into cantons.

2. French citizens are:

Those who are born in France of a French father;

Those who, born in France of a foreign father, have fixed their residence in the kingdom;

Those who, born in a foreign country of a French father. have become established in France and have taken the civic oath;

Lastly, those who, born in a foreign country and descended in any degree whatsoever from a French man or a French woman expatriated on account of religion, may come to live in France and take the civic oath.

3. Those residing in France, who were born outside of the kingdom from foreign parents. become French citizens after five years of continued domicile in the kingdom, if they have in addition acquired real estate, or married a French woman, or formed an agricultural or commercial establishment, and have taken the civic oath.

4. The legislative power shall be able, for important considerations, to give to a foreigner a certificate of naturalization, without other conditions than the fixing of his domicile in France and the taking of the civic oath.

5. The civic oath is: *I swear to be faithful to the nation, the law, and the king, and to maintain with all my power the constitution of the kingdom decreed by the National Constituent Assembly in the years* 1789, 1790, and 1791.

6. The title to French citizenship is lost:

1st. By naturalization in a foreign country;

2d. By condemnation to the penalties which involve civic degradation, as long as the condemned is not rehabilitated;

3d. By a judgment of contempt of court, as long as the judgment is not annulled;

4th. By affiliation with any foreign order of knighthood, or with any foreign organization which would imply proofs of nobility or distinctions of birth, or which would demand religious vows.

7. The law considers marriage as only a civil contract.

The legislative power shall establish for all inhabitants, without distinction, the manner in which births, marriages, and deaths shall be recorded, and it shall designate the public officers who shall receive and preserve the records therof.

8. French citizens, considered in their local relations arising from their union into cities and into certain districts of rural territory, form *communes*.

The legislative power shall fix the extent of the district of each commune.

9. The citizens who compose each commune have the right to elect at stated times and according to the forms fixed by law those among themselves, who, under the title of *municipal officers*, are charged with carrying on the particular affairs of the commune.

Some functions related to the interests of the state may be delegated to the municipal officers.

10. The regulations which the municipal officers shall be required to follow in the exercise of their municipal functions, as well as those which have been delegated to them for the general interest, shall be fixed by the laws.

Title III. Of the Public Powers.

1. Sovereignty is one, indivisible, inalienable, and imprescriptible: it belongs to the nation: no section of the people nor any individual can attribute to himself the exercise thereof.

2. The nation, from which alone emanates all the powers, can exercise them only by delegation.

The French constitution is representative; the representatives are the legislative body and the king.

3. The legislative power is delegated to one National Assembly, composed of temporary representatives freely elected by the people, in order to be exercised by it with the sanction

of the king in the manner which shall be determined here-inafter.

4. The government is monarchical: the executive power is delegated to the king, in order to be exercised under his authority by ministers and other responsible agents, in the manner which shall be determined hereinafter.

5. The judicial power is delegated to judges elected at stated times by the people.

Chapter I. Of the National Legislative Assembly.

1. The National Assembly, forming the legislative body, is permanent and is composed of only one chamber.

2. It shall be formed every two years by new elections.

Each period of two years shall constitute a legislature.

3. The provisions of the preceding article shall not oper-ate with respect to the next legislative body, whose powers shall cease the last day of April, 1793.

4. The renewal of the legislative body takes place *ipso facto*.

5. The legislative body shall not be dissolved by the king.

Section I. Number of the representatives.—Basis of rep-resentation.

1. The number of representatives in the legislative body is seven hundred and forty-five, by reason of the eighty-three departments of which the kingdom is composed, and apart from those which may be granted to the colonies.

2. The representatives shall be distributed among the eighty-three departments, according to the three proportions of territory, population, and direct tax.

3. Of the seven hundred and forty-five representatives, two hundred and forty-seven are accredited for territory.

Each department shall select three of these, with the ex-ception of the department of Paris which shall select but one.

4. Two hundred and forty-nine are accredited for popula-tion.

The total mass of the population of the kingdom is divided into two hundred and forty-nine parts, and each department selects as many deputies as it has parts of population.

5. Two hundred and forty-nine representatives are ac-credited for the direct tax.

The sum total of the direct tax of the kingdom is likewise

divided into two hundred and forty-nine parts, and each department selects as many deputies as it pays parts of the tax.

Section II. Primary assemblies.—Selection of the electors.

1. In order to form the National Legislative Assembly the active citizens shall meet every two years in primary assemblies in the cities and cantons.

The primary assemblies shall constitute themselves *ipso facto* on the second Sunday of March, if they have not been convoked earlier by the public functionaries designated by the law.

2. In order to be an active citizen it is necessary to be born or to become a Frenchman; to be fully twenty-five years of age; to be domiciled in the city or in the canton for the time fixed by the law;

To pay in some place within the kingdom a direct tax at the least equal to the value of three days of labor, and to present the receipt therefor;

Not to be in a state of domestic service, that is to say, not to be a servant for wages;

To be registered upon the roll of the national guards in the municipality of his domicile;

To have taken the civic oath.

3. Every six years the legislative body shall fix the *minimum* and *maximum* of the value of a day's labor, and the department administrators shall make the local determination thereof for each department.

4. No one may exercise the rights of an active citizen in more than one place, nor cause himself to be represented by another.

5. The following are excluded from the exercise of the rights of active citizenship:

Those who are under indictment;

Those who, after having been declared to be in a state of bankruptcy or insolvency, proven by authentic documents, do not procure a general discharge from their creditors.

6. The primary assemblies shall select electors in proportion to the number of active citizens domiciled in the city or canton.

There shall be one elector selected at the rate of one hundred active citizens, whether present at the assembly or not.

There shall be two selected for one hundred and fifty-one up to two hundred, and so on.

7. No one can be chosen an elector if he does not unite with the conditions necessary to be an active citizen, the following:

In the cities over six thousand souls, that of being proprietor or usufructuary of an estate valued upon the tax rolls at a revenue equal to the local value of two hundred days of labor, or of being the occupant of a habitation valued upon the same rolls at a revenue equal to the value of a hundred and fifty days of labor;

In cities under six thousand souls that of being proprietor or usufructuary of an estate valued upon the tax rolls at a revenue equal to the local value of a hundred and fifty days of labor, or of being the occupant of a habitation valued upon the same rolls at a revenue equal to the value of a hundred days of labor;

And in the country, that of being the proprietor or usufructuary of an estate valued upon the tax rolls at a revenue equal to the local value of one hundred and fifty days of labor, or that of being the farmer or *métayer* of estates valued upon the same rolls at the value of four hundred days of labor.

With respect to those who shall at the same time be proprietors or usufructuaries for one part and occupants, farmers or *métayers* for another, their means by these different titles shall be cumulated up to the amount necessary to establish their eligibility.

Section III. Electoral assemblies.—Selection of representatives.

1. The electors chosen in each department shall assemble in order to elect the number of representatives whose selection shall be assigned to their department and a number of substitutes equal to a third of that of the representatives.

The electoral assemblies shall constitute themselves *ipso facto* on the last Sunday in March, if they have not been convoked earlier by the public functionaries designated by the law.

2. The representatives and the substitutes shall be elected

by majority of the votes, and they shall be chosen only from among the active citizens of the department.

3. All active citizens, whatever their condition, profession, or tax, can be elected representatives of the nation.

4. Nevertheless, the ministers and other agents of the executive power removable at pleasure, the commissioners of the national treasury, the collectors and receivers of the direct taxes, the overseers of the collection and administration of the indirect taxes and national domains, and those who, under any denomination whatsoever, are attached to the military and civil household of the king, shall be obliged to choose [between their offices and that of representative].

The administrators, sub-administrators, municipal officers, and commandants of the national guards shall likewise be required to choose [between their offices and that of representative].

5. The exercise of judicial functions shall be incompatible with that of representative of the nation, for the entire duration of the legislature.

The judges shall be replaced by their substitutes, and the king shall provide by commissionary warrants for the replacing of his commissioners before the tribunals.

6. The members of the legislative body can be re-elected to the following legislature, and they can be elected thereafter only after the interval of one legislature.

7. The representatives selected in the department shall not be the representatives of one particular department, but of the entire nation, and no instructions can be given them.

Section IV. Meeting and government of the primary electoral assemblies.

1. The functions of the primary and electoral assemblies are confined to election; they shall separate immediately after the elections have taken place and they shall not form themselves again unless they shall be convoked, except in the case of the 1st article of section II and of the 1st article of section III above.

2. No active citizen can enter or cast his vote in an assembly, if he is armed.

3. The armed force shall not be introduced into its midst without the express wish of the assembly, unless violence is

committed there; in that case the order of the president shall suffice to summon the public force.

4. Every two years there shall be drawn up in each district lists by cantons of the active citizens, and the list of each canton shall be published and posted there two months before the date of the primary assembly.

The complaints which shall arise, either to contest the qualifications of the citizens placed upon the list or on the part of those .who. shall allege that they are unjustly omitted, shall be brought before the tribunals in order to be passed upon there summarily.

The list shall serve as the rule for the admission of the citizens in the next primary assembly in everything that shall not have been rectified by the judgments rendered before the holding of the assembly.

5. The electoral assemblies have the right to verify the title and the credentials of those who shall present themselves there, and their decisions, shall be carried out provisionally, saving the judgment of the legislative body at the time of the verification of the credentials of the deputies.

6. In no case and under no circumstances shall the king or any of the agents appointed by him assume jurisdiction over questions relative to the regularity of the convocations, the holding of the assemblies, the form of the elections, or the political rights of the citizens, without prejudice to the functions of the commissioners of the king in the cases determined by the law where questions relative to the political rights of citizens must be brought before the tribunals.

Section V. Meeting of the representatives in National Legislative Assembly.

1. The representatives shall meet on the first Monday of the month of May in the place of the sittings of the last legislature.

2. They shall form themselves provisionally in assembly under the presidency of the oldest member in point of age, in order to verify the credentials of the representatives present.

3. As soon as there shall be verified members to the number of three hundred and seventy-three, they shall constitute themselves under the title of *National Legislative Assembly;*

it shall name a president, a vice-president, and secretaries, and shall begin the exercise of its functions.

4. During the entire course of the month of May, if the number of the representatives present is under three hundred and seventy-three, the assembly shall not be able to perform any legislative act.

It can pass an order requiring the absent members to repair to their duties within the period of fifteen days at the latest, upon penalty of 3,000 livres fine, if they do not present an excuse which shall be pronounced legitimate by the assembly.

5. On the last day of May, whatever may be the number of the members present, they shall constitute themselves into National Legislative Assembly.

6. The representatives shall pronounce in unison, in the name of the French people, the oath *to live free or to die.*

They shall afterwards individually take the oath to *maintain with all their power the constitution of the kingdom, decreed by the National Constituent Assembly, in the years 1789, 1790, and 1791; and not to propose nor to consent within the course of the legislature to anything which may injure it, and to be in everything faithful to the nation, the law, and the king.*

7. The representatives of the nation are inviolable; they cannot be questioned, accused, nor tried at any time for what they have said, written, or done in the exercise of their functions as representatives.

8. They can, for criminal acts, be seized in the very act or in virtue of a warrant of arrest; but notice shall be given thereof without delay to the legislative body; and the prosecution can be continued only after the legislative body shall have decided that there is occasion for accusation.

Chapter II. Of the Royalty, the Regency, and the Ministers.

Section I. Of the royalty and the king.

1. Royalty is indivisible and is delegated hereditarily to the ruling family, from male to male, by order of primogeniture, to the perpetual exclusion of females and their descendants.

(Nothing is presumed about the effect of renunciations in the actually ruling family.)

2. The person of the king is inviolable and sacred: his only title is *King of the French*.

3. There is no authority in France superior to that of the law; the king reigns only by it and it is only in the name of the law that he can demand obedience.

4. The king, upon his accession to the throne or as soon as he shall have attained his majority, shall take to the nation, in the presence of the legislative body, the oath *to be faithful to the nation and the law, to employ all the power which is delegated to him to maintain the constitution decreed by the National Constituent Assembly in the years* 1789, 1790, *and* 1791, *and to cause the laws to be executed.*

If the legislative body is not assembled, the king shall cause a proclamation to be published, in which shall be set forth this oath and the promise to reiterate it as soon as the legislative body shall assemble.

5. If, one month after the invitation of the legislative body, the king shall not have taken this oath, or if, after having taken it, he retracts it, he shall be considered to have abdicated the throne.

6. If the king puts himself at the head of an army and directs the forces thereof against the nation, or if he does not by a formal instrument place himself in opposition to any such enterprise which may be conducted in his name, he shall be considered to have abdicated the throne.

7. If the king, having left the kingdom, should not return after the invitation which shall be made to him for that purpose by the legislative body and within the period which shall be fixed by the proclamation, which shall not be less than two months, he shall be considered to have abdicated the throne.

The period shall begin to run from the day when the proclamation of the legislative body shall have been published in the place of its sittings; and the ministers shall be required under their responsibility to perform all the acts of the executive power, whose exercise shall be suspended in the hands of the absent king.

8. After the express or legal abdication, the king shall be in the class of citizens and can be accused and tried like them for acts subsequent to his abdication.

9. The individual estates which the king possesses upon his accession to the throne are irrevocably united to the domain of the nation: he has the disposal of those which he acquires by personal title; if he does not dispose of them they are likewise united at the end of the reign.

10. The nation provides for the splendor of the throne by a civil list, of which the legislative body shall determine the sum at each change of reign for the entire duration of the reign.

11. The king shall appoint an administrator of the civil list, who shall conduct the judicial actions of the king, and against whom all the actions against the king shall be directed and judgments pronounced. The judgments obtained by the creditors of the civil list shall be executable against the administrator personally and upon his own estates.

12. The king shall have, apart from the guard of honor which shall be furnished him by the citizen national guards of the place of his residence, a guard paid out of the funds of the civil list; it shall not exceed the number of twelve hundred infantrymen and six hundred cavalrymen.

The grades and the regulations for promotion in it shall be the same as in the troops of the line; but those who shall compose the guard of the king shall advance for all the grades exclusively among themselves, and they cannot obtain any of those in the army of the line.

The king can choose the men of his guard only from among those who are actually in active service in the troops of the line, or from among the citizens who for a year past have done service as national guards, provided they be residents of the kingdom and have previously taken the civic oath.

The guard of the king cannot be ordered or requisitioned for any other public service.

Section II. Of the regency.

1. The king is a minor until he is fully eighteen years old; and during his minority there is a regent of the kingdom.

2. The regency belongs to the kinsman of the king nearest in degree, according to the order of inheritance to the throne, and fully twenty-five years of age, provided that he be French and native born, that he be not heir presumptive

of another crown, and that he has previously taken the civic oath.

Women are excluded from the regency.

3. If a minor king has no kinsman uniting the qualifications above set forth, the regent of the kingdom shall be elected as provided in the following articles.

4. The legislative body cannot elect the regent.

5. The electors of each district shall meet at the head-town of the district, according to the proclamation which shall be made in the first week of the new reign by the legislative body, if it is assembled; and if it is separated, the minister of justice shall be required to issue this proclamation within the same week.

6. The electors in each district shall appoint, by individual ballot and majority of the votes, an eligible citizen domiciled within the district, to whom they shall give, by the minutes of the election, a special mandate limited to the single function of electing the citizen whom he shall judge, upon his soul and his conscience, the most worthy to be elected regent of the realm.

7. The mandatory citizens appointed by the districts shall be required to meet in the city where the legislative body is to hold its sitting, on the fortieth day at the latest from the accession of the minor king to the throne, and they shall form the electoral assembly which shall proceed to appointment of the regent.

8. The election of the regent shall be made by individual ballot and by majority of the votes.

9. The electoral assembly shall be able to occupy itself only with the election and shall separate as soon as the election shall be concluded; any other act which it may undertake to do is declared unconstitutional and void.

10. The electoral assembly shall cause the minutes of the election to be presented by its president to the legislative body, which, after having verified the regularity of the election, shall cause it to be published in all the kingdom by a proclamation.

11. The regent exercises, until the majority of the king, all the functions of royalty, and he is not personally responsible for acts of his administration.

12. The regent can begin the exercise of his functions only after having taken to the nation, in the presence of the legis-

lative body, the oath *to be faithful to the nation, the law, and
the king; to employ all the power delegated to the king, and
the exercise of which is confided to him during the minority
of the king, to maintain the constitution decreed by the National Constituent Assembly in the years 1789, 1790, and 1791,
and to cause the laws to be executed.*

If the legislative body is not assembled, the regent shall
cause a proclamation to be published in which shall be expressed his oath and the promise to repeat it as soon as the
legislative body shall be assembled.

13. As long as the regent has not entered upon the exercise of his functions, the sanction of the laws remains suspended; the ministers continue to perform under their responsibility all the acts of the executive power.

14. As soon as the regent shall have taken the oath, the
legislative body shall determine his stipend, which cannot be
changed during the continuance of the regency.

15. If, on account of the minority of the kinsman summoned to the regency, it shall have devolved upon a more
remote kinsman, or shall have been bestowed by election, the
regent who shall have entered upon the exercise of it shall
continue his functions until the majority of the king.

16. The regency of the kingdom does not confer any right
over the person of the minor king.

17. The custody of the minor king shall be confided to his
mother; and if he has no mother, or if she has been married
again at the time of the accession of her son to the throne,
or if she marries again during the minority, the custody shall
be bestowed by the legislative body.

Neither the regent and his descendants, nor women, can be
elected to the guardianship of the minor king.

18. In case of notoriously recognized insanity of the king,
legally established and declared by the legislative body after
three deliberations taken successively from month to month,
there shall be occasion for a regency as long as the insanity
lasts.

Section III. Of the family of the king.

1. The heir presumptive shall bear the name of *Prince
Royal.*

He cannot leave the kingdom without a decree of the legislative body and the consent of the king.

If he does leave it, and if, having reached the age of eighteen years, he does not return to France after having been required to do so by a proclamation of the legislative body, he is considered to have abdicated the right of succession to the throne.

2. If the heir presumptive is a minor, the kinsman of full age first summoned to the regency is required to reside within the kingdom.

In case he may have left it and should not return upon the requisition of the legislative body, he shall be considered to have abdicated his right to the regency.

3. The mother of the minor king, having his custody, or the elected guardian, if they leave the kingdom, are deprived of the custody.

If the mother of the minor heir presumptive should leave the realm, she cannot, even after her return, have the custody of her minor son who has become king, except by a decree of the legislative body.

4. A law shall be made to govern the education of the minor king and that of the heir presumptive.

5. The members of the family of the king entitled to the eventual succession to the throne enjoy the rights of active citizenship, but they are not eligible to any of the places, employments, or functions which are at the disposal of the people.

With the exception of the departments of the ministry, they are eligible to the places and employments at the disposal of the king; nevertheless, they shall not command in chief any military or naval forces, nor fulfill the functions of ambassadors, except with the consent of the legislative body, granted upon the proposal of the king.

6. The members of the family of the king entitled to eventual succession to the throne shall add the denomination of *French Prince* to the name which shall have been given them in the civil certificate attesting their birth, and this name cannot be patronymical nor formed from any of the titles abolished by the present constitution.

The denomination of *prince* shall not be given to any other person and it shall not bestow any privileges nor any exception to the rights common to all Frenchmen.

7. The certificates by which shall be attested the births, marriages, and deaths of the French princes shall be presented to the legislative body, which shall order the deposit of them in its archives.

8. No real estate appanage shall be granted to members of the family of the king.

The younger sons of the king shall receive at the age of twenty-one years, or at the time of their marriage, an appanaged income which shall be fixed by the legislative body and shall terminate with the extinction of their masculine posterity.

Section IV. Of the ministers.

1. The choice and dismissal of the ministers shall belong to the king alone.

2. The members of the present National Assembly and of the legislatures following, the members of the tribunal of cassation, and those who shall serve on the high jury, cannot be promoted to the ministry, nor receive any place, gift, pension, stipend, or commission from the executive power or from its agents, during the continuance of their functions, nor for two years after having ceased the exercise of them.

It shall be the same with those who are only enrolled upon the list of the high jury, during the time that their enrollment shall continue.

3. No one can enter upon the exercise of any employment either in the offices of the ministry or in those of the management or administration of the public revenues, nor in general any employment at the nomination of the executive power, without taking the civic oath, or without proving that he has taken it.

4. No order of the king can be executed unless it is signed by him and countersigned by the minister or administrator of the department.

5. The ministers are responsible for all the offences committed by themselves against the national security and the constitution;

For every attack upon property and personal liberty;

For all waste of monies appropriated for the expenses of their departments.

6. In no case can the order of the king, verbal or in writing, shield a minister from his responsibility.

7. The ministers are required to present each year to the legislative body at the opening of the session an estimate of the expenditures to be made in their departments, to render account of the employment of the sums which were appropriated for them, and to indicate the abuses which may have been able to introduce themselves into the different parts of the government.

8. No minister, in office or out of office, can be prosecuted for any acts of his administration, without a decree of the legislative body.

Chapter III. Of the Exercise of the Legislative Power.

Section I. Powers and functions of the National Legislative Assembly.

1. The constitution delegates exclusively to the legislative body the following powers and functions:

1st. To propose and enact the laws; the king can only invite the legislative body to take the matter under consideration;

2d. To fix the public expenditures;

3d. To establish the public taxes, to determine the nature of them, the quota, the duration, and the mode of collection;

4th. To make the apportionment of the direct tax among the departments of the kingdom, to supervise the employment of all the public revenues, and to cause an account of them to be rendered;

5th. To decree the creation or suppression of public offices;

6th. To determine the title, weight, stamp, and denomination of the monies;

7th. To permit or forbid the introduction of foreign troops upon French soil and foreign naval forces in the ports of the kingdom;

8th. To determine annually, after the proposal of the king, the number of men and vessels of which the land and naval forces shall be composed; the pay and the number of persons of each grade; the rules for admission and promotion, the forms of enrollment and discharge, the formation of ship crews; the admission of troops or foreign forces into the service of France, and the treatment of troops in case of disbandment;

9th. To determine upon.the administration and to order the alienation of the national lands;

10th. To institute before the High National Court legal proceedings for securing the responsibility of the ministers and the principal agents of the executive power;

To accuse and to prosecute before the same court those who shall be charged with attacks and conspiracies against the general security of the state or against the constitution;

11th. To establish laws according to which purely personal marks of honor or decorations shall be granted to those who have rendered services to the state;

12th. The legislative body alone has the right to award public honors to the memory of great men.

2. War can be declared only by a decree of the legislative body, rendered upon the formal and indispensable proposal of the king, and sanctioned by him.

In case hostilities are imminent or already begun, or in case of an alliance to sustain or a right to preserve by force of arms, the king shall give notification of it without delay to the legislative body and shall make known the causes thereof. If the legislative body is in recess the king shall convoke it immediately.

If the legislative body decides that war ought not to be made, the king shall take measures immediately to cause the cessation or prevention of all hostilities, the ministers remaining responsible for delays.

If the legislative body finds the hostilities already commenced to be a culpable aggression on the part of the ministers or of any other agent of the executive power, the author of the aggression shall be prosecuted criminally.

During the entire course of the war the legislative body can require the king to negotiate for peace; and the king is required to yield to this requisition.

As soon as the war shall have ceased the legislative body shall fix the period within which the troops raised in excess of the peace footing shall be discharged and the army reduced to its usual condition.

3. The ratification of treaties of peace, alliance, and commerce belongs to the legislative body; and no treaty shall have effect except by this ratification.

4. The legislative body has the right to determine the place of its sittings, to continue them as long as it shall judge necessary, and to adjourn. At the beginning of each reign, if it is not in session, it shall be required to reassemble without delay.

It has the right of police over the place of its sittings, and over the environs which it shall have determined.

It has the right of discipline over its members; but it cannot impose punishment more severe than censure, arrest for eight days, or imprisonment for three days.

It has the right, for its security and for the maintenance of the respect that is due to it, to dispose of the forces, which with its own consent shall be established in the city where it shall hold its sittings.

5. The executive power cannot cause any body of troops of the line to pass or sojourn within thirty thousand toises of the legislative body, except upon its requisition or with its authorisation.

Section II. Holding of the meetings and the form of deliberation.

1. The deliberations of the legislative body shall be public and the minutes of its sittings shall be printed.

2. The legislative body, nevertheless, may at any time form itself into committee of the whole.

Fifty members shall have the right to require it.

During the continuance of the committee of the whole the clerks shall retire, the chair of the president shall be vacant; order shall be maintained by the vice-president.

3. No legislative act shall be deliberated upon or decreed, except in the following form.

4. There shall be three readings of the project for a decree at three intervals, each of which shall not be less than eight days.

5. The discussion shall be open after each reading; nevertheless, after the first or second reading, the legislative body

may declare that there is need for adjournment or that there is no need for consideration of it; but in this last case, the project for a decree can be presented again in the same session.

Every project for a decree shall be printed and distributed before the second reading of it can be given.

6. After the third reading, the president shall be required to put in deliberation and the legislative body shall decide whether it finds itself in condition to render a definitive decree or whether it wishes to postpone the decision to another time in order to receive more ample enlightenment.

7. The legislative body cannot deliberate unless the sitting is composed of at least two hundred members, and no decree shall be passed except by a majority of the votes.

8. No project of law which, submitted to discussion, shall have been rejected after the third reading can be presented again in the same session.

9. The preamble of every definitive decree shall announce expressly: 1st, the dates of the sittings at which the three readings of the project shall have occurred; 2d, the decree by which, after the third reading, it shall have been determined to decide definitively.

10. The king shall refuse his sanction to a decree whose preamble does not attest the observation of the above forms: if any of these decrees be sanctioned, the ministers shall not seal it and promulgate it, and their responsibility in this respect shall last for six years.

11. The decrees recognized and declared urgent by a prior declaration of the legislative body are excepted from the above provisions; but they can be modified or revoked in the course of the same session.

The decree by which the matter shall have been declared urgent shall set forth the motives thereof; and there shall be mention made of this prior decree in the preamble of the definitive decree.

Sction III. Of the royal sanction.

1. The decrees of the legislative body are presented to the king, who can refuse his consent to them.

2. In the case where the king refuses his consent, this refusal is only suspensive.

When the two legislatures following that which shall have presented the decree shall have again presented the same decree in the same terms, the king shall be considered to have given the sanction.

3. The consent of the king is expressed upon each decree by this formula signed by the king: *The king consents and will cause it to be executed.*

The suspensive refusal is expressed by this: *The king will examine.*

4. The king is required to express his consent or his refusal upon each decree within two months from the presentation.

5. No decree to which the king has refused his consent can be presented again by the same legislature.

6. The decrees sanctioned by the king and those which shall have been presented by three consecutive legislatures have the force of law, and bear the name and title of *laws.*

7. The following are executed as laws, without being subject to the sanction: The acts of the legislative body concerning its constitution in deliberative assembly;

Its internal police, and that which it is allowed to exercise in the environs which it shall have determined;

The verification of the credentials of its members in attendance;

Orders to the absent members;

The convocation of the primary assemblies which are late;

The exercise of the constitutional police over the administrators and the municipal officers;

Questions either of eligibility or of the validity of elections.

In like manner, neither the acts relative to the responsibility of the ministers, nor the decrees providing that there is cause for accusation are subject to the sanction.

8. The decrees of the legislative body concerning the establishment, the promulgation, and the collection of the public taxes shall bear the name and the title of *laws.* They shall be promulgated and executed without being subject to the sanction, except for the provisions which establish penalties other than fines and pecuniary constraints.

These decrees cannot be rendered except in accordance with the formalities prescribed by articles 4, 5, 6, 7, 8 and

9 of section II of the present chapter; and the legislative body shall not insert in them any provision foreign to their purpose.

Section IV. Relations of the Legislative Body with the King.

1. When the legislative body is definitely constituted, it sends to the king a deputation in order to inform him thereof. The king can each year open the session and can bring forward the matters which he believes ought to be taken into consideration in the course of that session, without this formality, nevertheless, being considered as necessary for the activity of the legislative body.

2. When the legislative body wishes to adjourn beyond fifteen days, it is required to notify the king thereof by a deputation, at least eight days in advance.

3. At least eight days before the end of each session, the legislative body sends to the king a deputation, in order to announce to him the day whereon it proposes to terminate its sittings. The king can come to close the session.

4. If the king thinks it important for the welfare of the state that the session be continued, or that the adjournment should not occur, or that it should occur only for a shorter time, he can send a message to that effect, upon which the legislative body is required to deliberate.

5. The king shall convoke the legislative body during the intermission of its sessions, whenever the interests of the state appear to him to require it, as well as in the cases which have been provided for and determined by the legislative body before its adjournment.

6. Whenever the king repairs to the place of the sittings of the legislative body, he shall be received and conducted by a deputation; he cannot be accompanied within the interior of the hall except by the prince royal and the ministers.

7. In no case can the president make up part of a deputation.

8. The legislative body shall cease to be a deliberative body as long as the king shall be present.

9. The documents of the correspondence of the king with the legislative body shall always be countersigned by a minister.

10. The ministers of the king shall have entrance into

the National Legislative Assembly; they shall have a designated place there.

They shall be heard, whenever they shall demand it, upon matters relative to their administrations or when they shall be required to give information.

They shall likewise be heard upon matters foreign to their administrations when the National Assembly shall grant them the word.

Chapter IV. Of the Exercise of the Executive Power.

1. The supreme executive power resides exclusively in the hands of the king.

The king is the supreme head of the general administration of the kingdom; the task of looking after the maintenance of public order and tranquility is confided to him.

The king is the supreme head of the army and navy.

The task of looking after the external security of the kingdom and of mantaining its rights and possessions is delegated to the king.

2. The king appoints the ambassadors and other agents of political negotiations.

He confers the command of the armies and fleets, and the grades of marshal and admiral.

He appoints two-thirds of the rear-admirals, half of the lieutenant generals, camp-marshals, ship-captains, and colonels of the national *gendarmerie*.

He appoints two-thirds of the colonels and lieutenant colonels, and a sixth of the ship-lieutenants.

All of these conforming to the laws upon promotion.

He appoints in the civil administration of the navy the managers, comptrollers, treasurers of the arsenals, heads of the works, under-chiefs of civil buildings, and half of the heads of administration and under-chiefs of construction.

He appoints the commissioners before the tribunals.

He appoints the officers-in-chief for the administrations of the indirect taxes and for the administration of the national lands.

He superintends the coining of monies, and appoints the officers charged with the exercise of this surveillance in the general commission and in the mints.

The image of the king is stamped upon all the monies of the kingdom.

3. The king causes to be delivered the letters-patent, warrants, and commissions, to public functionaries or others who ought to receive them.

4. The king causes to be drawn up the list of the pensions and gratuities, in order to be presented to the legislative body at each of its sessions and to be decreed, if there is need thereof.

Section I. Of the promulgation of the laws.

1. The executive power is charged to cause the laws to be sealed with the seal of the state and to cause them to be promulgated.

It is likewise charged to cause to be promulgated and to be executed the acts of the legislative body which do not need the sanction of the king.

2. There shall be made two original copies of each law, both signed by the king, countersigned by the minister of justice, and sealed with the seal of the state.

One shall remain on deposit in the archives of the seal, and the other shall be placed in the archives of the legislative body.

3. The promulgation shall be thus expressed:

"N. (*the name of the king*), by the grace of God, and by the constitutional law of the state, King of the French, to all present and to come, greeting. The National Assembly has decreed, and we wish and order as follows:"

(*A literal copy of the decree shall be inserted without any change.*)

"We command and order to all the administrative bodies and the tribunals that they cause these presents to be recorded in their registers, read, published, and posted in their respective departments and jurisdictions, and executed as law of the kingdom. In testimony whereof we have signed these presents, to which we have caused to be affixed the seal of the state."

4. If the king is a minor, the laws, proclamations, and other documents emanating from the royal authority during the regency shall be expressed as follows:

"N. (*the name of the regent*), regent of the kingdom, in

the name of N. (*the name of the king*), by the grace of God and by the constitutional law of the state, King of the French, etc., etc."

5. The executive power is required to send the laws to the administrative bodies and the tribunals, to cause the transmission to be certified, and to give proof thereof to the legislative body.

6. The executive power cannot make any law, even provisionally, but only proclamations in conformity with the laws to order or call to mind the execution of them.

Section II. Of the internal administration.

1. In each department there is a superior administration, and in each district a subordinate administration.

2. The administrators do not have any representative character.

They are agents elected at stated times by the people to exercise, under the surveillance and authority of the king, the administrative functions.

3. They cannot interfere in the exercise of the legislative power, nor suspend the execution of the laws, nor encroach in any manner upon the judiciary, nor upon the military arrangements or operations.

4. The administrators are essentially charged with the apportionment of the direct taxes and the surveillance of the monies arising from all the public taxes and revenues in their territory.

It belongs to the legislative power to determine the regulations and the mode of their functions, upon the matters above expressed as well as upon all the other parts of the internal administration.

5. The king has the right to annul the acts of the department administrators which are contrary to the laws or to the orders which shall have been addressed to them.

He can suspend them from their functions, in case of persistent disobedience, or if they compromise by their acts the public security or tranquility.

6. The department administrators, likewise, have the right to annul the acts of the district sub-administrators which are contrary to the laws, or to the decisions of the department administrators, or to the orders which these latter shall have

given or transmitted. They can, likewise, suspend them from their functions in case of persistent disobedience, or if these latter compromise by their acts the public security or tranquility, provided that notification thereof be given to the king who can remove or confirm the suspension.

7. When the department administrators shall not have used the power which is delegated to them in the article above, the king can annul directly the acts of the sub-administrators and suspend them in the same cases.

8. Whenever the king shall have pronounced or confirmed the suspension of administrators or sub-administrators, he shall give notice thereof to the legislative body.

This [body] may remove the suspension or confirm it, or even dissolve the guilty administration and, if there is need, send all the administrators or any of them to the criminal tribunals, or bring against them the decree of accusation.

Section III. Of the external relations.

1. The king alone can enter upon political relations abroad, conduct negotiations, make preparations for war proportioned to those of the neighboring states, distribute the forces of the army and the navy as he shall deem suitable and control the direction thereof in case of war.

2. Every declaration of war shall be made in these terms: *On the part of the King of the French, in the name of the nation.*

3. It belongs to the king to conclude and sign with all foreign powers all treaties of peace, alliance, and commerce, and all other conventions which he shall deem necessary for the welfare of the state, subject to the ratification of the legislative body.

Chapter V. Of the Judicial Power.

1. The judicial power cannot in any case be exercised by the legislative body nor by the king.

2. Justice shall be rendered gratuitously by judges elected at stated times by the people and instituted by letters patent of the king, who cannot refuse them.

They cannot be removed except for duly pronounced forfeiture, nor suspended save by an accepted accusation.

The public accuser shall be chosen by the people.

3. The tribunals cannot interfere in the exercise of the legislative power, nor suspend the execution of the laws, nor encroach upon the administrative functions, nor cite before them the administrators on account of their functions.

4. Citizens cannot be deprived of the judges whom the law assigns to them by any commission, nor by other attributions and evocations than those determined by the laws.

5. The right of citizens to terminate definitively their controversies by means of arbitration cannot be impaired by the acts of the legislative power.

6. The ordinary tribunals cannot entertain any civil action unless it should be shown to them that the parties have appeared, or that the plaintiff has cited the adverse party before mediators, in order to obtain a conciliation.

7. There shall be one or several justices of the peace in the cantons and cities; the number thereof shall be determined by the legislative power.

8. It belongs to the legislative power to regulate the number and the districts of the tribunals, and the number of the judges of which each tribunal shall be composed.

9. In criminal matters no citizen can be tried except upon an accusation received by the jurors or decreed by the legislative body, in the cases where the preferring of the accusation belongs to it.

After the accusation has been accepted, the facts shall be recognized and declared by the jurors.

The accused shall have the right to reject up to twenty of these without giving reasons.

The jurors who shall declare the facts shall not be less than twelve in number.

The application of the law shall be made by the judges.

The proceedings shall be public and the assistance of counsel shall not be refused to the accused.

No man acquitted by a legal jury can be taken again or accused on account of the same act.

10. No man can be seized except in order to be brought before the police officer; and no man can be put under arrest or detained, except in virtue of a warrant from police officers, an order of arrest from a tribunal, a decree of accusation of the legislative body, in case the decision belongs to it, or of

a sentence of condemnation to prison or correctional detention.

11. Every man seized and brought before the police officers shall be examined immediately, or at the latest within twenty-four hours.

If the examination shows that there is no ground for incrimination, he shall be set at liberty immediately; or if there is occasion for sending him to jail, he shall be taken there within the briefest possible interval, which in any case shall not exceed three days.

12. No arrested man can be kept in confinement in any case in which the law permits remaining free under bail, if he gives sufficient bail.

13. No man, in a case in which his detention is authorised by law, can be brought to or confined anywhere except in the places legally and publicly designated to serve as jail, court house, or prison.

14. No custodian nor jailer can receive or confine any man, except in virtue of a warrant or order of arrest, decree of accusation or sentence mentioned in article 10 above, and unless the transcript thereof has been made upon his register.

15. Every custodian or jailer is required, without any order being able to dispense therewith, to present the person of the prisoner to the civil officer having the police of the jail, whenever it shall be required by him.

In like manner the presentation of the person of the prisoner cannot be refused to his kinsmen and friends bearing the order of the civil officer, who shall always be required to grant it, unless the custodian or jailer presents an order of the judge, transcribed upon his register, to keep the accused in secret.

16. Any man, whatever may be his place or his employment, other than those to whom the law gives the right of arrest, who shall give, sign, execute or cause to be executed an order or arrest for a citizen, or anyone, who, even in the case of arrest authorised by law, shall conduct, receive, or retain a citizen in a place of detention not publicly and legally designated, and any custodian or jailer who shall contravene the provisions of articles 14 and 15 above, shall be guilty of the crime of arbitrary imprisonment.

17. No man can be questioned or prosecuted on account

of writings which he shall have caused to be printed or published upon any matter whatsoever, unless he has intentionally instigated disobedience to the law, contempt for the constituted authorities, resistance to their acts, or any of the acts declared crimes or offences by the law.

Criticism upon the acts of the constituted authorities is permitted; but wilful calumnies against the probity of the public functionaries and the rectitude of their intentions in the exercise of their functions can be prosecuted by those who are the object of them.

Calumnies and injuries against any persons whatsoever relative to acts of their private life shall be punished upon their prosecutions.

18. No one can be tried either by civil or criminal process for written, printed, or published facts, unless it has been recognized and declared by a jury: 1st, whether there is an offence in the writing denounced; 2d, whether the prosecuted person is guilty.

19. There shall be for all the kingdom a single tribunal of cassation, established near the legislative body. Its functions shall be to pronounce:

Upon petitions in cassation against the judgments rendered in the last resort by the tribunals;

Upon petitions for transfer from one tribunal to another, on account of legitimate suspicion;

Upon orders of judges and the charges of prejudice against an entire tribunal.

20. In matters of cassation the tribunal of cassation shall never be able to take jurisdiction over the facts of suits; but after having quashed the judgment rendered upon a proceeding in which the forms shall have been violated, or which shall contain an express contravention of the law, it shall remand the facts of the trial to the tribunal which ought to have jurisdiction therein.

21. When after two cassations, the judgment of the third tribunal shall be attacked by the same means as the first two, the question shall not be further discussed in the tribunal of cassation without having been submitted to the legislative body, which shall pass a decree declaratory of the law, to which the tribunal of cassation shall be required to conform.

22. Each year the tribunal of cassation shall be required

to send to the bar of the legislative body a deputation of eight of its members, who shall present to it the list of the judgments rendered, along with each of which shall be a condensed account of the suit and the text of the law which shall have determined the decision.

23. A high national court, formed of members of the tribunal of cassation and of high jurors, shall have jurisdiction over the offences of the ministers and principal agents of the executive power, and over crimes which shall assail the general security of the state, when the legislative body shall have rendered a decree of accusation.

It shall not assemble except upon the decree of the legislative body, and only at a distance of at least thirty thousand toises from the place where the legislative body shall hold its sittings.

24. The writs of execution of the tribunals shall be expressed as follows:

"N. (*the name of the king*), by the grace of God and by the constitutional law of the state, King of the French, to all present and to come, greeting. The tribunal of . . . . . has rendered the following judgment:

(*Here shall be copied the judgment, in which mention shall be made of the names of the judges.*)

"We command and order to all bailiffs, upon this requisition, to put the said judgment into execution; to our commissioners before the tribunals, to support them; and to all commandants and officers of the public forces, to lend assistance, when they shall be legally summoned thereto. In testimony of which, the present judgment has been signed by the president of the tribunal and the clerk."

25. The functions of the commissioners of the king before the tribunals shall be to require the observation of the laws in the judgments rendered, and to cause the judgments rendered to be executed.

They shall not be public accusers, but they shall be heard upon all accusations and shall make demand for the regularity of the forms, during the course of the proceedings, and for the application of the law before the sentence.

26. The commissioners of the king before the tribunals shall denounce to the foreman of the jury, either *ex-officio* or

in consequence of the orders which shall be given them by the king:

Attacks upon the personal liberty of the citizens, against the free circulation of provisions and other articles of commerce, and against the collection of the taxes;

Offences by which the execution of the orders given by the king in the exercise of the functions which are delegated to him may be disturbed or interfered with;

Attacks upon international law;

And revolts against the execution of the judgments and of all the executory acts emanating from the constituted authorities.

27. The minister of justice shall denounce to the tribunal of cassation, by means of the commissioner of the king, and without prejudice to the rights of the interested parties, the acts in which the judges may have exceeded the limits of their power.

The tribunal shall annul them; and, if they give occasion for forfeiture, the fact shall be denounced to the legislative body, which shall render the decree of accusation, if there is need, and shall send the accused before the high national court.

Title IV. Of the Public Force

1. The public force is instituted in order to defend the state against enemies from abroad, and to assure within the maintenance of order and the execution of the laws.

2. It is composed of the army and the navy, of the troops especially intended for internal service, and subsidiarily of the active citizens and their children, in condition to bear arms, registered upon the roll of the national guard.

3. The national guards form neither a military body nor an institution within the state; they are the citizens themselves summoned to service in the public force.

4. The citizens shall never take the form nor act as national guards, except in virtue of a requisition or of a legal authorisation.

5. They are subject in this capacity to an organization determined by the law.

They can have but one common discipline and one common uniform in the whole kingdom.

The distinctions of rank and subordination exist only in relation to the service and during its continuance.

6. The officers are elected at stated times and they can be re-elected only after an interval of service as soldiers.

No one shall command the national guard of more than one district.

7. All parts of the public force employed for the security of the state against enemies from abroad shall act under the orders of the king.

8. No corps nor detachment of troops of the line can act in the interior of the kingdom without a legal requisition.

9. No agent of the public force can enter into the house of a citizen, except for the execution of the warrants of police and justice, or in the cases expressly provided for by law.

10. The requisition of the public force within the interior of the realm belongs to the civil officers, according to the regulations determined by the legislative power.

11. If disorders disturb an entire department, the king, under the responsibility of his ministers, shall give the necessary orders for the execution of the laws and for the re-establishment of order, but subject to informing the legislative body thereof, if it is assembled, and of convoking it, if it is in recess.

12. The public force is essentially obedient; no armed body can deliberate.

13. The army and navy and the troops designed for the internal security are subject to special laws, in the matter of military offences, both for the maintenance of discipline and for the form of the trials and the nature of the penalties.

Title V. Of the Public Taxes

1. The public taxes are considered and fixed each year by the legislative body and they shall not remain in force beyond the last day of the following session, unless they have been expressly renewed.

2. Under no pretext shall the funds necessary for the discharge of the national debt and the payment of the civil list be refused or suspended.

The compensation of the ministers of the Catholic worship, pensioned, maintained, elected, or appointed in virtue of the decrees of the National Assembly, makes part of the national debt.

The legislative body shall not in any case charge the nation with the payment of the debts of any person.

3. The detailed accounts of the expenditure of the ministerial departments, signed and certified by the ministers or ordainers-general, shall be made public by being printed at the beginning of the sessions of each legislature.

Likewise there shall be lists of the receipts from the different taxes and of all the public revenues.

The lists of these expenses and receipts shall be distinguished according to their nature, and shall show the sums received and expended year by year in each district.

The-particular expenses of each department relative to the tribunals, the administrative bodies and other establishments, shall likewise be made public.

4. The department administrators and sub-administrators shall not establish any public tax, nor make any apportionment beyond the time and sums fixed by the legislative body, nor consider or permit, without being authorised by it, any local loan at the expense of the citizens of the department.

5. The executive department directs and supervises the collection and disbursement of the taxes and gives all the necessary orders for that purpose.

Title VI. Of the Relation of the French Nation with Foreign Nations

The French nation renounces the undertaking of any war with a view to making conquests, and will never employ its forces against the liberty of any people.

The constitution does not admit the right of *aubaine*.

Foreigners, established in France or not, inherit from their French or foreign kinsmen.

They can contract for, acquire, and receive estates situated in France and dispose of them just as any French citizen by all the methods authorised by the laws.

Foreigners who chance to be in France are subject to the same criminal and police laws as the French citizens, saving the conventions arranged with the foreign powers; their persons, their estates, their business, their religion, are likewise protected by the law.

Title VII. Of the Revision of the Constitutional Decrees

1. The National Constituent Assembly declares that the nation has the imprescriptible right to change its constitution: nevertheless, considering that it is more conformable to the national interests to make use of the right only to reform, by the means provided in the constitution itself, the articles of which experience shall have made the inconveniences felt, decrees that it shall proceed by an assembly of revision in the following form.

2. When three consecutive legislatures shall have expressed a uniform wish for the amendment of some constitutional article, the revision demanded shall take place.

3. The next legislature and the one following shall not propose the alteration of any constitutional article.

4. Of the three legislatures which may one after another propose any changes, the first two shall occupy themselves with that matter only in the last two months of their last session and the third only at the end of its first session or at the beginning of the second.

Their deliberations upon this matter shall be subject to the the same forms as the legislative acts; but the decrees by which they shall have expressed their wish shall not be subject to the sanction of the king.

5. The fourth legislature, augmented by two hundred and forty-nine members elected in each department by doubling the usual number which it furnishes for its population, shall form the assembly of revision.

These two hundred and forty-nine members shall be elected after the selection of the representatives of the legislative body shall have been concluded and there shall be a separate record made of it.

The assembly of revision shall be composed of only one chamber.

6. The members of the third legislature which shall have requested the alteration cannot be elected to the assembly of revision.

7. The members of the assembly of revision, after having

pronounced in unison the oath to *live free or to die,* shall take individually that "to confine themselves to pass upon the matters which shall have been submitted to them by the uniform wish of the three preceding legislatures; to maintain, besides. with all their power the constitution of the kingdom, decreed by the National Constituent Assembly in the years 1789, 1790, and 1791, and in everything to be faithful to the nation, the law, and the king."

8. The assembly of revision shall be required to occupy itself afterwards and without delay with the matters which shall have been submitted to its examination: as soon as its work shall be concluded, the two hundred forty-nine members in augmentation shall retire, without power to take part in any case in legislative acts.

[Miscellaneous Provisions.]

The French colonies and possessions in Asia, Africa, and America, although they form part of the French dominion, are not included in the present constitution.

None of the authorities instituted by the constitution has the right to change it in its entirety or in its parts, saving the alterations which may be made in it by way of revision in conformity with the provisions of title VII above.

The National Constituent Assembly delivers it as a trust to the fidelity of the legislative body, the king, and the judges, to the vigilance of the fathers of families, to the wives and the mothers, to the affection of the young citizens, to the courage of all the French.

The decrees rendered by the National Constituent Assembly which are not included in the constitutional act, shall be executed as laws, and the prior laws which have not been abrogated shall likewise be observed, in so far as the one or the other have not been revoked or modified by the legislative power.

The National Assembly having heard the reading of the above constitutional act, and after having approved it, declares that the constitution is completed and that it cannot be further changed.

There shall be appointed immediately a deputation of sixty members to offer, within the day, the constitutional act to the king.

16. The King's Acceptance of the Constitution.

September 13, 1791. *Moniteur,* September 14, 1791 (*Réimpression,* IX, 655).

This document was read to the Constituent Assembly in explanation of the king's acceptance of No. 15. Three features call for particular notice: (1) the official defence of the king's flight, (2) the interpretation placed upon the revision recently effected in the final draft of the constitution, (3) the attitude of the king towards the general course of the revolution and especially towards the new constitution.

REFERENCE.   Aulard, *Révolution française,* 164-166.

Gentlemen: I have examined attentively the constitutional act which you have presented to me for my acceptance; I accept it and shall cause it to be executed. This declaration might have sufficed at another time; today I owe it to the interests of the nation, I owe it to myself, to make known my reasons.

.   .   .   .

Let everyone recall the moment at which I went away from Paris: the constitution was on the point of completion, nevertheless the authority of the laws seemed to become enfeebled every day. Opinion, far from becoming fixed, was subdividing into a multitude of parties. The most extreme opinions alone seemed to obtain favor, the license of the press was at the highest pitch, no authority was respected. I could no longer recognize the mark of the general will in the laws which I saw everywhere without force and without execution. At that time, I am bound to declare, if you had presented the constitution to me, I should not have believed that the interest of the people (the constant and sole rule of my conduct) would permit me to accept it. I had only one feeling, I formed only one project; I wished to isolate myself from all the parties and to know what was truly the will of the nation.

The considerations which were controlling me no longer remain today; since then the inconveniences and evils of which I was complaining have impressed you as they did me; you have manifested a desire to re-establish order, you have directed your attention to the lack of discipline in the army, you have recognized the necessity of repressing the abuses of the press. The revision of your work has put in the number of the regulative laws several articles which had been presented to me as constitutional. You have established legal forms for the revision of those which you have placed in the constitution. Finally, the opinion of the people is to me no longer doubtful; I have seen it manifested both in their adhesion to your work and their attachment to the maintenance of the monarchical government.

I accept then the constitution. I take the engagement to maintain it within, to defend it against attacks from without, and to cause it to be executed by all the means which it places in my power. I declare that, instructed by the adhesion which the great majority of the people give to the constitution, I renounce the co-operation which I had claimed in that work; and that, being responsible only to the nation, no other, when I renounce it, has the right to complain thereof. I should be lacking in sincerity, however, if I said that I perceived in the means of execution and administration, all the energy which may be necessary in order to give motion to and to preserve unity in all the parts of so vast an empire; but since opinions at present are divided upon these matters, I consent that experience alone remain judge therein. When I shall have loyally caused to operate all the means which have been left to me, no reproach can be aimed at me, and the nation, whose interest alone ought to serve as rule, will explain itself by the means which the constitution has reserved to it.

. . . .

Signed,   LOUIS.

17. The Rejected Decrees.

The Legislative Assembly began its sittings October 1, 1791. Among the many difficult questions confronting it were those of the *émigrés* and the non-juring clergy. These decrees represent the assembly's solution of these problems. Both were rejected by the king. This rejection was a leading factor in producing both the declaration of war against Austria and the overthrow of the monarchy.

REFERENCES. Gardiner, *French Revolution,* 100-102; Stephens, *French Revolution,* II, 31-39 ; *Cambridge Modern History,* VIII. 218-219 ; Lavisse and Rambaud, *Histoire générale,* VIII, 125-126 ; Jaurès, *Histoire socialiste,* II, 842-845, 848-860.

A. Decree upon the *Émigrés.* November 9, 1791. Duvergier, *Lois,* IV, 14-15.

The National Assembly, considering that the tranquility and security of the kingdom require it to take prompt and effective measures against Frenchmen who, despite the amnesty, do not cease to plot abroad against the French constitution, and that it is time finally to repress severely those whom indulgence has not been able to reclaim to the duties and sentiments of free citizens, has declared that there is urgency for the following decree, and the decree of urgency being previously rendered, has decreed as follows:

1. The Frenchmen mustered beyond the frontiers of the kingdom are from this moment declared suspects for conspiracy against the fatherland.

2. If on the 1st of January next they are still in a state of muster, they shall be declared guilty of conspiracy, they shall be prosecuted as such and punished with death.

3. As to the French princes and public functionaries, civil and ecclesiastical, and those who were such at the date of their departure from the kingdom, their absence at the above cited date of the 1st of January, 1792, shall make them guilty of the same crime of conspiracy against the fatherland; they shall be punished with the penalty provided in the preceding article.

.   .   .   .

5. The incomes of the conspirators condemned in contumacy shall be collected during their lifetime for the benefit of the nation, without prejudice to the rights of their wives, children, and lawful creditors.

.   .   .   .

13. Every Frenchman who, outside of the kingdom, shall engage and enroll persons to repair to the musters mentioned in articles 1 and 2 of the present decree shall be punished with death, in conformity with the law of October 6, 1790. The same penalty shall apply to every person who shall commit the same crime in France.

14. The National Assembly charges its diplomatic committee to propose to it the measures which the king shall be requested to take in the name of the nation with respect to the adjacent foreign powers which permit upon their territories the musters of French fugitives.

.   .   .   .

B. Decree upon the Non-Juring Clergy. November 29, 1791. Duvergier, *Lois,* IV, 20-22.

The National Assembly, after having heard the report of the civil commissioners sent into the department of the Vendée, the petitions of a large number of citizens, and the report of the committee of civil and criminal legislation upon the disturbances excited in several departments of the kingdom by the enemies of the public welfare, under pretext of religion;

Considering that the social contract ought to bind, as it ought equally to protect, all the members of the state;

That it is important to define, without ambiguity, the terms of that engagement, in order that a confusion in its words may not effect one in its ideas; that the oath, purely civic, is the surety which every citizen ought to give of his fidelity to the law and of his attachment to society, and that difference of religious opinions cannot be an impediment to the taking of the oath, since the constitution secures to every citizen complete liberty of his opinions in the matter of religion, provided that *their expression does not disturb order,* or involve *acts injurious to the public security;*

That the minister of a religion in refusing to recognize the constitutional act which authorises him to profess his religious opinions, without setting over against him any other obligation than respect for *the order established by the law* and for *the public security,* would announce, by this refusal itself, that it was his intention not to respect them;

That in determining not to recognize the law, he voluntarily renounces the advantages which that law alone can guarantee;

That the National Assembly, eager to devote itself to the great matters which invite attention for the consolidation of credit and the system of finances, with regret sees itself obliged to turn its attention first to the disorders which have a tendency to compromise all parts of the public service, by preventing the prompt assessment and peaceable collection of the taxes;

That in tracing to their origin these disorders it has heard the voice of all the citizens clearly proclaiming the authority of this great truth, that religion is for the enemies of the constitution only a pretext of which they make an ill use, and an instrument of which they venture to avail themselves, in order to disturb the earth in the name of heaven;

That their mysterious offences easily escape ordinary measures, which do not get hold of the clandestine ceremonies in which their plots are enveloped and by which they exercise over consciences an invisible authority;

That it is time finally to pierce these obscurities, in order that the peaceable and well intentioned citizen may be distinguished from the turbulent priest and contriver who mourns for the ancient abuses and does not pardon the revolution for having destroyed them;

That these considerations imperatively demand that the legislative body should take ample political measures to repress the factious who cover their conspiracies with a sacred veil;

That the efficiency of these measures depends in great part upon the patriotism, prudence and firmness of the municipal and administrative bodies and the energy which their impetus can communicate to all the other constituted authorities;

That the department administrations, especially, can under the circumstances render the greatest service to the nation and cover themselves with glory by making haste to respond to the confidence of the National Assembly, which will always be pleased to take notice of their zeal, but which at the same time will punish severely the public functionaries whose lack of zeal in the execution of the law may have the appearance of a tacit connivance with the enemies of the constitution;

That, finally, it is especially to the progress of sane reason and well directed public opinion that it is reserved to achieve the triumph of the law, to open the eyes of the inhabitants of the country districts to the perfidious interest of those who wish to make them believe that the constituent legislators have laid hands upon the religion of their fathers, and to prevent for French honor, in the age of enlightenment, the renewal of the horrible scenes by which superstition has unhappily only too often soiled their history in the ages in which the ignorance of the people was one of the forces of the government;

The National Assembly, having previously decreed urgency, decrees as follows:

1. Within a week, dating from the publication of this decree, all ecclesiastics other than those who have conformed to the decree of November 27 last shall be required to present themselves before the municipality of the place of their domicile, to take there the civic oath in the terms of article 5 of title II of the constitution, and to sign the record, which shall be signed without expense to them.

.   .   .   .

3. Those of the clergymen of the catholic religion who have given the example of submission to the laws and of attachment to their fatherland in taking the civic oath, according to the form prescribed by the decree of November 27, 1790, and who have not retracted it, are dispensed from any new formality; they are to be without exception maintained in all the rights which have been attributed to them by preceding decrees.

4. As to the other ecclesiastics, none of them may henceforth receive, claim, or obtain pension or salary out of the public treasury, except by presenting proof of the taking of the civic oath, in conformity with article 1 above.

.   .   .   .

6. Besides the forfeiture of all salary and pension, the ecclesiastics who shall have refused to take the civic oath, or who shall retract it after having taken it, by this refusal or this retraction shall be reputed suspects of revolt against the law and of bad intention against the fatherland, and as such shall be more especially subjected to and recommended to the surveillance of all the constituted authorities.

7. In consequence, every ecclesiastic having refused to take the civic oath (or who shall retract it after having taken it) who is present in a commune wherein there shall occur disturbances of which religious opinions shall be the cause or pretext may be provisionally removed from the place of his usual domicile, in virtue of an order of the department directory, upon the notification of that of the district, without prejudice to the denunciation to the tribunals, according to the gravity of the circumstances.

8. In case of disobedience to the order of the department directory the offenders shall be prosecuted in the tribunals and

punished by imprisonment in the head-town of the department. The term of this imprisonment shall not exceed one year.

.   .   .   .

18. Letter of Louis XVI to the King of Prussia.

December 3, 1791.   Feuillet De Conches, *Louis XVI, Marie Antoinette, et Madame Elizabeth,* IV, 269-271.

This letter is selected out of many written from the French court in 1791-1792, suggesting or soliciting outside interference in behalf of the authority of the king. At the time, the existence of this correspondence, though strongly suspected, was not positively known.

Paris, December 3, 1791.

Monsieur my Brother, I have learned through M. du Moustier of the interest which Your Majesty had expressed not only for my person, but also for the welfare of my kingdom. The disposition of Your Majesty towards me in giving these proofs in all the cases where that interest might be useful for the welfare of my people, has warmly aroused my sensibility. I lay claim to it with confidence in this moment, wherein, despite the acceptance which I have made of the new constitution, the factions openly exhibit the project of destroying entirely the remnants of the monarchy. I have just addressed myself to the Emperor, the Empress of Russia, the kings of Spain and Sweden, and presented to them the idea of a congress of the principal powers of Europe, supported by an armed force, as the best manner to check the factions here, to give the means to establish a more desirable order of things, and to prevent the evil which afflicts us from being able to take possession of the other states of Europe. I hope that Your Majesty will approve of my ideas and that you will preserve the most absolute secrecy upon the step that I have taken with you. You will easily realize that the circumstances in which I find myself compel the greatest circumspection on my part. That is why only the Baron de Breteuil is informed of my projects, and Your Majesty can communicate to him what you shall wish. I take this occasion to thank Your Majesty for the acts of kindness which you have shown to M. Heyman, and I experience a real delight in giving to Your Majesty the assurances of esteem and affection with which I am,

LOUIS.

19.   Declaration of War against Austria.

April 20, 1792.   Duvergier, *Lois*, IV, 117-118.

The outbreak of the war between France and Austria in 1792 was one of the turning points of the revolution. This document contains a concise statement of one class of the causes which produced the war, i.e., the avowed causes from the French standpoint.

REFERENCES. Gardiner, *French Revolution*, 101-105 ; Mathews, *French Revolution*, 191-193 ; *Cambridge Modern History*, VIII, 219-220, 398-400 : Clapham, *Cause of the War of 1792*, Chs. VI-IX : Lavisse and Rambaud, *Histoire générale*, VIII, 126-128 ; Sorel, *L'Europe et la révolution française*, II, 516-520.

The National Assembly, deliberating upon the formal proposition of the king; considering that the court of Vienna, in contempt of the treaties, has not ceased to grant an open protection to the French rebels; that it has instigated and formed a concert with several powers of Europe against the independence and security of the French nation;

That Francis I, King of Hungary and Bohemia, has, by his notes of March 18 and April 7 last, refused to renounce this concert;

That, despite the proposition which has been made to him by the note of March 11, 1792, to reduce on both sides to the peace basis the troops upon the frontiers, he has continued and augmented hostile preparations;

That he has formally attacked the sovereignty of the French nation, in declaring his determination to support the pretentions of the German princes to possessions in France, for which the French nation has not ceased to offer indemnities;

That he has sought to divide the French citizens and to arm them against each other, by offering to the malcontents a support in the concert of the powers;

Considering, finally, that the refusal to reply to the last despatches of the King of the French leaves no longer any hope of obtaining, by way of an amicable negotiation, the redress of these different grievances and is equivalent to a declaration of war;

Decrees that there is urgency.

The National Assembly declares that the French nation, faithful to the principles consecrated by its constitution, *not to undertake any war with a view to making conquests, and never to employ its forces against the liberty of any people,* takes arms only to maintain its liberty and its independence;

That the war which it is forced to sustain is not a war of nation against nation, but the just defence of a free people against the unjust aggression of a king.

That the French will never confound their brothers with their real enemies; that they will neglect nothing in order to alleviate the scourge of war, to spare and preserve property, and to cause to return upon those alone, who shall league themselves against its liberties, all the miseries inseparable from war;

That it adopts in advance all foreigners, who, abjuring the cause of its enemies, shall come to range themselves under its banners and to consecrate their efforts to the defence of its liberty; that it will favor also, by all the means which are in its power, their establishment in France.

Deliberating upon the formal proposition of the King, and after having decreed urgency, [the National Assembly] decrees war against the King of Hungary and Bohemia.

20. The Three Revolutionary Decrees.

These three decrees were passed by the Legislative Assembly amid the excitement produced by the unexpected Austrian victories on the French frontier. Inspired by doubt regarding the king's competency and loyalty to the nation, they became important factors in producing the movement which finally resulted in the suspension of Louis XVI on the 10th of August. To document B the king gave a reluctant consent; the other two were rejected.

REFERENCES. Gardiner, *French Revolution*, 111-112; Mathews, *French Revolution*, 193-195; *Cambridge Modern History*, VIII, 227; Aulard, *Révolution française*, 189; Stephens, *French Revolution*, II, 78-82; Jaurès, *Histoire socialiste*, II, 1175-1202.

A. Decree for the Deportation of the Non-Juring Priests. May 27, 1792. Duvergier, *Lois,* IV, 177-178.

The National Assembly, after having heard the report of its committee of twelve, considering that the troubles excited within the kingdom by the non-juring ecclesiastics require that it should apply itself without delay to the means of suppressing them, decrees that there is urgency;

The National Assembly, considering that the efforts to overthrow the constitution, to which the non-juring ecclesiastics are continually devoting themselves, do not permit it to be supposed that these ecclesiastics desire to unite in the social compact, and that it would compromise the public safety to regard for a longer time as members of society the men who evidently are seeking to dissolve it; considering that the laws are without force against these men, who, operating upon the consciences in order to mislead them, nearly always conceal their criminal maneuvers from the attention of those who might be able to cause them to be repressed and punished; after having decreed urgency, decrees as follows:

1. The deportation of the non-juring ecclesiastics shall take place as a measure of public security and of general police, in the case and according to the forms hereinafter set forth.

2. All those are considered as non-juring ecclesiastics, who, being liable for the oath prescribed by the law of December 26, 1790, may not have taken the oath; also those who, not being subject to that law, have not taken the civic oath subsequent to September 3 last, the day whereon the French constitution was declared completed; finally, those who shall have retracted either oath.

3. When twenty active citizens of the same canton shall unite to ask for the deportation of a non-juring ecclesiastic, the department directory shall be required to pronounce the deportation, if the opinion of the district directory is in conformity with the petition.

4. When the opinion of the district directory shall be in conformity with the petition, the department directory shall be required to cause commissioners to ascertain by examination whether the presence of the ecclesiastic or ecclesiastics denounced is injurious to the public tranquility, and upon the opinion of these commissioners, if it is in conformity with the petition, the department directory shall be required to pronounce the deportation.

5. In case a non-juring ecclesiastic may have excited

disturbances by overt acts, the facts may be denounced to the department directory by one or several active citizens, and after the verification of the facts, the deportation shall likewise be pronounced.

. . . .

16. Those of the ecclesiastics against whom deportation shall have been pronounced, who may remain within the kingdom after having declared their retirement, or who may return after their departure, shall be condemned to the penalty of imprisonment for ten years.

. . . .

B. Decree for Disbanding the King's Body Guard. May 29, 1792. Duvergier, *Lois*, IV, 180-181.

The National Assembly, considering that the admission into the existing paid guard of the king of a large number of persons who do not meet the conditions required for that service by the constitutional act; that the spirit of incivism with which that body is generally animated and the conduct of its higher officers excite just alarms and may compromise the personal security of the king and the public tranquility, decrees as follows:

1. The existing paid guard of the king is disbanded, and it shall be renewed without delay in conformity with the laws.

2. Until this renewal of the paid guard of the king, the Parisian guard shall do service about his person, just as and in the same manner as it did before the establishment of the paid guard.

C. Decree for Establishing a Camp of *Fédérés*. June 8, 1792. *Moniteur*, June 9, 1792. (*Réimpression*, XII, 607.)

The National Assembly, deliberating upon the proposal of the minister of war converted into a motion by a member, and after having heard the report of its military committee, considering that it is urgent to convey to the frontiers the troops of the line who are in the capital; considering that it is important to remove every hope of the enemies of the public weal who are devising conspiracies in the interior; consid·

ering that it is advantageous to draw still closer at the time of the 14th of July the ties which unite the national guards of all the other departments with those of Paris, who have served the revolution so well and merited so well of the fatherland by an unlimited devotion and an arduous and constant service, decrees that there is urgency.

The National Assembly, after having decreed urgency, decrees as follows:

1. The armed force already decreed shall be augmented by 20,000 men.

.   .   .   .

3. The 20,000 additional men shall assemble at Paris on the 14th of July next.

.   .   .   .

8. No citizen shall be allowed to enroll himself who has not done personal service in the national guard since July 14, 1790, or since the formation of the national guard of the canton of his commune, or lastly since he has reached the age of 18 years, unless, however, upon leaving the troops of the line with a discharge in regular form he has directly entered the national guard.

He shall be required, besides, upon presenting himself for enrollment, to deliver to the municipality a certificate of civism of the officers, under-officers and national guards of the company in which he served.

.   .   .   .

21. The Petition of the 20th of June.

June 20, 1792. *Moniteur*, June 22, 1792 (*Réimpression*, XII, 717).

This petition was carried to the Legislative Assembly by the great crowd which after presenting it broke into the Tuileries on June 20, 1792. Two features of it deserve attention: (1) what it shows as to the state of mind of the people of Paris, (2) the precise character of its demand in regard to the king. The progress of events may be traced by comparing it with No. 23.

REFERENCES. Gardiner, *French Revolution*, 111-114; Mathews, *French Revolution*, 195-197; Stephens, *French Revolution*, II, 82-97; *Cambridge Modern History*, VIII, 228-230; Jaurès, *Histoire socialiste*, II, 1203-1210.

Legislators, the French people come today to present to you

their fears and their anxieties; it is in your midst that they
set forth their alarms and that they hope to find at last the
remedy for their ills. This day recalls the memorable date of
the 20th of June, the tennis court in which the representatives
of the people met and swore in the face of heaven not to
abandon our cause and to die in defence of it.

Recall, gentlemen, that sacred oath and allow these same
people, afflicted in their turn, to ask you if you will abandon
them. In the name of the nation, which has fixed its eyes
upon this city, we come to assure you that the people are
aroused, that they are equal to the occasion and are ready to
make use of unusual methods in order to avenge the majesty
of the outraged people. These extreme means are justified
by article 2 of the Declaration of the Rights of Man, *resistance to oppression.*

What a misfortune, however, for the free men who have entrusted to you all their powers to see themselves reduced to
the cruel necessity of steeping their hands in the blood of
the conspirators! It is no longer time to conceal it: the plot
is discovered; the hour has arrived. Blood will flow or the
tree of liberty which we are about to plant will blossom in
peace.

Legislators, do not let this language astonish you. We do
not belong to any party; we do not wish to adopt anything
other than what shall be in accord with the constitution. Did
the enemies of the fatherland imagine that the men of the
14th of July are asleep? If they had that appearance, their
awakening is terrible; they have lost none of their energy.
The immortal Declaration of the Rights of Man is too profoundly graven upon their hearts. That precious boon, that
boon of all the nations, will be defended by them and nothing
will be capable of depriving them of it. It is time, gentlemen, to put in execution that article 2 of the Rights of Man.
Follow the example of the Ciceros and Demosthenes and un-
veil in open senate the perfidious machinations of the Cata-
lines. You have men animated by the sacred fire of patriotism: let them speak, and we will act. It is in you that the
public safety now resides. We have always believed that our
union made our strength. Union and general harmony ought
to rule in a still greater degree among you; we have always
believed that when the interests of the state were under dis-

cussion they alone ought to be looked to, and that the legislator ought to have a heart inaccessible to any individual interest. The image of the fatherland being the sole divinity
which it is permissible to adore, could that divinity so dear
to all Frenchmen exist even in its temple, for deserters from
its worship? could it live? Let the friends of arbitrary power
speak! let them make themselves known! The people, the
true sovereign, is there to judge them. Their place is not
here; let the land of liberty be purged of them; let them go
to Coblentz to join the *émigrés*. Near them, their hearts will
expand; there they will distill their venom; they will plot
without regret; there they will conspire against their fatherland which will never tremble.

It was thus that Cicero spoke in the senate of Rome, when
he was pressing the traitor Cataline to go to join the camp of
the traitors to the fatherland. Then cause to be carried into
effect the constitution and the will of the people who sustain
you, and who will perish in order to defend you. Unite, act;
it is time. Yes, it is time, legislators, that the French people
show themselves worthy of the character which they have assumed. They have overthrown prejudices; they intend to remain free and to deliver themselves from the tyrants leagued
against them. You know the tyrants; do not yield before
them, since a simple declaration often overwhelms the will of
despots.

The executive power is not in accord with you. We do not
wish for any other proof of it than the dismissal of the patriotic ministers. Is it thus then that the welfare of a free
people shall depend upon the caprice of a king? but ought
this king to have any other will than that of the law? The
people willed him thus; and their head is indeed worth that
of the crowned despots. That head is the genealogical tree
of the nation; and before that robust oak, the feeble reed
must bend.

We complain, gentlemen, of the inaction of our armies.
We ask that you ascertain the cause of it. If it springs from
the executive power, let it be abolished! The blood of the
patriots ought not to flow to satisfy the arrogance and ambition of the perfidious château of the Tuileries.

Who then can stop us in our march? Shall we behold our
armies perish by parts? The cause being a common one, the

action ought to be general; and if the first defenders of liberty had thus temporised, would you have been sitting today in this august areopagus?

Reflect well herein: nothing can stop you; liberty cannot be suspended. If the executive power does not act, there can be no other alternative; it is that which must cease to be; a single man must not influence the determination of 25 millions of men. If, out of respect, we maintain him in his post, it is on condition that he will fill it constitutionally; if he deviates therefrom he is no longer anything to the French people.

We complain, finally, of the delays of the high national court: you have entrusted to it the sword of the law; why does it wait to lay a heavy hand upon the head of the guilty? Has the civil list here again some influence? Are there privileged criminals whom it may with impunity shelter from the vengeance of the law? Shall the people be forced to go back to the date of the 14th of July, to take up that sword again themselves, to avenge at a single stroke the outraged law, and to punish the guilty and pusillanimous depositories of that same law? No, gentlemen, no; you see our fears and our alarms, and you will dissipate them.

We have set forth in your midst a great anguish; we have opened our long since embittered hearts; we hope that the last cry which we address to you will make itself felt among you. The people are there; they await in silence a response worthy of their sovereignty. Legislators, we ask for the permanence of our arms until the constitution be put into execution.

This petition is not that of the inhabitants of the faubourg Saint-Antoine alone, but of all the sections of the capital and of the environs of Paris. The petitioners of this address ask to have the honor of filing before you.

22. Addresses to the Legislative Assembly.

These addresses are typical of the many sent to the Legislative Assembly from all parts of France between June 20 and August 10, 1792. From them much may be learned about the character of the movement which finally resulted in the suspension of the king. Both the reasons assigned for action against him and the measures demanded should receive attention.

REFERENCE. Aulard. *Révolution française*, 192-205, has a careful study of the entire series of addresses.

A. Address of the Commune of Marseilles, June 27, 1792. *Archives parlementaires,* XLVI, 383-384.

Legislators, the nation entrusts to you the maintenance and defence of its liberty, its independence, and the sovereignty of its rights. The law relative to royalty, which your predecessors established, without any regard for the objections and complaints of the nation, is contrary to the rights of man. It is time that that tyrannical law should be finally abolished, that the nation should make use of all its rights, and that it should govern itself.

Legislators, the principles of the constitution of every free nation, which your predecessors have decreed, which the French have adopted, and which they have sworn to defend, give us the right to these. These are: *"Men are born and remain free and equal in rights.* Social distinctions can be based only upon public utility."

"The aim of every political association is the preservation of the natural and imprescriptible rights of man. These rights are liberty, property, security, and resistance to oppression."

"All citizens are equal in the eyes of the law; all are equally admissible to all the dignities, public places and employments, according to their capacities, and without any other distinction than that of their virtues and their talents."

Such, legislators, are the eternal foundations of all political principles. Anything which is contrary to these principles ought to be rejected from a free constitution. How then could our Constituents, your predecessors, establish upon these foundations that monstrous pretension of a special family to which should be delegated hereditarily the crown, from male to male, by order of primogeniture? How can there be that reigning family in a time in which everything must be regenerated? What has that reigning family done to be preferred to every other? Is it necessary to make a law for the inviolability of one person? Does that inviolability guarantee him against the steel of assassins? Is not the privilege subversive of every principle? Who would recognize there the principles of that sovereign reason which had consecrated the imprescriptible rights of man, in decreeing that there should no longer exist any hereditary distinction? Is this supreme distinction founded upon public utility? Who is the

wise Constituent who can assure and guarantee that the son
or the greatest and most just of kings will be like his father?
that he will not be a traitor, a scoundrel? Would it be necessary, then, in conformity with that pernicious law, that although he should be depraved, he might with impunity bring
wretchedness upon men whom that same law submitted to the
fury of his crimes? No, legislators, it is only the hired abettors of tyranny who have been capable of abandoning themselves to that delirium! and it is in the sanctuary destined
for the triumph of liberty, reason, and justice, that that
usurped pretension has obtained the force of law! What in-
famy! The nation cannot subscribe to it. It once made vain
objections; it desires today that they may be effective. It
has the incontestable right to approve or to reject the laws
which its representatives impose upon it, since it is the only
sovereign.

What has this ruling family done to be elevated to this
post? Was it the ruin of our finances, was it the sceptre of
iron with which it ruled us who had prepared that homage,
while robbing us of our gold and exhausting our substance?
or, indeed, was it the hereditary descendants of that family,
prolific of rebellious *émigrés,* who, charged with debts, accusations and crimes, our Constituents would have wished to
force us to recognize as master? Do not be offended by that
word, legislators, it signifies nothing for us. But such is
the pretension of kings, such is the intention of cowards and
slaves.

.   .   .   .

May not the gold of that enormous civil list, which cannot
be diminished before the date of each change of reign, per-
petuate the means of corruption? and may not these means
ruin the nation before it has the right to abolish them? And
that independent guard which our Constituents have granted
to their king and which the nation pays by keeping up the
civil list, can there be a private force by the terms of the Rights
of Man? And if it is a public force, can it serve the king alone?
And that law, by which the choice and dismissal of the ministers belong to the king alone, is it not, despite their pretended responsibility, an inexhaustible source of abuses, crimes
and disorders, a source of eternal divisions and contradictions?
And, finally, that suspensive *veto,* put in opposition to our

best laws by the authority of a single person and contrary to the general will, does it not radically destroy our constitution? Can the legislative power exist in the presence of that destructive law of the absolute executive power? And can the judicial power, to which the legislative power gives existence and life, continue to be effective, if the executive power paralyzes our laws?

Avow, legislators, that our Constituents have settled nothing at all; and if you wish to be something, if you wish to be useful to the nation, abrogate a law which renders null the national will.

We all know the history of our disasters, it would be useless to recall it. The indignation which it provokes has reached its climax. Let us make haste to destroy the cause and to re-establish ourselves in our rights. Let the executive power be appointed and renewed by the people, as are, with some slight differences, the other two powers, and soon all will be re-established.

Done at Marseilles, at the communal building, June 27, the fourth year of liberty.

B. Address of the *Fédérés* at Paris, July 23, 1792. *Archives parlementaires,* XLVII, 69-70.

Representatives elected by the people to defend and preserve their rights, listen to-day once more to the cry of their grief.

Some weeks have passed since you declared that the fatherland was in danger and you do not indicate to us any means of saving it. Can you still ignore the cause of our evils, or ignore the remedies for them? Well, legislators, we citizens of the 83 departments, we, whom love of liberty alone has brought here, we, who are strong in the deliberate and strongly pronounced opinion of all the French, point out to you that remedy. We say to you that the source of our evils is in the abuse which the head of the executive power has made of his authority; we say to you that it is also in the staffs of the army, in a large portion of the department and district directories and in the tribunals. Let us say to you once more, with the frankness of a free people and one which holds itself ready to defend its rights, that it exists in part in your midst.

Legislators, the peril is imminent, it can no longer be dissimulated, it is necessary that the reign of the truth commence; we are courageous enough to come to tell it to you, be courageous enough to hear it.

Deliberate, during the sitting and without leaving the place, upon the one means to remedy our evils; suspend the executive power as was done last year; thereby you will cut the root of all our evils. We know that the constitution does not speak of deposition; but in order to declare that the king has forfeited the throne it is necessary to try him, and in order to try him it is necessary that the king should be temporarily suspended. Convoke the primary assemblies, in order to put yourselves in a position to learn, in an indirect manner, the desire of the majority of the people for the national convocation upon the so-called constitutional articles relative to the executive power.

Legislators, there is not an hour nor a second to lose, the evil is at its height, avert from your fatherland a universal shock, make use of all the power which is entrusted to you and save it yourselves. Would you fear to call down upon your heads a terrible responsibility, or indeed (what we cannot believe) would you wish to give to the nation a proof of impotency? There would remain to it no more than one resource, that of displaying all its strength and sweeping away its tyrants. We have all, both you and we, sworn a hundred times to live free and to die in defending our rights. Well, we have come to renew that oath which makes despots tremble when it is pronounced by men who know how to feel strongly. We shall either emerge from this conflict free or else the tomb of liberty shall be ours.

C. Address of the Paris Sections. August 3, 1792. *Archives parlementaires,* XLVII, 425-427.

Legislators, it is when the fatherland is in danger that all its children ought to press around it; and never has so great a peril threatened the fatherland. The commune of Paris sends us to you; we come to bring into the sanctuary of the laws the opinion of an immense city. Filled with respect for the representatives of the nation, full of confidence in their courageous patriotism, it has not despaired of the public safety; but it believes that to cure the ills of France it is necessary to attack them in their source and not to lose a moment. It is with grief that it denounces to you, through our agency, the head of the executive power. Without doubt, the people have the right to be indignant with him; but the language of anger does not befit brave men. Compelled by Louis XVI to accuse him before you and before all France, we shall accuse him without bitterness as without pusillanimous deference. It is no longer time to listen to that protracted indulgence which befits generous peoples, but which encourages kings to perjury; and the most respectable passions must be silent when the saving of the state is in question.

We shall not retrace for you the entire conduct of Louis XVI since the first days of the revolution, his sanguinary projects against the city of Paris, his predilection for nobles and priests, the aversion which he exhibited to the body of the people, the National Constituent Assembly outraged by court valets, invested by men of arms, wandering in the midst of a royal city and finding an asylum only in a tennis court. We shall not retrace for you the oaths so many times violated, the protestations renewed incessantly and incessantly contradicted by actions, up to the moment at which a perfidious flight came to open the eyes of the citizens most blinded by the fanaticism of slavery. We shall leave at one side everything which is covered by the pardon of the people; but pardon is not oblivion. It would be in vain, moreover, should we be able to forget these delinquencies; they will soil the pages of history and posterity will remember them.

Meanwhile, legislators, it is our duty to remind you in rapid terms of the favors conferred by the nation upon Louis XVI and of the ingratitude of that prince. How many reasons there were for depriving him of the throne at the moment in which the people reconquered the sovereignty! The memory of an imperious and devouring dynasty, in which scarcely one king is reckoned against twenty tyrants, the hereditary despotism increasing from reign to reign with the misery of the people, the public finances entirely ruined by Louis XVI and his two predecessors, infamous treaties ruining the national honor, the eternal enemies of France becoming its allies and its masters: these are what constituted the rights of Louis XVI to the constitutional sceptre. The nation, faithful to its character, has preferred to be generous rather than prudent; the despot of an enslaved land has become the king of a free people: after having attempted to flee from France, in order to reign at Coblentz, he has been replaced upon the throne, perhaps contrary to th'e wish of the nation which ought to have been consulted.

Favors without number have followed that great favor. We have seen in the last days of the Constituent Assembly the rights of the people enfeebled in order to streng'h'n the royal authority, the first public functionary become an hereditary representative, a military establishment created for the splendor of his throne, and his legal authority supported by a civil list which has no other limits than those which he has wished to prescribe for it.

And we have speedily seen the favors of the nation turned against it. The power delegated to Louis XVI for the maintenance of liberty takes arms in order to overthrow it. Let us cast a glance over the interior of the kingdom. Perverse ministers are removed by the irresistible force of public contempt; they are the ones for whom Louis XVI mourns. Their successors notify the nation and the king of the danger which surrounds the fatherland; they are dismissed by Louis XVI for having shown themselves citizens. The royal inviolability and the perpetual change of the ministry each day elude the responsibility of the agents of the executive power. A conspiring guard is dissolved in appearance; but it still exists: it is still paid by Louis XVI; it sows trouble and promotes civil war. Turbulent priests, abusing their power over timid consciences, arm children against their fathers; and from the land of liberty they send forth new soldiers under the banners of servitude. These enemies *of the people* are protected by the appeal *to the people,* and Louis XVI maintains for them the right to conspire. Coalesced department directories dare to constitute themselves arbiters between the National Assembly and the king. They form a species of dispersed high chamber in the midst of the kingdom; some even usurp the legislative authority; and in consequence of a profound ignorance, while declaiming against the republicans, they seem to wish to organize France into a federative republic. It is in the name of the king that they inflame intestinal divisions; and the king does not disavow with indignation two hundred stupid and guilty administrators repudiated from one end of France to the other by the immense majority of the administrations!

Abroad, armed enemies threaten our territory. Two despots publish against the French nation a manifesto as insolent as absurd. French parricides, led by the brothers, kinsmen and connections of the king, prepare to rend the bosom of their fatherland. Already the enemy upon our frontiers places executioners in opposition to our warriors. And it is to avenge Louis XVI that the national sovereignty is impudently outraged; it is to avenge Louis XVI that the execrable house of Austria adds a new chapter to the history of its cruelties; it is to avenge Louis XVI that the tyrants have renewed the wish of Caligula, and that they would wish to destroy at a single blow all the citizens of France!

The flattering promises of a minister have caused the declaration of war, and we have commenced it with armies incomplete and destitute of everything.

Belgium calls upon us in vain; perverse orders have restrained the ardor of our soldiers; our first steps into those fair countries have been marked by conflagration; and the incendiary is still in the midst of the camp of the French! All the decrees which the National Assembly have rendered for the purpose of re-enforcing our troops are annulled by the refusal of the sanction or by perfidious delays. And the enemy advances with rapid steps, while patricians command the armies of equality, while our generals leave their posts in the face of the enemy, permit the armed force to deliberate, come to present to the legislators their opinions which cannot be legally expressed, and calumniate a free people whom it is their duty to defend.

The head of the executive power is the first link in the counter revolutionary chain. He seems to participate in the conspiracies of Pilnitz, which he has made known so lately. His name contends each day against that of the nation; his name is a signal of discord between the people and their magistrates, between the soldiers and the generals. He has separated his interests from those of the nation. Let us separate them as he has done. Far from putting himself by a formal act in opposition to the enemies within and without.

his conduct is a formal and perpetual act of disobedience to the constitution. As long as we shall have such a king, liberty cannot strengthen itself; and we are determined to remain free. By a stretch of indulgence we might have desired authority to ask you for the suspension of Louis XVI as long as the danger of the fatherland shall continue; but the constitution precludes that. Louis XVI invokes the constitution incessantly; we invoke it in our turn and ask for his deposition.

That great measure once taken, since it is very doubtful whether the nation can have confidence in the present dynasty, we ask that ministers, jointly and severally responsible, selected by the National Assembly, but outside of its own body, according to the constitutional law, selected by the open vote of free men, exercise provisionally the executive power, while waiting for the will of the people, our sovereign and yours, to be legally pronounced in a national convention, as soon as the security of the state may permit it. Meanwhile let our enemies, whoever they may be, all range themselves beyond our frontiers; let dastards and perjurers abandon the soil of liberty; let 300,000 slaves advance; they will find before them 10 millions of free men, as ready for death as for victory, fighting for equality, for the paternal roof, for their wives, their children and their aged ones. Let each of us be soldiers in turn; and if it is necessary to have the honor of dying for the fatherland, before yielding the last breath, let each of us make his memory illustrious by the death of a slave or a tyrant.

23.   The Duke of Brunswick's Manifesto.

July 25, 1792. *Archives parlementaires*, XLVII, 372-373.

This document sealed the fate of the old monarchy. Reaching Paris at the time when the agitation for the suspension of the king had already attained great strength, it gave the final impulse to that movement. Its authorship has been much discussed and it is now clear that the document was substantially the work of *émigrés*.

REFERENCES. Gardiner, *French Revolution*, 114-115; Mathews, *French Revolution*, 198-199; Stephens, *French Revoluton*, II, 105-106; Lavisse and Rambaud, *Histoire générale*, VIII. 139-140; Sorel, *L'Europe et la révolution française*, II, 503-515; Jaurès, *Histoire socialiste*, II, 1269-1274.

Their Majesties, the Emperor and the King of Prussia, having committed to me the command of the united armies which they have caused to assemble on the frontiers of France, I have wished to announce to the inhabitants of this kingdom, the motives which have determined the measures of the two sovereigns and the intentions which guide them.

After having arbitrarily suppressed the rights and possessions of the German princes in Alsace and Lorraine, disturbed and overthrown good order and legitimate government in the interior; exercised against the sacred person of the king and his august family outrages and brutalities which are still carried on and renewed day by day; those who have usurped the reins of the administration have at last completed their work by declaring an unjust war against His Majesty the Emperor and by attacking his provinces situated in the Low Countries. Some of the possessions of the Germanic Empire have been enveloped in this oppression, and several others have only escaped the same danger by yielding to the imperious threats of the dominant party and of its emissaries.

His Majesty the King of Prussia, united with his Imperial Majesty by the bonds of a strict defensive alliance and himself the preponderant member of the Germanic body, could not excuse himself from marching to the help of his ally and his co-state; and it is under this double relationship that he takes up the defence of this monarch and of Germany.

To these great interests is added another aim equally important and very dear to the hearts of the two sovereigns; it is to put an end to the anarchy in the interior of France, to stop the attacks carried on against the throne and the altar, to re-establish the legal power, to restore to the king the security and liberty of which he is deprived, and to put him in a position to exercise the legitimate authority which is his due.

Convinced that the sound part of the French nation abhors the excesses of a faction which dominates it, and that the greatest number of the inhabitants look forward with impatience to the moment of relief to declare themselves openly against the odious enterprises of their oppressors, His

Majesty the Emperor and His Majesty the King of Prussia, call upon them and invite them to return without delay to the ways of reason, justice, order and peace. It is in accordance with these views, that I, the undersigned, the General, commanding in chief the two armies, declare:

1. That, drawn into the present war by irresistible circumstances, the two allied courts propose to themselves no other aim than the welfare of France and have no intention of enriching themselves by conquests;

2. That they do not intend to meddle with the internal government of France, but that they merely wish to deliver the king, the queen and the royal family from their captivity, and to procure for His Most Christian Majesty the necessary security that he may make without danger or hindrance the conventions which he shall judge suitable and may work for the welfare of his subjects, according to his promises and as far as it shall depend upon him;

3. That the combined armies will protect the towns, boroughs and villages and the persons and goods of those who shall submit to the king and who shall co-operate in the immediate re-establishment of order and of the police in the whole of France;

4. That the national guard will be called upon to watch provisionally over the peace of the towns and country districts, the security of the persons and goods of all Frenchmen, until the arrival of the troops of their Imperial and Royal Majesties, or until otherwise ordered, under pain of being personally responsible; that on the contrary, those of the national guard who shall fight against the troops of the two allied courts, and who shall be taken with arms in their hands, will be treated as enemies and punished as rebels to their king and as disturbers of the public peace;

5. That the generals, officers, under officers and troops of the French line are likewise summoned to return to their former fidelity and to submit themselves at once to the king, their legitimate sovereign;

6. That the members of the departments, of the districts and municipalities shall likewise answer with their heads and their goods for all offences, fires, murders, pillaging, and acts of violence, which they shall allow to be committed, or which

they have not manifestly exerted themselves to prevent within their territory; that they shall likewise be required to continue their functions provisionally, until His Most Christian Majesty, being once more at liberty, may have provided for them subsequently or until it shall have been otherwise ordained in his name in the meantime;

7. That the inhabitants of the towns, boroughs and villages who may dare to defend themselves against the troops of their Imperial and Royal Majesties and fire on them either in the open country, or through the windows, doors and openings of their houses, shall be punished immediately according to the strictness of the law of war, and their houses destroyed or burned. On the contrary, all the inhabitants of the said towns, boroughs and villages, who shall submit to their king, opening their doors to the troops of their Majesties, shall at once be placed under their immediate protection; their persons, their property, and their effects shall be under the protection of the laws, and the general security of all and each of them shall be provided for;

8. The city of Paris and all its inhabitants without distinction shall be required to submit at once and without delay to the king, to put that prince in full and perfect liberty, and to assure him as well as the other royal personages the inviolability and respect which the law of nations and men requires of subjects toward their sovereigns; their Imperial and Royal Majesties declare personally responsible with their lives for all events, to be tried by military law and without hope of pardon, all the members of the National Assembly, of the department, district, municipality and national guard of Paris, the justices of the peace and all others that shall be concerned; their said Majesties also declare on their honor and on their word as Emperor and King, that if the château of the Tuileries be entered by force or attacked, if the least violence or outrage be offered to their Majesties, the king, queen and royal family, if their preservation and their liberty be not immediately provided for, they will exact an exemplary and ever-memorable vengeance, by delivering the city of Paris over to a military execution and to complete ruin, and the rebels guilty of these outrages to the punishments they shall have deserved. Their Imperial and

Royal Majesties, on the contrary, promise the inhabitants of Paris to employ their good offices with His Most Christian Majesty to obtain pardon for their misdeeds and errors, and to take the most vigorous measures to assure their lives and property, if they obey promptly and exactly all the above mentioned order.

Finally, their Majesties being able to recognize as laws in France only those which shall emanate from the king, in the enjoyment of a perfect liberty, protest beforehand against the authenticity of any declarations which may be made in the name of His Most Christian Majesty, so long as his sacred person, that of the queen, and those of the royal family shall not be really in security, for the effecting of which their Imperial and Royal Majesties beg His Most Christian Majesty to appoint the city in his kingdom nearest the frontiers, to which he would prefer to retire with the queen and his family under good and sufficient escort, which will be furnished him for this purpose, so that his most Christian Majesty may in all security summon such ministers and councillors as he may see fit, hold such meetings as he deems best, provide for the re-establishment of good order and regulate the administration of his kingdom.

Finally, I declare and bind myself, moreover, in my own private name and in my above capacity, to cause the troops entrusted to my command to observe a good and exact discipline, promising to treat with kindness and moderation all well intentioned subjects who show themselves peaceful and submissive, and only to use force against those who shall make themselves guilty of resistance and ill-will.

It is for these reasons that I call upon and exhort all the inhabitants of the kingdom in the strongest and most urgent manner not to oppose the march and the operations of the troops which I command, but rather to grant them everywhere a free passage and with every good will to aid and assist as circumstances shall require.

Given at the head-quarters at Coblentz, July 25, 1792.

Signed, CHARLES-WILLIAM FERDINAND,
Duke of Brunswick-Lunebourg.

24. Decree for Suspending the King.

August 10, 1792. Duvergier, *Lois*, IV, 290-291.

This decree was passed by the Legislative Assembly after the storming of the Tuileries. Every feature of it is important. The precise action with reference to the king, the character of the provisional arrangements, and the phraseology of the document should receive careful attention.

REFERENCES. Stephens, *French Revolution*, II, 130-131; Aulard, *Révolution française*, 215-220.

The National Assembly, considering that the dangers of the fatherland have reached their height;

That it is for the legislative body the most sacred of duties to employ all means to save it;

That it is impossible to find efficacious ones, unless they shall ocupy themselves with removing the source of its evils;

Considering that these evils spring principally from the misgivings which the conduct of the head of the executive power has inspired, in a war undertaken in his name against the constitution and the national independence;

That these misgivings have provoked from different parts of the kingdom a desire tending to the revocation of the authority delegated to Louis XVI;

Considering, nevertheless, that the legislative body ought not to wish to aggrandize itself by any usurpation;

That in the extraordinary circumstances wherein events unprovided for by any of the laws have placed it, it cannot reconcile what it owes, in its unshaken fidelity to the constitution, with the firm resolve to be buried under the ruins of the temple of liberty rather than to permit it to perish, except by recurring to the sovereignty of the people and by taking at the same time the precautions which are indispensable, in order that this recourse may not be rendered illusory by treasons; decrees as follows:

1. The French people are invited to form a national convention; the extraordinary commission shall present tomorrow a proposal to indicate the method and the time of this convention.

2. The head of the executive power is provisionally suspended from his functions until the national convention has

pronounced upon the measures which it believes ought to be adopted in order to assure the sovereignty of the people and the reign of liberty and equality.

3. The extraordinary commission shall present within the day a method for organizing a new ministry; the ministers actually in service shall continue provisionally·the exercise of their functions.

4. The extraordinary commission shall present, likewise, within the day, a proposal for a decree upon the selection of a governor for the prince royal.

5. The payment of the civil list shall continue suspended until the decision of the national convention. The extraordinary commission shall present, within twenty-four hours, a proposal for a decree upon the stipend to be granted to the king during the suspension.

6. The registers of the civil list shall be deposited in the office of the National Assembly, after having been numbered and attested by two commissioners of the assembly, who shall repair for that purpose to the intendant of the civil list.

7. The king and his family shall reside within the precincts of the legislative body until quiet may be re-established in Paris.

8. The department shall give orders to cause to be prepared for them within the day a lodging at the Luxembourg, where they shall be put under the custody of the citizens and the law.

9. Every public functionary, every soldier, under-officer, officer, of whatever grade he may be, and general of an army, who, in these days of alarm shall abandon his post, is declared infamous and traitorous to the fatherland.

10. The department and the municipality of Paris shall cause the present decree to be immediately and solemnly proclaimed.

11. It shall be sent by extraordinary couriers to the eighty-three departments, which shall be required to cause it to reach the municipalities of their jurisdiction within twenty-four hours, in order to be proclaimed with the same solemnity.

25. Decree for Electing the Convention.

August 11, 1792. Duvergier, *Lois,* IV, 297.

This decree was the work of the Legislative Assembly, which continued in session until the Convention met on September 21. The kind of authority to which the assembly laid claim and the points in which the electoral arrangements of this decree differ from those of the constitution of 1791 should be noted.

REFERENCE. Aulard, *Révolution française,* 221-222.

The National Assembly, considering that it has not the right to submit to imperative regulations the exercise of the sovereignty in the formation of a national convention, and that, nevertheless, it is important for the public safety that the primary and electoral assemblies should form themselves at the same time, should act with uniformity, and that the national convention should be promptly assembled,

Invites the citizens, in the name of liberty, equality, and the fatherland, to conform themselves to the following regulations :

1. The primary assemblies shall select the same number of electors as they have selected in the last elections.

2. The distinction of Frenchmen into active and non-active citizens shall be suppressed; and in order to be admitted to them, it shall suffice to be French, twenty-one years of age, domiciled for a year, living from his income or the product of his labor, and not being in the status of a household servant. As to those who, meeting the conditions of activity, were summoned by the law to take the civic oath, they shall be bound, in order to be admitted, to give proof of the taking of that oath.

3. The conditions of eligibility demanded for the electors or for the representatives not being applicable to a national convention, it shall suffice, in order to be eligible as deputy or as elector, to be twenty-five years of age and to unite the conditions demanded by the preceding article.

4. Each department shall select the number of deputies and alternates which it has selected for the existing legislature.

5. The elections shall take place according to the same method as for the legislative assemblies.

6. The primary assemblies are invited to invest their representatives with an unlimited confidence.

7. The primary assemblies shall meet on Sunday, August 26, in order to choose the electors.

8. The electors chosen by the primary assemblies shall meet on Sunday, September 2, in order to proceed to the election of the deputies to the national convention.

9. The electoral assemblies, shall sit in the places indicated by the table which shall be annexed to the present decree.

10. On account of the necessity of hastening the elections, the presidents, secretaries, and tellers, both in the primary assemblies and in the electoral assemblies, shall be chosen by plurality and by a single ballot.

11. The choice of the primary assemblies and the electoral assemblies may fall upon any citizen uniting the conditions above restored, whatever may be the public functions which he exercises or which he may have formerly exercised.

12. The citizens in the primary assemblies, and the electors in the electoral assemblies, shall take the oath *to maintain liberty and equality or to die in defending them.*

13. The deputies shall repair to Paris on September 20, and they shall cause themselves to be enrolled at the archives of the National Assembly. When they shall be two hundred in number, the National Assembly shall indicate the day of the opening of their sittings.

14. The National Assembly, after having indicated to the French citizens the regulations to which it believes it ought to invite them to conform themselves, considering that circumstances and justice alike urge a compensation in favor of the electors, decree that the electors who shall be obliged to go away from their domicile shall receive twenty *sous* per league, and three livres per day of sojourn.

The principal administration of the place where the electoral assemblies shall meet is authorised to deliver the necessary orders for the payment of the compensation due to the electors, subject to causing the replacement of it in the coffers of the district, upon the production of the additional *sous* from the department.

The above instruction and decree shall be, for more prompt

dispatch, addressed directly to both the district administrations and the department administrations; there shall be sent to each district administration a sufficient number of copies in order that they may transmit it without delay to each municipality.

26. The Jacobin Club Address.

September 12, 1792. Aulard, *Jacobins,* IV, 280-281.

During the interval between the 10th of August and the meeting of the Convention of September 21, 1792, the Jacobin Club closely followed and accurately expressed the tendency of public opinion in France upon the question of permanent form of government. This address, representing the final position of the club, had considerable influence in the way of preparing for the Republic.

REFERENCE. Aulard, *Révolution française,* 239-241.

The mother society has been itself obliged to interrupt its correspondence since the 10th of August; this is not because it has thought that that famous day was the end of all the conspiracies and of all the intrigues; a large portion of its members have received from the public confidence places in the provisional administrations, juries, etc. But the society, become a little more numerous, has expressed its desire to resume an active correspondence with its brothers of the departments, persuaded that circumstances demand more than ever fraternal communications between all the patriotic societies.

Since the 10th of August conspirators have expiated their offences; the public spirit has risen again; the sovereign, recovering possession of its rights, triumphs at length over the scoundrels leagued against its liberty and its welfare. Nevertheless, the people of Paris have felt the necessity of preserving an imposing attitude and of exercising a strict surveillance over the minions and agents of the traitor, Louis the Last. Be apprehensive, brothers and friends, lest new intrigues shall follow the baffled intrigues. The head, the cause and the pretext of the machinations still lives! Despotism moves in the darkness: let us be ready to engage in a combat to the death with it, under whatever form it presents itself.

The great interests of the people are about to be considered in the national convention; let us not lose a moment in preparing and making heard the national opinion, which alone ought to direct its actions. Especially let us prevent by firm measures the danger of seeing these new legislators oppose with impunity their personal interests or their opinions to the sovereign will of the nation. Let there be henceforth no inviolability except the law; let all the public functionaries always see the penalty alongside of the offence; recollect how small is the number of legislators who have resisted corruption: only a very few of them are counted in each legislature.

Let us impress our minds then with the spirit of the orders of the electoral body of Paris; they alone can save us from all sorts of despotism and the dangers of convulsions too long a time prolonged, etc.

These orders are in substance:

The purgatorial examination of the national convention, in order to reject from its midst the suspected members who may have escaped the sagacity of the primary assemblies;

The revocability of the deputies to the national convention who have attacked or who attack by any motions the rights of the sovereign;

The sanction, or the popular revision of all the constitutional decrees of the national convention;

The entire abolition of royalty and the penalty of death against those who may propose to re-establish it;

The form of a republican government.

These, friends, and brothers, are the important matters which the electors, the commune, and the primary assemblies of Paris, invite us to discuss earnestly in order to fortify and encompass the national convention with your opinion upon these matters.

27. Documents upon the Transition to the Republic.

From these documents something can be learned of the manner in which the Republic came to be established. The precise effect of each measure should be noted.

REFERENCES. Aulard. *Révolution française*, 268-274; Jaurès, *Histoire socialiste*, III, 171-179.

A. Declaration upon the Constitution. September 21, 1792. Duvergier, *Lois*, V, 1.

The National Convention declares: 1st, there cannot be any constitution except that which is accepted by the people: 2d, that persons and property are under the safeguard of the nation.

B. Decree for Provisional Enforcement of the Laws. September 21, 1792. *Moniteur,* September 22, 1792 *(Réimpression,* XIV, 8.)

The National Convention declares that all the laws not abrogated and all the powers not revoked or suspended are maintained.

The National Convention declares that the taxes at present actually existing shall be collected as in the past.

C. Decree for Abolishing Monarchy. September 21, 1792. Duvergier, *Lois,* V, 1.

The National Convention decrees unanimously, that monarchy is abolished in France.

D. Decree upon the Dating of Public Documents. September 22, 1792. Duvergier, *Lois,* V, 2.

A member demanded that henceforth documents be dated, *the first year of the French Republic.*

Another member proposed to join to that the era in use, *the fourth of liberty.*

This amendment is rejected, and it is decreed that all the public documents shall bear henceforth the date of the *first year of the French Republic.*

E. Decree upon the Unity and Indivisibility of the Republic. September 25, 1792. Duvergier, *Lois,* V, 4.

The National Convention declares that the French Republic is one and indivisible.

28. Documents upon the Convention and Foreign Policy.

The adoption of the policy set forth in the first two of these decrees marks a great turning point in the history of the revolution. Document A, passed hastily amid the enthusiasm following the French victory at Jemmapes, may be regarded as representing the Girondist theory of foreign policy. In contrast, document B may be called the Montagnard theory. Document C represents the more practical and moderate policy of Danton. Special attention should be given to the effect of each of these decrees in foreign countries.

REFERENCES. Gardiner, *French Revolution*, 130-135 ; Stephens, *French Revolution*, II, 204-206 ; Lecky, *England in the Eighteenth Century*, VI, 58, 81-83 (*French Revolution*, 457-458, 487-489) ; Von Sybel, *French Revolution*, II, 235-237, 257-259, III, 41-43 ; *Cambridge Modern History*, VIII, 300 ; Lavisse and Rambaud, *Histoire générale*, VIII, 242-245, 282-285 ; Jaurès, *Histoire socialiste*, III, 567-569, IV, 964-976.

A. Declaration for Assistance and Fraternity to Foreign Peoples. November 19, 1792. *Moniteur,* November 19, 1792 (*Réimpression,* XIV, 517).

The National Convention declares, in the name of the French people, that it will accord fraternity and assistance to all peoples who shall wish to recover their liberty, and charges the executive power to give to the generals the necessary orders to furnish assistance to these peoples and to defend the citizens who may have been or who may be harassed for the cause of liberty. The present decree shall be translated and printed in all languages.

B. Decree for Proclaiming the Liberty and Sovereignty of all Peoples. December 15, 1792. Duvergier, *Lois,* V, 82-84.

The National Convention, after having heard the report of its united committees of finances, war, and diplomacy, faithful to the principles of the sovereignty of the people, which do not permit it to recognize any of the institutions that constitute an attack thereon, and wishing to settle the rules to be followed by the generals of the armies of the Republic in the countries where they shall carry its arms, decrees:

1. In the countries which are or shall be occupied by the armies of the Republic, the generals shall proclaim immediately, in the name of the French nation, the sovereignty of the people, the suppression of all the established authorities and of the existing imposts and taxes, the abolition of the tithe, of feudalism, of seignioral rights, both feudal and *censuel,* fixed or precarious, of *banalités,* of real and personal

servitude, of the privileges of hunting and fishing, of *corvées*, of the nobility, and generally of all privileges.

2. They shall announce to the people that they bring them peace, assistance, fraternity, liberty and equality, and that they will convoke them directly in primary or communal assemblies in order to create and organize an administration and a provisional judiciary; they shall look after the security of persons and property; they shall cause the present decree and the proclamation herewith annexed to be printed in the language or idiom of the country, and to be posted and executed without delay in each commune.

3. All the agents and civil and military officers of the former government, as well as the persons formerly reputed noble, or the members of any formerly privileged corporation, shall be, for this time only, inadmissable to vote in the primary or communal assemblies, and they shall not be elected to administrative positions or to the provisional judicial power.

4. The generals shall directly place under the safeguard and protection of the French Republic all the movable and immovable goods belonging to the public treasury, to the prince, to his abettors, adherents and voluntary satellites, to the public establishments, to the lay and ecclesiastical bodies and communities; they shall cause to be prepared without delay a detailed list thereof which they shall dispatch to the executive council, and shall take all the measures which are in their power that these properties may be respected.

5. The provisional administration selected by the people shall be charged with the surveillance and control of the goods placed under the safeguard and protection of the French Republic; it shall look after the security of persons and property; it shall cause to be executed the laws in force relative to the trial of civil and criminal suits and to the police and the public security; it shall be charged to regulate and to cause the payment of the local expenses and those which shall be necessary for the common defence; it may establish taxes, provided, however, that they shall not be borne by the indigent and laboring portion of the people.

6. When the provisional administration shall be organized the National Convention shall appoint commissioners from within its own body to go to fraternise with it.

7. The executive council shall also appoint national commissioners, who shall repair directly to the places in order to co-operate with the generals and the provisional administration selected by the people upon the measures to be taken for the common defence, and upon the means employed to procure the clothing and provisions necessary for the armies, and to meet the expenses which they have incurred and shall incur during their sojourn upon its territory.

8. The national commissioners appointed by the executive council shall every fifteen days render an account to it of their operations. The executive council shall approve, modify or reject them and shall render an account thereof directly to the Convention.

9. The provisional administration selected by the people and the functions of the national commissioners shall cease as soon as the inhabitants, after having declared the sovereignty and independence of the people, liberty and equality, shall have organized a free and popular form of government.

10. There shall be made a list of the expenses which the French Republic shall have incurred for the common defence and of the sums which it may have received, and the French nation shall make arrangements with the government which shall have been established for that which may be due; and in case the common interest should require that the troops of the Republic remain beyond that time upon the foreign territory, it shall take suitable measures to provide for their subsistence.

11. The French nation declares that it will treat as enemies the people who, refusing liberty and equality, or renouncing them, may wish to preserve, recall, or treat with the prince and the privileged castes; it promises and engages not to subscribe to any treaty, and not to lay down its arms until after the establishment of the sovereignty and independence of the people whose territory the troops of the Republic have entered upon and who shall have adopted the principles of equality, and established a free and popular government.

12. The executive council shall dispatch the present decree by extraordinary couriers to all the generals and shall take the necessary measures to assure the execution of it.

The French People to the . . . People.

Brothers and friends, we have conquered liberty and we shall maintain it. We offer to cause you to enjoy this inestimable blessing, which has always belonged to us and which our oppressors have not been able to take away from us without crime.

We have driven out your tyrants: show yourselves free men and we will guarantee you from their vengeance, their projects, and their return.

From this moment the French nation proclaims the sovereignty of the people, the suppression of all the civil and military authorities which have governed you up to this day and of all the imposts which you support under whatever form they exist; the abolition of the tithe, of feudalism, of seigniorial rights, both feudal and *censuel,* settled or precarious, of *banalités,* of real and personal servitude, of the privileges of hunting and fishing, of the *corvées,* of the *gabelle,* of the tolls, of the *octrois,* and generally of every species of taxes with which you have been charged by your usurpers; it also proclaims the abolition among you of every noble corporation, sacerdotal and others, of all prerogatives and privileges contrary to equality. You are from this moment, brothers and friends, all citizens, all equal in rights, and all equally called to govern, to serve, and to defend your fatherland.

Form yourselves immediately into primary and communal assemblies, make haste to establish your provisional administrations and judiciaries, in conformity with the provisions of article 3 of the above decree. The agents of the French Republic will co-operate with you in order to assure your welfare and the fraternity which ought to exist henceforth between us.

C. Decree upon Non-Intervention. April 13, 1793. Duvergier, *Lois,* V, 248.

The National Convention declares, in the name of the French people, that it will not interfere in any manner in the government of the other powers; but it declares at the same time, that it will sooner be buried under its own ruins than suffer that any power should interfere in the internal régime of the Republic, or should influence the creation of the constitution which it intends to give itself.

The National Convention decrees the penalty of death against anyone who may propose to negotiate or treat with the hostile powers which may not have previously recognized in a solemn manner the independence of the French Republic, its sovereignty, and the indivisibility and unity of the Republic, founded upon liberty and equality.

29. Documents upon the Convention and Religion.

Document A shows the original attitude of the Convention towards religion, which was substantially that of the Constituent Assembly. (See No. 6.) Under various influences that attitude was gradually changed. The royalist sympathies of the non-juring priests led to document B, the Girondist sympathies of the constitutional clergy to document C. At the end of the year 1793 the anti-Christianity movement was very strong outside of the Convention. Document D represents the attitude of the Convention towards that movement and also marks the first step towards the establishment of a new system upon the relations between the state and religion. The remaining documents represent other steps in the process and its final position. The system outlined in document I continued as the legal basis until the Concordat.

REFERENCES. Sloane, *French Revolution and Religious Reform*, 211-217 ; *Cambridge Modern History*, VIII, 382-383 ; Aulard, *Révolution française*, 466-487, 532-542 ; Lavisse and Rambaud, *Histoire générale*, VIII, 514-525 ; Debidour, *L'Église et l'État*, 112-152.

A. Decree upon Religious Policy. January 11, 1793. Duvergier, *Lois*, V, 111.

The National Convention, after having heard a deputation of the citizens of the departments of Eure, Orne and Eure-et-Loir, who ask in the name of more than a hundred thousand of their fellow citizens that they be not disturbed in the exercise of their worship, and who protest that they wish to live and die good catholics as well as good republicans, and upon the proposal of one of its members, passes to the order of the day, giving as the reason the existence of its decree of the 30th of November, in which it orders that a notification to the people shall be made in order to explain to them that the National Convention never had an intention of depriving them of the ministers of the catholic sect whom the Civil Constitution of the Clergy has given them.

It decrees, besides, that a copy of this decree and of that of the 30th of November shall be sent to the petitioners.

B. Decree upon the Non-Juring Priests. April 23, 1793. Duvergier, *Lois*, V, 256.

1. The National Convention decrees that all the secular and regular ecclesiastics and converts and lay brothers, who have not taken oath to maintain liberty and equality in conformity with the law of August 15, 1792, shall be embarked and transferred without delay to French Guiana.

2. Those who shall be denounced because of incivism by six citizens in the canton shall be subject to the same penalty.

. . . .

5. Those deported in execution of articles 1 and 2 above who may return to the territory of the Republic shall be punished by death within twenty-four hours.

. . . .

C. Decree upon Dangerous Priests. October 20-21, 1793. (29-30 Vendémiaire, Year II). Duvergier, *Lois*, VI, 241-242.

1. Priests subject to deportation and taken with arms in their hands, either upon the frontiers or in the country of the enemy;

Those who shall have been or shall be discovered in possession of permits or passports delivered by French *émigré* leaders, or by commanders of enemies' armies, or by leaders of the rebels;

And those who shall be provided with any counter-revolutionary symbols, shall be delivered within twenty-four hours to the executioner of condemned criminals and put to death, after the facts shall have been declared proven by a military commission formed by the officers of the staff of the division within the area of which they shall have been arrested.

2. Those who have been or who shall be arrested without arms in the countries occupied by the troops of the Republic shall be tried in the same form and punished by the same penalty, if they have been previously in the armies of the enemy or in the musters of *émigrés* or insurgents, or if they were there at the moment of their arrest.

. . . .

5. Those of these ecclesiastics who shall return and those

who have returned to the territory of the Republic shall be
sent to the court house of the criminal tribunal of the department within the area of which they shall have been or shall be
arrested; and, after having undergone examination, of which
record shall be kept, they shall be delivered within twenty-
four hours to the executioner of condemned criminals and put
to death, after the judges of the tribunal shall have declared
that the prisoners are convicted of having been subjects of
deportation.

.   .   .   .

10. Those declared subjects for deportation, trial and punishment, as such, are the bishops, former archbishops, *curés*
kept in place, vicars of these bishops, superiors and directors of seminaries, vicars of the *curés*, professors of seminaries and colleges, public instructors, and those who shall
have preached in any churches whatsoever since the decree of
February 5, 1791, who shall not have taken the oath prescribed
by article 39 of the decree of July 24, 1790......or who have
retracted it, although they may have taken it again since their
retraction;

All secular or regular ecclesiastics and convert and lay
brothers, who have not complied with the decrees of August
14, 1792, and April 21st, last, or who have retracted their oath;

And finally all those who have been denounced because of
incivism, when the denunciation shall have been pronounced
valid, in conformity with the decree of the said 21st day of
April.

.   .   .   .

12. The ecclesiastics who have taken the oath prescribed
by the decrees of July 24 and November 27, 1790, as well as
that of liberty and equality, within the fixed time, and who
shall be denounced because of incivism, shall be embarked
without delay and transferred to the east coast of Africa from
the twenty-third to the twenty-eighth degree south.

.   .   .   .

17. Priests deported voluntarily and with passports . .
are reputed *émigrés*.

18. Every citizen is required to denounce the ecclesiastic
whom he shall know to be subject to deportation, to
arrest him or cause him to be arrested and conducted before

the nearest police officer; he shall receive a hundred livres reward.

19. Every citizen who shall conceal a priest subject to deportation shall be condemned to the same penalty.

D. Decree upon Religious Freedom. December 8, 1793. (18 Frimaire, Year II). Duvergier, *Lois*, VI, 333.

1. All violence and measures in constraint of the liberty of worship are forbidden.

2. The surveillance of the constituted authorities and the action of the public force shall confine themselves in this matter, each for what concerns it, to measures of police and public security.

3. The National Convention, by preceding provisions, does not mean to derogate in any manner from the laws or precautions of public safety against the refractory or turbulent priests, or against all those who may attempt to take advantage of the pretext of religion to compromise the cause of liberty; no more does it intend to disapprove of what has been done up to this day in virtue of the orders of the representatives of the people, nor to furnish or for diminishing the free text for disturbing patriotism or for diminishing the free scope of the public spirit. The Convention invites all good citizens, in the name of the fatherland, to abstain from all disputes that are theological or foreign to the great interests of the French people, in order to co-operate by all methods in the triumph of the Republic and the ruin of all its enemies.

. . . .

E. Decree for Establishing the Worship of the Supreme Being. May 7, 1794 (18 Floréal, Year II). Aulard, *Révolution française*, 489-490.

1. The French people recognize the existence of the Supreme Being and the immortality of the soul.

2. They recognize that the worship worthy of the Supreme Being is the practice of the duties of man.

3. They place in the first rank of these duties, to detest bad faith and tyranny, to punish tyrants and traitors, to relieve the unfortunate, to respect the weak, to defend the oppressed,

to do to others all the good that is possible and not to be unjust to anyone.

4. Festivals shall be instituted to remind man of the thought of the divinity and of the dignity of his being.

5. They shall take their names from the glorious events of our revolution, from the virtues most cherished and most useful to man, and from the great gifts of nature.

6. The French Republic shall celebrate every year the festival of July 14, 1789, August 10, 1792, January 21, 1793, and May 31, 1793.

7. It shall celebrate on the days of *décadi* the list of festivals that follows: to the supreme being and to nature; to the human race: to the French people; to the benefactors of humanity; to the martyrs of liberty; to liberty and equality; to the republic: to the liberty of the world; to the love of the fatherland; to the hatred of tyrants and of traitors; to truth; to justice; to modesty; to glory and immortality; to friendship; to frugality; to courage; to good faith; to heroism; to disinterestedness; to stoicism; to love; to conjugal love; to paternal love; to maternal tenderness; to filial affection; to childhood; to youth; to manhood; to old age; to misfortune; to agriculture; to industry; to our forefathers; to posterity; to happiness.

8. The committees of public safety and of public instruction are charged to present a plan of organization for these festivals.

9. The National Convention summons all the talents worthy to serve the cause of humanity to the honor of contributing to its establishment by hymns and patriotic songs and by all the means which can enhance its beauty and utility.

10. The Committee of Public Safety shall confer distinction upon those works which seem the best adapted to carry on these purposes and shall reward their authors.

11. Liberty of worship is maintained, in conformity with the decree of 18 Frimaire.

12. Every gathering that is aristocratic and contrary to public order shall be suppressed.

13. In case of disturbances of which any worship whatsoever may be the occasion or motive, those who may excite them by fanatical preaching or by counter-revolutionary in-

sinuations, those who may provoke them by unjust and gratuitous violence, shall likewise be punished with all the severity of the law.

14. A special report upon the provisions of detail relative to the present decree shall be made.

15. A festival in honor of the Supreme Being shall be celebrated upon 20 Prairial next.

David is charged to present the plan thereof to the National Convention.

F. Decree upon Expenditures for Religion. September 18, 1794 (2 Sans-Culottides, Year II). Duvergier, *Lois*, VII, 281.

1. The French Republic no longer pays the expenses or salaries of any sect.

.   .   .   .

G. Decree upon Religion. February 21, 1795 (3 Ventôse, Year III). Duvergier, *Lois*, VIII, 25-26.

1. In conformity with article 7 of the *Declaration of the Rights of Man* and with article 122 of the constitution, the exercise of any worship cannot be disturbed.

2. The Republic does not pay salaries for any of them.

3. It does not furnish an edifice, either for the exercise of worship or the lodging of the ministers.

4. The ceremonies of every worship are forbidden outside of the premises chosen for their exercise.

5. The law does not recognize any minister of religion: nobody can appear in public with garments, ornaments or costumes set apart for religious ceremonies.

6. Every gathering of citizens for the exercise of any worship is subject to the surveillance of the constituted authorities. That surveillance confines itself to measures of police and public security.

7. No symbol peculiar to a religion can be put in or upon the outside of a public place, in any manner whatsoever. No inscription can designate the place which is set aside for it. No proclamation or public summons can be made in order to call the citizens there.

8. The communes and communal sections in collective

name shall not acquire nor loan buildings for the exercises of religious organizations.

9. No perpetual or life time endowment can be formed or any tax established in order to provide for the expenses of them.

. . . .

H. Decree for Restoring Church Buildings. May 30, 1795 (11 Prairial, Year III). Duvergier, *Lois,* VIII, 127.

1. The citizens of the communes and communal sections of the Republic shall have the free use provisionally of the non-alienated edifices originally set apart for the exercises of one or more worships and of which they were in possession on the first day of the year 11 of the Republic. They can make use of them under the surveillance of the constituted authorities, both for the assemblies ordered by the law and for the exercise of their worship.

. . . .

5. Nobody shall perform the duties of the ministry of any religious organization in the said edifices, unless he has made acknowledgment, before the municipality of the place in which he shall wish to exercise it, of submission to the laws of the Republic. Ministers of religion who shall have contravened the present article, and citizens who shall have summoned or admitted them, shall each be punished with a thousand livres fine by way of correctional police.

. . . .

I. Organic Act upon Religion. September 29, 1795 (7 Vendémiaire, Year IV). Duvergier, *Lois,* VIII, 293-296.

The National Convention, after having heard the report of its committee of legislation;

Considering that by the terms of the constitution, nobody can be prevented from exercising, in conformity with the laws, the worship which he has chosen; that nobody can be forced to contribute to the expenses of any religious organization, and that the Republic does not pay salaries for any of them;

Considering that, these fundamental bases of the free exercise of worship being thus laid down, it is important, on the one hand, to reduce into laws the necessary consequences which are derived therefrom, and, for that purpose, to unite them into a single body and to modify or complete those which have been rendered; and, on the other hand, to add to them the penal provisions which may assure the execution of them;

Considering that the laws to which it is necessary to conform in the exercise of worship do not legislate upon what belongs to the domain of thought only, or upon the relations of man with the objects of his worship, and that they have and can have for their purpose only a surveillance restricted to measures of police and public security;

That thus they ought to guarantee the free exercise of worship by the punishment of those who disturb the ceremonies or outrage the ministers in their functions;

To demand of the ministers of every religious organization a purely civic guarantee against the abuse which they may make of their ministry in order to excite disobedience to the laws of the state;

To anticipate, prevent, or punish everything which may tend to render a religious organization exclusive or dominant and persecuting, such as acts of the communes in the collective name, endowments, forced contributions, acts of violence relative to the expenses of religious organizations, the exposure of special symbols in certain places, the exercise of ceremonies and the use of costumes outside of the premises designated for the said exercises, and the undertakings of the ministers relative to the civil condition of the citizens;

To repress offences which may be committed by occasion or abuse of the exercise of worship;

And, finally, to regulate the competency and procedure [of the courts] in these classes of cases;

Decrees as follows:

Title I. Surveillance of the Exercise of Worship
Preliminary and General Provision.

1. Every gathering of citizens for the exercise of any worship whatsoever is subject to the surveillance of the constituted authorities.

This surveillance is confined to measures of police and public security.

Title II. Guarantee of the Free Exercise of Every Worship

2. Those who shall insult the objects of any worship whatsoever in the places designated for its exercise, or its ministers on duty, or shall interrupt by a public disturbance the religious ceremonies of any other worship whatsoever, shall be condemned to a fine, which shall not exceed five hundred livres, nor less than fifty livres per person, and an imprisonment which shall not exceed two years nor be less than one month; without prejudice to the penalties provided by the penal code, if the nature of the act may give occasion thereto.

. . . .

Title III. Of the Civic Guarantee Required of the Ministers of Every Sect

5. Nobody can discharge the duties of the ministry of any religious organization, in any place whatever, unless he has previously made before the municipal administration or the municipal deputy of the place in which he shall wish to exercise it, a declaration, the model of which is in the following article. The declarations already made shall not dispense with that ordered by the present article. . . .

6. The formula of the declaration required above is this:
"The . . . . before us . . . has appeared N. (*the name and prenomens only*) resident of . . . who has made the declaration whose tenor is as follows:

"*'I recognize that the totality of the French citizens is the sovereign, and I promise submission and obedience to the law of the Republic.'*

"We have given to him an acknowledgment of this declaration and he has signed with us."

The declaration which shall contain anything more or less shall be null and void: . . .

. . . .

Title IV. Of the Guarantee against Any Religious Organization Which May Attempt to Become Exclusive or Dominant

Section 1. Concerning the expenses of the religious organizations.

9. Communes or communal sections shall neither acquire nor loan in the collective name premises for the exercise of worship.

10. No perpetual or lifetime endowment can be formed nor any tax established in order to provide for the expenses of any religious organization or the lodgment of its ministers.

.   .   .   .

Section II. Of the places in which it is forbidden to place the special symbols of a religious organization.

13. No special symbol of a religious organization can be raised, affixed or attached in any place whatsoever in such a manner as to be exposed to the eyes of the citizens, except within the premises designated for the exercises of that same religious organization, or within the interior of private houses, within the studios or magazines of artists and merchants, or the public edifices set apart to receive works of art.

.   .   .   .

Section III. Of the places in which the ceremonies of religious organizations are forbidden.

16. The ceremonies of all religious organizations are forbidden outside of the precincts of the edifice chosen for their exercise.

This prohibition does not apply to the ceremonies which take place within the precincts of private houses, provided, that, besides the persons who have that domicile, there shall not be on the occasion of the said ceremonies a gathering in excess of ten persons.

17. The premises chosen for the exercise of a worship shall be indicated and declared to the municipal deputy, in the communes above five thousand souls, and in others to the municipal administrations of the canton or district.

.   .   .   .

19. Nobody . . . can appear in public with the garments, ornaments or costumes set apart for religious ceremonies or for a minister of a religious organization.

.   .   .   .

Title V. Of Certain Offences Which Can Be Committed on the Occasion or by the Abuse of the Exercise of Worship

. . . .

22. Every minister of a religious organization who, outside of the premises of the edifice set apart for the ceremonies or exercises of a worship, shall read or cause to be read in an assembly of persons, or who shall post or cause to be posted, shall distribute or cause to be distributed, a writing emanating from or announced as emanating from a minister of worship who shall not be resident within the French Republic, or even from a minister of worship residing in France who declares himself the delegate of another who does not reside here, shall be condemned to six months in prison, independently of the tenor of the said writing, and in case of repetition, to two years.

23. Any minister of worship who shall commit any one of the following offences shall be condemned to prison forever, whether it be by his discourses, exhortations, sermons, invocations or prayers, in any language whatsoever, either by reading, publishing, posting, distributing, or causing to be read, published, posted and distributed, within the premises of the edifice set part for the ceremonies, or outside, a writing of which he shall be or any other shall be the author;

To wit: if, by the said writing or discourse, he has urged the re-establishment of monarchy in France, or the overthrow of the Republic, or the dissolution of the national representation;

Or if he has incited murder, or excited the defenders of the fatherland to desert their flags; or their fathers and mothers to recall them;

Or if he has reproached those who may wish to take arms for the maintenance of the republican constitution and the defence of liberty:

Or if he has summoned persons to cut down the trees consecrated to liberty, or has torn down or treated disrespectfully its symbols and colors;

Or, finally, if he has exhorted or encouraged any persons to treason or rebellion against the government.

24. If, by writings, placards or discourses, a minister of

worship seeks to mislead the citizens, in presenting to them as unjust or criminal the sales or acquisitions of national lands possessed formerly by the clergy or the *émigrés,* he shall be condemned to a thousand livres fine and two years in prison;

In addition, he shall be forbidden to continue his functions as a minister of worship;

If he infringes this prohibition, he shall be punished by ten years of imprisonment.

.   .   .   .

30. Documents upon the Emigres.

The *émigrés* were an important factor in the revolution. Their absence from France deprived Louis XVI of support which he needed ; their intrigues abroad and their threats of vengeance did much to arouse the fears of all Frenchmen who sympathized with the revolution. Document A, although much less virulent in tone than others, is a typical *émigré* manifesto. Document B may be called an organic act, codifying earlier legislation against the *émigrés.*

REFRENCES. Stephens, *French Revolution,* II, 496-513 ; *Cambridge Modern History,* VIII, 501-503 ; Aulard, *Révolution française,* 361-362.

A. Declaration of the Regent of France. January 28, 1793. *Moniteur,* February 26, 1793 (*Réimpression,* XV, 545-546).

Louis-Stanislas-Xavier of France, son of France, uncle of the king, regent of the kingdom, to all those to whom these presents shall come, greeting.

Filled with horror upon learning that the most criminal of men have just reached the climax of their numerous outrages by the greatest of crimes, we have first implored heaven to obtain its assistance in surmounting the feelings of a profound grief and the impulses of our indignation, to the end that we may give ourselves up to the fulfilling of the duties which, under such grave circumstances, are the first in order of those which the immutable laws of the French monarchy impose upon us,

Our very dear and honored brother and sovereign lord, King Louis, the sixteenth of that name, having died on the 21st of the present month of January, beneath the parricidal sword which the ferocious usurpers of the sovereign authority in France raised against his august person,

We declare that the dauphin Louis-Charles, born on the 27th day of March, 1785, is King of France and Navarre, under the name of Louis XVII, and that by right of birth, as well as by the provisions of the fundamental laws of the kingdom, we are and shall be regent of France during the minority of the king, our nephew and lord.

Invested, in that capacity, with the exercise of the rights and powers of the sovereignty and of the higher ministry of royal justice, we undertake them, as we are required to do in the discharge of our obligations and duties, for the purpose of employing ourselves, with the aid of God and the assistance of good and loyal Frenchmen of all the orders of the kingdom and of the powers recognized as sovereign allies of the crown of France.

1st. For the liberation of King Louis XVII, our nephew; 2d, of the queen, his august mother and guardian; of the Princess Elizabeth, his aunt, our very dear sister, all kept in the most distressing captivity by the leaders of the factious; and at the same time for the re-establishment of the monarchy upon the unalterable bases of its constitution, the reformation of the abuses introduced in the system of public administration, the re-establishment of the religion of our fathers in the purity of its worship and of the canonical discipline, the restoration of the magistracy for the maintenance of public order and the dispensing of justice, the restoration of Frenchmen of all orders, in the exercise of legitimate rights and in the enjoyment of their invaded and usurped properties, the severe and exemplary punishment of crimes, the re-establishment of the authority of the laws and of peace, and, finally, the fulfilling of the solemn engagements which we were pleased to take in conjunction with our very dear brother, Charles-Philippe of France, Count of Artois, with whom are united our very dear nephews, grandsons of France, Louis-Antoine, Duke of Angoulême, and Charles-Ferdinand, Duke of Berry, and our cousins of the royal blood, Louis-Joseph of Bourbon, Prince of Condé, Louis-Henry-Joseph of Bourbon, Duke of Bourbon, and Louis-Antoine-Henri of Bourbon, Duke of Enghein, by our resolutions addressed to the late king, our brother, September 11, 1791, and other acts emanating from us, declarations of our principles, feelings and wishes, in which acts we persist and shall constantly persist.

For these purposes, we command and order all Frenchmen and subjects of the king to obey the commands which they shall receive from us in the name of the king and the commands of our very dear brother Charles-Philippe of France, Count of Artois, whom we have appointed and designated lieutenant general of the kingdom, when our said brother and lieutenant general shall give orders in the name of the king and the regent of France. Our present declaration shall be notified to whomsoever it shall concern and shall be published by all the officers of the king, military or magisterial, to whom we shall give commission and charge thereto, in order that the said declaration may have all the publicity which it shall be possible to give it in France at present, and until it may be addressed in the usual form to the courts of the kingdom, as soon as they shall have resumed the exercise of their jurisdictions, in order to be there notified, published, registered and executed.

Given at Hamm, in Westphalia, under our signature and ordinary seal, of which we are making use for transactions of sovereignty until the seals of the kingdom, destroyed by the factious, may have been re-established, and under the counter signature of the ministers of state, the marshals Broglie and Castries. This 28th of January, 1793, and of the reign of the king, the first.

B. Decree against the *Émigrés*.   March 28, 1793. Duvergier, *Lois*, V, 218-228.

.   .   .   .

1. The *émigrés* are forever banished from French territory; *they are civilly dead;* their estates are acquired by the Republic.

2. Infraction of the banishment pronounced by article 1 shall be punished by death.

.   .   .   .

6. *Émigrés* are:

1st. Every Frenchman of either sex who, after having left the territory of the Republic since July 1, 1789, has not made proof of his return to France within the periods fixed by the decree of March 30-April 8, 1792. The said decree shall continue to be executed in that which has to do with the pecuniary penalties pronounced against those who shall have returned within the period which it has prescribed;

2d. Every Frenchman of either sex, absent from the place of his domicile, who shall not prove, in the form which is about to be prescribed, an uninterrupted residence in France since May 9, 1792;

3d. Every Frenchman of either sex who, although actually present, has been absent from the place of his domicile and shall not make proof of an uninterrupted residence in France since May 9, 1792;

4th. Those who shall leave the territory of the Republic without fulfilling the formalities prescribed by the decree;

5th. Every agent of the government who, having been charged with a mission to foreign powers, may not return to France within three months from the day of notification of his recall;

6th. Every Frenchman of either sex who, during invasion made by foreign armies, has left non-invaded French territory in order to reside upon territory occupied by the enemy;

7th. Those who, although born in foreign countries, have exercised the rights of citizens in France, or who, having a double domicile, to wit, one in France and the other in foreign countries, shall not make proof of an uninterrupted residence in France since May 9, 1792.

31. Declaration of War against Great Britain.

February 1, 1793. Duvergier, *Lois*, V, 134-135.

The great war begun by this declaration lasted until 1814, save for one interval of about fifteen months in 1802-3, being protracted for reasons very different from those which had originally caused it. From the document a tolerably complete list of the circumstances which the Convention regarded as justifying the war can be made out.

REFERENCES. Lecky, *England in the Eighteenth Century*, VI, 45-135 (*French Revolution*, 441-556) : Browning, *Flight to Varennes and Other Essays*, 170-201 ; *Cambridge Modern History*, VIII, 295-305 ; Lavisse and Rambaud, *Histoire générale*, VIII, 248-249 ; Sorel, *L'Europe et la révolution française*, III, 212-230, 240-245, 271-280.

The National Convention, after having heard the report of its committee of general defence upon the conduct of the English government towards France;

Considering that the King of England has not ceased, especially since the revolution of August 10, 1792, to give to the French nation proofs of his malevolence and of his attachment to the coalition of the crowned heads;

That at that time he ordered his ambassador to withdraw from Paris, because he did not wish to recognize the provisional executive council created by the Legislative Assembly;

That the cabinet of Saint James discontinued at the same time its correspondence with the ambassador of France at London, under pretext of the suspension of the former king of the French;

That, since the opening of the National Convention, it has not been willing to resume its accustomed correspondence nor to recognize the powers of this Convention;

That it has refused to recognize the ambassador of the French Republic, although furnished with letters of credence in its name;

That it has sought to thwart the various purchases of grain, arms, and other merchandise ordered in England, whether by French citizens or by the agents of the French Republic;

That it has caused the arrest of several barges and vessels loaded with grain for France, while, contrary to the tenor of the treaty of 1786, the exportation thereof to other foreign countries has continued;

That, in order to hamper still more effectively the commercial operations of the Republic in England, it has caused the circulation of the *assignats* to be prohibited by an act of parliament;

That, in violation of article 4 of the treaty of 1786, it has caused to be enacted by the same parliament, in the course of the month of January last, an act which subjects all French citizens going to or residing in England to forms that are most inquisitorial, most vexatious, and most dangerous to their security;

That, within the same time and against the tenor of article

1 of the treaty of peace of 1783, it has granted open protection
and financial relief to the *émigrés* and even to the rebel leaders who have already fought against France; that it maintains with them a daily correspondence evidently directed
against the French revolution;

That it likewise welcomes the leaders of the rebels of the
French western colonies;

That, in the same spirit, without any provocation being
given it, and when all the maritime powers are at peace with
England, the cabinet of Saint James has ordered a considerable armament by sea and an augmentation of its land forces;

That this augmentation was ordered at the moment when
the English ministry was persecuting with blind fury those
who were supporting in England the principles of the French
revolution, and was employing all possible means, whether in
parliament or outside, to cover the French Republic with
ignominy and to draw upon it the execration of the English
nation and of all Europe;

That the purpose of this armament, intended against
France, has not even been disguised in the parliament of England;

That, although the provisional executive council has employed all means to preserve peace and fraternity with the
English nation and has not responded to the calumnies and
the violations of the treaties, except by complaints founded
upon the principles of justice and expressed with the dignity
of free men, the English ministry has persevered in its system of malevolence and hostility, continued the armaments,
and sent a fleet towards the Scheldt to interfere with the
operations of France in Belgium;

That at the news of the execution of *Louis* it carried outrage against the French Republic to the point of giving an
order to the ambassador of France to leave the soil of Great
Britain within eight days;

That the King of England has manifested his attachment
to the cause of that traitor and his intention to sustain it by
various resolutions taken at the moment of his death, as well
in appointing generals for his army, as in askng the parliament of England for a considerable addition of land and naval
forces and in ordering the equipment of gunboats;

That his secret coalition with the enemies of France, and especially with the Emperor and with Prussia, has just been confirmed by a treaty effected with the first in the month of January last;

That he has drawn into the same coalition the Stadtholder of the United Provinces; that this prince, whose servile devotion to the orders of the cabinets of Saint James and of Berlin is only too notorious, has in the course of the French revolution and despite the neutrality which he was protesting, treated with contempt the agents of France, welcomed the *émigrés,* harassed the French patriots, interfered with their operations, released, despite the accepted usage and despite the request of the French minister, the counterfeiters of false *assignats;*

That, most recently in order to co-operate with the hostile designs of the court of London, he has ordered a naval armament, appointed an admiral, ordered the Dutch vessels to join the English fleet, opened a loan to supply the expenses of war, prevented exportations to France while he favored the supplying of the Prussian and Austrian magazines with provisions;

Considering, finally, that all these circumstances no longer allow the French Republic to hope to obtain, by means of amicable negotiations, the redress of its grievances, and that all the acts of the British court and of the Stadtholder are acts of hostility and equivalent to a declaration of war;

The National Convention decrees as follows:

1. The National Convention declares, in the name of the French nation, that in view of all these acts of hostility and aggression, the French Republic is at war with the King of England and the Stadtholder of the United Provinces.

2. The National Convention charges the provisional executive council to deploy the forces which shall appear to it necessary to repulse their aggression and to support the independence, the dignity and the interests of the Republic.

3. The National Convention authorizes the provisional executive council to dispose of the naval forces of the Republic, as the safety of the state shall appear to it to require; it revokes all the particular provisions ordered in this matter by preceding decrees.

32. Documents upon the Revolutionary Tribunal of Paris.

These documents are intended to show the evolution and general character of the Revolutionary Tribunal, one of the chief institutions of the Terror. Between the dates of the two documents the tribunal was divided into four sections, in order that its business might be despatched more rapidly, and its name was changed to Revolutionary Tribunal. Something of the methods by which it was supplied with cases can be ascertained from No. 41.

REFERENCES. Mathews, *French Revolution*, 231-232, 262 ; Stephens, *French Revolution*, II, 330-343, 544-548 ; *Cambridge Modern History*, VIII, 267-268, 366, 372 ; Aulard, *Révolution française*, 362-366 ; Jaurès, *Histoire socialiste*, IV, 1115-1121, 1808-1814.

A. Decree for Creating an Extraordinary Criminal Tribunal, March 10, 1793. Duvergier, *Lois*, V, 190-191.

Title I. Of the Composition and Organization of an Extraordinary Criminal Tribunal.

1. There shall be established at Paris an extraordinary criminal tribunal, which shall have jurisdiction over every counter-revolutionary enterprise, over all attacks against liberty, equality, unity, and the indivisibility of the Republic, the internal and external security of the state, and over all conspiracies tending to re-establish monarchy or to establish any other authority which makes an attack upon the liberty, equality, and sovereignty of the people, whether the accused be civil or military functionaries or simply citizens.

2. The tribunal shall be composed of a jury, and of five judges, who shall direct the examination and shall apply the law after the declaration of the jurors upon the facts.

3. The judges shall not render any decision unless they are at least three in number.

.   .   .   .

5. The judges shall be appointed by the National Convention by plurality of the votes, which, nevertheless, shall not be less than a fourth of the votes.

6. There shall be before the tribunal a public accuser and two assistants or alternates, who shall be appointed by the National Convention, as are the judges and according to the same method.

7. There shall be appointed by the National Convention in the sitting of tomorrow twelve citizens, of the department of Paris and of the four departments which environ it, who shall discharge the duties of jurors, and four alternates of the same department, who shall replace the jurors in case of absence, challenge or illness. The jurors shall discharge their duties until May 1st next; and there shall be provision made by the National Convention for their replacement and for the formation of a jury taken from among the citizens of all the departments.

8. The functions of the police of the general security, assigned to the municipalities and the administrative bodies by the decree of August 11th last, shall be extended to all the crimes and offences mentioned in article 1 of the present decree.

9. All the records of denunciations, informations, and arrests shall be addressed, in copy, by the administrative bodies, to the National Convention, which shall send them to a commission of its members charged to make examination of them and to make a report thereof.

10. There shall be formed a commission of six members of the National Convention, who shall be charged with the examination of all the papers, to make a report thereof, and to draw up and present the documents of accusation, to look after the examination which shall be made in the extraordinary tribunal, to maintain a constant correspondence with the public accuser and the judges upon all the public matters which shall be sent to the tribunal, and to render an account thereof to the National Convention.

11. The accused who shall wish to challenge one or more jurors shall be required to state the causes of challenge by one and the same document, and the tribunal shall pronounce upon the validity thereof within twenty-four hours.

12. The jurors shall vote and frame their declaration publicly, speaking aloud and acting by majority of the votes.

13. The judgments shall be carried out without recourse to the tribunal of cassation.

14. The accused fugitives who shall not present themselves within three months from the trial shall be treated as

émigrés, and shall be subject to the same penalties, whether in relation to their persons or to their estates.

. . . .

Title II. Of the Penalties.

1. The judges of the extraordinary tribunal shall pronounce the penalties provided by the penal code and the subsequent laws against the accused who are convicted; and when the offences which shall remain shall continue to be in the class of those which ought to be punished by penalties of the correctional police, the tribunal shall pronounce these penalties, without sending the accused to the police tribunals.

2. The estates of those who shall be condemned to the penalty of death shall be acquired by the Republic and there shall be provision made for the support of the widows and children, if they have no estates besides.

3. Those who may be convicted of crimes or offences which have not been provided for by the penal code and the subsequent laws, or whose punishment has not been determined by the laws, and whose incivism and residence upon the territory of the Republic have been a matter of public trouble and disturbance, shall be condemned to the penalty of deportation.

. . . .

B. Law of 22 Prairial. June 10, 1794 (22 Prairial, Year II). Duvergier, *Lois,* VII, 190-192.

1. The revolutionary tribunal shall have a president and four vice-presidents, one public accuser, four substitutes for the public accuser and twelve judges.

2. The jurors shall be fifty in number.

3. The different functions shall be discharged by the citizens whose names follow: . . .   (The omission relates exclusively to the *personnel* of the court.)

The revolutionary tribunal shall divide itself into sections composed of twelve members, to wit: three judges and nine jurors, which jurors cannot give judgment at a number less than that of seven.

4. The revolutionary tribunal is instituted in order to punish the enemies of the people.

5. The enemies of the people are those who seek to destroy the public liberty, either by force or by artifice.

6. Those are reputed enemies of the people who shall have promoted the re-establishment of royalty or sought to depreciate or dissolve the National Convention and the revolutionary and republican government of which it is the centre;

Those who shall have betrayed the Republic in the command of places and armies, or in any other military function; carried on correspondence with the enemies of the Republic; labored to make the supplies or the service of the armies fail;

Those who shall have sought to impede the supplies for Paris or to cause scarcity within the Republic;

Those who shall have seconded the projects of the enemies of France, either in aiding the withdrawal and the impunity of conspirators and the aristocracy, or in persecuting and calumniating patriotism, or in corrupting the servants of the people, or in abusing the principles of the revolution, the laws or the measures of the government, by false and perfidious applications;

Those who shall have deceived the people or the representatives of the people, in order to lead them into operations contrary to the interests of liberty;

Those who shall have sought to promote discouragement, in order to favor the enterprises of the tyrants leagued against the Republic;

Those who shall have spread false news in order to divide or disturb the people;

Those who shall have sought to mislead opinion and to prevent the instruction of the people, to deprave morals and to corrupt the public conscience, to impair the energy and the purity of the revolutionary and republican principles, either by stopping the progress of them, or by counter-revolutionary or insidious writings, or by any other machination;

The contractors whose bad faith compromises the safety of the Republic, and the wasters of the public fortune, other than those included in the provisions of the law of 7 Frimaire;

Those who, being charged with public functions, abuse them in order to serve the enemies of the revolution, to distress the patriots or to oppress the people;

Finally, all those who are designated in the preceding laws

relative to the punishment of the conspirators and counter-revolutionaries, and who, whatever the means or the appearances with which they cover themselves, shall have made an attack upon the liberty, unity, and security of the Republic, or labored to prevent the strengthening of them.

7. The penalty provided for all offences, the jurisdiction of which belongs to the revolutionary tribunal, is death.

8. The proof necessary to convict the enemies of the people is every kind of evidence, either material or moral or verbal or written, which can naturally secure the approval of every just and reasonable spirit; the rule of judgment is the conscience of the jurors enlightened by love of the fatherland; their aim, the triumph of the Republic and the ruin of its enemies; the procedure, the simple means which good sense dictates in order to come to the knowledge of the truth, in the forms which the law determines.

It is confined to the following points:

9. Every citizen has the right to seize and to arraign before the magistrates conspirators and counter-revolutionaries. He is required to denounce them when he knows of them.

10. Nobody can arraign a person before the revolutionary tribunal, except the National Convention, the committee of public safety, the committee of general security, the representatives of the people who are commissioners of the Convention, and the public accuser of the revolutionary tribunal.

11. The constituted authorities in general cannot exercise this right without having notified the committee of public safety and the committee of general security and obtained their authorisation.

12. The accused shall be examined in public session: the formality of the secret examination which precedes is suppressed as superfluous; it shall occur only under special circumstances in which it shall be judged useful for a knowledge of the truth.

13. If proofs exist, either material or moral, independently of the testified proof. there shall be no further hearing of testimony, unless that formality appears necessary, either to discover the accomplices or for other important considerations of public interest.

14. In a case in which there shall be occasion for this

proof, the public accuser shall cause to be summoned the witnesses who can show the way to justice, without distinction of witnesses for or against.

15. All the proceedings shall be conducted in public and no written deposition shall be received, unless the witnesses are so situated that they cannot be brought before the tribunal, and in that case an express authorisation of the committees of public safety and general security shall be necessary.

16. The law gives sworn patriots to calumniated patriots for counsel; it does not grant them to conspirators.

17. The pleadings finished, the jurors shall formulate their verdicts and the judges shall pronounce the penalty in the manner determined by the laws.

The president shall propound the question with lucidity, precision and simplicity. If it was presented in an equivocal or inexact manner, the jury may ask that it be propounded in another manner.

18. The public accuser may not on his own authority discharge a prisoner bound over to the tribunal or one whom he shall have caused to be arraigned there; in a case in which there is no matter for an accusation before the tribunal, he shall make a written report of it, with a statement of the reasons, to the chamber of the council, which shall pronounce. But no prisoner may be discharged from trial before the decision of the chamber has been communicated to the committees of public safety and general security, who shall examine it.

19. A double register shall be kept of the persons arraigned before the revolutionary tribunal, one for the public accuser and the other for the tribunal, upon which shall be enrolled all the prisoners, according as they shall be arraigned.

20. The Convention modifies all those provisions of the preceding laws which may not be in agreement with the present law and does not intend that the laws concerning the organization of the ordinary tribunals should apply to the crimes of counter-revolution and to the action of the revolutionary tribunal.

21. The report of the committee shall be joined to the present decree as instruction.

33. Decree for Establishing the Revolutionary Committees.

March 21, 1793. Duvergier, *Lois*, V, 206-207.

The revolutionary committees created by this decree were among the most characteristic and potent agencies in the service of the revolutionary government. The powers granted in this decree were subsequently much increased in various ways, chiefly by additional decrees and by authorisation of the committee of public safety. For these powers at their greatest extent see No. 45.

REFERENCE. Aulard, *Révolution française*, 350-355.

1. There shall be formed in each commune of the Republic and in each section of the communes divided into sections, at the hour which shall be indicated in advance by the general council, a committee composed of twelve citizens.

2. The members of this committee, who cannot be chosen from the ecclesiastics, former nobles, former seigneurs of the locality, and agents of the former seigneurs, shall be chosen by ballot and by plurality of the votes.

.   .   .   .

4. The committee of the commune, or each of the committees of the sections of the commune, shall be charged to receive for its district the declarations of all the strangers actually residing within the commune or who may arrive there.

5. These declarations shall contain the names, age, profession, place of birth and means of existence of the declarer.

6. They shall be made within eight days after the publication of the present decree; the list thereof shall be printed and posted.

7. Every foreigner who shall have refused or neglected to make his declaration before the committee of the commune or of the section in which he shall reside, within the period above prescribed, shall be required to leave the commune within twenty-four hours and the territory of the Republic within eight days.

.   .   .   .

34. Decree upon the Press.

March 29, 1793. Duvergier, Lois, V, 230.

During the earlier stages of the revolution the freedom of the press was accepted both in principle and in practice. Without formally abandoning the principle, the royalist newspapers were suppressed after the establishment of the Republic, and Girondist newspapers after the proscription of the Girondist deputies. This decree illustrates the method employed against the royalist newspapers and is typical of all decrees affecting the press.

REFERENCE. Aulard, *Révolution française*, 359-361.

The National Convention decrees:

1. Whoever shall be convicted of having composed or printed works or writings which incite to the dissolution of the national representation, the re-establishment of monarchy or of any other power which constitutes an attack upon the sovereignty of the people, shall be arraigned before the extra-ordinary tribunal and punished with death.

2. The vendors, distributors and hawkers of these works or writings shall be condemned to an imprisonment which shall not exceed three months, if they declare the authors, printers or other persons from whom they have obtained them; if they refuse this declaration, they shall be punished by two years in prison.

35. Decree for Establishing the Committee of Public Safety.

April 6, 1793. Duvergier, *Lois*, V, 240.

This document shows the Committee of Public Safety in its original character, that of a ministry responsible to the Convention. (See Aulard, *Révolution française*, 334-335.) Through changes in its membership and the multiplication of its powers and duties, in part by decree of the Convention, in part by mere custom, it gradually became a very different institution. For its later character see Nos. 43 and 45.

REFERENCES. Gardiner, *French Revolution*, 145-146; Mathews, *French Revolution*, 228-231; Stephens, *French Revolution*, II, Ch. ix; Aulard, *Révolution française*, 329-342.

The National Convention decrees:

1. There shall be formed, by the call of names, a committee of public safety, composed of nine members of the National Convention.

2. The committee shall deliberate in secret; it shall be charged to supervise and accelerate the action of the administration entrusted to the provisional executive council, of which it may even suspend the orders, when it shall believe them

contrary to the national interest, subject to giving information thereof to the Convention without delay.

3. It is authorised to take, under urgent circumstances, measures of external and internal defence; and the orders signed by the majority of its deliberating members, which cannot be less than two-thirds, shall be executed without delay by the provisional executive council. It shall not in any case issue warrants of capture or arrest, except against the executive agents, and subject to rendering an account thereof without delay to the Convention.

4. The National Treasury shall hold at the disposal of the committee of public safety [a sum of money] to the amount of a hundred thousand livres for secret expenses, which shall be disbursed by the committee and paid upon its commands, which shall be signed as are the orders.

5. It shall make each week in writing a general report of its operations and of the situation of the Republic.

6. A register of all its deliberations shall be kept.

7. This committee is established only for one month.

8. The national treasury shall remain independent of the committee of execution and subject to the immediate sur-veillance of the Convention, according to the method determined by the decrees.

36.   Robespierre's Proposed Declaration of Rights.

April 24, 1793. *Moniteur*, May 5, 1793. (*Réimpression*, XVI, 294-296).

This document was brought forward in the Convention by Robespierre during the debates over the constitution of the Year I. Although not actually adopted it possesses great interest as a profession of faith of its author. The economic tendency of the document and its implications in regard to foreign policy should be particularly noticed.

REFERENCES.   Von Sybel. *French Revolution*, III. 64 ; Aulard, *Révolution française*, 290-292 ; Jaurès, *Histoire socialiste*, IV, 1563-1572.

The representatives of the French people, met in National Convention, recognizing that human laws which do not flow from the eternal laws of justice and reason are only the outrages of ignorance and despotism upon humanity; convinced that neglect and contempt of the natural rights of man are the sole causes of the crimes and misfortunes of the world; have resolved to set forth in a solemn declaration these sacred and inalienable rights, in order that all citizens, being enabled to compare constantly the acts of the government with the purpose of every social institution, may never permit themselves to be oppressed and disgraced by tyranny; and in order that the people may always have before their eyes the foundations of their liberty and their welfare; the magistrate, the rule of his duties; the legislator, the purpose of his mission.

In consequence, the National Convention proclaims in the face of the world and under the eyes of the Immortal Legislator the following declaration of the rights of man and citizen.

1. The purpose of every political association is the maintenance of the natural and imprescriptible rights of man and the development of all his faculties.

2. The principal rights of man are those of providing for the preservation of his existence and his liberty.

3. These rights belong equally to all men, whatever may be the difference of their physical and mental powers.

4. Equality of rights is established by nature: society, far from impairing it, exists only to guarantee it against the abuse of power which renders it illusory.

5. Liberty is the power which belongs to man to exercise at his will all his faculties; it has justice for rule, the rights of others for limits, nature for principle, and the law for safeguard.

6. The right to assemble peaceably, the right to express one's opinions, either by means of the press or in any other manner, are such necessary consequences of the principle of the liberty of man, that the necessity to enunciate them supposes either the presence or the fresh recollection of despotism.

7. The law can forbid only that which is injurious to society; it can order only that which is useful.

8. Every law which violates the imprescriptible rights of man is essentially unjust and tyrannical; it is not a law.

9. Property is the right which each citizen has, to enjoy

and dispose of the portion of goods which the law guarantees to him.

10. The right of property is restricted, as are all the others, by the obligation to respect the possessions of others.

11. It cannot prejudice the security, nor the liberty, nor the existence, nor the property of our fellow creatures.

12. All traffic which violates this principle is essentially illicit and immoral.

13. Society is under obligation to provide for the support of all its members either by procuring work for them or by assuring a means of existence to those who are not in condition to work.

14. The relief indispensable for those who lack the necessities of life is a debt of those who possess a superfluity; it belongs to the law to determine the manner in which this debt must be discharged.

15. The citizens whose incomes do not exceed what is necessary for their subsistence are exempted from contributing to the public expenses; the others shall support them progressively, accordingly to the extent of their fortunes.

16. Society ought to favor with all its power the progress of public reason and to put instruction at the door of all the citizens.

17. Law is the free and solemn expression of the will of the people.

18. The people are the sovereign, the government is their creation, the public functionaries are their agents; the people can, when they please, change their government and recall their mandatories.

19. No portion of the people can exercise the power of the entire people; but the opinion which it expresses shall be respected as the opinion of a portion of the people who ought to participate in the formation of the general will. Each section of the assembled sovereign ought to enjoy the right to express its will with entire liberty; it is essentially independent of all the constituted authorities and is capable of regulating its police and its deliberations.

20. The law ought to be equal for all.

21. All citizens are admissable to all public offices, without any other distinction than those of their virtues and talents

and without any other title than the confidence of the people.

22. All citizens have an equal right to participate in the selection of the mandatories of the people and in the formation of the law.

23. In order that these rights may not be illusory and the equality chimerical, society ought to give salaries to the public functionaries and to provide so that all the citizens who live by their labor can be present in the public assemblies to which the law calls them, without compromising their existence or that of their families.

24. Every citizen ought to obey religiously the magistrates and the agents of the government, when they are the organs or the executors of the law.

25. But every act against the liberty, security, or property of a man, committed by anyone whomsoever, even in the name of the law, outside of the cases determined by it and the forms which it prescribes, is arbitrary and void; respect for the law even forbids submission to it; and if an attempt is made to execute it by violence, it is permissible to repel it by force.

26. The right to present petitions to the depositories of the public authority belongs to every person. Those to whom they are addressed ought to pass upon the points which are the object thereof; but they can never interdict, nor restrain, nor condemn their use.

27. Resistance to oppression is a consequence of the other rights of man and citizen.

28. There is oppression against the social body when one of its members is oppressed. There is oppression against each member of the social body when the social body shall be oppressed.

29. When the government violates the rights of the people, insurrection is for the people and for each portion of the people the most sacred of rights and the most indispensable of duties.

30. When the social guarantee is lacking to a citizen he re-enters into the natural right to defend all his rights himself.

31. In either case, to tie down to legal forms resistance to oppression is the last refinement of tyranny. In every free state the law ought especially to defend public and personal

liberty against the abuse of the authority of those who gov ern; every institution which is not based upon the assumption that the people are good and the magistrate is corruptible is vicious.

32. The public offices cannot be considered as distinctions, nor as rewards, but only as duties.

33. The offences of the mandatories of the people ought to be severely and quickly punished. No one has the right to claim for himself more inviolability than other citizens. The people have the right to know all the transactions of their mandatories; these ought to render to them a faithful account of their own administration and to submit to their judgment with respect.

34. Men of all countries are brothers and the different peoples ought to aid one another, according to their power, as if citizens of the same state.

35. The one who oppresses a single nation declares himself the enemy of all.

36. Those who make war on a people in order to arrest the progress of liberty and to destroy the rights of man ought to be pursued by all, not as ordinary enemies, but as assassins and rebellious brigands.

37. Kings, aristocrats and tyrants, whoever they may be, are slaves in rebellion against the sovereign of the earth, which is mankind, and against the legislator of the universe, which is nature.

37. Decree upon the Deputies on Mission.

April 30, 1793. *Moniteur*, May 3, 1793. (*Réimpression*, XVI, 281-283).

Among the institutions of the revolutionary government there was none more characteristic than the deputies on mission. (They are also known as the representatives on mission.) The first appearance of the system was at the time of the king's flight; after the 10th of August it developed rapidly. This decree applied only to the deputies sent on mission to the armies, but their powers were typical of all those sent out. It simply defined what had already grown up in practice. In No. 45 the duties and powers of the deputies on mission are more fully set forth.

REFERENCES. Gardiner, *French Revolution*, 146-147; Stephens, *French Revolution*, II, 320, 364-371, 548-554; Aulard, *Révolution française*, 342-348.

The National Convention, after having heard the report of its Committee of Public Safety . . . decrees:

1. All the powers delegated by the Convention to the commissioners whom it has appointed to repair to the departments for recruiting, to the armies, upon the frontiers, coasts and in the harbors, are revoked. All the deputies who are on mission, except those hereinafter named, shall return directly to the body of the assembly.

. . . .

9. The commissioners of the Convention to the armies shall bear the titles of representatives of the people sent to such army; they shall wear the costume decreed the current April 3.

10. The representatives of the people sent to the armies and the generals shall co-operate in order to make appointments immediately for all the posts vacant or which shall come to be vacant, whether by death, resignation or dismissal, in conformity with the method of promotion which has been decreed; and in cases of urgency and the lack of persons who have the qualifications required by law, they can appoint provisionally and for fifteen days only.

11. The representatives of the people sent to the armies shall exercise the most active surveillance over the operations of the agents of the executive council, all contractors and dealers for the armies, and over the conduct of the generals, officers and soldiers; they may suspend all civil agents and appoint [others] provisionally.

12. They can also suspend the military agents, but they can replace them only provisionally until after the approval of the Convention for suspension or until the persons appointed or elected in virtue of the law have arrived at their posts.

13. They shall look after the condition as regards defence and supply of provisions for all places, forts, harbors, coasts, armies and fleets of their district; they shall cause inventories to be prepared for all the magazines of the Republic, and they shall cause an account to be rendered daily of the condition of all the descriptions of supplies, arms, provisions and munitions.

14. They shall cause inspection to be made of all the

armies and fleets of the republic; they shall cause to be returned every fifteen days lists of the effectives of each corps, signed by the civil and military agents; they shall take all measures which they shall deem suitable to accelerate the armament, equipment and incorporation of the volunteers and recruits in the existing organizations, and the armament and equipment of the fleets of the Republic; in these operations they shall co-operate with the admirals, generals and division commanders, and other agents of the executive council.

15. In case of insufficiency of the forces decreed, they may make requisition upon the national guards of the departments, whom they shall cause to be organized into battalions after the method which shall be decreed; they shall also make requisition for the mounted national guards, in order to complete the existing organizations; and when the organizations shall be complete, they can form new squadrons of them, making use of pleasure horses and those of the *émigrés* or those which can be procured.

16. They shall take all measures to discover and to cause to be arrested the generals, and to cause to be arrested and arraigned before the revolutionary tribunal every military man, civil agent and other citizen who may have aided, favored or advised a conspiracy against the liberty and security of the Republic, or who may have plotted for the disorganization of the armies and fleets and squandered the public funds.

17. They shall cause to be distributed to the troops the bulletins, addresses, proclamations and instructions of the Convention, which shall be addressed to the armies by the committee of correspondence; they shall employ all the means of instruction which are in their power, in order to maintain there the republican spirit.

18. The representatives of the people sent to the armies are invested with unlimited powers for the exercise of the powers which are delegated to them; they can make requisition upon the administrative bodies and all civil and military agents; they can act in the number of two and can employ the number of agents which shall be necessary for them. Their orders shall be executed provisionally.

.   .   .   .

20. The representatives of the people sent to the armies

shall render account of their operations, at least each week, to the Convention; they shall be required to address each day to the Committee of Public Safety the record of their operations, copies of their orders and proclamations, and of all inventories and lists of supplies, which they shall have caused to be drawn up; they shall also address each day to the committee of finance and to the national treasury a detailed account of the lists of expenses which they shall have examined and endorsed.

21. The Committee of Public Safety shall present each week to the Convention a summary report of the operations of the various commissioners; the committee of finance shall also make each week a report of the expenses examined and approved by them; these reports shall be printed and distributed.

22. The representatives of the people sent to the armies shall be renewed by half each month; they shall return to the Convention only after an authorization given by it, except in urgent cases, and in virtue of a decree of the commission with a statement of reasons.

23. The Committee of Public Safety shall furnish instructions to the representatives of the people sent to the armies, in order to secure uniformity in their operations.

.   .   .   .

26. The representatives of the people sent to the armies, who are appointed by the present decree, shall continue, each in his district, the supervision over the recruiting and the organization into departments and districts of the countries recently united to the Republic.   .   .   .

27. The Committee of Public Safety shall send the present decree to the commissioners of the Convention at present on mission. Those who are appointed by the present decree shall repair directly to their new posts, and those who are at present with the armies shall remain there until they may be replaced.

38. Documents upon the Convention and Education.

The Convention was greatly interested in education. Much time was devoted to the formulation of educational plans, even at the most critical stages of national danger. The plans first adopted were frequently changed. Of the plans here given the first two represent the most ambitious schemes of the Convention for primary and secondary schools respectively. Document C is the final scheme for the whole educational system.

REFERENCES. Stephens, *Yale Review*, IV, 314-323 ; Lavisse and Rambaud, *Histoire générale*, VIII, 534-556 ; Rambaud, *Civilisation contemporaine*, 162-168 ; Jaurès, *Histoire socialiste*, IV, 1465-1490, V, 186-206.

A. Decree upon Primary Education. May 30, 1793. Duvergier, *Lois*, V, 309.

1. There shall be a primary school in all places which have from four hundred to fifteen hundred persons.

This school shall serve for all the inhabitants except people who shall be more than a thousand toises distant.

2. There shall be in each of these schools a teacher charged to instruct the pupils in the branches of knowledge necessary to citizens in order to exercise their rights, to discharge their duties and to administer their domestic affairs.

3. The committee of public instruction shall present the proportional method for the more populous communes and the cities.

4. The teachers shall be charged to give lectures and instruction once per week to citizens of every age and of both sexes.

5. The project of the present decree presented by the committee of public instruction shall be irrevocably placed as the order of the day for every Thursday.

B. Decree upon Secondary Education. February 25, 1795 (7 Ventôse, Year III). Duvergier, *Lois*, VIII, 29-30.

Chapter I. Institution of the Central Schools.

1. For instruction in the sciences, letters and arts there shall be established in the entire extent of the Republic central schools distributed on the basis of population; the proportional basis shall be one school for three hundred thousand inhabitants.

2. Each central school shall be composed of, 1st, a professor of mathematics; 2d, a professor of experimental physics and chemistry; 3d, a professor of natural history; 4th, a

professor of agriculture and commerce; 5th, a professor of the method of the sciences or logic; 6th, a professor of political economy and legislation; 7th, a professor of the philosophical history of peoples; 8th, a professor of hygiene; 9th, a professor of arts and crafts; 10th, a professor of general grammar; 11th, a professor of *belles-lettres;* 12th, a professor of ancient languages; 13th, a professor of the living languages most appropriate to the localities; 14th, a professor of the arts of design.

3. In all the central schools the professors shall give their lessons in French.

4. They shall have every month a public conference upon matters which affect the progress of the sciences, letters and arts most useful to society.

5. At each central school there shall be, 1st, a public library; 2d, a garden and a cabinet of natural history; 3d, a cabinet of experimental physics; 4th, a collection of machines and models for the arts and crafts.

6. The committee of public instruction remains charged to cause to be composed the elementary books which must serve for the instruction in the central schools.

. . . .

Chapter III. Pupils of the Fatherland.

1. The pupils who at the *Festival of Youth* shall be most distinguished and shall have obtained more especially the approbation of the people shall receive, if they are of small fortune, an annual pension in order to procure for them the opportunity to attend the central schools.

2. Prizes of encouragement shall be distributed every year in the presence of the people at the *Festival of Youth.*

The professor of the pupils who shall have won the prize shall receive a civic crown.

3. In consequence of the present law, all the establishments devoted to public instruction under the name of *colleges* and paid stipends by the nation, are and shall remain suppressed within the entire extent of the Republic.

4. The committee of public instruction shall make a report upon the buildings and establishments already devoted to public instruction in the sciences and arts, such as botanical gardens, cabinets of natural history, fields intended for

experiments in cultivation, observations, and societies of scholars and artists which it may be well to preserve in the new plan of national instruction.

C. Organic Act upon Education. October 25, 1795. (3 Brumaire, Year IV). Duvergier, *Lois*, VIII, 357-360.

.　　.　　.　　.　　.　　.　　.　　.

Title III. Of the Special Schools.

1. There shall be in the Republic schools especially intended for the study of: 1st, astronomy; 2d, geometry and mechanics; 3d, natural history; 4th, medicine; 5th, the veterinary art; 6th, rural economy; 7th, antiquities; 8th, the political sciences; 9th, painting, sculpture and architecture; 10th; music.

.　　.　　.　　.　　.　　.　　.　　.

Title IV. National Institute of the Sciences and Arts.

1. The National Institute of the Sciences and Arts belongs to the whole Republic; it is located at Paris; it is intended: 1st, to improve the sciences and arts by uninterrupted researches, by the publication of discoveries, by correspondence with foreign learned societies; 2d, to pursue, in conformity with the laws and orders of the Executive Directory, literary and scientific works which shall have for their purpose the general advantage and the glory of the Republic.

2. It is composed of members residing at Paris and of an equal number scattered in the different parts of the Republic; it associates with itself foreign scholars, of whom the number is twenty-four, eight for each of the three classes.

.　　.　　.　　.　　.　　.　　.

6. Each class of the Institute shall publish every year its discoveries and works.

.　　.　　.　　.　　.　　.　　.

10. The Institute being once organized, the appointments to vacant places shall be made by the Institute out of a list, at least triple, presented by the class in which a place shall have become vacant.

39. Constitution of the Year I.

June 24, 1793.   Duvergier, *Lois*, V, 352-358.

This constitution was drawn up by the Convention and was submitted to the people. Although accepted by them, it was never put in operation, being first temporarily suspended and afterwards set aside. It possesses decided interest, nevertheless, since it represents the ideas of the Montagnards as to the best permanent form of government. It should be compared with their schemes of provisional government (Nos. 43 and 45) and with the constitutions of 1791 and of the Year III (Nos. 15 and 50), especially with respect to the executive and legislative branches of the government.

REFERENCES. Mathews, *French Revolution*, 227-229 ; Stephens, *French Revolution*, II, 530-535 ; *Cambridge Modern History*, VIII, 342 ; Aulard, *Révolution française*, Part II, Ch. IV ; Lavisse and Rambaud, *Histoire générale*, VIII, 179-180.

Declaration of the Rights of Man and Citizen.

The French people, convinced that forgetfulness and contempts of the natural rights of man are the sole causes of the miseries of the world, have resolved to set forth in a solemn declaration these sacred and inalienable rights, in order that all the citizens, being able to compare unceasingly the acts of the government with the aim of every social institution, may never allow themselves to be oppressed and debased by tyranny; and in order that the people may always have before their eyes the foundations of their liberty and their welfare, the magistrate the rule of his duties, the legislator the purpose of his commission.

In consequence, it proclaims in the presence of the supreme being the following declaration of the rights of man and citizen.

1. The aim of society is the common welfare.

Government is instituted in order to guarantee to man the enjoyment of his natural and imprescriptible rights.

2. These rights are equality, liberty, security, and property.

3. All men are equal by nature and before the law.

4. Law is the free and solemn expression of the general will; it is the same for all, whether it protects or punishes; it can command only what is just and useful to society; it can forbid only what is injurious to it.

5. All citizens are equally eligible to public employments. Free peoples know no other grounds for preference in their elections than virtue and talent.

6. Liberty is the power that belongs to man to do whatever is not injurious to the rights of others; it has nature for its principle, justice for its rule, law for its defence; its moral limit is in this maxim: Do not do to another that which you do not wish should be done to you.

7. The right to express one's thoughts and opinions by means of the press or in any other manner, the right to assemble peaceably, the free pursuit of religion, cannot be forbidden.

The necessity of enunciating these rights supposes either the presence or the fresh recollection of despotism.

8. Security consists in the protection afforded by society to each of its members for the preservation of his person, his rights, and his property.

9. The law ought to protect public and personal liberty against the oppression of those who govern.

10. No one ought to be accused, arrested, or detained except in the cases determined by law and according to the forms that it has prescribed. Any citizen summoned or seized by the authority of the law, ought to obey immediately; he makes himself guilty by resistance.

11. Any act done against man outside of the cases and without the forms that the law determines is arbitrary and tyrannical; the one against whom it may be intended to be executed by violence has the right to repel it by force.

12. Those who may incite, expedite, subscribe to, execute or cause to be executed arbitrary legal instruments are guilty and ought to be punished.

13. Every man being presumed innocent until he has been pronounced guilty, if it is thought indispensable to arrest him, all severity that may not be necessary to secure his person ought to be strictly repressed by law.

14. No one ought to be tried and punished except after having been heard or legally summoned, and except in virtue of a law promulgated prior to the offence. The law which would punish offences committed before it existed would be

a tyranny: the retroactive effect given to the law would be a crime.

15. The law ought to impose only penalties that are strictly and obviously necessary: the punishments ought to be proportionate to the offence and useful to society.

16. The right of property is that which belongs to every citizen to enjoy, and to dispose at his pleasure of his goods, income, and of the fruits of his labor and his skill.

17. No kind of labor, tillage, or commerce can be forbidden to the skill of the citizens.

18. Every man can contract his services and his time, but he cannot sell himself nor be sold: his person is not an alienable property. The law knows of no such thing as the status of servant; there can exist only a contract for services and compensation between the man who works and the one who employs him.

19. No one can be deprived of the least portion of his property without his consent, unless a legally established public necessity requires it, and upon condition of a just and prior compensation.

20. No tax can be imposed except for the general advantage. All citizens have the right to participate in the establishment of taxes, to watch over the employment of them, and to cause an account of them to be rendered.

21. Public relief is a sacred debt. Society owes maintenance to unfortunate citizens, either in procuring work for them or in providing the means of existence for those who are unable to labor.

22. Education is needed by all. Society ought to favor with all its power the advancement of the public reason and to put education at the door of every citizen.

23. The social guarantee consists in the action of all to secure to each the enjoyment and the maintenance of his rights: this guarantee rests upon the national sovereignty.

24. It cannot exist if the limits of public functions are not clearly determined by law and if the responsibility of all the functionaries is not secured.

25. The sovereignty resides in the people; it is one and indivisible, imprescriptible, and inalienable.

26. No portion of the people can exercise the power of

the entire people; but each section of the sovereign, in assembly, ought to enjoy the right to express its will with entire freedom.

27. Let any person who may usurp the sovereignty be instantly put to death by free men.

28. A people has always the right to review, to reform, and to alter its constitution. One generation cannot subject to its law the future generations.

29. Each citizen has an equal right to participate in the formation of the law and in the selection of his mandatories or his agents.

30. Public functions are necessarily temporary; they cannot be considered as distinctions or rewards, but as duties.

31. The offences of the representatives of the people and of its agents ought never to go unpunished. No one has the right to claim for himself more inviolability than other citizens.

32. The right to present petitions to the depositories of the public authority cannot in any case be forbidden, suspended, nor limited.

33. Resistance to oppression is the consequence of the other rights of man.

34. There is oppression against the social body when a single one of its members is oppressed: there is oppression against each member when the social body is oppressed.

35. When the government violates the rights of the people, insurrection is for the people and for each portion of the people the most sacred of rights and the most indispensable of duties.

Constitutional Act.

Of the Republic.

1. The French Republic is one and indivisible.

Of the Division of the People.

2. The French people is divided, for the exercise of its sovereignty, into cantonal primary assemblies.

3. It is divided for administration and for justice into departments, districts and municipalities.

Of the Conditions of Citizenship.

4. Every man born and living in France fully twenty-one years of age;

Every foreigner fully twenty-one years of age, who, domiciled in France for a year,

Lives there by his own labor,

Or acquires property,

Or marries a French woman,

Or adopts a child,

Or supports an aged man,

Finally, every foreigner who shall be thought by the legislative body to have deserved well of humanity,

Is admitted to the exercise of the rights of French citizenship.

5. The exercise of the rights of citizenship is lost:

By naturalization in a foreign country;

By the acceptance of employments or favors proceeding from a non-popular government;

By condemnation to ignominious or afflictive penalties until rehabilitation.

6. The exercise of the rights of citizenship is suspended:

By the condition of accusation;

By a judicial order for contempt of court until the order is abrogated.

Of the Sovereignty of the People.

7. The sovereign people is the totality of French citizens.

8. It selects its deputies directly.

9. It delegates to electors the choice of administrators, the public arbitrators, criminal judges, and judges of cassation.

10. It deliberates upon the laws.

Of the Primary Assemblies.

11. The primary assemblies are composed of the citizens domiciled for six months in each canton.

12. They are composed at the least of two hundred and at the most of six hundred citizens summoned to vote.

13. They are constituted by the selection of a president, secretaries and tellers.

14. Their policing belongs to themselves.

15. No one can appear in them with arms.

16. The elections are conducted by either secret or open voting at the choice of each voter.

17. A primary assembly cannot in any case prescribe a uniform method of voting.

18. The tellers attest the vote of citizens who, not knowing how to write, prefer to vote by ballot.

19. Votes upon the laws are given by *yes* or *no*.

20. The will of the primary assembly is proclaimed as follows: *The citizens met in primary assembly . . . to the number of . . . voters, vote for or vote against, by a majority of . . .*

Of the National Representation.

21. Population is the sole basis of the national representation.

22. There is one deputy for every forty thousand persons.

23. Each union of primary assemblies aggregating a population of thirty-nine to forty-one thousand souls selects directly one deputy.

24. The selection is made by the majority of the votes.

25. Each assembly counts the votes and sends a commissioner for the general recording to the place designated as the most central.

26. If the first return does not give a majority, a second appeal is made and a vote is taken upon the two citizens who have received the greatest number of votes.

27. In case of an equality of votes the most aged has the preference, either as the one to be voted upon or as the one elected. In case of an equality of age, lot decides.

28. Every Frenchman exercising the rights of citizenship is eligible throughout the extent of the Republic.

29. Each deputy belongs to the entire nation.

30. In case of the non-acceptance, resignation, forfeiture, or death of a deputy, his replacement is provided for by the primary assemblies which selected him.

31. A deputy who has resigned cannot leave his post until after the admittance of his successor.

32. The French people assembles every year on the first of May for the elections.

33. They proceed to them, whatever may be the number of citizens there having the right to vote.

34. The primary assemblies meet in extraordinary session upon the request of one-fifth of the citizens who have the right to vote there.

35. The summons is issued in that case by the municipality of the usual place of meeting.

36. These extraordinary assemblies transact business only if a half plus one of the citizens who have the right to vote there are present.

Of the Electoral Assemblies.

37. The citizens meet in primary assemblies and select one elector for every two hundred citizens, whether present or not; two for three hundred-one to four hundred; three for five hundred-one to six hundred.

38. The holding of electoral assemblies and the method of election are the same as in the primary assemblies.

Of the Legislative Body.

39. The legislative body is one, indivisible, and permanent.

40. The session is for one year.

41. It meets the first of July.

42. The National Assembly cannot constitute itself if it is not composed of at least one-half of the deputies plus one.

43. The deputies cannot be questioned, accused, or tried at any time for the opinions that they have expressed within the legislative body.

44. They can be arrested for criminal acts, if taken in the act; but the warrant of arrest and the warrant of apprehension can be issued against them only with the authorisation of the legislative body.

Holding of the Sittings of the Legislative Body.

45. The sittings of the National Assembly are public.

46. The minutes of its sittings are printed.

47. It cannot deliberate unless it is composed of at least two hundred members.

48. It cannot refuse the word to its members in the order that they have claimed it.

49. It decides by the majority of those present.

50. Fifty members have the right to require a vote by roll call.

51. It has the right of discipline upon the conduct of its members within its own midst.

52. The policing of the place of its sittings and of the environs of which it has fixed the extent belongs to it.

Of the Functions of the Legislative Body.

53. The legislative body proposes laws and issues decrees.

54. Included under the general name of *law* are the acts of the legislative body in regard to:

Civil and criminal legislation;

The general administration of the revenues and ordinary expenses of the Republic;

The national domains;

The title, weight, impress, and denomination of the monies;

The nature, amount, and collection of the taxes;

The declaration of war;

Every new general division of the French territory;

Public instruction;

Public honors to the memory of great men.

55. Included under the special name of *decree* are the acts of the legislative body in regard to:

The annual establishment of the land and sea forces;

Permission or prohibition of the passage of foreign troops over French soil;

The introduction of foreign naval forces into the ports of the Republic;

Measures of general security and tranquility;

The annual and occasional distribution of public relief and work;

Orders for the coining of money of every sort;

Unforeseen and extraordinary expenses;

The local and special measures for an administration, a commune, or a class of public works;

The defence of the soil;

Ratification of treaties;

The appointment and dismissal of commanders-in-chief of the armies;

Proceedings to enforce the responsibility of members of the council and of public officials:

Accusation of those accused of plots against the general security of the republic;

Every alteration in the division of French territory into parts;

National rewards.

Of the Formation of the Law.

56. Projects of law are preceded by a report.

57. The discussion cannot begin and the law cannot be provisionally decreed until fifteen days after the report.

58. The project is printed and sent to all the communes of the Republic under this title: *Proposed law.*

59. Forty days after the sending of the proposed law, if in one-half of the departments plus one, a tenth of the regularly constituted primary assemblies of each of them do not object, the project is accepted and becomes *law.*

60. If there is objection, the legislative body convokes the primary assemblies.

Of the Title of the Laws and Decrees.

61. The laws, the decrees, the judicial orders, and all public acts are superscribed: *In the name of the French people, the year . . . of the French Republic.*

Of the Executive Council.

62. There is an executive council composed of twenty-four members.

63. The electoral assembly of each department selects a candidate. The legislative body chooses the members of the council from the general list.

64. It is renewed by a half at each legislature in the last month of its session.

65. The council is charged with the direction and supervision of the general administration; it can act only in the execution of the laws and decrees of the legislative body.

66. It appoints, from outside of its own body, the principal agents of the general administration of the Republic.

67. The legislative body determines the number and the duties of these agents.

68. These agents do not form a council; they are separate and are without direct relations with each other; they do not exercise any personal authority.

69. The council appoints, from outside its own body, the foreign agents of the Republic.

70. It negotiates the treaties.

71. The members of the council, in cases of betrayal of trust, are accused by the legislative body.

72. The council is responsible for the non-execution of the laws and decrees and for the abuses of which it does not give notice.

73. It recalls and replaces the agents within its appointment.

74. It is required to denounce them, if there is occasion, to the judicial authorities.

Of the Relations of the Executive Council with the Legislative Body.

75. The executive council resides near the legislative body; it has admittance and a separate position in the place of its meetings.

76. It is heard whenever it has a statement to make.

77. The legislative body summons it into its presence, in whole or in part, whenever it thinks expedient.

Of the Administrative and Municipal Bodies.

78. There is in each commune of the Republic a municipal administration;

In each district, an intermediate administration;

In each department, a central administration.

79. The municipal officers are elected by the communal assemblies.

80. The administrators are appointed by the department and district electoral assemblies.

81. The municipalities and the administrations are renewed each year by half.

82. The administrators and municipal officers have no representative character.

They cannot in any case alter the acts of the legislative body nor suspend the execution of them.

83. The legislative body fixes the duties of the municipal officers and the administrators, the rules of their subordination, and the penalties that they may incur.

Of the Tribunal of Cassation.

98. There is a tribunal of cassation for the whole Republic.

99. This tribunal does not have jurisdiction over the facts of cases.

It passes upon the violation of forms and upon clear infractions of the law.

100. The members of this court are appointed every year by the electoral assemblies.

Of the Public Taxes.

101. No citizen is exempt from the honorable obligation to contribute to the public expenses.

Of the National Treasury.

102. The national treasury is the central point of the receipts and expenditures of the Republic.

103. It is administered by responsible agents appointed by the executive council.

104. These agents are watched over by commissioners appointed by the legislative body, taken from outside of itself, and responsible for the abuses of which they do not give notice.

Of the Book-Keeping.

105. The accounts of the agents of the national treasury and of the administrators of the public monies are rendered annually to responsible commissioners appointed by the executive council.

106. These auditors are watched over by commissioners appointed by the legislative body, taken from outside of itself, and responsible for the abuses and errors of which they do not give notice.

The legislative body approves the accounts.

Of the Forces of the Republic.

107. The general force of the Republic is composed of the entire people.

108. The Republic supports, even in time of peace, a paid army and navy.

109. All Frenchmen are soldiers; they are all trained in the handling of arms.

84. The sittings of the municipalities and the administrations are public.

Of Civil Justice.

85. The code of civil and penal law is uniform for the whole Republic.

86. No attack can be made upon the right that the citizens have to cause their differences to be passed upon by arbitrators of their own choice.

87. The decision of these arbitrators is final, if citizens do not reserve the right to object.

88. There are justices of the peace elected by the citizens of the districts fixed by the law.

89. They conciliate and pass judgment without expense.

90. Their number and competency are regulated by the legislative body.

91. There are public arbitrators elected by the electoral assemblies.

92. Their number and their districts are fixed by the legislative body.

93. They have jurisdiction over cases which have not been finally terminated by the private arbitrators or by justices of the peace.

94. They deliberate in public.

They deliver their opinions orally.

They decide in the last resort, upon oral pleas or simple memorial, without proceedings and without expense.

They state the grounds for their decisions.

95. The justices of the peace and the public arbitrators are elected every year.

Of Criminal Justice.

96. No citizen can be tried upon a criminal charge except upon an accusation received by the jurors or decreed by the legislative body.

The accused have counsel chosen by themselves or officially appointed.

The examination is public.

The facts and the intent are declared by a trial jury.

The penalty is awarded by a criminal tribunal.

97. The criminal judges are elected every year by the electoral assemblies.

110. There is no commander-in-chief.

111. Distinctions of rank, their distinguishing marks and subordination exist only in relation to the service and during its continuance.

112. The public force employed for the maintenance of order and peace within the country acts only upon the written requisition of the constituted authorities.

113. The public force employed against enemies from abroad acts under the orders of the executive council.

114. No armed body can deliberate.

Of the National Conventions.

115. If, in one-half of the departments plus one, one-tenth of the regularly constituted primary assemblies of each of them request the revision of the constitutional act or the alteration of some of its articles, the legislative body is required to convoke all the primary assemblies of the Republic, in order to ascertain if there is occasion for a national convention.

116. The national convention is formed in the same manner as the legislatures and annexes the powers thereof.

117. It occupies itself, in relation to the constitution, only with the objects that have led to its convocation.

Of the Relations of the French Republic with Foreign Nations.

118. The French people is the friend and natural ally of the free peoples.

119. It does not interfere in the government of other nations; it does not permit other nations to interfere in its own.

120. It gives asylum to foreigners banished from their fatherland for the cause of liberty.

It refuses it to tyrants.

121. It does not make peace with an enemy that occupies its territory.

Of the Guaranty of Rights.

122. The constitution guarantees to all Frenchmen equality, liberty, security, property, the public debt, the free exercise of worship, a public education, public relief, unlimited freedom of the press, the right of petition, the right to meet in the popular societies, and the enjoyment of all the rights of man.

123. The French Republic honors loyalty, courage, old age,

filial devotion, and misfortune. It places the trust of the constitution under the guardianship of all the virtues.

124. The declaration of rights and the constitutional act are graven upon tablets in the midst of the legislative body and in public places.

40. Decree for the Levy en Masse.

August 23, 1793. Duvergier, *Lois,* VI, 107-108.

This document exhibits something of the spirit with which France met the invasion of its territory, and may serve to indicate how it was possible for her to accomplish so much against such overwhelming odds. It was, perhaps, never intended that the decree should be everywhere put in force. It was enforced in the invaded departments and those adjacent. The precise effects of the measure is a matter of dispute.

REFERENCES. Gardiner, *French Revolution,* 170-171 ; Von Sybel, *French Revolution,* III, 165-169 ; *Cambridge Modern History,* VIII, 348 : *American Historical Review,* IX, 525-532 ; Lavisse and Rambaud, *Histoire générale,* VIII, 267-269 ; Jaurès, *Histoire socialiste,* IV, 1644-1646.

1. From this moment until that in which the enemy shall have been driven from the soil of the Republic, all Frenchmen are in permanent requisition for the service of the armies.

The young men shall go to battle; the married men shall forge arms and transport provisions; the women shall make tents and clothing and shall serve in the hospitals; the children shall turn old linen into lint; the aged shall betake themselves to the public places in order to arouse the courage of the warriors and preach the hatred of kings and the unity of the Republic.

2. The national buildings shall be converted into barracks, the public places into workshops for arms, the soil of the cellars shall be washed in order to extract therefrom the saltpetre.

3. The arms of the regulation calibre shall be reserved exclusively for those who shall march against the enemy; the service of the interior shall be performed with hunting pieces and side arms.

4. The saddle horses are put in requisition to complete the cavalry corps; the draught-horses, other than those employed in agriculture, shall convey the artillery and the provisions.

5. The Committee of Public Safety is charged to take all

the necessary measures to set up without delay an extraordinary manufacture of arms of every sort which corresponds with the ardor and energy of the French people. It is, accordingly, authorised to form all the establishments, factories, workshops and mills which shall be deemed necessary for the carrying on of these works, as well as to put in requisition, within the entire extent of the Republic, the artists and workingmen who can contribute to their success. For this purpose there shall be put at the disposal of the Minister of War a sum of thirty millions, to be taken out of the four hundred ninety-eight million two hundred thousand livres in *assignats* which are in reserve in the fund of the three keys. The central establishment of this extraordinary manufacture shall be fixed at Paris.

6. The representatives of the people sent out for the execution of the present law shall have the same authority in their respective districts, acting in concert with the Committee of Public Safety; they are invested with the unlimited powers assigned to the representatives of the people to the armies.

7. Nobody can get himself replaced in the service for which he shall have been requisitioned. The public functionaries shall remain at their posts.

8. The levy shall be general. The unmarried citizens and widowers without children, from eighteen to twenty-five years, shall march first; they shall assemble without delay at the head-town of their districts, where they shall practice every day at the manual of arms while awaiting the hour of departure.

.   .   .   .

41. The Law of Suspects.

September 17, 1793. Duvergier, *Lois*, VI, 172-173.

This famous law was one of the numerous exceptional measures taken in August and September, 1793, which mark the beginning of the reign of terror. To understand why it was enacted the precise status of both the foreign and civil wars then in progress should be noted. The terms in which the classes of suspects are defined call for special attention. The "committees of surveillance" to which the arrest of suspects is entrusted were those commonly called the revolutionary committees. (See No. 33.)

REFERENCES. Stephens, *French Revolution*, II, 324-325; Aulard, *Révolution française*, 351; Lavisse and Rambaud, *Histoire générale*, VIII, 191.

1. Immediately after the publication of the present decree all the suspect-persons who are in the territory of the Republic and who are still at liberty shall be placed under arrest.

2. These are accounted suspect-persons: 1st, those who by their conduct, their connections, their remarks, or their writings show themselves the partisans of tyranny or federalism and the enemies of liberty; 2d, those who cannot, in the manner prescribed by the decree of March 21st last, justify their means of existence and the performance of their civic duties; 3d, those who have been refused certificates of civism; 4th, public functionaries suspended or removed from their functions by the National Convention or its commissioners and not reinstated, especially those who have been or shall be removed in virtue of the decree of August 14th last; 5th, those of the former nobles, all of the husbands, wives, fathers, mothers, sons or daughters, brothers, or sisters, and agents of the *émigrés* who have not constantly manifested their attachment to the revolution; 6th, those who have emigrated from France in the interval from July 1, 1789, to the publication of the decree of March 30,-April 8, 1792, although they may have returned to France within the period fixed by that decree or earlier.

3. The committees of surveillance established according to the decree of March 21st last, or those which have been substituted for them, either by the orders of the representatives of the people sent with the armies and into the departments, or in virtue of special decrees of the National Convention, are charged to prepare, each in its district, the list of suspect-persons, to issue warrants of arrest against them, and to cause seals to be put upon their papers. The commanders of the public force to whom these warrants shall be delivered shall be required to put them into execution immediately, under penalty of removal.

4. The members of the committee without being seven in number and an absolute majority of votes cannot order the arrest of any person.

5. The persons arrested as suspects shall be first conveyed

to the jail of the place of their imprisonment: in default of jails, they shall be kept from view in their respective dwellings.

6. Within the eight days following they shall be transferred to the national building, which the administrations of the department, immediately after the receipt of the present decree, shall be required to designate and to cause to be prepared for that purpose.

7. The prisoners can cause to be transferred to these buildings the movables which are of absolute necessity to them; they shall remain there under guard until the peace.

8. The expenses of custody shall be at the charge of the prisoners and shall be divided among them equally; this custody shall be confided preferably to the fathers of families and the parents of the citizens who are upon or shall go to the frontiers. The salary for it is fixed for each man of the guard at the value of a day and a half of labor.

9. The committees of surveillance shall send without delay to the committee of general security of the National Convention the list of the persons whom they shall have caused to be arrested, with the reasons for their arrest and the papers which shall have been seized with them as suspect-persons.

10. The civil and criminal tribunals can, if there is need, cause to be arrested and sent into the above mentioned jails persons accused of offences in respect of whom it may have been declared that there was no ground for accusation, or who may have been acquitted of the accusations brought against them.

42. Law of the Maximum.

September 29, 1793. Duvergier, *Lois*, VI, 193-195.

Among the exceptional measures of August and September, 1793, the most important from the economic standpoint were those fixing maximum prices of wages and of many articles of necessity. The law here given is the most comprehensive in a series of such measures. The idea of fixing prices in this manner was not new, but was simply an extension of the practices of the government of the old régime and of measures taken in the spring of 1793. In connection with this law the operation of the Parisian revolutionary army and the system of requisitions should be noted. The law was not repealed until December 24, 1794.

REFERENCES. Mathews, *French Revolution*, 245-246; Stephens, *French Revolution*, II, 353-354; Lavisse and Rambaud, *Histoire générale*, VIII, 190-191, 626-627; Jaurès, *Histoire socialiste*, IV, 1668-1680, 1776-1786.

1. The articles which the Convention has decided to be of prime necessity and for which it has believed that it ought to fix the *maximum* or highest price are: fresh meat, salt meat and bacon, butter, sweet-oil, cattle, salt fish, wine, brandy, vinegar, cider, beer, fire-wood, charcoal, mineral coal, candles, combustible oil, salt, soda, sugar, honey, white paper, skins, iron, brass, lead, steel, copper, hemp, linen, wool, woolens, fabrics, the raw materials which serve for fabrics, sabots, shoes, cabbages and turnips, soap, potash, and tobacco.

2. For the articles included in the above list, the *maximum* price for fire-wood of the first quality, that of charcoal and of mineral coal, are the same as in 1790, plus a twentieth of the price. The decree of August 19th upon the determination by the departments of the prices of fire-wood, coal and peat is repealed.

The *maximum* or highest price of tobacco in rolls is twenty *sous* per pound, *poids de marc;* in that of smoking tobacco is ten *sous;* that of salt per pound is two *sous;* that of soap is twenty-five *sous.*

3. The *maximum* of the price of all the other commodities and articles of merchandise included in article 1 for the whole extent of the Republic, until the month of September next, shall be the price which each of them had in 1790, such as is established by the official price-lists or the market price of each department, and a third over and above this same price, deduction being made of fiscal and other duties to which they were then subject, under whatever denomination they may have existed.

. . . .

7. All persons who may sell or purchase the articles of merchandise included in article 1 above the *maximum* of the price settled and posted in each department shall pay by way of the municipal police a fine, for which they shall be jointly and severally liable, of double the value of the article sold and payable to the informer: they shall .be enrolled upon the list of suspected persons and treated as such. The purchaser shall not be subject to the penalties provided above, if he denounces the offence of the seller; and each merchant shall be required to have a list displayed in his shop, bearing the *maximum* or highest price of his merchandise.

8. The *maximum* or highest price belonging to salaries, wages, and manual labor by the day in each place, shall be fixed, to commence from the publication of this law until the month of September next, by the general councils of the communes at the same amount as in 1790, to which there shall be added half of that price in addition.

9. The municipalities shall put into requisition and punish, according to circumstances, with three days' imprisonment the workingmen, factory operatives and various laboring persons who may refuse without legitimate reasons to engage in their accustomed labors.

.   .   .   .

17. During the war all exportation of articles of merchandise or commodities of prime necessity, under any name or commission whatsoever, is prohibited upon all the frontiers, salt excepted.

.   .   .   .

43. Decree upon the Revolutionary Government.

October 10, 1793 (19 Vendémiaire, Year II). Duvergier, *Lois*, VI, 219-220.

This decree was adopted by the Convention at the time when it decided, on account of the critical condition of the country, not to put the constitution of the Year I into operation immediately. As a sort of provisional constitution it served as the basis of government until replaced by the great decree of 14 Frimaire (December 4, 1793). See No. 45. The meaning of the term *revolutionary government* can be deduced from the character of the arrangements here provided and should be carefully noted.

REFERENCES. Stephens, *French Revolution*, II, 280-281; Lavisse and Rambaud, *Histoire générale*, VIII, 196-197; Aulard, *Révolution française*, 314-315, 366-368.

Of the Government.

1. The provisional government of France is revolutionary until the peace.

2. The provisional executive council, the ministers, the generals, and the constituted bodies are placed under the surveillance of the committee of public safety, which shall render account of them to the Convention every eight days.

3. Every measure of security must be taken by the pro-

visional executive council, under the authorisation of the committee, which shall render an account thereof to the Convention.

4. The revolutionary laws must be executed rapidly. The government shall correspond immediately with the districts upon the measures of public safety.

5. The generals-in-chief shall be appointed by the National Convention, upon the presentation of the Committee of Public Safety.

6. The inertia of the government being the cause of the reverses, the limits for the execution of the decrees and measures of public safety are fixed. Violation of these limits shall be punished as an attack upon liberty.

Subsistences.

7. The table of the production of grain for each district, made by the Committee of Public Safety, shall be printed and distributed to all the members of the Convention, in order to be put into operation without delay.

8. The needs of each department shall be estimated by approximation and secured. The surplus shall be subject to the requisitions.

9. The table of the productions of the Republic shall be addressed to the representatives of the people, the ministers of the navy and the interior, and the administrators of subsistences. They must make requisitions in the districts which shall have been assigned to them. Paris shall be a special district.

10. The requisitions in behalf of the unfruitful departments shall be authorised and regulated by the provisional executive council.

11. Paris shall be supplied with provisions on March 1st for one year.

General Security.

12. The direction and employment of the revolutionary army shall be constantly regulated in a way to put down the counter-revolutionaries.

The Committee of Public Safety shall present a plan for this purpose.

13. The council shall send garrisons into the cities where

counter-revolutionary movements shall arise. The garrisons shall be paid and supported by the rich of these cities until the peace.

Finances.

14. There shall be created a tribunal and a jury of accounts. This tribunal and this jury shall be appointed by the National Convention; they shall be charged to proceed against all those who have managed the public funds since the revolution and to demand of them an account of their fortunes.

The organization of this tribunal is recommitted to the committee of legislation.

44. Decree for the Republican Calendar.

November 24, 1793 (4 Frimaire, Year II). Duvergier, *Lois*, VI, 294-301.

This is the first of two decrees by which the republican calendar displaced the Gregorian calendar. The later decree provided additional details, but did not essentially modify the scheme here presented. Until about 1801 the new calendar was used to the entire exclusion of the old; then for a time the two were used together. The republican calendar was not altogether abandoned until January 1, 1806. Both the general scheme of the calendar and the reasons given for its adoption should be noticed.

REFERENCES. Stephens, *Yale Review*, IV, 326-330; *Cambridge Modern History*, VIII, 358; Lavisse and Rambaud, *Histoire générale*, VIII, 193-194; Jaurès, *Histoire socialiste*, IV, 1685-1690; Stephens, *French Revolution*, II, 561, has a concordance of the two calendars to the end of the year VIII.

1. The era of the French counts from the foundation of the Republic, which occurred September 22, 1792, of the common era, the day when the sun arrived at the true equinox of autumn, in entering into the sign of Libra, at nine o'clock, eighteen minutes, thirty seconds, A. M., for the observatory of Paris.

2. The common era is abolished for civil uses.

3. Each year commences at midnight with the day on which the true equinox of autumn falls for the observatory of Paris.

4. The first year of the Republic commenced at midnight September 22, 1792, and ended at midnight, separating the 21st from the 22d of September, 1793.

5. The second year commenced September 22d, 1793, at

midnight, the true equinox of autumn being reached that day for the observatory of Paris at three o'clock, eleven minutes, thirty-eight seconds, P. M.

6. The decree which fixed the commencement of the second year of the Republic at January, 1, 1793, is repealed; all documents dated the second year of the Republic, passed within the current 1st of January to September 21st inclusive, are regarded as belonging to the first year of the Republic.

7. The year is divided into twelve equal months of thirty days each; after the twelve months follow five days in order to complete the ordinary year; these five days do not belong to any month.

8. Each month is divided into three equal parts of ten days each, which are called *décades*.

9. The names of the days of the *décade* are: *primidi, duodi, tridi, quatridi, quintidi, sextidi, septidi, octidi, nonidi, décadi.*

The names of the months are, for the autumn, *Vendémiaire, Brumaire, Frimaire;* for the winter, *Nivôse, Pluviôse, Ventôse;* for the spring, *Germinal, Floréal, Prairial;* for the summer, *Messidor, Thermidor, Fructidor.*

The last five days are called *the San-Culottides.*

10. The ordinary year receives one day more, according as the position of the equinox requires it, in order to maintain the coincidence of the civil year with the celestial movements. This day, called *Day of the Revolution,* is placed at the end of the year, and forms the sixth of the *Sans-Culottides.*

The period of four years, at the end of which this addition of a day is ordinarily necessary, is called *the Franciade,* in memory of the revolution, which, after four years of effort, has brought France to a republican government.

The fourth year of the *Franciade* is called *Sextile.*

11. The day from midnight to midnight is divided into ten parts or hours, each part into ten others, and so on to the smallest commensurable portion of its duration. The hundredth part of the hour is called decimal minute; the hundredth part of a minute is called second decimal. This article shall be in force for public documents only to count from 1 Vendémiaire, Year III of the Republic.

12. The committee of public instruction is charged to cause the new calendar to be printed in different forms, with

simple instructions in order to explain the principles and usage of it.

13. The calendar, as well as the instruction, shall be sent to the administrative bodies, the municipalities, the tribunals, the justices of the peace and all public officers, the armies, the popular societies and all colleges and schools. The provisional executive council shall cause it to be transmitted to the ministers, consuls, and other agents of France in foreign countries.

14. All public acts' shall be dated according to the new organization of the year.

15. The professors, schoolmasters and schoolmistresses, fathers and mothers of families, and all those who direct the education of children shall be diligent in explaining to them the new calendar, in conformity with the instructions which are herewith annexed.

16. Every four years, or every Francaide, *upon the Day of the Revolution,* republican games shall be celebrated, in memory of the French revolution.

Instructions upon the era of the Republic and upon the division of the year, decreed by the National Convention, in order to be put at the end of the decree:

First Part.

Of the motives which have determined the decree.

The French nation, oppressed and debased during a great many centuries by the most insolent despotism, has finally risen to a perception of its rights and the power to which its destinies call it. Each day for five years of a revolution, of which the annals of the world do not afford a parallel, it has been purging itself of all that defiles it or impedes its progress, which must be as majestic as rapid. It wishes that its regeneration should be complete, in order that its years of liberty and glory may be distinguished even more by their duration in the history of peoples than its years of slavery and humiliation in the history of kings.

Soon the arts are going to be called to new progress by the uniformity of weights and measures, whose exclusive and invariable standard, taken in the measure even of the earth, will cause the disappearance of the diversity, incoherence, and inexactitude which have existed up to the present in that part of the national industry.

The arts and history, for which time is a necessary element, were also demanding a new measure of duration disengaged from all the errors which credulity and a superstitious routine have handed down to us from the centuries of ignorance.

It is this new standard which the National Convention to-day presents to the French people; it ought to show at the same time both the impress of the intelligence of the nation and the character of our revolution by its exactitude, its simplicity, and its disengagement from every opinion which may not be approved by reason and philosophy.

. . . [The remainder of the instruction explains in the same vein the details of the calendar.]

45. Organic Decree upon the Government of the Terror.

December 4, 1793 (14 Frimaire, Year II). Duvergier, *Lois*, VI, 317-322.

This document may be called the constitution of the reign of terror. It co-ordinated and amended a large number of earlier decrees, by which the leading institutions of the revolutionary government had been created or regulated, e.g., Nos. 33, 37, 43. A careful study of the document will bring out how the government was carried on by the Convention and the great Committee of Public Safety and its agents. The manner in which the elected local authorities were divested of all power and replaced by agents of the Committee of Public Safety calls for particular notice.

REFERENCES. Stephens, *French Revolution*, II, 316-318; *Cambridge Modern History*, VIII. 359-360; Lavisse and Rambaud, *Histoire générale*, VIII, 197-199; Aulard, *Révolution française*, 355-357.

Section I. Dispatch and promulgation of the laws.

1. The laws which concern the public interest or which are of general operation shall be printed separately in a numbered bulletin, which shall serve henceforth for their notification to the constituted authorities. This bulletin shall bear the title: *Bulletin of the Laws of the Republic.*

. . . [The omitted articles relate to the preparation of the bulletin.]

8. This bulletin shall be addressed directly day by day to all the constituted authorities and to all the public authorities charged either with supervising the execution or causing the application of the laws. This bulletin shall be distributed to the members of the Convention.

9. At each place the promulgation of the law shall be made, within twenty-four hours after its receipt, by a publication at the sound of the trumpet or the drum; and the law shall become binding counting from the day of promulgation.

10. Independently of this proclamation in each commune of the Republic, the laws shall be read to the citizens in a public place each *décadi* by the mayor, a municipal officer, or the president of the section.

'   '   .   .   .   .

Section II. Execution of the laws.

1. The National Convention is the sole centre of impulsion of the government.

2. All the constituted bodies and the public functionaries are put under the immediate supervision of the Committee of Public Safety for the measures of government and of public safety, in conformity with the decree of the 19 Vendémiaire; and for all that relates to persons and to the general and internal police, this special supervision belongs to the Committee of General Security of the Convention, in conformity with the decree of September 17th, last: these two committees are required to render account of the results of their labors at the end of each month to the National Convention. Each member of these two committees is personally responsible for the fulfillment of this requirement.

3. The execution of the laws is divided into surveillance and application.

4. The active surveillance relative to the military laws and measures and to the administrative laws, civil and criminal, is delegated to the executive council, which shall render an account thereof in writing every ten days to the Committee of Public Safety, in order to inform it of delays and negligencies in the execution of the civil and criminal laws, acts of government and military and administrative measures, as well as the violations of these laws and measures, and the agents who make themselves guilty of these negligences and infractions.

5. Each minister, moreover, is required to personally render, every ten days, a detailed and summarized account of the operations of his department to the Committee of Public Safety, and to denounce all the agents that it employs who may not have discharged their duties exactly.

6. The surveillance of the execution of the revolutionary laws and the measures of government, of general security and public safety within the departments, is assigned exclusively to the districts, with the requirement to render exact account thereof every ten days to the Committee of Public Safety for the measures of government and of public safety, and to the committee of surveillance of the Convention for that which concerns the general and internal police as well as individuals.

7. The application of the military measures belongs to the generals and other agents attached to the service of the armies; the application of the military laws belongs to the military tribunals; that of the laws relative to the taxes, manufactures, highways, public canals, and surveillance over the national domains, belongs to the department administrations; that of the civil and criminal laws to the tribunals, with the express requirement of rendering account thereof every ten days to the executive council.

8. The application of the revolutionary laws and the measures of general security and public safety is confided to the municipalities and the surveillance or revolutionary committees, with the like requirement of rendering account every ten days of the execution of these laws in the territory of their district, as required of their immediate surveillance.

9. Nevertheless, in order that at Paris the action of the police may encounter no impediment, the revolutionary committees shall continue to correspond directly and without any intermediary with the Committee of General Security of the Convention, in conformity with the decree of September 17th last.

10. All the constituted bodies shall send also, at the end of each month, the outline of their deliberations and of their correspondence to the authority which is especially charged by this decree with their immediate supervision.

11. Every authority and every public functionary is expressly forbidden to issue proclamations or to promulgate extensive orders in limitation of or contrary to the literal sense of the law, under pretext of interpretation or supplementing it.

The right to give the interpretation of decrees belongs to the Convention alone, and it alone can be looked to for that purpose.

12. The intermediate authorities charged with surveillance over the execution and application of the laws are likewise forbidden to pronounce any decision and to order the release of citizens under arrest. This right belongs exclusively to the National Convention, the committees of public safety and of general security, the representatives of the people in the departments and with the armies, and the tribunals in making application of the criminal and police laws.

13. All the constituted authorities shall be sedentary and they can deliberate only in the usual place for their sittings, except in cases of superior force, with the sole exceptions of the justices of the peace and their assessors, and the criminal tribunals of the departments, in conformity with the laws which sanction their moving about.

14. In the place of the district procureurs-syndics, the commune procureurs and their substitutes, who are abolished by this decree, there shall be national agents especially charged with requiring and seeking to obtain the execution of the laws, as well as to denounce the negligences that occur in this execution and the infractions which may be committed. These national agents are authorised to leave their stations and to move about the circuit of their districts in order to be on the lookout and to satisfy themselves more thoroughly that the laws are exactly executed.

15. The functions of the national agents shall be performed by the citizens who now occupy the places of district procureurs-syndics, procureurs of the communes and their substitutes, with the exception of those who have given occasion for their removal.

16. The national agents attached to the districts, as well as every other public functionary personally charged by this decree either to require the execution of the law or to supervise it more particularly, are required to maintain an accurate correspondence with the committees of public safety and of general security. These national agents shall write to the two committees every ten days, according to the requirements established by article 10 of this section, in order to attest the diligence displayed in the execution of each law and to give information of delays and of negligent and double-dealing public functionaries.

17. The national agents attached to the communes are required to render the same account for the district of their jurisdiction, and the presidents of the surveillance and revolutionary committees shall carry on the same correspondence, as well with the Committee of General Security as with the district charged with surveillance over them.

18. The committees of public safety and of general security are required to denounce to the Convention the national agents and every other public functionary personally charged with the supervision of the application of the laws in order to cause them to be punished in conformity with the provisions set forth in the present decree.

19. The number of the national agents, whether in the districts or in the communes, shall be equal to that of the district procureurs-syndics and their substitutes and the commune procureurs and their substitutes actually on duty.

20. After the process of sifting out the citizens summoned by this decree to discharge the functions of national agents for the districts, each of these [districts] shall cause to be transmitted to the National Convention, within twenty-four hours after the process the names of those who shall have been retained or appointed in that place; and the list shall be read at the tribune, in order that the members of the Convention may explain about those they are able to recognize.

21. The replacing of the national agents for the districts who shall be rejected shall be made provisionally by the National Convention.

22. After the same sifting-out process shall have been effected in the communes, they shall send, within the same period, a similar list to the district which has jurisdiction, in order to be publicly proclaimed there.

Section III. Competence of the constituted authorities.

1. The Committee of Public Safety is especially charged with the conduct of the chief transactions in diplomacy and it shall deal directly with what springs from these same transactions.

2. The representatives of the people shall correspond every ten days with the Committee of Public Safety. They can suspend and replace the generals only provisionally, with the re-

quirement of informing the Committee of Public Safety of it within twenty-four hours; they cannot counteract nor arrest the execution of the orders and measures of government taken by the Committee of Public Safety; they shall conform themselves in all their missions to the provisions of the decree of 6 Frimaire.

3. The functions of the executive council shall be determined according to the principles established in the present decree.

4. The Convention reserves for itself the appointment of the generals-in-chief of the land and naval forces. As to the other general officers, the ministers of war and of the navy cannot make any promotion without having presented the list or the appointment, with a statement of reasons, to the Committee of Public Safety, in order to be accepted or rejected by it. These two ministers, likewise, cannot remove any of the military agents appointed provisionally by the representatives of the people sent to the armies, unless the proposal has been made in writing, with a statement of reasons, to the Committee of Public Safety and the committee has accepted it.

5. The department administrations remain especially charged with the apportionment of the taxes among the districts, the establishment of manufactures, of highways and public canals, and surveillance over the national domains. All that relates to the revolutionary laws and to the measures of government and of public safety is no longer within their jurisdiction. In consequence, the hierarchy which placed the districts, the municipalities, or any other authority, under the dependence of the departments is suppressed for what concerns the revolutionary and military laws, and the measures of government, of public safety, and of general security.

6. The general councils, the presidents, and the procureur-syndics-general are likewise abolished. The duties of the president shall be discharged by the members of the directory in turn and cannot continue more than one month. The president shall be charged with the correspondence and requisition and special surveillance in the portion of the execution confided to the department directories.

7. The presidents and secretaries of the revolutionary and surveillance committees, likewise, shall be renewed every fifteen

days, and can be re-elected only after an interval of one month.

8. No citizen already employed in the service of the Republic can exercise or assist in the exercise of an authority charged with the direct or indirect surveillance of his functions.

9. Those who unite or assist in the cumulative exercise of similar authorities are required to make their choice within twenty-four hours after the publication of this decree.

10. All the changes ordered by the present decree shall be put in execution within three days, counting from the publication of this decree.

11. The rules of the formerly established order in which nothing has been changed by this decree shall be followed until it has been otherwise ordered. However, the functions of the district of Paris are assigned to the department, as having become incompatible by this new organization with the operations of the municipality.

12. The power to send agents belongs exclusively to the Committee of Public Safety, the representatives of the people, the executive council, and the commission of subsistences. The object of their mission shall be expressed in precise terms in their commission.

These missions shall be confided strictly to effecting the execution of the revolutionary and general safety measures, and the requisitions and orders issued by those who shall have appointed them.

None of these commissioners can set aside the limitations of his commission; and in no case is the delegation of powers permitted.

13. The members of the executive council are required to present to the Committee of Public Safety for its verification and acceptance the list of the agents whom they are about to send into the departments, to the armies, and abroad, and to accompany it with a statement of the reasons.

14. The agents of the executive council and of the commission of subsistences are required to render exact account of their operations to the representatives of the people who are present in the same place. The powers of the agents appointed by the representatives with the armies and in the departments shall expire when the mission of the representa-

tives shall be terminated or they shall have been recalled by decree.

15. Every constituted authority, every public functionary, and every agent employed in the service of the Republic, is expressly forbidden to extend the exercise of his functions beyond the territory which is assigned to him, to perform acts which are not within his competency, to encroach upon other authorities, to exceed the functions delegated to him, or to arrogate to himself those which are not confided to him.

16. Every constituted authority is also expressly forbidden to alter the essence of its organization by unions with other authorities, by delegates charged to form separate assemblies, or by commissioners sent to other constituted authorities. All relations between public functionaries can take place only in writing.

17. All congresses or central unions established either by the representatives of the people or by the popular societies, whatever the denomination they may bear, even that of central committee of surveillance or of central revolutionary or military commission, are revoked and expressly forbidden by this decree, as subversive of the unity of action of the government and as *tending to federalism;* and those in existence shall dissolve themselves within twenty-four hours, counting from the publication of the present decree.

18. Every revolutionary army other than that established by the Convention and common to the whole Republic is disbanded by the present decree; and all citizens incorporated in similar military institutions are enjoined to separate within twenty-four hours, counting from the publication of the present decree, under penalty of being regarded by the law as rebels and treated as such.

19. Every armed force, whatever its institution or its denomination, and every leader of one is expressly forbidden to perform acts which belong exclusively to the constituted civil authorities, even domiciliary visits, without a written order issued by these authorities, which order shall be executed in the forms prescribed by the decrees.

20. No armed force, tax, forced or voluntary loan can be levied except in virtue of a decree. The revolutionary taxes of the representatives of the people shall be put into operation

only after having been approved by the Convention, except they be in enemy or rebel country.

21. Every constituted authority is forbidden to dispose of the public funds, or to change the destination of them, without being authorised to do so by the Convention or by an express requisition of the representatives of the people, under penalty of being personally responsible for them.

Section IV. Reorganization and purification of the constituted authorities.

1. The Committee of Public Safety is authorised to take all the necessary measures in order to proceed to the change of organization of the constituted authorities provided in the present decree.

2. The representatives of the people are charged to secure and accelerate the execution of them; also to accomplish without delay the complete purification of all the constituted authorities and to render a special account of these two operations to the National Convention before the end of the next month.

Section V. Of the penal law for public functionaries and other agents of the Republic.

1. Members of the executive council guilty of negligence in the surveillance and execution of the laws for the part which is assigned to them, as well individually as collectively, shall be punished by deprivation of citizenship for six years and the confiscation of half of the goods of the condemned.

2. Public functionaries on salary and charged personally by this decree to require and to follow up the execution of the laws, or to make the application of them, and to denounce negligences, infractions, functionaries, and other guilty agents, placed under their surveillance, and who shall not have rigorously fulfilled these duties, shall be deprived of citizenship for five years, and condemned for the same time to the confiscation of one-third of their incomes.

3. The penalty for public functionaries not on salary, personally charged with the same duties and guilty of the same offences, shall be deprivation of citizenship for four years.

4. The penalty inflicted upon the members of the judicial, administrative, municipal, and revolutionary bodies, guilty of negligence in the surveillance or the application of the laws,

shall be, for the salaried functionaries, deprivation of citizenship for four years and a fine equal to one-fourth of the annual income of each condemned person, and for those who do not receive any salary, exclusion from the exercise of the rights of citizenship for three years.

5. The general officers and all agents attached to the different services of the army who are guilty of negligence in the surveillance, execution, and application of the operations which are entrusted to them, shall be punished with deprivation of the rights of citizenship for eight years and the confiscation of half of their goods.

6. The commissioners and special agents appointed by the committees of public safety and of general security, the representatives of the people with the armies and in the departments, the executive council and commission of subsistences, who are guilty of having exceeded the limits of their commission, or of having neglected to execute it, or of not submitting to the provisions of the present decree, and especially to article 13 of section II in that which affects them, shall be punished by five years in prison.

7. The minor agents of the government, even those who have no public character, such as the heads of bureaus, secretaries, clerks of the Convention, the executive council, the different public administrations, every constituted authority, or any public functionary who has employes, shall be punished by suspension of citizenship for three years and by a fine of one-third of the income of the condemned person for the same space of time, for personal cause of all negligences, voluntary delays, or infractions committed in the execution of the laws, orders and measures of government, public safety and administration with which they can be entrusted.

8. Every infraction of the law, every betrayal of trust, every abuse of authority, committed by a public functionary or by any other principal or minor agent of the government and of the civil and military administration who receives a salary, shall be punished by five years in prison and the confiscation of one-half of the goods of the condemned person; and for those not salaried and guilty of the same offences, the penalty shall be deprivation of citizenship for six years and the confiscation of one-fourth of their incomes for the same time.

9. Every counterfeiter of the Bulletin of the Laws shall be punished by death.

10. The penalties inflicted for delays and negligences in the dispatch, sending, and reception of the Bulletin of the Laws are, for the members of the commission for the dispatch of the laws and for the letter-post agents, condemnation to five years in prison, except in the case where the use of violence is legally proven.

11. Public functionaries or any other agents subject to a joint responsibility, and who shall have notified the Convention of the lack of exact surveillance or of the non-execution of a law, within the space of fifteen days, shall be excepted from the penalties pronounced by this decree.

12. The confiscations ordered by the preceding articles shall be turned into the public treasury, after the indemnity due to a citizen injured by the non-execution or violation of a law has been deducted.

46. Decree upon Slavery.

February 4, 1794 (16 Pluviôse, Year II). Duvergier, *Lois,* VII, 30.

Of recent years historians have come to see that the work of the assemblies of the revolution was much less the result of attachment to abstract principles than was formerly supposed. Nevertheless, much of their legislation was prompted by what is vaguely called the revolutionary spirit. A prominent feature of that spirit was its passionate enthusiasm for the extension of human liberty. This decree is typical of many passed by the Convention at the prompting of that enthusiasm. Its immediate effects were unquestionably disastrous.

REFERENCES. Stephens, *French Revolution,* II, 468-471; *Cambridge Modern History,* VIII, 727-729, 790.

The National Convention declares that negro slavery in all the colonies is abolished; in consequence, it decrees that all men, without distinction of color, who are domiciled in the colonies are French citizens and shall enjoy all the rights guaranteed by the constitution.

It sends again to the Committee of Public Safety to prepare for it immediately a report upon the measures to be taken in order to assure the execution of the present decree.

47. Decree upon Assignats.

May 10, 1794 (21 Floréal, Year II). Duvergier, *Lois,* VII, 162.

This is a sort of organic law upon *assignats* co-ordinating and amending much earlier legislation on the subject. From it can be made up a tolerably complete list of the actions in relation to *assignats* which were regarded as crimes. The penalties, for which it refers to previous decrees, were exceptionally severe. In many cases the penalty was death.

REFERENCE. Lavisse and Rambaud, *Histoire générale,* VIII, 631-632, for some data in concise form upon the amount of *assignats* issued and their value at different dates.

1. The provisions of the decrees of 7 and 30 Frimaire and 14 Germinal relative to those accused of embezzlement of national lands, of engaging, manufacturing, distributing, or introducing false *assignats* or false money, shall likewise regulate the method of procedure against persons accused of having sold or purchased coin; of having agreed upon or proposed different prices according to payment in coin or in *assignats;* of having refused *assignats* in payment; of having given or received them at any loss whatever, or of having demanded, before concluding or even entering upon a bargain, in what money the payments shall be effected.

.   .   .   .

5. The above provisions shall be observed even with regard to those accused of offences previous to the publication of the present decree, who shall not yet have been definitely tried.

6. Articles 2 and 3 of the decree of April 11, 1793, shall continue to be executed against those who shall be convicted of having sold or purchased coin, or having given or sold *assignats* at any loss whatever, of having agreed upon or proposed different prices according to payment of coin or *assignats,* of having demanded, before concluding or even entering upon a bargain, in what money the payment may be effected.

7. The penalty provided by the decree of August 1, 1793, shall continue restricted to those who refuse *assignats* in payment; and nobody within the extent of the territory of the Republic can shelter himself in this under the allegation that he is not a Frenchman.

8. Every discourse tending to discredit the *assignats* shall likewise be punished in the same way.

9. In conformity with article 4 of the decree of September 5, 1793, there shall be occasion for the death penalty and for confiscation of goods, wherever the offences mentioned in the three preceding articles shall have been committed with the intention of assisting the undertakings of the internal or external enemies of the Republic.

.   .   .   .

48. Treaties with Prussia.

Through the first of these agreements Prussia withdrew from the coalition against France. Document B is the complement of document A. Particular attention should be given to the arrangements in regard to the territory upon the left bank of the Rhine, the compensation for the dispossessed princes and the neutrality line in Germany.

REFERENCES. Gardiner, *French Revolution*, 238-241 ; Fyffe, *Modern Europe*, I, 95-98 (Popular ed., 64-66) ; Von Sybel, *French Revolution*, IV, Book XI, Ch. III ; *Cambridge Modern History*, VIII, 441-442 ; Lavisse and Rambaud. *Histoire générale* VIII, 301-305 ; Sorel, *L'Europe et la révolution française*, IV, 281-292 ; Jaurès, *Histoire socialiste*. V, 115-119, 377-378.

MAPS. Droysen, *Historischer Hand-Atlas*, 48 ; Lane-Poole, *Historical Atlas of Modern Europe*, XI-XII ; Vidal-Lablache, *Atlas général*, 40.

A. Treaty of Basle. April 5, 1795 (16 Germinal, Year III). De Clercq, *Traités*, I, 232-236.

The French Republic and His Majesty, the King of Prussia, equally prompted by the desire to put an end to the war which divides them, by a firm peace between the two nations,

.   .   .   .

1. There shall be peace, amity and good understanding between the French Republic and the King of Prussia, considered as such and in the capacity of Elector of Brandenburg and of co-state of the Germanic Empire.

2. Accordingly, all hostilities between the two contracting powers shall cease, dating from the ratification of the present treaty; and neither of them, dating from the same time, shall furnish against the other, in any capacity or by any title whatsoever, any assistance or contingent, whether in men, in horses, provisions, money, munitions of war, or otherwise.

3. Neither of the contracting powers shall grant passage over its territory to troops of the enemies of the other.

4. The troops of the French Republic shall evacuate, within the fifteen days which follow the ratification of the present treaty, the parts of the Prussian states which they may occupy upon the right bank of the Rhine. .   .   .

5. The troops of the French Republic shall continue to occupy the part of the states of the King of Prussia situated upon the left bank of the Rhine. All definitive arrangement with respect to these provinces shall be put off until the general pacification between France and the German Empire.

.   .   .   .

11. The French Republic shall accept the good offices of His Majesty the King of Prussia in favor of the princes and states of the Germanic Empire who shall desire to enter directly into negotiation with it, and who, for that purpose, have already requested or shall yet request the intervention of the king. The French Republic, in order to give to the King of Prussia a signal proof of its desire to co-operate for the re-establishment of the former bonds of amity which have existed between the two countries, consents not to treat as hostile countries, during the space of three months after the ratification of the present treaty, those of the princes and states of the said empire situated upon the right bank of the Rhine and in favor of whom the king shall interest himself.

.   .   .   .

Separate and Secret Articles.

.   .   .   .

2. If, at the general pacification between the Germanic Empire and France, the left bank of the Rhine remains with France, His Majesty, the King of Prussia, will come to an agreement with the French Republic upon the method of the cession of the Prussian States situated upon the left bank of this river, in exchange for such territorial indemnification as shall be agreed upon. In this case the king shall accept the guarantee which the Republic offers him for this indemnification.

3. In order to remove the theatre of war from the frontiers of the states of the King of Prussia, to preserve the tranquility of the north of Germany, and to establish entire freedom of commerce between that part of the Empire and France

as before the war, the French Republic consents not to extend the operations of war, nor to cause its troops to enter, either by land or sea, into the countries and states situated beyond the following line of demarcation:

. . . [The omitted passage relates exclusively to the demarcation line. One portion of it, running south from near the mouth of the Ems river to the Rhine and along that stream to about the point where the Neckar joins it, separated that part of Germany which had fallen under French domination during the war from the unaffected region further east. Another portion was so drawn that northern and southern Germany were separated by a line running from about the junction of the Neckar and the Rhine eastwardly to the southeast corner of Prussian Silesia.]

The French Republic will regard as neutral countries and states all those which are situated beyond this line, on condition that His Majesty, the King of Prussia, undertakes to cause them to observe a strict neutrality, of which the first point shall be to recall their contingents and not to contract any new engagements which can authorise them to furnish troops to the powers at war with France. The king charges himself with the guarantee that no troops hostile to France shall pass this line, nor set out from the countries which are here included, in order to fight French armies; and for this purpose the two contracting powers, after having planned together, shall agree upon the essential points for sufficient corps of observation to cause this neutrality to be respected.

.   .   .   .

B. Secret Convention. August 5, 1796 (18 Thermidor, Year IV). De Clercq, *Traités*, I, 281-283.

The French Republic and His Majesty the King of Prussia prompted by an equal desire to see the baneful war which afflicts Europe cease shortly, and flàttering themselves that the accomplishment of this salutary desire cannot be far distant, have believed that they ought in advance to enter into amicable communications upon several matters relative to this pacification, which they hope is approaching.

.   .   .   .

1. The intention of the two contracting powers being, first of all, to agree upon a territorial indemnification for the

loss of the Prussian provinces upon the left bank of the
Rhine, in case the said bank shall be ceded to France at the
time of the peace with the Empire, . . . His Prussian Majesty, in order to give to the French Republic a proof
of his feelings of amity, declares that when the question of
the cession of the left bank of the Rhine to France shall arise,
he will not oppose it; and, as in that case, in order to indemnify the secular princes who will lose by that arrangement,
the principle of secularizations becomes absolutely indispensable, His Majesty consents to accept the said principle and
he shall receive as indemnity for the said Trans-Rhenish
provinces, including the enclave of Sevenaer, which in this
case will be ceded to France, the remainder of the bishopric of
Munster, with the county of Recklinghausen, making deduction of the part mentioned above and on condition of their
prior secularization; His Majesty still reserving to himself
to add to these what may be suitable to complete his idem-
nification, upon which matter the two powers shall come to an
agreement.

.   .   .   .

49. Treaty of the Hague.

May 16, 1795 (27 Floréal, Year III). De Clercq, *Traités*, I.
236-242.

This treaty illustrates the relationship between France and
countries such as Holland which it revolutionized but did not
annex.

REFERENCES. Lavisse and Rambaud, *Histoire générale*, VIII.
303-304; Jaurès, *Histoire socialiste*, V, 124.

The French Republic and the Republic of the United
Provinces, equally animated by the desire to put an end to
the war which had divided them, to repair the evils of it by
a just distribution of reciprocal damages and advantages, and
to unite themselves forever by an alliance founded upon the
true interests of the two peoples, ...

1. The French Republic recognizes the Republic of the
United Provinces as a free and independent power and guarantees to it its liberty, its independence, and the abolition of
the stadtholderate decreed by the states-general and by each
province on its own part.

2. There shall be forever between the two republics,

the French and the United Provinces, peace, friendship, and good understanding.

3. There shall be between the two republics, until the end of the war, an offensive and defensive alliance against all their enemies without distinction.

4. This offensive and defensive alliance shall exist against England, whenever either of the two republics shall be at war with her.

5. Neither of the two republics shall make peace with England, nor treat with her, without the co-operation and consent of the other.

6. The French Republic shall not make peace with any of the other coalesced powers without including the Republic of the United Provinces.

7. The Republic of the United Provinces shall furnish for its contingent during this campaign twelve line-of-battle ships and eighteen frigates, to be employed principally in the German Ocean, the North and Baltic Seas. These forces shall be increased for the next campaign, if one occurs. The Republic of the United Provinces shall furnish besides, if it is requested to do so, at least half of the land forces which it shall have on foot.

8. The land and sea forces of the United Provinces, which shall be expressly intended to act with those of the French Republic, shall be under the orders of the French generals.

.   .   .   [Articles 11-12 provide for the transfer to France of Flanders, Maestrecht, Venloo, and other districts in the vicinity of the river Meuse. By article 16 compensation of an equal extent of territory is to be provided at the general peace "out of the country conquered and retained by France."]

17. The French Republic shall continue to occupy militarily, during the present war only, but by a number of troops determined and agreed upon between the two nations, the places and positions which it will be useful to guard for the defence of the country.

.   .   .   .

20. The Republic of the United Provinces shall pay to the French Republic, as indemnity and damages for the ex-

penses of the war, one hundred million *florins* current money of Holland, either in coin or in good foreign bills of exchange, in conformity with the method of payment agreed upon between the two republics.

. . . .

22. The Republic of the United Provinces pledges itself not to give asylum to any French *émigré;* likewise the French Republic will not give asylum to Orangist emigrants.

. . . .

Separate and Secret Articles.

1. [Reduces the naval forces mentioned in number 1 of the open articles to three line-of-battle ships and four frigates.]

2. The districts named in article 12 of the open treaty are reserved [by France] only in order to be united to the French Republic and not to other powers.

3. A month after the exchange of the ratifications of the present treaty, the French army in the United Provinces shall be reduced, in execution of article 17 of the open treaty, to 25,000 men, who shall be paid in coin, equipped and clothed by the Republic of the United Provinces upon the footing of war, in conformity with a rule which shall be agreed upon between the two governments. This army shall be left after the peace, in whole or in part, to the Republic of the United Provinces as long as she shall desire and it shall be maintained upon the footing that shall be determined for that purpose.

. . . .

5. The requisitions made directly to the States-General by the Representatives of the People before the signing of the present treaty shall be fulfilled *in toto* without delay. The repayment of this outlay taken in its totality is reduced and fixed at the sum of ten million *florins.* . . .

6. The two contracting republics mutually guarantee the possessions which they had before this war in the two Indies and upon the coasts of Africa. The harbors of the Cape of Good Hope, Colombo and Trincomali shall be open to French vessels as well as to vessels of the United Provinces and upon the same terms.

. . . .

50. Constitution of the Year III.

August 22, 1795 (5 Fructidor, Year III). Duvergier, *Lois*, VIII, 223-242.

This constitution was drawn up after the suppression of the insurrection of Prairial, which had demanded that the constitution of the Year I should be put in operation. It was referred to the people, but coupled with the requirement that at least two-thirds of the members of the Convention must be elected to the two legislative councils. This "decree of the two-thirds" led to the unsuccessful royalist insurrection of Vendémiaire. The new constitution was then put into effect (October 26, 1795). It remained in operation until 18 Brumaire. The general plan for the legislative and executive branches of the government calls for notice; the former should be compared with those of the constitution of 1791 and of the Year I (see Nos. 15 and 39), the latter with those of the same documents and of No. 45. The basis for suffrage and office-holding should also be compared with the earlier constitutions.

REFERENCES. Gardiner, *French Revolution*, 247-250; Mathews, *French Revolution*, 277-280; Fyffe, *Modern Europe*, I, 100-103 (Popular ed., 68-69); Fournier, *Napoleon*, 54; Lanfrey, *Napoleon*, I, 48-50; Von Sybel, *French Revolution*, IV, 394-404; *Cambridge Modern History*, VIII, 392-397, 487-488; Lavisse and Rambaud, *Histoire générale*, VIII, 227-230, 374-376; Aulard, *Révolution française*, Part III, Ch. I; Jaurès, *Histoire socialiste*, V, 128-134.

Declaration of the Rights and Duties of Man and Citizen.

The French people proclaim in the presence of the Supreme Being the following declaration of the rights of man and citizen:

Rights.

1. The rights of man in society are liberty, equality, security, property.

2. Liberty consists in the power to do that which does not injure the rights of others.

3. Equality consists in this, that the law is the same for all, whether it protects or punishes.

Equality does not admit of any distinction of birth, nor of any inheritance of authority.

4. Security results from the co-operation of all in order to assure the rights of each.

5. Property is the right to enjoy and to dispose of one's goods, income, and the fruit of one's labor and industry.

6. The law is the general will expressed by the majority of the citizens or their representatives.

7. That which is not forbidden by the law cannot be prevented.

No one can be constrained to do that which it does not ordain.

8. No one can be summoned into court, accused, arrested, or detained except in the cases determined by the law and according to the forms which it has prescribed.

9. Those who incite, promote, sign, execute, or cause to be executed arbitrary acts are guilty and ought to be punished.

10. Every severity which may not be necessary to secure the person of a prisoner ought to be severely repressed by the law.

11. No one can be tried until after he has been heard or legally summoned.

12. The law ought to decree only such penalties as are strictly necessary and proportionate to the offence.

13. All treatment which increases the penalty fixed by the law is a crime.

14. No law, either civil or criminal, can have retroactive effect.

15. Every man can contract his time and his services, but he cannot sell himself nor be sold; his person is not an alienable property.

16. Every tax is established for the public utility; it ought to be apportioned among those liable for taxes, according to their means.

17. Sovereignty resides essentially in the totality of the citizens.

18. No individual nor assembly of part of the citizens can assume the sovereignty.

19. No one can without legal delegation exercise any authority or fill any public function.

20. Each citizen has a legal right to participate directly or indirectly in the formation of the law and in the selection of the representatives of the people and of the public functionaries.

21. The public offices cannot become the property of those who hold them.

22. The social guarantee cannot exist if the division of powers is not established, if their limits are not fixed, and if the responsibility of the public functionaries is not assured.

Duties.

1. The declaration of rights contains the obligations of

the legislators; the maintenance of society requires that those who compose it should both know and fulfill their duties.

2. All the duties of man and citizen spring from these two principles graven by nature in every heart:

Not to do to others that which you would not that they should do to you.

Do continually for others the good that you would wish to receive from them.

3. The obligations of each person to society consist in defending it, serving it, living in submission to the laws, and respecting those who are the agents of them.

4. No one is a good citizen unless he is a good son, good father, good brother, good friend, good husband.

5. No one is a virtuous man unless he is unreservedly and religiously an observer of the laws.

6. The one who violates the laws openly declares himself in a state of war with society.

7. The one who, without transgressing the laws, eludes them by stratagem or ingenuity wounds the interests of all; he makes himself unworthy of their good will and their esteem.

8. It is upon the maintenance of property that the cultivation of the land, all the productions, all means of labor, and the whole social order rest.

9. Every citizen owes his services to the fatherland and to the maintenance of liberty, equality, and property whenever the law summons him to defend them.

Constitution.

1. The French Republic is one and indivisible.

2. The totality of the French citizens is the sovereign.

Title I.

3. France is divided into — departments.
These departments are   .   .   .   [list omitted].

4. The boundaries of the departments can be changed or rectified by the legislative body; but in that case, the area of a department cannot exceed one hundred square myriameters (four hundred common square leagues).

5. Each department is divided into cantons, each canton into communes.

The cantons preserve their present circumscriptions.

Their boundaries, nevertheless, can be changed or rectified by the legislative body; but in that case there shall not
be more than one myriameter (two common leagues of two
thousand five hundred and sixty-six toises each) of the commune the most remote from the head-town of the canton.

6. The French colonies are integral parts of the Republic
and are subject to the same constitutional law.

7. *They are divided into departments as follows:

The island of Saint Domingo, of which the legislative
body shall determine the division, into four departments at
least and into six at most;

Guadaloupe, Marie Galante, Désirade, the Saintes, and the
French part of Saint Martin;

Martinique;

French Guiana and Cayenne;

Saint Lucia and Tabago.

The Isle of France, the Seychelles, Rodriguez, the settlements of Madagascar;

The Island of Réunion;

The East Indies, Pondicherry, Chandernagor, Mahé, Kar-
ikal and other settlements.

Title II. Political Condition of the Citizens.

8. Every man born and residing in France, fully twenty-
one years of age, who has had himself enrolled upon the
civic register of his canton, who has lived for a year past
upon the soil of the Republic, and who pays a direct land or
personal property tax, is a French citizen.

9. Frenchmen who shall have made one or more campaigns for the establishment of the Republic are citizens,
without condition as to tax.

10. A foreigner becomes a French citizen when, after having fully reached the age of twenty-one years and having declared an intention to settle in France, he has resided here for
seven consecutive years; provided he pays a direct tax, and in
addition possesses real estate or an agricultural or commercial
establishment, or has married a French woman.

11. Only French citizens can vote in the primary assemblies and be summoned to the offices established by the constitution.

12. The exercise of the rights of citizenship is lost:

1st. By naturalization in a foreign country;

2d. By affiliation with any foreign corporation which may imply distinctions of birth or which may demand religious vows;

3d. By the acceptance of positions or pensions offered by a foreign government;

4th. By condemnation to afflictive or infamous penalties until rehabilitation.

13. The exercise of the rights of citizenship is suspended:

1st. By judicial inhibition because of delirium, insanity, or imbecility;

2d. By the condition of bankruptcy or by the direct inheritance by gratuitous title of the whole or of part of the succession of a bankrupt;

3d. By the condition of domestic service for wages either for a person or a household;

4th. By the condition of accusation;

5th. By a judgment of contempt of court, as long as the judgment is not annulled.

14. The exercise of the rights of citizenship is neither lost nor suspended except in the cases enumerated in the two preceding articles.

15. Every citizen who shall have resided for seven consecutive years outside of the territory of the Republic, without commission or authorisation given in the name of the Republic, is reputed a foreigner; he becomes a French citizen again only after having conformed to the conditions prescribed in article 10.

16. Young men cannot be enrolled upon the civic register unless they prove that they know how to read and write and to follow a mechanical calling.

The manual operations of agriculture belong to the mechanical callings.

This article shall have effect only dating from the Year XII of the Republic.

Title III. Primary Assemblies.

17. The primary assemblies are composed of the citizens residing in the same canton.

The domicile requisite for voting in these assemblies is

acquired only by residence for one year and is lost only by a year of absence.

18. No one can act by proxy in the primary assemblies or vote upon the same matter in more than one of these assemblies.

19. There is at least one primary assembly per canton.

When there are several of them, each is composed of four hundred citizens at least, of nine hundred at most.

These numbers include the citizens, present or absent, having the right to vote there.

20. The primary assemblies constitute themselves provisionally under the presidency of the most aged; the youngest discharges provisionally the duties of secretary.

21. They are definitely constituted through the selection by ballot of a president, secretary, and three tellers.

22. If difficulties arise over the qualifications requisite for voting, the assembly decides provisionally, reserving recourse to the civil tribunal of the department.

23. In every other case the legislative body alone pronounces upon the validity of the operations of the primary assemblies.

24. No one can appear in arms in the primary assemblies.

25. Their policing belongs to themselves.

26. The primary assemblies meet:

1st. In order to accept or reject changes in the constitutional act proposed by the assemblies of revision;

2d. To conduct the elections which belong to them according to the constitutional act.

27. They meet with perfect right upon 1 Germinal of each year and proceed, according as there is occasion, to the selection:

1st. Of the members of the electoral assembly;

2d. The justice of the peace and his assessors;

3d. The president of the municipal administration of the canton, or the municipal officers in the communes of above five thousand inhabitants.

28. Immediately after these elections, in the communes of under five thousand inhabitants, the communal assemblies are held, which elect the agents of each commune and their assistants.

29. Whatever is done in a primary or communal assembly that is beyond the purpose of its convocation and contrary to the forms settled by the constitution is null.

30. The assemblies, whether primary or communal, carry on no elections other than those which are assigned to them by the constitutional act.

31. All the elections are carried on by secret ballot.

32. Every citizen who is legally convicted of having sold or purchased a vote is excluded from the primary and communal assemblies and from every public office for twenty years; in case of repetition, forever.

Title IV.   Electoral Assemblies.

33. Each primary assembly selects one elector for each two hundred citizens, present or absent, having the right to vote in the said assembly. For citizens up to the number of three hundred inclusive, only one elector is chosen.

Two of them are selected for three hundred-one up to five hundred;

Three for five hundred-one up to seven hundred;

Four for seven hundred-one up to nine hundred.

34. The members of the electoral assemblies are selected each year and can be re-elected only after an interval of two years.

35. No one can be chosen elector unless he is fully twenty-five years of age and unites to the qualifications necessary for the exercise of the rights of French citizenship one of the following conditions, to wit:

In the communes of above six thousand inhabitants, that of being proprietor or usufructuary of a property valued at an income equal to the local value of two hundred days of labor, or that of being occupant either of a habitation valued at an income equal to the value of one hundred and fifty days of labor, or of a rural property valued at two hundred days of labor;

In the communes of under six thousand inhabitants, that of being proprietor or usufructuary of a property valued at an income equal to the local value of one hundred and fifty days of labor, or that of being occupant either of a habitation valued at an income equal to the value of one hundred days of labor or of rural property valued at one hundred days of labor;

And in the country that of being proprietor or usufructuary of a property valued at an income equal to the local value of one hundred and fifty days of labor, or that of being the farmer or *métayer* of properties appraised at the value of two hundred days of labor.

With respect to those who shall be at the same time proprietors or usufructuaries for one part and occupants, farmers, or *métayers* for the other, their properties by these different titles shall be cumulated to the amount necessary to establish their eligibility.

36. The electoral assembly of each department meets on 20 Germinal of each year and concludes, in a single session of ten days at most and without power to adjourn, all the elections which are to occur; after that it is dissolved *ipso facto*.

37. The electoral assemblies cannot busy themselves with any matter foreign to the elections with which they are charged; they cannot send or receive any address, any petition, or any deputation.

38. The electoral assemblies cannot correspond among themselves.

39. No citizen, having been a member of an electoral assembly, can take the title of elector or meet in that capacity with those who have been with him members of that same assembly.

Infraction of the present article is an attempt against the general security.

40. Articles 18, 20, 21, 23, 24, 25, 29, 30, 31 and 32 of the preceding title, upon the primary assemblies, are common to the electoral assemblies.

41. The electoral assemblies elect, according as there is occasion:

1st. The members of the legislative body; to wit, the members of the Council of Ancients, then the members of the Council of the Five Hundred;

2d. The members of the tribunal of cassation;

3d. The high jurors;

4th. The department administrators;

5th. The president, public accuser, and recorder of the criminal tribunal;

6th. The judges of the civil tribunals.

42. When a citizen is elected by the electoral assemblies in order to replace a deceased, resigned, or dismissed functionary, this citizen is elected only for the time which remained to the replaced functionary.

43. The commissioner of the Executive Directory near the administration of each department is required, under penalty of dismissal, to inform the Directory of the opening and closing of the electoral assemblies: this commissioner can neither stop nor suspend the operations, nor enter into the place of the sittings; but he has the right to call for communication of the minutes of each session within the twenty-four hours which follow it, and he is required to inform the Directory of the infractions which may be made of the constitutional act.

In all cases the legislative body alone passes upon the validity of the operations of the electoral assemblies.

Title V. Legislative Power.
General Provisions.

44. The legislative body is composed of a Council of Ancients and a Council of the Five Hundred.

45. In no case can the legislative body delegate to one or several of its members, nor to anybody whomsoever, any of the functions which are assigned to it by the present constitution.

46. It cannot itself or by delegates discharge the executive or the judicial power.

47. The position of member of the legislative body and the discharge of any other public function, except that of archivist of the Republic, are incompatible.

48. The law determines the method of permanently or temporarily replacing the public functionaries who have been elected members of the legislative body.

49. Each department contributes, in proportion to its population alone, to the selection of the members of the Council of Ancients and of the members of the Council of the Five Hundred.

50. Every ten years the legislative body, according to the lists of population which are sent to it, determines the num-

ber of members of each council which each department shall furnish.

51. No change can be made in this apportionment during this interval.

52. The members of the legislative body are not representatives of the department which has selected them, but of the entire nation, and no instructions can be given to them.

53. Both councils are renewed every year by a third.

54. The members retiring after three years can be immediately re-elected for the three following years, after which there must be an interval of two years before they can be elected again.

55. No one in any case can be a member of the legislative body during more than six consecutive years.

56. If through extraordinary circumstances either of the two councils finds itself reduced to less than two-thirds of its members, it gives notice thereof to the Executive Directory, which is required to convoke without delay the primary assemblies of the departments, which have members of the legislative body to replace through the effect of these circumstances: the primary assemblies immediately select the electors, who proceed to the necessary replacements.

57. The newly elected members for both of the councils meet upon 1 Prairial of each year in the commune which has been indicated by the preceding legislative body, or in the same commune where it has held its last sittings, if it has not designated another.

58. The two councils always reside in the same commune.

59. The legislative body is permanent; nevertheless, it can adjourn for periods which it designates.

60. In no case can the two councils meet in a single hall.

61. Neither in the Council of Ancients nor in the Council of the Five Hundred can the functions of president and secretary exceed the duration of one month.

62. The two councils respectively have the right of police in the place of their sittings and in the environs which they have determined.

63. They have respectively the right of police over their members; but they cannot pronounce any penalty more severe than censure, arrests for eight days, or imprisonment for three.

64. The sittings of both councils are public: the specta·
tors cannot exceed in number half of the members of each
council respectively.

The minutes of the sittings are printed.

65. Every decision is taken by rising and sitting; in case
of doubt, the roll call is employed, but in that case the votes
are secret.

66. Upon the request of one hundred of its members each
council can form itself into secret committee of the whole
but only in order to discuss, not to resolve.

67. Neither of these councils can create any permanent
committee within its own body.

But each council has the power, when a matter seems to
it susceptible of a preparatory examination, to appoint from
among its members a special commission, which confines itself
exclusively to the matter that led to its formation.

This commission is dissolved as soon as the council has
legislated upon the matter with which it was charged.

68. The members of the legislative body receive an annual compensation; it is fixed for both councils at the value
of three thousand myriagrams of wheat (six hundred and
thirty quintals, thirty-two pounds).

69. The Executive Directory cannot cause any body of
troops to pass or to sojourn within six myriameters (twelve
common leagues) of the commune where the legislative body
is holding its sittings, except upon its requisition or with its
authorisation.

70. There is near the legislative body a guard of citizens
taken from the reserve national guard of all the departments
and chosen by their brothers in arms.

This guard cannot be less than fifteen hundred men in
active service.

71. The legislative body fixes the method of this service
and its duration.

72. The legislative body is not to be present at any public ceremony nor does it send deputations to them.

Council of the Five Hundred.

73. The Council of the Five Hundred is unalterably fixed
at that number.

74. In order to be elected a member of the Council of the Five Hundred it is necessary to be fully thirty years of age and to have been domiciled upon the soil of France for the ten years which shall have immediately preceded the election.

The condition of thirty years of age shall not be required before the seventh year of the Republic: until that date the age of twenty-five shall be sufficient.

75. The Council of the Five Hundred cannot deliberate, unless the sitting is composed of at least two hundred members.

76. The proposal of the laws belongs exclusively to the Council of the Five Hundred.

77. No proposition can be considered or decided upon in the Council of the Five Hundred, except in observance of the following forms.

There shall be three readings of the proposal; the interval between two of these readings cannot be less than ten days.

The discussion is open after each reading; nevertheless, the Council of the Five Hundred can declare that there is cause for adjournment, or that there is no occasion for consideration.

Every proposal shall be printed and distributed two days before the second reading.

After the third reading the Council of the Five Hundred decides whether or not there is cause for adjournment.

78. No proposition, which after having been submitted to discussion, has been definitely rejected after the third reading, can be renewed until after a year has elapsed.

79. The propositions adopted by the Council of the Five Hundred are called *Resolutions.*

80. The preamble of every resolution states:

1st. The dates of the sittings upon which the three readings of the proposition shall have occurred;

2d. The act by which after the third reading it has been declared that there was not cause for adjournment.

81. The propositions recognized as urgent by a previous declaration of the Council of the Five Hundred are exempt from the forms prescribed by article 77.

This declaration states the motives for urgency and mention shall be made of them in the preamble of the resolution.

Council of Ancients.

82. The Council of Ancients is composed of two hundred and fifty members.

83. No one can be elected a member of the Council of Ancients,

Unless he is fully forty years of age;

Unless, moreover, he is married or a widower;

And unless he has been domiciled upon the soil of the Republic for the fifteen years which shall have immediately preceded the election.

84. The condition of domicile required by the preceding article and that prescribed by article .74 do not affect the citizens who are away from the soil of the Republic upon a mission of the government.

85. The Council of Ancients cannot deliberate unless the sitting is composed of at least one hundred and twenty-six members.

86. It belongs exclusively to the Council of Ancients to approve or reject the resolutions of the Council of the Five Hundred.

87. As soon as a resolution of the Council of the Five Hundred has reached the Council of Ancients the president directs the reading of the preamble.

88. The Council of Ancients refuses to approve the resolutions of the Council of the Five Hundred which have not been taken in the forms prescribed by the constitution.

89. If the proposition has been declared urgent by the Council of the Five Hundred, the Council of Ancients decides to approve or reject the act of urgency.

90. If the Council of Ancients rejects the act of urgency it does not pass upon the matter of the resolution.

91. If the resolution is not preceded by an act of urgency there shall be three readings of it: the interval between two of these readings cannot be less than five days.

The debate is open after each reading.

Every resolution is printed and distributed at least two days before the second reading.

92. The resolutions of the Council of the Five Hundred adopted by the Council of Ancients are called *Laws*.

93. The preamble of the laws states the dates of the sit-

tings of the Council of Ancients upon which the three readings have occurred.

94. The decree by which the Council of Ancients recognizes the urgency of a law is adduced and mentioned in the
preamble of that law.

95. The proposition for a law made by the Council of the
Five Hundred embraces all the articles of a single project:
the council shall reject them all or approve them in their entirety.

96. The approval of the Council of Ancients is expressed
upon each proposition of law by this formula signed by the
president and the secretaries: *The Council of Ancients approves* . . .

97. The refusal to adopt because of the omission of the
forms indicated in article 77 is expressed by this formula,
signed by the president and the secretaries: *The Constitution
annuls* . . .

98. The refusal to approve the principle of the law is expressed by this formula, signed by the president and secretaries: *The Council of Ancients cannot adopt* . . . .

99. In the case of the preceding article, the rejected project of law cannot be again presented by the Council of the
Five Hundred until after a year has elapsed.

100. The Council of the Five Hundred, nevertheless, can
present at any date whatsoever a project of law which contains articles included in a project which has been rejected.

101. The Council of Ancients within the day sends the
laws which it has adopted to the Council of the Five Hundred as well as to the Executive Directory.

102. The Council of Ancients can change the residence
of the legislative body; it indicates in this case a new place
and the date at which the two councils are required to repair
thence.

The decree of the Council of Ancients upon this subject
is irrevocable.

103. Upon the day of this decree neither of the councils
can deliberate any further in the commune where they have
until then resided.

The members who may continue their functions there make
themselves guilty of an attempt against the security of the
Republic.

104. The members of the Executive Directory who may retard or refuse to seal, promulgate, and dispatch the decree of transfer of the legislative body are guilty of the same offence.

105. If, within the twenty days after that fixed by the Council of Ancients, the majority of each of the two councils have not made known to the Republic their arrival at the new place indicated or their meeting in some other place, the department administrators, or in their default, the department civil tribunals, convoke the primary assemblies in order to select the electors who proceed forthwith to the formation of a new legislative body by the election of two hundred and fifty deputies for the Council of Ancients and five hundred for the other council.

106. The department administrators, who, in the case of the preceding article may be remiss in convoking the primary assemblies, make themselves guilty of high treason and of an attempt against the security of the Republic.

107. All citizens who interpose obstacles to the convocation of the primary and electoral assemblies in the case of article 106 are guilty of the same offence.

108. The members of the new legislative body assemble in the place to which the Council of Ancients had transferred its sittings.

If they cannot meet in that place, in whatever place there is a majority there is the legislative body.

109. Except in the case of article 102 no proposition of law can originate in the Council of Ancients.

Of the Guaranty of the Members of the Legislative Body.

110. The citizens who are or have been members of the legislative body cannot be questioned, accused, or tried at any time for what they have said or written in the discharge of their functions.

111. The members of the legislative body, from the moment of their selection to the thirtieth day after the expiration of their functions, cannot be put on trial except in the forms prescribed by the articles that follow.

112. For criminal acts they can be seized in the very act; but notice thereof is given without delay to the legislative body and the prosecution shall be continued only after the

Council of the Five Hundred shall have proposed proceeding with the trial and the Council of Ancients shall have decreed it.

113. Outside of the case of *flagrante delicto* the members of the legislative body cannot be brought before the police officers nor put in a state of arrest until after the Council of the Five Hundred has proposed proceeding with the trial and the Council of Ancients has decreed it.

114. In the case of the two preceding articles a member of the legislative body cannot be brought before any other tribunal than the high court of justice.

115. They are brought before the same court for acts of treason, squandering, maneuvers to overthrow the constitution, and attempts against the internal security of the Republic.

116. No denunciation against a member of the legislative body can give rise to a prosecution unless it is reduced to writing, signed, and addressed to the Council of the Five Hundred.

117. If, after having deliberated in the form prescribed by article 77, the Council of the Five Hundred accepts the denunciation, it so declares in these terms:

*The denunciation against . . . for the act of . .
dated . . . signed . . . is accepted.*

118. The accused is then summoned: he has a period of three full days in which to make his appearance, and when he appears, he is heard in the interior of the place of the sittings of the Council of the Five Hundred.

119. Whether the accused be present or not, the Council of the Five Hundred declares after this period whether there is occasion or not for the examination of his conduct.

120. If the Council of the Five Hundred declares that there is occasion for an examination, the accused is summoned by the Council of Ancients: he has a period of two full days in which to appear: and if he appears, he is heard in the interior of the place of the sittings of the Council of Ancients.

121. Whether the accused be present or not, the Council of Ancients, after this period, and after having deliberated in the forms prescribed by article 91, pronounces the accusation

if there is occasion and sends the accused before the high court of justice, which is required to proceed with the trial without any delay.

122. All discussion in either council relative to complaint against or accusation of a member of the legislative body takes place in committee of the whole.

Every decision upon the same matters is taken by roll call and secret ballot.

123. Accusation pronounced against a member of the legislative body entails suspension.

If he is acquitted by the judgment of the high court of justice he resumes his functions.

Relations of the Two Councils between Themselves.

124. When the two councils are definitively constituted they give notice thereof reciprocally by a messenger of state.

125. Each council appoints four messengers of state for its service.

126. They carry the laws and acts of the legislative body to each of the councils and to the Executive Directory; they have entrance for that purpose into the place of the sittings of the Executive Directory.

They go preceded by two ushers.

127. Neither of the two councils can adjourn beyond five days without the consent of the other.

Promulgation of the Laws.

128. The Executive Directory causes the laws and other acts of the legislative body to be sealed and published within two days after their reception.

129. It causes to be sealed and promulgated, within a day, the laws and acts of the legislative body which are preceded by a decree of urgency.

130. The publication of the law and the acts of the legislative body is prescribed in the following form:

"In the name of the French Republic, (law) or (act of the legislative body) . . . the Directory orders that the above law or legislative act shall be published, executed, and that it shall be provided with the seal of the Republic."

131. Laws whose preambles do not attest the observation of the forms prescribed by articles 77 and 91 cannot be pro-

mulgated by the Executive Directory, and its responsibility in this respect lasts six years.

Laws are excepted for which the act of urgency has been approved by the Council of Ancients.

Title VI. Executive Power.

132. The executive power is delegated to a Directory of five members appointed by the legislative body, performing then the functions of an electoral body in the name of the nation.

133. The Council of the Five Hundred forms by secret ballot a list of ten times the number. of the members of the Directory to be appointed and presents it to the Council of Ancients, which chooses, also by secret ballot, within this list.

134. The members of the Directory shall be at least forty years of age.

135. They can be taken only from among the citizens who have been members of the legislative body or ministers.

The provision of the present article shall be observed only commencing with the ninth year of the Republic.

136. Counting from the first day of the Year V of the Republic the members of the legislative body cannot be elected members of the Directory or ministers, either during the continuance of their legislative functions or during the first year after the expirations of these same functions.

137. The Directory is renewed in part by the election of one new member each year.

During the first four years, the lot shall decide upon the order of retirement of those who shall have been appointed for the first time.

138. None of the retiring members can be re-elected until after an interval of five years.

139. The ancestor and the descendant in the direct line, brothers, uncle and nephew, cousins of the first degree, and those related by marriage in these various degrees, cannot be at the same time members of the Directory, nor can they succeed them until after an interval of five years.

140. In case of the removal of one of the members of the Directory by death, resignation or otherwise, his successor is elected by the legislative body within ten days at the latest.

The Council of the Five Hundred is required to propose the candidates within the first five days and the Council of Ancients shall complete the election within the last five days.

The new member is elected only for the term of office which remained to the one whom he replaces.

Nevertheless, if this time does not exceed six months, the one who is elected remains in office until the end of the fifth year following.

141. Each member of the Directory presides over it in his turn for three months only.

The president has the signature and the keeping of the seal.

The laws and the acts of the legislative body are addressed to the Directory in the person of its president.

142. The Executive Directory cannot deliberate if there are not at least three members present.

143. It chooses for itself outside of its own body a secretary who countersigns the despatches and records the transactions in a register, where each member has the right to cause to be inscribed his opinion with his motives.

two years which immediately follow the expiration of these without the presence of its secretary; in this case the transactions are recorded in a special register by one of the members of the Directory.

144. The Directory provides, according to the laws, for the external and internal security of the Republic.

It can issue proclamations in conformity with the laws and for their execution.

It disposes of the armed force, without the Directory collectively or any of its members being able in any case to command them during the time of their functions or during the two years which immediately follow the expiration of these same functions.

145. If the Directory is informed that some conspiracy is being plotted against the external or internal security of the state, it can issue warrants of apprehension and arrest against those who are presumed to be authors or the accomplices thereof; it can question them: but it is required under the penalties provided for the crime of arbitrary imprisonment to send them into the presence of the police officer within the

period of two days, in order to proceed according to the laws.

146. The Directory appoints the generals-in-chief; it cannot choose them from among the blood or marriage relations of its members within the degrees expressed in article 139.

147. It supervises and secures the execution of the laws in the administrations and tribunals by commissioners of its appointment.

148. It appoints, from outside of its own body, the ministers and dismisses them when it thinks expedient.

It cannot choose those under the age of thirty years, nor from among the blood or marriage relations of its members within the degrees set forth in article 139.

149. The ministers correspond directly with the authorities who are subordinate to them.

150. The legislative body determines the prerogatives and the number of the ministers.

This number is from six at the least to eight at the most.

151. The ministers do not form a council.

152. The ministers are individually responsible for the non-execution of the laws as well as for the non-execution of the orders of the Directory.

153. The Directory appoints the receiver of direct taxes of each department.

154. It appoints the superintendents in chief for the administrations of the indirect taxes and for the administration of the national lands.

155. All the public functionaries in the French colonies, except the departments of the islands of France and Réunion, shall be appointed by the Directory until the peace.

156. The legislative body can authorise the Directory to send into any of the French colonies, according to the need of the case, one or several special agents appointed by it for a limited time.

The special agents shall exercise the same functions as the Directory and shall be subordinate to it.

157. No member of the Directory can leave the soil of the Republic until two years after the cessation of his functions.

158. He is required during that interval to furnish to the legislative body proofs of his residence.

Article 112 and the following to article 123 inclusive, relative to the guarantee of the legislative body, are common to the members of the Directory.

159. In the case where more than two of the Directory may be put on trial, the legislative body shall provide in the usual forms for their provisional replacement during the trial.

160. Outside of the cases of articles 119 and 120 the Directory or any of its members cannot be summoned by the Council of the Five Hundred nor by the Council of Ancients.

161. The reports and explanations called for by either of the councils are furnished in writing.

162. The Directory is required to present to both councils each year in writing a statement of the expenses, the situation of the finances, and the list of the existing pensions, as well as a project for those which it believes ought to be established.

It shall indicate the abuses which have come to its knowledge.

163. The Directory can at any time in writing invite the Council of the Five Hundred to take a subject into consideration; it can propose measures to it, but not drawn up in the form of projects of law.

164. No member of the Directory can be absent more than five days nor go away beyond four myriameters (eight common leagues) from the place of the residence of the Directory without the authorisation of the legislative body.

165. The members of the Directory, when engaged in the exercise of their functions, whether upon the outside or within the interior of their residences, can appear only in the costume which is appropriate for them.

166. The Directory has its guard, paid and clothed at the expense of the Republic, composed of one hundred and twenty infantry and one hundred and twenty cavalry.

167. The Directory is accompanied by its guard in the public ceremonies and processions, where it has always the first rank.

168. Each member of the Directory when abroad is accompanied by two guards.

169. Every army post owes to the Directory and to each of its members the higher military honors.

170. The Directory has four messengers of state whom it appoints and whom it can dismiss.

They carry to the two legislative councils the letters and memoirs of the Directory; they have entrance for that purpose into the place of the sittings of the legislative councils.

They go preceded by two ushers.

171. The Directory resides in the same commune as the legislative body.

172. The members of the Directory are lodged at the expense of the Republic and in a single edifice.

173. The compensation of each of them for each year is fixed at the value of fifty thousand myriagrammes of wheat (ten thousand two hundred and twenty-two quintals).

Title VII. Administrative and Municipal Bodies.

174. There is in each department a central administration and in each canton at least one municipal administration.

175. Every member of a department or municipal administration shall be at least twenty-five years of age.

176. The ancestor and the descendant in the direct line, brothers, uncle and nephew, and those related by marriage in the same degrees, cannot be at the same time members of the same administration, nor can they succeed them until after an interval of two years.

177. Each department administration is composed of five members; it is renewed by a fifth each year.

178. Every commune whose population runs from five thousand to a hundred thousand inhabitants has a municipal administration of its own.

179. There are in every commune whose population is less than five thousand inhabitants a municipal agent and an assistant.

180. The union of the municipal agents from each commune forms the cantonal municipality.

181. There is, moreover, chosen in every canton a president of the municipal administration.

182. In the communes whose population runs from five to ten thousand inhabitants there are five municipal officers;

Seven for ten thousand to fifty thousand.

. Nine for fifty thousand to one hundred thousand.

183. In the communes whose population exceeds one

hundred thousand there are at least three municipal administrations.

In these communes the division of the municipalities is made in such a manner that the population of the district of each does not exceed fifty thousand persons and is not less than thirty thousand.

The municipality of each district is composed of seven members.

184. There is, in the communes which are divided into several municipalities, a central bureau for the subjects considered indivisible by the legislative body.

This bureau is composed of three members appointed by the department administration and confirmed by the executive power.

185. The members of every municipal administration are appointed for two years and renewed each year by half or the part nearest a half and by the larger and the smaller fraction alternately.

186. The department administrators and the members of the municipal administrations can be re-elected once without an interval.

187. Any citizen who has been elected department administrator or member of a municipal administration twice in succession and who has discharged the duties in virtue of both elections cannot be elected again until after an interval of two years.

188. In case a department or municipal administration should lose one or several of its members by death, resignation, or otherwise, the remaining administrators in filling the places can add to themselves temporary administrators who act in that capacity until the following elections.

189. The department and municipal administrators cannot alter the acts of the legislative body, nor those of the Executive Directory, nor suspend the execution of them.

They cannot meddle with matters belonging to the judicial body.

190. The administrators are particularly charged with the apportionment of the direct taxes and with surveillance over the monies accruing from the public revenues in their territory.

The legislative body determines the regulations and the method of their functions upon these subjects as well as upon other parts of the internal administration.

191. The Executive Directory appoints over each department and municipal administration a commissioner whom it recalls when it deems expedient.

This commissioner watches over and requires the execution of the laws.

192. The commissioner for each local administration shall be taken from among the citizens domiciled for a year past in the department where that administration is established.

He must be at least twenty-five years of age.

193. The municipal administrations are subordinate to the department administrations and these to the ministers.

In consequence, the ministers can annul, each on his part, the acts of the department administrations, and these the acts of the municipal administrations, when these acts are contrary to the laws or the orders of the higher authorities.

194. The ministers can also suspend the department administrations which have contravened the laws or the orders of the higher authorities, and the department administrators have the same right with respect to the members of the municipal administrations.

195. No suspension or annulment becomes definitive without the formal confirmation of the Executive Directory.

196. The Directory can also annul directly the acts of department or municipal administrations.

It can also suspend or dismiss directly when it thinks necessary either the department or the canton administrators and send them before the tribunals of the department when there is occasion.

197. Every order providing for the annulment of acts, suspension, or dismissal of an administrator must include a statement of the reasons.

198. When five members of a department administration are dismissed, the Executive Directory provides for their replacement until the following election; but it can choose their substitutes only from among the former administrators of the same department.

199. The administrations, whether department or canton, can correspond among themselves only upon matters as-

signed to them by the law and not upon the general interests of the Republic.

200. Every administration shall annually render an account of its management.

The reports rendered by the department administrations are to be printed.

201. All the acts of the administrative bodies are made public by the deposit of the register wherein they are recorded, which is open to all persons under the administration.

This register is closed every six months and is deposited only from that day that it has been closed.

The legislative body can postpone, according to circumstances, the day fixed for this deposit.

Title VIII. Judicial Power.
General Provisions.

202. The judicial functions cannot be exercised by the legislative body nor by the executive power.

203. The judges cannot interfere in the exercise of the legislative power nor make any regulation.

They cannot stop or suspend the execution of any law nor cite before them the administrators on account of their functions.

204. No one can be deprived of the judges that the law assigns to him by any commission nor by other authorities than those which are fixed by a prior law.

205. Justice is rendered gratuitously.

206. The judges cannot be dismissed except for legally pronounced forfeiture, nor suspended except by an accepted accusation.

207. The ancestor and the descendant in the direct line, brothers, uncle and nephew, cousins of the first degree, and those related by marriage in these various degreees, cannot be at the same time members of the same tribunal.

208. The sittings of the tribunal are public; ·the judges deliberate in secret; the judgments are pronounced orally; they include a statement of reasons and in them is set forth the terms of the law applied.

209. No citizen, unless he is fully thirty years of age, can be elected judge of a department tribunal, or justice of the peace, or assessor of a justice of the peace, or judge of a tri-

bunal of commerce, or member of the tribunal of cassation, or juror, or commissioner of the Executive Directory before the tribunals.

Of Civil Justice.

210. The right to have differences passed upon by arbitrators chosen by the parties cannot be impaired.

211. The decision of these arbitrators is without appeal and without recourse in cassation, unless the parties have expressly reserved it.

212. There are in each district fixed by law a justice of the peace and his assessors.

They are all elected for two years and can be immediately and indefinitely re-elected.

213. The law determines the matters over which the justices of the peace and the assessors have jurisdiction in the last resort.

It assigns to them the others over which they pronounce judgment subject to appeal.

214. There are special tribunals for land and maritime commerce; the law fixes the places where it is permissible to establish them.

Their power to pronounce judgment in the last resort cannot be extended beyond the value of five hundred myriagrams of wheat (a hundred and two quintals, twenty-two pounds).

215. Cases of which the trial belongs neither to the justices of the peace nor to the tribunals of commerce, either in the last resort or subject to appeal, are brought directly before the justice of the peace and his assessors in order to be conciliated.

If the justice of the peace cannot conciliate them, he sends them before the civil tribunal.

216. There is one civil tribunal per department.

Each civil tribunal is composed of twenty judges at least, one commissioner and one substitute approved and removable by the Executive Directory, and one recorder.

The election of all the members of a tribunal takes place every five years.

The judges can be re-elected.

217. At the time of the election of the judges five substitutes are selected, three of whom are taken from among the

citizens residing in the commune where the tribunal sits.

218. The civil tribunal pronounces in the last resort, in the cases determined by law, upon appeals from judgments, either of justices of the peace, or of the arbitrators, or of the tribunals of commerce.

219. The appeal from the judgments pronounced by the civil tribunal goes to the civil tribunal of one of the three nearest departments, as is determined by law.

220. The civil tribunal is divided into sections.

A section with less than five judges cannot pronounce judgment.

221. The assembled judges in each tribunal select among themselves by secret ballot the president of each section.

Of Correctional and Criminal Justice.

222. No one can be seized except in order to be brought before the officer of police; and no one can be put under arrest or detained except in virtue of a warrant of arrest from the officers of police or from the Executive Directory, in the case of article 145, or an order of arrest either from a tribunal or the foreman of the jury of accusation, or of a decree of accusation from the legislative body in the case where it has authority to pronounce, or of a judicial judgment of condemnation to prison or correctional detention.

223. In order that the warrant which orders the arrest may be executed, it is necessary:

1st. That it set forth formally the cause for the arrest and the law in conformity with which it is ordered;

2d. That it has been made known to the one who is the subject of it and that he has been left a copy thereof.

224. Every person seized and brought before the officer of police shall be examined immediately or within a day at the latest.

225. If the examination discloses that there is no matter for inculpation against him, he shall be put at liberty at once; or, if there is occasion to send him to jail, he shall be brought there within the shortest period possible, which in any case shall not exceed three days.

226. No arrested person can be detained, if he gives sufficient bail, in any of the cases where the law permits him to remain free under bail.

227. No person, in a case in which his detention is authorised by the law, can be brought to or detained except in the places legally and publicly designated to serve for jails, court houses, or houses of detention.

228. No custodian or jailer can receive or retain any person except in virtue of a warrant of arrest according to the forms prescribed by articles 222 and 223, an order for the taking of the body, a decree of accusation, or a judicial decision of condemnation to prison or correctional detention, and unless the transcript of it has been entered upon his register.

229. Every custodian or jailer is required, without any order being able to dispense therewith, to present the detained person to the civil officer having the police of the house of detention, whenever he shall be so required by that officer.

230. Production of the detained person cannot be refused to his relatives and friends who are bearers of an order of the civil officer, who shall always be required to accord it, unless the custodian or jailer presents an order of the judge, transcribed upon his register, to keep the arrested person in secret.

231. Any man, whatever his place or employment, other than those to whom the law has given the right of arrest, who shall give, sign, execute or cause to be executed an order for the arrest of any person, or whoever, even in the case of an arrest authorised by the law, shall bring to, receive, or detain a person in a place of detention not publicly and legally designated, and all custodians of jailers who shall contravene the provisions of the three preceding articles, shall be guilty of the crime of arbitrary imprisonment.

232. All severities employed in arrests, detention, or executions, other than those prescribed by the law, are crimes.

233. In each department there are at least three and not more than six correctional tribunals for the trial of offences for which the punishment is neither afflictive nor infamous.

These tribunals cannot pronounce penalties more severe than imprisonment for two years.

Jurisdiction over offences for which the penalty does not exceed the value of three days of labor or imprisonment for three days is delegated to the justice of the peace, who pronounces in the last resort.

234. Each correctional tribunal is composed of a president,

two justices of the peace or assessors of justices of the peace of the commune where it is established, a commissioner of the executive power, and a recorder.

235. The president of each correctional tribunal is taken every six months and in turn from among the members of the sections of the civil tribunal of the department, the presidents excepted.

236. There is an appeal from the judgment of the correctional tribunal before the department criminal tribunal.

237. In the matter of offences involving afflictive or infamous punishment, no person can be tried except upon an accusation accepted by the jurors or decreed by the legislative body, in case it belongs to that body to decree accusation.

238. A first jury declares whether the accusation ought to be accepted or rejected: the facts are passed upon by a second jury, and the penalty fixed by the law is applied by the criminal tribunals.

239. The jurors vote only by secret ballot.

240. There are in each department as many accusation juries as there are correctional tribunals.

The presidents of the correctional tribunals are the foremen thereof, each in his own district.

In the communes of over fifty thousand souls there can be established by law, besides the president of the correctional tribunal, as many foremen of accusation juries as the transaction of business shall require.

241. The functions of commissioner of the executive power and recorder for the foreman of the accusation jury are discharged by the commissioner and recorder of the correctional tribunal.

242. Each foreman of the accusation jury has the immediate surveillance over all the police officers of his district.

243. The foreman of the accusation jury, as police officer, on account of the denunciations made to him by the public accuser, whether ex-officio or in accordance with the orders of the Executive Directory, immediately prosecutes:

1st. Attacks upon the liberty or personal security of the citizens;

2d. Those committed against the laws of nations;

3d. Resistance to the execution of the judicial decisions or any of the executive acts emanating from the constituted authorities;

4th. Disturbances caused and assaults committed in order to hinder the collection of taxes and the free circulation of provisions and other articles of commerce.

244. There is one criminal tribunal for each department.

245. The criminal tribunal is composed of a president, a public accuser, four judges taken from the civil tribunal, the commissioner of the executive power before the tribunal or his substitute, and a recorder.

There is in the criminal tribunal of the department of the Seine, a vice-president and a substitute for the public accuser; this tribunal is divided into two sections; eight members of the civil tribunal discharge there the duties of judges.

246. The presidents of the sections of the civil tribunals cannot fill the positions of judges upon the criminal tribunal.

247. The other judges, each in his turn for six months in the order of his appointment, perform their duty there and they cannot discharge any functions in the civil tribunal during that time.

248. The public accuser is charged:

1st. To prosecute the offences according to the warrants of accusation accepted by the first juries;

2d. To transmit to the police officers the denunciations which are addressed directly to him;

3d. To watch over the police officers of the department and to proceed against them, according to the law, in cases of negligence or more serious acts.

249. The commissioner of the executive power is charged:

1st. To require regularity of forms in the course of the proceedings before the decision, and the application of the law.

2d. To obtain the execution of the decisions rendered by the criminal tribunal.

250. The judges cannot propound to the jurors any complex question.

251. The trial jury consists of at least twelve jurors: the accused has the right to reject the number of them which the law determines.

252. The proceedings before the trial jury are public and the accused cannot be denied the assistance of counsel whom he has chosen or who has been selected for him ex-officio.

253. No person acquitted by a legal jury can be re-arrested or accused for the same offence.

Tribunal of Cassation.

254. There is in the whole republic one tribunal of cassation.

It decides:

1st. Upon the petitions in cassation against the judicial decisions in the last resort rendered by the tribunals;

2d. Upon petitions for removal from one court to another, on account of legitimate suspicion or public security;

3d. Upon the orders of judges and the complaints of partiality of a whole court.

255. The tribunal of cassation can never have jurisdiction over the facts of the actions; but it reverses the judgments rendered upon proceedings in which the forms have been violated or which contain any express contravention of the law, and it sends back the facts of the suit to the tribunal which shall have jurisdiction therein.

256. When after one cassation the second judgment upon the matter is attacked by the same means as the first, the question cannot be discussed again before the tribunal of cassation without having been submitted to the legislative body, which provides a law to which the tribunal of cassation is required to conform itself.

257. Each year the tribunal of cassation is required to send to each of the sections of the legislative body a deputation which presents to it the list of the judgments rendered, with marginal notes and the text of the laws which have determined the judgment.

258. The number of the judges of the tribunal of cassation cannot exceed three-fourths of the number of the departments.

259. This tribunal is renewed every year by a fifth.

The electoral assemblies of the departments select successively and alternately the judges who shall replace those who retire from the tribunal of cassation.

The judges of this tribunal can always be re-elected.

260. Each judge of the tribunal of cassation has a substitute elected by the same electoral assembly.

261. There are before the tribunal of cassation a commissioner and substitutes appointed and removable by the Executive Directory.

262. The Executive Directory informs the tribunal of cassation, by means of its commissioner and without prejudice to the right of the interested parties, of the acts in which the judges have exceeded their powers.

263. The tribunal annuls these acts; and if they give cause for forfeiture the fact is announced to the legislative body, which renders the decree of accusation, after having heard or summoned the accused.

264. The legislative body can annul the judgments of the tribunal of cassation, reserving the personal prosecution of the judges who may have incurred forfeiture.

High Court of Justice.

265. There is a high court of justice to try the accusations accepted by the legislative body against either its own members or those of the Executive Directory.

266. The high court of justice is composed of five judges and two national accusers drawn from the tribunal of cassation and of high jurors selected by the electoral assemblies of the departments.

267. The high court of justice constitutes itself only in virtue of a proclamation of the legislative body drawn up and published by the Council of the Five Hundred.

268. It constitutes itself and holds its sittings in the place designated by the proclamation of the Council of the Five Hundred.

This place cannot be nearer than twelve myriameters to that where the legislative body resides.

269. When the legislative body has proclaimed the formation of the high court of justice, the tribunal of cassation in a public sitting draws by lot fifteen of its members; it selects in the same sitting five of these fifteen, one after another, by means of secret ballot; the five judges thus selected are the judges of the high court of justice; they choose a president from among themselves.

270. The tribunal of cassation selects by ballot, in the same sitting and by majority, two of its members to discharge

for the high court of justice the functions of national accusers.

271. The bills of accusation are drawn up and put into form by the Council of the Five Hundred.

272. The electoral assemblies of each department select every year a jury for the high court of justice.

273. The Executive Directory causes to be printed and published, one month after the date of the elections, the list of the jurors appointed by the high court of justice.

Title IX.   Of the Armed Force.

274. The armed force is established in order to defend the state against enemies from without and to assure within the maintenance of order and the execution of the laws.

275. The armed force is essentially obedient: no armed force can deliberate.

276. It is divided into the reserve national guard and the active national guard.

Of the Reserve National Guard.

277. The reserve national guard is composed of all citizens and sons of citizens in condition to bear arms.

278. Its organization and its discipline are the same for the whole Republic; they are fixed by law.

279. No Frenchman can exercise the rights of citizenship if he is not registered upon the roll of the reserve national guard.

280. The distinctions of rank and subordination exist there only in relation to the service and during its continuance.

281. The officers of the reserve national guard are elected at stated times by the citizens who compose it and can be reelected only after an interval.

282. The command of the national guard of an entire department cannot be entrusted ordinarily to a single citizen.

283. If it is deemed necessary to assemble the whole national guard of a department, the Executive Directory can appoint a temporary commander.

284. The command of the reserve national guard in a city of a hundred thousand and upwards cannot ordinarily be entrusted to a single man.

Of the Active National Guard.

285. The Republic maintains in its pay, even in time of peace, under the name of the active national guards, an army and a navy.

286. The army is formed by voluntary enlistment, and in case of need, by the method which the law determines.

287. No foreigner who has not acquired the rights of French citizenship can be admitted into the French armies, unless he has made one or more campaigns for the establishment of the Republic.

288. The commanders or heads of the army or navy are appointed only in case of war. They receive from the Directory commissions revocable at will. The duration of these commissions is confined to one campaign; but they can be continued.

289. The command of the armies of the Republic cannot be confided to a single man.

290. The army and navy are subject to special laws for discipline, for the form of trials, and for the nature of the penalties.

291. No part of the reserve national guard or of the active national guard can act in the internal service of the Republic except upon the written requisition of the civil authority in the forms prescribed by the law.

292. The public force cannot be requisitioned by the civil authorities except within the extent of their territory; it cannot be transported from one canton to another, without this being authorised by the administration of the department, nor from one department into another without the orders of the Executive Directory.

293. Nevertheless, the legislative body determines the methods to secure by the armed force the execution of the judicial decisions and the prosecution of the accused upon all the French territory.

294. In case of imminent danger the municipal administration of the canton can make requisition upon the national guard of the neighboring cantons; in this case, the administration which has made requisition and the leaders of the national guards who have been requisitioned are likewise required to make instant report of it to the department administration.

295. No foreign troops can be introduced upon French territory without the previous consent of the legislative body.

Title X. Public Instruction.

296. There are in the Republic primary schools where the pupils may learn reading, writing, the elements of computation and those of morality. The Republic provides for the expense of the lodgings of the instructors who preside over these schools.

297. There are in the different parts of the Republic schools higher than the primary schools, the number of which shall be such that there shall be at least one of them for every two departments.

298. There is for the whole Republic a national institute charged with the collection of discoveries and the perfecting of the arts and sciences.

299. The different establishments of public instruction have between them no relation of subordination nor of administrative correspondence.

300. Citizens have the right to form private establishments for education and instruction as well as free societies to promote the progress of science, letters, and the arts.

301. There shall be national festivals established in order to maintain fraternity among the citizens and to attach them to the constitution, the fatherland, and the laws.

Title XI. Taxes.

302. The public taxes are considered and fixed each year by the legislative body. The imposition of them belongs to it alone. They cannot continue more than one year unless they are expressly renewed.

303. The legislative body can create any kind of tax that it shall believe necessary; but it shall establish each year a land tax and a personal property tax.

304. Every person, who, not being included in the case of articles 12 and 13 of the constitution, has not been included on the roll of the direct taxes, has the right to present himself to the municipal administration of his commune and to be enrolled there for a personal tax equal to the local value of three days of agricultural labor.

305. The registration mentioned in the preceding article

can be effected only in the month of Messidor of each year.

306. Taxes of every sort are apportioned among those liable for taxes, in accordance with their means.

307. The Executive Directory directs and watches over the collection and the deposit of the taxes and gives all the orders necessary for that purpose.

308. The detailed accounts of the expenditure of the ministers, signed and certified by them, are made public at the commencement of each year.

The same thing shall be done for the lists of receipts for the different taxes and all the public revenues.

309. The accounts of these expenses and receipts are distinguished according to their nature; they show the sums received and expended year by year in each part of the general administration.

310. The accounts of the special expenses of the departments and those which relate to the tribunals, administrations, the progress of the sciences, and all public works and establishments are likewise published.

311. The department administrations and the municipalities cannot make any assessment beyond the sums fixed by the legislative body, nor, without being authorized by it, consider or allow any local loan at the expense of the citizens of the department, commune or canton.

312. The right to regulate the manufacture and issue of every sort of monies, to fix the values and weights thereof. and to determine the type thereof, belongs to the legislative body alone.

313. The Executive Directory watches over the manufacture of the monies and appoints the officers charged with the immediate conduct of this inspection.

314. The legislative body determines the taxes of the colonies and their commercial relations with the mother country.

National Treasury and Book-keeping.

315. There are five commissioners of the national treasury elected by the Council of Ancients from a triple list presented by that of the Five Hundred.

316. The duration of their functions is five years: one of them is renewed every year and can be re-elected indefinitely without interval.

317. The commissioners of the treasury are charged to watch over the receipt of all the national monies;

To order the movements of funds and the payment of all the public expenses consented to by the legislative body;

To keep an open expense and receipt account with the receiver of the direct taxes of each department, with the different national customs-administrations, and with the paymasters who may be established in the departments;

To maintain with the said receivers and paymasters, with the customs-administrations, the correspondence necessary to secure exact and regular returns regarding the funds.

318. Under penalty of forfeiture they cannot make any payment except in virtue:

1st. Of a decree of the legislative body and to the amount of the funds decreed by it for each purpose;

2d. Of a decision of the Directory;

3d. Of the signature of the minister who orders the expenditure.

319. Under penalty of forfeiture also, they cannot approve any payment, unless the warrant, signed by the minister whom that kind of expenditure concerns, sets forth the date of the decision of the Executive Directory, as well as of the decrees of the legislative body which authorise the payment.

320. The receivers of the direct taxes in each department, the different national customs-administrations, and the paymasters in the departments remit to the national treasury their respective reports; the treasury verifies and allows them.

321. There are five commissioners of the national book-keeping, elected by the legislative body at the same dates and according to the same forms and conditions as the commissioners of the treasury.

322. The general report of the receipts and expenditures of the Republic, supported by the special reports and the vouchers, is presented by the commissioners of the treasury to the commissioners of the book-keeping, who verify and allow it.

323. The commissioners of the book-keeping give information to the legislative body of the abuses, defalcations, and all cases of responsibility which they discover in the course of their operations; they propose on their part the measures suitable to the interests of the Republic.

324. The result of the accounts allowed by the commissioners of the book-keeping is printed and made public.

325. The commissioners, both of the national treasury and of the book-keeping, cannot be suspended or removed except by the legislative body.

But during the adjournment of the legislative body the Executive Directory can provisionally suspend and replace the commissioners of the national treasury to the number of two at most, subject to the reference of it to one or the other council of the legislative body as soon as they have resumed their sittings.

Title XII. Foreign Relations.

326. War can be declared only by a decree of the legislative body upon the formal and urgent proposal of the Executive Directory.

327. The two councils unite in the usual forms upon the decree by which war is declared.

328. In case of imminent or actually begun hostilities, of threats or preparations for war against the French Republic, the Executive Directory is required to employ, for the defence of the state, the means placed at its disposal, subject to giving information thereof without delay to the legislative body. Also, it can indicate in this case the augmentations of force and the new legislative measures which the circumstances may require.

329. The directory alone can maintain political relations abroad, conduct negotiations, distribute the forces of the army and the navy as it deems suitable and determine the direction of them in case of war.

330. It is authorised to make preliminary stipulations such as armistices and neutralizations; it can also arrange secret conventions.

331. The Executive Directory negotiates, signs or causes to be signed all the treaties of peace, alliance, truce, neutrality, commerce and other conventions with foreign powers which it deems necessary for the welfare of the state.

These treaties and conventions are negotiated in the name of the French Republic by the diplomatic agents appointed by the Executive Directory and subject to its instructions.

332. In case a treaty includes secret articles, the provisions of these articles cannot be destructive of the open articles nor contain any alienation of the territory of the Republic.

333. Treaties are valid only after having been examined and ratified by the legislative body; nevertheless the secret conditions can receive their execution provisionally from the very moment when they are arranged by the Directory.

334. Neither of the legislative councils deliberates over war or peace except in committee of the whole.

335. Foreigners, whether established in France or not, inherit from their kinsmen, whether French or foreign; they contract for, acquire, and receive estates situated in France, and dispose of them, just as French citizens, by all the means authorised by law.

Title XIII. Revision of the Constitution.

336. If experience makes known inconveniences from any articles of the constitution, the Council of Ancients may propose the revision of them.

337. The proposal of the Council of Ancients is in this case submitted for ratification to the Council of the Five Hundred.

338. When, within a space of nine years, the proposal of the Council of Ancients, ratified by the Council of the Five Hundred, has been made at three dates removed from one another by at least three years, an assembly of revision is convoked.

339. This assembly is formed of two members per department, all elected in the same manner as the members of the legislative body and meeting the same conditions as those demanded for the Council of Ancients.

340. The Council of Ancients designates, for the meeting of the assembly of revision, a place at least twenty myriameters distant from that where the legislative body sits.

341. The assembly of revision has the right to change the place of its residence, observing the distance prescribed in the preceding article.

342. The assembly of revision does not exercise any legislative or governmental function; it confines itself to the revision of the articles alone which have been designated by the legislative body.

343. All the articles of the constitution, without exception, continue in force until the changes proposed by the assembly of revision have been accepted by the people.

344. The members of the assembly of revision deliberate in common.

345. The citizens who are members of the legislative body at the moment when an assembly of revision is convoked cannot be elected members of this assembly.

346. The assembly of revision despatches directly to the primary assemblies the project of reform which it has agreed upon. It is dissolved when this project has been despatched to them.

347. The duration of the assembly of revision cannot in any case exceed three months.

348. The members of the assembly of revision cannot be questioned, accused, nor tried at any time for what they have said or written in the exercise of their functions.

During the continuance of these functions they cannot be put on trial except by a decision of their fellow members of the assembly of revision.

349. The assembly of revision does not participate in any public ceremony; its members receive the same compensation as that of the members of the legislative body.

350. The assembly of revision has the right to exercise or to cause to be exercised the police power in the commune where it resides.

Title XIV. General Provisions.

351. There exists among the citizens no other superiority than that of the public functionaries and that only in relation to the exercise of their functions.

352. The law does not recognize religious vows nor any obligation contrary to the natural rights of man.

353. No one can be prevented from speaking, writing, printing, or publishing his ideas.

Writings cannot be made subject to any censorship before their publication.

No one can be held responsible for what he has written or published, except in the cases provided for by law.

354. No one can be prevented from engaging in the worship which he has chosen, while he conforms to the laws.

No one can be forced to contribute to the expenses of a religion. The Republic does not pay a stipend to any of them.

355. There is neither privilege, nor mastership, nor *jurande*, nor limitation upon the liberty of the press, of commerce, and the pursuit of industry and the arts of every kind.

Every prohibitive law of this sort, when circumstances render it necessary, is essentially provisional and has effect only for one year at most, unless it be formally renewed.

356. The law particularly watches over the professions which affect the public morals, the security and the health of the citizens; but admission to the practice of these professions cannot be made dependent upon any pecuniary payment.

357. The law shall provide for the reward of inventors or for the maintenance of an exclusive property in their discoveries or their productions.

358. The constitution guarantees the inviolability of all properties or just indemnification for those of which legally established public necessity may demand the sacrifice.

359. The house of each citizen is an inviolable asylum; during the night no one has the right to enter it except in the case of fire, flood, or call from the interior of the house.

During the day the orders of the constituted authorities can be put into execution there.

No domiciliary visit can take place except in virtue of a law and for the person or object expressly designated in the document which orders the visit.

360. Corporations or associations contrary to the public order cannot be formed.

361. No assembly of citizens can style itself a popular society.

362. No private society occupying itself with political questions can correspond with another, or affiliate with it, or hold public sittings composed of the members of the society and of associates distinguished from one another, or impose conditions of admission and eligibility, or arrogate to itself rights of exclusion, or cause its members to wear any external sign of their association.

363. Citizens cannot exercise their political rights except in the primary or communal assemblies.

364. All persons are free to address petitions to the public authorities; but they shall be individual; no association can present them collectively, except the constituted authorities, and only for matters appropriate to their province.

The petitioners must never forget the respect due to the constituted authorities.

365. Every armed mob is an attack upon the constitution; it shall be dispersed immediately by force.

366. Every unarmed mob shall likewise be dispersed, at first by way of verbal command, and if necessary by the display of armed force.

367. Several constituted authorities can never unite in order to deliberate together; any document emanating from such a meeting cannot be executed.

368. No one can wear distinctive badges which recall functions formerly exercised or services rendered.

369. The members of the legislative body and all the public functionaries wear in the discharge of their functions the costume or symbol of the authority with which they are invested: the law determines the form thereof.

370. No citizen can renounce in whole or in part compensation or salary which is assigned to him by law, on account of public functions.

371. There is uniformity of weights and measures in the Republic.

372. The French era commences September 22, 1792, the day of the foundation of the Republic.

373. The French nation declares that in any case it will not permit the return of the French who, having abandoned their fatherland since July 15, 1789, are not included in the exceptions contained in the laws against the *émigrés;* and it forbids the legislative body to create new exceptions upon this point.

The estates of the *émigrés* are irrevocably acquired for the profit of the Republic.

374. The French nation likewise proclaims, as a guarantee of the public faith, that after a legally consummated award of national lands, whatever the origin thereof, the lawful acquirer cannot be dispossessed of them; saving to third claimants, if there be need, indemnification by the national treasurer.

375. None of the powers instituted by the constitution has the right to change it in its entirety or in any of its parts, saving the reforms which can be effected by way of revision in accordance with the provisions of the title xiii.

376. The citizens shall recall without ceasing that it is upon the wisdom of the choices in the primary and electoral assemblies that the duration, preservation and prosperity of the Republic principally depend.

377. The French people entrust the safe keeping of the present constitution to the fidelity of the legislative body, the Executive Directory, the administrators and the judges; to the vigilance of the fathers of families; to the husbands and the mothers; to the affection of the young citizens; to the courage of all the French.

51. Law against Public Enemies.

April 16, 1796 (27 Germinal, Year IV), Duvergier, *Lois*, IX, 79-80.

The period of the Directory (1795-1799) was marked by numerous harsh measures against the classes denominated public enemies. This law shows some of the classes which were regarded as public enemies and the character of the penalties employed against them. See also No. 56.

REFERENCE. Aulard, *Révolution française,* 580-581.

1. All those are guilty of crime against the internal security of the Republic and against the personal security of the citizens, and shall be punished with death, in conformity with article 612 of the code of offences and penalties, who, by their discourses or by their printed writings, whether distributed or posted, seek to effect the dissolution of the national representation or that of the Executive Directory, or the murder of all or any of the members who compose them, or the re-establishment of the monarchy, or that of the constitution of 1793, or that of the constitution of 1791, or of any government other than that established by the constitution of the Year III, as accepted by the French people, or the invasion of public properties, or the pillage or partition of individual properties, under the name of an agrarian law, or in any other manner.

The penalty of death mentioned in the present article shall be commuted to that of deportation, if the jury declares that there were extenuating circumstances in the offence.

. . . .

5. Every gathering in which provocations of the nature of those mentioned in article 1 are made takes the character of a *seditious mob* . . .

. . . .

9. Every person who shall appear in public wearing a rallying symbol other than the national cockade shall be arrested and punished with one year of imprisonment, by way of correctional police. . . .

52. Treaties with the Pope.

In 1796-7 during the intervals between his Italian campaigns against the Austrians Napoleon Bonaparte turned his attention to the states of northern and central Italy. Some he revolutionized, others he did not. These documents show how the states which were not revolutionized were treated.

REFERENCES. Fyffe, *Modern Europe*, I, 135-136 (Popular ed., 91-92) ; Fournier, *Napoleon*, 84-85, 93-95 ; Rose, *Napoleon*, I, 93-95, 125-126 ; Sloane, *Napoleon*, I, 211, 260-262 ; Lanfrey, *Napoleon*, I, 101-104, 124-127, 155-157 ; Lavisse and Rambaud, *Histoire générale*, VIII, 436-439 ; Jaurès, *Histoire socialiste*, V, 348, 352-354.

A. Suspension of Hostilities. June 23, 1796 (5 Messidor Year IV). De Clercq, *Traités*, I, 276-277.

1. Wishing to give proof of the regard which the French government has for His Majesty, the King of Spain, the general-in-chief and the undersigned commissioners grant a suspension of hostilities to His Holiness, dating from to-day until five days after the end of the negotiations which are about to be entered upon at Paris for the conclusion of a definitive peace between the two states.

2. The Pope shall send as soon as possible a plenipotentiary to Paris in order to obtain from the Executive Directory the definitive peace, offering for it the necessary reparations for outrages and losses, and especially the murder of Basseville and the damages due to his family.

3. All persons imprisoned in the states of the Pope on account of their political opinions shall be immediately set at liberty and their property shall be restored.

4. The ports of the states of the Pope shall be closed to the vessels of the powers at war with France and open to French vessels.

5. The French army shall continue to remain in posssession of the legations of Bologna and Ferrara, and shall evacuate that of Faenza.

6. The citadel of Ancona, with its artillery, supplies and provisions, shall be put in the hands of the French army within six days.

7. The city of Ancona shall continue to remain under the civil government of the Pope.

8. The Pope shall deliver to the French Republic one hundred pictures, busts, vases or statues at the choice of the commissioners who shall be sent to Rome, among which articles shall be particularly included the bronze bust of Junius Brutus and that in marble of Marcus Brutus, the two placed upon the capitol, and five hundred manuscripts at the choice of the same commissioners.

9. The Pope shall pay to the French Republic 21 million livres French money, of which 15,500,000 livres shall be in specie or ingots of gold or silver and the remaining 5,500,000 in commodities, merchandise, horses, and cattle, according to the requisition which shall be made for them by the agents of the French Republic.

The 15,500,000 livres shall be paid in three periods, to wit: 5 million within 15 days, 5 within a month, and the 5,500,000 within three months. The 5,500,000 in commodities, merchandise, horses, and cattle, as fast as demands are made, shall be delivered in the ports of Genoa, Leghorn, and other places occupied by the army, which shall be designated.

The sum of 21 millions mentioned in the present article is independent of the contributions which are or shall be levied in the legations of Bologna, Ferrara, and Faenza.

10. The Pope shall be required to give passage to the troops of the French Republic, whenever it shall be demanded of him. The provisions which shall be furnished them shall be paid for by mutual agreement.

B. Treaty of Tolentino, February 19, 1797 (1 Ventôse, Year V). De Clercq. *Traités*. I, 313-316.

The General-in-Chief Bonaparte, commanding the army of Italy, and Citizen Cacault, agent of the French Republic in Italy . . . and . . . plenipotentiaries of His Holiness, have agreed upon the following articles·

1. There shall be peace, friendship, and good understanding between the French Republic and Pope Pius VI.

2. The Pope revokes every written or secret adhesion, consent, and accession given by him to the armed coalition against the French Republic and to every treaty of offensive or defensive alliance with any power or state whatsoever. He binds himself, as well for the existing war as for wars in the future, not to furnish to any of the powers in arms against the French Republic any assistance in men, vessels, arms, munitions of war, provisions and money by any title or under any denomination whatsoever.

.   .   .   .

4. The warships or privateers of powers in arms against the Republic shall not be permitted to enter, and still less to remain, during the present war, in the ports and roadsteads of the Ecclesiastical State.

5. The French Republic shall continue to enjoy, as before the war, all the rights and prerogatives which France had at Rome, and in everything shall be treated as are the most favored powers, and especially in respect to its ambassador, or minister, consuls, and vice-consuls.

6. The Pope renounces unconditionally all the rights to which he could lay claim upon the cities and territory of Avignon, the County of Venaissin and its dependencies, and transfers, cedes, and abandons the said rights to the French Republic.

7. The Pope also forever renounces, cedes, and transfers to the French Republic all his rights to the territories known under the names of the *Legations of Bologna, Ferrara* and *Romagna;* no attack shall be made upon the catholic religion in the said legations.

8. The city, citadel, and villages forming the territory of the city of Ancona shall remain with the French Republic until the continental peace.

.   .   .   .

12. . . . The Pope shall pay to the French Republic

in coin, diamonds, or other valuables, the sum of 15,000,000 Tours livres of France, of which 10,000,000 shall be in the course of the month of March and 5,000,000 in the course of the following April.

.   .   .   .

53. Law upon British Products.

October 31, 1796 (10 Brumaire, Year V). Duvergier, *Lois*, IX, 210-213.

This document has a double interest. It shows one of the methods employed by the directory in the war against England and it contains the germ of that policy which Napoleon subsequently developed into the continental system. The states dependent upon France were easily induced to adopt similar measures.

REFERENCES. Rose. *Napoleon*, I, 134-137 and *English Historical Review*, VIII, 704-725 ; Sloane, *Napoleon*, II, 95-96 ; Mahan, *Sea Power* and *French Revolution*, II, 248-251.

1. The importation of manufactured merchandise, the product of English manufacture or commerce, is prohibited, both by land and by sea, within the entire extent of the French Republic.

2. No vessel loaded in whole or in part with the said merchandise shall enter into the ports of the Republic under any pretext whatsoever, on penalty of being seized immediately; saving, nevertheless, the application of the law of 23 Brumaire, Year III, in the cases for which it has provided.

.   .   .   .

5. Whatever may have been their origin, the following articles imported from abroad are reputed to be the product of English manufactures:

1st. Every kind of cotton velvet and all fabrics and cloths of wool, cotton and hair or mixtures of these materials; every sort of piqués, dimities, nankinettes and muslinettes; woolen, cotton and hair thread and the carpets called English;

2d. Every kind of hosiery, cotton or wool, single or mixed;

3d. Buttons of every kind;

4th. Every sort of plate, all products in fine hardware, cutlery, toys, clock-making, and other products in iron, steel, copper, brass, cast-iron, sheet-iron, tin, or other metals, polished or not polished, pure or mixed;

5th. Hides tanned, curried or prepared, worked up or not worked up; carriages, set up or not set up, harness and all other articles of harness-making;

6th. Ribbons, hats, veils and shawls known under the denomination of English;

7th. Every sort of skin for gloves, small-clothes, and waistcoats, and these same articles manufactured;

8th. Every kind of glass ware and crystal other than the glasses serving for the making of spectacles and in watch-making;

9th. Refined sugars, in lump or in powder;

10th. Every kind of faience or pottery known under the denomination of earthen or stone ware of England.

6. Dating from the publications of the law, it is forbidden to all persons to sell or expose for sale any article the product of English manufactures or commerce, and to all printers to print any notice which may announce these sales.

.   .   .   .

54. Secret Convention with Genoa.

June 5 and 6, 1797 (17 and 18 Prairial, Year V). De Clercq, *Traités*, XV, 138-140.

The ancient and oligarchical Republic of Genoa was one of the Italian states revolutionized by Napoleon Bonaparte in 1796-7. The revolution was effected through this document. From it the character of the new government and its relationship to France can be seen. In both respects it is typical for all of the republics established at that time by the French in Italy.

REFERENCES. Rose, *Napoleon*, I, 134-137; Sloane, *Napoleon*, II, 7; Lanfrey, *Napoleon*, I, 204-208; Lavisse and Rambaud, *Histoire générale*, VIII, 775-776; Jaurès, *Histoire socialiste*, V, 350, 394-395.

The French Republic and the Republic of Genoa, wishing to consolidate the union and harmony which of all time has existed between them, and the government of Genoa believing that the welfare of the Genoese nation, in the present circumstances, requires that it should return to her the deposit of the sovereignty of the nation, with which it has been entrusted, the French Republic and the Republic of Genoa have agreed upon the following articles:

1. The government of the Republic of Genoa recognizes that the sovereignty resides in the body of all the citizens of the Genoese territory.

2. The legislative power shall be confided to two representative councils, one of 300, the other of 150 members. The
executive power shall be the attribute of a senate of twelve
members presided over by a Doge. The Doge and the senators shall be selected by the two councils.

3. Each commune shall have a municipality, each district
an administration.

4. The methods of election of all the authorities, the circumscription of the districts, the portion of authority entrusted
to each body, the organization of the judicial power and of
the military forces, shall be determined by a legislative commission, which shall be charged to draw up the constitution
and all the organic laws of the government, having care in
this to do nothing which may be contrary to the catholic
religion, to guarantee the consolidated debts, to preserve the
free port of the city of Genoa, the bank of St. George, and to
take measures that there may be provision, as far as means
will permit it, for the maintenance of the poor nobles now
living.

This commission shall be obliged to complete its work
within a month, counting from the day of its formation.

5. The people finding themselves replaced in possession
of their rights, every kind of privilege or particular organization which breaks up the unity of the state finds itself necessarily dissolved.

6. The provisional government shall be confided to a
commission of government composed of 22 members, presided
over by the present Doge, which shall be installed on the
14th of the present month of June, 26 Prairial, Year V of
the French Republic.

7. The citizens who shall be called upon to compose the
provisional government of the Republic of Genoa cannot refuse these functions without being considered as indifferent to
the safety of the fatherland and condemned to a fine of two
thousand crowns.

8. As soon as the provisional government shall be constituted, it shall determine the necessary rules for the manner
of its deliberations. It shall select, within the week of its
installation, the legislative commission charged to draw up
the constitution.

9. The provisional government shall provide for the just indemnities due to the French who were plundered on the days of 3 and 4 Prairial (May 22 and 23.)

10. The French Republic, wishing to give a proof of the interest which it takes in the welfare of the people of Genoa, and desiring to see them united and exempt from factions, grants an amnesty to all the Genoese of whom it had occasion to make complaint, whether by reason of 3 and 4 Prairial or by occasion of the various events which occurred within the imperial fiefs.

The provisional government shall show the most lively solicitude to extinguish all the factions, to unite all the citizens, and to imbue them with the need of uniting about the public liberty, granting for this purpose a general amnesty.

11. The French Republic shall grant to the Republic of Genoa protection and, likewise, the aid of its armies, in order to facilitate, if it be necessary, the execution of the said articles, and to maintain the integrity of the territory of the Republic of Genoa.

.   .   _   .   .   .   .   .

55. Treaty of Campo Formio.

October 17, 1797 (26 Vendémiaire, Year VI). De Clercq, *Traités*, I, 335-343.

This treaty terminated the war against Austria begun in 1792. It left France at war only with England. The new boundaries of France, the changes in Italy, and the arrangements for the reorganization of Germany are the features of the treaty of most importance.

REFERENCES. Fyffe, *Modern Europe*, I, 146-151 (Popular edition, 98-101) ; Fournier, *Napoleon*, 99-100, 108-110 ; Rose, *Napoleon*, I, 128-130, 155-157 ; Sloane, *Napoleon*, II, 12-16 ; Lanfrey, *Napoleon*, I, Ch. IX ; Lavisse and Rambaud, *Histoire générale*, VIII, 439-440 ; Jaurès, *Histoire socialiste*, V, 391-399.

MAPS. Droysen, *Historischer Hand-Atlas*, 48 ; Schrader, *Atlas de geographie historique*, 48 ; Vidal-Lablache, *Atlas général*, 40.

His Majesty the Emperor of the Romans, King of Hungary and of Bohemia, and the French Republic, wishing to consolidate the peace of which the foundations were laid in the preliminaries signed at the château of Ekenwald near Léoben in Styria, April 18, 1797 (29 Germinal, Year V, of the

French Republic, one and indivisible), have appointed for their plenipotentiaries, to wit:

. . . .

1. There shall be for the future and forever a firm and inviolable peace between His Majesty the Emperor of the Romans, King of Hungary and of Bohemia, his heirs and successors, and the French Republic.

. . . .

3. His Majesty the Emperor, King of Hungary and of Bohemia, renounces for himself and his successors, in favor of the French Republic, all his rights and titles to the former Belgic Provinces, known under the name of the *Austrian Low Countries*. The French Republic shall possess these countries forever, in complete sovereignty and proprietorship, and with all the territorial advantages which result therefrom.

. . . .

5. His Majesty the Emperor, King of Hungary and of Bohemia, consents that the French Republic possess in complete sovereignty the former Venetian islands of the Levant, to wit: Corfu, Zante, Cephalonia, Santa Maura, Cerigo, and other islands dependent upon them, as well as Butrinto, Arta, Vonizza, and in general all the former Venetian establishments in Albania, which are situated below the Gulf of Drin.

6. The French Republic consents that His Majesty the Emperor and King should possess in complete sovereignty and proprietorship the countries hereinafter designated, to wit: Istria, Dalmatia, the former Venetian islands of the Adriatic, the mouths of the Cattaro, the city of Venice, the lagunes and countries included between the hereditary states of His Majesty the Emperor and King, the Adriatic sea, and a line which setting out from Tyrol shall follow the stream beyond Gardola, and shall cross the Lake of Garda, to Cise; from there a military line to San Giocomo, offering an equal advantage to the two parties, which shall be marked out by engineering officers appointed by both parties before the exchange of the ratifications of the present treaty. The line of limitation shall then pass the Adige at San Giocomo, shall follow the left bank of that river to the mouth of the Blanc canal, including the part of Porto Lignano which is upon the right bank of the Adige, with the district to a radius of three thousand toises. The line shall continue by the left

bank of the Blanc canal, the left bank of the Tartaro, the left bank of the canal called the Polisella to its juncture with the Po, and the left bank of the great Po to the sea.

7. His Majesty the Emperor, King of Hungary and of Bohemia, renounces forever, for himself, his successors and assigns, in favor of the Cisalpine Republic, all rights and titles springing from these rights, which his said Majesty could lay claim to over the countries which he possessed before the war, and which now make part of the Cisalpine Republic, which shall possess them in complete sovereignty and proprietorship, with all the territorial advantages which result therefrom.

8. His Majesty the Emperor, King of Hungary and of Bohemia, recognizes the Cisalpine Republic as an independent power.   .   .   .   .

18. His Majesty the Emperor, King of Hungary and of Bohemia, binds himself to cede to the Duke of Modena, as indemnity for the countries which that prince and his heirs had in Italy, the Breisgau, which he shall possess upon the same conditions as those in virtue of which he possessed Modena.

.   .   .   .

20. There shall be held at Rastadt a congress composed exclusively of the plenipotentiaries of the Germanic Empire and of those of the French Republic for the pacification between these two powers. This shall be opened one month after the signature of the present treaty, or sooner if it is possible.

.   .   .   .

Secret Articles.

1. His Majesty the Emperor, King of Hungary and of Bohemia, consents that the limits of the French Republic shall extend to the line designated below and pledges himself to use his good offices in order that, in establishing peace with the German Empire, the French Republic may obtain this same boundary, to wit:

The left bank of the Rhine from the Swiss frontier below Basle to the confluence of the Nette above Andernach, including the *tête de Pont* at Mannheim on the right bank of the Rhine and the town and fortress of Mainz, both banks of the Nette, from its mouth to its source near Bruch, from here a line passing through Senscherode and Borlei to Kerpen and from this town to Udelhofen, Blankenheim, Marmagen, Jactenigt, Cale and Gmünd, including the suburbs and surrounding districts of these places, then the two banks of the Olff to its junction with the Roer, the two banks of the Roer, including Heimbach, Niedeggen, Düren, and Jülich, with their suburbs and surrounding districts as well as the villages on the river and their surrounding districts as far as Limnich; from here a line passing Roffems and Thalens, Dalen, Hilas Papdermod, Laterforst, Radenberg, Haversloo (if this lies upon the line), Anderheide, Kalderkirchen, Wambach, Herringen and Grobray with the town of Venloo and its surrounding territory. If, in spite of the good offices of His Majesty the Emperor, King of Hungary and of Bohemia, the German Empire should not consent to the acquisition by the French Republic of the frontier above indicated, His Majesty the Emperor and King formerly engages not to furnish more than his contingent to the army of the Empire, which may not be employed in the fortresses without thereby interfering with the peace and amity just established between his said Majesty and the French Republic.

2. His Majesty the Emperor, King of Hungary and of Bohemia, will further use his good offices at the time of the pacification with the German Empire:

1st. In order that the navigation of the Rhine shall be free to the French Republic, and to the states of the Empire situated on the right bank of this river, from Hüningen to the point where it reaches the Batavian Republic;

2d. To arrange that the one in possession of that part of Germany opposite the mouth of the Moselle shall never upon any pretext whatsoever hinder the free navigation and exit of boats or other craft from the mouth of the river;

3d. That the French Republic shall enjoy the free navigation of the Meuse, and that all tolls and other dues which may be established from Venloo to the point where the river enters Batavian territory, shall be suppressed.

3. His Majesty the Emperor and King, renounces, on his

own part and for his successors, the sovereignty over, and possession of, the county of Falkenstein and its dependencies, in favor of the French Republic.

4. The territories which His Majesty the Emperor, King of Hungary and of Bohemia, is to possess in virtue of article VI of the open, definitive treaty signed this day, shall serve as an indemnity for those territories which he cedes by articles III and VII of the open treaty and by the preceding article. This cession shall not, however, have force until the troops of His Majesty the Emperor and King shall occupy the territory acquired by the said article.

5. The French Republic will employ its good offices in order that His Majesty the Emperor may acquire in Germany the archbishopric of Salzburg, and that portion of the circle of Bavaria situated between the archbishopric of Salzburg, the rivers Inn and Salzach and Tyrol, including the city of Wasserburg on the right bank of the Inn, with the surrounding territory within a radius of 3,000 toises.

6. His Majesty the Emperor and King agrees to cede to the French Republic, when peace shall be concluded with the Empire, the sovereignty and possession of the Frickthal, as well as all the possessions of the House of Austria on the left bank of the Rhine between Zurzach and Basle, provided that in the above-mentioned peace His Majesty shall obtain a proportionate compensation in Germany which shall be satisfactory.

The French Republic shall unite the said districts to the Helvetian Republic, according to an arrangement to be made between the said countries, without prejudice, however, to His Majesty the Emperor and King, or to the Empire.

7. It is understood between the two contracting powers that if, in arranging the pending peace with the German Empire, the French Republic shall make an acquisition in Germany, His Majesty the Emperor, King of Hungary and of Bohemia, shall obtain an equivalent there, and conversely if His Royal and Imperial Majesty make an acquisition of this kind, the French Republic shall similarly receive an equivalent.

8. A territorial indemnity shall be given to the Prince of Nassau-Dietz, formerly Stadtholder of Holland, but this ter-

ritorial indemnity shall not be chosen in the neighborhood of
the Austrian possessions nor of the Batavian Republic.

9. The French Republic will find no trouble in restoring
to the King of Prussia his possessions on the left bank of
the Rhine.   Hence there will be no question of any new acquisitions on the part of the King of Prussia.   To this the
contracting parties mutually pledge themselves.

10. If the King of Prussia consents to cede to the French
Republic and to the Batavian Republic certain small portions
of his possessions upon the left bank of the Meuse, as well as
the enclave of Zevenaar and other possessions toward the
Yssel, His Majesty the Emperor, King of Hungary and of
Bohemia, will employ his good offices to render the said cessions practicable, and to cause them to be recognized by the
German Empire.   The failure to carry out the present article
shall not affect the preceding one.

11. His Majesty the Emperor will not oppose the disposition which the French Republic has made in favor of the
Ligurian Republic of the imperial fiefs.   His Majesty the
Emperor will unite his efforts with those of the French Republic to induce the German Empire to renounce such rights
of suzerainty as it may have in Italy, especially over the
districts which form a part of the Cisalpine and Ligurian
republics, as well as over the imperial fiefs, such as Lusig-
nana and all those lying between Tuscany and the possessions
of Parma, the Ligurian and Luccan republics, and the former
territory of Modena, the which fiefs shall form a part of the
Cisalpine Republic.

12. His Majesty the Emperor, King of Hungary and of
Bohemia, and the French Republic, will unite their efforts in
order that, in negotiating peace with the German Empire, the
different princes and states of the Empire which shall suffer
losses of territory and of rights in consequence of the stipulations of the present treaty of peace, or later, in consequence
of the treaty which shall be concluded with the German
Empire, shall obtain appropriate indemnities in Germany;
which indemnities shall be determined in common accord with
the French Republic.   This applies especially to the electors
of Mainz, Trier and Cologne, the Elector Palatine of Bavaria,
the Duke of Würtemburg and Teck, the Margrave of Baden,

the Duke of Zweibrücken, the Landgraves of Hesse-Cassel and of Hesse-Darmstadt, the Princes of Nassau-Saarbrücken, of Salm-Kryburg, Löwenstein-Wertheim and of Wiedrunkel and the Count of Leyen.

13. The troops of His Majesty the Emperor shall evacuate within twenty days after the exchange of the ratifications of the present treaty, the city and fortress of Mainz, Ehrenbreitstein, Phillippsburg, Mannheim, Königsstein, Ulm and Ingolstadt, as well as all the territory belonging to the Germanic Empire as far as his hereditary possessions.

. . . .

17. The present secret articles shall have the same force as if they were inserted word for word in the open treaty of peace signed to-day. These shall be ratified at the same time by the contracting parties and the acts of ratification shall be exchanged in due form at Rastadt.

56. Law of Hostages.

July 12, 1799 (24 Messidor, Year VII). Duvergier. *Lois*, XI, 278-281.

This document is the complement of No. 51. That shows what measures might be employed against certain classes of persons denominated public enemies; this shows the measures which might be employed against regions where disturbances had occurred.

REFERENCES. *Cambridge Modern History*, VIII, 670-671; Lavisse and Rambaud, *Histoire générale*, VIII, 397-398; Jaurès, *Histoire socialiste*, V, 535-536.

The Council of the Five Hundred, considering that it is time to take effective measures to arrest the progress of the system of assassination and brigandage organized at different points of the Republic against public functionaries, acquirers or possessors of national lands, and all citizens attached to the constitution of the Year III,

Approves the act of urgency and the following resolution:

1. When a department, canton or commune is notoriously in a state of civil disturbance, the Executive Directory proposes to the legislative body to declare it included in the following provisions.

2. The kinsmen of *émigrés*, their relatives by marriage, and the former nobles included in the laws of 3 Brumaire,

Year IV, and 9 Frimaire, Year VI, the grandfathers, grandmothers, fathers and mothers of the persons who, without being ex-nobles or kinsmen of *émigrés,* are nevertheless notoriously known as making up part of the gatherings or bands of assassins, are personally and civilly responsible for assassinations and acts of brigandage committed in the interior out of hatred of the Republic, in the departments, cantons and communes declared in a state of disturbance.

3. Immediately after the publication of the law rendered in execution of article 1, the central administrations shall take hostages within the classes above designated, in the communes, cantons and departments declared in a state of disturbance:

.   .   .   .

9. If an assassination is committed upon a citizen who actually is or has been since the revolution a public functionary, or defender of the fatherland, or acquirer or possessor of the national domains, the Executive Directory, after having consulted the central administrations, is charged to cause to be deported outside of the territory of the Republic within two *décades* of the assassination, four of the persons designated in article 2 for each person assassinated, taking in the first place from among the noble kinsmen of *émigrés,* secondly from among the former nobles, and successively from among the kinsmen of persons taking part in the gatherings.

.   .   .   .

57. The Brumaire Decree.

November 10, 1799 (19 Brumaire, Year VIII) . Duvergier, *Lois,* XII, 1-2.

By the *coup d'état* of Brumaire the government of the Directory was overthrown. This decree was passed by remnants of the councils of the Five Hundred and of the Ancients after the dispersion of those bodies. Thereby some semblance of legality was imparted to the *coup d'état.*

REFERENCES. Fyffe, *Modern Europe,* I, 197-207 (Popular ed., 133-139) ; *Cambridge Modern History,* VIII, Ch. 22 ; Fournier, *Napoleon.* 166-182 : Rose, *Napoleon* I, Ch. x ; Sloane, *Napoleon,* II, Chs. X-XI ; Lanfrey. *Napoleon,* I, Ch. XII ; Lavisse and Rambaud. *Histoire générale,* VIII, 403-411 ; Aulard, *Révolution française,* Part III, Ch. v ; Jaurès, *Histoire socialiste,* V, Ch. 22.

The Council of the Five Hundred, considering the situation of the Republic, approves the act of urgency and the following resolution:

1. The Directory is no more, and the following named persons, owing to the excesses and the crimes in which they have constantly engaged, and especially as regards the majority of them in the session of this morning, are no longer members of the national representation: . . . [Here follow the names of sixty-one persons.]

2. The legislative body creates provisionally a consular executive commission, consisting of Citizens Siéyès, Roger-Ducos, and General Bonaparte, who shall bear the name of Consuls of the French Republic.

3. This commission is invested with the plentitude of directorial power and is particularly charged to organize order in all parts of the administration, to re-establish internal tranquility, and to procure honorable and enduring peace.

4. It is authorized to send out delegates having powers which are fixed and are within the limits of its own [powers].

5. The legislative body adjourns to the following 1 Ventôse [Feb. 20, 1800]; it shall reassemble of full right upon that date in its palace at Paris.

6. During the adjournment of the legislative body the adjourned members preserve their indemnity and their constitutional guarantee.

7. Without loss of their character as representatives of the people, they can be employed as ministers, diplomatic agents, delegates of the consular executive commission, and in all other civil functions. They are even invited in the name of the public welfare to accept these [employments].

8. Before its separation and during the sitting, each council shall appoint from its own body a commission consisting of twenty-five members.

9. The commissions appointed by the two councils with the formal and requisite proposal of the consular executive commission, shall decide upon all urgent matters of police, legislation, and finance.

10. The commission of the Five Hundred shall exercise the initiative; the commission of the Ancients, the approval.

11. The two commissions are further charged, in the same order of labor and co-operation, to prepare the changes to be brought about in the organic arrangements of the constitution of which experience has made known the faults and inconveniences.

12. These changes shall have for their object only to consolidate, guarantee, and consecrate inviolably the sovereignty of the French people, the republic one and indivisible, the representative system, the division of powers, liberty, equality, security and property.

13. The consular executive commission can present its views to them in this respect.

14. Finally, the two commissons are charged to prepare a civil code.

15. They shall sit at Paris in the place of the legislative body and they can convoke it in extraordinary session for the ratification of peace or in a great public danger.

16. The present [document] shall be printed, sent by extraordinary couriers into the departments, and solemnly published and posted in all the communes of the Republic.

58. Constitution of the Year VIII.

December 13, 1799. Duvergier, *Lois,* XII, 20-30.

This constitution although nominally framed by the two legislative commissions appointed by No. 57 was actually imposed upon them by Napoleon Bonaparte. It was submitted to the people and accepted by over three million votes against about fifteen hundred.

REFERENCES. Fournier, *Napoleon,* 183-187 ; Dickinson, *Revolution and Reaction in Modern France,* 36-41 ; Rose, *Napoleon,* I, 209-214 ; Sloane, *Napoleon,* II, 84-86 ; Lanfrey, *Napoleon,* I, Ch. XIII ; *Cambridge Modern History,* IX, 3-7 ; Lavisse and Rambaud, *Histoire générale,* IX, 5-12 ; Aulard, *Révolution française,* 704-711 ; Jaurès, *Histoire socialiste,* VI, 28-43.

Constitution of the French Republic.

Title I. Of the Exercise of the Rights of Citizenship.

1. The French Republic is one and indivisible.

Its European territory is divided into departments and communal districts.

2. Every man born and residing in France fully twenty-one years of age, who has caused his name to be inscribed upon the civic register of his communal district and has since lived for one year upon the soil of the Republic, is a French citizen.

3. A foreigner becomes a French citizen when, after having reached the full age of twenty-one years and having de-

clared his intention to settle in France, he has resided there for ten consecutive years.

4. The title to French citizenship is lost:

By naturalization in a foreign country;

By the acceptance of appointments or pensions tendered by a foreign government;

By affiliation with any foreign corporation which may imply distinctions of birth;

By condemnation to afflictive or infamous punishments.

5. The exercise of the rights of French citizenship is suspended by the state of bankruptcy or of direct inheritance, with gratuitous title, to the succession, in whole or in part, of a bankrupt;

By the condition of domestic service for wages, either for a person or a household;

By the condition of judicial interdiction, of accusation, or of contempt of court.

6. In order to exercise the rights of citizenship in a communal district, it is necessary to have acquired domicile there by one year of residence and not to have lost it by one year of absence.

7. The citizens of each communal district designate by their votes those among them whom they believe the most fit to conduct public affairs. Thus the result is a list of the trustworthy, containing a number of names equal to one-tenth of the number of citizens having the right to co-operate there. It is from this first communal list that the public functionaries of the district must be taken.

8. The citizens included in the communal lists of a department designate likewise a tenth of themselves. Thus there results a second list, known as the departmental list, from which the public functionaries of the department must be taken.

9. The citizens comprised in the departmental list designate in like manner a tenth of themselves: thus there results a third list which comprises the citizens of that department eligible to the national public functions.

10. The citizens who have the right to co-operate in the formation of one of the lists mentioned in the three preceding articles, are called upon every three years to provide for re-

placing those of the enrolled who have died or are absent for any other cause than the exercise of a public function.

11. They can, at the same time, remove from the lists the enrolled whom they judge unfit to remain there, and replace them by other citizens in whom they have greater confidence.

12. No one is removed from a list except by the votes of the majority of the citizens who have the right to co-operate in its formation.

13. No one is removed from a list of eligibles by the mere fact that he is not kept upon another list of higher or superior degree.

14. Inscription upon a list of eligibles is necessary only with reference to those of the public officers for which that condition is expressly required by the constitution or the law. The list of eligibles shall be formed for the first time during the course of the Year IX.

Citizens who shall be selected for the first formation of the constituted authorities, shall form a necessary part of the first lists of eligibles.

Title II. Of the Conservative Senate.

15. The Conservative Senate is composed of eighty members, irremovable and for life, of at least forty years of age.

For the formation of the Senate, there shall at first be chosen sixty members: that number shall be increased to sixty-two in the course of the Year VIII, to sixty-four in the Year IX, and it shall thus be gradually increased to eighty, by the addition of two members in each of the first ten years.

16. Appointment to the place of senator is made by the Senate, which chooses among three candidates presented, the first by the Legislative Body, the second by the Tribunate, the third by the First Consul.

It chooses between only two candidates if one of them is proposed by two of the three presenting authorities: it is required to admit that one who may be proposed at the same time by the three authorities.

17. The First Consul, upon leaving his place, either by expiration of his office or by resignation, becomes a senator *ipso facto* and necessarily.

The other two consuls, during the month following the

expiration of their duties, can take seats in the Senate, but they are not required to make use of this right.

They do not have it if they leave their consular duties by resignation.

18. A senator is forever ineligible to any other public office.

19. All the lists made in the departments, in virtue of article 9, are despatched to the Senate: they constitute the national list.

20. It chooses from this list the legislators, the tribunes, the consuls, the judges of cassation, and the commissioners of accounts.

21. It sustains or annuls all the acts which are referred to it as unconstitutional by the Tribunate or the government: the lists of eligibles are included among these acts.

22. Fixed revenues from the national domains are set apart for the expenses of the Senate. The annual stipend of each of its members is taken from these revenues, and is equal to a twentieth of that of the First Consul.

23. The sittings of the Senate are not public.

24. Citizens Siéyès and Roger-Ducos, retiring consuls, are appointed members of the Conservative Senate: they shall join to themselves the second and third consuls appointed by the present constitution. These four citizens appoint the majority of the Senate, which then completes itself and proceeds to the elections that are entrusted to it.

Title III. Of the Legislative Power.

25. New laws shall be promulgated only when the project for them shall have been proposed by the government, communicated to the Tribunate, and decreed by the Legislative Body.

26. The projects that the government proposes are drawn up in articles. In any stage of the discussion of these proposals, the government can withdraw them; it can reproduce them in modified form.

27. The Tribunate is composed of one hundred members, at least twenty-five years of age; they are renewed by a fifth each year and are indefinitely re-eligible as long as they remain upon the national list.

28. The Tribunate discusses the projects for laws: it votes for their adoption or their rejection.

It sends three orators taken from its own body, by whom the grounds for the view that it has taken upon each of these proposals are set forth and defended before the Legislative Body.

It refers to the Senate, on account of unconstitutionality only, the lists of eligibles, the acts of the Legislative Body and those of the government.

29. It expresses its opinion upon the laws made and to be made, the abuses to be corrected, and the improvements to be undertaken in all parts of the public administration, but never upon civil or criminal matters pending before the tribunals.

The opinions that it expresses by virtue of the present article have no necessary consequence and do not compel any constituted authority to a deliberation.

30. When the Tribunate adjourns, it can appoint a commission of from ten to fifteen of its members, charged to convoke it if it deems expedient.

31. The Legislative Body is composed of three hundred members of at least thirty years of age; they are renewed each year by a fifth.

It must always contain at least one member from each department of the Republic.

32. A member retiring from the Legislative Body cannot re-enter it until after an interval of one year; but he can be immediately elected to any other public office, including that of tribune, if he is otherwise eligible to it.

33. The session of the Legislative Body commences each year upon 1 Frimaire, and continues only four months; it can be convoked in extraordinary session during the other eight months by the government.

34. The Legislative Body makes a law by deciding through secret ballot, and without any discussion on the part of its members, upon the projects of law discussed before it by the orators of the Tribunate and the government.

35. The sittings of the Tribunate and those of the Legislative Body are public; the number of spectators at either of them cannot exceed two hundred.

36. The annual stipend of a tribune is fifteen thousand francs; that of a legislator, ten thousand francs.

37. Every decree of the Legislative Body is promulgated by the First Consul the tenth day after its passage unless within that period it has been referred to the senate upon the ground of unconstitutionality. This recourse cannot be taken against promulgated laws.

38. The first renewal of the Legislative Body and of the Tribunate shall take place only in the course of the Year X.

Title IV. Of the Government.

39. The government is confided to three Consuls appointed for ten years and indefinitely re-eligible.

Each of them is elected individually with the distinguishing title of First, Second or Third Consul.

The constitution appoints as First Consul, Citizen Bonaparte, former provisional consul; as Second Consul, Citizen Cambacérès, former minister of justice; and as Third Consul, Citizen Lebrun, former member of the commission of the Council of Ancients.

For this time the Third Consul is appointed only for five years.

40. The First Consul has special duties and prerogatives in which he is temporarily replaced by one of his colleagues, when there is need.

41. The First Consul promulgates the laws; he appoints and dismisses at will the members of the Council of State, the ministers, the ambassadors and other foreign agents of high rank, the officers of the army and navy, the members of the local administrations, and the commissioners of the government before the tribunals. He appoints all criminal and civil judges, other than the justices of the peace and the judges of cassation, without power to remove them.

42. In the other acts of the government, the Second and Third Consuls have a consultative voice: they sign the register of these acts in order to attest their presence; and if they wish, they there record their opinions; after that the decision of the First Consul suffices.

43. The stipend of First Consul shall be five hundred thousand francs in the Year VIII. The stipend of each of the

other two consuls is equal to three-tenths of that of the First Consul.

44. The government proposes the laws and makes the regulations necessary to secure their execution.

45. The government controls the receipts and expenses of the state in conformity with the annual law which fixes the amount of both of them; it superintends the coinage of money, of which the law alone orders the emission and fixes the denomination, weight, and stamp.

46. If the government is informed that some conspiracy is laid against the state, it can issue decrees of apprehension and arrest against the persons who are supposed to be the authors or accomplices of it; but if, within a period of ten days after their arrest, they are not set at liberty or put upon trial, the minister who signed the decree has committed the crime of arbitrary imprisonment.

47. The government provides for the internal security and the external defence of the state; it distributes the land and sea forces and controls their direction.

48. The active national guard is subject to the rules of the public administration: the reserve national guard is subject only to the law.

49. The government has charge of the foreign political relations, conducts negotiations, makes preliminary stipulations, signs and causes to be signed and concluded all treaties of peace and alliance, truce, neutrality, commerce, and other conventions.

50. Declarations of war and treaties of peace, alliance, and commerce are proposed, discussed, decreed, and promulgated as are the laws.

But the discussions and deliberations upon these matters, in the Tribunate as well as in the Legislative Body, take place in secret committee when the government demands it.

51. The secret articles of a treaty cannot be destructive of the open articles.

52. Under the direction of the consuls, a council of state is charged with drawing up projects of law and regulations of public administration, and with the settlement of difficulties which arise in administrative matters.

53. The orators charged to take the word, in the name of the government, before the Legislative Body, are always

taken from among the members of the Council of State.

These orators are never sent to the number of more than three for the defence of a single project of law.

54. The ministers procure the execution of the laws and regulations of public administration.

55. No edict of the government can have effect unless it is signed by a minister.

56. One of the ministers is especially charged with the administration of the public treasury: he provides for the security of the receipts, and orders the transfer of funds and the payments authorised by law. He cannot make any payment except in virtue of: 1st, a law, and to the amount of the funds which it has fixed for that kind of expenses; 2d, an order of the government; 3d, a warrant signed by a minister.

57. The detailed accounts of the expenses of each minister, signed and certified by him, are made public.

58. The government can select or retain as councillors of state and as ministers, only the citizens whose names are enrolled upon the national list.

59. The local administrations established either for each communal district or for more extended portions of territory are subordinate to the ministers. No one can become or remain a member of these administrations unless he is placed or kept upon one of the lists mentioned in articles 7 and 8.

Title V. Of the Tribunals.

60. Each communal district has one or more justices of the peace, elected directly by the citizens for three years.

Their principal duty consists in conciliating the parties, whom they urge, in case of non-conciliation, to get judgment by arbitrators.

61. In civil matters there are tribunals of first instance and tribunals of appeal. The law determines the organization of each of them, their competency, and the territory forming the jurisdiction of each.

62. In criminal matters involving afflictive or ignominious punishments, a first jury accepts or rejects the accusation: if it is accepted, a second jury passes upon the facts, and the judges forming a criminal tribunal impose the penalty. Their judgment is without appeal.

63. The duty of public prosecution before a criminal tri-

bunal is performed by the commissioner of the government.

64. Crimes that do not involve afflictive or ignominious punishments are tried by tribunals of correctional police, subject to appeal to the criminal tribunals.

65. There is for the whole Republic a tribunal of cassation, which passes upon the appeals in cassation against the judgments rendered in the last resort by the tribunals, upon applications for the removal from one tribunal to another on account of legitimate suspicion or public security, and upon complaints of prejudice against a whole tribunal.

66. The tribunal of cassation does not take cognizance of the facts of actions; but it quashes the judgments rendered upon proceedings in which the forms have been violated, or which contain some express contravention of the law; and it sends back the facts of the action of the tribunal which ought to have jurisdiction thereon.

67. The judges composing the tribunals of first instance and the commissioners of the government assigned to these tribunals, are taken from the communal list or the departmental list.

The judges constituting the tribunals of appeal and the commissioners placed with them are taken from the departmental list.

The judges composing the tribunal of cassation and the commissioners assigned to that tribunal, are taken from the national list.

68. The judges, other than the justices of the peace, keep their offices for life unless they should be condemned to forfeiture or should not be kept upon the lists of eligibles.

Title VI. Of the Responsibility of the Public Functionaries.

69. The positions of members of the Senate, Legislative Body, Tribunate, and those of the consuls and the councillors of state do not give occasion for any responsibility.

70. Personal crimes involving afflictive or ignominious punishments, committed by a member of the Senate, Tribunate, Legislative Body, or Council of State, are prosecuted before the ordinary tribunals only after a decision of the body to which the accused belongs has authorised that prosecution.

71. Ministers accused of private crimes involving afflictive or ignominious punishment are considered as members of the Council of State.

72. The ministers are responsible: 1st, for every act of the government signed by them and declared unconstitutional by the Senate; 2d, for the non-execution of the laws and regulations of the public administration; 3d, for the special orders which they have given, if these orders are contrary to the constitution, the laws, or the regulations.

73. In the case of the preceding article, the Tribunate accuses the minister by an act upon which the Legislative Body deliberates in the usual forms, after having heard or summoned the accused. The minister placed on trial by a decree of the Legislative Body is tried by a high court, without appeal and without recourse in cassation.

The high court is composed of judges and jurors. The judges are chosen by the tribunal of cassation and from its own body; the jurors are taken from the national list: the whole following the forms which the law determines.

74. Civil and criminal judges are prosecuted for crimes connected with their duties before the tribunals to which that of cassation sends them, after having annulled their acts.

75. The agents of the government, other than the ministers, cannot be prosecuted for acts relating to their duties except by virtue of a decision of the Council of State; in that case the prosecution takes place before the ordinary tribunals.

Title VII. General Provisions.

76. The house of every person dwelling upon French soil is an inviolable asylum.

During the night no one has the right to enter it except in case of fire, inundation, or a call coming from the interior of the house.

During the day it can be entered for a special purpose, determined either by law or by an order issued by a public authority.

77. In order that the instrument which orders the arrest of a person may be executed, it is necessary: 1st, that it set forth explicitly the ground for the arrest and the law in execution of which it is ordered; 2d, that it be issued by an official to whom the law has explicitly given that power; 3d,

that it be made known to the person arrested and that he be provided with a copy of it.

78. A warden or jailer cannot receive or detain any person except after having copied upon his register the document which orders the arrest: this document must be a warrant given in the forms prescribed by the preceding article, or an order of arrest, or a decree of accusation, or a judgment.

79. Every warden or jailer is required, without any order being able to dispense therewith, to present the arrested person to the civil officer having in charge the police of the prison, whenever he shall be required to do so by that officer.

80. The production of the arrested person cannot be refused to his kinsmen and friends bearing the order of the civil officer, who shall always be required to grant it, unless the warden or jailer presents an order of the judge to keep the person in secret.

81. All those who, not having received from the law the power to make arrests, shall cause, sign or execute the arrest of any person; all those who, even in cases of arrests authorised by law, shall receive or retain the arrested person in a place of confinement not publicly and legally designated as such; and all the wardens or jailers who shall contravene the provisions of the three preceding articles, shall be guilty of the crime of arbitrary imprisonment.

82. All severities employed in arrests, imprisonments or executions, other than those authorised by the laws, are crimes.

83. Any person has the right to present individual petitions to any constituted authority, and especially to the Tribunate.

84. The public force is essentially obedient; no armed body can deliberate.

85. Military offences are subject to special tribunals and to special forms of trial.

86. The French nation declares that pensions shall be granted to all soldiers wounded in the defence of the fatherland, as well as to the widows and children of soldiers dying upon the battlefield or from the effects of their wounds.

87. National rewards shall be conferred upon the warriors who shall have rendered distinguished services in fighting for the Republic.

88. A national institute is charged with the collection of the discoveries and the improvement of the sciences and the arts.

89. A commission of national book-keeping regulates and verifies the accounts of the receipts and expenditures of the Republic. This commission is composed of seven members chosen by the Senate from the national list.

90. A constituted body can deliberate only in a sitting when at least two-thirds of the members are present.

91. The form of government of the French colonies is determined by special laws.

92. In case of rebellion by armed force or of disturbances that threaten the security of the state, the law can suspend in the places and for the time which it determines, the authority of the constitution.

This suspension can be declared provisionally, in the same cases, by an order of the government, the Legislative Body being on vacation, provided that this body be convoked within the shortest possible time by an article of the same order.

93. The French nation declares that in any case it will not permit the return of the French, who, having abandoned their fatherland since July 14, 1789, are not included in the exceptions allowed by the laws made against the *émigrés;* it forbids any new exception upon this matter.

The goods of the *émigrés* are irrevocably acquired for the profit of the Republic.

94. The French nation declares that after a legally consummated sale of national lands, whatever be the cause thereof, the lawful purchaser cannot be dispossessed thereof, reserving to their claimants, if there is need, indemnification by the public treasury.

95. The present constitution shall be offered immediately for the acceptance of the French people.

59. Order for Suppressing the Newspapers.

January 17, 1800 (27 Nivôse, Year VIII). *Moniteur,* January 19, 1800 (29 Nivôse, Year VIII).

Shortly after the Constitution of the Year VIII went into effect the First Consul began a series of vigorous measures against possible oppositon to his rule. This document is typical of the series.

REFERENCES. *Cambridge Modern History,* IX, 14-15 : Fournier, *Napoleon,* 238 ; Sloane, *Napoleon,* II, 96 ; Lavisse and Rambaud, *Histoire générale,* IX, 15-16 ; Aulard, *Révolution française,* 714-716 ; Jaurès, *Histoire socialiste,* VI, 55-57.

The consuls of the Republic, considering that a part of the newspapers which are printed in the department of the Seine are instruments in the hands of the enemies of the Republic; that the government is particularly charged by the French people to look after their security, orders as follows:

1. The minister of police shall permit to be printed, published, and circulated during the whole course of the war only the following newspapers: . . . [Here follows the names of thirteen newspapers], and newspapers devoted exclusively to science, arts, literature, commerce, announcements and notices.

2. The minister of the general police shall immediately make a report upon all the newspapers that are printed in the other departments.

3. The minister of the general police shall see that no new newspaper be printed in the department of the Seine, as well as in all the other departments of the Republic.

4. The proprietors and editors of the newspapers preserved by the present order shall present themselves to the minister of the police in order to attest their character as French citizens, their residences and signatures, and they shall promise fidelity to the constitution.

5. All newspapers which shall insert articles opposed to the respect that is due to the social compact, to the sovereignty of the people and the glory of the armies, or which shall publish invectives against the governments and nations who are the friends or allies of the Republic, even when these articles may be extracts from foreign periodicals, shall be immediately suppressed.

6. The minister of the general police is charged with the execution of the present order, which shall be inserted in the *Bulletin of the Laws.*

60. Law for Reorganizing the Administrative System.

February 17, 1800 (28 Pluviôse, Year VIII). Duvergier, *Lois*, XII, 78-116.

This was a sort of organic act upon the administrative system. It deserves careful attention for three reasons: (1) the system here established has been one of the most substantial of Napoleon's institutions, existing to the present day with but little change; (2) under all French governments the administrative system is one of the most important features; (3) political scientists are now giving more attention to administration than ever before. This document may be profitably compared with No. 7.

REFERENCES. Dickinson, *Revolution and Reaction in Modern France*, 41-42; *Cambridge Modern History*, IX, 11-13; Fournier, *Napoleon*, 223-225; Rose, *Napoleon*, I, 246-249; Sloane, *Napoleon*, II, 139-140; Lanfrey, *Napoleon*, I, 436-441; Rambaud, *Civilisation contemporaine*, 69-72; Lavisse and Rambaud, *Histoire générale*, IX, 16-18; Aulard, *Révolution française*, 716-719; Jaurès, *Histoire socialiste*, VI, 57-60.

Title I. Division of the Territory.

1. The European territory of the Republic shall be divided into departments and communal districts, in conformity with the table annexed to the present law. [This table made but one change in the existing departments.]

Title II. Administration.

Section I. Department administration.

2. There shall be in each department a prefect, a council of prefecture, and a department general council, which shall discharge the functions now performed by the administrations and department commissioners.

[The remainder of the article provides for the number of members in the councils of prefecture and the department general councils. The former have three, four, or five members; the latter have sixteen, twenty, or twenty-four members.]

3. The prefect alone shall be charged with the administration.

4. The council of prefecture shall pronounce:

Upon the requests of individuals seeking to obtain the discharge or the reduction of their share of the direct taxes;

Upon disputes which may arise between the contractors

for public works and the administration over the meaning
or execution of articles in their contracts;

Upon the claims of individuals who shall complain of
injuries and damages proceeding from the personal acts of
the contractors and not the acts of the administration;

Upon requests and contests over indemnities due to individuals by reason of lands taken or excavated for the making
of roads, canals, and other public works;

Upon disputes which may arise in the matter of the
great highway commission;

Upon requests which shall be presented by city, town or
village communities to be authorised to litigate;

Finally, upon litigation over the national lands.

5. When the prefect shall attend the council of prefecture,
he shall preside; in case of equal division, he shall have the
casting vote.

6. The department general council shall meet each year:
the time of its meeting shall be determined by the government; the duration of its session cannot exceed fifteen days.

It shall appoint one of its members for president, another
for secretary.

It shall make the division of the direct taxes among the
communal districts of the department.

It shall decide upon the requests for reductions made by
the councils of the districts, cities, towns, and villages.

It shall determine, within the limits fixed by the law, the
number of additional centimes, the imposition of which shall
be requested for the expenses of the department.

It shall hear the annual account which the prefect shall
render of the employment of the additional centimes which
shall have been set aside for these expenses.

It shall express its opinion upon the condition and the
needs of the department and shall address it to the minister of
the interior.

7. A general secretary for the prefecture shall have the
custody of the papers and shall sign the documents.

Section II. Communal administration.

8. In each communal district there shall be a sub-prefect
and a district council composed of eleven members.

9. The sub-prefect shall discharge the functions now performed by the municipal administrations and the cantonal

commissioners, with the exception of those which are assigned hereafter to the district council and the municipalities

10. The district council shall meet each year: the time of its meeting shall be determined by the government; the duration of its session cannot exceed fifteen days.

It shall appoint one of its members for president and another for secretary.

It shall make the division of the direct taxes among the cities, towns, and villages of the district.

It shall give its opinion, with a statement of reasons, upon the requests for discharge which shall be formulated by the cities, towns and villages.

It shall hear the annual account which the sub-prefect shall render of the employment of the additional centimes set apart for the expenses of the district.

It shall express an opinion upon the condition and the needs of the district and shall address it to the prefect.

11. In the communal districts in which the head-town of the department shall be situated, there shall not be any sub-prefect.

Section III. Municipalities.

12. In the cities, towns, and other places for which there are now a municipal agent and deputy, and whose population shall not exceed two thousand five hundred inhabitants, there shall be a mayor and a deputy; in the cities or towns of two thousand five hundred to five thousand inhabitants, a mayor and two deputies; in the cities of five thousand to ten thousand inhabitants, a mayor, two deputies, and a commissioner of police; in the cities whose population shall exceed ten thousand inhabitants, besides the mayor, two deputies and a commissioner of police, there shall be a deputy for each twenty thousand inhabitants in excess and a commissioner for each ten thousand in excess.

13. The mayors and deputies shall discharge the administrative functions now performed by the municipal agent and the deputy: in relation to the police and the civil state, they shall discharge the functions now performed by the municipal administrations of the canton, the municipal agents, and the deputies.

14. In the cities of one hundred thousand inhabitants and upwards, there shall be a mayor and a deputy in the

place of each municipal administration; there shall be in addition a commissioner-general of police, to whom the commissioners of police shall be subordinate, and who shall be subordinate to the prefect: nevertheless, he shall execute the orders which he shall receive directly from the minister in charge of the police.

15. There shall be a municipal council in each city, town, or other place for which there is now a municipal agent and a deputy.

The number of its members shall be ten in the places whose population does not exceed two thousand five hundred inhabitants; twenty, in those in which it does not exceed five thousand; thirty, in those in which the population is more numerous.

This council shall meet each year on 15 Pluviôse and can remain in session fifteen days.

It can be assembled extraordinarily by order of the prefect.

It shall hear and can discuss the account of the municipal receipts and expenditures which shall be rendered by the mayor to the sub-prefect, who shall determine it definitively.

It shall control the division of the common woods, pastures, harvests, and fruits.

It shall regulate the division of labor necessary for the maintenance and repair of the property which is under the control of the inhabitants.

It shall deliberate upon the particular and local needs of the municipality, the loans, the *octrois* or taxes of additional centimes which may be necessary in order to supply these needs, and the lawsuits which it shall be expedient to institute or sustain for the exercise and preservation of the common rights.

16. At Paris, in each of the municipal districts, a mayor and two deputies shall be charged with the administrative part and with the functions relative to the civil state.

A prefect of police shall be charged with what concerns the police and shall have under his orders commissioners distributed in the twelve municipalities.

17. At Paris the department council shall discharge the functions of municipal council.

Section IV. Of the appointments.

18. The First Council shall appoint the prefects, the councillors of prefecture, the members of the general councils of the departments, the general secretary for the prefecture, the sub-prefects, the members of the district councils, the mayors and deputies of the cities of more than five thousand inhabitants, the commissioners-general of police and prefects of police in the cities in which they shall be established.

19. The members of the general councils of departments and those of the councils of the communal districts shall be appointed for three years: they can be continued.

20. The prefects shall appoint and can suspend from their functions the members of the municipal councils; they shall appoint and can suspend the mayors and deputies in cities whose population is less than five thousand inhabitants. The members of the municipal councils shall be appointed for three years: they can be continued.

Section V. Of the salaries.

21. In the cities whose population does not exceed fifteen thousand inhabitants, the salary of the prefect shall be eight thousand francs;

In those of fifteen to thirty thousand inhabitants, it shall be twelve thousand francs;

In those of thirty to forty-five thousand inhabitants, it shall be sixteen thousand francs;

In those of forty-five thousand to one hundred thousand, it shall be twenty thousand francs;

In those of one hundred thousand and upwards, twenty-four thousand francs.

At Paris it shall be thirty thousand francs.

22. The salary of the councillors for the prefecture shall be in each department one-tenth of that of the prefect; it shall be twelve hundred francs in the departments in which the salary of the prefect shall be only eight thousand francs.

23. The salary of the sub-prefects in the cities whose population shall exceed twenty thousand inhabitants shall be four thousand francs, and three thousand francs in the others.

24. The government shall fix for each department the amount of the office expenses which shall be used for the administration.

[The table of the departments and communal districts is omitted.]

61. Law for Reorganizing the Judicial System.

March 18, 1800 (27 Ventôse, Year VIII). Duvergier, *Lois*, XII, 151-163.

By this measure Napoleon introduced some important changes in the judicial system of France and gave it substantially the form which it has borne ever since.

REFERENCES. Dickinson, *Revolution and Reaction in Modern France*, 44-45 ; Lanfrey, *Napoleon*, I, 441-446.

For an adequate idea of what Napoleon did in the way of judicial reform his codification of French law must also be noticed. This cannot be shown here by documents, but some of the following acounts of it should be read : Dickinson, *Revolution and Reaction in Modern France*, 46 ; Fyffe, *Modern Europe*, I, 258-260 (Popular ed., 173-175) ; *Cambridge Modern History*, IX, Ch. VI ; Fournier, *Napoleon*. 230-232 : Rose, *Napoleon*, I, 265-271 ; Sloane, *Napoleon*, II, 142-144 ; Lavisse and Rambaud, *Histoire générale*, IX, 241-248.

Title I. General Provisions.

1. The department civil and criminal tribunals and the tribunals of correctional police are suppressed; nevertheless, they shall continue their functions until the installation of the new tribunals.

2. There is nothing changed, however, in the laws concerning the justices of the peace and the commercial judges, who shall continue to exercise their functions until it has been otherwise ordered.

.   .   .   .

Title II. Of the Tribunals of First Instance.

6. There shall be established a tribunal of first instance per communal district.

7. The tribunals of first instance shall have original and final jurisdiction of civil matters in the cases determined by law; they shall likewise have jurisdiction in matters of correctional police; they shall pass upon appeals from the judgments rendered in the first instance by the justices of the peace.

.   .   .   .

Title III. Of the Tribunals of Appeal.

21. There shall be established twenty-nine tribunals of appeal, in the places and for the departments as follows: . . .

22. The tribunals of appeal shall decide upon appeals from judgments in first instance rendered in civil matters by the district tribunals and upon appeals from judgments of first instance rendered by the commercial tribunals.

. . . .

Title IV. Of the Criminal Tribunals.

32. There shall be a criminal tribunal in each department.

. . . .

33. The criminal tribunals shall have jurisdiction, as in the past, over all criminal cases; they shall decide upon the appeals from the judgments rendered by the tribunals of the first instance in matters of correctional police.

. . . .

Title VI. Of the Tribunal of Cassation.

58. The tribunal of cassation shall sit at Paris in the place determined by the government.

It shall be composed of forty-eight judges.

. . . .

60. The tribunal shall be divided into three sections, each of sixteen judges.

The first shall decide upon the admission or rejection of petitions in cassation or as to prejudice, and definitively upon the applications as to the rulings of judges and as to transfers from one tribunal to another.

The second shall pronounce definitively upon applications in cassation or as to prejudice, when the petitions shall have been accepted.

The third shall pronounce upon the applications in cassation in criminal, correctional and police matters, unless there should be need of prior judgment of admission.

. . . .

76. Besides the functions given to the tribunal of cassation by article 65 of the constitution, it shall pronounce upon the rulings of the judges when conflict arises between several

tribunals of appeal or between several tribunals of first instance not resorting to the same tribunal of appeal.

77. There is no opportunity for cassation against the judgments in the last resort of the justices of the peace, except for cause of incompetency or of excess of power, nor against the judgments of military and naval tribunals, except, likewise, for cause of incompetency ·or excess of power proposed by a non-military citizen, or [one] assimilated to the military by the laws, on account of his functions.

. . . .

62. Treaty of Luneville.

February 9, 1801 (20 Pluviôse, Year IX). De Clercq, *Traités.* I, 424-429. Translation, James Harvey Robinson, *University of Pennsylvania Translations and Reprints.*

This treaty terminated the war with Austria which had been renewed while Napoleon Bonaparte was in Egypt. It should be compared with No. 55.

REFERENCES. Fyffe, *Modern Europe,* I, 225-226 (Popular ed., 152) ; *Cambridge Modern History,* IX, 69-70 ; Fournier, *Napoleon,* 206-208 ; Sloane, *Napoleon,* II, 125-126 ; Lavisse and Rambaud, *Histoire générale,* IX, 51-52 ; Jaurès, *Histoire socialiste,* VI, 114-115.

MAPS. Droysen, *Historischer Hand-Atlas,* 48 ; Lane-Poole, *Historical Atlas of Modern Europe,* XI ; Schrader, *Atlas de geographie historique,* 48.

His Majesty the Emperor, King of Hungary and of Bohemia, and the First Consul of the French Republic, in the name of the French people, induced by a common desire to put an end to the evils of war, have resolved to proceed to the conclusion of a definitive treaty of peace and amity. His said Imperial and Royal Majesty desiring no less sincerely to extend the benefits of peace to the German Empire, and the existing conditions not affording the necessary time for consulting the Empire, or permitting its representatives to take part in the negotiations, has resolved, in view of the concessions made by the deputation of the Empire at the recent Congress of Rastadt, to treat in the name of the German body, as has happened before under similar circumstances.

. . . .

1. Peace, amity and a good understanding shall hereafter exist forever between His Majesty the Emperor, King of Hungary and of Bohemia, acting both in his own name and in that of the German Empire, and the French Republic; His Majesty agreeing that the said Empire shall ratify the present treaty in due form. The contracting parties shall make every effort to maintain a perfect agreement between themselves, and to prevent the commission of any acts of hostility by land or sea upon any ground or pretence whatsoever; striving in every way to maintain the concord thus happily re-established. No aid or protection shall be given either directly or indirectly to any one attempting to injure either of the contracting parties.

2. The cession of the former Belgian Provinces to the French Republic, stipulated in Article 3 of the treaty of Campo Formio, is renewed here in the most solemn manner. His Majesty the Emperor and King therefore renounces for himself and his successors, as well on his own part as on that of the German Empire, all right and title to the above specified provinces, which shall be held in perpetuity by the French Republic in full sovereignty and proprietary right, together with all territorial possessions belonging to them.

His Imperial and Royal Majesty cedes likewise to the French Republic, with the due consent of the Empire:

1. The county of Falkenstein with its dependencies.

2. The Frickthal and all the territory upon the left bank of the Rhine between Zurzach and Basle belonging to the House of Austria; the French Republic reserving the future cession of this district to the Helvetian Republic.

3. Moreover, in confirmation of Article 6 of the treaty of Campo Formio, His Majesty the Emperor and King shall possess in full sovereignty and proprietary right the countries enumerated below, to wit:

Istria, Dalmatia and the islands of the Adriatic, formerly belonging to Venice, dependent upon them; the mouths of the Cattaro, the city of Venice, the Lagunes, and the territory included between the hereditary States of His Majesty the Emperor and King, the Adriatic Sea and the Adige from the point where it leaves Tyrol to that where it flows into the Adriatic, the thalweg of the Adige forming the boundary line. And since by this line the cities of Verona and

Porto-Legnago are separated into two parts, draw-bridges indicating the frontier shall be established in the middle of the bridges connecting the two parts of the said towns.

4. Article 18 of the treaty of Campo Formio is likewise renewed, whereby His Majesty the Emperor and King agrees to cede to the Duke of Modena, as an indemnity for the territory which this prince and his heirs possessed in Italy, the Breisgau, which he shall possess upon the same conditions as those upon which he held Modena.

5. It is further agreed that His Royal Highness the Grand Duke of Tuscany shall renounce for himself, his successors or possible claimants, the Grand Duchy of Tuscany and that part of the island of Elba belonging to it, as well as all rights and titles resulting from the possession of the said states, which shall hereafter be held in full sovereignty and proprietary right by His Royal Highness the Infante Duke of Parma. The Grand Duke shall receive a complete and full indemnity in Germany for the loss of his state in Italy. . . .

6. His Majesty the Emperor and King consents not only on his part but upon the part of the German Empire, that the French Republic shall hereafter possess in full sovereignty and proprietary right the territory and domains lying on the left bank of the Rhine and forming a part of the German Empire, so that, in conformity with the concessions granted by the deputation of the Empire at the Congress of Rastadt and approved by the Emperor, the thalweg of the Rhine shall hereafter form the boundary between the French Republic and the German Empire from that point where the Rhine leaves Helvetian territory to the point where it reaches Batavian territory.

In view of this the French Republic formally renounces all possessions whatsoever upon the right bank of the Rhine and agrees to restore to their owners the following places: Düsseldorf, Ehrenbreitstein, Philippsburg, the fortress of Cassel and other fortifications across from Mainz on the right bank of the stream, and the fortress of Kehl and Alt Breisach, under the express provision that these places and forts shall continue to exist in the condition in which they are left at the time of the evacuation.

7. Since in consequence of this cession made by the Empire to the French Republic various princes and states of

the Empire find themselves individually dispossessed in part or wholly of their territory, while the German Empire should collectively support the losses resulting from the stipulations of the present treaty, it is agreed between His Majesty the Emperor and King (both on his part and upon the part of the German Empire) and the French Republic that, in accordance with the principles laid down at the congress of Rastadt, the Empire shall be bound to furnish the hereditary princes who have lost possession upon the left bank of the Rhine an indemnity within the Empire, according to such arrangements as shall be determined later in accordance with the stipulations here made.

. . . .

11. The present treaty of peace . . . is declared to be common to the Batavian, Helvetian, Cisalpine and Ligurian republics. The contracting parties mutually guarantee the independence of the said republics and the freedom of the inhabitants of the said countries to adopt such form of government as they shall see fit.

12. His Majesty the Emperor and King renounces for himself and for his successors in favor of the Cisalpine Republic all rights and titles depending upon such rights, which His Majesty might assert over the territories in Italy which he possessed before the war and which, according to the terms of article 8 of the treaty of Campo Formio, now form a part of the Cisalpine Republic which shall hold them in full sovereign and proprietary right together with all the territorial possessions dependent upon them.

13. His Majesty the Emperor and King confirms both in his own name and in the name of the German Empire the sanction already given by the treaty of Campo Formio to the union of the former imperial fiefs to the Ligurian Republic and renounces all claims and titles resulting from these claims upon the said fiefs.

. . . .

63. Treaty of Amiens.

March 27, 1802. Hansard, *Parliamentary History*, XXXVI,
558-563.

As the result of this treaty France was left at peace with all
Europe, for the first time in ten years. The peace, however, lasted only fifteen months. A careful study of the document, with due
attention to the situation of Europe at the time, should do much
to show why the war was so soon renewed. Both the omissions
of the document and the vague character of some of its provisions
call for attention.

REFERENCES. Fyffe, *Modern Europe*, I, 236-238 (Popular ed.,
159-160) ; *Cambridge Modern History*, IX, 70-80 ; Fournier, *Napoleon*, 214-220 ; Rose, *Napoleon*, I, Ch. XIV ; Sloane, *Napoleon*. II.
135-136, 167-169 ; Lanfrey, *Napoleon*, II. 129-148, 187-189 ; Lavisse
and Rambaud, *Histoire générale*, IX, 60-62 ; Jaurès, *Histoire socialiste*, VI, 120-134.

His Majesty the King of the United Kingdom of Great
Britain and Ireland, and the First Consul of the French Republic, in the name of the French people, being animated with
an equal desire to put an end to the calamities of war, have
laid the foundation of peace in the preliminary articles signed
at London the 1st of October, 1801 (9 Vendémiaire, Year
X) ; . . .

1. There shall be peace, friendship and good understanding, between His Majesty the King of the United Kingdom of
Great Britain and Ireland, his heirs and successors, on the
one part ; and the French Republic, His Majesty the King of
Spain, his heirs and successors, and the Batavian Republic, on
the other part. . . .

3. His Britannic Majesty restores to the French Republic
and her allies, namely, His Catholic Majesty and the Batavian
Republic, all the possessions and colonies which belonged
to them respectively, and which had been occupied or conquered by the British forces in the course of the war, with the
exception of the island of Trinidad, and the Dutch possessions in the island of Ceylon.

4. His Catholic Majesty cedes and guarantees, in full right
and sovereignty, to his Britannic Majesty, the island of Trinidad.

5. The Batavian Republic cedes and guarantees in full right
and sovereignty to his Britannic Majesty, all the possessions
and establishments in the island of Ceylon, which belonged

before the war to the Republic of the United Provinces, or
to their East India company.

6. The Cape of Good Hope remains in full sovereignty to
the Batavian Republic, as it was before the war. . . .

7. The territories and possessions of Her Most Faithful
Majesty [of Portugal] are maintained in their integrity, such
as they were previous to the commencement of the war. . .

8. The territories, possessions and rights of the Ottoman
Porte, are hereby maintained in their integrity, such as they
were previous to the war.

9. The Republic of the Seven Islands is hereby acknowl-
edged.

10. The islands of Malta, Gozo, and Comino, shall be restored to the order of St. John of Jerusalem, and shall be
held by it upon the same conditions on which the order held
them previous to the war, and under the following stipulations:

.   .   .   .

4th. The forces of his Britannic Majesty shall evacuate
the island and its dependencies within three months after
the exchange of ratifications, or sooner if it can be done. At
that period the island shall be delivered up to the order in
the state in which it now is, provided that the grand master,
or commissioners fully empowered, according to the statutes
of the order, be upon the island to receive possession, and
that the force to be furnished by His Sicilian Majesty, as hereafter stipulated, be arrived there.

.   .   .   .

18. The branch of the House of Nassau, which was established in the republic, formerly called the Republic of the
United Provinces, and now the Batavian Republic, having
suffered losses there, as well in private property as in consequence of the change of constitution adopted in that country, an adequate compensation shall be procured for the said
branch of the House of Nassau for the said losses.

19. The present definitive treaty of peace is declared common to the Sublime Ottoman Porte, the ally of His Britannic Majesty and the Sublime Porte shall be invited to
transmit its act of accession thereto in the shortest delay
possible.

.   .   .   .

64. Documents upon Napoleon and the Reorganization of Religion.

At the beginning of the consulate the religious institutions of France were in a state of hopeless confusion. These documents show the general character of the reorganization effected by Napoleon. Document A is the compact between France and the papacy which until 1906 controlled the position of the Roman catholic church in France. The two dates ascribed to it represent those of its signature by the French and papal envoys and of its promulgation in France. Document B was purely a French legislative act; the consent of the Pope was neither asked nor given. Document D did for the two recognized protestant sects what the other documents did for the Roman catholic church. In 1808 a similar arrangement was made for the Jews.

REFERENCES. Fyffe, *Modern Europe*, I, 260-265 (Popular ed., 175-178); *Cambridge Modern History*, IX, Ch. VII; Fournier, *Napoleon*, II, 211-213; Rose, *Napoleon*, I, 249-262; Lanfrey, *Napoleon*, II, 153-173; Wells, *American Historical Association, Annual Report* for 1895, 469-485; Aulard, *Révolution française*, Part IV, Ch. III; Lavisse and Rambaud, *Histoire générale*, IX, 255-272; Debidour. *L'Église et l'État*, Part I, Ch. VI; Jaurès, *Histoire socialiste*, VI, 75-98.

A. The Concordat. July 15, 1801-April 8, 1802 (26 Messidor, Year IX-18 Germinal, Year X). Duvergier, *Lois*, XIII, 89-91.

The First Consul of the French Republic and His Holiness the Sovereign Pontiff Pius VII have appointed as their respective plenipotentiaries: . . .

Who, after the exchange of their respective full powers, have arranged the following convention:

Convention between the French Government and His Holiness Pius VII.

The government of the French Republic recognizes that the Roman, catholic and apostolic religion is the religion of the great majority of French citizens.

His Holiness likewise recognizes that this same religion has derived and in this moment again expects the greatest benefit and grandeur from the establishment of the catholic worship in France and from the personal profession of it which the consuls of the Republic make.

In consequence, after this mutual recognition, as well for the benefit of religion as for the maintenance of internal tranquility, they have agreed as follows:

1. The catholic, apostolic and Roman religion shall be freely exercised in France: its worship shall be public, and in conformity with the police regulations which the government shall deem necessary for the public tranquility.

2. A new circumscription of the French dioceses shall be made by the holy see in concert with the government.

3. His Holiness shall declare to the titular French bishops that he with firm confidence expects from them, for the benefit of peace and unity, every sort of sacrifice, even that of their sees.

After this exhortation, if they should refuse this sacrifice required for the welfare of the church (a refusal which His Holiness, nevertheless, does not expect), provision shall be made for the government of the bishoprics of the new circumscription by new titularies in the following manner:

4. The First Consul of the Republic shall make appointments, within the three months which shall follow the publication of the bull of His Holiness, to the archbishoprics and bishoprics of the new circumscription. His Holiness shall confer the canonical institution, following the forms established in relation to France before the change of government.

5. The nominations to the bishoprics which shall be vacant in the future shall likewise be made by the First Consul, and the canonical institution shall be given by the holy see, in conformity with the preceding article.

6. Before entering upon their functions, the bishops shall take directly, at the hands of the First Consul, the oath of fidelity which was in use before the change of government, expressed in the following terms:

"I swear and promise to God, upon the holy scriptures, to remain in obedience and fidelity to the government established by the constitution of the French Republic. I also promise not to have any intercourse, nor to assist by any counsel, nor to support any league, either within or without, which is inimical to the public tranquility; and if, within my diocese or elsewhere, I learn that anything to the prejudice of the state is being contrived, I will make it known to the government."

7. The ecclesiastics of the second rank shall take the same oath at the hands of the civil authorities designated by the government.

confer the canonical institution, following the forms established in relation to France before the change of Government.

5. The nominations to the bishoprics which shall be vacant in the future shall likewise be made by the First Consul, and the canonical institution shall be given by the Holy See, in conformity with the preceding article.

6. Before entering upon their functions, the bishops shall take directly, at the hands of the First Consul, the oath of fidelity which was in use before the change of Government, expressed in the following terms:

"I swear and promise to God, upon the Holy Scriptures, to remain in obedience and fidelity to the Government established by the constitution of the French Republic. I also promise not to have any intercourse, nor to assist by any counsel, nor to support any league, either within or without, which is inimical to the public tranquility; and if, within my diocese or elsewhere, I learn that anything to the prejudice of the State is being contrived, I will make it known to the Government."

7. The ecclesiastics of the second rank shall take the same oath at the hands of the civil authorities designated by the Government.

8. The following form of prayer shall be repeated at the end of divine service in all the Catholic churches of France: *Domine, salvam fac Rempublicam; Domine, salvos fac Consules.*

9. The bishops shall make a new circumscription of the parishes of their dioceses, which shall have effect only after the consent of the Government.

10. The bishops shall appoint the *cures.*

11. The bishops can have a chapter in their cathedrals and a seminary for their dioceses, without the Government being under obligation to endow them.

12. All the metropolitan, cathedral, parochial and other non-alienated churches needed for worship shall be again placed at the disposal of the bishops.

13. His Holiness, in the interest of peace and the happy re-establishment of the Catholic religion, declares that neither he nor his successors will disturb in any manner the purchasers of the alienated ecclesiastical estates, and that, in

B. Organic Articles for the Catholic Church. April 8, 1802 (18 Germinal, Year X). Duvergier, *Lois,* XIII, 91-101.

Title I. Of the Regime of the Catholic Church in its Relations with the Rights and the Police of the State.

1. No bull, brief, rescript, decree, injunction, provision, signature serving as a provision, nor other documents from the court of Rome, even concerning individuals only, can be received, published, printed, or otherwise put into effect, without the authorisation of the government.

2. No person calling himself nuncio, legate, vicar or apostolic commissioner, or taking advantage of any other denomination, without the same authorisation, can exercise upon French soil or elsewhere any function relative to the affairs of the Gallican church.

3. The decrees of foreign synods, even those of general councils, cannot be published in France before the government has examined their form, their conformity with the laws, rights, and liberties of the French Republic, and everything which, in their publication, may alter or affect the public tranquility.

4. No national or metropolitan council, no diocesan synod, no deliberative assembly, shall take place without the express permission of the government.

5. All the ecclesiastical offices shall be gratuitous, saving the offerings which may be authorised and fixed by the regulations.

6. There shall be recourse to the Council of State in every case of abuse on the part of the superiors and other ecclesiastical persons.

The cases of abuse are usurpation or excess of power, contravention of the laws and regulations of the Republic, infraction of the rules sanctioned by the canons received in France, attack upon the liberties, privileges and customs of the Gallican church, and every undertaking or any proceeding which in the exercise of worship can compromise the honor of the citizens, disturb arbitrarily their consciences, or degenerate into oppression or injury against them or into public scandal.

. . . .

Title II. Of the Ministers.

Section 1. General provisions.

9. The catholic worship shall be carried on under the direction of the archbishops and bishops in their dioceses, and under that of the *curés* in their parishes.

10. Every privilege involving exemption from or attribution of the episcopal jurisdiction is abolished.

11. The archbishops and bishops shall be able, with the authorisation of the government, to establish cathedral chapters and seminaries in their dioceses. All other ecclesiastical establishments are suppressed.

12. The archbishops and bishops shall be free to add to their name the title of *Citizen* or that of *Monsieur*. All other designations are forbidden.

Section 11. Of the archbishops and metropolitans.

13. The archbishops shall consecrate and install their suffragans. In case of hindrance or of refusal on their part, they shall be acted for by the senior bishop of the metropolitan district.

.   .   .   .

Section 111. Of the bishops, the vicars general and the seminaries.

16. No one can be appointed bishop before reaching thirty years of age, nor unless he is of French origin.

.   .   .   .

18. The priest appointed by the First Consul shall institute proceedings in order to procure investiture from the Pope.

He cannot exercise any function until the bull declaring his investiture has received the attestation of the government and until he has personally taken the oath prescribed by the convention agreed to by the French government and the holy see.

This oath shall be delivered to the First Consul; there shall be a record of it drawn up by the secretary of state.

19. The bishops shall appoint and install the *curés;* nevertheless, they shall not make known their appointment and they shall not give them the canonical investiture until after this appointment shall have been agreed to by the First Consul.

20. They shall be required to reside in their dioceses; they cannot leave them, except with the permission of the First Consul.

.   .   .   .

23. The bishops shall be charged with the organization of their seminaries, and the regulations for this organization shall be submitted to the approbation of the First Consul.

24. Those who shall be chosen to give instruction in the seminaries shall subscribe to the declaration made by the clergy of France in 1682 and published in an edict of the same year; they shall consent to teach in them the doctrine contained therein, and the bishops shall address a copy in due form to the councillor of state charged with all matters relating to worship.

.   .   .   .

26. They shall not ordain any ecclesiastic, unless he proves that he has property producing an annual revenue of at least three hundred francs, that he has reached the age of twenty-five years, and that he meets the qualifications required by the canons received in France.

The bishops shall not make any ordinations until the number of persons to be ordained has been submitted to the government and agreed to by it.

Section IV. Of the *curés*.

27. The *curés* shall enter upon their functions only after having taken at the hands of the prefect the oath prescribed by the convention agreed to by the government and the holy see. A minute of this oath-taking shall be drawn up by the general secretary of the prefecture and collated copies of it shall be delivered by them.

.   .   .   .

29. They shall be required to reside in their parishes.

.   .   .   .

32. No foreigner can be employed in the functions of the ecclesiastical ministry without the permission of the government.

33. All employment is forbidden to every ecclesiastic, even French, who does not belong to any one diocese.

.   .   .   .

Section V. Of the cathedral chapters, and the government of the dioceses during the vacancy of a see.

35. The archbishops and bishops who shall desire to make use of the privilege which is given them to establish chapters shall not do it without having procured the authorisation of the government, as well for the establishment itself as for the number and the choice of the ecclesiastics designated to constitute it.

.　　.　　.　　.　　.　　.　　.　　.　　.

Title III. Of the Worship.

39. There shall be only one liturgy and one catechism for all the catholic churches of France.

.　　.　　.　　.　　.　　.　　.

41. No religious festival, with the exception of the Sabbath, can be established without the permission of the government.

.　　.　　.　　.　　.　　.　　.

43. All the ecclesiastics shall be dressed in French fashion and in black.

The bishops can add to this costume the pastoral cross and violet stockings.

44. Family chapels and private oratories cannot be established without the express permission of the government, granted upon the request of the bishop.

45. In the cities in which there are temples set aside for different religious organizations, no catholic religious ceremony shall occur outside of the edifices consecrated to the catholic worship.

46. A single temple can be consecrated to only a single worship.

47. There shall be in the cathedrals and parish churches a place of distinction for catholic persons who occupy the civil and military posts.

48. The bishop shall co-operate with the prefect in order to regulate the manner of calling the faithful to divine service by the sound of the bells; no one can sound them for any other purpose without the permission of the local police.

49. When the government shall order public prayers the bishops shall co-operate with the prefect and the military commandant of the place as to the day, hour and manner of carrying into effect these orders.

50. The formal addresses called *sermons* and those known under the name of *stations* of Advent and of Lent shall be given only by the priests who have received a special authorisation for it from the bishop.

51. The *curés* at the sermons of the parochial masses shall pray and cause prayer to be offered for the French Republic and for the consuls.

52. They shall not permit themselves in their teaching any direct or indirect inculpation either of individuals or of the other religious organizations authorised in the state.

53. They shall not make in the sermon any publication foreign to the exercise of worship, except those .which shall be ordered by the government.

54. They shall give the nuptial benediction only to those who shall prove in good and due form that they have contracted marriage before the civil officer.

.   .   .   .

56. In all religious and ecclesiastical documents the employment of the equinoctial calendar, established by the laws of the Republic, shall be obligatory; the days shall be designated by the names which they had in the solstitial calendar.

57. The rest for the public functionaries shall be fixed upon Sunday.

Title IV. Of the Circumscription of the Archbishoprics, Bishoprics, and Parishes; of the Edifices Intended for Worship and of the Stipend of the Ministers.

Section 1. Of the circumscription of the archbishoprics and bishoprics.

58. There shall be in France ten archbishoprics or metropolitanates and fifty bishoprics.

.   .   .   .

Section 111. Of the compensation of the ministers.

64. The stipend of the archbishops shall be fifteen thousand francs.

65. The stipend of the bishops shall be ten thousand francs.

66. The *curés* shall be divided into two classes:

The stipend of the *curés* of the first class shall be fixed at fifteen hundred francs and that of the *curés* of the second class at a thousand francs.

.   .   .   .

68. The vicars and officiating priests shall be chosen from among the ecclesiastics pensioned in carrying into effect the laws of the constituent assembly.

The amount of these pensions and the product of the offerings shall form their stipend.

69. The bishops shall draw up projects for the regulations relative to the offerings which the ministers of the religion are authorised to receive for the administration of the sacraments. The projects for regulations drawn up by the bishops cannot be published, nor otherwise put into effect, until after having been approved by the government.

70. Every ecclesiastic pensioned by the state shall be deprived of his pension if he refuses, without legitimate cause, the functions which shall be entrusted to him.

.   .   .   .

73. Endowments which have for their purpose the support of the ministers and the carrying on of worship shall consist only of revenues settled upon the state; they shall be accepted by the diocesan bishop and can be carried out only with the authorisation of the government.

74. Immovables other than buildings intended for dwellings and the attendant gardens cannot be invested with ecclesiastical titles, nor possessed by the ministers of the sect on account of their functions.

.   .   .   .

C. The Declaration of 1682. March 19, 1682. Debidour, *L'Eglise et l'Etat en France,* 651-652.

Many persons are striving in these times to subvert the decrees of the Gallican church and its liberties, which our ancestors have supported with so much zeal, and to overthrow their foundations, which rest upon the holy canons and the tradition of the fathers. Others, under pretence of defending them, are not afraid to excite an attack upon the primacy of Saint Peter and the Roman pontiffs, his successors, who were instituted by Jesus Christ, and the obedience which all christians owe them, and to diminish the majesty of the apostolic holy see, which is worthy of respect by all the nations in which the true faith is taught and in which the unity of the church is preserved. On the other hand, heretics are putting everything at work to make the authority, which maintains the peace of the church, appear odious and intolerable to kings and peoples, and, by these artifices, to remove simple souls from the communion of the church, their mother, and therefore from that of Jesus Christ.—In order to remedy these inconveniences, we, archbishops and bishops assembled at Paris by order of the king, representing with the other ecclesiastical deputies the Gallican church, after mature deliberation have decided that it is necessary to make the regulations and the declarations which follow:

1. That Saint Peter and his successors, vicars of Jesus Christ, and even the whole church have received authority from God only over things spiritual and which have to do with salvation, and not over things temporal and civil; Jesus Christ himself tells us *that His kingdom is not of this world,* and, in another place, *that it is necessary to render to Caesar that which belongs to Caesar, and to God that which belongs to God.* That it is necessary to hold to this precept of Saint Paul: *that every person should be subject to the higher powers, for there is no power which does not come from God, and it is He who ordains those which are upon earth, that is why he who opposes the powers resists the order of God.* In consequence, we declare that kings by order of God, are not subject to any ecclesiastical power, in things which have to do with the temporal, and that they cannot be deposed directly or indirectly by the authority of the heads of the church; that their subjects cannot be exempted from the submissions and obedience which are due to them, nor be dispensed from the oath of fidelity; that this doctrine, necessary for the public peace, and as advantageous to church as to state, ought to be regarded as in conformity with the holy scriptures and with the traditions of the fathers of the church and with the example of the saints.

2. That the plentitude of power which the apostolic holy see and the successors of Saint Peter, vicars of Jesus Christ, have over things spiritual is such, nevertheless, that the decrees of the holy œcumenical council of Constance, contained in sessions 4 and 5, approved by the apostolic holy see and confirmed by the practice of all the church and of the Roman pontiffs, and religiously observed of all time by the Gallican church, remain in their force and vigor, and that the church of France does not approve of the opinion of those who make

attack upon these decrees or enfeeble them by saying that their authority is not well established and that they are not approved or that their provision had regard only to the time of the schism.

3. That it is necessary to regulate the use of the apostolic authority through canons made by the spirit of God and consecrated by the general respect of all the world; that the rules, customs and constitutions received in the kingdom and in the Gallican church ought to have their force and their vigor, and that the usages of our fathers ought to remain unshaken; that it is also for the grandeur of the apostolic holy see that the laws and customs established with the consent of that see and of the churches should have the authority which they ought to have.

4. That, although the pope has the principal part in questions of faith, and although his decrees relate to all the churches, and each church in particular, his judgment is not irreformable, unless the consent of the church intervenes.

These are the maxims which we have received from our fathers and which we have ordered to be sent to all the Gallican churches and to the bishops whom the holy spirit has established there to govern them, in order that we may all say the same thing, that we may be of the same sentiments, and that we may all hold the same doctrine.

D. Organic Articles for the Protestant Sects. April 8, 1802 (18 Germinal, Year X). Duvergier, *Lois*, XIII, 101-103.

Title I. General Provisions for all the Protestant Communions.

1. No one can conduct the performance of worship except a Frenchman.

2. Neither the protestant churches nor their ministers shall have relations with any foreign power or authority.

3. The pastors and ministers of the different protestant communions in the recital of their worship shall pray for and cause to be prayed for the prosperity of the French Republic and the consuls.

4. No doctrinal or dogmatic decision nor any formulary, under the title of confession or under any other title, shall be

published or become matter of instruction untii the government has authorised the publication or promulgation of it.

5. No change in discipline shall take place without the same authorisation.

6. The Council of State shall be informed of all the undertakings of the ministers of the sect, and of all the dissensions which shall arise among these ministers.

7. A stipend shall be provided [by the government] for the pastors of the consistorial churches; it is understood that the estates whicn these churches possess and the product of the offerings established by usage or by the regulations shall be utilized towards this stipend.

8. The arrangements provided by the organic articles of the catholic worship upon the liberty of endowments, and upon the nature of the estates which can be the object thereof, shall be common to the protestant churches.

9. There shall be two academies or seminaries in the east of France for the instruction of ministers of the confession of Augsburg.

10. There shall be a seminary at Geneva for the instruction of the ministers of the reformed churches.

11. The professors of all the academies or seminaries shall be appointed by the First Consul.

12. No one can be elected minister or pastor of a church of the confession of Augsburg, unless he has studied for a determined time in one of the French seminaries intended for the instruction of the ministers of that confession, and unless he brings a certificate in good form attesting his time of study, his capacity and his good morals.

13. No one can be elected minister or pastor of a reformed church, without having studied in the seminary at Geneva, nor unless he brings a certificate in the form set forth in the preceding article.

14. The regulations upon the administration and the internal police of the seminaries, upon the number and the qualification of the professors, upon the manner of instructing, and upon the matter of instruction, as well as upon the form of the certificates or attestations of study, good conduct and capacity, shall be approved by the government.

65. Documents upon Napoleon and Education.

From these documents an excellent idea of the educational system of Napoleon can be obtained. Documents A and C, the two principal creative acts. show the plan of the system and incidentally throw some light upon its educational spirit and ideals. Document B, although an extract from a church text-book instead of a school text-book, will serve to convey some idea of the character of the teaching touching political matters.

REFERENCES. Dickinson, *Revolution and Reaction in Modern France*, 48-51; *Cambridge Modern History*, IX, 126-130; Fournier, *Napoleon*, 233-235, 406-410; Rose, *Napoleon*, I, 271-275; Lanfrey, *Napoleon*, II, 221-224, III, 139-141; Sloane, *Napoleon*, II, 144-147, III, 72-74; Lavisse and Rambaud, *Histoire générale*, IX, 248-253.

A. Law upon Public Instruction. May 1, 1802 (11 Floréal, Year X). Duvergier, *Lois*, XIII, 175-178.

Title I. Division of the Instruction.

1. Instruction shall be given:

1st. In the primary schools established by the communes;

2d. In the secondary schools established by the communes or kept by private masters;

3d. In the *lycées* and the special schools maintained at the expense of the public treasury.

Title II. Of the Primary Schools.

.   .   .   .

3. The instructors shall be chosen by the mayors and the municipal councils; their stipend shall consist of: 1st, the dwelling provided by the communes; 2d, a fee paid by the parents, and fixed by the municipal councils.

4. The municipal councils shall exempt from the fee those of the parents who may be unable to pay it; nevertheless, this exemption cannot exceed a fifth of the children received into the primary schools.

5. The sub-perfects shall be especially charged with the organization of the primary schools; they shall render monthly to the prefects an account of their condition.

Title III. Of the Secondary Schools.

6. Every school established by the communes or kept by individuals, in which instruction is given in the Latin and French languages, the first principles of geography, history, and mathematics, shall be considered a secondary school.

7. The government encourages the establishment of secondary schools and will recompense good instruction which shall be given there, either by the grant of a habitation or by the distribution of gratuitous places in the *lycées* to those of the pupils of each department who shall most distinguish themselves, and by the bounties granted to the fifty masters of those schools which shall have had the most pupils admitted to the *lycées*.

8. Secondary schools cannot be established without the authorisation of the government. The secondary schools, as well as all the private schools whose instruction shall be higher than that of the primary schools, shall be placed under the special surveillance and inspection of the prefects.

Title IV. Of the Lycees.

9. *Lycées* shall be established for instruction in letters and the sciences. There shall be at least one *lycée* for each tribunal of appeal district.

10. Instruction shall be given in the *lycées* in the ancient languages, rhetoric, logic, ethics, and the elements of the mathematical and physical sciences.

The number of professors in the *lycée* shall never be less than eight; but it can be increased by the government, as well as the number of the subjects of instruction, according to the number of pupils who shall attend the *lycées*.

11. There shall be in the *lycées,* study masters, and masters of drawing, military exercises, and of accomplishments, [i.e. music and dancing].

12. Instruction shall be given there:

To pupils whom the government shall place there;

To the pupils of the secondary schools who shall be admitted there by a competition;

To pupils whose parents shall have placed them there to board;

To day scholars.

13. The administration of each *lycée* shall be confided to a principal; he shall have immediately under him a study-critic and a proctor conducting the affairs of the school.

14. The principal, the critic, and the proctor shall be ap-

pointed by the First Consul: they shall form the council of administration for the school.

15. In each of the cities where a *lycée* is established there shall be a bureau of administration for that school. This bureau shall be composed of the prefect of the department, the president of the tribunal of appeal, the commissioner of the government before this tribunal, the commissioner of the government before the criminal tribunal, the mayor, and the principal.

.   .   .   .   .   .

17. The First Consul shall appoint three inspectors-general of studies who shall visit the *lycées* at least once a year, shall definitely settle their accounts, shall examine all parts of the instruction and administration, and shall render an account thereof to the government.

.   .   .   .   .   .

19. The first appointment of the professors of the *lycées* shall be in the following manner: three inspectors-general of studies, in conjunction with three members of the national institute, designated by the First Consul, shall go over the departments and shall there examine the citizens who present themselves to occupy the different places of professors. For each place they shall indicate to the government two persons, one of whom shall be appointed by the First Consul.

20. When the *lycées* are once organized and a chair becomes vacant, the three inspectors-general of studies shall present one person to the government; the bureau, in conjunction with the council of administration and the professors of the *lycées,* shall present another; the First Consul shall appoint one of the two candidates.

.   .   .   .   .   .

Title V. Of the Special Schools.

23. The last grade of instruction shall include in the special schools the complete and profound study of the sciences and the useful arts, as well as the perfecting thereof.

24. The special schools now in existence shall be preserved, without prejudice to the modifications which the government believes that it must order for the economy and the welfare of the service. When the place of a professor shall

become vacant, including the school of law which shall be established at Paris, it shall be filled by the First Consul from three candidates who shall be presented, the first by one of the classes of the national institute, the second by the inspectors-general of studies, and the third by the professors of the school in which the place shall be vacant.

25. The following new special schools shall be instituted:

1st. Ten law schools can be established: each of them shall have four professors at most;

2d. Three new schools of medicine can be created, which shall have at most eight professors each, and one of which shall be devoted especially to the study and treatment of the diseases of the troops of the army and navy;

3d. There shall be four schools of natural history, physics, and chemistry, with four professors in each;

4th. The mechanical and chemical arts shall be taught in two special schools; there shall be three professors in each of these schools;

5th. A school of transcendental mathematics shall have three professors;

6th. A special school of geography, history, and public economy shall be composed of four professors;

7th. In addition to the schools of the arts of design existing at Paris, Dijon, and Toulouse, there shall be formed a fourth one with four professors;

8th. The observatories in operation at present shall each have a professor of astronomy;

9th. There shall be in several *lycées* professors of the living languages;

10th. There shall be appointed eight professors of music and composition.

26. The first appointment of the professors for these new special schools shall be made in the following manner: The classes of the institute corresponding to the places which are to be filled shall present one person to the government; the three inspectors-general of studies shall present a second: the First Consul shall choose one of the two.

After the organization of the new special schools, the First Consul shall appoint to the vacant places from among the three persons who shall be presented to him as is provided in article 24.

.　　.　　.　　.　　.　　.　　.

Title VII. Of the National Pupils.

32. Six thousand four hundred boarding pupils shall be supported at the expense of the Republic at the *lycées* and the special schools.

33. Out of these six thousand four hundred pensioners, two thousand four hundred shall be chosen by the government from among the sons of military men and of civil, judicial, administrative, or municipal functionaries who shall have served the Republic well; and for ten years only, from among the children of citizens of the departments united with France, although they may have been neither military men nor public functionaries.

These two thousand four hundred pupils must be at least nine years of age and know how to read and write.

34. The other four thousand pupils shall be taken from a double number of pupils of the secondary schools, who shall be presented to the government in consequence of an examination and a competition.

Each department shall furnish a number of these latter pupils proportionate to its population.

35. The pupils supported in the *lycées* cannot remain there more than six years at the expense of the nation. At the end of their studies they shall undergo an examination, in consequence of which one-fifth of them shall be placed in the different special schools, according to the inclination of these pupils, in order to be supported there for from two to four years at the expense of the Republic.

.　　.　　.　　.　　.　　.　　.

B. Imperial Catechism. April 4, 1807. Extract, Larousse, *Grande Dictionaire Universel,* III, 567.

Lesson VII. Continuation of the Fourth Commandment.
Q. What are the duties of christians with respect to the princes who govern them, and what in particular are our duties towards Napoleon I, our Emperor?
A. Christians owe to the princes who govern them, and we owe in particular to Napoleon I, our Emperor, *love, re-*

spect, obedience, fidelity, military service and the tributes laid for the preservation and defence of the Empire and of his throne; we also owe to him fervent prayers for his safety and the spiritual and temporal prosperity of the state.

Q. Why are we bound to all these duties towards our Emperor?

A. First of all, because God, who creates empires and distributes them according to His will, in loading our Emperor with gifts, both in peace and in war, has established him as our sovereign and has made him the minister of His power and His image upon the earth. *To honor and to serve our Emperor is then to honor and to serve God himself.* Secondly, because our Lord Jesus Christ by his doctrine as well as by His example, has Himself taught us what we owe to our sovereign: He was born the subject of Caesar Augustus; He paid the prescribed impost; and just as He ordered to render to God that which belongs to God, so He ordered to render to Caesar that which belongs to Caesar.

Q. Are there not particular reasons which ought to attach us more strongly to Napoleon I, our Emperor?

A. Yes; for it is he whom God has raised up under difficult circumstances to re-establish the public worship of the holy religion of our fathers and to be the protector of it. He has restored and preserved public order by his profound and active wisdom; he defends the state by his powerful arm; he has become the anointed of the Lord through the consecration which he received from the sovereign pontiff, head of the universal church.

Q. What ought to be thought of those who may be lacking in their duty towards our Emperor?

A. According to the apostle Saint Paul, they would be resisting the order established by God himself and would render themselves *worthy of eternal damnation.*

Q. Will the duties which are required of us towards our Emperor be equally binding with respect to his lawful successors in the order established by the constitutions of the Empire?

A. Yes, without doubt; for we read in the holy scriptures, that God, Lord of heaven and earth, by an order of His supreme will and through His providence, gives empires not only to one person in particular, but also to his family.

C. Decree for Organizing the Imperial University, March 17, 1808. Duvergier, *Lois*, XVI, 238-248.

Title I. General Organization of the University.

1. Public instruction in the entire empire is intrusted exclusively to the University.

2. No school, no establishment for instruction whatsoever, can be formed outside of the Imperial University and without the authorisation of its head.

3. No one can open a school nor give instruction publicly without being a member of the Imperial University and graduated by one of its faculties. Nevertheless, the instruction in the seminaries is under the control of the archbishops and bishops, each for his own diocese. They appoint and dismiss the directors and professors thereof. They are only required to comply with the regulations for the seminaries, approved by us.

4. The Imperial University shall be composed of as many academies as there are courts of appeal.

5. The schools belonging to each academy shall be placed in the following order:

1st. The faculties for the sciences of investigation and the bestowal of degrees;

2d. The *lycées* for the ancient languages, history, rhetoric, logic, and the elements of the mathematical and physical sciences;

3d. The colleges, secondary communal schools, for the elements of the ancient languages and the first principles of history and the sciences;

4th. The institutions and schools conducted by private instructors, in which the instruction is allied to that of the colleges;

5th. The schools and boarding-schools belonging to private masters and devoted to studies less advanced than those of the institutions;

6th. The petty schools and primary schools, in which reading, writing, and the first principles of arithmetic are taught.

Title II. Of the Composition of the Faculties.

6. There shall be in the Imperial University five orders of faculties, to wit:

1st. The faculties of theology,
2d. The faculties of law,
3d. The faculties of medicine,
4th. The faculties of mathematical and physical sciences.
5th. The faculties of letters.

‘ ‘ . . . .

Title IV. Of the Order which shall be Established among the Members of the University; of the Ranks and the Title Attached to the Functions.

I. Of the Ranks among the Functionaries.

29. The functionaries of the Imperial University shall take rank among themselves in the following order:

Ranks.

	Of Administration.	Of Instruction.
1st.	The grand master.	
2d.	The chancellor.	
3d.	The treasurer.	
4th.	The councillors for life.	
5th.	The ordinary councillors.	
6th.	The inspectors of the University.	
7th.	The rectors of the academy.	
9th.	The deans of the faculties.	
10th.		The professors of the facultles
11th.	The head-masters of the *lycées*.	
12th.	The critics of the *lycées*.	
13th.		The professors of the *lycées*.
14th.	The principals of the colleges.	
15th.		The fellows.
16th.		Regents of the colleges.
17th.	The heads of the institutions.	
18th.	The masters of the boarding schools.	
19th.		The masters of studies.

30. After the first formation of the Imperial University, the order of the ranks shall be followed in the selection of the functionaries, and no one can be appointed to a place until after having passed through the subordinate places.

The places shall form also a field of action which shall present, for knowledge and good conduct, the promise of rising to the highest ranks of the Imperial University.

Title V. Of the Principles of Instruction in the Schools of the University.

. . . .

38. All the schools of the Imperial University shall take for the basis of their instruction:

1st. The precepts of the catholic religion;

2d. Fidelity to the Emperor, to the imperial monarchy, the depository of the welfare of the peoples, and to the Napoleonic dynasty, the conservator of the unity of France and of all the liberal ideas proclaimed by the constitutions;

3d. Obedience to the rules of the teaching corps, which have for their object the uniformity of instruction, and which tend to train for the state citizens attached to their religion, to their prince, to their fatherland, and to their family;

4th. All the professors of theology shall be required to conform themselves to the provisions of the edict of 1682, concerning the four propositions contained in the declaration of the clergy of France of the said year.

Title VI. Of the Obligations which the Members of the University Contract.

39. By the terms of article 2 of the law of May 10, 1806, the members of the Imperial University at the time of their installation shall contract by oath the civil obligations, special and temporary, which shall bind them to the instructional corps.

40. They shall bind themselves to the precise observance of the rules and regulations of the University.

41. They shall promise obedience to the grand master in all that he shall command them for our service and for the good of the instruction.

42. They shall bind themselves not to leave the instructional corps and their functions until after having obtained the consent of the grand master therefor in the forms which shall be prescribed.

43. The grand master can release a member of the University from his obligations and permit him to leave the corps: in case of refusal by the grand master, and of persistence on the part of the member of the University in the reso-

lution to leave the corps, the grand master shall be required to deliver to him a letter of *exeat* after three consecutive demands repeated at intervals of two months.

44. Whoever shall have left the instructional body without having fulfilled these formalities shall be removed from the roll of the University and shall incur the penalty attached to that removal.

45. The members of the University shall not be able to accept any salaried public or private position without the properly attested permission of the grand master.

46. The members of the University shall be required to inform the grand master and his officers of everything in the establishments of public instruction which may come to their knowledge that is contrary to the doctrine and the principles of the instructional corps.

47. The disciplinary penalties which the violation of the duties and obligations may entail shall be:

1st. Arrests;

2d. Reprimand in the presence of an academic council;

3d. Censure in the presence of the council of the University;

4th. Change to a subordinate employment;

5th. Suspension from duty for a fixed time, with or without total or partial deprivation of stipend;

6th. Reform or retirement given before the time of emeritation, with a stipend less than the pension of the emerited;

7th. Lastly, removal from the roll of the University.

48. Every person who shall have incurred removal shall be disqualified for employment in any public administration.

49. The relations between the penalties and the infraction of duties, as well as the grading of these penalties according to the different employments, shall be established by rules.

Title VII. Of the Functions and Prerogatives of the Grand Master of the University.

50. The Imperial University shall be administered and governed by the grand master, who shall be appointed and dismissed by us.

51. The grand master shall have the selection to the administrative places and to the chairs of the colleges and the

lycées; he shall likewise appoint the officers of the academies and those of the University, and he shall make all the promotions in the instructional corps.

52. He shall install the persons who shall have obtained the chairs of the faculties, according to the competition whose method shall be determined by the council of the University.

. . . . . .

54. He shall grant permission to instruct and to open houses of instruction to the graduates of the University who shall ask it from him and who shall have fulfilled the condition required by the regulations in order to obtain this permission.

55. The grand master shall be presented to us each year by the minister of the interior, in order to submit to us: 1st, the list of the establishments of instruction, and particularly of the boarding schools, institutions, colleges and *lycées;* 2d, that of the officers of the academies and of the officers of the University; 3d, the promotion list of the members of the instructional corps who shall have merited it by their services. He shall cause these lists to be published at the opening of the academic year.

56. He can transfer from one academy to another the regents and principals of the colleges maintained by the communes, as well as the functionaries and the professors of the *lycées,* upon taking the opinion of three members of the council.

57. He shall have the authority to impose arrests, reprimand, censure, the change and suspension of functions (article 47) upon members of the University who shall have been delinquent enough in their duties to incur these penalties.

. . . .

60. He shall give to the different schools the regulations for discipline, which shall be discussed by the council of the University.

61. He shall convoke and preside over this council, and he shall appoint its members, as well as those of the academic councils, as shall be provided in the following titles.

. . . .

Title IX. Of the Council of the University.

Of the Formation of the Council.

69. The council of the University shall be composed of thirty members.

70. Ten of these members, of whom six shall be chosen from among the inspectors and four from among the rectors, shall be councillors for life or titular councillors of the University. They shall be commissioned by us.

The ordinary councillors, to the number of twenty, shall be taken from among the inspectors, the deans and professors of the faculties, and the head-masters of the *lycées*.

71. Every year the grand master shall make up the list of the twenty ordinary councillors, who shall complete the council for the year.

. . . .

75. The council shall be divided for work into five sections:

The first shall occupy itself with the condition and the improvement of the studies;

The second with the administration and the police of the schools;

The third with their accounts;

The fourth with litigious matters;

And the fifth with affairs of the seal of the University.

Each section shall examine the matters which shall be sent to it by the grand master, and shall make report thereof to the council, which shall deliberate thereon.

Of the Prerogatives of the Council.

76. The grand master shall propose for the discussion of the council all the projects for regulations and rules which may be made for the schools of different degrees.

77. All questions relative to the police, the accounting and the general administration of the faculties, the *lycées,* and the colleges shall be decided by the council, which shall fix the budgets of these schools upon the report of the treasurer of the University.

78. It shall pass judgment upon the accusations of the superiors and the complaints of the subordinates.

79. It alone can impose upon the members of the Uni-

versity the penalties for reformation or removal (article 47) after investigation and examination of the offences which shall involve condemnation to these penalties.

80. The council shall admit or reject the works which shall have been or ought to be put into the hands of the pupils or placed in the libraries of the *lycées* or colleges; it shall examine the new works which shall be proposed for the instruction of the same schools.

81. It shall hear the report of the inspectors upon return from their missions.

82. The litigious matters relative to the general administration of the academies and their schools, and in particular those which shall concern the members of the University in relation to their functions, shall be carried to the council of the University. The decisions, taken by majority of the votes and after an exhaustive discussion, shall be executed by the grand master. Nevertheless, in this he can have recourse to our Council of State against the decisions upon the report of our minister of the interior.

83. In conformity with the proposal of the grand master and upon the presentation of our minister of the interior, a commission of the council of the University can be admitted to our Council of State in order to solicit the reform of the regulations and the decisions interpretative of the law.

84. The minutes of the meetings of the council of the University shall be sent each month to our minister of the interior: the members of the council may cause to be inserted in these minutes the reasons for their opinions, when they differ from the opinion adopted by the council.

.   .   .   .

Title XI. Of the Inspectors of the University and of the Inspectors of the Academies.

90. The general inspectors of the University shall be appointed by the grand master, and taken from among the officers of the University; their number shall be at least twenty and cannot exceed thirty.

91. They shall be divided into five orders, as are the faculties; they shall not belong to any academy in particular; they shall visit them in turns and upon the order of the

grand master, in order to ascertain the condition of the studies and of the discipline in the faculties, the *lycées,* and the colleges, to make certain the accuracy and the talents of the professors, regents and masters of study, to examine the scholars, and lastly, to supervise their administration and accounts.

. . . .

Title XII. Of the Rectors of the Academies.

94. Each academy shall be governed by a rector under the immediate orders of the grand master, who shall appoint him for five years, and shall choose him from among the officers of the academies.

. . . .

97. They [the rectors] shall cause the deans of the faculties, head-masters of the *lycées,* and principals of the colleges to give accounts to them of the condition of these establishments; and they shall direct their administration, especially in relation to the severity of the discipline and economy in the expenses.

98. They shall cause to be inspected and looked after by the individual inspectors of academies, the schools, and especially the colleges, institutions, and boarding schools, and they themselves shall make visits as often as it is possible for them.

. . . .

Title XIII. Of the Regulations to be Given to the Lycees, Colleges, Institutions, Boarding Schools and Primary Schools.

. . . . . .

101. For the future, and after the complete organization of the University, the head-masters and critics of the *lycées,* the principals and regents of the colleges, as well as the masters of study of these schools, shall be bound to celibacy and to the life in common.

The professors of the *lycées* can be married and, in that case, they shall dwell outside of the *lycée.* The celibate professors can dwell therein, and take advantage of the life in common.

. . . .

104. There shall be nothing printed and published to announce the studies, the discipline, the boarding conditions, or upon the exercises of the pupils in the schools, unless the different programs have been submitted to the rectors and councils of the academies and approval has been obtained for them.

105. Upon the proposal of the rectors and the advice of the inspectors, and after an information made by the academic councils, the grand master, after having consulted with the council of the University, can cause the closing of the institutions and schools in which there shall have been discovered serious abuses and principles contrary to those which the University professes.

.   .   .   .   .   .

107. Measures shall be taken by the University in order that the art of instructing in reading, writing, and the first principles of arithmetic in the primary schools shall henceforth not be exercised except by masters sufficiently enlightened to impart readily and accurately these fundamental acquirements necessary for all men.

108. For that purpose there shall be established under the care of each academy, and within the precincts of the colleges or the *lycées,* one or several normal classes, for the purpose of training masters for the primary schools. The most suitable methods for improving the art of teaching reading, writing, and cyphering shall be set forth there.

.   .   .   .

Title XVI. Of the Costumes.

128. The common costume for all the members of the University shall be the black coat with a palm embroidered in blue silk upon the left part of the breast.

129. The regents and professors shall give their lectures in black tamine robes. Over the robe and upon the left shoulder shall be placed the shoulder knot, which shall vary in color according to the faculties, and in braiding only according to the grades.

.   .   .   .

Title XIX. General Provisions.

143. The Imperial University and its grand master, charged exclusively by us with the care of education and public instruction in all the empire, shall aim without respite to improve the instruction of all sorts, and to favor the composition of classical works; they shall particularly take care that the instruction of the sciences shall always be upon the level of acquired knowledge and that the spirit of system shall never arrest their progress.

144 and last. We reserve to ourselves to recognize and reward in a particular manner the great services which may be rendered by the members of the University for the instruction of our peoples; and also to reform, and that by decrees taken in our council, every decision, rule, or act emanating from the council of the University or the grand master, whenever we shall deem it useful for the good of the state.

66. Documents upon the Consulate for Life.

The first four of these documents show how the ten years' consulate was transformed into a life consulate. The enumeration of reasons in document B also shows something of the popular estimate put upon Napoleon's achievements. Document E was in fact a new constitution, being often called the Constitution of the Year X. It should be compared with the Constitution of the Year VIII (No. 58). The precise changes effected in all the more important institutions and methods for carrying on the government should be carefully noted.

REFERENCES. *Cambridge Modern History*, IX, 19; Fournier, *Napoleon*, 238-241; Rose, *Napoleon*, I, 283-305; Sloane, *Napoleon*, II, Ch. XXII; Lanfrey, *Napoleon*, II, 225-238; Lavisse and Rambaud, *Histoire générale*, IX, 24-30; Aulard, *Révolution française*, 748-758; Jaurès, *Histoire socialiste*, VI, 166-172.

A. Declaration of the Tribunate. May 6, 1802 (16 Floréal, Year X). *Moniteur*, May 7, 1802 (17 Floréal, Year X).

The Tribunate expresses the wish that there should be given to General Bonaparte, First Consul of the Republic, a striking token of national recognition.

The Tribunate orders that this wish shall be addressed by a messenger of state to the Conservative Senate, the Legislative Body and the government.

B. Re-election by the Senate. May 8, 1802 (18 Floréal, Year X.) *Moniteur,* May 11, 1802 (21 Floréal, Year X).

The Senate, assembled in the number of members prescribed by article 90 of the constitutional act;

In view of the message of the consuls of the Republic transmitted by three orators of the government, and relative to the peace of France with England;

After having heard its special commission, charged by its order of the 16th of this month to present to it views upon the testimonial of national recognition which the Senate has in mind to give to the First Consul of the Republic;

Considering that, under the circumstances in which the Republic finds itself, it is the duty of the Conservative Senate to employ all the means which the constitution has put in its power in order to give to the government the stability which alone multiplies resources, inspires confidence abroad, establishes credit within, reassures allies, discourages secret enemies, turns away the scourge of war, permits the enjoyment of the fruits of peace, and leaves to wisdom time to carry out whatever it can conceive for the welfare of a free people;

Considering, moreover, that the supreme magistrate who, after having so many times led the republican legions to victory, delivered Italy, triumphed in Europe, in Africa, in Asia, and filled the world with his renown, has preserved France from the horrors of anarchy which were menacing it, broken the revolutionary sickle, dispersed the factions, extinguished civil discords and religious disturbances, added to the benefits of liberty those of order and of security, hastened the progress of enlightenment, consoled humanity, and pacified the continent and the seas, has the greatest right to the recognition of his fellow citizens, as well as the admiration of posterity;

That the wish of the Tribunate, which has come to the Senate in the sitting of this day, under these circumstances, can be regarded as that of the French nation;

That the Senate cannot express more solemnly to the First Consul the recognition of the nation than in giving him a striking proof of the confidence which he has inspired in the French people;

Considering, finally, that the second and the third consuls

have worthily seconded the glorious labors of the First Consul of the Republic;

In consequence of all these motives, and the votes having been collected by secret ballot;

The Senate decrees as follows:

1. The Conservative Senate, in the name of the French people, testifies to its recognition of the consuls of the Republic.

2. The Conservative Senate re-elects Citizen Napoleon Bonaparte, First Consul of the French Republic for the ten years which shall immediately follow the ten for which he has been appointed by article 39 of the constitution.

3. The present senatus-consultum shall be transmitted by a message to the Legislative Body, the Tribunate, and the Consuls of the Republic.

C. Message of the First Consul to the Senate. May 9, 1802 (19 Floréal, Year X). *Moniteur*, May 11, 1802 (21 Floréal, Year X).

Senators:

The honorable proof of esteem contained in your resolution of the 18th will ever be graven upon my heart.

The suffrage of the people has invested me with the supreme magistracy. I should not think myself assured of their confidence, if the act which retained me there was not again sanctioned by their suffrage.

In the three years which have just passed away fortune has smiled upon the Republic; but fortune is inconstant, and how many men whom it had crowned with its favors have lived on some years too many.

The interest of my glory and that of my happiness would seem to have marked the termination of my public life at the moment in which the peace of the world is proclaimed.

But the glory and happiness of the citizen must be silent, when the interest of the state and the public well-being summon him.

You deem that I owe to the people a new sacrifice: I will make it, if the wish of the people commands what your suffrage authorises.

Signed,   BONAPARTE.

D.   Order of the Consuls. May 10, 1802 (20 Floréal, Year X). *Moniteur,* May 11, 1802 (21 Floréal, Year X).

The consuls of the Republic, upon the reports of the ministers, the Council of State having been heard;

In view of the act of the Conservative Senate of the 18th of this month;

The message of the First Consul to the Conservative Senate, by date of yesterday, the 19th;

Considering that the resolution of the First Consul is a striking homage rendered to the sovereignty of the people; that the people, consulted upon their dearest interests, ought not to know any other limits than their own interests, orders as follows:

1.   The French people shall be consulted upon this question:

Shall Napoleon Bonaparte be Consul for life?

2.   There shall be opened in each commune registers, in which the citizens shall be invited to express their wish upon that question.

.   .   .   .

E.   Senatus-Consultum. August 4, 1802 (16 Thermidor, Year X). Duvergier, *Lois,* XIII, 262-267.

Title I.

1.   Each justice of the peace jurisdiction has a cantonal assembly.

2.   Each communal district or sub-prefecture district has a district electoral college.

3.   Each department has a department electoral college.

Title II.   Of the Cantonal Assemblies.

4.   The cantonal assembly consists of all the citizens domiciled in the canton and who are enrolled there upon the district communal list.

Counting from the date at which, by the terms of the constitution, the communal lists must be renewed, the cantonal assembly shall be composed of all the citizens domiciled in the canton and who there enjoy the rights of citizenship.

5.   The First Consul appoints the president of the cantonal assembly.

His functions continue for five years: he can be reappointed indefinitely.

He is assisted by four tellers, two of whom are the eldest and the other two the most highly taxed of the citizens having the right to vote in the assembly of the canton.

The president and the four tellers appoint the secretary.

6. The cantonal assembly divides itself into sections in order to perform the operations which belong to it.

At the first meeting of each assembly its organization and forms shall be determined by a regulation issued by the government.

7. The president of the cantonal assembly appoints the presidents of the sections.

Their functions terminate with each sectional assembly.

They are each assisted by two tellers, one of whom is the eldest, and the other the most highly taxed of the citizens having the right to vote in the section.

8. The cantonal assembly selects two citizens from whom the First Consul chooses the justice of the peace of the canton.

It likewise selects two citizens for each vacant place of substitute justice of the peace.

9. The justices of the peace and their substitutes are appointed for ten years.

10. In cities of five thousand souls, the cantonal assembly presents two citizens for each of the places in the municipal council. In cities in which there are several justices of the peace or several cantonal assemblies, each assembly shall likewise present two citizens for each place in the municipal council.

11. The members of the municipal councils are taken by each cantonal assembly from the list of the one hundred largest tax-payers of the canton. This list shall be drawn up and printed by order of the prefect.

12. The municipal councils are renewed by half every ten years.

13. The First Consul chooses the mayors and deputies within the municipal councils; they are in office for five years: they can be reappointed.

14. The cantonal assembly appoints to the district electoral college the number of members assigned to it in ac-

cordance with the number of citizens of which it is composed.

15. It appoints to the department electoral college, out of a list to be spoken of hereafter, the number of members allowed to it.

16. The members of the electoral colleges must be domiciled in their respective districts and departments.

17. The government convokes the cantonal assemblies, and determines the time of their duration and the purpose of their meeting.

Title III. Of the Electoral Colleges.

18. The district electoral colleges have one member per five hundred inhabitants domiciled in the district.

Nevertheless, the number of members cannot exceed two hundred nor be less than one hundred and twenty.

19. The department electoral colleges have one member per thousand inhabitants domiciled in the department; nevertheless, these members cannot exceed three hundred nor be less than two hundred.

20. The members of the electoral colleges are for life.

21. If a member of an electoral college is denounced to the government as being implicated in some act prejudicial to honor or to the fatherland, the government summons the college to express its opinion; there must be three-fourths of the votes in order to cause a denounced member to lose his place in the college.

22. Places in the electoral college are lost for the same causes which entail loss of citizenship.

They are also lost when, without legitimate excuse, one has not participated in three successive meetings.

23. The First Consul appoints, at each session, the presidents of the electoral colleges.

The president alone has the policing of the electoral college when it is assembled.

24. The electoral colleges appoint, at each session, two tellers and a secretary.

25. In order to provide for the formation of the department electoral colleges, there shall be prepared in each department, under orders of the minister of finances, a list of the six hundred citizens most highly rated upon the land,

personal property, and sumptuary tax-rolls and upon the roll of licenses.

There is added to the amount of the tax in the domicile of the department that which can be proven to have been paid in the other parts of the territory of France and its colonies.

This list shall be printed.

26. The cantonal assembly shall take from this list the members whom it must appoint to the electoral college of the department.

27. The First Consul can add to the district electoral college ten members taken from among the citizens belonging to the Legion of Honor, or who have rendered the services.

He can add to each department electoral college twenty citizens, ten of them taken from among the thirty largest taxpayers of the department, and the other ten from among the members of the Legion of Honor or the citizens who have rendered services.

For these appointments he is not subject to the fixed periods.

28. The district electoral colleges present to the First Consul two citizens domiciled in the district for each vacant place in the district council.

At least one of the citizens must be taken from outside of the college which presents him.

The district councils are renewed by thirds every five years.

29. The district electoral colleges present at each meeting two citizens to make part of the list from which the members of the Tribunate must be chosen.

At least one of these citizens must necessarily be taken from outside of the college which presents him.

Both can be taken from the outside of the department.

30. The department electoral colleges present to the First Consul for each vacant place in the general council of the department two citizens domiciled in the department.

At least one of these citizens must necessarily be taken from outside of the electoral college that presents him.

The general councils of the department are renewed by thirds every five years.

31. The department electoral colleges present at each

meeting two citizens in order to form the list from which the members of the Senate are appointed.

At least one must necessarily be taken from outside the college which presents him; and both can be taken from outside the department.

They must have the age and qualifications required by the constitution.

32. The department and district electoral colleges each present two citizens domiciled in the department in order to form the list from which the members of the deputation in the Legislative Body must be appointed.

One of these citizens must necessarily be taken from outside the college that presents him.

There must be three times as many different candidates upon the list formed by the union of the presentations of the department and district electoral colleges as there are vacant places.

33. One can be a member of a communal council and of a district or department electoral college.

One cannot be at the same time a member of a district college and a department college.

34. The members of the Legislative Body and of the Tribunate cannot be present at the meetings of the electoral college to which they belong. All other public functionaries have the right to be present and to vote there.

35. No cantonal assembly proceeds to make appointments for the places which belong to it in an electoral college, except when these places are reduced to two-thirds.

36. The electoral colleges assemble only in virtue of an act of convocation issued by the government, and in the place which is assigned to them.

They cannot engage in any operations except those for which they are convoked, nor continue their sittings beyond the term fixed by the act of convocation.

If they exceed these limits the government has the right to dissolve them.

37. The electoral colleges cannot directly or indirectly, under any pretext whatever, correspond with each other.

38. The dissolution of an electoral body makes necessary the renewal of all its members.

Title IV. Of the Consuls.

39. The consuls are for life.

They are members of the Senate, and preside over it.

40.· The second and third consuls are appointed by the Senate upon the presentation of the first.

41. For that purpose, when one of the two places becomes vacant, the First Consul presents to the Senate a first choice; if he is not appointed, he presents a second; if the second is not accepted, he presents a third who is necessarily appointed.

42. When the First Consul thinks it seasonable, he presents a citizen to succeed him after his death, in the form indicated by the preceding article.

43. The citizen appointed to succeed the First Consul takes on oath to the Republic at the hands of the First Consul, assisted by the second and third consuls, in the presence of the Senate, the ministers, the Council of State, the Legislative Body, the Tribunate, the tribunal of cassation, the archbishops, the bishops, the presidents of the appellate tribunals, the presidents of the electoral colleges, the presidents of the cantonal assemblies, the grand officers of the Legion of Honor, and the mayors of the twenty-four principal cities of the Republic.

The secretary of state prepares the record of the taking of the oath.

44. The oath is thus expressed:

"I swear to maintain the constitution, to respect liberty of conscience, to oppose a return to feudal institutions, never to make war except for the defence and glory of the Republic, and to employ the authority with which I shall be invested only for the good of the people, from whom and for whom I shall have received it."

45. Having taken the oath, he takes a seat in the Senate immediately next to the Third Consul.

46. The First Consul can deposit in the archives of the government his opinion upon the appointment of his successor, in order to be presented to the Senate after his death.

47. In that case he summons the second and third consuls, the ministers, and the presidents of the sections of the Council of State.

In their presence he transfers to the secretary of state the paper, sealed with his seal, in which his opinion is contained.

This paper is attested by all those who are present at the act.

The secretary of state deposits it in the archives of the government in the presence of the ministers and the presidents of the sections of the Council of State.

48. The First Consul can withdraw his deposit, observing the formalities prescribed in the preceding article.

49. After the death of the First Consul, if his opinion remains on deposit, the paper which contains it is withdrawn from the archives of the government by the secretary of state, in the presence of the ministers and presidents of the sections of the Council of State. The integrity and authenticity of it is recognized in the presence of the second and third consuls. It is forwarded to the Senate with a message of the government, together with the dispatch of the records which have established its deposit, authenticity, and integrity.

50. If the person presented by the First Consul is not appointed, the second and third consuls each present one: in case of non-appointment, they each present another, and one of the two is necessarily appointed.

51. If the First Consul has not left any presentation, the second and third consuls make their separate presentations; one first and one second; and if neither of them obtains the appointment, a third. The Senate necessarily appoints from the third.

52. In any case the presentations and the appointment must be consummated within the twenty-four hours which shall follow the death of the First Consul.

53. The law fixes for the life of each First Consul the list of the expenses of the government.

Title V. Of the Senate.

54. The Senate regulates by an organic senatus-consultum:

1st. The constitution of the colonies:

2d. All which has not been provided for by the constitution and which is necessary for its operation:

3d. It interprets the articles of the constitution which give rise to different interpretations.

55. The Senate by the decrees entitled senatus-consulta:

1st. Suspends for five years the functions of juries ·in the departments in which that measure is necessary;

2d. Declares, when circumstances require it, the departments that are outside of the constitution;

3d. Determines the time within which the persons arrested in virtue of article 46 of the constitution must be brought before the tribunals, when they have not been within ten days after their arrest;

4th. Annuls the judgments of the tribunals when they are injurious to the security of the state;

5th. Dissolves the Legislative Body and the Tribunate;

6th. Appoints the consuls.

56. The organic senatus-consulta and the senatus-consulta are considered by the Senate, upon the initiative of the government.

A simple majority suffices for the senatus-consulta; there must be two-thirds of the votes of the members present for an organic senatus-consultum.

57. The proposals for senatus-consulta, made in consequence of articles 55 and 56, are discussed in a privy council, composed of the consuls, two ministers, two senators, two councillors of state, and two grand officers of the Legion of Honor.

The First Consul designates at each sitting the members who shall compose the privy council.

58. The first council ratifies treaties of peace and alliance after having taken the opinion of the privy council.

Before promulgating them, he gives notice of them to the Senate.

59. The decree of appointment of a member of the Legislative Body, the Tribunate, and the tribunal of cassation is entitled *arrêté*.

60. The decrees of the Senate relative to its police and its internal administration are entitled *délibérations*.

61. In the course of the year XI appointments shall be made of the forty citizens to complete the number of the eighty senators fixed by article 15 of the constitution.

These appointments shall be made by the Senate, upon the presentation of the First Consul, who, for this presentation and for the further presentations within the number of eighty, takes three persons from the list of citizens prepared by the electoral colleges.

62. The members of the grand council of the Legion of

Honor are members of the Senate, whatever may be their
ages.

63. The First Consul can, in addition, appoint to the
Senate without previous presentation by the department electoral colleges, citizens distinguished by their services, and their
talents, on condition, nevertheless, that they shall be of the
age required by the constitution, and that the number of senators shall in no case exceed one hundred and twenty.

64. The senators can be consuls, ministers, members of
the Legion of Honor, inspectors of public instruction, and
employees in extraordinary and temporary missions.

The Senate appoints each year two of its members to fill
the functions of secretaries.

65. The ministers have seats in the Senate, but without
deliberative voice unless they are senators.

Title VI. Of the Councillors of State.

66. The councillors of state shall never exceed the number of fifty.

67. The Council of State is divided into sections.

68. The ministers have rank, seats and deliberative voice
in the Council of State.

Title VII. Of the Legislative Body.

69. Each department shall have in the Legislative Body a
number of members proportionate to the extent of its population, in conformity with the appended table.

70. All members of the Legislative Body belonging to the
same deputation are appointed at the same time.

71. The departments of the Republic are divided into five
series, in conformity with the appended table.

72. The present deputies are classed in the five series.

73. They shall be renewed in the year to which shall belong the series in which the department shall be placed to
which they shall have been attached.

74. Nevertheless, the deputies who have been appointed
in the year X shall complete their five years.

75. The government convokes, adjourns and prorogues
the Legislative Body.

Title VIII. Of the Tribunate.

76. Dating from the Year XIII, the Tribunate shall be reduced to fifty members.

Half of the fifty shall retire every third year. Until this reduction, the retiring members shall not be replaced.

The Tribunate is divided into sections.

77. The Legislative Body and the Tribunate are renewed in their whole membership when the Senate has decreed their dissolution.

Title IX. Of Justice and the Tribunals.

78. There is a high-judge minister of justice.

79. He has a distinguished place in the Senate and the Council of State.

80. He presides over the tribunal of cassation and the tribunals of appeal, when the government thinks it desirable.

81. He has the right of surveillance and reproof over the tribunals, the members who compose them, and the justices of the peace.

82. The tribunal of cassation, presided over by him, has the right of censure and discipline over the tribunals of appeal and the criminal tribunals: it can, for grave cause, suspend the judges from their functions, and cite them before the high judge, in order to there render account of their conduct.

83. The tribunals of appeal have the right of surveillance over the civil tribunals of their jurisdiction, and the civil tribunals over the justices of the peace of their district.

84. The commissioner of the government to the tribunal of cassation supervises the commissioners to the tribunals of appeal and the criminal tribunals.

The commissioners to the tribunals of appeal supervise the commissioners to the civil tribunals.

85. The members of the tribunal of cassation are appointed by the Senate, upon the presentation of the First Consul.

The First Consul presents three persons for each vacant place.

Title X. Right of Pardon.

86. The First Consul has the right to pardon.

He exercises it after having heard in a privy council the high-judge, two ministers, two senators, two councillors of state, and two judges of the tribunal of cassation.

[The appended tables are omitted.]

67. Law for Organizing the Legion of Honor.

May 19, 1802 (29 Floréal, Year X). Duvergier, *Lois,* XIII, 199-200.

This law created one of the most enduring and characteristic of the institutions of Napoleon. It still exists and membership is highly prized. The provisions in relation to the admission of members and the oath of the legion should be particularly noticed.

REFERENCES. *Cambridge Modern History,* IX, 19-20 ; Rose, *Napoleon,* I, 262-265 ; Sloane, *Napoleon,* II, 158-159 ; Lanfrey, *Napoleon,* II, 231-234 ; Lavisse and Rambaud, *Histoire générale,* IX, 31-32.

Title I.   Creation and Organization of the Legion of Honor.

1. In fulfillment of article 87 of the constitution, concerning military rewards, and in order also to reward civil services and virtues, there shall be formed a Legion of Honor.

2. This legion shall be composed of a grand council or administration and fifteen cohorts, each of which shall have its own headquarters.

3. National lands providing two hundred thousand francs of income shall be appropriated for each cohort.

4. The grand council of administration shall be composed of seven grand officers, to wit: the three consuls, and four other members, one of whom shall be appointed from among the senators by the Senate, another from among the members of the Legislative Body by the Legislative Body, another from among the members of the Tribunate by the Tribunate, and, lastly, one from among the councillors of state by the Council of the State. The members of the grand council of administration shall retain during their lives the title of grand officer, even though they may be replaced as the result of new elections.

5. The First Consul is *ex-officio* head of the Legion and president of the grand council of administration.

6. Each cohort shall be composed of seven grand officers, twenty commandants, thirty officers, and three hundred and fifty legionaries.

Memberships in the legion are for life.

7. There shall be appropriated for each grand officer five thousand francs;

For each commandant, two thousand francs;

For every officer, a thousand francs;

For each legionary, two hundred and fifty francs.

These stipends shall be taken from the lands appropriated for each cohort.

8. Each person admitted to the legion shall swear upon his honor to devote himself to the service of the Republic, to the preservation of its territory in its integrity, to the defence of its government, its laws and the properties which they have consecrated; to combat with all the means that justice, reason and the laws authorise, every undertaking having a tendency to re-establish the feudal régime, or to reproduce the titles and qualties which were symbolical of it; lastly, to assist with all his power in the maintenance of liberty and equality.

9. There shall be established in each head-quarters of a cohort a hospital and dwellings to receive either the members of the legion whose age, infirmities or wounds may have made it impossible for them to serve the state, or the military men who, after having been wounded in the war for liberty, may find themselves in need.

Title II. Composition.

1. All military men who have received arms of honor are members of the legion.

The military men who have rendered important services to the state in the war for liberty;

The citizens who by their knowledge, their talents or their virtues, have contributed to the establishment or defence of the principles of the Republic, or have made justice or the public administration loved and respected shall be eligible for appointment.

2. The grand council of administration shall appoint the members of the legion.

3. During the ten years of peace which shall follow the

first formation, the places which become vacant shall remain vacant to the extent of a tenth, and in succession to the extent of a fifth. These places shall be filled only at the end of the first campaign.

4. In times of war there shall be no appointments to vacant places except at the end of each campaign.

5. In times of war distinguished acts shall furnish a title for all the grades.

6. In times of peace one must have had twenty-five years of military service in order to be appointed a member of the legion; the years of service in time of war shall count double and each campaign of the last war shall count for four years.

7. Great services rendered to the state in legislative functions, diplomacy, administration, justice or the sciences, shall also be titles for admission, provided the person who shall have rendered them has made part of the national guard of the place of his domicile.

8. After the first organization, no one can be admitted into the legion who has not performed his functions for twenty-five years with the requisite distinction.

9. After the first organization, no one can advance to a higher grade except after having passed through the lower grade.

10. The details of the organization shall be determined by the public regulations of administration: they must be made by 1 Vendémiaire, Year XII, and that time passed. nothing in them can be changed except through laws.

68. Law for Re-establishing Slavery in the French Colonies.

May 20, 1802 (30 Floréal, Year X). Duvergier, *Lois,* XIII, 208.

During the interval between the peace of Amiens and the renewal of the war with England, Napoleon was engaged upon a vast design for the restoration of the once extensive colonial empire of France. His plan included the establishment of French colonies in America, India and Australia. This law was intended to promote the first step towards the realization of the American branch of the scheme, the re-establishment of French authority in San Domingo. It had precisely the opposite effect.

REFERENCES. Rose. *Napoleon,* I, Ch. xv; Henry Adams. *History of the United States,* I, Chs. XIII-XVI, *passim,* for Napoleon's colonial plans: *Cambridge Modern History*, IX, 419-422; Jaurès, *Histoire socialiste*, VI, 129-130, 176-177.

1. In the colonies restored to France in fulfillment of the treaty of Amiens of 6 Germinal, Year X, slavery shall be maintained in conformity with the laws and regulations in force prior to 1789.

2. The same shall be done in the other French colonies beyond the Cape of Good Hope.

3. The trade in the blacks and their importation into the said colonies shall take place in conformity with the laws and regulations existing prior to the said date of 1789.

4. Notwithstanding all previous laws, the government of the colonies is subject for ten years to the regulations which shall be made by the government.

69. Declaration of France upon the Reorganization of Germany.

August 18, 1802. De Clercq, *Traités*, I, 596-603.

The reorganization of Germany through the *recez* adopted by the diet at Ratisbon on March 24, 1803, was substantially along the lines dictated by Napoleon in this document. The length of the passage containing the suggested changes has made necessary its omission; the chief feature was the elimination of the ecclesiastical princes, nearly all of the city republics, and the knights of the Empire, through the transfer of their territories to other states or princes who had lost possessions in the countries which France had revolutionized. The portion here given shows something of the circumstances which made possible the intervention of France and the manner in which the transaction was officially represented.

REFERENCES. Fyffe, *Modern Europe*, I, 247-257 (Popular ed., 166-173); *Cambridge Modern History*, IX, 91-95; Fournier, *Napoleon*, 257-262; Sloane, *Napoleon*, II, 169-171; Lavisse and Rambaud, *Histoire générale*, IX, 67-69; Jaurès, *Histoire socialiste*, VI, 174-175.

The First Consul of the French Republic, being animated by the desire to contribute to the consolidation of the repose of the Germanic Empire, no method has appeared to him more suitable for obtaining this object of his solicitude than that of formulating in a plan of indemnity, as well adapted to respective convenience as circumstances have permitted, an arrangement calculated to produce that salutary result; and an agreement of views having been established in this matter between the First Consul of the French Republic and His Imperial Majesty of all the Russias, he [the First Consul] has

authorised the minister of foreign affairs to co-operate with
the minister plenipotentiary of His Imperial Majesty of Russia upon the most suitable means of applying the principles
adopted regarding these indemnifications for the different
demands of the interested parties. The result of this effort
having obtained his approval, he has ordered the undersigned
to bring it to the knowledge of the diet of the Empire by the
present declaration, a measure to which the First Consul of
the French Republic, as well as His Imperial Majesty, have
been determined by the following considerations:

Article VII of the Treaty of Lunéville, having stipulated
that the hereditary princes, whose possessions were included
in the cession made to France of the countries situated upon
the left of the Rhine, should be indemnified, it has been
recognized that, in conformity with what had been formerly
decided upon at the congress of Rastadt, this indemnification
should be carried out by way of secularization; but, although
perfectly agreed upon the basis of indemnification, the interested states have continued so opposed in views upon the
distribution that it has appeared until now impossible to proceed to the execution of the aforesaid article of the treaty of
Lunéville.

And although the diet of the Empire has appointed a
commission especially charged to occupy itself with this important matter, it is well enough seen, by the obstacles which
its meeting encounters, how much the opposition of interests and the jealousy of pretensions place obstacles in the
way of that which the regulation of the indemnities in Empire derives from the spontaneous action of the Germanic
body.

It is this which has caused the First Consul of the Republic and His Majesty the Emperor of Russia to think that
it was fitting for two perfectly disinterested powers to present
their mediation and to offer for the deliberation of the Imperial diet a general plan of indemnity, drawn up according
to calculations of the most rigorous impartiality, and in
which an endeavor has been made both to compensate the
recognized losses and to preserve among the principal houses
in Germany the equilibrium which existed before the war.

In consequence, after having examined with the most
scrupulous attention, all the memoirs presented by the inter-

ested parties, as well upon the value of the losses as upon the demands for indemnity, they have remained agreed to propose that the indemnification should be accorded in the following manner:

. . . .

Such is the total of the arrangements and considerations which the undersigned has been ordered to present to the imperial diet, and upon which he believes that he ought to call for the most prompt and serious deliberation, expressing to it, in the name of his government, that the interest of Germany, the consolidation of the general peace and tranquility of Europe, demand that everything which concerns the regulation of the Germanic indemnities should be terminated within the space of two months.

Signed, Ch. Mau. Talleyrand.

70. Treaty with Spain.

October 19, 1803 (26 Vendémiaire, Year XII). De Clercq, *Traités,* II, 82-84.

Shortly after the renewal of the war with Great Britain, Napoleon made a series of treaties with the states dependent upon France. This document is typical of the series. It illustrates one of Napoleon's methods of supporting his wars and shows the character of the relationship existing between France and Spain.

References. Fournier, *Napoleon,* 268-269 ; Rose, *Napoleon,* I, 403-404 ; Sloane, *Napoleon,* II, 184 ; Lanfrey, *Napoleon,* II, 310-319.

The First Consul of the French Republic, in the name of the French people, and His Majesty the King of Spain, desiring to prevent the consequences of the misunderstanding to which the present difficulties between the two governments tend to give birth, and wishing at the same time to establish for the time of the present war, in a manner more conformable to circumstances and the interests of the two states, the interpretation of the treaties which unite them. . . .

. . . .

3. The First Consul consents that the obligations imposed upon Spain by the treaties which unite the two states shall be converted into a pecuniary subsidy of six millions per month, which shall be furnished by Spain to its ally, dating from the renewal of hostilites until the end of the present war.

. . . .

6. In consideration of the above stipulated clauses and during all the time in which they shall be carried out, France will recognize the neutrality of Spain, and it promises not to make opposition to any of the measures which may be taken with respect to the belligerent nations in virtue of the general principles and laws of neutrality.

7. His Most Catholic Majesty, having at heart to prevent all the difficulties which may arise with respect to the neutrality of his territory, in the event of a war between the French Republic and Portugal, binds himself to cause to be furnished by this latter power, and in virtue of a convention which shall be kept secret, the sum of one million per month . . . ; and in consideration of this subsidy, the neutrality of Portugal shall be consented to on the part of France.

. . . .

71. Constitution of the Year XII.

May 18, 1804 (28 Floréal, Year XII). Duvergier, *Lois*, XV, 1-12.

Through this measure the life consulate was transformed into the Empire. It should be studied in conjunction with the constitutions of the years VIII and X (Nos. 58 and 66 E), which it supplemented. Most of the institutions created by the two preceding constitutions were retained, but with important alterations which should be noticed. A number of new institutions also call for notice. The question of establishing the imperial dignity, but not the whole document, was submitted to popular vote.

REFERENCES. *Cambridge Modern History,* IX, 107-111; Fournier, *Napoleon,* 275-282; Rose, *Napoleon,* I, 429-432; Sloane, *Napoleon,* II, 203-207; Lanfrey, *Napoleon,* II, 398-402, 406-415; Lavisse and Rambaud, *Histoire générale,* IX, 35-37, 224-229; Aulard. *Révolution française,* 771-778; Jaurès, *Histoire socialiste,* VI, 195-204.

Title I.

1. The government of the French Republic is entrusted to an emperor, who takes the title of EMPEROR OF THE FRENCH.

Justice is administered in the name of the Emperor by the officers whom he appoints.

2. Napoleon Bonaparte, present First Consul of the Republic, is Emperor of the French.

Title II. Of the Inheritance.

3. The imperial dignity is hereditary in the direct natural

and legitimate lineage of Napoleon Bonaparte, from male to male, by order of primogeniture, and to the perpetual exclusion of women and their descendants.

4. Napoleon Bonaparte can adopt the children or grandchildren of his brothers, provided they have fully reached the age of eighteen years, and he himself has no male children at the moment of adoption.

His adopted sons enter into the line of his direct descendants.

If, subsequently to the adoption, male children come to him, his adopted sons can be summoned only after the natural and legitimate descendants.

Adoption is forbidden to the successors of Napoleon Bonaparte and their descendants.

5. In default of a natural and legitimate heir or an adopted heir of Napoleon Bonaparte, the imperial dignity is devolved and bestowed upon Joseph Bonaparte and his natural and legitimate descendants, by order of primogeniture, from male to male, to the perpetual exclusion of women and their descendants.

6. In default of Joseph Bonaparte and his male descendants, the imperial dignity is devolved and bestowed upon Louis Bonaparte, and his natural and legitimate descendants by order of primogeniture from male to male to the perpetual exclusion of women and their descendants.

7. In default of a natural and legitimate heir and of an adopted heir of Napoleon Bonaparte;

In default of natural and legitimate heirs of Joseph Bonaparte and his male descendants;

Of Louis Bonaparte and his male descendants;

An organic senatus-consultum, proposed to the Senate by the titular high dignitaries of the Empire and submitted for the acceptance of the people, appoints the emperor and controls in his family the order of inheritance, from male to male, to the perpetual exclusion of women and their descendants.

8. Until the moment in which the election of the new emperor is completed, the affairs of the state are directed by the ministers, who form themselves into a council of government and who make their decisions by a majority of

votes. The secretary of state keeps the register of the deliberations.

Title III. Of the Imperial Family.

9. The members of the imperial family within the order of inheritance bear the title of *French Princes*.

The eldest son of the Emperor bears that of *Prince Imperial*.

10. A senatus-consultum regulates the manner of the education of the French princes.

11. They are members of the Senate and of the Council of State when they have reached their eighteenth year.

12. They cannot marry without the authorisation of the Emperor.

The marriage of a French prince made without the authorisation of the Emperor entails deprivation of all right of inheritance, both for him who contracts it and for his descendants.

Nevertheless, if there is no child from this marriage, and it becomes dissolved, the prince who had contracted it recovers his rights of inheritance.

13. The documents which attest the birth, marriages, and decease of the members of the imperial family, are transmitted upon an order of the Emperor to the Senate, which orders their transcription upon its registers and their deposit in its archives.

14. Napoleon Bonaparte establishes by statutes, to which his successors are required to conform:

1st. The duties of the persons of both sexes, members of the imperial family, towards the Emperor;

2d. An organization of the imperial palace in conformity with the dignity of the throne and the grandeur of the nation.

15. The civil list remains as it has been regulated by articles 1 and 4 of the decree of May 26—June 1, 1791.

The French princes, Joseph and Louis Bonaparte, and, for the future, the younger natural and legitimate sons of the Emperor, shall be treated in conformity with articles 1, 10, 11, 12 and 13 of the decree of December 21, 1790—April 6, 1791.

The Emperor can fix the jointure of the Empress and assign it out of the civil list; his successors can change none of the dispositions which he shall have made in this respect.

16. The Emperor visits the departments: in consequence, imperial palaces are established at the four principal points of the Empire.

These palaces are designated and their appointments determined by a law.

Title IV. Of the Regency.

17. The Emperor is a minor until he has fully completed eighteen years; during his minority there is a regent of the Empire.

18. The regent must be at least fully twenty-five years of age.

Women are excluded from the regency.

19. The Emperor designates the regent from among the French princes who are of the age required by the preceding article, and in default of them, from among the titular grand dignitaries of the Empire.

20. In default of designation on the part of the Emperor, the regency is bestowed upon the prince the nearest in degree in the order of inheritance, who has fully completed twenty-five years.

21. If, the Emperor not having designated the regent, none of the French princes have fully completed twenty-five years, the Senate elects the regent from the titular grand dignitaries of the Empire.

22. If, by reason of the minority in age of the prince summoned to the regency in the order of heredity, it has been bestowed upon a more remote kinsman, or upon one of the titular grand dignitaries of the Empire, the regent who has entered upon his functions continues until the majority of the Emperor.

23. No organic senatus-consultum can be issued during the regency, nor before the end of the third year which follows the majority.

24. The regent exercises, until the majority of the Emperor, all the attributes of the imperial dignity.

Nevertheless, he cannot make appointments to the high dignities of the Empire, nor to the places of the grand officers, which may be vacant at the time of the regency, or which may become vacant during the minority, nor use the prerogative reserved to the Emperor to raise citizens to the rank of senator.

He cannot dismiss the grand judge nor the secretary of state.

25. He is not personally responsible for the acts of his administration.

26. All the acts of the regency are in the name of the minor Emperor.

27. The regent does not propose any project of law or of senatus-consultum, nor adopt any rule of public administration until after he has taken the opinion of the council of regency, composed of the titular high dignitaries of the Empire.

He cannot declare war, nor sign treaties of peace, alliance, or commerce until after deliberation over it in the council of regency, whose members, for this case alone, have deliberative voice. The decision is by a majority of the votes; and if there is an equal division, it passes, according to the opinion of the regent.

The minister of foreign affairs takes a seat in the council of regency, when this council deliberates over matters relative to his department.

The grand judge minister of justice can be summoned there by order of the regent.

The secretary of state keeps the register of its deliberations.

28. The regency does not confer any right over the person of the minor Emperor.

29. The stipend of the regent is fixed at one-fourth of the sum of the civil list.

30. The guardianship of the minor Emperor is confided to his mother, and in her default, to the prince designated for that purpose by the predecessor of the minor Emperor.

In default of the mother of the minor Emperor and of a prince designated by the Emperor, the Senate confides the guardianship of the minor Emperor to one of the titular grand dignitaries of the Empire.

Neither the regent and his descendants nor women can be chosen for the guardianship of the minor Emperor.

31. In case Napoleon Bonaparte shall make use of the power conferred upon him by article 4, title II, the document of adoption shall be drawn up in the presence of the

titular grand dignitaries of the Empire, received by the secretary of state and transmitted immediately to the Senate in order to be transcribed upon its registers and deposited in its archives.

When the Emperor designates either a regent for the minority or a prince for the guardianship of a minor Emperor, the same formalities are observed.

The documents of designation, either of a regent for the minority or a prince for the guardianship of a minor Emperor, are revocable at will by the Emperor.

Every document of adoption, of designation or of revocation of designation, which shall not have been transcribed upon the registers of the Senate before the decease of the Emperor shall be null and void.

Title V. Of the Grand Dignitaries of the Empire.

32. The grand dignitaries of the Empire are these:
Grand elector,
Archchancellor of the Empire,
Archchancellor of state,
Archtreasurer,
Constable,
Grand admiral.

33. The titular grand dignitaries of the Empire are appointed by the Emperor.

They enjoy the same honors as the French princes and take rank immediately after them.

The date of their reception determines the rank which they respectively occupy.

34. The high dignitaries of the Empire are irremovable.

35. The titular grand dignitaries of the Empire are senators and councillors of state.

36. They form the grand council of the Emperor;

They are members of the privy council;

They compose the grand council of the Legion of Honor.

The present members of the grand council of the Legion of Honor preserve their titles, functions and prerogatives for the duration of their lives.

37. The Senate and the Council of State are presided over by the Emperor.

When the Emperor does not preside over the Senate or the Council of State, he designates the one of the titular high dignitaries of the Empire who must preside.

38. All the decrees of the Senate and of the Legislative Body are rendered in the name of the Emperor and are promulgated or published under the imperial seal.

39. The grand elector performs the functions of chancellor;

1st, For the convocation of the Legislative Body, the electoral colleges and the cantonal assemblies; 2d, for the promulgation of the senatus-consulta providing for the dissolution either of the Legislative Body or of the electoral colleges.

The grand elector presides in the absence of the Emperor when the Senate proceeds to the appointment of senators, legislators, and tribunes.

He can reside in the palace of the Senate.

He brings to the knowledge of the Emperor the claims formulated by the electoral colleges or the cantonal assemblies, for the preservation of their prerogatives.

When a member of an electoral college is denounced, in conformity with article 21 of the organic senatus-consultum of 16 Thermidor, Year X, as being involved in some act prejudicial to honor or the fatherland, the grand elector invites the college to express its opinion. He brings the opinion of the college to the knowledge of the Emperor.

The grand elector presents to the members of the Senate, the Council of State, the Legislative Body, and the Tribunate, the oath which they take at the hands of the Emperor.

He receives the oath of the presidents of the department electoral colleges and the cantonal assemblies.

He presents the solemn deputations of the Senate, Council of State, Legislative Body, Tribunate, and the electoral colleges when they are admitted to the audience of the Emperor.

40. The archchancellor of the Empire performs the functions of chancellor for the promulgation of the organic senatus-consulta and the laws.

He performs, likewise, those of chancellor of the imperial palace.

He is present at the annual report in which the high judge

minister of justice gives an account to the Emperor of the abuses which may have been introduced into the administration of either civil or criminal justice.

He presides over the high imperial court.

He presides over the united sections of the Council of State, and of the Tribunate, in conformity with article 95, title XI.

He is present at the celebration of the marriages and at the birth of the princes, at the coronation and at the obsequies of the Emperor. He signs the record which the secretary of state draws up.

He presents to the titular grand dignitaries of the Empire, the ministers and the secretary of state, the grand civil officers of the crown, and the first president of the court of cassation, the oath which they take at the hands of the Emperor.

He receives the oath of the members and of the bar of the court of cassation, and of the presidents and procureurs-general of the courts of appeal and the criminal courts.

He presents the solemn deputations and the members of the courts of justice admitted to the audience of the Emperor.

He signs and seals the commissions and warrants of the members of the courts of justice and of the ministerial officers; he seals the commissions and warrants of civil functions, administrative and other certificates which shall be designated in the regulation providing for the organization of the seal.

41. The archchancellor of state performs the functions of chancellor for the promulgation of treaties of peace and alliance and for the declarations of war.

He presents to the Emperor and signs the letters of credence and the ceremonial correspondence with the different courts of Europe, drawn up according to the forms of the imperial formulary of which he is the keeper.

He is present at the annual report in which the minister of foreign affairs gives an account to the Emperor of the political situation of the state.

He presents to the ambassadors and ministers of the Emperor at foreign courts the oath which they take at the hands of His Imperial Majesty.

He receives the oath of the resident *chargés d'affaires,*

secretaries of embassy and legation, commissioners-general and commissioners of commercial relations.

He presents the extraordinary ambassadors and ambassadors, and French and foreign ministers.

42. The archtreasurer is present at the annual report in which the ministers of finance and of the public treasury render to the Emperor the accounts of the receipts and expenditures of the state and express their views upon the needs of the finances of the Empire.

The accounts of the annual receipts and expenditures are endorsed with his signature before being presented to the Emperor.

He receives, every three months, the statement of the report of the national accounting, and every year the general result and the views for reform and improvement in the different parts of the accounting; he brings them to the knowledge of the Emperor.

He audits every year the ledger of the public debt.

He signs the warrants for the civil pensions.

He presides over the united sections of the Council of State and of the Tribunate, in conformity with article 95, title XI.

He receives the oath of the members of the national accounting, of the finance administrations, and of the principal agents of the public treasury.

He presents the deputations of the national accountants and of the finance administrations admitted to the audience of the Emperor.

43. The constable is present at the annual report in which the minister of war and the director of the war administration render account to the Emperor of the provisions taken to complete the system of defence of the frontiers, the maintenance, repair, and supplying of the posts.

He lays the first stone of the fortresses whose construction is ordered.

He is governor of the military schools.

When the Emperor does not in person transmit the flags to the corps of the army, they are sent to them in his name by the constable.

In the absence of the Emperor, the constable presides over the grand review of the imperial guard.

When a *général d'armée* is accused of an offence specified in the military penal code, the constable can preside over the council of war, which must give judgment.

He presents to the marshals of the Empire, the colonels-general, the inspectors-general, the general officers and the colonels of all arms, the oaths which they take at the hands of the Emperor.

He receives the oaths of the majors, and leaders of battalions and squadrons of all arms.

He installs the marshals of the Empire.

He presents the general officers and the colonels, majors, and leaders of battalions and squadrons, when they are admitted to the audience of the Emperor.

He signs the warrants of the army and those of the military pensioners of the State.

44. The grand admiral is present at the annual report in which the minister of the navy renders account to the Emperor of the condition of the naval forces, arsenals, and supplies.

He receives annually and presents to the Emperor the accounts of the marine invalids' fund.

When an admiral, vice-admiral, or rear-admiral commanding in chief a naval force is accused of an offence specified in the marine penal code, the grand admiral can preside over the court martial which shall give judgment.

He presents to the admirals, vice-admirals, rear-admirals, and captains of vessels the oath which they take at the hands of the Emperor.

He receives the oaths of the members of the council of prizes and the captains of frigates.

He presents the admirals, vice-admirals, rear-admirals, captains of vessels and frigates, and the members of the council of prizes, when they are admitted to the audience of the Emperor.

He signs the warrants of the officers of the naval forces and those of the marine pensioners of the state.

45. Each of the titular grand dignitaries of the Empire presides over a department electoral college.

The electoral college sitting at Brussels is presided over by the grand elector.

The electoral college sitting at Bordeaux is presided over by the archchancellor of the Empire.

The electoral college sitting at Nantes is presided over by the archchancellor of state.

The electoral college sitting at Lyon is presided over by the archtreasurer of the Empire.

The electoral college sitting at Turin is presided over by the constable.

The electoral college sitting at Marseilles is presided over by the grand admiral.

46. Each of the titular grand dignitaries of the Empire receives annually by way of fixed stipend two-thirds of the sum appropriated for the princes, in conformity with the decree of December 21, 1790.

47. A statute of the Emperor regulates the functions of the titular grand dignitaries of the Empire near the Emperor and determines their costumes in the grand ceremonies. The successors of the Emperor can deviate from this statute only by a senatus-consultum.

Title VI.   Of the Grand Officers of the Empire

48. The grand officers of the Empire are:

First, the marshals of the Empire, chosen from among the most distinguished generals.

Their number cannot exceed that of sixteen.

The marshals of the Empire who are senators are not part of this number.

Secondly, eight general inspectors and colonels-general of artillery and engineers, of cavalry troops and of the navy.

Thirdly, the grand civil officers of the crown, such as are instituted by the statutes of the Emperor.

49. The positions of the grand officers are irremovable.

50. Each of the grand officers of the Empire presides over an electoral college which is especially set aside for him at the moment of his appointment.

51. If, by an order of the Emperor or by any other cause whatsoever, a titular grand dignitary of the Empire or a grand officer happens to discontinue his functions, he preserves his title, his rank, his privileges, and half of his stipend: he loses these only by a judgment of the high imperial court.

Title VII. Of the Oaths.

52. Within the two years which follow his accession or his majority, the Emperor, accompanied by
The titular grand dignitaries of the Empire,
The ministers,
The grand officers of the Empire,
Takes oath to the French people upon the gospel, in the presence of:
The Senate,
The Council of State,
The Legislative Body,
The Tribunate,
The court of cassation,
The archbishops,
The bishops,
The grand officers of the Legion of Honor,
The national accountants,
The presidents of the courts of appeal,
The presidents of the electoral colleges,
The presidents of the cantonal assemblies,
The presidents of the consistories,
And the mayors of the thirty-six principal cities of the Empire.
The secretary of state prepares the record of the taking of the oath.

53. The oath of the Emperor is thus expressed:
"I swear to maintain the integrity of the territory of the Republic, to respect and cause to be respected the laws of the concordat and the liberty of worship, to respect and cause to be respected equality of rights, political and civil liberty, the irrevocability of the sales of the national lands; not to raise any impost, nor to establish any tax except in virtue of the law; to maintain the institution of the Legion of Honor; to govern in the sole view of the interest, the welfare and the glory of the French people."

54. Before beginning the exercise of his functions, the regent, accompanied by:
The titular grand dignitaries of the Empire,
The ministers,
The grand officers of the Empire,
Takes oath upon the gospel, and in the presence of

The Senate,

The Council of State,

The president and questors of the Legislative Body,

The president and the questors of the Tribunate,

And the grand officers of the Legion of Honor.

The secretary of state prepares the record of the taking of the oath.

55. The oath of the regent is expressed in these terms:

"I swear to administer the affairs of the state, in conformity with the constitutions of the Empire, the senatus-consulta and the laws; to maintain in all their integrity the territory of the Republic, the rights of the nation and those of the imperial dignity, and to deliver up to the Emperor, at the moment of his majority, the authority, the exercise of which is confided to me."

56. The titular grand dignitaries of the Empire, the ministers and the secretary of state, the grand officers and the members of the Senate, the Council of State, the Legislative Body, the Tribunate, the electoral colleges and the cantonal assemblies, take oath in these terms:

"I swear obedience to the constitutions of the Empire and fidelity to the Emperor."

The public, civil, and judicial functionaries and the officers and soldiers of the army and navy take the same oath.

Title VIII. Of the Senate.

57. The Senate is composed:

1st, Of the French princes who have reached their eighteenth year;

2d, Of the titular grand dignitaries of the Empire;

3d, Of eighty members appointed upon the presentation of the candidates chosen by the Emperor from the lists formed by the department electoral colleges;

4th, Of citizens whom the Emperor deems suitable to be raised to the dignity of senator.

In case the number of the senators shall exceed that which has been fixed by article 63 of the organic senatus-consultum of 16 Thermidor, Year X, provision shall be made for this by a law for the execution of article 17 of the senatus-consultum of 14 Nivôse, Year XI.

58. The president of the Senate is appointed by the Emperor and chosen from among the senators.

His functions continue one year.

59. He convokes the Senate upon an order issued of his own accord by the Emperor and upon the request either of the commissioners, which will be spoken of hereafter in articles 60 and 64, or of a senator, in conformity with the provisions of article 70, or of an officer of the Senate for the internal affairs of the body.

He gives an account to the Emperor of the convocations made upon the request of the commissions or of a senator, of their object, and of the results of the deliberation of the Senate.

60. A commission of seven members, appointed by the Senate and chosen within its own body, takes cognizance, upon the communication made to it by the ministers, of the arrests effected in conformity with article 46 of the constitution, when the persons arrested have not been brought before the tribunals within ten days after their arrest.

This commission is called the *senatorial commission of personal liberty*.

61. All persons arrested and not put on trial within ten days after their arrest, can apply directly, by themselves, their relatives, or their representatives, and by way of petition, to the senatorial commission of personal liberty.

62. When the commission considers that detention prolonged beyond ten days after arrest is not warranted by the interest of the state, it invites the minister who has ordered the arrest to cause the detained person to be put at liberty or to send him before the ordinary tribunals.

63. If, after three consecutive invitations, renewed within the space of one month, the detained person is not put at liberty nor sent before the ordinary tribunals, the commission requests a meeting of the Senate, which is convoked by the president and which renders, if there is need, the following declaration:

"There are strong presumptions that N———is arbitrarily detained."

Thereafter proceedings are in conformity with the provisions of article 112, title XIII, *Of the high imperial court.*

64. A commission of seven members, appointed by the

Senate and chosen from within its own body, is charged to watch over the liberty of the press.

Periodical works printed and distributed by subscription are not included within its powers.

This commission is called the *senatorial commission of the liberty of the press.*

65. Authors, printers, or publishers who believe that there is ground for complaint over restrictions placed upon the printing or circulation of a work can have recourse directly and by way of petition to the senatorial commission of the liberty of the press.

66. When the commission thinks that the restrictions are not warranted by the interest of the state, it invites the minister who has given the order to revoke it.

67. If, after three consecutive invitations renewed within the space of one month, the restrictions remain, the commission asks for a meeting of the Senate, which is convoked by the president and which renders, if there is need, the following declaration:

"There are strong presumptions that the liberty of the press has been violated."

After that, proceedings are in conformity with the provision of article 112, title XIII, *Of the high imperial court.*

68. One member of each of these senatorial commissions discontinues his functions every four months.

69. The projects of law decreed by the Legislative Body are transmitted to the Senate on the day of their adoption, and deposited in its archives.

70. Every decree rendered by the Legislative Body can be denounced to the Senate by a Senator:

1st, As tending to the re-establishment of the feudal régime; 2d, as contrary to the irrevocability of the sales of the national lands; 3d, as not having been deliberated upon in the forms prescribed by the constitutions of the Empire, the regulations and the laws; 4th, as constituting an attack upon the prerogatives of the imperial dignity and those of the Senate; without prejudice to the execution of articles 21 and 37 of the *acte* of the constitutions of the Empire of the date of 22 Frimaire, Year VIII.

71. The Senate, within the six days which follow the

adoption of the project of law, deliberating upon the report of a special commission, and after having heard three readings of the decree in three sittings held on different days, can express the opinion that *there is no need to promulgate the law.*

The president conveys to the Emperor the resolution of the Senate with a statement of the motives for it.

72. The Emperor, after having heard the Council of State, either declares by a decree his adherence to the resolution of the Senate, or causes the promulgation of the law.

73. Any law whose promulgation under that circumstance has not taken place before the expiration of the interval of ten days, can no longer be promulgated, unless it has been newly deliberated upon and adopted by the Legislative Body.

74. The entire operations of an electoral college and the partial operations which are relative to the presentation of the candidates to the Senate, Legislative Body, and Tribunate cannot be annulled on account of unconstitutionality, except by a senatus-consultum.

Title IX. Of the Council of State.

75. When the Council of State deliberates upon projects of law or regulations of public administration, two-thirds of the members of the council in ordinary service must be present.

The number of the councillors of state present cannot be less than twenty-five.

76. The Council of State is divided into six sections, to wit:

Section of legislation,

Section of the interior,

Section of the finances,

Section of war,

Section of the navy,

And section of commerce.

77. When a member of the Council of State has been carried for five years upon the list of the members of the council in ordinary service he receives a commission of councillor of state for life.

When he ceases to be carried upon the list of the Council

of State in ordinary or extraordinary service, he has a right to but one-third of the stipend of councillor of state.

He loses his title and his rights only by a judgment of the high imperial court, involving afflictive or infamous penalty.

Title X. Of the Legislative Body.

78. The retiring members of the Legislative Body can be re-elected without interval.

79. The projects of law presented to the Legislative Body are sent back to the three sections of the Tribunate.

80. The sittings of the Legislative Body are divided into ordinary sittings and committees of the whole.

81. The ordinary sittings are composed of the members of the Legislative Body, the orators of the Council of State, and the orators of the three sections of the Tribunate.

The committees of the whole are composed only of the members of the Legislative Body.

The president of the Legislative Body presides over the ordinary sittings and over the committees of the whole.

82. In ordinary sitting, the Legislative Body hears the orators of the Council of State and those of the three sections of the Tribunate, and votes upon the project of law.

In committee of the whole, the members of the Legislative Body discuss among themselves the advantages and disadvantages of the project of law.

83. The Legislative Body forms itself into committee of the whole:

1st. Upon the invitation of the president, for the internal affairs of the body;

2d. Upon a request made to the president and signed by fifty members present;

In these two cases the committee of the whole is secret, and the discussions shall not be printed nor divulged.

3d. Upon the request of the orators of the Council of State, especially authorised for that purpose.

In this case the committee of the whole is necessarily public.

No decision can be reached in the committees of the whole.

84. When the discussion in committee of the whole is closed, the decision is adjourned to the next day in ordinary sitting.

85. The Legislative Body, on the day when it must vote upon the project of law, hears, in the same sitting, the *résumé* which the orators of the Council of State offer.

86. The decision over a project of law cannot in any case be deferred more than three days beyond that which has been fixed for the closing of the discussion.

87. The sections of the Tribunate constitute the only commissions of the Legislative Body, which can form others only in the case provided for in article 113, title XIII, *Of the high imperial court.*

Title XI. Of the Tribunate.

88. The functions of the members of the Tribunate continue ten years.

89. The Tribunate is renewed by half every five years.

The first renewal shall take place for the session of the Year XVII, in conformity with the organic senatus-consultum of 16 Thermidor, Year X.

90. The president of the Tribunate is appointed by the Emperor out of a presentation of three candidates made by the Tribunate by secret ballot and a majority.

91. The functions of the president of the Tribunate continue two years.

92. The Tribunate has two questors.

They are appointed by the Emperor out of a triple list of candidates chosen by the Tribunate by secret ballot and a majority.

Their functions are the same as those assigned to the questors of the Legislative Body by articles 19, 20, 21, 22, 23, 24 and 25 of the organic senatus-consultum of 24 Frimaire, Year XII.

One of the questors is renewed each year.

93. The Tribunate is divided into three sections, to wit:
Section of legislation.
Section of the interior.
Section of the finances.

94. Each section forms a list of three of its members from whom the president of the Tribunate designates the president of the section.

The functions of the president of a section continue one year.

95. When the respective sections of the Council of State and the Tribunate ask to unite, the conferences take place under the presidency of the archchancellor of the Empire or of the archtreasurer, according to the nature of the matters to be examined.

96. Each section discusses separately and in sectional meeting, the projects of law which are transmitted to it by the Legislative Body.

Two orators of each of the three sections carry to the Legislative body the opinion of their section, and explain the grounds for it.

97. In no case can the projects of law be discussed by the Tribunate in general assembly.

It unites in general assembly, under the presidency of its president, for the exercise of its other attributes.

Title XII. Of the Electoral Colleges.

98. Whenever a department electoral college meets for the formation of the list of candidates for the Legislative Body, the lists of candidates for the Senate are renewed.

Each renewal renders the former presentations of no effect.

99. The grand officers, the commandants, and the officers of the Legion of Honor are members of the electoral college of the department in which they have their domicile, or of one of the departments for the cohort to which they belong.

The legionaries are members of the electoral college of their district.

The members of the Legion of Honor are admitted to the electoral college, of which they shall form part, upon the presentation of a certificate which is delivered to them for that purpose by the grand elector.

100. The prefects and the military commandants of the departments cannot be elected candidates for the Senate by the electoral colleges of the departments in which they exercise their functions.

Title XIII. Of the High Imperial Court.

101. A high imperial court takes cognizance:

1st. Of the personal offences committed by the members of the imperial family, the titular grand dignitaries of the

Empire, the ministers and the secretary of state, the grand officers, the senators, and the councillors of state;

2d. Of crimes, attempts, and conspiracies against the internal and external security of the state, the person of the Emperor and that of the heir presumptive of the Empire;

3d. Of *offences of responsibility of office* committed by the ministers and councillors of state especially charged with a part of the public administration;

4th. Of betrayals of trust and abuse of power, committed either by the captains-general of the colonies, the colonial prefects and commandants of French establishments outside of the continent, or by the administrators-general employed extraordinarily, or by the generals of the army or navy; without prejudice, in respect to these, of prosecutions by the military jurisdiction in the cases determined by the laws;

5th. Of the fact of disobedience of the generals of the army or navy who disregard their instructions;

6th. Of the peculations and squandering of which the prefects of the interior make themselves guilty in the exercise of their functions;

7th. Of the forfeitures and complaints of prejudice which may be incurred by a court of appeal or by a court of justice or by members of the court of cassation.

8th. Of denunciations on account of arbitrary detentions and of violations of the liberty of the press.

102. The seat of the high imperial court is in the Senate.

103. It is presided over by the archchancellor of the Empire.

If he is ill, absent, or lawfully prevented, it is presided over by another of the titular grand dignitaries of the Empire.

104. The high imperial court is composed of the princes, the titular grand dignitaries and grand officers of the Empire, the high judge minister of justice, sixty senators, the six presidents of the sections of the Council of State, fourteen councillors of state, and twenty members of the court of cassation.

The senators, the councillors of state and members of the court of cassation are appointed by order of seniority.

105. There is before the high imperial court a procureur-general, appointed for life by the Emperor.

He performs the duties of the public ministry, being assisted by three tribunes, appointed each year by the Legislative Body out of a list of nine candidates presented by the Tribunate, and of three magistrates whom the Emperor appoints, also each year, from among the officers of the courts of appeal and of criminal justice.

106. There is before the high imperial court a recorder-in-chief appointed for life by the Emperor.

107. The president of the high imperial court can never be challenged; he can abstain for legitimate reasons.

108. The high imperial court can act only upon proceedings instituted by the public ministry in the offences committed by those whose rank makes them subject to the jurisdiction of the imperial court; if there is a complaint, the public ministry becomes necessarily joint and prosecuting party, and proceeds as is required hereinafter.

The public ministry is likewise the joint and prosecuting party in cases of forfeiture or of complaint of prejudice.

109. The security magistrates and the jury directors are required to draw up and transmit, within the period of eight days, to the procureur-general before the high imperial court all the documents of the proceedings, when, in the offences whose reparation they seek, it happens either from the quality of the persons, or the title of the accusation, or from circumstances, that the matter belongs to the jurisdiction of the high imperial court.

Nevertheless, the security magistrates continue to collect the proofs and indications of the offence.

110. The ministers or the councillors of state charged with any part whatsoever of the public administration can be denounced by the Legislative Body, if they have given orders contrary to the constitutions and the laws of the Empire.

111. The Legislative Body can likewise denounce:

The captains-general of the colonies, the colonial prefects, the commandants of French establishments outside of the continent, the administrators-general, when they have betrayed their trusts or abused their authority;

The generals of the army or navy who have disobeyed their instructions;

The prefects of the interior who have made themselves guilty of squandering or of peculation.

112. The Legislative Body denounces likewise the ministers or agents of authority when there has been, on the part of the Senate, declaration of *strong presumptions of arbitrary detention* or *of violation of the liberty of the press.*

113. The denunciation of the Legislative Body cannot be decreed except upon the demand of the Tribunate, or upon the application of fifty members of the Legislative Body, who require a secret committee for the purpose of causing the selection, by way of ballot, of ten from among themselves to draw up the instrument of denunciation.

114. In either case, the request or the demand shall be made in writing, and signed by the president and the secretaries of the Tribunate, or by the ten members of the Legislative Body.

If it is directed against a minister or a councillor of state charged with a part of the public administration, it is communicated to him within the period of a month.

115. The denounced minister or councillor of state does not appear there to reply.

The Emperor appoints three councillors of state to repair to the Legislative Body on the appointed day, and to give information upon the facts of the denunciation.

116. The Legislative Body discusses in secret committee the facts included in the request or the demand, and it decides by means of the ballot.

117. The document of denunciation shall be circumstantially stated and signed by the president and secretary of the Legislative Body.

It is addressed by a message to the archchancellor of the Empire, who transmits it to the procureur-general before the high imperial court.

118. Betrayals of trust or abuses of power of the captainsgeneral of the colonies, the colonial prefects, the commandants of the establishments outside of the continent, and the administrators-general; the facts of disobedience on the part of the generals of the army or the navy to the instructions which have been given them; and the squanderings and extravagances of the prefects are denounced by the ministers, each within his department, to the officers charged with the public ministry.

If the denunciation is made by the high judge minister of

justice, he cannot assist nor take part in the judgments which
follow upon his denunciation.

119. In the cases prescribed by articles 110, 111, 112, and
118, the procureur-general notifies the archchancellor of the
Empire, within three days, that there is need for the high
imperial court to meet.

The archchancellor, after having taken the orders of the
Emperor, fixes within eight days the opening of the sittings

120. At the first sitting of the high imperial court it shall
pass upon its jurisdiction.

121. When there is a denunciation or a complaint, the
procureur-general in concert with the tribunes and the three
magistrate-officers of the bar, considers whether there is need
for prosecutions.

The decision belongs to him; one of the magistrates of
the bar can be charged by the procureur-general with the
direction of the prosecutions.

If the public ministry thinks that the complaint or the denunciation ought not to be admitted, it states the grounds
for the conclusions, upon which the high imperial court pronounces, after having heard the magistrate charged with the
report.

122. When the conclusions are adopted, the high imperial
court brings the affair to an end by a definitive judgment.

When they are rejected, the public ministry is required
to continue the prosecutions.

123. In the second of the cases provided for by the preceding article, and also when the public ministry considers
that the complaint or denunciation ought to be admitted, it
is required to prepare the document of accusation within
eight days, and to communicate it to the commissioner and
the alternate whom the archchancellor of the Empire appoints from among the judges of the court of cassation who
are members of the high imperial court. The functions of
this commissioner, and, in his default, of the alternate, consist of making the examination and the report.

124. The reporter or his alternate submits the document
of accusation to twelve commissioners of the high imperial
court, chosen by the archchancellor of the Empire, six from
among the senators and six from among the other members

of the high imperial court. The members chosen do not participate in the judgment of the high imperial court.

125. If the twelve commissioners conclude that there is need for accusation, the commissioner-reporter prepares an ordinance in conformity therewith, issues the warrants of arrest, and proceeds to the examination.

126. If the commissioners, on the contrary, think that there is no need for accusation, the matter is referred by the reporter to the high imperial court, which pronounces definitively.

127. The high imperial court cannot give judgment with less than sixty members. Ten of the whole number of members can be challenged, without assignment of cause, by the accused and ten by the public party. The decision is rendered by majority of the votes.

128. The proceedings and the judgment take place in public.

129. The accused have counsel; if they do not present any, the archchancellor of the Empire officially gives them some one.

130. The high imperial court can pronounce only the penalties provided by the penal code.

It pronounces, if there is need, condemnation to damages and civil interests.

131. When it acquits, it can put those who are acquitted under the surveillance or at the disposal of the high police of the state, for the time which it determines.

132. The judgments rendered by the high imperial court are not subject to any appeal;

Those which pronounce condemnation to an afflictive or infamous penalty can be executed only when they have been signed by the Emperor.

133. A special senatus-consultum contains the remainder of the arrangements relative to the organization and action of the high imperial court.

Title XIV. Of the Judicial Class.

134. The judgments of the courts of justice are entitled *arrêts*.

135. The presidents of the court of cassation, of the courts of appeal and of criminal justice, are appointed for life

by the Emperor, and can be chosen from outside of the courts over which they shall preside.

136. The tribunal of cassation assumes the denomination of *court of cassation.*

The tribunals of appeal assume that of *court of appeal;*

The criminal tribunals, that of *court of criminal justice.*

The president of the court of cassation and those of the courts of appeal divided into sections assume the title of *first president.*

The vice-presidents assume that of *presidents.*

The commissioners of the government before the court of cassation, the courts of appeal and the courts of criminal justice, take the title of *imperial procureurs-general.*

The commissioners of the government before the other tribunals assume the title of *imperial procureurs.*

Title XV.   Of the Promulgation.

137. The Emperor causes the sealing and promulgation of the organic senatus-consulta,

The senatus-consulta,

The *actes* of the Senate,

The laws.

The organic senatus-consulta, the senatus-consulta, and the *actes* of the Senate are promulgated at the latest on the tenth day following their emission.

138. Two original copies are made of each of the documents mentioned in the preceding article.

Both are signed by the Emperor, attested by one of the titular grand dignitaries, each according to their rights and powers, countersigned by the secretary of state and the minister of justice, and sealed with the great seal of the state.

139. One of these copies is deposited in the archives of the seal, and the other is transmitted to the archives of the public authority from which the *acte* emanated.

140. The promulgation is thus expressed:

"N. (the prenomen of the Emperor), by the grace of God and the constitutions of the Republic, Emperor of the French, to all present and to come, greeting:

"The Senate, after having heard the orators of the Council of State, has decreed *or* resolved, and we order as follows:

"(And if a law is in question) The Legislative Body has

rendered   .   .   .   (the date) the following decree, in conformity with the proposal made in the name of the Emperor,
and after having heard the orators of the Council of State
and of the sections of the Tribunate, the   .   .   .

"We command and require that the presents, invested with
the seals of the State and inserted in the Bulletin of the
Laws, be addressed to the courts, tribunals and administrative
authorities, in order that they may inscribe them in their
registers, observe them and cause them to be observed; and
the high judge minister of justice is charged to supervise the
publication of them."

141. The executory copies of the judgments shall be
drawn up as follows:

"N. (the prenomen of the Emperor), by the grace of God
and the constitutions of the Republic, Emperor of the French,
to all present and to come, greeting:

"The court of   .   .   .   or the tribunal of   .   .   .   (if
it is a tribunal of first instance), has rendered the following judgment:"

(Here follows the *arrêt* or judgment.)

"We command and require of all bailiffs upon this requisition to put the said judgment into execution; of our procureurs-general and our procureurs before the tribunals of
the first instance, to take it in hand; of all commanders and
officers of the public forces, to lend assistance when it shall
be legally required of them.

"In testimony whereof the present judgment has been
signed by the president of the court *or* the tribunal, and
by the bailiff."

Title XVI and Last

142. The following proposition shall be presented for the
acceptance of the people, in the forms prescribed by the
arrêté of 20 Floréal, Year X:

"The people desire the inheritance of the imperial dignity
in the direct, natural, legitimate and adoptive lineage of
Napoleon Bonaparte, and in the direct, natural, and legitimate
lineage of Joseph Bonaparte and of Louis Bonaparte, as is
regulated by the organic senatus-consultum of this day."

72.　Documents upon the Kingdom of Italy.

A deputation from the Italian Republic was present at the coronation of Napoleon as Emperor. These documents show how the occasion was utilized to transform the Italian Republic into the Kingdom of Italy and the manner in which the transaction was officially explained. The address to Napoleon and the second and more elaborate constitution mentioned in the document are in the *Moniteur* for March 18 and 31, 1805. The general character of the constitution can be made out from what is given in these documents.

REFERENCES. Fournier, *Napoleon,* 293-295 ; *Cambridge Modern History,* IX, 247 ; Lavisse and Rambaud, *Histoire générale,* IX, 431-432.

A. Constitutional Statute. March 17, 1805. *Moniteur,* March 19, 1805 (28 Ventôse, Year XIII).

The Council of State, in view of the unanimous desire of the united council and the deputation of the 15th instant:

In view of article 60 of the constitution, upon the constitutional initiative:

Decrees:

1. The emperor of the French, Napoleon I, is King of Italy.

2. The crown of Italy is hereditary in his direct and legitimate lineage. natural or adopted, from male to male, and to the perpetual exclusion of women and their descendants, provided, nevertheless, that his right of adoption cannot be extended over any other person than a citizen of the French Empire or of the Kingdom of Italy.

3. At the moment in which foreign armies shall have evacuated the state of Naples, the Ionian Islands, and the island of Malta, the Emperor Napoleon shall transmit the hereditary crown of Italy to one of his legitimate, natural or adopted children.

4. Dating from that time, the crown of Italy shall no longer be united with the crown of France upon the same head, and the successors of Napoleon First in the Kingdom of Italy shall be obliged to reside constantly upon the territory of the Italian Republic.

5. Within the course of the present year, the Emperor Napoleon, with the advice of the Council of State and the deputations of the electoral colleges, shall give to the Italian monarchy constitutions founded upon the same bases as

those of the French Empire, and upon the same principles
as the laws which he has already given to Italy.

Signed,   NAPOLEON.

Melzi, Mareschalchi, Caprara, Paradisi,
Fenaroli, Costabili, Luosi, Guiccardi.

B. Proclamation of the Kingdom. March 19, 1805, *Moniteur,* March 23, 1805 (2 Germinal, Year XIII).

The Council of State to the Peoples of the Kingdom of Italy.

A new State, created in the midst of political commotions, could not arrive all at once at a degree of perfection, consistency and strength, capable of assuring forever its existence, its repose and its prosperity. The genius of the founder, however gigantic, however bold it might be, was bound to pause before insurmountable obstacles, and his wisdom exhibited itself in not going beyond what circumstances would permit. Such was the lot of our republic, when, for the first time, it appeared suddenly upon the political horizon of Europe.

It took a great step, when in the comitia of Lyons, under the auspices and under the direction of its creator, it gave itself a new constitution and proclaimed for its head the man whose power and enlightenment could elevate it most rapidly to the degree of consideration and welfare to which its destinies would permit it to aspire.

But this second organization could be only provisional, for it was then necessary to conform to the circumstances of the time and to wait for the result of the lessons of experience. Soon, indeed, experience proved that many things were lacking for the completion of the edifice; that its foundations were not solid enough; and the conduct of affairs, however skillful, however unsullied might be the hands which guided them, was so slow and so embarrassed that one could not but perceive that the means which might be made use of were not sufficiently effective.

Finally, the great example given by France served to carry conviction to all minds, and its happy results apprised us that the time had come to imitate it.

From that time, therefore, the Council of State, charged especially by its institution with looking after the security of the republic, has occupied itself with the means to effect a change which not only was rendered necessary by the events that were occurring about us, but was commanded by a still more pressing interest, that of our preservation.

Already it had made known its thoughts and addressed its desires to the august head of the state; already it had submitted to him the result of its meditations, when it was invited to repair to Paris, in company with a numerous deputation of members of all the constituted bodies, in order to be present at the grand solemnity of the coronation of Napoleon, Emperor of the French.

It was then that, having occasion to observe still more closely the splendid labors of that prodigious genius, admiring the state of glory and prosperity to which, as in an instant, he had again raised the nation of which he is the head, seeing confidence, good order and tranquility reigning everywhere, the Council of State turned its thoughts to the fatherland, and, by a very natural feeling, coveted for that so dear fatherland the felicity of which it had come to contemplate the spectacle.

Furthermore, tormented incessantly by the thought of the great dangers to be feared, the Council of State could not conceal the fact that these were bound to be always united in order to menace the state. It could not forget either the designs or interests of certain other powers, and not reflect with dismay upon the inequality of the forces, the danger of a precarious situation, and the power of the charms of our climate.

It therefore concluded that it was its duty to take up again the work which it had commenced, and uniting with the deputies, all alike distinguished no less by the places which they occupy than by their zeal and their enlightenment, and all with one voice have expressed the opinion which they have believed the most useful and which without any doubt was already formed by all hearts.

This opinion, which was dictated by love and investigation and was made a duty by the good of the fatherland, has been favorably received. Napoleon is King of Italy. . . .

It is our interest which has induced Napoleon to yield to our wishes; and in fact he did not wish to assume the crown, and he will keep it only as long as our interest shall be the law for it to his wisdom and the affection which he bears us; . . .

Finally, as he has wished to restrict the duration of his power, he will limit and regulate the extent and usage of it. He will give us a constitution, which will guarantee us our religion, the integrity of our territory, equality of rights, political and civil liberty, the irrevocability of the sales of the national lands, the exclusive right to fill offices of the state; which will reserve to the law alone the power to establish imposts, and which, in a word, will consecrate and consolidate all the grand principles upon which the welfare of peoples and their tranquility are founded. Napoleon has made promise of this. Who can doubt that he does not intend, that he will not seek to fulfill his promise?

Such are the results of the constitutional statute joined to this proclamation.

. . .

73. Treaty of Alliance Between Great Britain and Russia.

April 11, 1805. F. Martens, *Traités de la Russie,* II, 433-448.

This treaty presents numerous points of interest. Among those calling for particular notice are: (1) as the basis of the Third Coalition it shows the character of the arrangements by which the coalitions against France were built up; (2) in its stipulations regarding the general peace it foreshadows the meeting of the congress of Vienna and some of its decisions.

REFERENCES. Fyffe, *Modern Europe,* I, 278-279 (Popular ed., 187-188); *Cambridge Modern History,* IX, 245-246; Fournier, *Napoleon,* 295-297; Rose, *Napoleon,* II, 7-8; Lanfrey, *Napoleon,* III, 4-8; Lavisse and Rambaud, *Histoire générale,* IX, 94-95; Jaurès, *Histoire socialiste,* VI, 208-210.

In the name of the most holy and indivisible Trinity.

His Majesty the Emperor of all the Russias and His Majesty the King of the United Kingdom of Great Britain and Ireland, animated by the desire to secure for Europe the peace, independence and well being of which it is deprived through the unmeasured ambition of the French government and the degree of influence out of all proportion which it tends to arrogate to itself, have resolved to employ all the means which are in their power, in order to obtain this salutary aim and to prevent the renewal of such distressing circumstances, and in consequence they have appointed to arrange and agree to the measures which their magnanimous intentions demand. . . .

1. As the state of suffering in which Europe finds itself demands prompt remedies, their Majesties the Emperor of all the Russias and the King of the United Kingdom of Great Britain and Ireland have agreed to consult upon the means of causing its cessation, without waiting for the case of further encroachments on the part of the French government. They have agreed, in consequence, to employ the most prompt and efficacious measures in order to form a general league of the states of Europe, and to bind them to accede to the present concert and to gather, for the purpose of fulfilling the aim, a force which, independent of that which His Britannic Majesty shall furnish, shall amount to 500,000 effective men and to employ them with energy in order to bring the French government by inclination or by force to assent to the re-establishment of the peace and the equilibrium of Europe.

2. This league shall have for its aim the accomplishment of that which is proposed by the present concert, to wit:

A. The evacuation of the country of Hanover and of the north of Germany.

B. The establishment of the independence of the republics of Holland and Switzerland.

C. The re-establishment of the King of Sardinia in Piedmont, with an enlargement as considerable as circumstances will permit.

D. The future security of the Kingdom of Naples and the entire evacuation of Italy, including therein the island of Elba, by the French forces.

E. The establishment of an order of things which guarantees effectively the security and independence of the different states and presents a solid barrier against future usurpations.

3. His Britannic Majesty, in order to co-operate effectively on his side for the happy purposes of the present concert, agrees to contribute to the common efforts by the employment of his land and sea forces, including his vessels suitable for the transport of troops, according to what shall be

determined upon in this respect in the general plan of operations. He will aid, besides, the different powers which shall accede thereto by subsidies, the amount of which shall correspond to the respective forces which it is decided to employ; and in order that these pecuniary aids may be apportioned in the manner most suitable for the general welfare, and to assist the powers in the measure of the efforts which they shall make to contribute to the common success, it is agreed, that these subsidies shall be furnished (except by special arrangements) in the proportion of 1,250,000 pounds sterling per annum for each hundred thousand men of regular troops and thus in proportion for a greater or less number, payable under the conditions specified below.

6. Their Majesties agree that in case a league is formed such as has been specified in article 1, they will not make peace with France except with the consent of all the powers which shall be parties in the said league, and in case the continental powers shall not recall their forces until the peace, His Britannic Majesty agrees to continue the payment of the subsidies for the entire duration of the war.

Separate Articles.

3. The high contracting parties are agreed that it enters into the aim of the present concert to procure for Holland and for Switzerland, according to circumstances, suitable enlargements, such as the former Austrian Low Countries, in whole or in part, for the first and Geneva and Savoy for the second.

They likewise agree that the arrangements which shall be made as the result of the war shall include in favor of Austria an augmentation of territory, such as is stipulated for it by its convention with the Emperor of all the Russias, and in favor of other states which may co-operate in the aim of the present concert acquisitions proportioned to their efforts for the common cause and compatible with the equilibrium of Europe.

6. His Majesty the Emperor of all the Russias and His

Majesty the King of the United Kingdom of Great Britain and Ireland, having been induced to establish an energetic concert between themselves only with a view to assure to Europe a stable and solid peace founded upon the principles of justice, equity and international law, which are constantly guiding them, have recognized the necessity of agreeing even at present upon various principles which they shall bring forward according to a previous agreement as soon as the fortunes of war shall furnish the necessity therefor.

These principles are not to interfere in any manner with the national will in France relative to the form of the government, nor in the other countries in which the combined armies may come to act; not to appropriate in advance of the peace any .of the conquests which may be made by one or the other of the belligerent parties, and to take possession of the cities and territories which may be wrested from·the common enemy only in the name of the county or state to which they belong by recognized right and in every other case in the name of all the members of the league.

Finally, to assemble at the end of the war a general congress, in order to discuss and settle upon the most precise foundations, what unfortunately has not been possible until now, the precepts of international law, and to assure the observance of them by the establishment of a federative system based upon the situation of the different states of Europe.

. . . .

74. Treaty of Pressburg.

December 26, 1805 (5 Nivôse, Year XIV). De Clercq, *Traités,* II, 145-151.

Austria became a member of the Third Coalition upon the terms outlined in No. 73. Ulm and Austerlitz forced her to withdraw and to accept the terms granted by Napoleon in his treaty. It should be compared with the treaties of Campo Formio and Lunéville (Nos. 55 and 62), and the altered position in which it left Austria should be carefully noted.

REFERENCES. Fyffe. *Modern Europe,* I. 299-300, 307-308 (Popular ed., 201-202, 206-207) : *Cambridge Modern History,* IX, 261-262 : Fournier, *Napoleon,* 318-324 ; Rose, *Napoleon,* II, 41-46 ; Sloane, *Napoleon,* II, 251-252 ; Lanfrey. *Napoleon,* III, 101-106 ; Lavisse and Rambaud, *Histoire générale,* IX, 101-102 ; Jaurès, *Histoire socialiste,* VI, 215-218.

MAPS. Putzger, *Historischer Schul-Atlas,* 26 ; Schrader, *Atlas de geographie historique,* 48 ; Vidal-Lablache, *Atlas général,* 41.

His Majesty the Emperor of the French, King of Italy, and His Majesty the Emperor of Germany and of Austria, equally prompted by the desire to put an end to the calamities of the war, have resolved to proceed without delay to the conclusion of a definitive treaty of peace. . . .

. . . . . .

1. There shall be, dating from this day, peace and amity between His Majesty the Emperor of Germany and of Austria and His Majesty the Emperor of the French, King of Italy, their heirs and successors, their respective states and subjects, forever.

2. France shall continue to possess in complete ownership and sovereignty the duchies, principalities, lordships and territories beyond the Alps, which were, prior to the present treaty, united or incorporated with the French Empire, or ruled by French laws and administrations.

. . . .

4. His Majesty the Emperor of Germany and of Austria renounces, as well for himself as for his heirs and successors, the portion of the states of the Republic of Venice ceded to him in the treaties of Campo Formio and Lunéville, which shall be united forever with the Kingdom of Italy.

5. His Majesty the Emperor of Germany and of Austria recognizes His Majesty the Emperor of the French as King of Italy. But it is agreed that, in conformity with the declaration made by His Majesty the Emperor of the French at the time when he took the crown of Italy, as soon as the powers named in that declaration shall have fulfilled the conditions which are there set forth, the crowns of France and of Italy shall be separated forever, and they can no longer in any case be united upon the same head. His Majesty the Emperor of Germany and of Austria binds himself to recognize, at the time of the separation, the successor whom His Majesty the Emperor of the French shall give himself as King of Italy.

6. The present treaty of peace is declared common to their Most Serene Highnesses the electors of Bavaria, Wurtemburg, and Baden, and to the Batavian Republic, allies in the present war of His Majesty the Emperor of the French, King of Italy.

7. The electors of Bavaria and of Wurtemburg having

taken the title of king, without however ceasing to belong to the Germanic Confederation, His Majesty the Emperor of Germany and of Austria recognizes them in that capacity.

8. His Majesty the Emperor of Germany and of Austria, both for himself, his heirs and successors, and for the Princes of his house, their respective heirs and successors, renounces the principalities, lordships, domains and territories hereinafter designated:

Cedes and abandons to His Majesty the King of Bavaria, the Margravate of Burgau and its dependencies, the principality of Eichstadt, the portion of the territory of Passau belonging to His Royal Highness the Elector of Salzburg, and situated between Bohemia, Austria, the Danube and the Inn; the county of Tyrol, including the principalities of Brixen and Trent; the seven lordships of Vorarlburg with their enclaves; the county of Hohenems, the county of Konigsegg-Rothenfels, the lordships of Tettnang and Argen, and the city and territory of Lindau.

To His Majesty the King of Wurtemburg, the five so-called cities of the Danube, to wit: Ehingen, Munderkingen, Riedlingen, Mengen, and Sulgen, with their dependencies; the Upper and Lower county of Hohenberg; the landgravate of Nellenbourg and the prefecture of Altorf, with their dependencies (the city of Constance excepted); the portion of Breisgau constituting an enclave within the Wurtemburg possessions and situated to the east of a line drawn from Schlegelberg to Molbach, and the cities and territories of Willingen and Brentingen.

To His Serene Highness the Elector of Baden, the Breisgau (with the exception of the enclave and the separate portions above designated), the Ortenau and their dependencies, the city of Constance and the commandery of Meinau.

The principalities, lordships, domains and territories above said shall be possessed respectively by their Majesties the Kings of Bavaria and of Wurtemburg and by His Serene Highness the Elector of Baden, whether in suzerainty or in complete ownership and sovereignty, in the same manner, with the same titles, rights, and prerogatives as they were possessed by His Majesty the Emperor of Germany and of Austria, or the princes of His House, and not otherwise.

10. The countries of Salzburg and Berechtesgaden belonging to His Royal and Excellent Highness the Archduke Ferdinand shall be incorporated in the Empire of Austria; and His Majesty the Emperor of Germany and of Austria shall possess them in complete ownership and sovereignty, but with the title of duchy only.

11. His Majesty the Emperor of the French, King of Italy, engages to obtain in favor of His Royal Highness the Archduke Ferdinand, Elector of Salzburg, the cession, by His Majesty the King of Bavaria, of the principality of Würzburg, as it was given to his Majesty by the *recez* of the deputation of the Germanic Empire of February 25, 1803. . . .

   .   .   .   .   .

13. His Majesty the King of Bavaria may occupy the city of Augsburg and its territory, unite them with his states, and possess them in full ownership and sovereignty. His Majesty the King of Wurtemburg may likewise occupy, unite with his states, and possess in full ownership and sovereignty the county of Bondorff; and His Majesty the Emperor of Germany and of Austria agrees not to make any opposition thereto.

14. Their Majesties the Kings of Bavaria and Wurtemburg and His Most Serene Highness the Elector of Baden shall enjoy, over the territories ceded to them, as over their former states, the plenitude of sovereignty and of all the rights which are derived therefrom and which have been guaranteed by His Majesty the Emperor of the French, King of Italy, like and. in the same manner as His Majesty the Emperor of Germany and of Austria and His Majesty the King of Prussia enjoy over their German states. His Majesty the Emperor of Germany and of Austria, whether as head of the Empire or as co-state, agrees not to impose any obstacle to the execution of the acts which have been done or may be done in consequence thereof.

15. His Majesty the Emperor of Germany and of Austria, as well for himself, his heirs and successors, as for the princes of his House, their heirs and successors, renounces without exception all rights, whether of sovereignty or of suzerainty, all claims whatsoever, present or contingent, upon all the states of their Majesties the kings of Bavaria and Wurtemburg and His Serene Highness the Elector of Baden,

and generally upon all the states, domains and territories included in the circles of Bavaria, Franconia and Swabia, as well as every title taken from the said domains and territories; and reciprocally all present or contingent claims of the said states at the expense of the House of Austria or of its princes are and shall remain extinguished forever: . . .

17. His Majesty the Emperor Napoleon guarantees the integrity of the Empire of Austria in the condition wherein it shall be in consequence of the present treaty of peace, likewise the integrity of the possessions of the princes of the House of Austria designated in the eleventh and twelfth articles.

Separate Article.

There shall be paid by His Majesty the Emperor of Germany and of Austria, for redemption of all the contributions imposed upon the different hereditary states occupied by the French army and not yet collected, a sum of forty million francs (metallic value) . . .

75. Documents upon Napoleon and the Kingdom of Naples.

These documents show the manner and official justification of the transfer of the Neapolitan crown from its Bourbon sovereign to Joseph Bonaparte. This event was the first of a series by which the Grand Empire was created. Something of the conception of this empire can be learned from document B.

REFERENCES. Fyffe, *Modern Europe*, I, 300-303 (Popular ed., 202-204) : Fournier, *Napoleon*, 327-329 ; Rose, *Napoleon*, II, 56-59 ; Sloane, *Napoleon*, II, 255-256 ; Lanfrey, *Napoleon*, III, 106-108.

A. Proclamation to the Army. December 30, 1805. *Moniteur*, February 1, 1806.

At my Imperial Camp at Schoenbrünn,
6 Nivôse, Year XIV (December 30, 1805).
Soldiers,

For ten years past I have done everything to save the King of Naples; he has done everything to ruin himself.

After the battles of Dego, Mondovi and Lodi he could

oppose to me only a feeble resistance. I trusted the words of that prince and was generous towards him.

When the second coalition was dissolved at Marengo, the King of Naples, who had first commenced that unjust war, abandoned at Lunéville by his allies, remained alone and without defence. He implored me; I pardoned him a second time.

A few months ago you were at the gates of Naples. I had plenty of legitimate reasons to suspect the treason which was meditated and to avenge the outrages which had been committed. I was again generous. I recognized the neutrality of Naples; I ordered you to evacuate that kingdom; and for the third time the House of Naples was saved and strengthened.

Shall we pardon a fourth time? shall we confide for a fourth time in a heart without faith, without honor, and without reason? No! no! the dynasty of Naples has ceased to reign; its existence is incompatible with the repose of Europe and the honor of my crown.

Soldiers, march; cast into the waves, supposing that they await you, those debilitated battalions of the tyrant of the seas. Show to the world in what manner we punish perjurers. Be not slow to understand that all Italy is subject to my laws or to those of my allies; that the most beautiful country of the world is liberated from the yoke of the most perfidious men; that the sanctity of treaties is avenged, and that the manes of my brave soldiers butchered in the harbors of Sicily on their return from Egypt, after having escaped the perils of shipwreck, of the deserts, and of a hundred battles, are at length appeased.

Soldiers, my brother will march at your head; he knows my plans; he is the depository of my authority; he has my entire confidence; encompass him with yours.

NAPOLEON.

B. Imperial Decree making Joseph Bonaparte King of Naples. March 30. 1806. Duvergier, *Lois*, XV, 323.

Napoleon, by the grace of God and the constitutions, Emperor of the French, King of Italy, to all those to whom these presents shall come, greeting.

The interests of our people, the honor of our crown, and the tranquility of the continent of Europe, requiring that we should assure in a stable and definitive manner the fate of the peoples of Naples and of Sicily, who have fallen into our power by the right of conquest, and who moreover make up part of the Grand Empire, we have declared and do declare by these presents that we recognize as King of Naples and of Sicily our well beloved brother Joseph Napoleon, grand elector of France. That crown shall be hereditary, by order of primogeniture, in his masculine, legitimate and natural lineage. Should his said lineage become extinct, which God forbid, we intend to call thereto our legitimate and natural male children, by order of primogeniture, and in default of our legitimate and natural male children, those of our brother Louis and his masculine, legitimate and natural lineage, by order of primogeniture; reserving to ourselves, if our brother Joseph Napoleon should die during our lifetime, without leaving legitimate and natural male children, the right to designate for the succession to the said crown a prince of our house, or even to call thereto an adopted child, according as we shall judge expedient for the interest of our peoples and for the advantage of the grand system which Divine Providence has destined us to establish.

We institute in the said Kingdom of Naples and of Sicily six grand fiefs of the Empire, with the title of duchy and with the same advantages and prerogatives as those which have been instituted in the Venetian provinces united to our crown of Italy, in order that the said duchies may be grand fiefs of the Empire forever, appointments thereto, if there is occasion, falling to us or our successors. All the details of the formation of the said fiefs are remitted to the care of our said brother Joseph Napoleon.

We reserve from the said Kingdom of Naples and of Sicily the disposal of one million of income, in order to be distributed to the·generals, officers and soldiers of our army, who have rendered the most services to the fatherland and the throne, and whom we shall designate for that purpose, under the express condition of the said generals, officers and soldiers not having power before the expiration of ten years to sell or alienate the said incomes, except with our authorisation.

The King of Naples shall be forever a grand dignitary of the Empire, under the title of grand elector; reserving to ourselves, however, when we shall deem suitable, to create the dignity of prince vice-grand-elector.

We intend that the crown of Naples and of Sicily, which we place upon the head of our brother Joseph Napoleon and his discendants, shall not affect injuriously in any manner their rights of succession to the throne of France. But it is likewise within our wish that the crowns of France, Italy, and Naples and Sicily, may never be united upon the same head.

76. Treaty between France and Holland.

May 24, 1806. De Clercq, *Traités*, II, 165-167.

The event shown in this document belongs to the series by which the republics dependent upon France were transformed into monarchies and made, in effect if not in name, parts of the Grand Empire. The reasons given for the change and the relationship with France should be particularly noticed.

REFERENCES. Fournier, *Napoleon*, 331-334; Sloane, *Napoleon*, II, 256; Lanfrey, *Napoleon*, III, 114-116; Lavisse and Rambaud, *Histoire générale*, IX, 488-493.

His Imperial and Royal Majesty Napoleon, Emperor of the French, King of Italy, and the assembly of their High Mightinesses representing the Batavian Republic, presided over by His Excellency the Grand Pensionary, accompanied by the Council of State and the ministers and secretaries of state, considering:

1st. That in view of the general tendency of opinion and the actual organization of Europe, a government without stability and certain duration cannot fulfill the aim of its institution;

2d. That the periodical renewal of the head of the state will always be in Holland a source of dissensions, and abroad a constant subject of agitation and discord between the powers friendly or hostile to Holland;

3d. That an hereditary government alone can guarantee the tranquil possession of everything which is dear to the people of Holland, the free exercise of their religion, the preservation of their laws, their political independence and their civil liberty;

4th. That the first of their interests is to assure themselves of a powerful protection, under the shelter of which they can freely exercise their industry and maintain themselves in the possession of their territory, their commerce and their colonies;

5th. That France is essentially interested in the welfare of the people of Holland, the prosperity of the state and the stability of their institutions, as well in consideration of the northern frontier of the Empire, open and stripped of fortified places, as under the aspect of the principles and interests of general policy;

. . . . . .

1. His Majesty the Emperor of the French, King of Italy, both for himself and for his heirs and successors forever, guarantees to Holland the maintenance of its constitutional rights, its independence, the integrity of its possessions in the two worlds, its political, civil and religious liberty, as it is consecrated by the actually established laws, and the abolition of every privilege in the matter of taxation.

2. Upon the formal request made by their High Mightinesses representing the Batavian Republic, that Prince Louis Napoleon should be appointed and crowned hereditary and constitutional King of Holland, His Majesty defers to this opinion and authorises Prince Louis Napoleon to accept the crown of Holland, to be possessed by him and his natural, legitimate and masculine descendants, by order of primogeniture, to the perpetual exclusion of women and their descendants.

In consequence of this authorisation, Prince Louis Napoleon shall possess that crown under the title of king, and with all the power and all the authority which shall be determined by the constitutional laws which the Emperor Napoleon has guaranteed in the preceding article.

Nevertheless, it is declared that the crowns of France and of Holland can never be united upon the same head.

. . . . . .

4. In case of a minority, the regency belongs of right to the queen; and in her default, the Emperor of the French, in his capacity as perpetual head of the imperial family, appoints the regent of the kingdom; he chooses from among the princes of the royal family, and, in their default, from

among the nationals. The minority of the king ends at the age of eighteen completed years.

. . . .

6. The King of Holland shall be in perpetuity a grand dignitary of the Empire, under the title of grand constable.

. . . . . .

7. The members of the reigning house of Holland shall remain personally subject to the provisions of the constitutional statute of March 30th last, forming the law of the imperial family of France.

8. The posts and employments of state, other than those appertaining to the personal service of the palace of the king, shall be conferred only upon nationals.

9. The arms of the king shall be the ancient arms of Holland, quartered with the imperial eagle of France and surmounted by the royal crown.

10. There shall be immediately concluded between the contracting powers a treaty of commerce, in virtue of which the subjects of Holland shall be treated at all times in the harbors and upon the territory of the French Empire as the most specially favored nation.

. . . .

Paris, this May 24, 1806.

77. Documents upon the Continental System.

The first five of these documents exhibit the steps whereby the neutral trade of the world was destroyed during the great commercial war between France and England. Document F shows a subsequent adjustment of the English system. Document G illustrates the methods employed by Napoleon in the application of his system. The idea of conquering England by destroying her commerce was an old French conception which the Directory had begun to apply. Napoleon resumed the policy at the renewal of the war in 1803 and his measures led to document A.

REFERENCES. The best consecutive account of the whole system is in Mahan, *Sea Power and French Revolution*, II, 265-357. Henry Adams, *History of the United States*, IV, Ch. IV, should be read with reference to documents C and D; valuable comment upon the other documents may also be obtained through the index. See also *Cambridge Modern History*, IX, 361-380; Fournier, *Napoleon*, 503-507; Rose, *Napoleon*, II, 95-99, 195-206, 215-216; Lanfrey, *Napoleon*, III, 179-183, 357-358, IV, 269-278; Jaurès, *Histoire socialiste*, VI, 303-340.

A. British Note to the Neutral Powers. May 16, 1806.
American State Papers, Foreign Relations, III, 267.

Downing Street, May 16, 1806.

The undersigned, His Majesty's principal Secretary of State for Foreign Affairs, has received His Majesty's commands to acquaint Mr. Monroe, that the king, taking into consideration the new and extraordinary means resorted to by the enemy for the purpose of distressing the commerce of his subjects, has thought fit to direct that the necessary measures should be taken for the blockade of the coast, rivers and ports, from the river Elbe to the port of Brest, both inclusive; and the said coast, rivers and ports are and must be considered as blockaded; but that His Majesty is pleased to declare that such blockade shall not extend to prevent neutral ships and vessels laden with goods not being the property of His Majesty's enemies, and not being contraband of war, from approaching the said coast, and entering into and sailing from the said rivers and ports (save and except the coast, rivers and ports from Ostend to the river Seine, already in a state of strict and rigorous blockade, and which are to be considered as so continued), provided the said ships and vessels so approaching and entering (except as aforesaid), shall not have been laden at any port belonging to or in the possession of any of His Majesty's enemies; and that the said ships and vessels so sailing from said rivers and ports (except as aforesaid) shall not be destined to any port belonging to or in possession of any of His Majesty's enemies, nor have previously broken the blockade.

Mr. Monroe is therefore requested to apprise the American consuls and merchants residing in England, that the coasts, rivers and ports above mentioned, must be considered as being in a state of blockade, and that from this time. all the measures authorised by the law of nations and the respective treaties between His Majesty and the different neutral powers, will be adopted and executed with respect to vessels attempting to violate the said blockade after this notice.

The undersigned requests Mr. Monroe, etc.

C. J. Fox.

B. The Berlin Decree. November 21, 1806. *Correspondance de Napoleon I*, XIII, 555-557. Translation, based upon that of James Harvey Robinson, *University of Pennsylvania Translations and Reprints*.

From our Imperial Camp at Berlin, November 21, 1806.

Napoleon, Emperor of the French and King of Italy, in consideration of the fact:

1. That England does not recognize the system of international law universally observed by all civilized nations;

2. That she regards as an enemy every individual belonging to the enemy's state, and consequently makes prisoners of war not only of the crews of armed ships of war but of the crews of ships of commerce and merchantmen, and even of commercial agents and of merchants travelling on business;

3. That she extends to the vessels and commercial wares and to the property of individuals the right of conquest, which is applicable only to the possessions of the belligerent power;

4. That she extends to unfortified towns and commercial ports, to harbors and the mouths of rivers, the right of blockade, which, in accordance with reason and the customs of all civilized nations, is applicable only to fortified places;

That she declares places in a state of blockade, before which she has not even a single ship of war, although a place may not be blockaded except it be so completely guarded that no attempt to approach it can be made without imminent danger. That she declares also in a state of blockade places which all her united forces would be unable to blockade, such as entire coasts and the whole of an empire.

5. That this monstrous abuse of the right of blockade has no other aim than to prevent communication among the nations and to raise the commerce and the industry of England upon the ruins of that of the continent.

6. That, since this is the obvious aim of England, whoever deals on the continent in English goods, thereby favors and renders himself an accomplice of her designs.

7. That this policy of England, worthy of the earliest stages of barbarism, has profited that power to the detriment of every other nation.

8. That it is a natural right to oppose such arms against

an enemy as he makes use of, and to fight in the same way that it fights; when it disregards all ideas of justice and every high sentiment, due to the civilization among mankind.

We have resolved to apply to her the usages which she has sanctioned in her maritime legislation.

The provisions of the present decree shall continue to be looked upon as embodying the fundamental principles of the Empire until England shall recognize that the law of war is one and the same on land and sea, and that the rights of war cannot be extended so as to include private property of any kind or the persons of individuals unconnected with the profession of arms, and that the right of blockade should be restricted to fortified places actually invested by sufficient forces.

We have consequently decreed and do decree that which follows:

1. The British Isles are declared to be in a state of blockade.

2. All commerce and all correspondence with the British isles are forbidden. Consequently letters or packages directed to England or to an Englishman or written in the English language shall not pass through the mails and shall be seized.

3. Every individual who is an English subject, of whatever state or condition he may be, who shall be discovered in any country occupied by our troops or by those of our allies, shall be made a prisoner of war.

4. All warehouses, merchandise or property of whatever kind belonging to a subject of England shall be regarded as lawful prize.

5. Trade in English goods is prohibited, and all goods belonging to England or coming from her factories or her colonies are declared lawful prize.

6. Half of the product resulting from the confiscation of the goods and possessions declared lawful prize by the preceding articles shall be applied to indemnify the merchants for the losses they have experienced by the capture of merchant vessels taken by English cruisers.

7. No vessel coming directly from England or from the English colonies or which shall have visited these since the publication of the present decree shall be received in any port.

8. Any vessel contravening the above provision by a false

declaration shall be seized, and the vessel and cargo shall be confiscated as if it were English property.

9. Our court of prizes at Paris shall pronounce final judgment in all cases arising in our Empire or in the countries occupied by the French army relating to the execution of the present decree. Our court of prizes at Milan shall pronounce final judgment in the said cases which may arise within our Kingdom of Italy.

10. The present decree shall be communicated by our minister of foreign affairs to the kings of Spain, of Naples, of Holland and of Etruria, and to our other allies whose subjects, like ours, are the victims of the unjust and barbarous maritime legislation of England.

11. Our ministers of foreign affairs, of war, of the navy, of finance and of the police and our directors-general of the port are charged with the execution of the present decree so far as it affects them.

Signed, NAPOLEON.

C. British Order in Council, January 10, 1807. *American State Papers, Foreign Relations,* III, 5.

Note communicated by Lord Howick to Mr. Monroe, dated
Downing Street, January 10, 1807.

The undersigned, His Majesty's principal Secretary of State of Foreign Affairs, has received His Majesty's commands to acquaint Mr. Monroe that the French government having issued certain orders, which, in violation of the usages of war, purport to prohibit the commerce of all neutral nations with His Majesty's dominions, and also to prevent such nations from trading with any other country in any articles, the growth, produce, or manufacture of His Majesty's dominions. And the said government having also taken upon itself to declare all His Majesty's dominions to be in a state of blockade, at a time when the fleets of France and her allies are themselves confined within their own ports by the superior valor and discipline of the British navy.

Such attempts, on the part of the enemy, giving to His Majesty an unquestionable right of retaliation, and warranting His Majesty in enforcing the same prohibition of all commerce with France, which that Power vainly hopes to effect against the commerce of His Majesty's naval subjects, a prohibition which the superiority of His Majesty's naval forces might enable him to support, by actually investing the ports and coasts of the enemy with numerous squadrons and cruisers, so as to make the entrance or approach thereto manifestly dangerous.

His Majesty, though unwilling to follow the example of his enemies by proceeding to an extremity so distressing to all nations not engaged in the war, and carrying on their accustomed trade, yet feels himself bound, by a due regard to the just defence of the rights and interests of his people, not to suffer such measures to be taken by the enemy, without taking some steps, on his part, to restrain this violence; and to retort upon them the evils of their own injustice. Mr. Monroe is, therefore, requested to apprise the American consuls and merchants residing in England, that His Majesty has, therefore, judged it expedient to order that no vessel shall be permitted to trade from one port to another, both which ports shall belong to, or be in the possession of, France or her allies, or shall be so far under their control as that British vessels may not freely trade thereat; and that the commanders of His Majesty's ships of war and privateers have been instructed to warn every neutral vessel coming from any such port, and destined to another port, to discontinue her voyage, and not to proceed to any such port; and every vessel after being so warned, or any vessel coming from any such port, after a reasonable time shall have been afforded for receiving information of this His Majesty's order, which shall be found proceeding to another such port, shall be captured and brought in, and, together with her cargo, shall be condemned as lawful prize. And that, from this time, all the measures authorised by the law of nations, and the respective treaties between His Majesty and the different neutral powers, will be adopted and executed with respect to vessels attempting to violate the said order after this notice.   HOWICK.

D.   British Order in Council. November 11, 1807. *American State Papers, Foreign Relations*, III, 269-270.

*At the Court at the Queen's Palace, the 11th of November,
1807: Present, the King's Most Excellent
Majesty in Council.*

Whereas certain orders establishing an unprecedented system of warfare against this kingdom, and aimed especially at the destruction of its commerce and resources, were some time since issued by the government of France, by which "the British islands were declared to be in a state of blockade," thereby subjecting to capture and condemnation all vessels, with their cargoes, which should continue to trade with His Majesty's dominions:

And, whereas, by the same order, "all trading in English merchandise is prohibited, and every article of merchandise belonging to England, or coming from her colonies, or of her manufacture, is declared lawful prize:"

And, whereas, the nations in alliance with France, and under her control, were required to give, and have given, and do give, effect to such orders:

And, whereas, His Majesty's order of the 7th of January last has not answered the desired purpose, either of compelling the enemy to recall those orders, or of inducing neutral nations to interpose, with effect, to obtain their revocation, but on the contrary, the same have been recently enforced with increased rigor:

And, whereas, His Majesty, under these circumstances, finds himself compelled to take further measures for asserting and vindicating his just rights, and for supporting that maritime power which the exertions and valor of his people have, under the blessings of Providence, enabled him to establish and maintain; and the maintenance of which is not more essential to the safety and prosperity of His Majesty's dominions, than it is to the protection of such states as still retain their independence, and to the general intercourse and happiness of mankind:

His Majesty is therefore pleased, by and with the advice of his privy council, to order, and it is hereby ordered, that all the ports and places of France, and her allies, or of any other country at war with His Majesty, and all other ports or places in Europe, from which, although not at war with His Majesty, the British flag is excluded, and all ports or places in the colonies belonging to His Majesty's enemies, shall, from henceforth, be subject to the same restrictions in point of trade and navigation, with the exceptions hereinafter mentioned, as if the same were actually blockaded by His Majesty's naval forces, in the most strict and rigorous manner: And it is hereby further ordered and declared, that all trade in articles which are of the produce or manufacture of the said countries or colonies shall be deemed and considered to be unlawful; every vessel trading from or to the said countries or colonies, together with all goods and merchandise on board and all articles of the produce or manufacture of the said countries or colonies, shall be captured and condemned as a prize to the captors.

But, although His Majesty would be fully justified by the circumstances and considerations above recited, in establishing such system of restrictions with respect to all the countries and colonies of his enemies, without exception or qualification, yet His Majesty being, nevertheless, desirous not to subject neutrals to any greater inconvenience than is absolutely inseparable from the carrying into effect His Majesty's just determination to counteract the designs of his enemies, and to retort upon his enemies themselves the consequences of their own violence and injustice; and being yet willing to hope that it may be possible (consistently with that object) still to allow to neutrals the opportunity of furnishing themselves with colonial produce for their own consumption and supply, and even to leave open, for the present, such trade with His Majesty's enemies as shall be carried on directly with the ports of His Majesty's dominions, or of his allies, in the manner hereinafter mentioned.

His Majesty is, therefore, pleased further to order and it is hereby ordered, that nothing herein contained shall extend to subject to capture or condemnation any vessel, or the cargo of any vessel, belonging to any country not declared by this order to be subjected to the restrictions incident to a state of blockade, which shall have cleared out with such cargo from some port or place of the country to which she belongs, either in Europe or America, or from some free port in His Majesty's colonies, under circumstances in which such trade, from such free ports, is permitted, direct to some port or place in the colonies of His Majesty's enemies, or from those colonies direct to the country to which such vessel belongs, or to some free port in His Majesty's colonies, in such cases, and with such articles, as it may be lawful to import into such free port; nor to any vessel, or the cargo of any vessel, belonging to any country not at war with His Majesty, which shall have cleared out under such regulations as His Majesty may think fit to prescribe, and shall be proceeding direct from some port or place in this kingdom, or from Gibraltar, or Malta, or from any port belonging to His Majesty's allies, to the port specified in her clearance; nor to any vessel, or the cargo of any vessel, belonging to any country not at war with His Majesty, which shall be coming from any port or place in Europe which is declared by this order to be subject to the restrictions incident to a state of blockade, destined to some port or place in Europe belonging to His Majesty, and which shall be on her voyage direct thereto; but these exceptions are not to be understood as exempting from capture or confiscation any vessel or goods which shall be liable thereto in respect to having entered or departed from any port or place actually blockaded by His Majesty's squadrons or ships of war, or for being enemy's property, or for any other cause than the contravention of his present order.

And the commanders of His Majesty's ships of war and privateers, and other vessels acting under His Majesty's commission, shall be, and are hereby, instructed to warn every vessel which shall have commenced her voyage prior to any notice of this order, and shall be destined to any port of France or of her allies or of any other country at war with His Majesty or any port or place from which the British flag, as aforesaid, is excluded, or to any colony belonging to His Majesty's enemies, and which shall not have cleared out as is hereinbefore allowed, to discontinue her voyage, and to proceed to some port or place in this kingdom, or to Gibraltar, or Malta; and any vessel which, after having been so warned or after a reasonable time shall have been afforded for the arrival of information of this His Majesty's order at any port or place from which she sailed, or which, after having notice of this order, shall be found in the prosecution of any voyage contrary to the restrictions contained in this order, shall be captured, and, together with her cargo, condemned as lawful prize to the captors.

And, whereas, countries not engaged in the war have acquiesced in these orders of France, prohibiting all trade in any articles the produce or manufacture of His Majesty's dominions; and the merchants of those countries have given countenance and effect to those prohibitions by accepting from persons, styling themselves commercial agents of the enemy, resident at neutral ports, certain documents, termed "certificates of origin," being certificates obtained at the ports of shipment, declaring that the articles of the cargo are not of the produce or manufacture of His Majesty's dominions, or to that effect.

And, whereas, this expedient has been directed by France, and submitted to by such merchants, as part of the new system of warfare directed against the trade of this kingdom, and as the most effectual instrument of accomplishing the same, and it is therefore essentially necessary to resist it.

His Majesty is therefore pleased, by and with the advice of his privy council, to order, and it is hereby ordered, that if any vessel, after reasonable time shall have been afforded for receiving notice of this His Majesty's order, at the port or place from which such vessel shall have cleared out shall be found carrying any such certificate or document as aforesaid, or any document referring to or authenticating the same, such vessel shall be adjudged lawful prize to the captor, together with the goods laden therein, belonging to the person or persons by whom, or on whose behalf, any such document was put on board.

And the right honourable the Lords Commissioners of His Majesty's Treasury, His Majesty's principal Secretaries of State, the Lords Commissioners of the Admiralty, and the Judges of the High Court of Admiralty, and Courts of Vice-Admiralty, are to take the necessary measures herein as to them shall respectively appertain.   W. FAWKENER.

E. The Milan Decree. December 17, 1807. *Correspondance de Napoleon I,* XVI, 192-193. Translation, James Harvey Robinson, *University of Pennsylvania Translations and Reprints.*

At Our Royal Palace at Milan, December 17, 1807.
Napoleon, Emperor of the French, King of Italy, Protector of the Confederation of the Rhine. In view of the measures

adopted by the British government on the 11th of November last by which vessels belonging to powers which are neutral or are friendly and even allied with England are rendered liable to be searched by British cruisers, detained at certain stations in England, and subject to an arbitrary tax of a certain per cent. upon their cargo to be regulated by English legislation.

Considering that by these acts the English government has denationalized the vessels of all the nations of Europe, and that no government may compromise in any degree its independence or its rights—all the rulers of Europe being jointly responsible for the sovereignty and independence of their flags,—and that, if through unpardonable weakness which would be regarded by posterity as an indelible stain, such tyranny should be admitted and become consecrated by custom, the English would take steps to give it the force of law, as they have already taken advantage of the toleration of governments to establish and to give the right of blockade an arbitrary extension which threatens the sovereignty of every state: We have decreed and do decree as follows:

1. Every vessel of whatever nationality which shall submit to be searched by an English vessel or shall consent to a voyage to England, or shall pay any tax whatever to the English government is *ipso facto* declared denationalized, loses the protection afforded by its flag and becomes English property.

2. Should such vessels which are thus denationalized through the arbitrary measures of the English government enter our ports or those of our allies or fall into the hands of our ships of war or of our privateers they shall be regarded as good and lawful prizes.

3. The British Isles are proclaimed to be in a state of blockade both by land and sea. Every vessel of whatever nation or whatever may be its cargo, that sails from the ports of England or from those of the English colonies or of countries occupied by English troops, or is bound for England or for any of the English colonies or any country occupied by English troops, becomes, by violating the present decree, a lawful prize, and may be captured by our ships of war and adjudged to the captor.

4. These measures, which are only a just retaliation

against the barbarous system adopted by the English government, which models its legislation upon that of Algiers, shall cease to have any effect in the case of those nations which shall force the English to respect their flags. They shall continue in force so long as that government shall refuse to accept the principles of international law which regulate the relations of civilized states in a state of war. The provisions of the present decree shall be *ipso facto* abrogated and void so soon as the English government shall abide again by the principles of the law of nations, which are at the same time those of justice and honor.

All our ministers are charged with the execution of the present decree, which shall be printed in the *Bulletin des lois.*

F. British Order in Council, April 26, 1809. *American State Papers, Foreign Relations,* III, 241.

At the Court at the Queen's Palace, the 26th of April, 1809; Present, the King's Most Excellent Majesty in council.

Whereas, His Majesty, by his order in council of the 11th of November, 1807, was pleased, for the reasons assigned therein, to order that "all the ports and places of France and her allies, or of any other country at war with His Majesty, and all other ports or places in Europe, from which, although not at war with His Majesty, the British flag is excluded, and all ports or places in the colonies belonging to His Majesty's enemies, should from henceforth be subject to the same restrictions in point of trade or navigation as if the same were actually blockaded in the most strict and vigorous manner;" and also to prohibit "all trade in articles which are the produce or manufacture of the said countries or colonies;" and whereas, His Majesty, having been nevertheless desirous not to subject those countries which were in alliance or amity with His Majesty to any greater inconvenience than was absolutely inseparable from carrying into effect His Majesty's just determination to counteract the designs of his enemies, did make certain exceptions and modifications expressed in the said order of the 11th of November, and in certain subsequent orders of the 25th of November, declaratory of the aforesaid order of the 11th of November and of the 18th of December, 1807, and of the 30th of March, 1808;

And whereas, in consequence of diverse events which have taken place since the date of the first-mentioned order, affecting the relations between Great Britain and the territories of other powers, it is expedient that sundry parts and provisions of the said orders should be ordered or revoked;

His Majesty is therefore pleased, by and with the advice of his privy council, to revoke and annul the said several orders, except as hereinafter expressed; and so much of the said orders, except as aforesaid, is hereby revoked accordingly. And His Majesty is pleased, by and with the advice of his privy council, to order, and it is hereby ordered, that all the ports and places as far north as the river Ems, inclusively, under the government styling itself the Kingdom of Holland, and all ports and places under the government of France, together with the colonies, plantations, and settlements in the possession of those governments, respectively, and all ports and places in the northern parts of Italy, to be reckoned from the ports of Orbitello and Pesaro, inclusively, shall continue, and be subject to the same restrictions, in point of trade and navigation, without any exception, as if the same were actually blockaded by His Majesty's naval forces in the most strict and rigorous manner; and that every vessel trading from and to the said countries or colonies, plantations or settlements, together with all goods and merchandise on board, shall be condemned as prize to the captors.

And His Majesty is further pleased to order, and it is hereby ordered, that this order shall have effect from the day of the date thereof with respect to any ship, together with its cargo, which may be captured subsequent to such day, on any voyage which is and shall be rendered legal by this order, although such voyage, at the time of the commencement of the same, was unlawful, and prohibited under the said former orders; and such ships, upon being brought in, shall be released accordingly; and with respect to all ships, together with their cargoes, which may be captured in any voyage which was permitted under the exceptions of the orders above mentioned, but which is not permitted according to the provisions of this order, His Majesty is pleased to order, and it is hereby ordered that such ships and their cargoes shall not be liable to condemnation, unless they shall have received actual notice of the present order, as were allowed for constructive notice in the orders of the 25th of November, 1807, and the 18th of May, 1808, at the several places and latitudes therein specified.

And the right honorable the Lords Commissioners of His Majesty's Treasury, His Majesty's principal Secretary of State, the Lords Commissioners of the Admiralty, and the Judge of the High Court of Admiralty, and judges of the courts of vice-admiralty, are to give the necessary directions herein as to them may respectively appertain.

STEPHEN COTTRELL.

G. The Rambouillet Decree. March 23, 1810, Duvergier, *Lois,* XVII, 59.

Napoleon . . . considering that the government of the United States, by an act dated March 1, 1809, which forbids the entrance of the ports, harbors and rivers of the said states to all French vessels, orders:

1st. That, dating from the 20th of May following, the vessels under the French flag which shall arrive in the United States shall be seized and confiscated, as well as their cargoes;

2d. That, after the same date, no merchandise and productions coming from the soil or manufactures of France or of its colonies can be imported into the said United States, from any port or foreign place whatsoever, under penalty of seizure, confiscation and fine of three times the value of the merchandise;

3d. That American vessels cannot repair to any port of France, its colonies or dependencies,

We have decreed and do decree as follows:

1. That all vessels navigating under the flag of the United States, or possessed in whole or in part by any citizen or subject of that power, which, dating from May 20, 1809, may have entered or shall enter into the ports of our Empire, our colonies or the countries occupied by our armies, shall be seized, and the products of the sales shall be deposited in the surplus fund.

Vessels which may be charged with despatches or commissions of government of the said states and which have not cargo or merchandise on board are excepted from this provision.

2. Our grand judge, minister of justice, and our minister of finance, are charged with the execution of the present decree.

78. Documents upon the Dissolution of the Holy Roman Empire.

The destruction of the Holy Roman Empire, begun in the treaties of Basel and Campo Formio (Nos. 48 and 55), was finally completed by the organization of the Confederation of the Rhine. The most important feature of document A is the relationship which it creates between France and each of the confederated states. By subsequent acts of accession nearly all the German states, except Austria and Prussia, became members. In the other documents the important features are the explanations for the action that is taken.

REFERENCES. Fyffe, *Modern Europe*, I, 303-306 (Popular ed., 204-206) ; *Cambridge Modern History*, IX, 268-269 ; Fisher, *Napoleonic Statesmanship, Germany*, ch. v ; Fournier, *Napoleon*, 335-340 ; Rose. *Napoleon*. II, 69-72 ; Sloane, *Napoleon*, II, 259-262 ; Lavisse and Rambaud, *Histoire générale*, IX, 503-505.

MAPS. Droysen, *Historischer Hand-Atlas*, 48-49 ; Lane-Poole, *Historical Atlas of Modern Europe*, XII.

A. Treaty for Establishing the Confederation. July 12, 1806. De Clercq, *Traités*, II, 171-179.

His Majesty, the Emperor of the French, King of Italy, of the one part, and of the other part their Majesties the Kings of Bavaria and of Wurtemburg and their most Serene Highnesses the Electors, the Archchancellor of Baden, the Duke of Berg and of Cleves, the Landgrave of Hesse-Darmstadt, the princes of Nassau-Usingen and Nassau-Weilburg, the princes of Hohenzollern-Heckingen and Hohenzollern-Sigmaringen, the princes of Salm-Salm and Salm-Kirburg, the Prince of Isneburg-Birstein, the Duke of Aremberg and the Prince of Lichtenstein, and the Count of Leyen, wishing, by suitable stipulations, to assure the internal peace of the south of Germany, for which experience for a long time past, and again quite recently, has shown that the Germanic constitution can no longer offer any sort of guarantee. . . .

1. The states of . . . [names of the parties of the second part] shall be forever separated from the territory of

the Germanic Empire and united among themselves by a separate confederation, under the name of the Confederated States of the Rhine.

. . . .

3. Each of the kings and confederated princes shall renounce those of his titles which express any relations with the Germanic Empire; and on the 1st of August next he shall cause the diet to be notified of his separation from the Empire.

4. His Most Serene Highness the Archchancellor shall take the titles of Prince Primate and Most Eminent Highness. The title of prince primate does not carry with it any prerogative contrary to the plenitude of sovereignty which each of the confederates shall enjoy.

. . . .

6. The common interests of the confederated states shall be dealt with in a diet, of which the seat shall be at Frankfort, and which shall be divided into two colleges, to wit: the college of kings and the college of princes.

. . . .

12. His Majesty the Emperor of the French shall be proclaimed Protector of the Confederation, and in that capacity, upon the decease of each prince primate, he shall appoint the successor of that one.

[Articles 13-34 provide for a large number of territorial changes, principally consolidations in the interests of the larger states of the confederation.]

35. There shall be between the French Empire and the Confederated States of the Rhine, collectively and separately, an alliance in virtue of which every continental war which one of the high contracting parties may have to carry on shall immediately become common to all the others.

. . . .

38. The contingent to be furnished by each of the allies in case of war is as follows: France shall furnish 200,000 men of all arms; the Kingdom of Bavaria 30,000 men of all arms; the Kingdom of Wurtemburg 12,000; the Grand Duke of Baden 8,000; the Grand Duke of Berg 5,000; the Grand Duke of Darmstadt 4,000; Their Most Serene Highnesses the Dukes and the Prince of Nassau, together with the other confederated princes, shall furnish a contingent of 4,000 men.

39. The high contracting parties reserve to themselves the admission at a later time into the new confederation of other princes and states of Germany whom it shall be found for the common interest to admit thereto.

. . . .

B. Note of Napoleon to the Diet. August 1, 1806. De Clercq, *Traités*, II, 183-184. Translation, James Harvey Robinson, *University of Pennsylvania Translations and Reprints*

The undersigned, *chargé d'affaires* of His Majesty the Emperor of the French and King of Italy at the general diet of the German Empire, has received orders from His Majesty to make the following declarations to the diet:

Their Majesties the Kings of Bavaria and of Wurtemberg, the sovereign princes of Regensburg, Baden, Berg, Hesse-Darmstadt and Nassau, as well as the other leading princes of the south and west of Germany have resolved to form a confederation between themselves which shall secure them against future emergencies, and have thus ceased to be states of the Empire.

The position in which the treaty of Pressburg has directly placed the courts allied to France, and indirectly those princes whose territory they border or surround, being incompatible with the existence of an empire, it becomes a necessity for those rulers to reorganize their relations upon a new system and to remove a contradiction which could not fail to be a permanent source of agitation, disquiet and danger.

France, on the other hand, is directly interested in the maintenance of peace in southern Germany and yet must apprehend that, the moment she shall cause her troops to re-cross the Rhine, discord, the inevitable consequence of contradictory, uncertain and ill-defined conditions, will again disturb the peace of the people and reopen, possibly, the war on the continent. Feeling it incumbent upon her to advance the welfare of her allies and to assure them the enjoyment of all the advantages which the treaty of Pressburg secures them and to which she is pledged, France cannot but regard the confederation that they have formed as a natural result and a necessary sequel to that treaty.

For a long period successive changes have, from century to century, reduced the German constitution to a shadow ot its former self. Time has altered all the relations in respect to size and importance which originally existed among the various members of the confederation, both as regards each other and the whole of which they have formed a part.

The diet has no longer a will of its own. The sentences of the superior courts can no longer be executed. Everything indicates such serious weakness that the federal bond no longer offers any protection whatever and only constitutes a source of dissension and discord between the powers. The results of three coalitions have increased this weakness to the last degree. An electorate has been suppressed by the annexation of Hanover to Prussia. A king in the north has incorporated with his other lands a province of the Empire. The treaty of Pressburg assures complete sovereignty to their majesties the kings of Bavaria and of Wurtemburg and to His Highness the Elector of Baden. This is a prerogative which the other electors will doubtless demand, and which they are justified in demanding; but this is in harmony neither with the letter nor the spirit of·the constitution of the Empire.

His Majesty the Emperor and King is, therefore, compelled to declare that he can no longer acknowledge the existence of the German constitution, recognizing, however, the entire and absolute sovereignty of each of the princes whose states compose Germany to-day, maintaining with them the same relations as with the other independent powers of Europe.

His Majesty the Emperor and King has accepted the title of *Protector of the Confederation of the Rhine*. He has done this with a view only to peace, and in order that by his constant mediation between the weak and the powerful he may obviate every species of dissension and disorder.

Having thus provided for the dearest interests of his people and of his neighbors, and having assured, so far as in him lay, the future peace of Europe and that of Germany in particular, heretofore constantly the theatre of war, by removing a contradiction which placed people and princes alike under the delusive protection of the system contrary both to their political interests and to their treaties, His Majesty the Emperor and King trusts that the nations of Europe will at last close their ears to the insinuations of those who would maintain an eternal war upon the continent. He trusts that the French armies which have crossed the Rhine have done so for the last time, and that the people of Germany will no longer witness, except in the annals of the past, the horrible pictures of disorder, devastation and slaughter which war invariably brings with it.

His Majesty declared that he would never extend the limits of France beyond the Rhine, and he has been faithful to his promise. At present his sole desire is so to employ the means which Providence has confided to him as to free the seas, restore the liberty of commerce and thus assure the peace and happiness of the world.   BACHER.

Regensburg, August 1, 1806.

C. Declaration of the Confederated States. August 1, 1806. De Clercq, *Traités*, II, 185-186.

The undersigned, Ministers Plenipotentiary to the general diet of the Germanic Empire, have received orders to communicate to Your Excellencies, in the name of their most high principals, the following declaration:

The events of the last three wars which almost without interruption have disturbed the repose of Germany, and the political changes which have resulted therefrom, have put in broad daylight the sad truth that the bond which ought to unite the different members of the Germanic body is no longer sufficient for that purpose, or rather that it is already broken in fact; the feeling of this truth has been already a long time in the hearts of all Germans; and however painful may have been the experience of latter years, it has in reality served only to put beyond doubt the senility of a constitution respectable in its origin, but become defective through the instability inherent in all human institutions. Doubtless it is to that instability alone that the scission which was effected in the Empire in 1795 must be attributed, and which had for result the separation of the interests of the north from those of the south of Germany. From that moment all idea of a fatherland and of common interests was of necessity bound to disappear; the words *war of the Empire* and *peace of the Empire* became devoid of meaning; one sought in vain for Germany in the midst of the Germanic body. The princes who bordered upon France, left to themselves and exposed to all the evils of a war to which they could not seek to put an end by constitutional means, saw themselves forced to free themselves from the common bond by separate peace arrangements.

The treaty of Lunéville and still more the *recez* of the Empire of 1803, should no doubt have appeared sufficient to give new life to the Germanic constitution, by causing the feeble parts of the system to disappear and by consolidating its principal supports. But the events which have occurred in the last six months, under the eyes of the entire Empire, have destroyed that hope also and have again put beyond doubt the complete insufficiency of the existing constitution. The urgency of these important considerations has determined the sovereigns and princes of the south and west of Germany to form a new confederation suited to the circumstances of the time. In freeing themselves, by this declaration, from the bonds which have united them up to the present with the Germanic Empire, they are only following the systems established by anterior facts, and even by the declarations of the leading states of the Empire. It is true, they might have preserved the empty shadow of an extinct constitution; but they have believed that it was more in conformity with their dignity and with the purity of their intentions to make frank and open declaration of their resolution and of the motives which have influenced them.

Moreover, they would flatter themselves in vain upon attaining the desired aim, if they were not at the same time assured of a powerful protection. The monarch whose views are always found to be in conformity with the true interests of Germany charges himself with that protection. A guarantee so powerful is tranquilizing under a double aspect. It offers the assurance that His Majesty the Emperor of the French will have at heart, as well for the interest of his glory as for the advantage of his own French Empire, the maintenance of the new order of things and the consolidation of the internal and external tranquility. That precious tranquility is the principal object of the Confederation of the Rhine, of which the co-states of the sovereigns in whose name the present declaration is made will see the proof in the opportunity which is left to each of them to accede to it, if his position makes it desirable for him to do so.

In discharging this duty, we nave the honor to be, . . . (Signed by the representatives of thirteen sovereigns.)

D. Abdication of Francis II. August 7, 1806. *Moniteur.* August 14, 1806. Translation, James Harvey Robinson, *University of Pennsylvania Translations and Reprints.*

We, Francis the Second, by the Grace of God Roman Emperor Elect, Ever August, Hereditary Emperor of Austria, etc., King of Germany, Hungary, Bohemia, Croatia, Dalmatia, Slavonia, Galizia, Lodomeria and Jerusalem; Archduke of Austria, etc.

Since the peace of Pressburg all our care and attention has been directed towards the scrupulous fulfillment of all engagements contracted by the said treaty, as well as the preservation of peace so essential to the happiness of our subjects, and the strengthening in every way of the friendly relations which have been happily re-established. We could but await the outcome of events in order to determine whether the important changes in the German Empire resulting from the terms of the peace would allow us to fulfill the weighty duties which, in view of the conditions of our election, devolve upon us as the head of the Empire. But the results of certain articles of the treaty of Pressburg, which showed themselves immediately after and since its publication, as well as the events which, as is generally known, have taken place in the German Empire, have convinced us that it would be impossible under these circumstances farther to fulfill the duties which we assumed by the conditions of our election. Even if the prompt readjustment of existing political complications might produce an alteration in the existing conditions, the convention signed at Paris, July 12th, and approved later by the contracting parties, providing for the complete separation of several important states of the Empire and their union into a separate confederation, would entirely destroy any such hope.

Thus, convinced of the utter impossibility of longer fulfilling the duties of our imperial office, we owe it to our principles and to our honor to renounce a crown which could only retain any value in our eyes so long as we were in a position to justify the confidence reposed in us by the electors, princes, estates and other members of the German Empire, and to fulfill the duties devolving upon us.

We proclaim, accordingly, that we consider the ties which have hitherto united us to the body politic of the German Empire as hereby dissolved; that we regard the office and dignity of the imperial headship as extinguished by the formation of a separate union of the Rhenish states, and regard ourselves as thereby freed from all our obligations toward the German Empire; herewith laying down the imperial crown which is associated with these obligations, and relinquishing the imperial government which we have hitherto conducted.

We free at the same time the electors, princes and estates, and all others belonging to the Empire, particularly the members of the supreme imperial courts and other magistrates of the Empire, from the duties constitutionally due to us as the lawful head of the Empire. Conversely, we free all our German provinces and imperial lands from all their obligations of whatever kind, towards the German Empire, in uniting these, as Emperor of Austria, with the whole body of the Austrian state we shall strive, with the restored and existing peaceful relations with all the powers and neighboring states, to raise them to the height of prosperity and happiness, which is our keenest desire, and aim of our constant and sincerest efforts.

Done at our capital and royal residence, Vienna, August 6, 1806, in the fifteenth year of our reign as Emperor and hereditary ruler of the Austrian lands.

FRANCIS.

79. Documents upon the Peace of Tilsit.

By the Peace of Tilsit France broke up the fourth coalition, leaving herself at peace save with England. The first three of these documents show the arrangements made at Tilsit as the basis for continental peace. Document D shows the manner in which Napoleon took advantage of various omissions and vague expressions in document C. Among the numerous features which call for notice are: (1) the character of the alliance made between Russia and France; (2) the recent changes in Europe effected by Napoleon and sanctioned by these treaties; (3) the humiliation of Prussia through loss of territory, payment of indemnity, the stipulations as to its army, etc,

REFERENCES. Fyffe, *Modern Europe*, I, 346-349 (Popular ed.,

233-235) ; *Cambridge Modern History*, IX, 291-293, 307 ; Fournier, *Napoleon*, 383-390 ; Rose, *Napoleon*, II, 115-128 ; Sloane, *Napoleon*, III, Chs. v-vi; Lanfrey, *Napoleon*, III, 268-285 ; Fisher, *Napoleonic Statesmanship, Germany*, Chs. v-vi; Lavisse and Rambaud, *Histoire générale*, IX, 115-117 ; Jaurès, *Histoire socialiste*, VI, 224-225.

MAPS. Droysen, *Historischer Hand-Atlas*, 48-49, 53 ; Lane-Poole, *Historical Atlas of Modern Europe*, XII.

A. Treaty of Peace between France and Russia. July 7, 1807. De Clercq, *Traités*, II, 207-213, XV, 141-142.

His Majesty the Emperor of the French, King of Italy, Protector of the Confederation of the Rhine and His Majesty the Emperor of all the Russias, being prompted by an equal desire to put an end to the calamities of war. . . .

. . . .

1. There shall be, dating from the day of the exchange of the ratifications of the present treaty, perfect peace and amity between His Majesty the Emperor of the French, King of Italy, and His Majesty the Emperor of all the Russias.

. . . .

4. His Majesty the Emperor Napoleon, out of regard for His Majesty the Emperor of all the Russias, and wishing to give a proof of his sincere desire to unite the two nations by the bonds of an unalterable confidence and friendship, consents to restore to His Majesty the King of Prussia, the ally of His Majesty the Emperor of all the Russias, all the conquered countries, cities and territories denominated hereinafter, to wit: . . . [The omitted passage is practically identical with article 2 of document C.]

5. The provinces which on the 1st of January, 1772, made up part of the former Kingdom of Poland and which have since passed at different times under Prussian domination, with the exception of the countries that are named or designated in the preceding article and those specified in article 9 hereinafter, shall be possessed in complete ownership and sovereignty by His Majesty the King of Saxony, under the title of the Duchy of Warsaw, and shall be governed by constitutions which, while assuring the liberties and privileges of the peoples of this duchy, are consistent with the tranquility of the neighboring states.

6. The city of Dantzic, with a territory of two leagues radius from its circumference, shall be re-established in its

independence, under the protection of His Majesty the King
of Prussia and His Majesty the King of Saxony and shall be
governed by the laws which governed it at the time when it
ceased to govern itself.

.   .   .   .   .   .

12. Their Serene Highnesses the dukes of Saxe-Coburg,
Oldenburg, and Mechlinburg-Schwerin shall each be replaced
in the complete and peaceable possession of his states; but
the ports of the duchies of Oldenburg and Mechlinburg shall
continue to be occupied by French garrisons until the exchange of the ratifications of the future definitive treaty of
peace between France and England.

13. His Majesty the Emperor Napoleon accepts the
mediation of His Majesty the Emperor of all the Russias
for the purpose of negotiating and concluding a definitive
treaty of peace between France and England, upon the sup-
position that this mediation will also be accepted by England,
one month after the exchange of the ratifications of
the present treaty.

14. On his side, His Majesty the Emperor of all the Russias, wishing to prove how much he desires to establish the
most intimate and enduring relations between the two empires, recognizes His Majesty the King of Naples, Joseph
Napoleon, and His Majesty the King of Holland, Louis Napoleon.

15. His Majesty the Emperor of all the Russias likewise
recognizes the Confederation of the Rhine, the actual state of
possession of each of the sovereigns who compose it, and the
titles given to several of them, whether by the act of confederation or by the subsequent treaties of accession. His
said Majesty promises to recognize, upon the notifications
which shall be made to him on the part of His Majesty the
Emperor Napoleon, the sovereigns who shall subsequently
become members of the confederation, in the capacity which
shall be given them in the documents which shall bring about
their entrance to it.

.   .   .   .

17. The present treaty of peace and amity is declared common to their Majesties the Kings of Naples and of Holland,
and to the Confederated Sovereigns of the Rhine, allies of
His Majesty the Emperor Napoleon.

18. His Majesty the Emperor of all the Russias also recognizes His Imperial Highness, Prince Jerome Bonaparte, as King of Westphalia.

19. The Kingdom of Westphalia shall be composed of the provinces on the left of the Elbe ceded by His Majesty the King of Prussia and of other states actually possessed by His Majesty the Emperor Napoleon.

20. His Majesty the Emperor of all the Russias promises to recognize the arrangement which, in consequence of article 19 above and of the cessions of His Majesty the King of Prussia, shall be made by His Majesty the Emperor Napoleon (which shall be announced to His Majesty the Emperor of all the Russias) and the resulting state of possession for the sovereigns for whose profit it shall have been made.

. . . .

23. His Majesty the Emperor of all the Russias accepts the mediation of His Majesty the Emperor of the French, King of Italy, for the purpose of negotiating and concluding a peace advantageous and honorable to the two empires [of Russia and Turkey]. The respective plenipotentiaries shall repair to the place which the interested parties shall have agreed upon in order to open and to pursue the negotiations.

. . . .

25. His Majesty the Emperor of the French, King of Italy, and His Majesty the Emperor of all the Russias mutually guarantee the integrity of their possessions and those of the powers included in the present treaty of peace, such as they now are or shall be in consequence of the above stipulations.

. . . .

28. The ceremonial of the two courts of the Tuileries and of Saint Petersburg between themselves and with respect to the ambassadors, ministers and envoys whom they shall accredit to each other shall be established upon the principle of a perfect reciprocity and equality.

. . . .

Separate and Secret Articles.

. . . .

2. The Seven Islands shall be possessed in complete pro-

prietorship and sovereignty by His Majesty the Emperor Napoleon.

. . . .

4. His Majesty the Emperor of all the Russias engages to recognize His Majesty the King of Naples Joseph Napoleon, as King of Sicily as soon as King Ferdinand IV shall have an indemnity such as the Balearic islands or the island of Candia, or any other of like value.

5. If, at the time of the future peace with England, Hanover should come to be united with the Kingdom of Westphalia, a territory formed from the countries ceded by His Majesty the King of Prussia upon the left bank of the river Elbe, and having a population of from three to four hundred thousand souls, shall cease to make part of that kingdom and shall be retroceded to Prussia.

. . . .

B. Secret Treaty of Alliance between France and Russia, July 7, 1807. De Clercq, *Traités,* XV, 142-144.

His Majesty the Emperor of the French, King of Italy, Protector of the Confederation of the Rhine, and His Majesty the Emperor of all the Russias, having particularly at heart to re-establish the general peace in Europe upon substantial and, if it be possible, immovable foundations, have for that purpose resolved to conclude an offensive and defensive alliance. . . .

. . . .

1. His Majesty the Emperor of the French, King of Italy, and His Majesty the Emperor of all the Russias, undertake to make common cause, whether by land or by sea, or indeed by land and by sea, in every war which France or Russia may be under the necessity of undertaking against any European power.

2. The occasion for the alliance occurring, and each time that it shall occur, the high contracting parties shall regulate, by a special convention, the forces which each of them shall employ against the common enemy, and the points at which these forces shall act; but for the present they undertake to employ, if the circumstances require it, the totality of their land and sea forces.

3. All the operations of the common wars shall be carried on in concert and neither of the contracting parties in any case shall treat for peace without the co-operation or consent of the other.

4. If England does not accept the mediation of Russia or if having accepted it she does not by the first of November next consent to conclude peace, recognizing therein that the flags of all the powers shall enjoy an equal and perfect independence upon the seas and restoring therein the conquests made by it from France and its allies since the year eighteen hundred and five, when Russia made common cause with it, a note shall be sent to the cabinet of St. James in the course of the said month of November by the ambassador of His Majesty the Emperor of all the Russias. This note, expressing the interest that his said Imperial Majesty takes in the tranquility of the world and the purpose which he has of employing all the forces of his empire to procure for humanity the blessings of peace, shall contain the positive and explicit declaration that, upon the refusal of England to conclude peace upon the aforesaid conditions, His Majesty the Emperor of all the Russias will make common cause with France, and, in case the cabinet of St. James shall not have given upon the 1st of December next a categorical and satisfactory reply, the ambassador of Russia shall receive the contingent order to demand his passports on the said day and to leave England at once.

5. If the case provided for by the preceding article occurs, the high contracting parties shall act in concert and at the same moment summon the three courts of Copenhagen, Stockholm and Lisbon to close their ports to the English, to recall their ambassadors from London, and to declare war upon England. That one of the three courts which refuses this shall be treated as an enemy by the two high contracting parties, and, if Sweden refuses it, Denmark shall be constrained to declare war upon it.

6. The two high contracting parties shall likewise act in concert and shall urge with force upon the court of Vienna that it adopt the principles set forth in article four above, that it close its ports to the English, recall its ambassador from London and declare war on England.

7. If, on the contrary, within the period specified above,

England makes peace upon the aforesaid conditions (and His Majesty the Emperor of all the Russias shall employ all his influence to bring it about) Hanover shall be restored to the King of England in compensation for the French, Spanish and Dutch colonies.

8. Likewise, if in consequence of the changes which have just occurred at Constantinople, the Porte should not accept the mediation of France, or if, after it has been accepted, it should happen that within the period of three months after the opening of the negotiations they have not led to a satisfactory result, France will make common cause with Russia against the Ottoman Porte, and the two high contracting parties shall come to an agreement to remove all the provinces of the Ottoman Empire in Europe, the city of Constantinople and the Province of Roumalia excepted, from the yoke and the vexations of the Turks.

9. The present treaty shall remain secret and shall not be made public nor communicated to any cabinet by one of the two contracting parties without the consent of the other. It shall be ratified and the ratifications thereof exchanged at Tilsit within the space of four days.

Done at Tilsit, July 7, 1807 (June twenty-fifth, [Russian style]).

C. Treaty of Peace between France and Prussia. July 9, 1807. De Clercq, *Traités,* II, 217-223.

His Majesty the Emperor of the French, King of Italy, Protector of the Confederation of the Rhine, and His Majesty the King of Prussia, being prompted by an equal desire to put an end to the calamities of war. . . .

1. There shall be, dating from the day of the exchange of the ratifications of the present treaty, perfect peace and amity between His Majesty the Emperor of the French, King of Italy, and His Majesty the King of Prussia.

2. The portion of the Duchy of Magdeburg situated to the right of the Elbe; the Mark of Prignitz, the Unker-Mark, the middle and the new Mark of Brandenburg, with the exception of the Cotbuser-Kreis or circle of Cotbus in lower Lusace; the duchy of Pomerania; upper, lower and middle Silesia, with the county of Glatz; the portion of the

district of Netze situated to the north of the causeway running from Driesen to Schneidemühl and of a line running from Schneidemühl to the Vistula at Waldau, following the limits of the circle of Bromberg; Pommerellen; the island of Nogat; the countries to the right of Nogat and the Vistula, to the east of Old Prussia and the north of the circle of Kulm; Ermeland; and, lastly, the Kingdom of Prussia, such as it was on January 1, 1772, shall be restored to His Majesty the King of Prussia, with the places of Spandau, Stettin, Küstrin, Glogau, Braslau, Schweidnitz, Neisse, Brieg, Kosel, and Glatz, and generally all the places, citadels, châteaux and strongholds of the countries denominated above, in the condition in which the said places, citadels, châteaux and strongholds now are. The cities and citadels of Graudenz, with the villages of Neudorf, Parschken and Swirkorzy, shall also be restored to His Majesty the King of Prussia.

3. His Majesty the King of Prussia recognizes His Majesty the King of Naples, Joseph Napoleon; and His Majesty the King of Holland, Louis Napoleon.

4. His Majesty the King of Prussia likewise recognizes the Confederation of the Rhine, the actual state of possession of each of the sovereigns who compose it, and the titles given to several of them, whether by the act of confederation or by the subsequent treaties of accession. His Majesty promises to recognize the sovereigns who shall subsequently become members of the said confederation, in the capacity which shall be given them by the documents which shall bring about their entrance to it.

5. The present treaty of peace and amity is declared common to His Majesty the King of Naples, Joseph Napoleon, to His Majesty the King of Holland, and the Confederated Sovereigns of the Rhine, allies of His Majesty the Emperor Napoleon.

6. His Majesty the King of Prussia likewise recognizes His Imperial Highness Prince Jerome Napoleon as King of Westphalia.

7. His Majesty the King of Prussia cedes in complete ownership and sovereignty to the kings, grand dukes, duke or princes who shall be designated by His Majesty the Emperor of the French, King of Italy, all the duchies, marquisdoms, principalities, counties, lordships and generally all

the territories or parts of any territories, as well as all the domains and landed estates of every nature which His Said Majesty the King of Prussia possessed by any title whatsoever between the Rhine and the Elbe at the commencement of the present war.

8. The Kingdom of Westphalia shall be composed of provinces ceded by His Majesty the King of Prussia and of other states actually possessed by His Majesty the Emperor Napoleon.

9. The disposition which shall be made by His Majesty the Emperor Napoleon of the countries designated in the two preceding articles and the state of possession resulting therefrom to the sovereigns for whose profit it shall have been made, shall be recognized by His Majesty the King of Prussia, in the same manner as if it were already effected and were contained in the present treaty.

10. His Majesty the King of Prussia, for himself, his heirs and successors, renounces all present or contingent right which he can have or lay claim to: 1st. Upon all the territories, without exception, situated between the Rhine and the Elbe other than those designated in article 7; 2d. Upon those of the possessions of His Majesty the King of Saxony and of the House of Anhalt which are upon the right of the Elbe; reciprocally, every present or contingent right and every claim of the states included between the Elbe and the Rhine upon the possessions of His Majesty the King of Prussia, as they shall be in consequence of the present treaty, are and shall remain forever extinguished.

11. All agreements, conventions or treaties of alliance, open or secret, which may have been concluded between Prussia and any of the states situated to the left of the Elbe, and which the present war shall not have dissolved, shall remain without effect and shall be regarded as null and void.

12. His Majesty the King of Prussia cedes in complete ownership and sovereignty to His Majesty the King of Saxony the Cotbuser-Kreis or Circle of Cotbus in lower Lusatia.

13. His Majesty the King of Prussia renounces in perpetuity the possession of all the provinces which, having belonged to the Kingdom of Poland subsequent to the 1st of

January, 1772, have passed at various times under the domination of Prussia, with the exception of Ermeland and the
countries situated to the west of old Prussia, to the east of
Pomerania and the new mark, to the north of the circle of
Kulm and of a line running from the Vistula to Schneidemühl through Waldau, following the limits of the circle of
Bomberg and of the causeway running from Schneidemühl
to Drisen, which, with the city and citadel of Graudenz and
the villages of Neudorf, Parschken, and Swierkorzy, shall
continue to be possessed in complete ownership and sovereignty by His Majesty the King of Prussia.

14. His Majesty the King of Prussia likewise renounces
in perpetuity the possession of Danzig.

15. The provinces which His Majesty the King of Prussia
renounces by article 13 above (with the exception of the
territory specified in article 18 hereinafter) shall be possessed
in complete ownership and sovereignty by His Majesty the
King of Saxony, under the title of the Duchy of Warsaw,
and shall be governed by constitutions which, while assuring the liberties and privileges of the peoples of this duchy,
are consistent with the tranquility of the neighboring states.

. . . . .

19. The city of Danzig, with a territory of two leagues
radius around its circumference, shall be re-established in its
independence, under the protection of His Majesty the King
of Prussia and of His Majesty the King of Saxony and
shall be governed by the laws which governed it at the time
when it ceased to govern itself.

. . . . . .

21. The city, port and territory of Danzig, shall be closed
during the continuance of the present maritime war to the
commerce and navigation of the English.

. . . . .

27. Until the day of the exchange of the ratifications of
the future definitive treaty of peace between France and England, all the countries under the domination of His Majesty
the King of Prussia, without exception, shall be closed to the
navigation and commerce of the English. No shipment can
be made from Prussian ports for the British islands, nor
can any vessel coming from England or its colonies be received in the said ports.

28. A convention shall immediately be made having for
its object the regulation of everything relative to the method
and the time of the restoration of the places which must
be restored to His Majesty the King of Prussia, as well as
the details in regard to the civil and military administration
of the districts which must also be restored.

.　.　.　.　.　.　.　.　,　,

Secret Articles.

.　.　.　.　.　.

2. His Majesty the King of Prussia engages to make
common cause with France against England, if, on the 1st
of December, England has not consented to conclude a peace
upon conditions reciprocally honorable to the two nations
and conformable to the true principles of maritime law; in
such case, there shall be a special convention made to regulate the execution of the above stipulation.

.　.　.　.　.　.　.

D. Treaty between France and Prussia. September 8,
1808. De Clercq, *Traités*, II, 270-273.

His Majesty the Emperor of the French, King of Italy,
Protector of the Confederation of the Rhine and His Majesty
the King of Prussia, wishing to remove the difficulties which
have occured in the execution of the treaty of Tilsit, .　.　.

.　.　.　.　.　.

1. The amount of the sums due from the Prussian states
to the French army, as well for extraordinary contribution as
for arrears of revenues, is fixed at 140 million francs; and
by means of the payment of the said sum, every claim of
France upon Prussia, on the ground of war contributions,
shall be extinguished. This sum of 140 millions shall be
deposited within twenty days from the exchange of the ratifications of the present treaty in the counting house of the
receiver general of the army, to wit: half in ready money
or in good and acceptable bills of exchange, payable at the
rate of 6 millions per month dating from the day of the exchange of the ratifications and the payment of which shall
be guaranteed by the Prussian treasury. The other half
[shall be] in land notes of privileged mortgage upon the

royal domains, which shall be reimbursable within the space of from one year to eighteen months after the exchange of the ratifications of the present treaty.

.   .   .   .

5. The states of His Majesty the King of Prussia shall be evacuated by the French troops within the interval of thirty to forty days after the exchange of the ratifications, or sooner if possible.

6. The places of Glogau, Stettin and Custrin shall remain in the power of the French army until the entire discharge of the bills of exchange and the land notes given in payment of the contribution mentioned in the first article.

.   .   .   .

15. His Majesty the Emperor and King guarantees to His Majesty the King of Prussia the integrity of his territory, on condition that His Majesty the King of Prussia remains the faithful ally of France.

16. His Majesty the King of Prussia recognizes as King of Spain and of the Indies His Majesty Joseph Napoleon, and as King of the Two Sicilies His Majesty Joachim Napoleon.

.   .   .   .

Separate Articles.

1. His Majesty the King of Prussia, wishing to avoid everything which may give umbrage to France, makes engagement to mantain for ten years, dating from January 1, 1809, only the number of troops specified below, to wit:

10 Regiments of infantry, forming at most an effective of	22,000 men.
8 Regiments of cavalry or 32 squadrons forming at most an effective of	8,000 "
A corps of artillerymen, miners and sappers, at most of	6,000 "
Not included the guard of the king estimated, infantry and cavalry, at most	6,000 "
Total,.....	42,000 men.

2. At the expiration of the ten years, His Majesty the King of Prussia shall re-enter into the common right and shall maintain the number of troops which shall seem to him suitable, according to circumstances.

3. During these ten years there shall not be any extraordinary levy of militia or of citizen guards, nor any mustering that tends to augment the forces above specified.

.   .   .   .

5. In return for the guarantee stipulated in the treaty of this day, and as security of the alliance contracted with France, His Majesty the King of Prussia promises to make common cause with His Majesty the Emperor of the French if war comes to be declared between him and Austria, and in that case to place at his disposal a division of 16,000 men, infantry as well as cavalry and artillery.

The present engagement shall continue for ten years. Nevertheless, the King of Prussia, not having been able yet to form his military establishment, shall not be held for any contingent during the present year, and shall be bound to furnish in the year 1809, if war should break out, which the present amicable relations between France and Austria in no wise give occasion to fear, only a contingent of 12,000 men, infantry as well as cavalry.

.   .   .   .

80.   Senatus-Consultum for Suppressing the Tribunate.

August 19, 1807.   Duvergier, *Lois,* XVI, 151-152.

Before its suppression by this document the Tribunate had been the forum for the discussion of legislative measures. Although its meetings were not public this discussion was displeasing to Napoleon and he dissolved it, in order "to simplify and perfect the institutions." The manner of its suppression and the substitute arrangement should be noted.

REFERENCES. Lanfrey, *Napoleon,* III, 333-336; Lavisse and Rambaud, *Histoire générale,* IX, 228-229.

1. For the future, counting from the end of the session which is about to open, the preliminary discussion of the laws which is carried on by the sections of the Tribunate shall be performed, during the continuance of each session, by three commissions of the Legislative Body, under the titles:

The first, of commission of civil and criminal legislation;

The second, of commission of internal administration;

The third, of commission of the finances.

2. Each of these commissions shall deliberate separately and without spectators; they shall be composed of seven members selected by the Legislative Body through secret

ballot and a majority of the votes. The president shall be appointed by the Emperor, either from among the members of the commission or from among the other members of the Legislative Body.

3. The form of the ballot shall be arranged in such a manner that there may be, as far as shall be possible, *four jurisconsultes* upon the commission of legislation.

4. In case of disagreement of opinion between the section of the Council of State which shall have drawn up the project of law and the proper commission of the Legislative Body, both of them shall meet together in conference under the presidency of the archchancellor of the Empire or the archtreasurer, according to the nature of the matters to be examined.

5. If the councillors of state and the members of the commission of the Legislative Body are of the same opinion, the president of the commission shall be heard, after the orator of the Council of State shall have set forth before the Legislative Body the reasons for the law.

6. When the commission shall have decided against the project of law, all the members of the commission shall have power to set forth before the Legislative Body the reasons for their opinion.

7. The members of the commission who shall have discussed a project of law shall be admitted, as are the other members of the Legislative Body, to vote upon the project.

8. When circumstances shall give occasion for the examination of some project of particular importance, it shall be lawful for the Emperor, in the interval of two sessions, to summon the members of the Legislative Body necessary to form the commissions, who shall proceed immediately to the preliminary discussion of the project; these commissions shall be appointed for the next session.

9. The members of the Tribunate who, by the terms of the act of the Conservative Senate dated 17 Fructidor, Year X ought to remain until in the Year XIX, and whose powers, by article 89 of the act of the constitutions of the Empire of 28 Floréal, Year XII, have been extended until in the Year XXI, corresponding to the year 1812 of the Gregorian calendar, shall enter the Legislative Body and shall make

part of that body until the date at which their functions would have ceased in the Tribunate.

10. For the future, nobody can be chosen a member of the Legislative Body unless he is at least fully forty years of age.

81. Documents upon the Overthrow of the Spanish Monarchy.

The first of these documents shows the manner in which Napoleon secured the military position in Spain which enabled him to dictate terms to the Spanish king and heir apparent. Document B shows the terms forced upon the king. A similar agreement was also forced upon the heir apparent. In both documents B and C there is something shown in regard to the manner in which the transaction was effected and officially justified.

REFERENCES. Fyffe, *Modern Europe*, I, 367-387 (Popular ed., 247-261) ; *Cambridge Modern History*, IX, 301-304, 428-434 : Fournier, *Napoleon*, 425-436 ; Rose, *Napoleon*, II, Ch. XXVIII ; Sloane, *Napoleon*, III, 95-119 ; Lanfrey, *Napoleon*, III, 299-314, 362-433 ; Hume, *Modern Spain*, 78-134 ; Henry Adams, *History of the United States*, IV, 115-125, 290-291, 297-303, 315-316 ; Lavisse and Rambaud, *Histoire générale*, IX, 185-191, 200-208 ; Jaurès, *Histoire socialiste*, VI, 340-350.

A. Convention of Fontainebleau. October 27, 1807. De Clercq, *Traités*, II, 235-236.

His Majesty the Emperor of the French, King of Italy, etc., etc., etc., and His Majesty the King of Spain, desiring to regulate by a joint agreement the interests of the two states and to determine the future fate of Portugal, in a manner consistent with the policy of the two countries, . . .

1. The provinces between the Minho and the Duero, with the city of Oporto, shall be given in full ownership and sovereignty to His Majesty the King of Etruria, under the title of King of Northern Lusitania.

2. The Province of Alemte and the Kingdom of Algarve shall be given in full ownership and sovereignty to the *Prince of the Peace,* to be enjoyed under the title of Prince of Algarve.

3. The provinces of Beira, Tras-os-Montes and Portuguese Estremadura, shall remain in trust until the general peace, to be disposed of then according to circumstances.

and according to what shall be agreed upon between the two high contracting parties.

. . . . . .

9. His Majesty the King of Etruria cedes in complete ownership and sovereignty the Kingdom of Etruria to His Majesty the Emperor of the French, King of Italy.

. . . .

11. His Majesty the Emperor of the French, King of Italy, guarantees to His Majesty the King of Spain the possession of his states on the continent of Europe situated to the south of the Pyrenees.

12. His Majesty the Emperor of the French, King of Italy, agrees to recognize and to cause to be recognized His Majesty the King of Spain as Emperor of the Two Americas, when everything shall be prepared so that His Most Catholic Majesty can take that title, which shall be at the general peace or at the latest within three years.

13. The two high contracting parties shall agree to make an equal partition of the islands, colonies and other beyond-the-sea possessions of Portugal.

14. The present convention shall remain secret; it shall be ratified and the ratifications thereof shall be exchanged at Madrid at the latest twenty days after the signing.

B. Convention with Charles IV. May 5, 1808. De Clercq, *Traités*, II, 246-248.

Napoleon, Emperor of the French, King of Italy, Protector of the Confederation of the Rhine, and Charles IV, King of Spain and the Indies, animated by an equal desire to promptly put an end to the anarchy to which Spain is a prey and to save that valiant nation from the agitations of factions, wishing to spare it all the convulsions of civil and foreign war and to place it without disturbances in the only position which, under the extraordinary circumstances in which it finds itself, can preserve its integrity, guarantee it its colonies and enable it also to unite all its means with those of France in order to obtain a maritime peace, have resolved to unite all their efforts and to regulate in a special convention such precious interests . . .

. . . . . .

1. His Majesty King Charles having had in view during all his life only the welfare of his subjects, and rely-

ing upon the principle that all the acts of a sovereign ought to be done only in order to attain that aim; able to be under the existing circumstances only a source of dissensions, all the more fatal since the factions have divided his own family, has resolved to cede, as he does cede by the present [convention], to His Majesty the Emperor Napoleon all his right to the throne of Spain and the Indies, as to the only one who, at the point to which affairs therein have arrived, can re-establish order; intending that the said cession shall take place only in order to cause his subjects to enjoy the two following conditions.

2.   1st. The integrity of the kingdom shall be maintained; the prince whom the Emperor Napoleon shall decide that he ought to place upon the throne of Spain shall be independent, and the boundaries of Spain shall not suffer any alteration.

2d.   The catholic, apostolic and Roman religion shall be the only one in Spain; there cannot be tolerated there any reformed religion and still less infidelity, according to the usage established today.

.   .   .   .

[The omitted articles provide, *inter alia,* that the Spanish royal family shall have a refuge in France, a palace and grounds, a stipulated income and the enjoyment of their royal rank.]

11.   The present convention shall remain secret until the two high contracting parties shall see fit to make it known; it shall be ratified, and the ratification thereof shall be exchanged within eight days or as much sooner as shall be possible.

Done at Bayonne, May 5, 1808.

C.   Imperial Decree proclaiming Joseph Bonaparte King of Spain.   June 6, 1808.   *Moniteur,* June 22, 1808.

Napoleon, by the grace of God, Emperor of the French, King of Italy, Protector of the Confederation of the Rhine, to all those who shall see these presents, greeting.

The Junta of State, the Council of Castile, the city of Madrid, etc., etc., having made known to us by addresses that the welfare of Spain requires that an end should be promptly put to the interregnum, we have resolved to proclaim, as we do proclaim by the present [proclamation], that our well-beloved brother Joseph Napoleon, at present King of Naples and Sicily, is King of Spain and the Indies.

We guarantee to the King of Spain the integrity of his States, whether in Europe, Africa, Asia, or America.

We enjoin upon the lieutenant general of the kingdom, the ministers, and the Council of Castile, to cause the present proclamation to be despatched and published in the accustomed forms, in order that nobody can pretend grounds of ignorance of it.

Given at our imperial palace at Bayonne, June 6, 1808.

Signed, NAPOLEON.

82. The Erfurt Convention.

October 12, 1808. De Clercq, *Traités,* II, 284-286.

This document should be studied in connection with No. 79. The Spanish rising against Napoleon for a time threatened to produce a general movement against his domination. Napoleon, however, induced the Czar to meet him at Erfurt, where a series of conferences led to the signing of this convention. The consolidation of the Franco-Russian alliance prevented the threatened general rising. Both the general character and the special terms of this alliance, as set forth in the document, merit careful attention.

REFERENCES. *Cambridge Modern History,* IX, 314-321; Fournier, *Napoleon,* 438-444; Rose, *Napoleon,* II, 164-170; Sloane, *Napoleon,* III, 133-138; Lanfrey, *Napoleon,* III, 485-494; Lavisse and Rambaud, *Histoire générale,* IX, 135-147.

His Majesty the Emperor of the French, King of Italy, Protector of the Confederation of the Rhine, and His Majesty the Emperor of all the Russias, wishing to cause the alliance which unites them to be more and more close and forever durable, and reserving to themselves to agree subsequently, if there is need, upon the new determinations to be taken and the new means of attack to be directed against England, their common enemy and the enemy of the continent, have resolved to establish in a special convention the principles which they are determined to follow invariably in all their measures to obtain the re-establishment of peace. . . .

.   .   .   .

1. His Majesty the Emperor of the French, King of Italy, etc., and His Majesty the Emperor of all the Russias confirm and, in as far as there is need, renew the alliance concluded

between them at Tilsit; binding themselves, not only not to make any separate peace with the common enemy, but in addition not to enter into any negotiation with it, and not to listen to any of its proposals except by common consent.

2. Thus resolved to remain inseparably united for peace as well as for war, the high contracting parties agree to appoint plenipotentiaries to treat for peace with England and to send them for this purpose to the city of the continent which England shall designate.

3. In all the course of the negotiation, if it occurs, the respective plenipotentiaries of the high contracting parties shall constantly act with the most perfect accord, and it shall not be permissible for either of them to support, nor even to receive or approve contrary to the interests of the other contracting party any proposal or demand of the English plenipotentiaries, which, taken by itself and favorable to the interests of England, may also present some advantage to one of the contracting parties.

4. The basis of the treaty with England shall be the *uti possidetis.*

5. The high contracting parties bind themselves to consider as an absolute condition of peace with England that she shall recognize Finland, Wallachia, and Moldavia as making part of the Empire of Russia.

6. They agree to consider as an absolute condition of the peace that England shall recognize the new order of things established by France in Spain.

7. The high contracting parties agree not to receive from the side of the enemy during the continuance of fhe negotiations any proposal, offer or communication whatsoever, without immediately sharing it with the respective courts: and if the said proposals are made at the congress assembled for the peace, the respective plenipotentiaries shall be bound to communicate them.

8. His Majesty the Emperor of all the Russias, in consequence of all the revolutions and changes which disturb the Ottoman Empire and which do not leave any possibility of giving, and in consequence any hope of obtaining, sufficient guarantees for the persons and goods of the inhabitants of Wallachia and Moldavia, having already carried the limits of his Empire to the Danube on that side and united Wal-

lachia and Moldavia with his Empire, and being able only on that condition to recognize the integrity of the Ottoman Empire, the Emperor Napoleon recognizes the said union and the said limits of the Russian Empire, extended on that side to the Danube.

9. His Majesty the Emperor of all the Russias agrees to keep in the most profound secrecy the preceding article and to enter upon a negotiation, either at Constantinople or anywhere else, in order to obtain amicably, if that be possible, the cession of these two provinces. France renounces its mediation. The plenipotentiaries or agents of the two powers shall agree upon the language to be held, in order not to compromise the friendship existing between France and the Porte, as well as the security of the French who reside in the Turkish dominions in order to prevent the Porte throwing itself into the arms of England.

10. In case the war should happen to be rekindled, the Ottoman Porte refusing the cession of the two provinces, the Emperor Napoleon shall not take any part therein and shall confine himself to the employment of his good offices with the Ottoman Porte; but if it should happen that Austria or any other power should make common cause with the Ottoman Empire in the said war, His Majesty the Emperor Napoleon shall immediately make common cause with Russia, being obliged to consider this case as one of those of the general alliance which unites the two empires. In case Austria should engage in war against France, the Emperor of Russia agrees to declare himself against Austria and to make common cause with France, that case being likewise one of those to which the alliance that unites the two empires applies.

11. The high contracting parties bind themselves, moreover, to maintain the integrity of the other possessions of the Ottoman Empire, not wishing to undertake themselves or suffer that there should be undertaken any enterprise against any part of that empire, unless they should be previously informed of it.

12. If the measures taken by the two high contracting parties are unavailing, either because England evades the proposal which shall be made to it, or because the negotiations are broken off, their Imperial Majesties shall meet

again within the space of one year, in order to agree upon the operations of the common war and upon the means to pursue it with all the forces and all the resources of the two empires.

13. The two high contracting parties, wishing to recognize the loyalty and the perseverance with which the King of Denmark has supported the common cause, agree to procure for him an indemnification for his sacrifices and to recognize the acquisitions which he shall have been in a position to make in the present war.

14. The present convention shall be kept secret for at least the space of ten years.

83. Decree upon the Term, French Republic.

October 22, 1808. Duvergier, *Lois*, XVI, 312.

The time and manner in which the idea of the Republic disappeared from French institutions is a matter of much importance for the comprehension of the method whereby Napoleon built up his power. This document serves to fix the date of its final disappearance; something of the manner in which it was eliminated can be seen from an examination of Nos. 58, 66 E and 71.

REFERENCE. Aulard, *Révolution française*, 778-780.

1. The monies which shall be coined dating from January 1, 1809, shall bear for legend upon the reverse of the piece the words, *French Empire,* in lieu of those of *French Republic.*

2. Our Minister of Finance is charged with the execution of the present decree.

84. Documents upon the Annexations of 1809-1810.

In 1809-1810 Napoleon annexed to France a great deal of territory. All of it had for some time been dependent upon France. These documents show most of the territory taken, some of the reasons assigned for its annexation, something of the manner in which the former rulers were treated, and the kind of special arrangements made for the territory as part of France.

REFERENCES. Fyffe, *Modern Europe,* I, 436-441 (Popular ed., 294-297) ; *Cambridge Modern History,* IX, 195-196, 369-371, 374-375, 400-403 ; Fournier. *Napoleon,* 495-498. 506-511 ; Rose, *Napoleon,* II, 141-142, 195-198 ; Sloane, *Napoleon,* III, 201-204, 211-214 ; Lanfrey, *Napoleon*, IV, 252-264, 278-303, 341-343 ; Lavisse and Rambaud, *Histoire générale*, IX, 275-278, 766-767.

As the Empire of Napoleon was at its height following these annexations, its territorial extent and the relationship of the various parts may be profitably studied at this point.

Maps. Droysen, *Historischer Hand-Atlas*, 58-59 ; Lane-Poole, *Historical Atlas of Modern Europe*, LIX ; Schrader, *Atlas de geographie historique*, 43 ; Vidal-Lablache, *Atlas général*, 40-41.

A. Imperial Decree for the Annexation of the Papal States. May 17, 1809. *Correspondance de Napoleon I*, XIX, 15-16. Translation, James Harvey Robinson, *University of Pennsylvania Translations and Reprints.*

Napoleon, Emperor of the French, King of Italy, Protector of the Confederation of the Rhine, etc., in consideration of the fact that when Charlemagne, Emperor of the French and our august predecessor, granted several counties to the bishops of Rome he ceded these only as fiefs and for the good of his realm and Rome did not by reason of this cession cease to form a part of his empire; farther that since this association of spiritual and temporal authority has been and still is a source of dissensions and has but too often led the pontiffs to employ the influence of the former to maintain the pretensions of the latter, and thus the spiritual concerns and heavenly interests which are unchanging have been confused with terrestrial affairs which by their nature alter according to circumstances and the policy of the time; and since all our proposals for reconciling the security of our armies, the tranquility and the welfare of our people and the dignity and integrity of our Empire, with the temporal pretensions of the popes have failed, we have decreed and do decree what follows :

1. The Papal States are reunited to the French Empire.

2. The city of Rome, so famous by reason of the great memories which cluster about it and as the first seat of christianity, is proclaimed a free imperial city. The organization of the government and administration of the said city shall be provided by a special statute.

3. The remains of the structures erected by the Romans shall be maintained and preserved at the expense of our treasury.

4. The public debt shall become an imperial debt.

5. The lands and domains of the Pope shall be increased to a point where they shall produce an annual net revenue of two millions.

6. The lands and domains of the Pope as well as his palaces shall be exempt from all taxes, jurisdiction or visitation, and shall enjoy special immunities.

7. On the first of June of the present year a special *consultus* shall take possession of the Papal States in our name and shall make the necessary provisions in order that a constitutional system shall be organized and may be put in force on January first, 1810.

Given at our Imperial Camp at Vienna, May 17th, 1809.

NAPOLEON.

B. Organic Senatus-Consultum for the Annexation of the Papal States. February 17, 1810. Duvergier, *Lois*, XVII, 27.

Title I. Of the Union of the States of Rome with the Empire.

1. The state of Rome is united with the French Empire and makes an integral part thereof.

2. It shall form two departments, the department of Rome and the department of Trasimeno.

3. The department of Rome shall have seven deputies in the Legislative Body; the department of Trasimeno shall have four.

.   .   .   .

5. There shall be a senatorship established for the departments of Rome and Trasimeno.

6. The city of Rome is the second city of the Empire. The mayor of Rome is present at the taking of the oath by the Emperor at his accession: he takes rank, along with the deputation of the city of Rome, on all occasions immediately after the mayors and deputations of the city of Paris.

7. The prince imperial bears the title and receives the honors of King of Rome.

8. There shall be at Rome a prince of the blood or a grand dignitary of the Empire, who shall hold the court of the Emperor.

.   .   .   .

10. After having been crowned in the church of Notre Dame at Paris, the Emperors shall be crowned in the church of Saint Peter at Rome, before the tenth year of their reign.

11. The city of Rome shall enjoy the special privileges and immunities which shall be determined by the Emperor Napoleon.

Title II. Of the Independence of the Imperial Throne of Every Authority upon Earth.

12. Any foreign sovereignty is incompatible with the exercise of any spiritual authority within the interior of the Empire.

13. At the time of their elevation [to the papal dignity], the popes shall take oath never to do anything contrary to the four propositions of the Gallican church, decreed in the assembly of the clergy in 1682.

14. The four propositions of the Gallican church are declared common to all the catholic churches of the Empire.

Title III. Of the Temporal Position of the Popes.

15. Palaces shall be prepared for the Pope in the different places of the Empire in which he may wish to reside. There snall be necessarily one at Paris and one at Rome.

16. Two millions of revenue in rural estates, free from all taxation and situated in the different parts of the Empire, shall be assigned to the Pope.

17. The expenses of the Sacred College and of the Propaganda are declared imperial [expenses].

C. Treaty with Holland. March 16, 1810. De Clercq, *Traités*, II, 328-330.

His Majesty the Emperor of the French, King of Italy, Protector of the Confederation of the Rhine, Mediator of the Swiss Confederation, and His Majesty the King of Holland, wishing to put an end to the difficulties which have arisen between them and to reconcile the independence of Holland with the new circumstances in which the orders in council of England of 1807 have placed all the maritime powers, have

agreed to come to an understanding, and have appointed plenipotentiaries for that purpose, to wit: . . .

1. Until the British government has formally renounced
the methods comprised in its orders in council of 1807, all
commerce whatsoever between the ports of Holland and the
ports of England is forbidden. If there is occasion to give licenses, those given in the name of the Emperor shall be the
only valid ones.

2. A body of troops consisting of 18,000 men, of which
3,000 shall be cavalry, composed of 6,000 Frenchmen and
12,000 Hollanders, shall be placed at all the mouths of the
rivers with the employes of the French customs-houses, in
order to watch over the execution of the preceding article.

3. These troops shall be taken care of, fed and clothed
by the government of Holland.

4. Every prize taken upon the coasts of Holland by French
ships of war or privateers from vessels contravening article
1 shall be declared good prize; in case of doubt the difficulty
can be adjudged only by His Majesty the Emperor.

5. The provisions contained in the above articles shall be
annulled as soon as England shall have solemnly revoked its
orders in council of 1807, and from that moment the French
troops shall evacuate Holland and shall leave it to enjoy the
whole of its independence.

6. It being a constitutional principle in France that the
thalweg of the Rhine is the boundary of the French Empire,
and the ship yards of Antwerp, being unguarded and exposed
through the existing situation of the boundaries of the two
States, His Majesty the King of Holland cedes to His Majesty the Emperor of the French, etc., Dutch Brabant, the
whole of Zeeland, including therein the island of Schouwen,
and part of Gelderland upon the left bank of the Waal, in
such a manner that the boundary of France and of Holland
shall be henceforth the thalweg of the Waal, . . .

.   .   .   .

8. His Majesty the King of Holland, in order to co-operate with the forces of the French Empire, shall have at an-
chor a fleet of 9 ships of the line and 6 frigates, armed and
provisioned for six months and ready to put sail on July 1st
next, and a flotilla of 100 gunboats or other ships of war.

This force shall be kept up and made constantly disposable during the entire war.

.   .   .   .

10. All merchandise arriving upon American vessels entered into the ports of Holland since January 1, 1809, shall be placed in sequestration and shall belong to France to be disposed of according to circumstances and its political relations with the United States.

11. All merchandise of English manufacture is prohibited in Holland.

12. Police measures shall be taken to look after and to cause the arrest of insurers of contraband, contrabandists, their abettors, etc.; finally, the government of Holland agrees that it will destroy contraband.

.   .   .   .

15. Filled with confidence as to the manner in which the engagements resulting from the present treaty will be fulfilled, His Majesty the Emperor and King guarantees the integrity of the possessions of Holland as they shall be in virtue of this treaty.

16. The present treaty shall be ratified and the ratifications thereof shall be exchanged at Paris within the space of fifteen days or sooner if it is possible to do so.

Done at Paris, March 16, 1810.

D. Organic Senatus-Consultum for the Annexation of Holland and North Germany, December 13th, 1810. Duvergier, *Lois*, XVII, 235.

1. Holland, the Hanseatic cities, Lauenburg, and the countries situated between the North Sea and a line drawn from the confluence of the Lippe with the Rhine to Haltern, from Haltern to the Ems below Telgte; from the Ems to the confluence of the Werre with the Weser, and from Stozenau upon the Weser to the Elbe below the confluence of the Steckenitz, shall make an integral part of the French Empire.

2. The said countries shall form ten departments to wit:

.   .   .   .

3. The number of deputies of these departments in the Legislative Body shall be . . . [29 in all].

.   .   .   .

8. One senatorship shall be established for the departments forming the jurisdiction of the imperial court of the Hague, and another for the departments forming the jurisdiction of the imperial court of Hamburg.

9. The cities of Amsterdam, Rotterdam, Hamburg. Bremen, and Lubeck, are included among the good cities of which the mayors are present at the taking of the oath of the Emperor at his accession.

. . . .

85. Treaty of Vienna.

October 14, 1809. De Clercq, *Traités,* II, 293-299.

This treaty came at the end of the fourth war which Austria had fought against France since the beginning of the revolution. Its terms should be compared with those of the three preceding treaties, Campo Formio. Lunéville and Pressburg (Nos. 55, 62, 74).

REFERENCES. Fyffe, *Modern Europe,* I, 430-433 (Popular ed., 289-292) ; *Cambridge Modern History,* IX, 359-360 ; Fournier, *Napoleon,* 477-482 ; Lanfrey, *Napoleon,* IV, 213-224 ; Sloane, *Napoleon,* III, 182-185 ; Lavisse and Rambaud, *Histoire générale,* IX, 176-177.

MAP. Schrader, *Atlas de geographie historique,* 48.

His Majesty the Emperor of the French, King of Italy, Protector of the Confederation of the Rhine, Mediator of the Swiss Confederation, and His Majesty the Emperor of Austria, King of Hungary and of Bohemia, equally prompted by the desire to put an end to the war that has been kindled between them, have resolved to proceed without delay to the conclusion of a definitive treaty of peace, . . .

. . . .

1. There. shall be, dating from the day of the exchange of the ratifications of the present treaty, peace and amity between His Majesty the Emperor of the French, King of Italy, Protector of the Confederation. of the Rhine, and His Majesty the Emperor of Austria, King of Hungary and of Bohemia, their heirs and successors, their respective States and subjects, forever.

. . . .

3. His Majesty the Emperor of Austria, King of Hungary and of Bohemia, both for himself, his heirs and successors, and for the princes of his house, their respective heirs and successors, renounces the principalities, lordships, domains and

territories hereinafter designated, as well as every title whatsoever which may be derived from their possession, and the properties, whether domanial or possessed by them under personal title, which these countries include.

1st. He cedes and abandons to His Majesty the Emperor of the French, in order to make part of the Confederation of the Rhine and to be disposed of in favor of the sovereigns of the confederation: the countries of Salzburg and Berechtesgaden, the portion of Upper Austria situated beyond a line setting out from the Danube near the village of Strass and taking in Weissenkirchen, Wiedersdorf, Michelbach, Greist, Muckenhoffen, Helft, Jeding, from there the road to Schwanenstadt, the city of Schwanenstadt upon the Kammer, and in continuation reascending the course of that river and of the lake of that name to the point at which that lake touches the frontier of the country of Salzburg. . . .

2d. He likewise cedes to His Majesty the Emperor of the French, King of Italy, the County of Görz, the territory of Montefalcone, the Government of the city of Trieste, Carniola with its enclaves upon the gulf of Trieste, the circle of Vilach in Carinthia, and all the countries situated to the right of the Save, in setting out from the point at which that river leaves Carniola and following it to the frontier of Bosnia, to wit: part of provincial Croatia, six districts of military Croatia, Fiume and the Hungarian littoral, the Austrian Istria or district of Küsten, the dependent islands of these ceded countries and all the other countries under whatsoever denomination upon the right bank of the Save, the thalweg of that river serving as boundary between the two States; lastly, the lordship of Razuns, enclave within the country of the Grisons.

3d. He cedes and abandons to His Majesty the King of Saxony the enclaves dependent upon Bohemia and included within the territory of the Kingdom of Saxony, to wit: . .

4th. He cedes and abandons to His Majesty the King of Saxony, in order to be united to the Duchy of Warsaw, all eastern or new Galicia, a district about Cracow upon the right bank of the Vistula, which shall be determined hereafter, and the circle of Zamoste in eastern Galicia.

. . . .

5th. He cedes and abandons to His Majesty the Emperor

of Russia, in the most eastern part of former Galicia, a territory comprising four hundred thousand souls of population, in which the city of Brody shall be included. This territory shall be determined by agreement between commissioners of the two Empires.

.   .   .   .

14. His Majesty the Emperor of the French, King of Italy, Protector of the Confederation of the Rhine, guarantees the integrity of the possessions of His Majesty the Emperor of Austria, King of Hungary and of Bohemia, in the state in which they are according to the present treaty.

15. His Majesty the Emperor of Austria recognizes all the changes which have occurred or which may occur in Spain, in Portugal, and in Italy.

16. His Majesty the Emperor of Austria, wishing to contribute to the return of maritime peace, adheres to the prohibitive system adopted by France and Russia in opposition to England for the present maritime war. His Imperial Majesty will cause all relations with Great Britain to cease and will put himself, as regards the English Government, in the position in which he was before the present war.

.   .   .   .

Separate Article.

1. In virtue of the authorisation given by His Majesty the Emperor of Russia, the treaty of peace of this day is declared to be common to Russia, the ally of France.

2. His Majesty the Emperor of Austria, in consequence of the diminution of his possessions and being anxious to remove everything which might give birth to uneasiness and distrust between the two states, as well as to manifest his political intentions, binds himself to reduce the rolls of his troops in such a manner that the total number of the troops of all arms and of every sort shall not rise above 150,000 men during the continuance of the maritime war.

.   .   .   .

5. His Majesty the Emperor of Austria, King of Hungary and of Bohemia, shall discharge in coin that which remains to be paid of the two hundred millions of contributions imposed upon the different states occupied by the French armies, whether in bank notes or in metallic value. In order to

facilitate the payment of this sum, His Majesty the Emperor of the French consents to reduce it to 85,000,000 francs. . . .

. . . .

86. Decree upon Printing and Bookselling.

February 5, 1810. Duvergier, *Lois*, XVII, 19-23.

This law is a sort of organic act upon the press. It co-ordinates and consolidates a number of earlier measures in restraint of freedom of printing. The system delineated in the document had existed, substantially as here shown, from about 1804.

REFERENCES. Dickinson, *Revolution and Reaction in Modern France*, 46-48 ; Lanfrey, *Napoleon*, IV, 316-326.

Title I. Of the Directorship of Printing and Bookselling.

1. There shall be a director general charged, under the orders of our minister of the interior, with everything that relates to printing and bookselling.

. . . .

Title II. Of the Occupation of Printer.

3. Dating from January 1, 1811, the number of printers in each department shall be fixed and that of the printers of Paris shall be reduced to sixty.

. . . .

5. The printers shall be commissioned and sworn.
6. At Paris they shall be required to have four presses, in the departments two.

. . . .

9. The commission of printer shall be given by our director general of printing, and shall be subject to the approval of our minister of the interior ; it shall be registered at the civil tribunal of the place of residence of the grantee, who shall there take oath not to print anything which is contrary to the duties towards the sovereign and the interest of the state.

Title III. Of the Police for Printing.

Section 1. Of the guarantee for the administration.

10. Printing or causing to be printed anything which may involve injury to the duties of subjects towards the sovereign or the interests of the state is forbidden. . . .

11. Each printer shall be required to have a book numbered and lettered by the prefect of the department, in which he shall register, by order of dates, the title of each work which he shall wish to print, and the name of the author, if it is known. This book shall be presented at every requisition, and examined and endorsed, if it is thought desirable, by any officer of police.

12. The printer shall immediately deliver or address to the director general of printing and bookselling, and also to the prefects, a copy of the transcript made upon his book: and the declaration that he has an intention of printing the work: he shall be given a receipt therefor.

The prefects shall give information of each of these declarations to our minister of the general police.

13. The director general can order, if it seems good to him, the communication and examination of the work, and can suspend the printing.

14. When the director general shall have suspended the printing of a work, he shall send it to a censor chosen from among those whom we, upon the advice of the director general and the proposal of our minister of the interior, shall have appointed to discharge that function.

15. Our minister of the general police, and the prefects in their departments, shall cause to be suspended the printing of all works which shall appear to them to be in contravention to article 10: in that case, the manuscript shall be sent within twenty-four hours to the director general, as is said above.

16. Upon the report of the censor, the director general shall indicate to the author the changes or suppressions deemed appropriate, and, upon his refusal to make them, shall forbid the sale of the work, shall cause the forms to be broken, and shall seize the sheets or copies already printed.

.   .   .   .

Title IV. Of Booksellers.

29. Dating from January 1, 1811, booksellers shall be commissioned and sworn.

30. The commissions for booksellers shall be given by our director general of printing, and shall be subject to the approval of our minister of the interior. They shall be registered at the civil tribunal of the place of residence of the grantee, who shall there take oath not to sell, circulate or distribute any work contrary to the duties towards the sovereign and the interest of the state.

. . . .

33. For the future, commissions shall not be granted to booksellers who shall wish to establish themselves, except after they shall have furnished proof of their good life and morals and of their attachment to the fatherland and the sovereign.

Title V. Of Books Printed Abroad.

34. No book . in the French or Latin languages printed abroad shall enter France without paying import duty.

35. This duty shall not be less than fifty per cent. of the value of the work.

. . . .

36. Independently of the provisions of article 34, no book printed or reprinted outside of France can be introduced into France without a permit from the director general of bookselling designating the custom house at which it shall enter.

. . . .

87. The Frankfort Declaration.

December 1, 1813. *British and Foreign State Papers*, I, 911.

This manifesto of the allied powers was issued just as their armies were about to enter France. Its purpose, as shown by various expressions in the document, should be noticed. Its phraseology upon such points as the future of France and its boundaries also requires attention. The latter may be compared with that of the first draft as quoted by Fournier.

REFERENCES. Fournier, *Napoleon*, 648-650; Rose, *Napoleon*, II, 346-347; Lavisse and Rambaud, *Histoire générale*, IX, 848-849; Sorel, *L'Europe et la révolution française*, VIII, 224-224.

The French government has just ordered a new levy of 300,000 conscripts. The reasons of the senatus-consultum contain a provocation to the allied powers. They find themselves again called upon to promulgate in the face of the world the views which govern them in the present war, the principles which constitute the basis of their conduct, their views and their determinations.

The allied powers are not at war with France, but with that haughtily announced preponderance, that preponderance which, to the misfortune of Europe and of France, the Emperor Napoleon has for too long a time exercised outside of the boundaries of his empire.

Victory has led the allied armies to the Rhine. The first use which their Imperial and Royal Majesties have made of victory has been to offer peace to His Majesty the Emperor of the French. An attitude reinforced by the accession of all the sovereigns and princes of Germany has not had any influence upon the conditions of peace. These conditions are founded upon the independence of the French Empire, as well as upon the independence of the other states of Europe. The views of the powers are just in their object, generous and liberal in their application, reassuring for all, and honorable for each.

The allied sovereigns desire that France should be great, strong and happy, because the great and strong French power is one of the fundamental bases of the social edifice. They desire that France should be happy, that French commerce should rise again, and that the arts, those blessings of peace, should flourish again, because a great people cannot be tranquil except in as far as it is happy. The powers confirm to the French Empire an extent of territory which France never knew under its kings, because a valiant nation should not lose rank for having in its turn experienced reverse in an obstinate and bloody conflict, in which it has fought with its usual daring.

But the powers also wish to be free, happy and tranquil. They desire a state of peace which, by a wise distribution of power and a just equilibrium, may preserve henceforth their peoples from the innumerable calamities which for the past twenty years have weighed upon Europe.

The allied powers will not lay aside their arms without having attained that great and beneficent result, that noble object of their efforts. They will not lay aside their arms until the political condition of Europe shall be again consol-

idated, until immutable principles shall have resumed their
rights over vain pretensions, until the sanctity of treaties shall
have finally assured a real peace for Europe.

Frankfort, December 1, 1813.

88. Address of the Legislative Body to Napoleon.

December 28, 1813. Buchez and Roux, *Histoire parlementaire*, XXXIX, 456-458.

This address was drawn up after Napoleon had submitted to
the Legislative Body a portion of his correspondence with the allies. Napoleon dissolved the chamber and forbade the publication
of the address. The document throws some light upon the state
of France, its attitude towards Napoleon and the war.

·REFERENCES. Fournier, *Napoleon*, 650-652; Sloane, *Napoleon*,
IV, 85-86; Rose, *Napoleon*, II, 347-348; Lavisse and Rambaud,
Histoire générale, IX, 849-853; Sorel, *L'Europe et la révolution
française*, VIII, 226-228.

We have examined with a scrupulous attention the official
documents which the Emperor has deigned to place before
our eyes. We consider ourselves then as the representatives
of the nation itself, speaking with open hearts to a father who
hears us with benevolence. Filled with that sentiment, so
adapted to the elevation of our souls and to disengaging us
from every personal consideration, we have dared to bring
the truth to the foot of the throne; our august sovereign
could not suffer any other language.

[The omitted passage reviews the course of events from
the outbreak of the war with Russia to the end of the campaign of 1813.]

. . . .

Here, gentlemen, we must avow it, the enemy carried along
by victory to the banks of the Rhine has offered to our august monarch a peace which a hero accustomed to so much
success must have found strange indeed. But if a manly and
heroic sentiment dictated to him a refusal before the deplorable state of France had been ascertained, that refusal cannot
be reiterated without imprudence when the enemy is already
breaking the frontiers of our territory. If the matter here in
question had been the discussion of disgraceful conditions,
His Majesty would have deigned to reply only by making

known to his people the projects of the foreigners; there is no wish, however, to humiliate us, but to confine us within our limits and to repress the soaring of an ambitious activity so fatal for twenty years past to all the peoples of Europe.

Such proposals seem to us honorable for the nation, since they prove that the foreigner fears and respects us. It is not he who sets limits to our power, it is the terrified world which invokes the common right of nations. The Pyrenees, the Alps and the Rhine enclose a vast territory of which several provinces were not held by the Empire of the Lilies, and yet the royal crown of France was radiant with glory and majesty among all the diadems.

Furthermore, the protectorate of the Rhine ceases to be a title of honor for a crown, from the moment when the peoples of that confederation disdain that protection.

It is obvious that here there is no question of a right of conquest, but of a title of alliance useful only to the Germans. A powerful hand was assuring them of its assistance; they wish to slip away from that benefaction as from an insupportable burden; it is consistent with the dignity of His Majesty to abandon to themselves those peoples who are hastening to range themselves under the yoke of Austria. As for Brabant, since the allies propose to adhere to the bases of the treaty of Lunéville, it seems to us that France could sacrifice without loss provinces difficult to retain, in which the English spirit dominates almost exclusively, and for which, finally, commerce with England is a necessity so indispensable that these districts have been languishing and impoverished as long as our dominion has lasted. Have we not seen patrician families exiling themselves from Dutch soil, as if devastating scourges had pursued them, and taking to the enemy the wealth and industry of their fatherland. Doubtless it does not take courage to make the heart of our sovereign hear the truth; but we should be bound to expose ourselves to all perils, we should prefer to incur disgrace from him rather than to betray his confidence, and to expose our lives rather than the safety of the nation which we represent.

Let us not dissemble: our ills are at their height; the fatherland is threatened at all points upon its frontiers; commerce is annihilated, agriculture languishes, industry is expiring;

and there is not a Frenchman who has not in his family or
his fortune a cruel wound to heal. Let us not be weighed
down by these facts; the agriculturist has not prospered for
five years past; he barely lives, and the fruits of his labors serve to augment the treasure which is annually exhausted in the supplies which the constantly ruined and fam-
ished armies demand. The conscription has become for all
France an odious scourge, because that measure has always
been overdone in execution. For the past two years the
gathering in has occurred three times per year; a barbarous
and aimless war has swallowed up youths torn away from
education, agriculture, commerce and the arts. Are the tears
of mothers and the pains of the people then the patrimony of
kings? It is time that the nations should be in repose; it is
time that the powers should cease clashing and tearing each
others entrails; it is time that the thrones should be strengthened and that France should cease to be reproached with wishing to carry into all the world revolutionary torches. Our
august monarch, who shares the zeal that animates us and
who is burning to consolidate the welfare of his peoples, is
the only one capable of performing that great work. Love
of military honor and of conquests may seduce a magnanimous heart; but the genius of a true hero, who spurns a
glory achieved at the expense of the blood and repose of the
people, finds his true grandeur in the public felicity which
is his work. French monarchs have always gloried in holding their crown from God, the people and their sword, because peace, morality and power are, with liberty, the firmest
support of empires.

89. Treaty of Chaumont.

March 1, 1814. De Clercq, *Traités*, II, 395-399; XV, 144-145.
Translation based upon Hertslet, *Map of Europe by Treaty*, 2043-
2048.

This treaty in terms includes only Austria and Russia, but
Great Britain and Prussia were included in similar treaties
formed at the same time. Although dated March 1 the treaty
was not actually signed until March 9. The terms alluded to in
article 1 were those offered to Napoleon at the Congress of Châ-
tillon. As the most comprehensive and typical of the series of
treaties which created and controlled the alliance against France
the terms of this document should be carefully noted.

REFERENCES. Fournier, *Napoleon*, 665-666 ; Rose, *Napoleon*, II, 370-371 ; Sorel, *L'Europe et la révolution française*, VIII, 289-291.

His Imperial Majesty and Royal Highness the Emperor of Austria, King of Hungary and of Bohemia, His Majesty the Emperor of all the Russias, His Majesty the King of the United Kingdom of Great Britain and Ireland, His Majesty the King of Prussia, having forwarded to the French government proposals for the conclusion of a general peace, and desiring, in case France should refuse the conditions of that peace, to draw closer the bonds which unite them for the vigorous prosecution of a war undertaken with the salutary purpose of putting an end to the misfortunes of Europe by assuring future repose through the re-establishment of a just equilibrium of the powers, and wishing at the same time, if Providence blesses their pacific intentions, to settle the methods of maintaining against every attack the order of things which shall have been the happy result of their efforts, have agreed to sanction by a solemn treaty, signed separately by each of the four powers with the other three, this double engagement.

.   .   .   .

1. The high contracting parties above named solemnly engage by the present treaty, and in the event of France refusing to accede to the conditions of peace now proposed, to apply all the means of their respective states to the vigorous prosecution of the war against that power, and to employ them in perfect concert, in order to obtain for themselves and for Europe a general peace, under the protection of which the rights and liberties of all nations shall be established and secured.

This engagement shall in no respect affect the stipulations which the several powers have already contracted relative to the number of troops to be kept against the enemy; and it is understood that the courts of England, Austria, Russia, and Prussia engage by the present treaty to keep in the field, each of them, 150,000 effective men, exclusive of garrisons, to be employed in active service against the common enemy.

2. The high contracting parties reciprocally engage not to treat separately with the common enemy, nor to sign peace, truce, nor convention, but with common consent. They, more-

over, engage not to lay down their arms until the object of the war, mutually understood and agreed upon, shall have been attained.

3. In order to contribute in the most prompt and decisive manner to fulfill this great object, His Britannic Majesty engages to furnish a subsidy of £5,000,000 for the service of the year 1814, to be divided in equal proportions amongst the three powers; and his said Majesty promises, moreover, to arrange before the 1st of January in each year, with their Imperial and Royal Majesties, the further succours to be furnished during the subsequent year, if (which God forbid) the war should so long continue.

.   .   .   .

5. The high contracting parties, reserving to themselves to concert together, on the conclusion of a peace with France, as to the means best adapted to guarantee to Europe, and to themselves, reciprocally, the continuance of the peace, have also determined to enter without delay into defensive engagements for the protection of their respective states in Europe against every attempt which France might make to infringe the order of things resulting from such pacification.

6. To effect this, they agree that in the event of one of the high contracting parties being threatened with an attack on the part of France, the others shall employ their most strenuous efforts to prevent it, by friendly interposition.

7. In case of these endeavours proving ineffectual, the high contracting parties promise to come to the immediate assistance of the power attacked, each with a body of 60,000 men.

.   .   .   .

9. As the situation of the seat of war, or other circumstances, might render it difficult for Great Britain to furnish the stipulated succours in English troops within the term prescribed, and to maintain the same on a war establishment, His Britannic Majesty reserves the right of furnishing his contingent to the requiring power in foreign troops in his pay, or to pay annually to that power a sum of money, at the rate of £20 per man for infantry, and of £30 for cavalry, until the stipulated succour shall be complete.

.   .   .   .

13. The high contracting parties mutually promise, that in case they shall be reciprocally engaged in hostilities, in con-

sequence of furnishing the stipulated succours, the party requiring and the parties called upon, and acting as auxiliaries in the war, shall not make peace but by common consent.

.   .   .   .

15. In order to render more effectual the defensive engagements above stipulated, by uniting for their common defence the powers the most exposed to a French invasion, the high contracting parties engage to invite those powers to accede to the present treaty of defensive alliance

16. The present treaty of defensive alliance having for its object to maintain the equilibrium of Europe, to secure the repose and independence of its states, and to prevent the invasions which during so many years have desolated the world, the high contracting parties have agreed to extend the duration of it to twenty years, to take date from the day of its signature; and they reserve to themselves to concert upon its ulterior prolongation three years before its expiration, should circumstances require it.

.   .   .   .

Secret Articles.

1. The re-establishment of an equilibrium of the powers and a just distribution of forces among them being the aim of the present war, their Imperial and Royal Majesties obligate themselves to direct their efforts toward the actual establishment of the following system in Europe, to wit:

Germany composed of sovereign princes united by a federative bond which assures and guarantees the independence of Germany.

The Swiss Confederation in its former limits and in an independence placed under the guarantee of the great powers of Europe, France included.

Italy divided into independent states, intermediaries between the Austrian possessions in Italy and France.

Spain governed by King Ferdinand VII in its former limits.

Holland, free and independent state, under the sovereignty of the Prince of Orange, with an increase of territory and the establishment of a suitable frontier.

2. The high confederated parties agree, in execution of article 15 of the open treaty, to invite the accession to the pres-

ent treaty of defensive alliance of the monarchies of Spain, Portugal, Sweden, and His Royal Highness the Prince of Orange, and to admit to it likewise other sovereigns and states according to the exigency of the case.

3. Considering the necessity which may exist after the conclusion of a definitive treaty of peace with France, to keep in the field during a certain time sufficient forces to protect the arrangements which the allies must make among themselves for the re-establishment of the situation of Europe, the high confederated powers have decided to concert among themselves, not only over the necessity, but over the sum and the distribution of the forces to be kept upon foot, according to the need of the circumstances. None of the high confederated powers shall be required to furnish forces, for the purpose set forth above, during more than one year, without its express and voluntary consent, and England shall be at liberty to furnish its contingent in the manner stipulated in article 9.

90. Documents upon the Transition to the Restoration Monarchy.

As a group these documents show how the government of France passed from Napoleon to Louis XVIII. Taken separately several of them are of additional interest. Document A should be compared with No. 87. The indictment of the Napoleonic régime drawn in document C deserves careful attention. Documents D and F should be compared. The character of the system of government which the Senate in document E proposed to establish should be compared with that actually established by No. 93.

REFERENCES. Fournier. *Napoleon*, 672-678 ; Rose, *Napoleon*, II, 389-398 ; Seignobos. *Europe Since* 1814. 104-105 ; *Cambridge Modern History*. IX. 555-559 ; Lavisse and Rambaud, *Histoire générale*, IX. 881-888 ; Sorel. *L'Europe et la révolution française*, VIII, 316-325 ; Jaurès, *Histoire socialiste*, VII, 6-25.

A. Proclamation of the Allies. March 31, 1814. De Clercq, *Traités*, II, 400-401.

The armies of the allied powers have occupied the capital of France. The allied sovereigns honor the wish of the French nation; they declare:

That if the conditions of peace must indeed include some strong guarantees when dealing with the enchaining of the ambition of Bonaparte, they must be more favorable when, by a return to a wise government, France itself shall offer assurance of repose. The sovereigns proclaim in consequence:

That they will no longer treat with Napoleon Bonaparte, nor with any member of his family.

That they respect the integrity of old France, as it was under its legitimate kings; they can even do more, because they will always respect the principle, that for the welfare of Europe it is necessary that France should be great and strong.

They will recognize and guarantee the constitution which the French nation shall give itself. In consequence, they invite the senate to designate immediately a provisional government which can look after the needs of the administration and prepare the constitution which shall be appropriate for the French people.

The intentions which I have just expressed are common to all the allied powers.

ALEXANDER.

Paris, March 31, 1814.

B. Act of the Senate. April 1, 1814. Duvergier, *Lois,* XIX, 1-2.

The Senate resolves:

1. That there shall be established a provisional government charged to look after the needs of the administration and to present to the Senate a project for a constitution which may be suitable for the French people;

2. That this government shall be composed of five members.

.   .   .   .

C. Decree for Deposing Napoleon. April 3-4, 1814. Duvergier, *Lois,* XIX, 3-4.

The Conservative Senate,

Considering that, in a constitutional monarchy, the monarch exists only in virtue of the constitution or of the social compact:

That Napoleon Bonaparte, during a short time of firm and prudent government, gave to the nation grounds for counting upon acts of wisdom and justice in the future; but that afterwards he broke the compact which united him with the French people, especially in raising imposts and in establishing taxes otherwise than in virtue of the law, contrary to the express tenor of the oath which he had taken at his accession to the throne, in conformity with article 53 of the constitutions of 28 Floréal, Year XII;

That he has committed this attack upon the rights of the people also when he proceeded to adjourn the Legislative Body without necessity, and caused to be suppressed as criminal a report of that body, in which his title and his part in the national representation were contested;

That he has undertaken a series of wars in violation of article 50 of the act of the constitutions of 22 Frimaire, Year VIII, which provides that a declaration of war shall be proposed, discussed, decreed and promulgated as are the laws;

That he has unconstitutionally rendered several decrees involving the death penalty, especially the two of March 5th last, the tendency of which was to cause to be considered as national a war which had occurred only in the interest of his unmeasured ambition;

That he has violated the constitutional laws by his decrees upon the state prisons;

That he has destroyed the responsibility of the ministers, confounded all the powers, and destroyed the independence of the judicial bodies;

Considering that the liberty of the press, established and consecrated as one of the rights of the nation, has been constantly subjected to the arbitrary censorship of his police, and that at the same time he has always made use of the press in order to fill France and Europe with imaginary facts, false maxims, doctrines favorable to despotism, and outrages against foreign governments;

That the acts and reports agreed to by the Senate have sustained alterations in the publication which has been made of them;

Considering that instead of reigning with a sole view to the interest, welfare and glory of the French people, according to the terms of his oath, Napoleon has put the capstone to the misfortunes of the fatherland by his refusal to treat for conditions which the national interest would oblige him to accept and which did not compromise French honor;

By the abuse which he has made of all the means in men and money which have been confided to him;

By the abandonment of the wounded without the dressing of their wounds, without relief, and without food;

By different measures of which the results were the ruin of the cities, the depopulation of the country, famine and contagious diseases;

Considering that by all these causes the imperial government, established by the senatus-consultum of 28 Floréal, Year XII, has ceased to exist, and that the express wish of all Frenchmen calls for an order of things of which the first result may be the re-establishment of the general peace, and which may be also the epoch of a solemn reconciliation among all the states of the great European family;

The Senate declares and decrees as follows:

1. Napoleon Bonaparte has forfeited the throne, and the right of inheritance established in his family is abolished.

2. The French people and army are absolved from the oath of fidelity to Napoleon Bonaparte.

3. The present decree shall be transmitted by a message to the provisional government of France, sent at once to all the departments and to the armies, and proclaimed immediately in all the quarters of the capital.

D. First Abdication of Napoleon. April 4, 1814. Helie, *Constitutions*, 878.

The allied powers having proclaimed that the Emperor Napoleon was the sole obstacle to the re-establishment of peace in Europe, the Emperor Napoleon, faithful to his oath, declares that he is ready to descend from the throne, to leave France and even to lay down his life for the welfare of the fatherland, which cannot be separated from the rights of his son, those of the regency of the Empress, and the laws of the Empire.

Done at our palace of Fontainebleau, April 4, 1814.

NAPOLEON.

E. The Senate's Proposed Constitution. April 6, 1814. Duvergier, *Lois,* XIX, 6-8.

The Conservative Senate, deliberating upon the project of a constitution which has been presented to it by the provisional government, in execution of the act of the Senate of the 1st of this month.

After having heard the report of a special commission of seven members,

Decrees as follows:

1. The French government is monarchical and hereditary from male to male, by order of primogeniture.

2. The French people freely summon to the throne of France Louis-Stanislas-Xavier of France, brother of the late king, and, after him, the other members of the house of Bourbon in the old order.

3. The old nobility resume their titles: the new retain theirs hereditarily. The Legion of Honor is maintained with its prerogatives; the king shall determine the decoration.

4. The executive power belongs to the king.

5. The king, the Senate and the Legislative Body co-operate in the formation of the laws.

Projects of law can be proposed both in the Senate and in the Legislative Body.

Those relative to taxes can be proposed only in the Legislative Body.

The king can likewise invite the two bodies to occupy themselves with matters which he deems in need of consideration.

The sanction of the king is necessary for the completion of the law.

6. There are at least one hundred and fifty senators and two hundred at most.

Their rank is irremovable and hereditary from male to male, by order of primogeniture. They are appointed by the king.

The present senators, with the exception of those who may renounce the attribute of French citizenship, are retained and make part of that number. The present endowment of the Senate and of the senatorships belong to them. The revenues thereof are likewise divided among them and pass to their successors. In case of the death of a senator without direct male posterity, his portion returns to the public treasury. The senators who shall be appointed in the future cannot have part in this endowment.

7. The princes of the royal family and the princes of the blood are by right members of the Senate.

They cannot exercise the functions of a senator until after they have reached the age of majority.

8. The Senate determines the cases in which the discussion of the matters that it treats shall be public or secret.

9. Each department shall select the same number of deputies to the Legislative Body which it was sending there. The deputies who were sitting in the Legislative Body at the time of its last adjournment shall continue to sit there until their replacement. All shall retain their stipend.

For the future they shall be directly chosen by the electoral colleges, which are retained, subject to the changes which may be made by a law upon their organizaton.

The duration of the functions of the deputies of the Legislative Body is fixed at five years.

New elections shall take place for the session of 1816.

10. The Legislative Body assembles of right October 1st of each year. The king can convoke it extraordinarily. He can adjourn it; he can also dissolve it; but in this last case, another Legislative Body must be formed, within three months at the latest, by the electoral colleges.

11. The Legislative Body has the right of discussion. The sittings are public, except in the case in which it thinks that it is expedient to form itself into committee of the whole.

12. The Senate, the Legislative Body, the electoral colleges, and the cantonal assemblies, elect their presidents from within their own midst.

13. No member of the Senate or of the Legislative Body can be arrested without a prior authorisation of the body to which he belongs.

The trial of an accused member of the Senate or of the Legislative Body belongs exclusively to the Senate.

14. The ministers can be members either of the Senate or of the Legislative Body.

15. Equality of proportion in taxation is a matter of right. No tax can be established or collected, unless it has been freely consented to by the Legislative Body and the Senate. The land tax can be established only for one year. The budget of the following year and the accounts of the preceding year are presented each year to the Legislative Body and the

Senate at the opening of the session of the Legislative Body.

16. The law shall determine the mode and the quota of the recruiting for the army.

17. The independence of the judicial authority is guaranteed. Nobody can be deprived of his natural judges.

The jury system is retained, as well as publicity of proceedings in criminal matters.

The penalty of confiscation of goods is abolished.

The king has the right to grant pardons.

18. The ordinary courts and tribunals actually in existence are retained; their number cannot be increased nor diminished except in virtue of a law. The judges are for life and are irremovable, with exception of the justices of the peace and the commercial judges. The extraordinary commissions and tribunals are suppressed, and they cannot be re-established.

19. The court of cassation, the courts of appeal and the tribunals of first instance propose to the king three candidates for each position as judge which is vacant in their body: the king chooses one of the three. The king appoints the first presidents and the public minister of the courts and tribunals.

20. Military men in active service, officers and soldiers in retirement, pensioned widows and officers, preserve their ranks, their honors and their pensions.

21. The person of the king is inviolable and sacred. All acts of the government are signed by a minister. The ministers are responsible for everything which these acts may contain which is injurious to the laws, to public and private liberty, and to the rights of citizens.

22. Liberty of worship and of conscience is guaranteed. The ministers of the religious bodies are likewise paid and protected.

23. The liberty of the press is complete, saving the legal repression of offences which might result from the abuse of that liberty. The senatorial commissions of liberty of the press and of personal liberty are retained.

24. The public debt is guaranteed. The sales of the national lands are irrevocably maintained.

25. No Frenchman can be called to account for the opinions or votes which he may have given.

26. Any person has the right to address individual petitions to any constituted authority.

27. All Frenchmen are equally eligible to all civil and military employments.

28. All actually existing laws remain in force until they may be legally altered. The code of civil laws shall be entitled *Civil Code of the French.*

29. The present constitution shall be submitted for the acceptance of the French people in the form which shall be regulated. Louis-Stanislas-Xavier shall be proclaimed *King of the French,* as soon as he shall have sworn and signed by an act declaring: *I accept the constitution; I swear to observe it and cause it to be observed.* This oath shall be reiterated in the solemn ceremony by which he shall receive the oath of fidelity of the French.

F. Second Abdication of Napoleon. April 11, 1814. De Clercq, *Traités,* II, 402.

The allied powers having proclaimed that the Emperor Napoleon was the sole obstacle to the re-establishment of peace in Europe, the Emperor Napoleon, faithful to his oath, declares that he renounces, for himself, and for his heirs, the thrones of France and Italy, and that there is no personal sacrifice, even that of life, which he would not be ready to make in the interest of France.

Done at the palace of Fontainebleau, April 11, 1814.

NAPOLEON.

G. Treaty of Fontainebleau. April 11, 1814. De Clercq, *Traités,* II, 402-405.

His Majesty the Emperor Napoleon of the one part, and their Majesties the Emperor of Austria, the King of Prussia and the Emperor of all the Russias, stipulating both in their names and in those of their allies, . . .

.   .   .   .

1. His Majesty the Emperor Napoleon renounces for himself, his successors and descendants, as well as for all the members of his family, all right of sovereignty and dominion, as well to the French Empire and the Kingdom of Italy as to every other country.

2. Their Majesties the Emperor Napoleon and the Empress Maria Louisa shall retain their titles and ranks, to be enjoyed during their lives. The mother, brothers, sisters, nephews and nieces of the Emperor shall retain, wherever they may be, the title of princes of his family.

3. The island of Elba, adopted by His Majesty the Emperor Napoleon as the place of his residence, shall form, during his life, a separate principality, which shall be possessed by him in full sovereignty and ownership. There shall be given besides, in full property, to the Emperor Napoleon, an annual revenue of 2,000,000 francs in *rentes* upon the ledger of France of which 1,000,000 shall be in reversion to the Empress.

. . . .

5. The Duchies of Parma, Piacenza, the Guastalla shall be given in full ownership and sovereignty to Her Majesty the Empress Maria Louisa. They shall pass to her son, and to his descendants in the direct line. The prince, her son, shall take from this moment the title of Prince of Parma, Piacenza and Guastalla.

6. There shall be reserved in the countries which the Emperor Napoleon renounces for himself and his family domains or dower of *rentes* upon the ledger of France producing a net annual income, after deduction of all charges is made, of 2,500,000 francs. These domains or *rentes* shall belong in full ownership, and to be disposed of as shall seem good to them, to the princes and princesses of his family and shall be apportioned among them in such a manner that the income of each may be in the following proportion:

. . . .

91. Treaty of Paris.

May 30, 1814. Hertslet, *Map of Europe by Treaty*, 1-20.

Two features of this treaty call for particular notice. (1) The territorial limits of France should be compared with those existing prior to 1789, those of various subsequent dates such as 1795 and 1810, and those which on different occasions during 1813 and 1814 were offered to Napoleon. (2) The stipulations relative to the congress which subsequently met at Vienna may be compared with those in No. 73 and the arrangements effected by the Congress of Vienna. The negative features of the treaty may be profitably noticed.

REFERENCES. Andrews, *Modern Europe*, I, 89-90; Fyffe, *Modern Europe*, I, 536-541 (Popular ed., 360-364); Rose, *Napoleon*, II, 401; *Cambridge Modern History*, IX, 563-564, 576-577; Lavisse and Rambaud, *Histoire générale*, X, 1-4; Sorel, *L'Europe et la révolution française*, VIII, 346-353.

In the Name of the Most Holy and Undivided Trinity.

His Majesty, the King of the United Kingdom of Great Britain and Ireland, and his allies on the one part, and His Majesty the King of France and Navarre on the other part, animated by an equal desire to terminate the long agitations of Europe, and the sufferings of mankind, by a permanent peace, founded upon a just repartition of force between its states, and containing in its stipulations the pledge of its durability and His Britannic Majesty, together with his allies, being unwilling to require of France, now that, replaced under the paternal government of her kings, she offers the assurance of security and stability to Europe, the conditions and guarantees which they had with regret demanded from her former government, their said Majesties have named plenipotentiaries to discuss, settle, and sign a treaty of peace and amity; namely,

. . . .

1. There shall be from this day forward perpetual peace and friendship between His Britannic Majesty and his allies on the one part, and His Majesty the King of France and Navarre on the other, their heirs and successors, their dominions and subjects, respectively.

The high contracting parties shall devote their best attention to maintain, not only between themselves, but, inasmuch as depends upon them, between all the states of Europe, that harmony and good understanding which are so necessary for their tranquility.

2. The Kingdom of France retains its limits entire, as they existed on the 1st of January, 1792. It shall further receive the increase of territory comprised within the line established by the following article:

3. On the side of Belgium, Germany, and Italy, the ancient frontiers shall be re-established as they existed on the 1st of January, 1792, extending from the North Sea, between Dunkirk and Nieuport to the Mediterranean between Cagnes and Nice, with the following modifications:

. . . .

[This line is shown by maps in Hertslet, *Map of Europe by Treaty*, 28-29.]

France on her part renounces all rights of sovereignty, *suzerainty,* etc., and of possession, over all the countries, districts, towns, and places situated beyond the frontier above described, the principality of Monaco being replaced on the same footing on which it stood before the 1st of January, 1792.

The allied powers assure to France the possession of the principality of Avignon, of the Comitat Venaissin, of the Comté of Montbéliard, together with the several insulated territories which formerly belonged to Germany, comprehended within the frontier above described, whether they have been incorporated with France before or after the 1st of January, 1792.

.   .   .   .

5. The navigation of the Rhine, from the point where it becomes navigable unto the sea, and *vice versa,* shall be free, so that it can be interdicted to no one:—and at the future congress attention shall be paid to the establishment of the principles according to which the duties to be raised by the states bordering on the Rhine may be regulated, in the mode the most impartial and the most favourable to the commerce of all nations.

The future congress, with a view to facilitate the communication between nations and continually to render them less strangers to each other, shall likewise examine and determine in what manner the above provisions can be extended to other rivers, which in their navigable course, separate or traverse different states.

6. Holland, placed under the sovereignty of the house of Orange, shall receive an increase of territory. The title and exercise of that sovereignty shall not in any case belong to a prince wearing, or destined to wear, a foreign crown.

The states of Germany shall be independent, and united by a federative bond.

Switzerland, independent, shall continue to govern herself.

Italy, beyond the limits of the countries which are to revert to Austria, shall be composed of sovereign states.

7. The island of Malta and its dependencies shall belong in full right and sovereignty to His Britannic Majesty.

8. His Britannic Majesty, stipulating for himself and his

allies, engages to restore to His Most Christian Majesty, within the term which shall be hereafter fixed, the colonies, fisheries, factories, and establishments of every kind which were possessed by France on the 1st of January, 1792, in the seas and on the continents of America, Africa, and Asia; with the exception, however, of the Islands of Tobago and St. Lucia, and of the Isle of France and its dependencies, especially Rodrigues and Les Séchelles, which several colonies and possessions His Most Christian Majesty cedes in full right and sovereignty to His Britannic Majesty, and also the portion of St. Domingo ceded to France by the Treaty of Basle, and which His Most Christian Majesty restores in full right and sovereignty to His Catholic Majesty.

32. All the powers engaged on either side in the present war, shall, within the space of two months, send plenipotentiaries to Vienna, for the purpose of regulating, in general congress, the arrangements which are to complete the provisions of the present treaty.

Additional, Separate, and Secret Articles.

1. The disposal of the territories given up by His Most Christian Majesty, under the 3d article of the public treaty, and the relations from whence a system of real and permanent balance of power in Europe is to be derived, shall be regulated at the congress upon the principles determined upon by the allied powers among themselves, and according to the general provisions contained in the following articles.

2. The possessions of His Imperial and Royal Apostolic Majesty in Italy, shall be bounded by the Po, the Tessino, and the Lago Maggiore. The King of Sardinia shall return to the possession of his ancient dominions, with the exception of that part of Savoy secured to France by the 3d article of the present treaty. His Majesty shall receive an increase of territory from the state of Genoa.

The Port of Genoa shall continue to be a free port; the powers reserving to themselves the right of making arrangements upon this point with the King of Sardinia.

France shall acknowledge and guarantee, conjointly with the allied powers, and on the same footing, the political organization which Switzerland shall adopt under the auspices of the said allied powers, and according to the basis already agreed upon with them.

3. The establishment of a just balance of power in Europe requiring that Holland should be so constituted as to be enabled to support her independence through her own resources, the countries comprised between the sea, the frontiers of France, such as they are defined by the present treaty, and the Meuse, shall be given up forever to Holland,

The frontiers upon the right bank of the Meuse shall be regulated according to the military convenience of Holland, and her neighbours.

The freedom of the navigation of the Scheldt shall be established upon the same principle which has regulated the navigation of the Rhine, in the 5th Article of the present treaty.

4. The German territories upon the left bank of the Rhine, which have been united to France since 1792, shall contribute to the aggrandizement of Holland, and shall be further applied to compensate Prussia, and other German states.

.   .   .   .

92. Declaration of St. Ouen.

May 2, 1814. Duvergier, *Lois*, XIX, 23.

The Count of Artois, acting for Louis XVIII, declined to accept the constitution prepared by the Senate (No. 97 E). He was, however, prevailed upon to promise that he would accept "the basis" of it. This declaration was promulgated in redemption of that promise. It should be compared with both the Senate's constitution and the Constitutional Charter (No. 93).

REFERENCES. Seignobos, *Europe Since 1814*, 106; Lavisse and Rambaud, *Histoire générale*, IX, 890-891.

Louis, by the grace of God, King of France and of Navarre, to all those to whom these presents come, greeting.

Recalled by the love of our people to the throne of our fathers, enlightened by the misfortunes of the nation, which we are destined to govern, our first thought is to invoke that mutual confidence so necessary to our repose and to its welfare.

After having read attentively the plan for a constitution proposed by the Senate at its sitting of the 6th of April last, we have recognized that the principles thereof were good, but that a great number of articles bear the impress of the haste with which they were drawn up and they cannot in their present form become fundamental laws of the state.

Resolved to adopt a liberal constitution, we wish that it should be wisely drawn up; and not being able to accept one which it is necessary to rectify, we convoke, for the 10th of the month of June of the present year, the Senate and the Legislative Body, and engage to put before their eyes the work which we shall have done with a commission chosen from among these two bodies; and to give as a basis for this constitution the following guarantees:

Representative government shall be maintained such as it is to-day, divided into two bodies, to wit:

The Senate and the Chamber composed of the deputies of the departments;

Taxes shall be freely consented to;

Public and personal liberty are guaranteed;

Liberty of the press shall be respected, saving the precautions necessary for the public tranquility;

Liberty of worship is guaranteed;

Property shall be inviolable and sacred; the sale of the national lands shall remain irrevocable.

Responsible ministers may be prosecuted by one of the legislative chambers and judged by the other.

Judges shall be irremovable, and the judicial power independent;

The public debt shall be guaranteed; pensions, ranks and military honors shall be preserved, as also the old and the new nobility.

The Legion of Honor, of which we will fix the decoration, shall be maintained.

Every Frenchman shall be eligible to civil and military employments.

Finally, no person shall be disturbed on account of his opinions or his vote.

Given at St. Ouen, May 2, 1814.

Signed,   LOUIS.

93. Constitutional Charter of 1814.

June 4, 1814, Duvergier, *Lois,* XIX, 59-73.

This famous document presents many points of interest. Two features of it are particularly worthy of notice. (1) As a statement of what the restored Bourbons would accept, it exhibits some of the most important permanent gains of the revolution. This may be brought out by comparing it with typical *cahiers* of 1789 or with the constitution of 1791 (No. 15). As the frame of government under which France lived until 1830, it is an excellent starting point for a study of that period. The phraseology of the document requires careful attention.

REFERENCES. Fyffe, *Modern Europe,* II, 14-15, (Popular ed., 376-377) ; Seignobos. *Europe Since 1814,* 106-108 ; Andrews, *Modern Europe,* I, 135-137 ; *Cambridge Modern History,* IX, 563 ; Jaurès, *Histoire socialiste,* VII, 35-36.

Louis, by the grace of God, King of France and Navarre, to all those to whom these presents come, greeting.

Divine Providence, in recalling us to our estates after a long absence, has laid upon us great obligations. Peace was the first need of our subjects: we have employed ourselves thereto without relaxation; and that peace, so necessary for France, as well as for the remainder of Europe, is signed. A constitutional charter was called for by the actual condition of the kingdom; we promised it, and we now publish it. We have taken into consideration that, although all authority in France resides in the person of the king, our predecessors have not hesitated to alter the exercise thereof in accordance with the change of the times: that it was in this manner that the communes owed their emancipation to Louis, the Fat, the confirmation and extension of their rights to Saint Louis and Philip the Fair; that the judicial system was established and developed by the laws of Louis XI, Henry II and Charles IX; and finally, that Louis XIV regulated almost all parts of the public administration by various ordinances whose wisdom nothing has yet surpassed.

We are bound, by the example of the kings, our predecessors, to estimate the effects of the ever increasing progress of enlightenment, the new relations which these advances have introduced into society, the direction impressed upon opinions during the past half century, and the significant alterations which have resulted therefrom: we have recognized that the wish of our subjects for a constitutional charter was the expression of a real need; but, in yielding to this wish, we have taken every precaution that this charter should be worthy of us and of the people over whom we are proud to rule. Sagacious men taken from the highest body of the state met with commissioners of our council to labor upon this important work.

While we have recognized that a free and monarchical constitution was necessary to meet the expectation of enlightened Europe, we have also been constrained to remember that our first duty towards our subjects was to preserve, in their own interest, the rights and prerogatives of our crown. We have hoped that, taught by experience, they may be convinced that only the supreme authority can give to institutions which it establishes the strength, permanence, and majesty with which it is itself invested; that thus, when the wisdom of the king freely coincides with the wish of the people, a constitutional charter can be of long duration; but that, when violence wrests concessions from the feebleness of the government, public liberty is not less in danger than the throne itself. In a word, we have sought the principles of the constitutional charter in the French character and in the enduring examples of past ages. Thus, we have seen, in the renewal of the peerage, an institution truly national and one which must bind all the recollections with all the hopes, in bringing together former and present times.

We have replaced by the Chamber of Deputies those former assemblies of the fields of March and May, and those chambers of the Third Estate, which so often gave at the same time proof of zeal for the interests of the people and of fidelity and respect for the authority of the king. In thus attempting to renew the chain of the times, which disastrous errors have broken, we have banished from our recollection, as we could wish it were possible to blot out from history, all the evils which have afflicted the fatherland during our absence. Happy to find ourselves once more in the bosom of our great family, we have felt that we could respond to the love of which we have received so many testimonials, only by pronouncing words of peace and consolation. The dearest wish of our heart is that all Frenchmen should live as brothers, and that no bitter recollection should ever disturb the security that must follow the solemn act which we grant them to-day.

Assured of our intentions, and strengthened by our conscience, we pledge ourselves, in the presence of the assembly which hears us, to be faithful to this constitutional charter, reserving to ourselves to swear to maintain it with a new solemnity, before the altars of Him who weighs in the same balance kings and nations.

For these reasons,

We have voluntarily, and by the free exercise of our royal authority, accorded and do accord, grant and concede to our subjects, as well for us as for our successors forever, the constitutional charter which follows:

Public Law of the French.

1. Frenchmen are equal before the law, whatever may be their titles and ranks.

2. They contribute without distinction, in proportion to their fortunes, towards the expenses of the state.

3. They are all equally admissible to civil and military employments.

4. Their personal liberty is likewise guaranteed; no one can be prosecuted nor arrested save in the cases provided by law and in the form which it prescribes.

5. Every one may profess his religion with equal freedom, and shall obtain for his worship the same protection.

6. Nevertheless, the catholic, apostolic and Roman religion is the religion of the state.

7. The ministers of the catholic, apostolic and Roman religion and those of the other christian sects alone receive stipends from the royal treasury.

8. Frenchmen have the right to publish and to have printed their opinions, while conforming with the laws, which are necessary to restrain abuses of that liberty.

9. All property is inviolable, without any exception for that which is called *national*, the law making no distinction between them.

10. The state can require the sacrifice of a property on account of a legally established public interest, but with a previous indemnity.

'11. All investigations of opinions and votes given prior to the restoration are forbidden. The same oblivion is required from the tribunals and from citizens.

12. The conscription is abolished. The method of recruiting for the army and navy is determined by a law.

Form of the Government of the King.

13. The person of the king is inviolable and sacred. His ministers are responsible. To the king alone belongs the executive power.

14. The king is the supreme head of the state, commands the land and sea forces, declares war, makes treaties of peace, alliance and commerce, appoints to all places of public administration, and makes the necessary regulations and ordinances for the execution of the laws and the security of the state.

15. The legislative power is exercised collectively by the king, the Chamber of Peers, and the Chamber of the Deputies of the departments.

16. The king proposes the laws.

17. The proposition for a law is sent, at the pleasure of the king, to the Chamber of Peers or to that of the Deputies, except a law for the imposition of taxes, which must be sent first to the Chamber of Deputies.

18. Every law shall be freely discussed and voted by the majority of each of the two chambers.

19. The chambers have the power to petition the king to propose a law upon any subject whatsoever and to indicate what seems suitable for the law to contain.

20. This request can be made by either of the two chambers, but only after having been discussed in secret committee; it shall be sent to the other chamber by that which shall have proposed it, only after an interval of ten days.

21. If the proposal is adopted by the other chamber, it shall be laid before the king; if it is rejected, it cannot be presented again in the same session.

22. The king alone sanctions and promulgates the laws.

23. The civil list is fixed, for the entire duration of the reign, by the first legislature assembled after the accession of the king.

Of the Chambers of Peers.

24. The Chamber of Peers is an essential part of the legislative power.

25. It is convoked by the king at the same time as the Chamber of the Deputies of the departments. The session of the one begins and ends at the same time as that of the other.

26. Every meeting of the Chamber of Peers which may be held outside of the time of the session of the Chamber of Deputies, or which may not be ordered by the king, is unlawful and of no validity.

27. The appointment of peers of France belongs to the king. Their number is unlimited: he can at his pleasure alter their dignities, appoint them for life, or make them hereditary.

28. Peers have entrance to the chamber at twenty-five years and a deliberative voice only at thirty years.

29. The Chamber of Peers is presided over by the chancellor of France, and in his absence, by a peer appointed by the king.

30. Members of the royal family and princes of the blood are peers by right of their birth. They sit next to the president; but they have no deliberative voice until twenty-five years of age.

31. The princes can take their places in the chamber only upon the order of the king, expressed for each session by a message, under penalty of invalidating everything which may have been done in their presence.

32. All the deliberations of the Chamber of Peers are secret.

33. The Chamber of Peers has jurisdiction over the crimes of high treason and attacks against the security of the state, which shall be defined by law.

34. No peer can be arrested except by the authority of the chamber, nor tried in a criminal matter except by it.

Of the Chamber of Deputies of the Departments.

35. The Chamber of Deputies shall be composed of the deputies elected by electoral colleges, whose organization shall be determined by law.

36. Each department shall have the same number of deputies that it has had up to the present time.

37. The deputies shall be elected for five years and in such a manner that the chamber may be renewed each year by a fifth.

38. No deputy can be admitted to the chamber unless he is forty years of age and pays a direct tax of one thousand francs.

39. Nevertheless, if there cannot be found in the department fifty persons of the requisite age, who pay at least one thousand francs of direct taxes, their number shall be filled up from the largest taxpayers under one thousand francs, and these shall be elected together with the first.

40. Electors who meet for the naming of deputies cannot have the right of suffrage, unless they pay a direct tax of three hundred francs and are not less than thirty years of age.

41. The presidents of the electoral colleges shall be appointed by the king, and are ex-officio members of the college.

42. At least one-half of the deputies shall be chosen from among the eligibles who have their political domicile in the department.

43. The president of the Chamber of Deputies is appointed by the king, from a list of five members presented by the chamber.

44. The sittings of the chamber are public, but the request of five members suffices for it to form itself into secret committee.

45. The chamber divides itself into *bureaux* in order to discuss the propositions which have been presented to it by the king.

46. No amendment can be made in a law unless it has been proposed or consented to by the king, and unless it has been sent back to the *bureaux* and discussed there.

47. The Chamber of Deputies receives all proposals in regard to taxes; only after these proposals have been accepted can they be carried to the Chamber of Peers.

48. No tax can be imposed or collected, unless it has been consented to by the two chambers and sanctioned by the king.

49. The land tax is consented to only for one year. Indirect taxes can be established for several years.

50. The king convokes the two chambers each year: he prorogues them, and can dissolve that of the deputies of the departments; but, in that case, he must convoke a new one within the space of three months.

51. No bodily constraint can be exercised against a mem-

ber of the chamber during the session nor in the preceding or following six weeks.

52. No member of the chamber, during the course of the session, can be prosecuted or arrested upon a criminal charge, unless he should be taken in the act, except after the chamber has permitted his prosecution.

53. No petition can be made or presented to either of the chambers, except in writing. The law forbids any personal presentation of them at the bar.

Of the Ministers.

54. The ministers can be members of the Chamber of Peers or of the Chamber of Deputies. They have, besides, their entrance into either chamber, and they must be heard when they demand it.

55. The Chamber of Deputies has the right to accuse the ministers and to arraign them before the Chamber of Peers, which alone has that of trying them.

56. They can be accused only for acts of treason and peculation. Special laws shall determine the nature of this offence and shall fix the method of prosecution.

Of the Judiciary.

57. All justice emanates from the king. It is administered in his name by judges whom he appoints and whom he invests.

58. The judges appointed by the king are irremovable.

59. The courts and regular tribunals actually existing are continued. They shall not be in any wise changed except by virtue of a law.

60. The existing commercial court is retained.

61. The justice of the peace, likewise, is retained. Justices of the peace, although appointed by the king, are not irremovable.

62. No one can be deprived of the jurisdiction of his natural judges.

63. In consequence, extraordinary commissions and tribunals cannot be created. Provost-courts are not included under this denomination, if their re-establishment is deemed necessary.

64. Criminal trials shall be public, unless such publicity

should be dangerous to order and morality; and in that case, the tribunal shall declare it by a judicial order.

65. The system of juries is retained. Changes which a longer experience may cause to be thought necessary can be made only by a law.

66. The penalty of confiscation of property is abolished and cannot be re-established.

67. The king has the right of pardon, and that of commuting penalties.

68. The Civil Code, and the laws actually existing which are not in conflict with the present charter, remain in force until legally abrogated.

Special Rights Guaranteed by the State.

69. Persons in active military service, retired officers and soldiers, pensioned widows, officers and soldiers, retain their ranks, honors and pensions.

70. The public debt is guaranteed. Every form of engagement made by the state with its creditors is inviolable.

71. The old nobility resume their titles. The new retain theirs. The king makes nobles at will, but he grants to them only ranks and honors, without any exemption from the burdens and duties of society.

72. The Legion of Honor is maintained. The king shall determine its internal regulations and its decoration.

73. The colonies shall be governed by special laws and regulations.

74. The king and his successors shall swear, at the solemnizing of their coronation, to observe faithfully the present constitutional charter.

Temporary Articles.

75. The deputies of the departments of France who sat in the Legislative Body at the time of its last adjournment shall continue to sit in the Chamber of Deputies until replaced.

76. The first renewal of a fifth of the Chamber of Deputies shall take place in the year 1816, at the latest, according to the order established in the series.

We command that the present constitutional charter, laid before the Senate and the Legislative Body, in conformity with our proclamation of May 2, shall be sent forthwith to the Chamber of Peers and that of the Deputies.

Given at Paris, in the year of grace, 1814, and of our reign the nineteenth.

Signed, Louis.

94. Proclamation of Napoleon.

March 1, 1815. Duvergier, *Lois*, XIX, 373.

This proclamation, dated on the day of his arrival in France from Elba, is typical of the declarations and addresses made by Napoleon during the course of his journey to Paris. A similar proclamation was addressed to the army. The manner in which the disasters of 1814 are explained and the skill with which appeal is made to the memories of the Empire should be noticed.

REFERENCE. Lavisse and Rambaud, *Histoire générale*, IX, 903-904.

Frenchmen, the defection of the Duke of Castiglione delivered Lyon without defence to our enemies; the army, of which I had confided to him the command, was, by the number of its battalions, and the bravery and patriotism of the troops who composed it, in a condition to fight the Austrian army which was opposing it and to reach the rear of the left flank of the hostile army which was threatening Paris.

The victories of Champ-Aubert, Montmirail, Château-Thierry, Vauchamp, Mormans, Montereau, Craone, Reims, Arcy-sur-Aube and Saint-Dizier, the rising of the brave peasants of Lorraine, Champagne, Alsace, Franche-Comté and Bourgogne, and the position which I had taken at the rear of the hostile army, separating it from its magazines, its reserve parks, its convoys and all its equipment, had placed it in a desperate position. Frenchmen were never at the point of being more powerful, and the flower of the hostile army was lost beyond recovery; it would have found its grave in those vast countries which it has so pitilessly plundered, but that the treason of the Duke of Raguse gave up the capital and disorganized the army. The unexpected conduct of these two generals, who betrayed at one and the same time their fatherland, their prince and their benefactor, changed the destiny of the war. The disastrous situation of the enemy was such, that at the end of the affair which took place be-

fore Paris, they were without ammunition, through separation from their reserve parks.

Under these new and difficult circumstances my heart was
torn, but my soul remained steadfast. I only thought of the
interest of the fatherland; I exiled myself upon a rock in the
midst of the sea; my life was and must still be useful to you.
I did not allow the greater part of those who wished to accompany me to share my lot; I thought their presence was
useful in France, and I only took with me a handful of valiant men as my guard.

Raised to the throne by your choice, everything that has
been done without you is illegitimate. During the last twenty-five years, France has acquired new interests, new institutions, and a new glory, which can only be guaranteed by a
national government and by a dynasty born under these new
circumstances. A prince who would reign over you, who
would be seated upon my throne by the power of the very
armies who have devastated our territory, would seek in vain
to support himself by the principles of feudal rights and he
could only assure the honor and the rights of a small number of individuals, enemies of the people, who, for twenty-
five years past, have condemned them in our national assemblies. Your internal peace and your foreign prestige would
be forever lost.

Frenchmen! In my exile I have heard your complaints and
your desires; you were claiming that government of your
choice, which alone is legitimate. You were complaining of
my long sleep, you reproached me with sacrificing to my own
repose the great interests of the fatherland.

I have crossed the seas in the midst of perils of every sort;
I arrive among you in order to reclaim my rights, which are
yours. Everything which individuals have done, written or
said since the taking of Paris, I will forever ignore; that
will not in the least influence the recollection which I have
of the important services that they have rendered; for there
are events of such a nature that they are beyond human organization.

Frenchmen! There is no nation, however small it may be,
which has not had the right to withdraw and which may not
be withdrawn from the dishonor of obeying a prince imposed
upon it by a momentarily victorious enemy. When Charles

VII re-entered Paris and overthrew the ephemeral throne of
Henry VI he recognized that he held his throne by the bravery of his soldiers and not from a prince regent of England.

It is therefore to you alone; and to the brave men of the
army, that I consider and shall always consider it glorious to
owe everything.

Signed,   NAPOLEON.

95. Decree for Convoking an Extraordinary Assembly.

March 13, 1815. Duvergier, *Lois,* XIX, 375-376.

This decree is typical of the series issued by Napoleon while
at Lyon on his journey to Paris. The list of reasons for dissolving the Senate and Legislative Body contains many of the popular grievances against the restored Bourbon régime for things
actually done or anticipated.

REFERENCES. Fournier, *Napoleon,* 692 ; Rose, *Napoleon,* II,
408.

Napoleon by the grace of God and the constitutions of
the Empire, Emperor of the French, considering that the
Chamber of Peers is in part composed of persons who have
borne arms against France, and who have an interest in the
re-establishment of feudal rights, in the destruction of equality among the different classes, in the setting aside of the
sales of the national lands, and, in short, in depriving the people of the rights which they have acquired by twenty-five
years of conflict against the enemies of the national glory;

Considering that the powers of the deputies to the Legislative Body have expired, and that, therefore, the Chamber
of the Commons has no longer any national character; that
a portion of that chamber has shown itself unworthy of the
confidence of the nation by adhering to the re-establishment
of the feudal nobility, abolished by constitutions that the people have accepted; in causing France to pay debts contracted
abroad for the purpose of organizing coalitions and hiring
armies against the French people; in giving to the Bourbons
the title of legitimate king, thereby declaring that the French
people and armies were rebels, and proclaiming that the only
good Frenchmen were the *émigrés,* who have for twenty-five

years rent the bosom of the fatherland and violated all the rights of the people by consecrating the principle that the nation was made for the throne and not the throne for the nation,

We have decreed and do decree as follows:

1. The Chamber of Peers is dissolved.

2. The Chamber of the Commons is dissolved; each of its members summoned and arrived at Paris since the seventh of March is ordered to return to his domicile without delay.

3. The electoral colleges of the departments of the Empire shall meet at Paris during the course of the approaching month of May *in extraordinary assembly of the Champ-de-Mai,* for the purpose of taking suitable measures to correct and modify our constitutions in accordance with the interest and the will of the nation, and at the same time to assist at the coronation of the Empress our very dear and well-beloved wife and at that of our dear and well-beloved son.

. . . .

96. Declaration of the Powers against Napoleon.

March 13, 1815. *British and Foreign State Papers,* II, 665.

This declaration was issued by the Congress of Vienna upon learning that Napoleon had left Elba. It shows the precise attitude of the Powers of Europe towards him.

REFERENCES. Fournier. *Napoleon,* 697-699; Rose, *Napoleon,* II, 410-411; *Cambridge Modern History,* IX, 617-618; Lavisse and Rambaud. *Histoire générale,* X, 47.

The powers who have signed the treaty of Paris reassembled in congress at Vienna having been informed of the escape of Napoleon Bonaparte, and of his entrance into France with an armed force, owe to their dignity and the interest of social order a solemn declaration of the sentiments which that event has inspired in them.

In thus violating the convention which established him in the island of Elba, Bonaparte destroyed the only legal title for his existence. By reappearing in France with projects of disorder and destruction, he has cut himself off from the protection of the law and has shown in the face of the world that there can be neither peace nor truce with him.

Accordingly, the powers declare that Napoleon Bonaparte

is excluded from civil and social relations, and, as an enemy and disturber of the tranquility of the world, that he has incurred public vengeance.

At the same time, being firmly resolved to preserve intact the treaty of Paris of May 30, 1814, and the arrangements sanctioned by that treaty, as well as those which have been or shall be arranged hereafter in order to complete and consolidate it, they declare that they will employ all their resources and will unite all their efforts in order that the general peace, the object of the desires of Europe and the constant aim of their labors, may not be again disturbed, and in order to secure themselves from all attempts which may threaten to plunge the world once more into the disorders and misfortunes of revolutions.

And although fully persuaded that all France, rallying around its legitimate sovereign, will strive unceasingly to bring to naught this last attempt of a criminal and impotent madman, all the sovereigns of Europe, animated by the same feeling and guided by the same principles, declare that if, contrary to all expectation, there shall result from that event any real danger, they will be ready to give to the King of France. and the French nation or to any government which shall be attacked, as soon as shall be required, all the assistance necessary to re-establish the public tranquility, and to make common cause against all who may attempt to compromise it.

The present declaration, inserted in the protocol of the Congress assembled at Vienna, March 13, 1815, shall be made public.

97.   Treaty of Alliance against Napoleon.

March 25, 1815.   De Clercq, *Traités,* II, 474-476.

This treaty was framed for the purpose of giving effect to the declaration of March 13 (see No. 96). It shows the strength, purpose and general character of the alliance against which Napoleon had to contend.

REFERENCES.   Fournier, *Napoleon,* 698-699 ; Rose, *Napoleon,* II, 412 ; Lavisse and Rambaud, *Histoire générale,* IX, 922, X, 47-49.

In the Name of the Most Holy and Indivisible Trinity. His Majesty the King of Prussia   and His Majesty the

King of the United Kingdom of Great Britain and Ireland,
having taken into consideration the result which the invasion
of France by Napoleon Bonaparte and the present situation
of that kingdom may have for the security of Europe, have
resolved of one accord with His Majesty the Emperor of
all the Russias and His Majesty the Emperor of Austria,
King of Hungary and of Bohemia, to apply to that important
circumstance the principles consecrated by the treaty of Chaumont. In consequence, they have agreed to renew by a solemn
treaty, signed separately by each of the four powers with
each of the other three, the engagement to preserve against
every attack the order of things so happily re-established in
Europe and to determine the most effective means to put this
engagement into execution, as well as to give it all the extension which, under the present circumstances, it imperatively requires.

.   .   .   .   .

1. The above named high contracting parties solemnly
agree to unite the means of their respective states, in order to
maintain in all their integrity the conditions of the treaty of
peace concluded at Paris on May 30, 1814, as well as the
stipulations agreed to and signed at the Congress of Vienna
with the purpose of completing the dispositions of that treaty
and of guaranteeing them against every attack and particularly
against the designs of Napoleon Bonaparte. For that purpose
if the case should demand it and in the sense of the declaration of March 13 last, they agree to direct in concert and in
common accord all their efforts against him and against all
who may have already rallied to his faction or who may unite
with it hereafter, in order to force them to desist from that
project and to render them unable to disturb in the future the
tranquility of Europe and the general peace, under the protection of which the rights, the liberty and the independence of
the nations have just come to be placed and assured.

2. Although so great and so beneficent an aim does not
permit the means destined for its attainment to be measured,
and although the high contracting parties have resolved to
consecrate to it all those of which, according to their respective situations, they can dispose, they have each agreed to keep
constantly in the field an hundred fifty thousand men complete,
including at least the proportion of one-tenth of cavalry and a

just proportion of artillery, without counting garrisons, and to employ them actively and in concert against the common enemy.

3. The high contracting parties reciprocally agree not to lay aside their arms except by a common accord and not until the object of the war designated in article 1 of the present treaty has been attained, and not until Bonaparte shall have been put absolutely beyond the possibility of exciting disturbances and of renewing his attempts to seize upon the supreme power in France.

4. The present treaty being principally applied to the present circumstances, the stipulations of the treaty of Chaumont, and especially those contained in article 14, shall again have all their force and vigor as soon as the present purpose shall have been attained.

.   .   .   .

7. The engagements stipulated in the present treaty having for their purpose the maintenance of the general peace. the high contracting parties agree among themselves to invite all the powers of Europe to accede to it.

8. The present treaty being solely intended for the purpose of supporting France, or any other invaded country against the enterprises of Bonaparte and his adherents, His Most Christian Majesty shall be specially invited to give his adherence to it and to make known, for the case in which the forces stipulated in article 2 should be required, what assistance circumstances will permit him to bring to the object of the present treaty.

.   .   .   .   .   .

Separate, Additional and Secret Article.

As circumstances may prevent His Majesty the King of the United Kingdom of Great Britain and Ireland from keeping constantly in the field the number of troops specified in article 2, it is agreed that His Britannic Majesty shall have the right either to furnish his contingent or to pay at the rate of thirty pounds sterling per annum for each infantryman, to the extent of the number stipulated in article 2.

.   .   .   .   .   .

98. The Act Additional.

April 22, 1815. Duvergier, *Lois*, XIX, 403-410.

Upon returning to France Napoleon promised that political liberty should be secured. This document was promulgated in consequence of that promise. It was in the main the work of Benjamin Constant, a liberal and former opponent of the Empire. It should be compared with the constitutions of the Empire which it supplemented and modified (see Nos. 58, 66 E, 71) and the Constitutional Charter which it replaced (No. 93). As with the preceding imperial constitutions, it was submitted to popular vote. The interest in it, however, was slight. It was never actually put into operation.

REFERENCES. Fyffe, *Modern Europe*, II, 42-45. (Popular ed., 395-397) ; Fournier, *Napoleon*, 702-705 ; Rose, *Napoleon*, II, 414-415 ; Sloane, *Napoleon*, IV, 167-168 ; *Cambridge Modern History*, IX, 619-620 ; Lavisse and Rambaud, *Histoire générale*, IX, 919-921 ; Jaurès, *Histoire socialiste*, VII, 47-49.

Napoleon, by the grace of God and the constitutions, Emperor of the French. Since we were called fifteen years ago by the will of France to the government of the state we have sought at different times to improve the constitutional forms, according to the needs and desires of the nation and by profiting from the lessons of experience. The constitutions of the Empire have thus been formed by a series of acts which have received the acceptance of the people. We had then for our aim to organize a great European federative system which we had adopted as in conformity with the spirit of the age and favorable to the progress of civilization. In order to bring it to completion and to give to it all the extent and all the stability of which it was susceptible, we had postponed the establishment of several internal institutions, more especially designed to protect the liberty of the citizens. Our aim henceforth is nothing else than to increase the prosperity of France by strengthening public liberty. From this springs the necessity of several important alterations in the constitutions, senatus-consulta, and other acts which govern the Empire.

For these reasons, wishing, on the one hand, to retain from the past whatever is good and salutary, and on the other, to make the constitutions of the Empire entirely conformable to the national wishes and needs, as well as to the state of peace which we shall desire to maintain with Europe, we have resolved to propose to the people a series of provisions tending to alter and improve these constitutional acts, to surround the rights of citizens with all their guarantees, to give to the representative system its full extent, to invest the intermediary bodies with desirable importance and power; in a word, to combine the highest point of political liberty and individual security with the strength and centralization necessary to make the independence of the French people and the dignity of our crown respected by foreigners. In consequence, the following articles, forming an act supplementary to the constitutions of the Empire, shall be submitted for the free and solemn acceptance of all citizens throughout the whole extent of France.

Title I. General Provisions.

1. The constitutions of the Empire, particularly the constitutional act of 22 Frimaire, Year VIII, the senatus-consulta of 14 and 16 Thermidor, Year X, and that of 28 Floréal, Year XII, shall be altered by the following provisions. All of their other provisions are confirmed and maintained.

2. The legislative power is exercised by the Emperor and by two chambers.

3. The first chamber, called Chamber of Peers, is hereditary.

4. The Emperor appoints its members, who are irremovable, they and their male descendants in the direct line from eldest to eldest. The number of peers is unlimited. Adoption does not transmit the dignity of a peer to one who is the object of it.

Peers take seats at twenty-one years of age, but have a deliberative voice only at twenty-five.

5. The Chamber of Peers is presided over by the archchancellor of the Empire, or, in the case provided for by article 51 of the senatus-consultum of 28 Floréal, Year XII, by one of the members of that chamber especially designated by the Emperor.

6. The members of the imperial family within the order of succession are peers by right. They sit beside the president. They take seats at eighteen years of age, but have a deliberative voice only at twenty-one years.

7. The second chamber, called Chamber of Representatives, is elected by the people.

8. The members of this chamber are in number six hun-

dred and twenty-nine. They must be at least twenty-five years of age.

9. The president of the Chamber of Representatives is appointed by the chamber at the opening of the first session. He remains in office until the renewal of the chamber. His appointment is submitted to the approval of the Emperor.

10. The Chamber of Representatives verifies the credentials of its members and pronounces upon the validity of contested elections.

11. The members of the Chamber of Representatives receive for the expenses of travel and during the session the compensation decreed by the Constituent Assembly.

12. They are indefinitely re-eligible.

13. The Chamber of Representatives is of right renewed entire every five years.

14. No member of either chamber can be arrested, saving in the case of *flagrante delicto,* nor prosecuted for a criminal or correctional matter, during the sessions, except in virtue of a resolution of the chamber of which he is a part.

15. None can be arrested or imprisoned for debts from the beginning of the convocation nor for forty days after the session.

16. Peers are tried by their chamber in criminal and correctional matters in the forms which shall be regulated by law.

17. The character of peer or of representative is compatible with any public position, except those of accountants.

Nevertheless, the prefects and sub-prefects cannot be elected by the electoral college of the department or the district which they administer.

18. The Emperor sends into the chamber ministers of state and councillors of state, who sit there and take part in the discussions, but have a deliberative voice only in case they are members of the chamber as peers or as representatives of the people.

19. The ministers who are members of the Chamber of Peers or of that of the representatives, or who sit by direction of the government, give to the chambers the explanations which are deemed necessary when their publicity does not compromise the interest of the state.

20. The sittings of the two chambers are public. Nevertheless they can form themselves into secret committee, the

Chamber of Peers upon the request of ten members, that of the representatives upon the request of twenty-five. The government can also require secret committees for communications which it has to make. In any case the decisions and the votes can take place only in public session.

21. The Emperor can prorogue, adjourn and dissolve the Chamber of Representatives. The proclamation which pronounces the dissolution convokes the electoral colleges for a new election, and directs the meeting of the representatives within six months at the latest.

22. During the interval between sessions of the Chamber of Representatives, or in case of dissolution of that chamber, the Chamber of Peers cannot assemble.

23. The government has the proposing of the laws; the chambers can propose amendments; if these amendments are not adopted by the government, the chambers are required to vote upon the law as it has been proposed.

24. The chambers have the power to invite the government to propose a law upon a defined subject and to draw up what seems to it suitable to insert in the law. This request may be made by each of the two chambers.

25. When a bill is adopted in one of the two chambers, it is sent to the other; and if it is approved there, it is sent to the Emperor.

26. No written speech, except reports of commissions, reports of the ministers upon the laws which are presented and the accounts which are rendered, can be read in either of the chambers.

Title II. Of the Electoral Colleges and of the Manner of Election.

27. The department and district electoral colleges are maintained, in conformity with the senatus-consultum of 16 Thermidor, Year X, except for the modifications that follow.

28. The cantonal assemblies shall fill each year by annual elections all the vacancies in the electoral colleges.

29. Dating from the year 1816, a member of the Chamber of Peers, designated by the Emperor, shall be president, for life and irremovable, of each department electoral college.

30. Dating from the same time, the electoral college of each

department shall appoint from among the members of each district college, the president and two vice-presidents. For this purpose the meeting of the department college shall precede that of the district college by fifteen days.

31. The colleges of the department and of the district shall appoint the number of representatives fixed for each by the act and the table herewith annexed, number one.

32. Representatives may be chosen without distinction of residence from the whole extent of France.

Each department or district college which shall choose a representative outside of the department or the district shall select a substitute, who shall be taken necessarily from within the department or the district.

33. Industry and manufacturing and commercial property shall have a special representation.

The election of the commercial and manufacturing representatives shall be made by the electoral college of the department out of a list of eligibles prepared by the chamber of commerce and the consultative chambers assembled together, according to the act and table herewith annexed.

Title III.　Of the Law of Taxation.

34. The general direct tax, upon either real estate or personal property, is voted only for one year; the indirect taxes can be voted for several years.

In case of the dissolution of the Chamber of Representatives, the taxes voted in the preceding session are continued until the new meeting of the chamber.

35. No direct or indirect tax, in money or in kind, can be collected, no loan can be made, no entry of credits upon the ledgers of the public debt can be made, no domain can be alienated or exchanged, no levy of men for the army can be ordered, no portion of the territory can be exchanged, except in virtue of a law.

36. No proposal for taxation, loan or the levy of men, can be made except by the Chamber of Representatives.

37. To the Chamber of Representatives also is first brought: 1st, the general budget of the state, containing the estimate of the receipts and the amount of money proposed to be assigned for the year to each department of the ministry;

2d, the account of the receipts and expenses of the year or the preceding years.

Title IV. Of the Ministers and of Responsibility.

38. All the acts of the government must be countersigned by a minister having a department.

39. The ministers are responsible for the acts of the government signed by them, as well as for the execution of the laws.

40. They can be accused by the Chamber of Representatives and are tried by that of the peers.

41. Any minister or any commander of the army or navy can be accused by the Chamber of Representatives and tried by the Chamber of Peers for having compromised the safety or the honor of the nation.

42. The Chamber of Peers in this case exercises a discretionary power, either to characterise the offence or to inflict the penalty.

43. Before pronouncing for the indictment of a minister, the Chamber of Representatives must declare that there is occasion to investigate the proposal of accusation.

44. This declaration can be made only after the report of a commission of sixty members drawn by lot. This commission does not make its report sooner than ten days after its appointment.

45. When the chamber has declared that there is occasion to investigate, it can call before it the minister to ask for explanations from him. This call cannot take place until ten days after the report of the commission.

46. In no other case can ministers having departments be called or sent for by the chambers.

47. When the Chamber of Representatives has declared that there is occasion to investigate a minister, there is formed a new commission of sixty members, drawn by lot, as was the first, and this commission makes a new report upon the indictment. This commission cannot make its report until ten days after its appointment.

48. The indictment cannot be pronounced until ten days after the reading and the distribution of the report.

49. The accusation being pronounced, the Chamber of Rep-

resentatives appoints five commissioners taken from its body, to prosecute the accusation before the Chambers of Peers.

50. Article 75 of title VIII of the constitutional act of 22 Frimaire, Year VIII, providing that the agents of the government can be prosecuted only in virtue of a decision of the Council of State, shall be altered by a law.

Title V. Of the Judicial Power.

51. The Emperor appoints all the judges. They are irremovable, and are appointed for the remainder of their lives, except the appointments of justices of the peace and judges of commerce, which shall take place as in the past. The present judges appointed by the Emperor upon the terms of the senatus-consultum of October 12, 1807, and whom he shall think proper to retain, shall receive life nominations before the first of January next.

52. The jury system is retained.

53. Trials in criminal matters are public.

54. Military offences only are under the jurisdiction of the military tribunals.

55. All other offences, even if committed by soldiers, are under the jurisdiction of the civil tribunals.

56. All crimes and offences over which the imperial high court had jurisdiction and the trial of which is not reserved by the present act to the Chamber of Peers, shall be brought before the ordinary tribunals.

57. The Emperor has the right to pardon, even in correctional matters, and to grant amnesties.

58. The interpretations of the laws asked for by the court of cassation shall be given in the form of a law.

Title VI. Rights of Citizens.

59. Frenchmen are equal before the law, whether for contribution to public taxes and charges, or for admission to civil and military employments.

60. No one under any pretext can be deprived of the judges who are assigned to him by law.

61. No one can be prosecuted, arrested, detained or exiled except in the cases provided for by law and according to the prescribed forms.

62. Liberty of worship is guaranteed to all.

63. All property possessed or acquired by virtue of the laws, and all state-credits, are inviolable.

64. Every citizen has the right to print and publish his thoughts in signed form, without any prior censorship, subject to legal responsibilty, after publication, by jury trial, even when there may be occasion for the application of only a correctional penalty.

65. The right of petition is secured to all citizens. Every petition is individual. These petitions can be addressed either to the government or to the two chambers: but these last also must be entitled: *To his Majesty the Emperor*. They shall be presented to the chambers under the guarantee of a member who recommends the petition. They are read publicly; and if the chamber takes them into consideration, they are brought to the Emperor by the president.

66. No place nor any part of the territory can be declared in a state of siege, except in the case of invasion on the part of a foreign force, or of civil disturbances.

In the first case, the declaration is made by an act of the government.

In the second case, it can be made only by a law.

Yet, the case occurring, if the chambers are not assembled, the act of the government declaring the state of siege must be converted into a proposal for a law within the first fifteen days of the meeting of the chambers.

67. The French people declare that, in the delegation which it has made and which it makes of its powers, it has not intended and does not intend to give the right to propose the re-establishment of the Bourbons or any prince of that family upon the throne, even in the case of the extinction of the imperial dynasty, nor the right to re-establish either the ancient feudal nobility, or the feudal and seignioral rights, or the tithes, or any privileged and ruling worship, or the power to bring any attack upon the irrevocability of the sale of the national domains; it especially forbids to the government, the chambers and the citizens any proposition of this kind.

[The tables mentioned in articles 31 and 33 are omitted. These tables regulated the apportionment of the deputies.]

99. Treaty of Paris.

November 20, 1815. Hertslet, *Map of Europe by Treaty*, 342-350.

This treaty contains the terms imposed upon France by the allies at the end of the Hundred Days. By comparing it with the treaty of the previous year (No. 91) a large part of what that episode cost France can be ascertained.

REFERENCES. Fyffe, *Modern Europe*, II, 60-63 (Popular ed., 406-408) ; Andrews, *Modern Europe*, I, 111-113 ; Seignobos, *Europe Since 1814*, 113-114 ; *Cambridge Modern History*, IX, 663-666 ; Lavisse and Rambaud, *Histoire générale*, IX, 930-931 ; Sorel, *L'Europe et la révolution française*, VIII, 469-481, 490 ; Jaurès, *Histoire socialiste*, VII, 76-80.

In the Name of the Most Holy and Undivided Trinity.

The allied powers having by their united efforts, and by the success of their arms, preserved France and Europe from the convulsions with which they were menaced by the late enterprise of Napoleon Bonaparte, and by the revolutionary system reproduced in France, to promote its success : participating at present with His Most Christian Majesty in the desire to consolidate, by maintaining inviolate the royal authority, and by restoring the operation of the Constitutional Charter, the order of things which had been happily re-established in France, as also in the object of restoring between France and her neighbours those relations of reciprocal confidence and good will which the fatal effects of the revolution and of the system of conquest had for so long a time disturbed ; persuaded, at the same time, that this last object can only be obtained by an arrangement framed to secure to the allies proper indemnities for the past and solid guarantees for the future, they have, in concert with His Majesty the King of France, taken into consideration the means of giving effect to this arrangement ; and being satisfied that the indemnity due to the allied powers cannot be either entirely territorial or entirely pecuniary, without prejudice to France in one or other of her essential interests, and that it would be more fit to combine both the modes, in order to avoid the inconvenience which would result, were either resorted to separately, their Imperial and Royal Majesties have adopted this basis for their present transactions ; and agreeing alike as to the necessity of retaining for a fixed time in the frontier provinces of France, a certain number of allied troops, they have determined to combine their different arrangements, founded upon these bases, in a definitive treaty.

. . . .

1. The frontiers of France shall be the same as they were in the year 1790, save and except the modifications on one side and on the other, which are detailed in the present article.

. . . .

[This line is indicated in the maps facing p. 350 of Hertslet, *Map of Europe by Treaty*.]

4. The pecuniary part of the indemnity to be furnished by France to the allied powers is fixed at the sum of 700,-000,000 francs. . . .

5. The state of uneasiness and fermentation, which after so many violent convulsions, and particularly after the last catastrophe, France must still experience, notwithstanding the paternal intentions of her king, and the advantages secured to every class of his subjects by the Constitutional Charter, requiring for the security of the neighbouring states, certain measures of precaution and of temporary guarantee, it has been judged indispensable to occupy, during a fixed time, by a corps of allied troops certain military positions along the frontiers of France, under the express reserve, that such occupation shall in no way prejudice the sovereignty of His Most Christian Majesty, nor the state of possession, such as it is recognized and confirmed by the present treaty. The number of these troops shall not exceed 150,000 men. . . . As the maintenance of the army destined for this service is to be provided by France, a special convention shall regulate everything which may relate to that object. . . . The utmost extent of the duration of this military occupation is fixed at 5 years. It may terminate before that period if, at the end of 3 years, the allied sovereigns, after having, in concert with His Majesty the King of France, maturely examined their material situation and interests, and the progress which shall have been made in France in the re-establishment of order and tranquility, shall agree to acknowledge that the motives which led them to that measure have ceased to exist. But whatever may be the result of this deliberation, all the fortresses and positions occupied by the allied troops shall, at the expiration of 5 years, be evacuated without further delay,

and given up to His Most Christian Majesty, or to his heirs and successors.

. . . . . .

11. The treaty of Paris of the 30th of May, 1814, and the final act of the Congress of Vienna of the 9th of June, 1815, are confirmed, and shall be maintained in all such of their enactments which shall not have been modified by the articles of the present treaty.

. . . . . .

100.   Treaty of Alliance against France.

November 20, 1815.   Hertslet, *Map of Europe by Treaty*, 372-375.

This secret treaty was signed at Paris on the same day as the treaty of peace with France (No. 99). It shows what Europe still feared from France and the measures which the allies believed to be necessary in order to avert that danger. It is also important in connection with that concert of powers later known as the Holy Alliance. Its relationship towards the Holy Alliance treaty of September 26, 1815, and the actual alliance should receive careful attention.

REFERENCES. Fyffe, *Modern Europe*, II, 63-66 (Popular ed., 408-411) ; Andrews. *Modern Europe*, I, 117-121 : *Cambridge Modern History*, IX. 666, X, 10-12 : Lavisse and Rambaud, *Histoire générale*, X, 65-68 ; Sorel, *L'Europe et la révolution française*, VIII, 490-492.

In the Name of the Most Holy and Undivided Trinity.

The purpose of the alliance concluded at Vienna the 25th day of March, 1815, having been happily attained by the re-establishment in France of the order of things which the last criminal attempt of Napoleon Bonaparte had momentarily subverted; Their Majesties the King of the United Kingdom of Great Britain and Ireland, the Emperor of Austria, King of Hungary and Bohemia, the Emperor of all the Russias, and the King of Prussia, considering that the repose of Europe is essentially interwoven with the confirmation of the order of things founded on the maintenance of the royal authority and the Constitutional Charter, and wishing to employ all their means to prevent the general tranquility (the object of the wishes of mankind and the constant end of their efforts), from being again disturbed; desirous moreover to draw closer the ties which unite them for the common interests of their people, have resolved to give to the principles solemnly laid down in the treaties of Chaumont of the 1st March, 1814, and of Vienna of the 25th of March, 1815, the application the most analogous to the present state of affairs, and to fix beforehand by a solemn treaty the principles which they propose to follow, in order to guarantee Europe from dangers by which she may still be menaced; . . .

. . . .

1. The high contracting parties reciprocally promise to maintain, in its force and vigour, the treaty signed this day with His Most Christian Majesty, and to see that the stipulations of the said treaty, as well as those of the particular conventions which have reference thereto, shall be strictly and faithfuly executed in their fullest extent.

2. The high contracting parties, having engaged in the war which has just terminated for the purpose of maintaining inviolably the arrangements settled at Paris last year, for the safety and interest of Europe, have judged it advisable to renew the said engagements by the present act, and to confirm them as mutually obligatory, subject to the modifications contained in the treaty signed this day with the plenipotentiaries of His Most Christian Majesty, and particularly those by which Napoleon Bonaparte and his family in pursuance of the Treaty of the 11th of April, 1814, have been forever excluded from supreme power in France, which exclusion the contracting powers bind themselves, by the present act, to maintain in full vigour, and, should it be necessary, with the whole of their forces. And as the same revolutionary principles which upheld the last criminal usurpation, might again, under other forms, convulse France, and thereby endanger the repose of other states; under these circumstances, the high contracting parties solemnly admitting it to be their duty to redouble their watchfulness for the tranquility and interests of their people, engage, in case so unfortunate an event should again occur, to concert among themselves, and with His Most Christian Majesty, the measures which they may judge necessary to be pursued for the safety of their respective states, and for the general tranquility of Europe.

3. The high contracting parties, in agreeing with His Most Christian Majesty that a line of military positions in France should be occupied by a corps of allied troops during

a certain number of years, had in view to secure, as far as lay in their power, the effect of the stipulations contained in articles 1 and 2 of the present treaty, and uniformly disposed to adopt every salutary measure calculated to secure the tranquility of Europe by maintaining the order of things re-established in France, they engage, in case the said body of troops should be attacked or menaced with an attack on the part of France, that the said powers should be again obliged to place themselves on a war establishment against that power, in order to maintain either of the said stipulations, or to secure and support the great interests to which they relate, each of the high contracting parties shall furnish, without delay, according to the stipulations of the treaty of Chaumont, and especially in pursuance of articles 7 and 8 of that treaty, its full contingent of 60,000 men, in addition to the forces left in France, or such part of the said contingent as the exigency of the case may require, should be put in motion.

4. If, unfortunately, the forces stipulated in the preceding article should be found insufficient, the high contracting parties will concert together, without loss of time, as to the additional number of troops to be furnished by each for the support of the common cause; and they engage to employ, in case of need, the whole of their forces, in order to bring the war to a speedy and successful termination, reserving to themselves the right to prescribe, by common consent, such conditions of peace as shall hold out to Europe a sufficient guarantee against the recurrence of a similar calamity.

5. The high contracting parties having agreed to the dispositions laid down in the preceding articles, for the purpose of securing the effect of their engagements during the period of the temporary occupation, declare, moreover, that even after the expiration of this measure, the said engagements shall still remain in full force and vigour, for the purpose of carrying into effect such measures as may be deemed necessary for the maintenance of the stipulations contained in articles 1 and 2 of the present act.

6. To facilitate and to secure the execution of the present treaty, and to consolidate the connections which at the present moment so closely unite the four sovereigns for the happiness of the world, the high contracting parties have agreed to renew their meetings at fixed periods, either under the im-

mediate auspices of the sovereigns themselves, or by their respective ministers, for the purpose of consulting upon their common interests, and for the consideration of the measures which at each of those periods shall be considered the most salutary for the repose and prosperity of nations, and for the maintenance of the peace of Europe.

. . . .

101. Press Laws and Ordinances of the Restoration.

The political battles of the restoration period. 1815-1830, centered largely about the regulation of the press and the method of electing the deputies. With each pronounced change of general policy there was usually some alteration of the measures regulating one or both of these matters. These document according-ly throw light upon both the fluctuations of gen. al policy and the measures taken for the control of the press. Document **A** was one of the "liberal" press laws of 1819 ; B represents the reaction following the assassination of the Duke of Berry ; C exhibits the still more pronounced reactionary policy of the Villèle ministry ; while D, which was promulgated after an even more repressive measure than C had been rejected by the Chamber of Peers, shows how the ordinance-making power of the king was used to put in operation a more reactionary policy than the Chambers would sanction.

REFERENCES. Seignobos, *Europe Since 1814*, 120-125, *passim ;* Andrews, *Modern Europe*, I, 150-166, *passim ; Cambridge Modern History*, X, 59-60, 63, 77, 89-90 ; Lavisse and Rambaud, *Histoire générale*, X, 107-109, 111, 115, 131-133 ; Rambaud, *Civilisation contemporaine*, 330-332 ; Jaurès, *Histoire socialiste*, VII, 134, 146-147, 180-182, 215-218.

A. Law upon the Press. June 9, 1819. Duvergier, *Lois*, XXII, 165-166.

1. The proprietors or editors of any newspaper or periodical work, devoted in whole or in part to news or political matters, and appearing, either on a fixed day or in parts, or irregularly but more than once per month, shall be required,

1st. To make a declaration setting forth the name of at least one proprietor or responsible editor, his residence and the duly authorised printing office at which the newspaper or periodical work must be printed ;

2d. To furnish a money deposit which shall be, in the departments of the Seine, Seine-et-Oise and Seine-et-Marne, ten thousand francs of yearly income for daily newspapers, and five thousand francs of yearly income for newspapers or periodical works appearing at less frequent intervals;

And in the other departments, the money deposit for daily newspapers shall be two thousand five hundred francs of *rentes* in cities of fifty thousand souls and upwards; fifteen hundred francs of *rentes* in the cities below [fifty thousand]; and of half these *rentes* for newspapers or periodical works which appear at less frequent intervals.

.   .   .   .

2. The responsibility of the authors or editors named in the declaration shall extend to all the articles inserted in the newspaper or periodical work, without prejudice to the joint liability of the authors or writers of the said articles.

.   .   .   .

5. At the moment of the publication of each sheet or part of a newspaper or periodical work a copy thereof, signed by a proprietor or responsible editor, shall be sent to the prefecture in the head-towns of the departments, to the subprefecture in those of the district, and in the others, to the *mairie*.

This formality shall not delay nor suspend the dispatching or distribution of the newspaper or periodical work.

6. Whoever shall publish a newspaper or periodical work without complying with the conditions prescribed by articles 1, 4 and 5 of the present law shall be punished correctionally with an imprisonment of from one month to six months and a fine of from two hundred francs to twelve hundred francs.

7. The editors of any newspaper or periodical work shall not render an account of the secret sessions of the chambers, nor of one of them, without their authorisation.

.   .   .   .

9. The proprietors or responsible editors of a newspaper or periodical work, or the authors or writers of articles printed in the said newspaper or work, accused of crimes or offences for act of publication, shall be prosecuted and tried in the forms and according to the distinctions prescribed with respect to all other publications.

.   .   .   .

B. Law upon the Press. March 31, 1820. Duvergier, *Lois.* XXII. 409-410.

1. The free publication of newspapers and periodical works devoted in whole or in part to news and to political matters,

and appearing either at a fixed day or irregularly and by parts, is temporarily suspended until the term hereinafter fixed.

2. None of the said newspapers and periodical works can be published except with the authorisation of the king.

However, the actually existing newspapers and periodical works shall continue to appear, upon conforming with the provisions of the present law.

3. The authorisation required by the preceding article can be accorded only to those which shall prove that they have conformed with the conditions prescribed in article 1 of the law of June 9, 1819.

4. Before the publication of any sheet or part, the manuscript must be submitted, by the proprietor or responsible editor, to a prior examination.

5. Any proprietor or responsible editor who may have caused to be printed a sheet or a part of a newspaper or periodical work without having communicated it to the censor before printing, or who may have inserted in one of the said sheets or parts an article not communicated or not approved, shall be punished correctionally by an imprisonment of from one month to six months, and by a fine of from two hundred francs to twelve hundred francs, without prejudice to the prosecutions to which the contents of these sheets, parts and articles may give occasion.

6. When a proprietor or responsible editor shall be prosecuted in virtue of the preceding article, the government can pronounce the suspension of the newspaper or periodical work until the judicial decision.

7. Upon inspection of the judgment of condemnation, the government can prolong for a term which shall not exceed six months, the suspension of the said newspaper or periodical work. In case of repetition it can pronounce definitively the suppression thereof.

8. No printed, engraved or lithographic design can be published, exposed, distributed or put on sale, without the prior authorisation of the government.

Those who may contravene this provision shall be punished with the penalties provided in article 5 of the present law.

9. The provisions of the laws of May 17, May 26, and

June 9, 1819, in which there is no alteration by the above articles shall continue to be executed.

10. The present law of right shall cease to have its effect at the end of the session of 1825.

C. Law upon the Press. March 17, 1822. Duvergier, *Lois,* XXIII, 478-480.

1. No newspaper or periodical work, devoted in whole or in part to news or to political matters, and appearing either regularly and at a fixed day, or by parts and irregularly, can be established and published without the authorisation of the king.

This provision is not applicable to the newspapers and periodical works existing January 1, 1822.

2. The first copy of each sheet or part of periodical works and newspapers, at the very instant of its issue from the press, shall be dispatched to and deposited at the office of the procureur of the king of the place of printing. This remittance shall take the place of that which was prescribed by article 5 of the law of June 9, 1819.

3. In the case in which the spirit of a newspaper or periodical work, resulting from a succession of articles, may be of a nature to constitute an attack upon the public peace, the respect due to the religion of the state or other religions legally recognized in France, the authority of the king, the stability of the constitutional institutions, the inviolability of the sales of the national lands and the tranquil possession of these properties, the royal courts in the jurisdiction of which they shall be established, in solemn audience of two chambers and after having heard the procureur-general and the parties, shall be able to pronounce the suspension of the newspaper or periodical work during a time which cannot exceed one month for the first time and three months for the second. After these two suspensions, in case of new repetition, definitive suppression can be ordered.

4. If, in the interval of the session of the chambers grave circumstances should render momentarily insufficient the established measures of guarantee and repression, the laws of March 31, 1820, and of July 26, 1821, can be immediately put into operation again, in virtue of an ordinance of the king deliberated in Council of State and countersigned by three ministers.

This provision *ipso facto* shall cease one month after the opening of the session of the two chambers, if, during that interval, it has not been converted into a law.

It, likewise *ipso facto,* shall cease the day on which may be published an ordinance which pronounces the dissolution of the Chamber of Deputies.

5. The provisions of previous laws in which there is no alteration by the present shall continue to be executed.

D. Royal Ordinance upon the Press. June 24, 1827. Duvergier, *Lois,* XXVII, 290.

Charles, etc., upon the report of our minister-secretary of state for the department of the interior, in view of our ordinance of this day, concerning the putting in operation of the laws of March 31, 1820, and of July 26, 1821, relative to the publication of newspapers and periodical works, etc.

1. There shall be at Paris, in the service of our minister-secretary of state for the department of the interior, a bureau charged with the prior examination of all newspapers and periodical works.

2. This bureau shall be composed of six censors, who shall be appointed by us, upon the presentation of our minister-secretary of state of the interior.

3. Every number of a newspaper or periodical work, before being printed, must have been furnished with the visa of this bureau, which shall authorise the publication thereof, in conformity with article 5 of the law of March 31, 1820.

.   .   .   .   .   .

6. In the departments, the prefects shall appoint, according to the needs, one or several censors charged with the prior examination of the newspapers which shall be published there.

.   .   .   .   .   .

102. Circular of the Keeper of the Seals.

About February 1, 1824. *Moniteur,* February 4, 1824.

In February, 1824, a general election for members of the Chamber of Deputies occurred. The reactionary ministry then in office left no stone unturned in its efforts to secure a large majority favorable to itself. This document, which was sent to all of the prefects, illustrates the kind of methods employed by the ministry in that election and is also typical of the manner in which the administrative officials were used throughout the period. The election produced an overwhelming majority for the ministry.

REFERENCES. Seignobos, *Europe Since 1814*, 123 : Lavisse and Rambaud, *Histoire générale*, X, 121-122 ; Jaurès, *Histoire social-iste*, VII, 196-198.

The king has deemed it useful for the welfare of the state to dissolve the Chamber of Deputies and to order the general elections.

The experience which you have acquired in affairs will not permit you to misunderstand the aim of that measure, and the knowledge which you have of the interests of France and of your duties will have long since apprised you of the zeal which you ought to display in order to assure the success of it. Instability cannot be an isolated accident in the state. When the systems of the government change, it soon descends to the lowest grades of the scale of public employments; and there is no functionary or magistrate, whatever may be his rank or his employment, who ought not to desire for himself that the general administration should receive and preserve a uniform and constant direction.

On the other hand, sir, the government confers public employments only in order that it may be served and supported. Whoever accepts a place contracts at the same time an obligation to consecrate his efforts, his talents, and his influence to the service of the government; it is a contract of which reciprocity forms the bond. If the government withdraws the place, the one who loses it recovers the right to dispose of himself and to regulate at his own will all the actions of his public life; if the functionary refuses to the government the services which it expects of him, he betrays his fidelity and breaks voluntarily the compact of which the position that he fills has been the object and the condition. It is the most certain and the most irrevocable of abdications; the government owes nothing further to one who does not render to it all that he owes it.

Make haste, sir, to recall these truths to your deputies, the officers of the judicial police and the ministerial officials of your jurisdiction, all those, in a word, of whom the law has made you the overseer and guide. Say to them that I demand of them a loyal, active and effective co-operation. Prescribe for them a prudent and uniform conduct. Condemn without qualification all division in voting, of which the most certain effect would be to offer chances of success to the opposition.

Announce to them that you will be attentive to their proceedings, and be particular to fulfil that promise. I like to persuade myself that you will have only favorable reports to transmit to me, and that I myself shall have to transmit to them only thanks and eulogies.

Receive, sir, assurance of a perfect consideration.

103. Documents upon the Dissolution of 1830.

The dissolution of the Chamber of Deputies in March, 1830, and the election that followed were the prelude to the July Revolution. These documents bring out clearly the reason why Charles X dissolved the Chamber of Deputies and the issue presented at the election, which was a complete triumph for the opposition to the king.

REFERENCES. Fyffe, *Modern Europe*, II, 364-368 (Popular ed., 608-611); Seignobos, *Europe Since 1814*, 128; Andrews, *Modern Europe*, I, 170-173; *Cambridge Modern History*, X, 98-99; Lavisse and Rambaud, *Histoire générale*, X, 278-282; Jaurès, *Histoire socialiste*, VII, 234-238.

A. The King's Speech. March 2, 1830. *Moniteur,* March 3, 1830.

Gentlemen:

It is always with confidence that I gather around my throne the peers of the kingdom and the deputies of the departments.

.   .   .   .   .   .

Gentlemen, the first longing is to see France, happy and respected, develop all the wealth of its soil and its industry, and enjoy in peace the institutions whose advantages I have firmly determined to consolidate. The Charter has placed the public liberties under the safeguard of the rights of my crown: these rights are sacred; my duty towards my people is to transmit them intact to my successors.

Peers of France and deputies of the departments, I do not doubt of your co-operation in order to secure the gain which I wish to effect; you will repulse the perfidious insinuations which malevolence seeks to propagate. If culpable maneuvers raise up against my government obstacles which I do not wish to anticipate, I will find the power to surmount them in my resolution to maintain the public peace, in the just confidence

of Frenchmen and the love which they have always borne for
their kings.

B. Reply of the Chamber of Deputies.   March 18, 1830.
Moniteur, March 19, 1830.

Sire,

It is with an enduring gratification that your faithful subjects, the deputies of the departments, assembled around your
throne, have heard from your august lips the flattering testimony of the confidence which you have accorded them. . . .

Summoned by your voice from all points of your kingdom, we bring you from all parts, sire, the homage of a
faithful people, once more aroused at having seen you the most
beneficent of all in the midst of universal beneficence, and who
revere in you the accomplished model of all the most touching virtues. Sire, this people cherish and respect your authority; fifteen years of peace and of liberty, which they owe to
your august brother and to you, have profoundly enrooted
in their hearts the gratitude which attaches them to your
royal family; their reason, matured by experience and by liberty of discussion, says to them that it is especially in matters
of authority that antiquity of possession is the most sacred of
all titles, and that it is for their welfare as well as for your
glory that the ages have placed your throne in a region inaccessible to storms. Their convictions, then, are in accord with
their duty in placing before themselves the most sacred rights
of your crown as the surest guarantee of their liberties and
the integrity of your prerogatives as necessary for the preservation of these rights.

Nevertheless, sire, in the midst of the unanimous sentiments of respect and affection with which your people surround you, there is manifested in their minds a lively disquie-
tude which disturbs the security that France had commenced
to enjoy, affects the sources of its prosperity, and, if it should
be prolonged, might become disastrous to its repose. Our
conscience, our honor, the fidelity to you which we have sworn
and which we shall always preserve, impose upon us the duty
of disclosing to you the cause of this.

Sire, the Charter, which we owe to the wisdom of your
august predecessor, and the advantages of which Your Majesty

is firmly determined to consolidate, consecrates, as a right, the participation of the country in the deliberation upon public interests. That participation ought to be, and is in fact, indirect, wisely measured and circumscribed within limits exactly traced, and which we shall never suffer that anyone should attempt to break; but it is positive in its results; for it is made by the permanent co-operation of the political views of your government with the wishes of your people, the indispensable condition of the regular progress of public affairs. Sire, our loyalty and our devotion to you condemn us to tell you that this co-operation does not exist.

An unjust contempt for the sentiments and the reason of France is to-day the fundamental thought of the administration. Your people are afflicted thereat, because it is injurious to them; they are disturbed thereat, because it is menacing to their liberties!

This contempt could not proceed from your noble heart. No, sire, *France no more wishes for anarchy than you wish for despotism;* it is fitting that you should have faith in its loyalty, as it has faith in your promises.

Between those who misunderstand a nation so calm and so faithful and us, who with a profound conviction come to set forth in your presence the grievances of a people anxious above everything else for the esteem and confidence of their king, let the lofty wisdom of Your Majesty pronounce! His [your] royal prerogatives have placed in his [your] hands the means of assuring among the powers of the state that constitutional harmony the first and necessary condition of the power of the throne and of the grandeur of France.

C. Response of the King. March 18, 1830. *Moniteur,* March 19, 1830.

Sir, I have heard the address which you present me in the name of the Chamber of Deputies.

I have a right to count upon the co-operation of the two chambers in order to accomplish all of the good which I was meditating; my heart is afflicted at seeing the deputies of the departments declare that on their part that co-operation does not exist.

Gentlemen, I have announced my determinations in my discourse at the opening of the session. Those determinations are immovable; the interest of my people forbids me to depart therefrom.

My ministers will make known to you my intentions.

D. Proclamation of the King. June 13, 1830. Duvergier, *Lois*, XXX, 56.

Charles, by the grace of God, King of France and of Navarre, to all those to whom these presents shall come, greeting.

Frenchmen,

The late Chamber of Deputies misconceived my intentions. I had the right to count upon its co-operation in order to accomplish the good which I was meditating: it refused that to me! As father of my people, my heart is afflicted thereat; as king, I have been offended at it: I have pronounced the dissolution of that chamber.

Frenchmen, your prosperity constitutes my glory; your welfare is mine. At the moment in which the electoral colleges are about to open at all points of my kingdom, you will hear the voice of your king.

To maintain the Constitutional Charter and the institutions which it has founded has been and ever shall be the aim of my efforts.

But, in order to attain that aim, I ought to exercise that judgment freely and to make respected the sacred rights which are the appanage of my crown.

It is in them that the guarantee of the public reposes and of your liberties lies. The nature of the government would be altered, if culpable attacks should enfeeble my prerogatives, and I would betray my oaths if I should suffer it.

Under the shelter of this government, France has become flourishing and free. She owes to it her liberties, her credit and her industry. France has nothing to envy in other states, and can aspire only to the preservation of the advantages which she enjoys.

Reassure yourselves then about your rights. I blend them with mine, and I will protect them with an equal solicitude.

Do not allow yourselves to be led astray through the language of the insidious enemies of your repose. Repel unworthy suspicions and false fears, which would disturb public confidence and might excite grave disorders.

The designs of those who propagate these fears will fail, whoever they may be, before my immovable resolution. Your security and your interests shall no more be compromised than your liberties; I watch over the one as over the others.

Electors, make haste to gather in your colleges. Do not let a reprehensible negligence deprive them of your presence! Let a single sentiment animate you, let a single flag rally you!

It is your king who asks it of you; it is a father who calls you.

Fulfil your duties; I shall know how to fulfil mine.

Given at our château of the Tuileries, the 13th day of the month of June of the year of grace, 1830, and of our reign the sixth.

Signed, CHARLES.

104. Documents upon the July Revolution.

The July Revolution passed through three quite distinct phases. In the first phase it was simply a protest against the July Ordinances and the popular cries were *"Vive la Charte,"* "Down with the ministers." In the second phase it became a movement for the overthrow of the Bourbon monarchy and the popular cry was "Down with the Bourbons." In the third phase it became a movement to make Louis Philippe king and the popular cry was *"Vive Louis Philippe."* Documents, A, B and C throw light upon the first phase, the remainder upon the third phase. From the documents much can be learned about the causes for the unpopularity of the Bourbon régime, why the candidacy of Louis Philippe was favorably received, and the real character of the change effected by the revolution.

REFERENCES. Fyffe, *Modern Europe*, II, 368-379 (Popular ed., 611-618) ; Seignobos, *Europe Since 1814*, 129-132 ; Andrews. *Modern Europe*, I, 173-179 ; *Cambridge Modern History*, X, 99-100, 475-479 ; Lavisse and Rambaud, *Histoire générale*, X, 282-292 ; Jaurès, *Histoire socialiste*, VII, 239-255.

A. The July Ordinances, July 25, 1830. Duvergier, *Lois*, XXX, 74-78.

I. Ordinance for Suspending Liberty of the Press.

Charles, etc.

Upon the report of our council of ministers,

We have ordained and do ordain as follows:

1st. The liberty of the periodical press is suspended.

2d. The provisions of articles 1, 2, and 9 of the 1st title of the law of October 2, 1814, are again put in force.

In consequence, no newspaper or periodical or semi-periodical work, established or to be established, without discrimination as to the matters which shall be treated therein, shall appear, either in Paris or in the departments, except in virtue of an authorisation, which the authors and the printer thereof shall have separately obtained from us.

This authorisation must be renewed every three months.

It can be revoked.

3d. The authorisation can be provisionally granted and provisionally withdrawn by the prefects for newspapers and periodicals or semi-periodical works published or to be published in their departments.

4th. Newspapers and works published in contravention of article 2, shall be immediately seized.

The presses and the type which shall have been used for their printing shall be placed in a public repository under seal or put out of service.

5th. No work of less than twenty printed sheets can appear without the authorisation of our minister-secretary of state of the interior at Paris, and of the prefects in the departments.

Any work of more than twenty printed pages which does not constitute a connected work, shall likewise be subject to the necessity of authorisation.

Works published without authorisation shall be immediately seized.

The presses and type which shall have been used for their printing shall be placed in a public repository under seal or put out of service.

6th. Proceedings upon law suits and the transactions of scientific or literary societies are subject to prior authorisation, if they treat in whole or in part of political matters, in which case the measures prescribed in article 5 shall be applicable to them.

7th. Any provision contrary to the present [provisions] shall remain without force.

8th. The execution of the present ordinance shall take place in conformity with article 4 of the ordinance of November 27, 1816, and of what is prescribed by that of January 18, 1817.

9th. Our ministers-secretaries of state are charged, etc.

II. Ordinance for Dissolving the Chamber of Deputies.

Charles, etc.

In view of article 50 of the Constitutional Charter;

Being informed of the maneuvers which have been practised as many points in our kingdom in order to deceive and mislead the electors during the late operations of the electoral colleges;

Our Council having been heard;

We have ordained and do ordain as follows:

1st. The Chamber of Deputies of the departments is dissolved.

2d. Our minister-secretary of state of the interior (Count de Peyronnet) is charged, etc.

III. Ordinance upon the Elections.

Charles, etc.

Having resolved to prevent the recurrence of the maneuvers which have exercised a pernicious influence during the late proceedings of the electoral bodies;

Wishing, therefore, to reform, in accordance with the principles of the Constitutional Charter, the rules of election of which experience has made the inconveniences felt;

We have recognized the necessity of making use of the right which belongs to us, to provide, by acts emanating from us, for the safety of the state and for the repression of any enterprise attacking the dignity of our crown;

For these reasons,

Our Council having been heard,

We ordain and do ordain as follows:

1st. In conformity with articles 15, 36 and 50 of the Constitutional Charter, the Chamber of Deputies shall be composed only of deputies of the departments.

2d. The electoral property qualification and the property qualification for eligibility shall be composed exclusively of the sums for which the elector or eligible person shall be personally enrolled, in the capacity of proprietor or usufructuary upon the roll of the land tax and of the personal property tax.

3d. Each department shall have the number of deputies

which is assigned to it by article 36 of the Constitutional Charter.

4th. The deputies shall be elected and the chamber shall be renewed in the form and for the time determined by article 37 of the Constitutional Charter.

5th. The electoral colleges shall be divided into district colleges and department colleges.

Nevertheless the electoral colleges of the departments to which only one deputy is assigned are excepted.

6th. The district electoral colleges shall be composed of all the electors whose political residence shall be established in the district.

The department electoral colleges shall be composed of the fourth of the electors of the department who are most heavily taxed.

7th. The existing circumscription of the district electoral colleges is maintained.

8th. Each district electoral college shall elect a number of candidates equal to the number of the deputies of the department.

9th. The district college shall be divided into as many sections as there are candidates to be selected.

This division shall be made in proportion to the number of sections and to the total number of electors of the college, having regard therein, as far as shall be possible, to the convenience of the localities and of the neighborhoods.

10th. The sections of the district electoral college can be assembled in different places.

11th. Each section of the district electoral college shall elect one candidate and shall proceed separately.

12th. The presidents of the sections of the district electoral colleges shall be appointed by the prefects from among the electors of the district.

13th. The department electoral college shall elect the deputies.

Half the deputies of the department must be chosen from the general list of the candidates proposed by the district electoral colleges.

Nevertheless, if the number of deputies of the department is odd, the division shall be made without abatement of the right reserved to the college of the department.

14th. In the case where, by reason of omissions, invalid nominations, or double nominations, the list of candidates proposed by the electoral bodies of the district may be incomplete, if this list is reduced to less than half the required number, the department electoral college can elect one more deputy from outside of the list; if the list is reduced to less than a quarter, the department college can elect from outside of the list the total number of the deputies of the department.

15th. The prefects, sub-prefects and general officers commanding the military division and the departments cannot be elected in the departments in which they exercise their functions.

16th. The list of the electors shall be drawn up by the prefect in the council of prefecture. It shall be posted five days before the meeting of the colleges.

17th. Complaints with regard to the right of voting to which justice has not been done by the prefects shall be judged by the Chamber of Deputies, at the same time that it decides on the validity of the proceedings of the college.

18th. In the department electoral colleges the two most aged electors and the two most heavily taxed shall discharge the duties of tellers.

The same arrangement shall be observed in the sections of the district colleges composed of more than fifty electors.

In the other college sections the duties of teller shall be discharged by the most aged and by the most heavily taxed of the electors.

The secretary in the colleges and college sections shall be appointed by the president and the tellers.

19th. Nobody shall be admitted into the college or college section, unless he is registered upon the list of the electors who have a right to participate therein. This list shall be sent to the president and shall remain posted in the place of the meetings of the college during the continuance of its proceedings.

20th. All discussion and all deliberation whatsoever in the midst of the electoral colleges shall be forbidden.

21st. The policing of the college belongs to the president. Without his request no armed force can be stationed near the place where the sittings are held. Military commanders shall be required to comply with his requests.

22d. The nominations shall be made in the colleges and college sections by a majority of the votes cast.

Nevertheless, if the selections are not decided after two ballots, the *bureau* shall draw up a list of the persons who have obtained the most votes at the second ballot. It shall contain a number of names double that of the selections which shall still remain to be made. At the third ballot votes can be given only for the persons enrolled upon this list, and the selection shall be made by plurality.

23d. The electors shall vote by ballot. Each ballot shall contain as many names as there are selections to be made.

24th. The electors shall write their vote at the desk or shall have it written there by one of the tellers.

25th. The name, title and domicile of each voter who shall deposit his ballot shall be entered by the secretary upon a list intended to authenticate the number of voters.

26th. Each ballot shall remain open for six hours and shall be canvassed forthwith.

27th. A record shall be drawn up for each sitting: this record shall be signed by all the members of the *bureau*.

28th. In conformity with article 46 of the Constitutional Charter, no amendment to any law can be made in the chamber, unless it has been proposed or consented to by us, and unless it has been sent back to and discussed in the *bureaux*.

29th. Any provisions contrary to the present ordinance shall remain without force.

30th. Our ministers-secretaries of state are charged, etc.

IV. Ordinance for Convoking the Electoral Colleges.

Charles, etc.

In view of the royal ordinance, dated this day, relative to the organization of the electoral colleges;

Upon the report of our minister-secretary of state of the department of the interior;

We have ordained and do ordain as follows:

1st. The electoral colleges shall meet as follows: the district electoral colleges September 6th next and the department electoral colleges the 13th of the same month.

2d. The Chamber of Peers and the Chamber of Deputies of the departments are convoked for the 28th of the month of September next.

3d. Our minister-secretary of state of the interior (Count de Peyronnet) is charged, etc.

B. Protest of the Paris Journalists. July 26, 1830. Lavisse and Rambaud, *Histoire générale*, X, 283.

The legal régime is interrupted, that of force is begun. The government has violated legality, we are absolved from obedience. We shall attempt to publish our papers without asking for the authorisation which is imposed upon us. The government has to-day lost the character which commands obedience. We are resisting it in that which concerns us; it is for France to decide how far its own resistance must extend.

C. Protest of the Paris Deputies. July 26, 1830. Duvergier, *Lois*, XXX, 81.

The undersigned, regularly elected [to the Chamber of Deputies] and at present in Paris, consider themselves absolutely obliged by their duty and their honor to protest against the measures which the councillors of the crown have recently made to prevail for the overthrow of the legal system of elections and the ruin of the liberty of the press.

The said measures, contained in the ordinances of July 25, are, in the eyes of the undersigned, directly contrary to the constitutional rights of the Chamber of Peers, to the public law of the French, to the prerogatives and decrees of the tribunals, and calculated to throw the whole state into a confusion which would compromise both present peace and future security.

In consequence, the undersigned, inviolably faithful to their oath, protest with one accord, not only against the said measures, but also against all the acts which may be the consequence of them.

And seeing, on the one hand, that the Chamber of Deputies, not having been constituted, cannot be legally dissolved; and on the other hand that the attempt to form another Chamber of Deputies by a new and arbitrary method is in formal contradiction to the Constitutional Charter and the acquired rights of the electors, the undersigned declare that they still consider themselves as legally elected to the deputation by the district and department colleges whose suffrages they have obtained, and that they cannot be replaced except in virtue of elections conducted according to the principles and forms determined by the laws.

And if the undersigned do not effectively exercise the rights and do not discharge all the duties which spring from their legal election, it is because they have been prevented from so doing by physical violence.

[Signatures.]

D. Thiers' Orleanist Manifesto. July 30, 1830. Lavisse and Rambaud, *Histoire générale*, X, 287-288.

Charles X can no longer return to Paris: he has caused the blood of the people to flow. The Republic would expose us to frightful divisions; it would embroil us with Europe. The Duke of Orleans is a prince devoted to the cause of the revolution. The Duke of Orleans did not fight against us. The Duke of Orleans was at Jemmapes. The Duke of Orleans is a citizen king. The Duke of Orleans has borne the tricolors with ardor. The Duke of Orleans alone can again bear them; we do not wish for any others. The Duke of Orleans does not declare himself. He awaits our will. Let us proclaim that will, and he will accept the Charter as we have always understood and wanted it. It is from the French people that he will hold the crown.

E. Proclamation of the Deputies, July 31, 1830. Duvergier, *Lois* XXX, 84-85.

Frenchmen,

France is free. The absolute power was raising its flag; the heroic population of Paris overthrew it. Paris attacked has made to triumph in arms the sacred cause which in the elections had just triumphed in vain. A power, the usurper of our rights and the disturber of our repose, was threatening at the same time order and liberty; we re-enter into possession of order and liberty. No more fear for acquired rights; no further barrier between us and the rights which we still lack.

A government which, without delay, will guarantee us these blessings is to-day the first need of the fatherland.

Frenchmen, those of your deputies who happen to be already at Paris have assembled; and, while awaiting the regular action of the chambers, they have invited a Frenchman who has never fought except for France, Monsieur, the Duke of Orleans, to exercise the functions of lieutenant-general of the kingdom. This is in their eyes the surest method to complete by peace the success of the most lawful defence.

The Duke of Orleans is devoted to the national and constitutional cause; he has always defended its interests and professed its principles. He will respect our rights, for he will hold his from us. We shall assure ourselves by laws all the necessary guarantees in order to render liberty strong and durable:

The re-establishment of the national guard, with the participation of the national guards in the choice of the officers;

The participation of the citizens in the formation of the department and municipal administrations;

The jury for press offences;

Legally organized responsibility of ministers and the subordinate agents of the administration;

The status of military men legally assured;

The re-election of the deputies promoted to public offices.

Finally, we shall in concert with the head of the state give to our institutions the development which they need.

Frenchmen, the Duke of Orleans himself has already spoken, and his language is that which befits a free country, "The chambers are about to meet," he tells you, "they will deliberate upon the means to assure the reign of the laws and the maintenance of the rights of the nation."

"The Charter shall henceforth be a reality."

Were present Messrs.:

[Here follow the names of eighty-nine deputies.]

F. Proclamation by Louis-Philippe. August 1, 1830. *Moniteur,* August 2, 1830.

Inhabitants of Paris,

The deputies of France, at this moment assembled in Paris, have expressed to me a desire that I should proceed into this capital in order to exercise here the functions of lieutenant-general of the kingdom.

I have not hesitated to come to share your dangers, to place myself in the midst of your heroic population, and to use all my endeavors to preserve you from the calamities of civil war and of anarchy.

In re-entering the city of Paris, I bear with pride the glorious colors which you have resumed and which I have myself for a long time borne.

The chambers are about to convene and will deliberate upon the means to assure the reign of the laws and the maintenance of the rights of the nation.

The Charter shall henceforth be a reality.

LOUIS-PHILIPPE D'ORLEANS.

G. Abdication of Charles X. August 2, 1830. Duvergier, *Lois,* XXX, 87-88.

My cousin, I am too profoundly pained at the evils which afflict or which may threaten my people not to have sought a method of preventing them. I have, therefore, taken the resolution to abdicate the crown in favor of my grandson, the Duke of Bordeaux.

The dauphin, who shares my feelings, also renounces his rights in favor of his nephew.

You will have, therefore, in your capacity of lieutenant-general of the kingdom, to cause to be proclaimed the accession of Henry V to the crown. You will in addition take all the measures which concern you in order to regulate the forms of the government during the minority of the new king. Here I confine myself to making known these arrangements; it is indeed a method to still escape evils.

You will communicate my intentions to the diplomatic corps, and you will make known to me as soon as possible the proclamation by which my grandson will be recognized under the name of Henry V.

I charge Lieutenant-General Viscount de Foissac-Latour to bring this letter to you. He has orders to come to an understanding with you about the arrangements to be taken in favor of the persons who have accompanied me, as well as about suitable arrangements for what concerns me and the remainder of my family.

We shall regulate afterwards the other measures which are the consequence of the change of reign.

I renew to you, my cousin, the assurance of the sentiments with which I am your affectionate cousin,

Signed, CHARLES, LOUIS-ANTOINE.

H. Declaration of the Chamber of Deputies. August 7, 1830. Duvergier, *Lois*, XXX, 93-101.

The Chamber of Deputies, taking into consideration the imperative necessity which results from the events of July 26, 27, 28, 29 and the days following and the general situation in which France is placed in consequence of the violation of the Constitutional Charter;

Considering besides that, in consequence of that violation and of the heroic resistance of the citizens of Paris, His Majesty Charles X, His Royal Highness Louis-Antoine, dauphin, and all the members of the elder branch of the royal house have at this moment left French territory;

Declares that the throne is vacant in fact and in right, and that it is indispensable to provide therefor.

The Chamber of Deputies declares secondly that,

In accordance with the wish and in the interest of the French people, the preamble of the Constitutional Charter is suppressed, as wounding the national dignity, in appearing to *grant* to Frenchmen the rights which essentially belong to them, and that the following articles of the same Charter must be suppressed or modified in the manner which is about to be indicated.

.   .   .   .   .   .

[These changes may be ascertained by comparison of Nos. 93 and 105.]

Special Provisions.

All the nominations and new creations of peers made during the reign of Charles X are declared null and void.

Article 27 of the Charter shall be subjected to a new examination in the session of 1831.

The Chamber of Deputies declares thirdly,

That it is necessary to provide successively, by separate laws and within the shortest possible space, for the objects which follow:

1st. The use of the jury for offences of the press and for political offences;

2d. The responsibility of ministers and other agents of authority;

3d. The re-election of deputies promoted to salaried public offices;

4th. The annual vote of the army contingent;

5th. The organization of the national guard, with the participation of the national guards in the choice of their officers;

6th. Provisions which assure in a legal manner the status of army and navy officers of every grade;

7th. Departmental and municipal institutions founded upon an elective system;

8th. Public instruction and liberty of education;

9th. The abolition of the double vote and the fixing of the electoral and eligibility conditions;

10th. To declare that all the laws and ordinances, in whatever they contain contrary to the provisions adopted for the reform of the Charter, are and shall remain annulled and abrogated.

On condition of the acceptance of these provisions and propositions, the Chamber of Deputies declares finally that the universal and pressing interest of the French people calls to the throne His Royal Highness Louis-Philippe d'Orleans, Duke of Orleans, Lieutenant-General of the Kingdom, and his descendants in perpetuity, from male to male, by order of primogeniture to the perpetual exclusion of women and their descendants.

In consequence. His Royal Highness Louis-Philippe d'Orleans shall be invited to accept and to swear to the clauses and engagements above set forth, the observation of the Constitutional Charter and the modifications indicated, and after having done it before the assembled chambers, to take the title of King of the French.

Resolved at the palace of the Chamber of Deputies, August 7, 1830.

105. Constitution of 1830.

August 14, 1830. Duvergier, *Lois*, XXX, 110-114.

This constitution should be carefully compared with the Constitutional Charter of 1814 (No. 93) of which it is a revision. The difference in the theories upon which the two documents are based calls for particular notice.

REFERENCES. Fyffe, *Modern Europe*, II, 379-381 (Popular ed., 618-619) ; Andrews, *Modern Europe*, I, 277-279 ; Seignobos, *Europe Since 1814*, 132-134 ; *Cambridge Modern History*, X, 478-479 ; Lavisse and Rambaud, *Histoire générale*, X, 290-291 ; Rambaud, *Civilisation contemporaine*, 324-325.

Louis-Philippe, King of the French, to all present and to come, greeting.

We have ordered and do order that the Constitutional Charter of 1814, such as it has been amended by the two chambers on August 7th and accepted by us on the 9th, shall be again published in the following terms:

Public Law of the French.

1. Frenchmen are equal before the law, whatever may be their titles and ranks.

2. They contribute, without distinction, in proportion to their fortunes, towards the expenses of the state.

3. They are all equally admissible to civil and military employments.

4. Their personal liberty is likewise guaranteed; no one can be prosecuted or arrested save in the cases provided by law and in the form which it prescribes.

5. Everyone may profess his religion with equal freedom and shall obtain for his worship the same protection.

6. The minister of the catholic, apostolic, and Roman religion, professed by the majority of the French, and those of the other christian sects, receive stipends from the state.

7. Frenchmen have the right to publish and to have printed their opinions, while conforming with the laws.

The censorship can never be re-established.

8. All property is inviolable, without any exception for that which is called national, the law making no distinction between them.

9. The state can require the sacrifice of a property on

account of a legally established public interest, but with a previous indemnity.

10. All investigations of opinions and votes given prior to the restoration are forbidden : the same oblivion is required from the tribunals and from citizens.

11. The conscription is abolished. The method of recruiting for the army and navy is determined by the law.

Forms of the Government of the King.

12. The person of the king is inviolable and sacred. His ministers are responsible. To the king alone belongs the executive power.

13. The king is the supreme head of the state; he commands the land and sea forces, declares war, makes treaties of peace, alliance and commerce, appoints to all places of public administration, and makes the necessary rules and ordinances for the execution of the laws, without the power ever to suspend the laws themselves or to dispense with their execution.

Moreover, no foreign troops can be admitted into the service of the state except in virtue of a law.

14. The legislative power is exercised collectively by the king, the Chamber of Peers, and the Chamber of Deputies.

15. The proposal of laws belongs to the king, the Chamber of Peers, and the Chamber of Deputies.

Nevertheless every taxation law must be first voted by the Chamber of Deputies.

16. Every law shall be freely discussed and voted by the majority of each of the two chambers.

17. If a project of law has been rejected by one of the three powers, it cannot be presented again in the same session.

18. The king alone sanctions and promulgates the laws.

19. The civil list is fixed for the entire duration of the reign by the first legislature assembled after the accession of the king.

Of the Chamber of Peers.

20. The Chambers of Peers is an essential part of the legislative power.

21. It is convoked by the king at the same time as the

Chamber of Deputies. The session of the one begins and ends at the same time as that of the other.

22. Every meeting of the Chamber of Peers which may be held outside of the time of the session of the Chamber of Deputies is unlawful and of no validity, except the single case in which it is assembled as a court of justice, and then it can exercise only judicial functions.

23. The appointment of peers of France belongs to the king. Their number is unlimited: he can at his pleasure alter their dignities, appoint them for life, or make them hereditary.

24. Peers have entrance to the chamber at twenty-five years of age, and a deliberative voice only at thirty years.

25. The Chamber of Peers is presided over by the chancellor of France, and, in his absence, by a peer appointed by the king.

26. The princes of the blood are peers by right of their birth: they sit next to the president.

27. The sittings of the Chamber of Peers are public, as are those of the Chamber of Deputies.

28. The Chamber of Peers has jurisdiction over the crimes of high treason and attacks against the security of the state, which shall be defined by law.

29. No peer can be arrested except by the authority of the chamber, nor be tried in a criminal matter except by it.

Of the Chamber of Deputies.

30. The Chamber of Deputies shall be composed of the deputies elected by electoral colleges, whose organization shall be determined by law.

31. The deputies are elected for five years.

32. No deputy can be admitted to the chamber unless he is thirty years of age and meets the other qualifications required by the law.

33. If, however, there cannot be found in the department fifty persons of the required age who pay the amount of taxes required by the law, their number shall be filled up from the largest tax-payers below this amount of tax, and these shall be elected together with the first.

34. No one is an elector, unless he is at least twenty-five

years of age and meets the other conditions required by the law.

35. The presidents of the electoral colleges are chosen by the electors.

36. At least one-half of the deputies shall be chosen from among the eligibles who have their political domicile in the department.

37. The president of the Chamber of Deputies is elected by it at the opening of each session.

38. The sittings of the chamber are public; but the request of five members suffices for it to form itself into secret committee.

39. The Chamber divides itself into *bureaux* in order to discuss the propositions which have been presented to it by the king.

40. No tax can be imposed or collected, unless it has been consented to by the two chambers and sanctioned by the king.

41. The land-tax is consented to only for one year. Indirect taxes can be established for several years.

42. The king convokes the two chambers each year: he prorogues them and can dissolve that of the deputies; but in that case he must convoke a new one within the space of three months.

43. No bodily constraint can be exercised against a member of the chamber during the session nor in the preceding or following six weeks.

44. No member of the chamber, during the course of the session, can be prosecuted or arrested upon a criminal charge, unless he should be taken in the act, except after the chamber has permitted his prosecution.

45. No petition can be made or presented to either of the chambers except in writing: the law forbids any personal presentation of them at the bar.

Of the Ministers.

46. The ministers can be members of the Chamber of Peers or of the Chamber of Deputies.

They have, besides, their entrance into either chamber and must be heard when they demand it.

47. The Chamber of Deputies has the right to accuse the ministers and to arraign them before the Chamber of Peers, which alone has that of trying them.

Of the Judiciary.

48. All justice emanates from the king: it is administered in his name by judges whom he appoints and whom he invests.

49. The judges appointed by the king are irremovable.

50. The courts and regular tribunals actually existing are continued; they shall not be anywise changed except by virtue of a law.

51. The existing commercial court is retained.

52. The justice of the peace, likewise, is retained. Justices of the peace, although appointed by the king, are not irremovable.

53. No one can be deprived of the jurisdiction of his natural judges.

54. In consequence, extraordinary commissions and tribunals cannot be created, under any title or under any denomination whatsoever.

55. Criminal trials shall be public unless such publicity would be dangerous to order and morality; and, in that case, the tribunal shall declare it by a judicial order.

56. The system of juries is retained. Changes which a longer experience may cause to be thought necessary can be made only by a law.

57. The penalty of confiscation of property is abolished and cannot' be re-established.

58. The king has the right of pardon and that of commuting penalties.

59. The Civil Code and the laws actually existing which are not in conflict with the present charter remain in force until legally abrogated.

Special Rights Guaranteed by the State.

60. Persons in active military service, retired officers and soldiers, pensioned widows, officers and soldiers, retain their ranks, honors and pensions.

61. The public debt is guaranteed. Every form of engagement made by the state with its creditors is inviolable.

62. The old nobility resume their titles, the new retain theirs. The king makes nobles at will; but he grants to them only ranks and honors, without any exemption from the burdens and duties of society.

63. The Legion of Honor is maintained. The king shall determine its internal regulations and its decoration.

64. The colonies are regulated by special laws.

65. The king and his successors shall swear, at their accession in the presence of the assembled chambers, to observe faithfully the Constitutional Charter.

66. The present charter and all the rights that it consecrates stand entrusted to the patriotism and the courage of the national guards and of all French citizens.

67. France resumes its colors. For the future, no other cockade shall be worn than the tricolor cockade.

Special Provisions.

68. All the new appointments and creations of peers made during the reign of Charles X are declared null and void.

Article 23 of the Charter shall be submitted to a new examination in the session of 1831.

69. The following subjects shall be provided for successively by separate laws within the shortest possible space of time:

1st. The use of the jury for political and press offences;

2d. The responsibility of the ministers and the other agents of the executive authority;

3d. The re-election of deputies appointed to public functions with salaries;

4th. The annual vote of the quota of the army;

5th. The organization of the national guards, with the participation of the national guards in the choice of their officers;

6th. Provisions which assure in a legal manner the status of the officers of every grade in the army and navy;

7th. Departmental and municipal institutions founded upon an elective system;

8th. Public instruction and the liberty of teaching;

9th. Abolition of the double vote and fixing of the electoral and eligibility conditions.

70. All laws and ordinances, wherein they are contrary to the provisions adopted for the reform of the charter, are forthwith and shall remain annulled and abrogated.

We command all our courts and tribunals, administrative

bodies, and all others that they keep and maintain, cause to be kept, observed and maintained the present Constitutional Charter, and to make it more known to all, that they cause it to be published in all the municipalities of the kingdom and wherever there shall be need; and in order that this may be firm and stable forever, we have caused our seal to be affixed thereto.

Done at the Palais Royal at Paris, the 14th day of the month of August, in the year 1830.

Signed, LOUIS-PHILIPPE.

106. Law upon Elections.

April 19, 1831. Duvergier, *Lois,* XXXI, 211-244.

The Constitutional Charter of 1814 fixed the tax-paying qualification for membership in the Chamber of Deputies at one thousand francs per annum and for the exercise of the suffrage of three hundred francs. (No. 93, articles 38 and 40.) When the revision of 1830 occurred there was an informal understanding that these qualifications should be revised. This law was enacted in fulfillment of that understanding and remained unchanged throughout the entire period of the July Monarchy. It raised the number of voters from about 94,000 to about 188,000. The population of France was approximately thirty millions. In connection with this measure notice should be taken of the laws of 1831 upon the Chamber of Peers, municipal government, and the organization of the national guards. The four constitute a sort of supplement to the Constitution of 1830.

REFERENCES. Lavisse and Rambaud, *Histoire générale,* X, 377-378; Rambaud, *Civilisation contemporaine,* 325-329; Jaurès, *Histoire socialiste,* VIII, 98-99.

Title I. Of Electoral Capacities.

1. Every Frenchman enjoying civil and political rights, fully twenty-five years of age, and paying two hundred francs of direct taxes is an elector, if he fulfils the other conditions required by the present law.

. . . .

Title IV. Of the Electoral Colleges.

38. The Chamber of Deputies is composed of four hundred fifty-nine deputies.

39. Each electoral college elects only one deputy.

The number of the deputies of each department, and the division of the departments into electoral districts, are regulated by the annexed table, making part of the present law.

40. The electoral colleges are convoked by the king. They meet in the city of the electoral or administrative district which the king designates. They cannot occupy themselves with other matters than the election of the deputies; all discussion and all deliberation are forbidden to them.

. . . .

Title V. Of Eligibles.

59. No one shall be eligible to the Chamber of Deputies, if, at the day of his election, he is not thirty years of age, and if he does not pay five hundred francs of direct taxes, saving the case provided for by article 33 of the Charter. . .

. . . .

107. Proclamations and Decrees of the Provisional Government.

The provisional government of 1848 exhibited prodigious activity in the promulgation of proclamations and decrees. These few are intended to show how some of the great problems were dealt with and the ideas of the period. Documents A, C, and H bear upon the problem of the form of government which should succeed the July Monarchy. Documents B, D, E and F show what was done to meet the demands of the socialists. Documents F and I illustrate the manner in which the maxim Liberty, Equality, Fraternity, was applied.

REFERENCES. Fyffe, *Modern Europe,* III, 34-37 (Popular ed., 728-731) ; Seignobos. *Europe Since 1814,* 159-162 ; Andrews. *Modern Europe,* I. 342-352 ; Dickinson, *Revolution and Reaction in Modern France,* 168-185 , *passim ;* Lavisse and Rambaud. *Histoire générale,* XI. 10-17 ; Jaurès. *Histoire socialiste,* IX. 2-11 ; La Gorce, *Seconde republique,* I, 99, 103-107, 115-119, 206.

A. Proclamation of the Overthrow of the July Monarchy. February 24, 1848. Duvergier, *Lois,* XLVIII, 49-56.

In the Name of the French People.

A retrograde and oligarchical government has just been overthrown by the heroism of the people of Paris. That government has fled, leaving behind it a trail of blood that forbids it ever to retrace its steps.

The blood of the people has flowed as in July; but this time this generous people will not be deceived. It has gained a national and popular government in harmony with the rights, the progress, and the will of this great and generous people.

A provisional government, issuing from acclamation and urgency by the voice of the people and of the deputies of the departments, in the sitting of February 24, is for the moment invested with the task of assuring and organizing the national victory. It is composed of:

MM. Dupont (de l'Eure), *Lamartine, Crémieux, Arago* (of the Institute), *Ledru-Rollin, Garnier-Pagès, Marie, Armand Marrast, Louis Blanc, Ferdinand Flocon, and Albert,* workingman.

These citizens have not hesitated a moment to accept the patriotic commission which is imposed upon them by the pressure of necessity. When the capital of France is on fire the warrant of the provisional government is in the public safety. All France will understand this and will lend to it the help of its patriotism. Under the popular government which proclaims the provisional government every citizen is a magistrate.

Frenchmen, give to the world the example which Paris has given to France; prepare yourselves by order and confidence in yourselves for the solid institutions which you are about to be called upon to give yourselves.

The provisional government resolves to have the Republic, subject to ratification by the people, who shall be immediately consulted.

The unity of the nation, constituted henceforth of all the classes of citizens who compose it; the government of the nation by itself;

Liberty, equality, and fraternity for principles, the people for emblem and watch-word, that is the democratic government which France owes to itself and which our efforts shall be directed to securing for it.

B. Declaration Relative to Workingmen. February 25, 1848. Duvergier, *Lois,* XLVIII, 59.

The provisional government of the French Republic engages to guarantee the existence of the workingman by labor;

It engages to guarantee work to all citizens;

It recognizes that workingmen ought to enter into associations among themselves in order to enjoy the advantage of their labor.

The provisional government returns to the workingmen, to whom it belongs, the million which was about to fall due upon the civil list.

C. Proclamation of the Republic. February 26, 1848. Duvergier, *Lois,* XLVIII, 60.

In the Name of the French People.

Citizens,

Royalty, under whatever form it may take, is abolished.

No more legitimism, no more Bonapartism, no regency.

The provisional government has taken all the measures necessary to render impossible the return of the former dynasty and the advent of a new dynasty.

The Republic is proclaimed.

The people are united.

All the forts which surround the capital are ours.

The brave garrison of Vincennes is a garrison of brothers.

Let us preserve that old republican flag whose three colors made with our fathers the tour of the world.

Let us show that this symbol of equality, liberty, and fraternity, is at the same time the symbol of order, and of order the more real, the more durable, since justice is its foundation and the whole people its instrument.

The people have already understood that the provisioning of Paris requires a freer circulation in the streets of Paris, and the hands which erected the barricades have in several places made in these barricades an opening large enough for the free passage of transportation wagons.

Let this example be followed everywhere; let Paris resume its accustomed appearance and commerce its activity and its confidence; let the people at the same time look to the maintenance of their rights, and let them continue to assure, as they have done until now, the public tranquility and security.

D. Decree for Establishing National Workshops. February 26, 1848. Duvergier, *Lois*, XLVIII, 60.

In the Name of the French People.

The provisional government of the Republic
Decrees the immediate establishment of national workshops.
The minister of public works is charged with the execution of the present decree.

E. Proclamation and Order for the Luxembourg Commission. February 28, 1848. Duvergier, *Lois*, XLVIII, 62.

In the Name of the French People.

Considering that the revolution, made by the people, ought to be made for them;

That it is time to put an end to the long and iniquitous sufferings of the laboring men;

That the labor question is one of supreme importance;

That there is none higher and more worthy of the attention of a republican government;

That it belongs especially to France to study intensely and to solve a problem propounded today to all the industrial nations of Europe;

That it is necessary without the least delay to see to the guaranteeing to the people the legitimate fruits of their labor,

The provisional government of the Republic resolves:

A permanent commission, which shall be called the government commission for the workingmen, is about to be appointed with the express and special mission of occupying itself with their condition.

In order to show what importance the provisional government of the Republic attaches to the solution of this great problem, it appoints as president of the *government commission for the workingmen* one of its members, M. Louis Blanc, and for vice-president another of its members, M. Albert, workingman.

Workingmen will be summoned to make up part of the commission.

The seat of the commission will be at the Luxembourg Palace.

F.   Decree for Abolishing Titles of Nobility.   February 29, 1848.   Duvergier, *Lois,* XLVIII, 64.

In the Name of the French People.

The provisional government,
Considering:
That equality is one of the three grand principies of the French Republic; that, in consequence, it ought to receive an immediate application,

Decrees:

All the former titles of nobility are abolished: the designations which were connected with them are interdicted; they cannot be taken in public nor figure in any public document.

G.   Decree upon Labor.   March 2, 1848.   Duvergier, *Lois,* XLVIII, 67.

In the Name of the French People.

Upon the report of the government commission for the workingmen,

Considering:

1.   That too prolonged manual labor ruins the health of the worker, but even more, in preventing him from cultivating his intelligence, impairs the dignity of man;

2.   That the exploitation of the workers by the working sub-contractors, called *marchandeurs* or *tâcherons,* is essentially unjust, vexatious, and contrary to the principle of fraternity;

The provisional government of the Republic decrees:

1.   The working day is diminished by one hour. In consequence, at Paris, where it was eleven hours, it is reduced to ten; and in the country where it has been until now twelve hours, it is reduced to eleven;

2.   The exploitation of the workers by the sub-contractors or *marchandage* is abolished.

It is understood that the associations of workers which have not for their purpose the exploitation of workers by each other are not considered as *marchandage.*

H. Decree for the National Assembly. March 5, 1848.
Duvergier, *Lois,* XLVIII, 70-71.

In the Name of the French People.

The provisional government of the Republic.

Wishing to transfer as soon as possible to the hands of a definitive government the powers which it exercises in the interest and by the command of the people.

Decrees:

1. The cantonal electoral assemblies are convoked for the ninth of April next in order to elect the representatives of the people to the National Assembly which shall decree the constitution.

2. The election shall have population for its basis.

3. The total number of the representatives of the people shall be nine hundred, including Algeria and the French colonies.

4. They shall be apportioned among the departments in the proportion indicated in the table annexed.

5. The suffrage shall be direct and universal.

6. All Frenchmen twenty-one years of age, residing in the commune for six months past, and not judically deprived nor suspended from the exercise of civic rights, are electors.

7. All Frenchmen twenty-five years of age and not deprived nor suspended from civic rights are eligible [to the National Assembly].

8. The ballot shall be secret.

9. All the electors shall vote at the head-town of their cantons by *scrutin de liste.*

Each ballot shall contain as many names as there are representatives to elect in the department.

The counting of the votes shall take place at the head-town of the canton and the verification at that of the department.

No one can be chosen a representative of the people if he does not obtain two thousand votes.

10. Each representative of the people shall receive a compensation of twenty-five francs per day during the continuance of the session.

11. An instruction of the provisional government shall

regulate the details of the execution of the present decree.

12. The National Constituent Assembly shall be opened on April 20.

13. The present decree shall be immediately sent into the departments and published and posted in all the communes of the Republic.

I. Decree upon Slavery. April 27, 1848. Duvergier, *Lois,* XLVIII, 194.

The provisional government, considering that slavery is an outrage against human dignity; that in destroying the free will of man it sets aside the natural principles of right and duty; that it is a flagrant violation of the republican dogma, *Liberty, Equality, Fraternity;* considering that if effective measures did not follow very closely the proclamation already made, of the principle of abolition, the most deplorable disorders in the colonies may result from it,

Decrees:

1. Slavery shall be entirely abolished in all the French colonies and possessions two months after the promulgation of the present decrees in each of them. From the promulgation of the present decree in the colonies, all corporal punishment and all sale of persons not free shall be absolutely forbidden.

2. The system of contracts for a term of years in Senegal is suppressed.

3. The governors and general commissioners of the Republic are charged to apply the whole of the measures appropriate to secure liberty to Martinique, Guadeloupe and dependencies, the island of Réunion, Guiana, Senegal and other French settlements on the west coast of Africa, the island of Mayotta and dependencies, and in Algeria.

4. Former slaves condemned to afflictive or correctional penalties for deeds which imputed to free men would not have entailed that punishment are amnestied. The persons deported by administrative act are recalled.

5. The National Assembly shall determine the amount of the indemnity which shall be granted to the colonists.

6. The colonies freed from servitude and the possessions in India shall be represented in the National Assembly.

7. The principle that the soil of France liberates the slave who touches it applies to the colonies and the possessions of the Republic.

8. For the future, even in a foreign country, every Frenchman is forbidden to possess, buy or sell slaves, or to participate, either directly or indirectly, in any traffic or exploitation of that kind. Any infraction of these provisions shall entail the loss of title to French citizenship. Nevertheless, the French who shall find themselves affected by these prohibitions at the moment of the promulgation of the present decree have a period of three years in which to conform to them. Those who shall become the possessors of slaves in foreign countries by inheritance, gift or marriage, shall, under the same penalty, liberate or alienate them within the same period from the day whereon their possession shall have commenced.

.   .   .   .   .   .

108. Petition of the 16th of April.

April 16, 1848. *Moniteur,* April 17, 1848.

This petition was presented to the provisional government by one of the monster demonstrations organized by the socialists for the purpose of bringing about a postponement of the elections for the Constituent Assembly. It exhibits in concise form some of the general demands of the socialists.

REFERENCES. Lavisse and Rambaud, *Histoire générale,* XI, 14-15; Jaurès, *Histoire socialiste,* IX, 31-39; La Gorce, *Seconde république,* I, 188-203, 207-208.

The Workingmen of the Department of the Seine to the Provisional Government.

Citizens,

Reaction raises its head; calumny, that favorite weapon of men without principles and without honor, from every side pours its contagious venom upon the true friends of the people. It is to us, men of the revolution, men of action and devotion, that it belongs to declare to the provisional government that the people wish the *Democratic Republic;* that the ·people wish the *abolition of the exploitation of man by man;* that the people wish the *organization of. labor through association.*

Vive la Republique! Vive le Gouvernment provisiore!

109. Declaration upon the Republic.

May 4, 1848. Duvergier, *Lois,* XLVIII, 278.

When the National Assembly met on May 4, 1848, this declaration was proposed by the representatives of the department of the Seine and adopted unanimously.

REFERENCE. La Gorce, *Seconde republique,* I, 224-228.

In the Name of the French People.

The National Assembly, as faithful interpreter of the sentiments of the people who have just selected it, before beginning its labors, declares,

In the name of the French people, and in the face of the entire world, that *THE REPUBLIC,* proclaimed February 24, 1848, is and shall remain the form of government of France.

The Republic which France chooses has for its motto: *Liberty, Equality, Fraternity.*

In the name of the fatherland, the National Assembly conjures all Frenchmen, of all opinions, to forget former dissensions and to constitute henceforth but a single family. The day on which the representatives of the people meet is for all citizens the festival of concord and fraternity. *Vive LA RE-PUBLIQUE.*

110. Constitution of 1848.

November 4, 1848. Duvergier, *Lois,* XLVIII, 560-609.

This constitution was drafted and promulgated by the National Assembly of 1848. It should be studied from two standpoints; (1) as a theoretical frame of government; (2) with reference to the political situation of France in 1848. Particular notice should be taken of the manner in which its two fundamental principles, popular sovereignty and separation of the powers, are applied.

REFERENCES. Seignobos, *Europe Since 1814,* 164-165 : Andrews, *Modern Europe,* I, 357-362; Dickinson, *Revolution and Reaction in Modern France,* 200-201 : Tocqueville, *Recollections,* Part II, Ch. XI : Lavisse and Rambaud, *Histoire générale,* XI, 20-22 ; Rambaud. *Civilisation contemporaine,* 516-517 : Jaurès, *Histoire social-iste,* IX, 100-124 ; La Gorce, *Seconde republique,* I, 431-456.

The National Assembly has adopted, and in conformity with article 6 of the decree of October 28, 1848, the president of the National Assembly promulgates the following constitution:

Preamble.

In the Presence of God, and in the Name of the French People, the National Assembly Proclaims:

I. France is constituted a republic. In definitely adopting that form of government, it proposes for its aim to move more freely in the path of progress and civilization, to assure a more and more equitable distribution of the burdens and advantages of society, to increase the comfort of each person by large reductions in the public expenditures and taxes, and without new commotion, through the successive and constant action of institutions and laws, to cause every one to reach a degree of morality, enlightenment and well-being constantly becoming more elevated.

II. The French Republic is democratic, one and indivisible.

III. It recognizes rights and duties existing before and superior to positive laws.

IV. It has for its maxim liberty, equality, and fraternity. It has for its basis the family, labor, property, and public order.

V. It respects foreign nationalities, as it intends to cause its own to be respected; it does not undertake any war for the purpose of conquest, and it never employs its forces against the liberty of any people.

VI. Reciprocal duties bind the citizens to the Republic, and the Republic to the citizens.

VII. The citizens ought to love the fatherland, to serve the Republic, to defend it at the price of their lives, and to share the expenses of the state in proportion to their fortunes; they ought to secure for themselves, by labor, means of subsistence, and, by foresight, resources for the future; they ought to contribute to the common well-being by fraternally co-operating with one another, and to the general order by observing the moral and the written laws which control society, the family, and the individual.

VIII. The Republic ought to protect the citizen in his person, his family, his religion, his property, his labor, and to put within the reach of each person the education indispensable for all men; it is bound to assure by fraternal assistance the maintenance of indigent citizens, either by furnishing work to them within the limits of its resources, or, in the absence of the family, by giving assistance to those who are unable to work.

For the purpose of fulfilling all these duties and for a guarantee of all these rights, the National Assembly, faithful to the traditions of the great assemblies which inaugurated the French revolution, decrees as follows, the constitution of the Republic.

Constitution.

Chapter I.   Of the Sovereignty.

1. Sovereignty resides in the totality of the French citizens. It is inalienable and imprescriptible.

No individual nor any part of the people can claim for themselves the exercise thereof.

Chapter II.   Rights of the Citizens Guaranteed by the Constitution.

2. No one can be arrested or held in custody except according to the provisions of the law.

3. The dwelling-place of every person living on French soil is inviolable; it can be entered only according to the forms and in the cases provided by law.

4. No one shall be removed from the jurisdiction of his natural judges.

No extraordinary commissions or tribunals can be created under any title or denomination whatsoever.

5. The death penalty for political offences is abolished.

6. Slavery cannot exist upon any French soil.

7. Every person freely professes his religion, and receives from the state, for the exercise of his worship, an equal protection.

Ministers, either of the sects now recognized by law or of those which may be recognized in the future, have the right to receive a stipend from the state.

8. Citizens have the right to form associations, to assemble peaceably and without arms, to petition, and to express their opinions by means of the press or otherwise.

The exercise of these rights has for limits only the rights and liberty of others and the public security.

The press cannot in any case be subjected to the censorship.

9. Instruction is free.

The liberty of instruction is exercised according to the conditions of capacity and morality that are determined by law and under the oversight of the state.

This oversight extends to all establishments for education and instruction, without any exception.

10. All citizens are equally eligible to all public employments, without any other grounds for preference than their own merits, and according to the conditions which shall be fixed by the laws.

All titles of nobility, all distinctions of birth, class or caste are forever abolished.

11. All property is inviolable. Nevertheless, the state can demand the sacrifice of a property on the ground of a legally established public utility, and by furnishing a just and prior indemnity.

12. The confiscation of property can never be re-established.

13. The constitution guarantees to citizens liberty of labor and of industry.

Society favors and encourages the development of labor by gratuitous primary education, professional education, equality of relations between the employer and the workingman, institutions of savings and of credit, agricultural institutions, voluntary associations, and the establishment by the state, the departments and the communes of public works suitable for the employment of unemployed hands; it furnishes assistance to abandoned children, the infirm, and the aged that are without resources and whose families cannot relieve them.

14. The public debt is guaranteed. Every form of engagement made by the state with its creditors is inviolable.

15. Every tax is imposed for the common utility.

Each person contributes thereto in proportion to his means and his fortune.

16. No tax can be imposed or collected except by virtue of the law.

17. Direct taxation is consented to only for one year. Indirect taxes can be consented to for several years.

Chapter III. Of the Public Powers.

18. All the public powers, whatever they may be, spring from the people.

They cannot be delegated hereditarily.

19. The separation of the powers is the fundamental principle of a free government.

Chapter IV. Of the Legislative Power.

20. The French people delegate the legislative power to a single assembly.

21. The total number of the representatives of the people shall be seven hundred and fifty, including the representatives of Algeria and the French colonies.

22. This number shall be increased to nine hundred for the assemblies which are called to alter the constitution.

23. The basis for election is population.

24. The suffrage is direct and universal. The ballot is secret.

25. All Frenchmen, twenty-one years of age and enjoying their civil and political rights, are electors, regardless of property.

26. All electors twenty-five years of age, regardless of their domicile, are eligible to election.

27. The electoral law shall determine the causes which can deprive a French citizen of the right to elect and to be elected.

It shall designate the citizens who, exercising or having exercised functions in a department or a territorial jurisdiction, cannot be elected there.

28. Every remunerated public employment is incompatible with the commission of representative of the people.

No member of the National Assembly, during the continuance of the legislature, can be appointed or preferred for public salaried employments of which the incumbents are appointed by the executive power.

The exceptions to the provisions of the two preceding paragraphs shall be determined by the organic electoral law.

29. The provisions of the preceding articles are not applicable to the assemblies elected to alter the constitution.

30. The election of the representatives shall be by departments and by *scrutin de liste*.

The electors shall vote in the head-town of the canton; nevertheless, on account of local conditions, the canton can be divided into several districts, in the form and upon the conditions that shall be determined by the electoral law.

31. The National Assembly is elected for three years, and is renewed in a body.

At least forty-five days before the end of the legislature, a law determines the time of the new elections.

If any law does not intervene within the limit fixed by the preceding article, the electors meet as if regularly convoked upon the thirtieth day preceding the end of the legislature.

The new assembly is convoked *ipso facto* upon the day following that upon which the commission of the preceding assembly expired.

32. It is permanent.

Nevertheless, it can adjourn for a period which it shall fix.

During the continuance of the prorogation, a commission, composed of members of the *bureau* and of twenty-five members appointed by the assembly through secret ballot and majority vote has the right to convoke it in case of urgency.

The President of the Republic also has the right to convoke the assembly.

The National Assembly determines the place of its meetings. It determines the extent of the military forces provided for its security, and it controls them.

33. Representatives are always re-eligible.

34. Members of the National Assembly are the representatives, not of the department which selects them, but of all France.

35. They cannot receive imperative instructions.

36. The representatives of the people are inviolable.

They cannot be questioned, accused nor condemned at any time for opinions that they have expressed in the National Assembly.

37. They cannot be arrested upon a criminal charge, unless taken in the act, nor prosecuted except after the assembly has authorised the prosecution.

In case of the arrest of one taken in the act, it shall be forthwith referred to the assembly, which shall authorise or forbid the continuance of the prosecution. This provision applies to the case in which a citizen under arrest is elected representative.

38. Each representative of the people receives a salary which he cannot refuse.

39. The sittings of the assembly are public. Nevertheless, the assembly can form itself into secret committee, upon the demand of the number of representatives fixed by the rule.

Each representative has the right of parliamentary initiative; he shall exercise it according to the forms determined by the rule.

40. The presence of half plus one of the members of the assembly is necessary for the valid enactment of laws.

41. No proposal for a law, unless in case of urgency, shall be voted definitively except after three deliberations at intervals which cannot be less than five days.

42. Every proposal whose purpose is to declare *urgency* is preceded by a statement of reasons.

If the assembly agrees to give effect to the proposal of urgency it orders the reference thereof to the *bureaux* and fixes the time at which the report upon the urgency shall be presented.

Upon this report, if the assembly recognizes the urgency, it makes declaration thereof, and fixes the time of the discussion.

If it decides that there is no urgency, the proposal follows the course of ordinary propositions.

Chapter V. Of the Executive Power.

43. The French people delegate the executive power to a citizen who receives the title of President of the Republic.

44. The President must be French born, at least thirty years of age, and never have lost the quality of Frenchman.

45. The President of the Republic is elected for four years and is re-eligible only after an interval of four years.

Furthermore, neither the Vice-President, nor any of the kinsmen or connections of the President to the sixth degree inclusive, can be elected after him.

46. The election takes place *ipso facto* upon the second Sunday of the month of May.

In case, owing to death, resignation or any other cause,

the President should be elected at any other time, his powers shall expire upon the second Sunday of the month of May of the fourth year following his election.

The President is selected, through secret ballot and majority of the votes, by the direct vote of all the electors of the French departments and of Algeria.

47. The minutes of the electoral proceedings are transmitted immediately to the National Assembly, which decides without delay upon the validity of the election and proclaims the President of the Republic.

If no candidate has obtained more than half of the vote cast, and at least two million votes, or if the conditions prescribed by article 44 are not fulfilled, the National Assembly elects the President of the Republic, by majority and secret ballot, from among the five eligible candidates who have received the most votes.

48. Before entering upon his duties, the President of the Republic in the presence of the National Assembly takes the following oath:

In the presence of God and before the French people, represented by the National Assembly, I swear to remain faithful to the democratic Republic one and indivisible, and to fulfil all the duties that the constitution imposes upon me.

49. He has the right to cause propositions of law to be presented by his ministers to the National Assembly.

He supervises and secures the execution of the laws.

50. He disposes of the armed force, without power ever to command in person.

51. He cannot cede any portion of the territory, nor dissolve or prorogue the National Assembly, nor suspend in any way the absolute authority of the constitution and the laws.

52. He presents each year, in a message to the National Assembly, a statement of the general condition of the affairs of the Republic.

53. He negotiates and ratifies treaties.

No treaty is definitive until after it has been ratified by the National Assembly.

54. He watches over the defence of the state, but he cannot undertake any war without the consent of the National Assembly.

55. He has the right to pardon, but he can exercise this right only after taking the opinion of the Council of State.

Amnesties can be accorded only by a law.

The President of the Republic, and the ministers, as well as all others persons condemned by the high court of justice, can be pardoned only by the National Assembly.

56. The President of the Republic promulgates the laws in the name of the French people.

57. The laws of urgency are promulgated within a period of three days, and the other laws within a period of one month, counting from the day on which they shall have been adopted by the National Assembly.

58. Within the period fixed for promulgation, the President of the Republic, by an explanatory message can request a new consideration.

The assembly deliberates; its resolution becomes definitive; it is transmitted to the President of the Republic.

In that case, the promulgation takes place within the time fixed for laws of urgency.

59. In default of promulgation by the President of the Republic, within the periods required by the preceding articles, the president of the assembly shall provide for it.

60. Envoys and ambassadors of foreign powers are accredited to the President of the Republic.

61. He presides at national solemnities.

62. He is housed at the expense of the Republic and receives a salary of six hundred thousand francs per annum.

63. He resides in the place in which the National Assembly sits, and cannot leave the continental territory of the Republic without being authorised thereto by a law.

64. The President of the Republic appoints and dismisses the ministers.

He appoints and dismisses, in council of the ministers, the diplomatic agents, the commanders-in-chief of the army and the navy, the prefects, the superior commandant of the national guards of the Seine, the governors of Algeria and the colonies, the procureurs-general and other officials of high rank.

He appoints and dismisses, upon the proposal of the proper minister and according to the regular conditions determined by law, the subordinate agents of the government.

65. He has the right to suspend, for a term that cannot exceed three months, the agents of the executive power elected by the citizens.

He can dismiss them only upon the advice of the Council of State.

The law determines the cases in which dismissed agents can be declared ineligible for the same employments.

This declaration of ineligibility can be pronounced only by a judicial order.

66. The number of the ministers and their prerogatives are fixed by the legislative power.

67. The acts of the President of the Republic, except those by which he appoints and dismisses ministers, are not valid unless they are countersigned by a minister.

68. The President of the Republic, the ministers, and the agents and depositories of public authority are responsible, each in that which concerns him, for all the acts of the government and the administration.

Every measure by which the President of the Republic dissolves the National Assembly, prorogues it or places an obstacle to the exercise of its commission, constitutes the crime of high treason.

By this act alone, the President is stripped of his functions; the citizens are required to refuse him obedience; the executive power passes *ipso facto* to the National Assembly. The judges of the high court of justice meet immediately upon pain of forfeiture: they convoke the jurors in the place that they designate, in order to proceed to the trial of the President and his accomplices; they themselves designate the public officers who shall be charged with performing the functions of the public ministry.

A law shall determine the other cases of responsibility, as well as the forms and the conditions of the prosecution.

69. The ministers have admission to the body of the National Assembly; they are heard whenever they demand it and can have the assistance of commissioners appointed by a decree of the President of the Rpublic.

70. There is a Vice-President of the Republic appointed by the National Assembly out of three candidates presented by the President within the month that follows his election.

The Vice-President takes the same oath as the President.

The Vice-President cannot be chosen from among the kinsmen and connections of the President to the sixth degree inclusive.

In case of the disability of the President, the Vice-President acts for him.

If the presidency becomes vacant by death, resignation of the President, or otherwise, an election for president takes place within a month.

Chapter VI.   Of the Council of State.

71. There shall be a Council of State of which the Vice-President of the Republic shall be president, *ex-officio*.

72. The members of this council are appointed for six years by the National Assembly. They are renewed by a half within the first three months of each legislature through secret ballot and majority.

They are re-eligible indefinitely.

73. Those of the members of this council who have been taken from the body of the National Assembly shall be replaced immediately as representatives of the people.

74. The members of the Council of State can be dismissed only by the assembly and upon the proposal of the President of the Republic.

75. The Council of State is consulted upon the government's proposals for laws, which according to law must be previously submitted for its examination and upon projects of parliamentary initiative which the assembly shall have submitted to it.

It prepares the regulations for public administration; of these regulations, it makes only those for which the National Assembly has given it a special authorisation.

It exercises over the public administration all the powers of control and supervision which are conferred upon it by law.

The law shall determine its other duties.

Chapter VII. Of the Internal Administration.

76. The division of the territory into departments, districts, cantons and communes is retained. The present limits can be changed only by a law.

77. There are: 1st. In each department, an administra-

tion composed of a prefect, a council-general and council of prefecture;

2d. In each district, a sub-prefect;

3d. In each canton, a cantonal council; nevertheless only one cantonal council shall be established in cities divided into several cantons;

4th. In each commune, an administration composed of a mayor, assistants, and a municipal council.

78. A law shall determine the composition and the prerogatives of the councils-general, the cantonal councils, the municipal councils, and the manner of selecting the mayors and the assistants.

79. The councils-general and the municipal councils are elected by the direct vote of all the citizens domiciled in the department or the commune. Each canton elects one member of the council-general.

A special law shall regulate the mode of election in the department of the Seine, in the city of Paris, and in cities of more than twenty thousand souls.

80. The councils-general, the cantonal councils, and the municipal councils can be dissolved by the President of the Republic upon the advice of the Council of State. The law shall fix the period within which a new election shall be held.

Chapter VIII. Of the Judicial Power.

81. Justice is administered gratuitously in the name of the French people.

Trials are public, unless publicity would be dangerous to order or morality; and in that case the tribunal declares it by a judicial order.

82. The jury shall continue to be employed in criminal trials.

83. Jurisdiction over all political offences and all offences committed by means of the press belongs exclusively to the jury.

The organic laws shall determine the jurisdiction in the matter of criminal libels against individuals.

84. The jury alone decides upon the damages claimed for acts or offences of the press.

85. The justices of the peace and their substitutes, the

judges of first instance and of appeal, the members of the court of cassation and the court of accounts are appointed by the President of the Republic, according to an order of candidature or conditions which shall be regulated by the organic laws.

86. The magistrates of the public ministry are appointed by the President of the Republic.

87. The judges of first instance and of appeal, the members of the court of cassation and of the court of accounts are appointed for life.

They cannot be dismissed or suspended except by a judicial order, nor retired except for the causes and in the forms determined by the laws.

88. The councils of war and of revision for the army and navy, the maritime tribunals, the tribunals of commerce, the trade councils and other special tribunals retain their organization and existing prerogatives until they have been altered by a law.

89. Conflicts of jurisdiction between the administrative and judicial authorities shall be regulated by a special tribunal of members of the court of cassation and councillors of state, selected every three years in equal number by their respective bodies.

This tribunal shall be presided over by the minister of justice.

90. Appeals for lack of jurisdiction and excess of power against the decrees of the court of accounts shall be carried before the magistracy of conflicts.

91. A high court of justice decides, without appeal or recourse in cassation, the accusation brought by the National Assembly against the President of the Republic or the ministers.

It likewise tries all persons accused of crimes, attempts or conspiracies against the internal or external security of the state, whom the National Assembly shall have sent before it.

Except in the case provided for by article 68, it cannot be assembled except by virtue of a decree of the National Assembly, which designates the city where the court shall hold its sittings.

92. The high court is composed of five judges and thirty-six jurors.

Each year, within the first fifteen days of the month of November, the court of cassation appoints from among its members by secret ballot and majority vote the judges of the high court, to the number of five, and two substitutes. The five judges called to sit choose their own president.

The magistrates filling the functions of the public ministry are selected by the President of the Republic, and, in case of the accusation of the President or the ministers, by the National Assembly.

The jurors, to the number of thirty-six, and four substitute jurors, are taken from among the members of the councils-general of the departments.

The representatives of the people cannot form part of them.

93. When a decree of the National Assembly has ordered the formation of the high court of justice, and, in the case provided for by article 68 upon the requisition of the president or of one of the judges, the president of the court of appeal, and, in default of the court of appeal, the president of the tribunal of first instance of the judicial head-town of the department, draws by lot in public audience the name of a member of the council-general.

94. Upon the day appointed for the trial if there are less than sixty jurors present, that number shall be completed by supplementary jurors drawn by lot by the president of the high court from among the members of the council-general of the department in which the court shall sit.

95. Jurors who shall not have furnished a valid excuse shall be condemned to a fine of from one thousand to ten thousand francs, and deprivation of political rights for five years at most.

96. The accused and the public prosecutor exercise the right of challenge as in other cases.

97. The verdict of the jury that the accused is guilty can be rendered only by a two-thirds majority.

98. In all cases of responsibility of the ministers, the National Assembly can, according to circumstances, send the accused minister before the high court of justice or before the ordinary tribunals for civil damages.

99. The National Assembly and the President of the Republic can in all cases turn over the examination of the

acts of any officer, other than the President of the Republic, to the Council of State, whose report is made public.

100. The President of the Republic is amenable only to the high court of justice.

With the exception of the case provided for by article 68, he cannot be prosecuted except upon the accusation brought by the National Assembly, and for crimes and offences which shall be determined by law.

Chapter IX. Of the Public Forces.

101. The public forces are established to defend the state against its enemies abroad and to secure within the maintenance of order and the execution of the laws.

It is composed of the national guard and of the army and the navy.

102. Every Frenchman, with the exceptions fixed by law, owes service to the army and the national guard.

The means by which a citizen may be freed from personal military service shall be regulated by the law of recruiting.

103. The organization of the national guard and the constitution of the army shall be regulated by law.

104. The public forces are of necessity obedient.

No armed body can deliberate.

105. The public forces employed to preserve internal order act only upon the requisition of the constituted authorities, according to the regulations determined by the legislative power.

106. A law shall determine the cases in which the state of siege can be declared and shall regulate the forms and consequences of that measure.

107. No foreign troops can be introduced upon French soil, without the previous consent of the National Assembly.

Chapter X. Special Provisions.

108. The Legion of Honor is retained; its statutes shall be revised and put in harmony with the constitution.

109. The territory of Algeria and of the colonies is declared to be French territory, and shall be ruled by separate laws until a special law places them under the régime of the present constitution.

110. The National Assembly confides the safe-keeping of

the present constitution, and the rights which it consecrates, to the guardianship and patriotism of all the French.

Chapter XI. Of the Revision of the Constitution.

111. Whenever, in the last year of a legislature, the National Assembly shall have expressed the wish that the constitution should be altered in whole or in part, such revision shall proceed in the following manner:

The wish expressed by the assembly shall be converted into a definitive decision only after three consecutive considerations, taken at intervals of a month each, and by three-fourths of the votes cast. The number of voters must be at least five hundred.

The assembly of revision shall be appointed only for three months.

It must occupy itself only with the revision for which it shall have been convoked.

Nevertheless, it can, in case of urgency, provide for necessary legislation.

Chapter XII. Temporary Provisions.

112. The provisions of the existing codes, laws and regulations, which are not in conflict with the present constitution, remain in force until they are legally altered.

113. All the authorities constituted by the existing laws continue in the exercise of their functions until the promulgation of organic laws affecting them.

114. The law for the organization of the judiciary shall determine the special method of appointment for the first composition of the new tribunals.

115. After the vote upon the constitution, the National Constituent Assembly shall proceed to frame the organic laws whose drafting shall be determined by a special law.

116. The first election of the President of the Republic shall occur in conformity with the special law passed by the National Assembly, October 28, 1848.

111. Documents upon the Coup d'Etat of December 2, 1851.

These documents throw light upon many features of the *coup d'état* of December 2, 1851, and the plebiscite which followed it. Among the features that call for notice are: (1) the official explanation of the events and conditions which had led up to the *coup d'état*; (2) the inducements offered in order to procure acquiescence or approval; (3) the fundamental principles of the government about to be established; (4) the change effected in the original scheme for conducting the plebiscite. All of these documents were signed, Louis-Napoleon Bonaparte.

REFERENCES. Fyffe, *Modern Europe*, III, 171-177 (Popular ed., 817-823); Seignobos, *Europe Since 1814*, 170-172; Andrews, *Modern Europe*, II, 27-37; Dickinson, *Revolution and Reaction in Modern France*, 212-218; Lavisse and Rambaud, *Histoire générale*, XI, 32-35; Jaurès, *Histoire socialiste*, X, 1-4; La Gorce, *Seconde republique*, II, 502, 507-510, 594-596.

A. Decree for Dissolving the National Assembly. December 2, 1851. Duvergier, *Lois,* LI, 475.

In the Name of the French People.

The President of the Republic decrees:

1. The National Assembly is dissolved.

2. Universal suffrage is re-established. The law of May 31 is abrogated.

3. The French people are convoked in their assemblies for December 14 to December 21 following.

4. The state of siege is decreed within the extent of the 1st military division.

5. The Council of State is dissolved.

6. The Minister of the Interior (M. de Morny) is charged, etc.

B. Proclamation to the People. December 2, 1851. Duvergier, *Lois,* LI, 475-476.

Frenchmen!

The present situation cannot last much longer. Each day that passes increases the dangers of the country. The assembly, which ought to be the firmest support of order, has become a centre of conspiracies. The patriotism of three hundred of its members could not arrest its fatal tendencies. Instead of making laws in the general interest, it forges weapons for civil war; it makes an attack upon the authority that I hold directly from the people; it encourages all the evil passions; it puts in jeopardy the repose of France: I have

dissolved it, and I make the whole people judge between it
and me.

The constitution, as you know, was made with the purpose of weakening in advance the power that you were about
to confer upon me. Six million votes were a striking protest against it, nevertheless I faithfully observed it. Provocations, calumnies, outrages, have found me unmoved. But
now that the fundamental compact is no longer respected
even by those who incessantly invoke it, and the men who
have already destroyed two monarchies wish to bind my
hands, in order to overthrow the Republic, it is my duty to
defeat their wicked designs and to save the country by in-
voking the solemn judgment of the only sovereign that I
recognize in France, the people.

I make, therefore, a loyal appeal to the whole nation, and
I say to you: If you wish to continue this state of uneasiness which degrades us and makes uncertain our future,
choose another in my place, for I no longer wish an authority which is powerless to do good, makes me responsible for
acts I cannot prevent, and chains me to the helm when I see
the vessel speeding toward the abyss.

If, on the contrary, you still have confidence in me, give
me the means to accomplish the great mission that I hold
from you.

This mission consists in bringing to a close the era of
revolutions by satisfying the legitimate wants of the people
and by protecting them against subversive passions. It consists, especially, in creating institutions that may survive men
and that may be at length foundations upon which something
durable can be established.

Persuaded that the instability of the executive authority
and the preponderance of a single assembly are permanent
causes of trouble and discord, I submit to you the following
fundamental bases of a constitution which the assemblies will
develop later.

1st. A responsible chief selected for ten years;

2d. Ministers dependent upon the executive power alone;

3d. A council of state composed of the most distinguished
men to prepare the laws and to discuss them before the legislative body;

4th. A legislative body to discuss and vote the laws,

elected by universal suffrage without *scrutin de liste,* which falsifies the election;

5th. A second assembly, composed of all the illustrious persons of the country, predominant authority, guardian of the fundamental compact and of the public liberties.

This system, created by the First Consul at the beginning of the century, once gave to France repose and prosperity; it will guarantee them to her again.

Such is my profound conviction. If you share it, declare the fact by your votes. If, on the contrary, you prefer a government without force, monarchical or republican, borrowed from I know not what past or from what chimerical future, reply in the negative.

Thus, therefore, for the first time since 1804, you will vote with knowledge of the case, knowing well for whom and for what.

If I do not obtain a majority of your votes I shall then bring about the meeting of a new Assembly, and I shall resign to it the mandate that I have received from you.

But if you believe that the cause of which my name is the symbol, that is, France regenerated by the revolution of '89 and organized by the Emperor, is always yours, proclaim it by sanctioning the powers that I ask of you.

Then France and Europe will be preserved from anarchy, obstacles will be removed, rivalries will have disappeared, for all will respect, in the decision of the people, the decree of Providence.

C. Proclamation to the Army. December 2, 1851. Duvergier, *Lois,* LI, 476.

Soldiers!

Be proud of your mission, you shall save the fatherland, for I count upon you, not to violate the laws but to make respected the first law of the country, the national sovereignty, of which I am the legitimate representative.

For a long time you suffered, as I did, from obstacles that opposed themselves to both the good which I wished to do for you and the demonstrations of your sympathy in my favor. Those obstacles are broken to pieces. The assembly sought to make an attack upon the authority that I hold from the entire nation; it has ceased to exist.

I make a loyal appeal to the people and the army, and I say to them: Either give me the means to assure your prosperity, or choose another in my place.

In 1830, as in 1848, you were treated as vanquished. After having flouted your heroic disinterestedness they disdain to consult your sympathies and views, although you are the élite of the nation. To-day, in this solemn moment, I desire that the army should make its voice heard.

Vote, then, freely as citizens; but as soldiers, do not forget that passive obedience to the orders of the head of the government is the strict duty of the army, from the general to the soldier. It is for me, responsible for my actions before the people and posterity, to take the measures that seem to me indispensable for the public welfare.

As for you, remain steadily within the rules of discipline and honor. By your impressive attitude help the country to express its will with calmness and reflection. Be ready to put down every attack upon the free exercise of the sovereignty of the people.

Soldiers, I do not speak to you of the memories which my name recalls. They are graven upon your hearts. We are united by indissoluble ties. Your history is mine. For the past, there is between us community of glory and misfortune; for the future, there will be community of sentiments and resolutions for the repose and grandeur of France.

D. First Decree for the Plebiscite. December 2, 1851. Duvergier, *Lois,* LI, 476-477.

The President of the Republic, considering that sovereignty resides in the whole body of citizens, and that no fraction of the people can assume for itself the exercise of it; in view of the laws and regulations which have hitherto regulated the mode of appeal to the people and especially the decrees of 5 Fructidor, Year III, 24 and 25 Frimaire, Year VIII, the regulation of 20 Floréal, Year X, the senatus-consultum of 28 Floréal, Year XII, decrees:

1. The French people are solemnly summoned in their assemblies for the fourteenth of the present month of December, in order, to accept or reject the following plebiscite:

"The French people desire the maintenance of the authority of *Louis-Napoleon Bonaparte,* and delegate to him the necessary powers in order to make a constitution upon the bases proposed in his proclamation of December 2."

2. All Frenchmen twenty-one years of age and enjoying their civil and political rights are summoned to vote.

.   .   .   .   .   .

3. Upon receipt of the present decree, the mayors of every commune shall open two registers upon unstamped paper, one of acceptance, the other of non-acceptance of the plebiscite.

.   .   .   .   .   .

E. Second Decree for the Plebiscite. December 4, 1851. Duvergier, *Lois*, LI, 479.

The President of the Republic, considering that the mode of election promulgated by the decree of the second of December had been adopted under other circumstances as guaranteeing the sincerity of election; but considering that the secret ballot actually carried out appears to guarantee better the independence of the votes; considering that the essential object of the decree of the second of December is to obtain the sincere and free expression of the will of the people, decrees:

Articles 2, 3 and 4 of the decree of the second of December are modified as follows:

Article 2. The election shall take place by universal suffrage. All Frenchmen twenty-one years of age and enjoying their civil and political rights are called upon to vote.

.   .   .   .   .   .

Article 4. The ballot shall be open during the days of the twentieth and twenty-first of December, in the head-town of each commune, from eight a. m. to four p. m. The voting shall be by secret ballot, yes or no, by means of a written or printed vote.

F. Election Appeal. December 8, 1851. Duvergier, *Lois,* LI, 479-480.

Frenchmen!

The disturbances are pacified. Whatever may be the decision of the people, society is saved. The first part of my task is accomplished. I know that the appeal to the nation, in order to terminate the conflict of parties, did not cause any serious risk to the public tranquility.

Why should the people rise against me?

If I no longer possess your confidence, if your ideas have changed, there is no need to shed precious blood; it suffices to deposit in the urn an adverse vote.

I shall always respect the decision of the people.

But until the nation has spoken, I shall not recoil before any effort nor before any sacrifice in order to defeat the attempts of the factions. This task, moreover, is made easy for me.

On the one hand, it has been seen how insensate it is to struggle against an army united by the ties of discipline and animated by the sentiment of military honor and by devotion to the fatherland.

On the other hand, the calm attitude of the inhabitants of Paris, the reprobation with which they have stigmatized the riot, have testified decisively enough for whom the capital pronounces:

In those populous quarters, where but lately insurrection recruited itself so quickly among the workingmen susceptible to its allurements, anarchy this time could find only a profound repugnance for those detestable excitements. Let thanks for this be rendered to the intelligent and patriotic population of Paris! Let it persuade itself more and more that my only ambition is to assure the repose and prosperity of France.

Let it continue to lend its assistance to authority, and soon the country will be able to carry through with calmness the solemn act which must inaugurate a new era for the Republic.

112. Constitution of 1852.

January 14, 1852. Duvergier, *Lois*, LII, 18-27.

This constitution was prepared and promulgated by Louis Napoleon in conformity with the authorisation given him by the plebiscite of December 20. 1851 (See No. 111 D). As a whole it should be compared with its model, the constitution of the Year VIII (No. 58). Numerous features of it may also be compared with the preceding constitutions, especially those of 1802, 1804, 1830 and 1848 (Nos. 66 E, 70, 105, 110). Features of it which seem to indicate a speedy reappearance of the Empire should be particularly noticed.

REFERENCES. Seignobos, *Europe Since 1814*, 171-172; Andrews, *Modern Europe*, II, 151-153; Dickinson, *Revolution and Reaction in Modern France*, 228-229; Lavisse and Rambaud, *Histoire générale*, XI, 35; Rambaud, *Civilisation contemporaine*, 518-519; Jaurès, *Histoire socialiste*, X, 32-33; La Gorce, *Second empire*, I, 24-35.

The President of the Republic,

Considering . . . [The omitted paragraphs recite the resolution submitted to the people, and the five bases for a constitution accepted at the same time, see pp. 539-540].

Considering that the people have responded in the affirmative by seven million one hundred thousand votes,

Promulgates the constitution of which the tenor follows:

Title I.

1. The constitution recognizes, confirms and guarantees the great principles proclaimed in 1789, and which are the basis of the public law of the French.

Title II. Form of the Government of the Republic.

2. The government of the French Republic is confided for ten years to Prince Louis-Napoleon Bonaparte, now President of the Republic.

3. The President of the Republic governs by means of the ministers, the Council of State, the Senate and the Legislative Body.

4. The legislative power is exercised by the President of the Republic, the Senate, and the Legislative Body collectively.

Title III. Of the President of the Republic.

5. The President of the Republic is responsible before the French people, to whom he has always the right to make appeal.

6. The President of the Republic is the head of the state, he commands the land and sea forces, declares war, makes treaties of peace, alliance and commerce, appoints to all the offices, and makes the regulations and decrees necessary for the execution of the laws.

7. Justice is administered in his name.

8. He alone has the proposal of the laws.

9. He has the right to grant pardons.

10. He sanctions and promulgates the laws and the senatus-consulta.

11. He presents every year to the Senate and the Legislative Body, by a message, the condition of the affairs of the Republic.

12. He has the right to declare the state of siege in one or several departments, provided that he reports it to the Senate with the least possible delay.

The results of the state of siege are regulated by law.

13. The ministers are subject to the head of the state only; they are not responsible for the acts of the government except each in that which concerns him; there is no solidarity among them; they can be accused only by the Senate.

14. The ministers, the members of the Senate, the Legislative Body, the Council of State, the officers of the army and the navy, the magistrates and the public functionaries take the following oath:

I swear obedience to the constitution and fidelity to the President.

15. A senatus-consultum fixes the sum annually allowed to the President of the Republic for the entire duration of his functions.

16. If the president of the Republic dies before the expiration of his commission, the Senate convokes the nation in order to proceed to a new election.

17. The Head of the State has the right, by a secret act deposited in the archives of the Senate, to designate the name of the citizen whom he recommends, in the interest of France, to the confidence of the people and for their votes.

18. Until the election of the new President of the Republic, the president of the Senate governs with the assistance of the ministers in office, who organize themselves into a council of government and act by the majority of votes.

Title IV. Of the Senate.

19. The number of senators cannot exceed one hundred and fifty; it is fixed for the first year at eighty.

20. The Senate is composed: 1st, of the cardinals, marshals and admirals; 2d, of the citizens whom the President of the Republic sees fit to elevate to the dignity of senator.

21. The senators are irremovable and for life.

22. The services of a senator are gratuitous; nevertheless the President of the Republic can grant to senators, by reason of services rendered and the condition of their fortunes, a personal allowance, which cannot exceed thirty thousand francs per annum.

23. The president and the vice-presidents of the Senate are appointed by the President of the Republic and are chosen from among the senators.

They are appointed for one year.

The stipend of the president of the Senate is fixed by a decree.

The sittings of the Senate are not public.

25. The Senate is the guardian of the fundamental compact and of the public liberties. No law can be promulgated until after having been submitted to it.

26. The Senate opposes the promulgation,

1st. Of laws which contravene or constitute an attack upon the constitution, religion, morality, freedom of worship, personal liberty, equality of the citizens before the law, the inviolability of property and the principle of the irremovability of the magistracy;

2d. Of those which can compromise the defence of the territory.

27. The Senate regulates by a senatus-consultum:

1st. The constitution of the colonies and of Algeria;

2d. Everything that has not been provided for by the constitution and which is necessary for its operation;

3d. The meaning of the articles of the constitution which occasion different interpretations.

28. These senatus-consulta shall be submitted to the sanction of the President of the Republic and shall be promulgated by him.

29. The Senate allows or annuls all the acts which are submitted to it by the government as unconstitutional or are denounced, for the same reason, by the petitions of citizens.

30. The Senate can, in a report addressed to the President of the Republic, propose the bases of proposals for laws of great national interest.

31. It can likewise propose alterations in the constitution.

If the proposal is adopted by the executive power, it is enacted by a senatus-consultum.

32. Nevertheless every alteration in the fundamental bases of the constitution, as they have been set forth in the proclamation of December 2 [1851], and adopted by the French people, shall be submitted to universal suffrage.

33. In case of the dissolution of the Legislative Body, and until a new convocation, the Senate, upon the proposal of the President of the Republic, provides by measures of urgency for whatever is necessary for the operation of the government.

Title V. Of the Legislative Body.

34. Population is the basis for election.

35. There shall be one deputy to the Legislative Body for every thirty-five thousand electors.

36. The deputies are elected by universal suffrage without *scrutin de liste*.

37. They do not receive any stipend.

38. They are selected for six years.

39. The Legislative Body discusses and votes upon proposals for laws and upon taxation.

40. Every amendment adopted by the commission charged to examine a proposal for a law shall be sent back, without discussion, to the Council of State by the president of the Legislative Body.

If the amendment is not adopted by the Council of State, it cannot be submitted to the consideration of the Legislative Body.

41. The report of the sessions of the Legislative Body by newspapers or any other means of publication shall consist only in the reproduction of the minutes drawn up at the close of each session under the direction of the President of the Legislative Body.

43. The president and the vice-presidents of the Legislative Body are appointed by the President of the Republic for one year; they are chosen from among the deputies. The stipend of the president of the Legislative Body is fixed by a decree.

44. The ministers cannot be members of the Legislative Body.

45. The right of petition is exercised before the Senate. No petition can be addressed to the Legislative Body.

Title VI. Of the Council of State.

46. The President of the Republic convokes, adjourns, prorogues and dissolves the Legislative Body. In case of dissolution, the President of the Republic must convoke it anew within a period of six months.

47. The number of councillors of state in regular service is from forty to fifty.

48. The councillors of state are appointed by the President of the Republic, and are dismissable by him.

49. The Council of State is presided over by the President of the Republic, and in his absence by the person whom he designates as vice-president of the Council of State.

50. The Council of State is charged, under the direction of the President of the Republic, to draw up the proposals for laws and the regulations for public administration, and to settle the difficulties that arise in affairs of administration.

51. It carries on, in the name of the government, the discussion of the proposals for laws before the Senate and Legislative Body.

The councillors of state charged to speak in the name of the government are designated by the President of the Republic

52. The salary of each councillor of state is twenty-five thousand francs.

53. The ministers have rank, sitting and deliberative voice in the Council of State.

Title VII. Of the High Court of Justice.

54. A high court of justice tries, without appeal or recourse in cassation, all persons who have been sent before it as accused of crimes, attempts or conspiracies against the President of the Republic and against the internal or external security of the state.

It can be called in session only in virtue of a decree of the President of the Republic.

55. A senatus-consultum shall determine the organization of this high court.

Title VIII. General and Temporary Provisions.

56. The provisions of the existing codes, laws and regulations, which are not contrary to the present constitution, remain in force until legally altered.

57. A law shall determine the municipal organization. The mayors shall be appointed by the executive power and can be taken from outside of the municipal council.

58. The present constitution shall be in force dating from the day on which the great bodies of the state which it organizes shall be constituted.

The decrees issued by the President of the Republic from December 2, 1851, to the present time, shall have the force of law. -

Done at the Palace of the Tuileries, January 14, 1852.

Signed,   LOUIS NAPOLEON.

113. Documents upon Louis Napoleon and the Press.

February 17, 1852. Duvergier, *Lois,* LII, 104-107.

One of the most characteristic of the governmental methods of Louis Napoleon was his policy toward the press. The system established in document A was followed without any essential change until the enactment of the law of 1868, document B. This was one of the "liberal laws" which accompanied the constitutional changes whereby the autocratic empire was transformed into the liberal empire. (See No. 117) The system revealed by these documents should be compared with those of the first Empire (No. 86) and of the restoration period (No. 101).

REFERENCES. Seignobos, *Europe Since 1814,* 174 ; Rambaud, *Civilisation contemporaine,* 536-538 ; La Gorce, *Second empire, 1,* 43-48, V, 346-362; Jaurès, *Histoire socialiste,* X, 44-48, 322.

Chapter I. Of the Prior Authorisation and Caution-Money of Newspapers and Periodical Works.

1. No newspaper or periodical work treating of political matters or of social economy, and appearing either regularly and at a fixed day or in parts and irregularly, can be produced or published without the prior authorisation of the government.

This authorisation can be granted only to a Frenchman who has reached his majority and enjoys all his civil and political rights.

The prior authorisation of the government shall likewise be necessary for all changes effected in the personnel of the conductors, editors-in-chief, proprietors or administrators of a newspaper.

2. Political or social economy newspapers published abroad cannot circulate in France except by virtue of an authorisation of the government.

The introducers or distributors of a foreign newspaper whose circulation has not been authorised shall be punished by an imprisonment of from one month to one year, and a fine of from one hundred francs to five thousand francs.

3. The proprietors of every newspaper or periodical work treating of political matters or of social economy are required. before its publication, to pay into the treasury a caution-money in coin, upon which interest to the regular amount for caution-monies shall be paid.

4. [This article fixes the amount of the caution-money, varying from fifteen to fifty thousand francs.]

. . . .

Chapter II. Of the Stamp-Duty of Periodical Journals.

6. Newspapers or periodical works and periodical collections of political engravings or lithographs of less than ten sheets of twenty-five to thirty-two square decimeters or of less than five sheets of fifty to seventy-two square decimeters shall be subject to a stamp-duty.

This duty shall be six centimes per sheet of seventy-two square decimeters or less in the departments of the Seine and of Seine-et-Oise, and three centimes for newspapers, engravings or periodical works published anywhere else.

. . . .

Chapter III. Offences and Contraventions not Provided for in Previous Laws. . . . Right of Suspension and Suppression.

. . . .

14. Every contravention of article 42 of the constitution upon the publication of the official reports of the sittings of the Legislative Body shall be punished by a fine of from one thousand to five thousand francs.

15. The publication or reproduction of false news and of

fabricated items, falsely or deceitfully attributed to third parties, shall be punished by a fine of from fifty to one thousand francs.

If the publication or reproduction is made in bad faith, or if it is of a nature to disturb the public peace, the penalty shall be from one month to one year imprisonment and a fine of from five hundred to one thousand francs. The maximum penalty shall be applied if the publication or reproduction was at the same time of a nature to disturb the public peace and was made in bad faith.

16. Reporting the sittings of the Senate otherwise than by the reproduction of the articles inserted in the official journal is forbidden.

Reporting the sittings of the Council of State which are not public is forbidden.

17. Reporting trials for press offences is forbidden. The prosecution alone can be announced; in every case, the decision can be published.

In all civil, correctional or criminal cases, the courts and tribunals can forbid the reporting of the trial. This interdiction cannot be applied to the decision, which can always be published.

. . . .

19. Every conductor shall be required to insert at the top of the paper official documents, authentic accounts, information, replies and corrections which are sent to him by a depository of the public authority.

The publication shall take place in the next number which shall appear after the day of the receipt of the documents.

The insertion shall be gratuitous.

. . . . . .

21. The publication of any article treating of political matters or of social economy, and emanating from an individual condemned to an afflictive and infamous punishment, or infamous only, is forbidden.

. . . . . .

22. No designs, no engravings, lithographs, medals, prints or emblems, of any nature or kind whatsoever, can be published, exposed or put on sale without the prior authorisation of the minister of police at Paris, or of the prefects in the departments.

23. The judicial notices required by the laws for the validity or publication of legal proceedings or contracts shall be inserted, on pain of the nullity of the insertion, in the newspaper or newspapers of the district which shall be designated each year by the prefect.

. . . .

The prefect shall regulate at the same time the scale of prices for the printing of these notices.

. . . . .

24. Any person who follows the business of bookseller without having obtained the warrant required by article II of the law of October 2, 1814, shall be punished by a penalty of from one month to two years imprisonment and a fine of from one hundred to two thousand francs. The establishment shall be closed.

. . . . . .

32. A condemnation for crime committed by means of the press, two condemnations for offences or contraventions committed within the space of two years, entails *ipso facto* the suppression of the newspapers whose conductors have been condemned.

After a condemnation for a press contravention or offence pronounced against the responsible conductor of a newspaper, the government has the right, during the two months which follow that condemnation, to pronounce either the temporary suspension or the suppression of the newspaper.

A newspaper can be suspended by ministerial decision, even when it has not been the subject of any condemnation, after two notices, with statements of reasons, and during a time which cannot exceed two months.

A newspaper can be suppressed either after a judicial or administrative suspension or as a measure of public safety, by a special decree of the President of the Republic, published in the Bulletin of the Laws.

. . . .

B. Law upon the Press. May 11, 1868. Duvergier, *Lois,* LXVIII. 125-170.

1. Any Frenchman of legal age and in the enjoyment of his civil and political rights can, without prior authorisation,

publish a newspaper or periodical work appearing either regularly and at a fixed day or in parts and irregularly.

2. No newspaper or periodical work can be published unless there has been made, at Paris at the prefecture of police and in the departments at the prefecture, and within at least fifteen days before the publication, a declaration containing:

1st. The title of the newspaper or periodical work and the periods at which it is due to appear;

2d. The name, residence and duties of the proprietors other than the silent partners;

3d. The name and residence of the conductor;

4th. The location of the printing office where it is to be printed.

.   .   .   .

3. The stamp duty, fixed by article 6 of the decree of February 17, 1852, is reduced to five centimes in the departments of the Seine and Seine-et-Oise, and to two centimes everywhere else.

4. Electoral posters of a candidate containing his profession of faith, a circular signed by him, or only his name, are free from the stamp duty.

.   .   .   .

7. At the moment of the publication of each sheet or part of a newspaper or periodical work, there shall be sent to the prefecture for the head-towns of the departments, to the subprefecture for those of the district, and for the other cities to the *mairie*, two copies signed by the responsible conductor or one of them, if there are several responsible conductors.

.   .   .   .

8. No newspaper or periodical work can be signed by a member of the Senate or Legislative body in the capacity of responsible conductor. . . .

9. The publication by a newspaper or periodical work of an article signed by a person deprived of his civil and political rights, or to whom admission to France is forbidden, is punished by a fine of one thousand to five thousand francs.

.   .   .   .

12. A condemnation for crime committed by means of the press entails *ipso facto* the suppression of the newspaper whose conductor has been condemned.

In case of repetition within two years from the first con-

demnation for a press offence, other than those committed
against individuals, the tribunals can, in punishing a new offence of the same nature, pronounce the suspenson of the
newspaper or periodical work for a time which shall not be
less than fifteen days or more than two months.

.   .   .   .

114. Documents upon the Evolution of the Second Empire.

These documents record some of the most important steps in
the process by which the restoration of the Empire was effected.
Incidentally they also throw light upon many other features of
the process. Document A is the speech made by Louis Napoleon
at the inauguration of the government created by the constitution of 1852. It may be called the manifesto of the reorganized
republic. Document B is a type of the hundreds of addresses
presented during the course of his famous tour in southern France
in September and October, 1852. Document C is often called the
manifesto of the Empire. Pronounced by Louis Napoleon at the
end of his southern tour, it contained the first direct intimation
from him that the Empire was to be re-established, and outlined
its policy. Document D effected the necessary changes to adapt
the constitution of 1852 to the Empire. The vote for acceptance
was nearly eight millions against about two hundred and fifty
thousand.

REFERENCES. Andrews, *Modern Europe*, II, 37-41 ; La Gorce,
Second empire, I, 59-61, 88-103.

A. Speech of the Prince-President to the Chambers.
March 29, 1852. *Moniteur*, March 30, 1852.

Messrs Senators, Messrs Deputies.

The dictatorship which the people confided to me ceases
to-day. Things are about to resume their regular course. It
is with a feeling of real satisfaction that I come to proclaim
here the putting into effect of the constitution; for my constant preoccupation has been not only to re-establish order,
but to render it durable by giving France institutions suitable
to its needs.

Only a few months ago, you will recall, the more I confined myself within the narrow circle of my attributes, the
more it was sought to restrict them, in order to deprive me of
movement and action. Often discouraged, I confess, I had
thought of abandoning an authority thus disputed. What restrained me was that I saw only one thing to succeed me:

anarchy. Everywhere, in fact, ardent passions, incapable of
establishing anything, were rising up to destroy. Nowhere
was there an institution or a man to whom to attach; nowhere
was there an incontestable right, or any organization, or system which could be realized.

So when, thanks to the co-operation of some courageous
men, thanks especially to the energetic attitude of the army,
all the perils were swept away in a few hours, my first care
was to ask the people for institutions. For too long a time
society had resembled a pyramid which someone had turned
over and sought to make rest upon its apex; I have replaced
it upon its base. Universal suffrage, the only source of right
in such conjunctures, was immediately re-established; order
reconquered its ascendancy; in fine, France adopting the principal provisions of the constitution which I submitted to it, I
was permitted to create political bodies whose influence and
consideration will be so much greater as their attributes
have been wisely regulated.

In fact, among political institutions those alone endure
which fix in an equitable manner the limits in which each
power must remain. There is no other means of arriving at
a useful and beneficent application of liberty; examples are
not far from us.

Why, in 1814, was the inauguration of a parliamentary
régime seen with satisfaction, despite our reverses? It was,
I do not fear to avow it, because the Emperor, on account
of war, had been led to a too absolute exercise of authority.

Why, on the contrary, in 1851, did France applaud the fall
of that same parliamentary régime? It was because the
chambers had abused the influence which had been given
them, and because, wishing to dominate everything, they
were compromising the general equilibrium.

Finally, why has France not risen against the restrictions
imposed upon the liberty of the press and personal liberty?
It is because one had degenerated into license and the other,
instead of being the orderly exercise of the right of each, by
odious excesses had menaced the rights of all.

This extreme danger, especially for democracies, of constantly seeing badly defined institutions sacrifice in turn authority or liberty, was perfectly appreciated by our fathers

half a century ago, when, upon emerging from the revolutionary turmoil and after vain trial of every kind of system, they proclaimed the constitution of the Year VIII, which has served as the model for that of 1852. Without doubt these do not sanction all, those liberties, to the abuses of which we had even become accustomed; but they also consecrate some very real ones. On the morrow of revolutions, the first of the guarantees for a people does not consist in the immoderate use of the tribune and the press; it is in the right to choose the government which is suitable for it. Now the French nation has given to the world, perhaps for the first time, the imposing spectacle of a great people voting in entire liberty the form of its government.

Thus the head of the state whom you have before you is indeed the expression of the popular will; and what do I see before me? two chambers, one elected in virtue of the most liberal law which exists in the world; the other appointed by me, it is true, but independent also, because it is irremovable.

Around me you will notice men of patriotism and of recognized merit, always ready to support me with their counsel and to enlighten me upon the needs of the country.

That constitution which from to-day is going to be in operation is not, then, the work of a vain theory nor of despotism: it is the work of experience and of reason. You will aid, me, gentlemen, to consolidate, extend and improve it.

    .   .   .   .

And now, gentlemen, at the moment in which you are about to associate yourselves patriotically with my labors, I desire to set forth frankly what shall be my conduct.

Seeing me re-establish the institutions and recollections of the Empire, it has been often repeated that I desire to re-establish the Empire itself. If such was my constant preoccupation, that transformation would have been accomplished long since; neither the means nor the occasions were lacking to me.

Thus in 1848, when six million votes elected me, in spite of the *Constituante*, I was not ignorant of the fact that by simple refusal to acquiesce in the constitution, I could have given myself a throne. But an elevation which must necessarily lead to grave disturbances did not seduce me.

On June 13. 1849. it would have been equally easy for me to change the form of the government; I did not wish it.

Finally, on the 2d of December, if personal considerations had outweighed the grave interests of the country, I might have first of all asked the people for a pompous title, which they would not have refused. I was content with what I had.

When, then, I draw examples from the Consulate and the Empire, it is because I find them there especially stamped with nationality and grandeur. Resolved to-day, as before, to do everything for France, and nothing for myself, I shall accept modifications of the present state of things only if I am constrained thereto by evident necessity. Whence can it arise? Only from the conduct of parties. If they are resigned, nothing will be changed. But if by their secret intrigues they seek to undermine the foundations of my government; if, in their blindness, they deny the legitimacy of the result of the popular election; if, in fine, they continue constantly to put in jeopardy the future of the country by their attacks, then, but only then, it may be reasonable to ask the people, in the name of the repose of France, for a new title which shall fix irrevocably upon my head the power with which I am invested. But let us not anticipate difficulties which doubtless have nothing of probability about them. Let us preserve the Republic; it threatens nobody, it can reassure everybody. Under its banner I wish to inaugurate again an era of oblivion and conciliation, and I call upon all, without distinction, who are willing to co-operate freely with me for the public welfare.

. . . . . .

B. Address of the Municipality of Vedennes to Louis-Napoleon. October, 1852. *Moniteur,* October 8, 1852.

The Municipal Council,

Considering that in destroying the hopes and baffling the projects of those perverse men who had dreamed of civil war, anarchy, and the overturning of society, Louis-Napoleon has done for the country and the peace of the entire world more than it has ever been given to any man to do;

Considering that by the repression of the anarchical attempts and the re-establishment of the principle of authority, he has rendered to society brilliant services and has merited well of France;

Considering that confidence in the stability of institutions is one of the most essential elements of the strength of states and of public prosperity;

Unanimously expresses the desire that the Empire should be re-established in the person of His Imperial Highness Prince Louis-Napoleon and his descendants, and for that purpose, in conformity with articles 31 and 32 of the constitution, a senatus-consultum should be proposed for the acceptance of the French people.

C. The Bordeaux Address. October 9, 1852. *Moniteur,* October 12, 1852.

Gentlemen,

The invitation of the chamber and of the tribunal of commerce of Bordeaux which I have cheerfully accepted furnishes me an opportunity to thank your grand city for its reception so cordial and its hospitality so replete with magnificence, and I am very glad also, towards the end of my tour, to share with you the impressions which it has left upon me.

The purpose of this tour, as you know, was that I might come to know for myself our beautiful provinces of the south, and that I might appreciate their needs. It has, however, given rise to a much more important result.

Indeed, I say it with a candor as far removed from arrogance as from a false modesty, never has a people testified in a manner more direct, spontaneous, and unanimous the desire to be freed from anxieties as to the future by consolidating in the same hands an authority which is in sympathy with them. It is because they know at this hour both the false hopes with which they deluded themselves and the dangers with which they are threatened. They knew that in 1852 society would hasten to its destruction, because each party was consoling itself in advance of the general ship-wreck with the hope of planting its banner upon the ruins which might float on the surface. They are thankful to me for having saved the ship, merely by raising the banner of France.

Disabused of absurd theories, the people have acquired the

conviction that the pretended reformers were only dreamers, because there was always inconsistency and disproportion between their means and the results promised.

To-day, France encompasses me with her sympathies, because I am not of the family of the ideologists. In order to secure the welfare of the country, it is not necessary to apply new systems; but, before everything else, to inspire confidence in the present and security for the future. That is why France seems to wish to return to the Empire.

There is, nevertheless, a fear which I must refute. In a spirit of distrust, certain persons declare: The Empire means war. But I say: The Empire means peace.

It means peace, because France desires it, and, when France is satisfied, the world is tranquil. Glory, indeed, is bequeathed by hereditary title, but not war. Did the princes who justly thought themselves honored in being the grandsons of Louis XIV recommence his struggles? War is not made for pleasure, but by necessity; and at these epochs of transition in which everywhere, by the side of so many elements of prosperity, as many causes of death shoot up, it can be said with truth: Woe to him who first should give in Europe the signal of a collision whose consequences would be incalculable!

I admit, however, that I, like the Emperor, have indeed conquests to make. I wish, like him, to conquer for conciliation the hostile parties and to bring into the current of the great popular stream the hostile factions which are now ruining themselves without profit to anybody.

I wish to conquer for religion, morality, and comfortable living that part of the population still so numerous, which, in the midst of a country of faith and belief, scarcely knows of the precepts of Christ; which, in the midst of the most fertile land in the world, can scarcely enjoy products of first necessity.

We have enormous uncultivated territories to clear, routes to open, harbors to deepen, rivers to make navigable, canals to finish, and our network of railroads to complete. We have opposite Marseilles an enormous kingdom to assimilate to France. We have to connect all of our great western ports with the American continent by those rapid communications which we still lack. In fine, we have everywhere ruins to raise again, false gods to cast down, and truths to make triumphant.

That is how I shall understand the Empire, if the Empire is to be re-established. Such are the conquests which I meditate, and all of you who surround me, who wish, like myself, the welfare of our fatherland, you are my soldiers.

D. Senatus-Consultum upon the Empire. November 7, 1852. Duvergier, *Lois,* LII, 680-682.

The Senate has deliberated, in conformity with articles 31 and 32 of the constitution, and voted the senatus-consultum whose tenor follows:

.1. The imperial dignity is re-established.

Louis-Napoleon Bonaparte is Emperor of the French, under the name of Napoleon III.

2. The imperial dignity is hereditary in the direct and legitimate descendants of Louis-Napoleon Bonaparte, from male to male, by order of primogeniture, and to the perpetual exclusion of women and their descendants.

3. Louis-Napoleon Bonaparte, if he has no male children can adopt legitimate children and descendants in the masculine line of the brothers of the Emperor Napoleon I.

The forms of adoption are regulated by a senatus-consultum.

If, after the adoption, male children should come to Louis-Napoleon, his adopted sons can be called to succeed him only after his legitimate descendants.

Adoption is forbidden to the successors of Louis-Napoleon and their descendants.

4. Louis-Napoleon Bonaparte regulates, by an organic decree addressed to the Senate and deposited in its archives, the order of succession to the throne within the Bonaparte family, for the case that he should not leave any direct heir, legitimate or adopted.

5. In default of a legitimate or adopted heir of Louis-Napoleon Bonaparte, and of successors in the collateral line who shall take their right in the above mentioned organic decree, a senatus-consultum, proposed to the Senate by the ministers formed into council of government with the addition of acting presidents of the Senate, the Legislative Body

and the Council of State, and submitted to the acceptance of the people, appoints the Emperor and regulates within his family the hereditary order from male to male, to the perpetual exclusion of women and their descendants.

Up to the moment at which the election of the new Emperor is consummated, the affairs of state are controlled by the ministers on duty, who form themselves into council of government and deliberate by majority of votes.

6. The members of the family of Louis-Napoleon Bonaparte summoned eventually to the inheritance and their descendants of both sexes, form part of the imperial family. A senatus-consultum regulates their position. They cannot marry without the authorisation of the Emperor. Marriage made by them without that authorisation involves loss of all right to the inheritance, both for the one who has contracted it and for his descendants.

Nevertheless, if there are no children from that marriage, in case of its dissolution because of death, the prince who had contracted it recovers his rights to the inheritance.

Louis-Napoleon Bonaparte fixes the titles and the station of the other members of his family.

The Emperor has full authority over all members of his family; he regulates their duties and their obligations by statutes which have the force of law.

The constitution of January 14, 1852, is maintained in all those of its provisions which are not contrary to the present senatus-consultum; modifications in it can be effected only in the forms and by the means which it has provided.

8. The following proposition shall be presented for the acceptance of the French people in the forms fixed by the decrees of December 2 and 4, 1851.

"The French people wish the re-establishment of the imperial dignity in the person of Louis-Napoleon Bonaparte, with inheritance in his direct descendants, legitimate or adopted, and give to him the right to regulate the order of succession, to the throne within the Bonaparte family, as is provided for by the senatus-consultum of November 7, 1852."

115. Documents upon the Congress of Paris.

These documents, representing the principal results of the international congress at the close of the Crimean war, are important from many standpoints. Three of these deserve special attention. (1) As the Crimean war was in large measure due to rivalry for international prestige, they may be examined to ascertain what direct and immediate advantages or disadvantages accrued to each state. (2) As a new settlement of the Eastern Problem was effected in these documents its various features should be carefully noted, e. g., the alteration in the position of Turkey, the status provided for the christian states of the Balkan peninsula, the control over the Black Sea and Dardanelles. (3) As a number of long-disputed international law questions were definitively settled, notice should be taken of what these were, the method provided for their settlement, and the principles finally accepted.

REFERENCES. Fyffe. *Modern Europe*, III, 227-240 (Popular ed., 856-865) ; Seignobos, *Europe Since 1814*, 789-792 ; Phillips, *Modern Europe*, 357-360 ; Andrews, *Modern Europe*, II, 77-90 ; Lavisse and Rambaud, *Histoire générale*, XI, 220-226.

A. Treaty of Paris. March 30, 1856. De Clercq, *Traités*, VII, 59-68. Translation based on that of Hertslet, *Map of Europe by Treaty*, 1250-1265.

Their Majesties the Queen of the United Kingdom of Great Britain and Ireland, the Emperor of the French, the Emperor of all the Russias, the King of Sardinia, and the Emperor of the Ottomans, animated by the desire to put an end to the calamities of war, and wishing to prevent the return of the complications which occasioned it, resolved to come to an understanding with His Majesty the Emperor of Austria as to the bases on which peace might be re-established and consolidated, by securing through effectual and reciprocal guarantees, the independence and integrity of the Ottoman Empire.

.   .   .   .

[The omitted passage names the plenipotentiaries and makes Prussia a party to the treaty.]

1. From the day of the exchange of the ratifications of the present treaty there shall be peace and friendship between Her Majesty the Queen of the United Kingdom of Great Britain and Ireland, His Majesty the Emperor of the French, His Majesty the King of Sardinia, His Imperial Majesty the Sultan, on the one part, and His Majesty the Emperor of all the Russias, on the other part; as well as be-

tween their heirs and successors, their respective dominions and subjects, in perpetuity.

. . . .

7. Her Majesty the Queen of the United Kingdom of Great Britain and Ireland, His Majesty the Emperor of Austria, His Majesty the Emperor of the French, His Majesty the King of Prussia, His Majesty the Emperor of all the Russias, and His Majesty the King of Sardinia, declare the Sublime Porte admitted to participate in the advantages of the public law and the concert of Europe. Their Majesties engage, each on his part, to respect the independence and the territorial integrity of the Ottoman Empire, guaranteeing in common the strict observance of that engagement; and will in consequence consider any act tending to its violation as a question of general interest.

8. If there should arise between the Sublime Porte and one or more of the other signatory powers any misunderstanding which might endanger the maintenance of their relations, the Sublime Porte and each of such powers, before having recourse to the use of force, shall afford the other contracting parties the opportunity of preventing such an extremity by means of their mediation.

9. His Imperial Majesty the Sultan having, in his constant solicitude for the welfare of his subjects, issued a firman, which, while ameliorating their condition without distinction of religion or of race, records his generous intentions towards the christian population of his empire, and wishing to give a further proof of his sentiments in that respect, has resolved to communicate to the contracting parties the said firman, emanating spontaneously from his sovereign will.

The contracting powers recognize the high value of this communication. It is clearly understood that it cannot, in any case, give to the said powers the right to interfere, either collectively or separately, in the relations of His Majesty the Sultan with his subjects, nor in the internal administration of his empire.

10. The convention of the 13th of July, 1841, which maintains the ancient rule of the Ottoman Empire relative to the closing of the straits of the Bosphorus and of the Dardanelles, has been revised by common consent.

The act concluded for that purpose and in conformity with that principle, between the high contracing paries, is and remains annexed to the present treaty, and shall have the same force and validity as if it formed an integral part thereof.

11. The Black Sea is neutralized; its waters and its ports. thrown open to the mercantile marine of every nation, are formally and in perpetuity interdicted to the flag of war, whether of the powers possessing its coasts, or of any other power, with the exceptions mentioned in Articles 14 and 19 of the present treaty.

.   .   .   .   .   .

15. The Act of the Congress of Vienna, having established the principles intended to regulate the navigation of rivers which separate or traverse different states, the contracting powers stipulate among themselves that those principles shall in future be likewise applied to the Danube and its mouths. They declare that its arrangement henceforth forms a part of the public law of Europe, and take it under their guarantee.

.   .   .   .

[Articles 13, 14, and 19 forbid Russia and Turkey to erect fortifications along the Black Sea or to maintain warships upon its waters except two vessels of each power for police purposes.]

20. [Provides for a rectification of the Russian frontier toward Bessarabia, whereby Russia lost some territory and was cut off from contact with the Danube.]

22. The Principalities of Wallachia and Moldavia shall continue to enjoy under the suzerainty of the Porte and under the guarantee of the contracting powers, the privilges and immunities of which they are in possession. No exclusive protection shall be exercised over them by any of the guaranteeing powers.

There shall be no separate right of interference in their internal affairs.

23. The Sublime Porte engages to preserve to the said principalities an independent and national administration, as well as full liberty of worship, legislation, commerce, and navigation.

.   .   .   .   .   .

28. The Principality of Servia shall continue to hold of the Sublime Porte, in conformity with the imperial hats which fix and determine its rights and immunities, placed henceforth under the collective guarantee of the contracting powers.

In consequence, the said principality shall preserve its independence and national administration, as well as full liberty of worship. legislation, commerce, and navigation.

30. His Majesty the Emperor of all the Russias and His Majesty the Sultan maintain in its integrity the state of their possessions in Asia, such as it legally existed before the rupture. . . .

B. The Dardanelles Convention. March 26, 1856. Hertslet, *Map of Europe by Treaty,* 1266-1269.

Their Majesties the Queen of the United Kingdom of Great Britain and Ireland, the Emperor of Austria, the Emperor of the French, the King of Prussia, the Emperor of all the Russias, signing parties to the convention of the 13th day of July, 1841, and His Majesty the King of Sardinia; wishing to record in common their unanimous determination to conform to the ancient rule of the Ottoman Empire, according to which the straits of the Dardanelles and of the Bosphorus are closed to foreign ships of war, so long as the Porte is at peace.

Their said Majesties, on the one part, and His Majesty the Sultan, on the other, have resolved to renew the convention concluded at London on the 13th day of July, 1841, with the exception of some modifications of detail which do not affect the principle upon which it rests;

.   .   .   .

His Majesty the Sultan, on the one part, declares that he is firmly resolved to maintain for the future the principle invariably established as the ancient rule of his Empire, and in virtue of which it has, at all times, been prohibited for the ships of war of foreign powers to enter the straits of the Dardanelles and of the Bosphorus; and that, so long as the Porte is at peace, His Majesty will admit no foreign ship of war into the said straits.

And their Majesties the Queen of the United Kingdom of

Great Britain and Ireland, the Emperor of Austria, the Emperor of the French, the King of Prussia, the Emperor of all the Russias, and the King of Sardinia, on the other part, engage to respect this determination of the Sultan, and to conform themselves to the principle above declared.

C. Declaration Respecting Maritime Power. April 16, 1856. De Clercq, *Traités*, VII, 91-92. Translation based on that of Hertslet, *Map of Europe by Treaty*, 1282-1284.

The plenipotentiaries who signed the treaty of Paris of the 30th of March, 1856, assembled in conference,—
Considering:
That maritime law, in time of war, has long been the subject of deplorable disputes;
That the uncertainty of the law and of the duties in such a matter, gives rise to differences of opinion between neutrals and belligerents which may occasion serious difficulties, and even conflicts;
That it is consequently advantageous to establish a uniform doctrine on so important a point;
That the plenipotentiaries assembled at the Congress of Paris cannot better respond to the intentions by which their governments are animated, than by seeking to introduce into international relations fixed principles in this respect;
The above-mentioned plenipotentiaries, being duly authorised, resolved to concert among themselves as to the means of attaining this object; and, having come to an agreement, have adopted the following solemn declaration:
1. Privateering is, and remains, abolished;
2. The neutral flag covers enemy's goods, with the exception of contraband of war:
3. Neutral goods, with the exception of contraband of war, are not liable to capture under the enemy's flag;
4. Blockades, in order to be binding, must be effective that is to say, maintained by a force sufficient really to prevent access to the coast of the enemy.
The governments of the undersigned plenipotentiaries engage to bring the present declaration to the knowledge of

the states which have not taken part in the Congress of Paris, and to invite them to accede to it.

Convinced that the maxims which they now proclaim cannot but be received with gratitude by the whole world, the undersigned plenipotentiaries doubt not that the efforts of their governments to obtain the general adoption thereof, will be crowned with full success.

The present declaration is not, and shall not be binding, except between those powers who have acceded, or shall accede, to it.

Done at Paris, the 16th of April, 1856.

116. Documents upon the Italian War of 1859.

The principal purpose of this group of documents is to throw light upon five features of the subject to which they relate. (1) Documents A and B show how the issue of war as between Austria and Piedmont was joined. (2) Document C may be regarded as an official defence and announcement of the purpose of French participation in the war. (3) From document D something may be learned of what the Italians expected from French assistance. (4) Documents E and F show the terms upon which the war was concluded and the settlement of the Italian question intended by Napoleon III. (5) Document G shows the compensation exacted by France for its participation in the war.

REFERENCES. Fyffe, *Modern Europe*, III, 251-281 (Popular ed., 873-892) ; Seignobos, *Europe Since 1814*, 793-797 ; Andrews, *Modern Europe*, II, 112-145 ; Cesaresco, *Cavour*, Chs. VIII-X ; Stillman, *Union of Italy*, Ch. XII ; King, *Italian Unity*, II, 45-51 ; 55-57, 61-70 , 77-82, 115-122 ; Lavisse and Rambaud, *Histoire générale*, XI, 263-276 ; La Gorce, *Second empire*, II, 436-440, 448, III, 109-113, 209-212.

A. The Austrian Ultimatum. April 19, 1859. Angeberg, *Traités concernant l'Autriche et l'Italie*, 775-776. Translation based upon that of Hertslet, *Map of Europe by Treaty*, 1359-1360.

The Imperial Government, as your excellency is aware, has hastened to accede to the proposal of the cabinet of St. Petersburg to assemble a congress of the five powers with the view to remove the complications which have arisen in Italy.

Convinced, however, of the impossibility of entering with any chance of success upon pacific deliberations in the midst of the noise of arms and of preparations for war carried on in a neighboring country, we have demanded the placing on a peace footing of the Sardinian army and the disbanding of the free corps or Italian volunteers, prior to the meeting of the congress.

Her Britannic Majesty's government finds this condition so just and so consonant with the exigencies of the situation that it did not hesitate to adopt it, at the same time declaring itself ready, in conjunction with France, to insist on the immediate disarmament of Sardinia, and to offer her in return a collective guarantee against any attack on our part, to which, of course, Austria would have done honor.

The cabinet of Turin seems to have answered only by a categorical refusal of the invitation to put her army on a peace footing, and to accept the collective guarantee which was offered her.

This refusal inspires us with regrets, so much the more deep as, if the Sardinian government had consented to the testimony of pacific sentiments which was demanded of her, we should have accepted it as a first indication of her intention to co-operate on her side, in bringing about an improvement in the relations between the two countries which have unfortunately been in such a state of tension for some years past. In that case, it would have been permitted us to furnish, by the breaking up of the imperial troops stationed in the Lombardo-Venetian kingdom, another proof that they were not assembled for the purpose of aggression against Sardinia.

Our hope having been hitherto deceived, the Emperor, my august master, has ordered me to make directly a last effort to cause the Sardinian government to reconsider the decision which it seems to have resolved on.

Such, Count, is the object of this letter. I have the honour to entreat your excellency to take its contents into your most serious consideration and to let me know whether the royal government consents, yes or no, to put its army on a peace footing without delay and to disband the Italian volunteers.

The bearer of this letter, to whom, Count, you will be so good as to give your answer, has orders to hold himself at your disposition for this purpose during three days.

If, at the expiration of this term, he should receive no answer, or if this answer should not be completely satisfactory, the responsibility for the grave events which that refusal will involve will fall entirely upon the government of His Sardinian Majesty. After having exhausted in vain all the means of conciliation in order to procure for his peoples the guarantee of peace, upon which the Emperor has the right to insist, His Majesty must, to his great regret, have recourse to force of arms to obtain it.

In the hope that the answer which I solicit of your Excellency will be congenial to our wishes for the maintenance of peace, I seize, &c.,

Signed,   BUOL.

To C. CAVOUR.

B. Reply of Sardinia. April 26, 1859. Angeberg, *Traités concernant l'Autriche et l'Italie, 777.* Translation based on that of Hertslet, *Map of Europe by Treaty,* 1361.

The question of the disarmament of Sardinia, which constitutes the basis of the demand which your Excellency addresses to me, has been the subject of numerous negotiations between the great powers and the government of the king. These negotiations led to a proposition drawn up by England, to which France, Prussia, and Russia adhered. Sardinia, in a spirit of conciliation, accepted it without reserve or afterthought. Since your Excellency can neither be ignorant either of the proposition of England nor the answer, I could add nothing in order to make known the intentions of the government of the king with regard to the difficulties which were opposed to the assembling of the Congress.

The decided conduct of Sardinia has been appreciated by Europe. Whatever may be the consequences which it entails, the king, my august master, is convinced that the responsibility will devolve upon them who first armed, who have refused the propositions made by a great power, and recognized as just and reasonable by the others, and who now substitute a menacing summons in its stead.

C. Proclamation of Napoleon III. May 3, 1859. De Clercq. *Traités,* VII, 606-607.

Frenchmen!

Austria, in causing its army to enter the territory of the

King of Sardinia, our ally, declares war upon us. It thus violates treaties and justice, and threatens our frontiers. All the great powers have protested against that aggression. Piedmont having accepted conditions which should have assured peace, it may be asked what can be the reason for this sudden invasion. It is because Austria has brought matters to that extremity, that it is necessary she should dominate to the Alps, or that Italy should be free to the Adriatic; for in that country, every corner of land that remains independent is in danger for its power.

Up to the present, moderation has been the rule of my conduct; now energy becomes my first duty.

Let France arm itself and say resolutely to Europe: I do not wish for conquest, but I am determined to maintain without feebleness my national and traditional policy; I observe treaties, on condition that they shall not be violated against me; I respect the territory and the rights of neutral powers, but I openly avow my sympathy for a people whose history is bound up with ours, and who groan under foreign oppression.

France has shown her hatred of anarchy; she has been pleased to give me an authority strong enough to reduce to impotence the abettors of disorder and the incorrigible men of those former parties who are seen incessantly making covenants with our enemies; but she has not for that abdicated her function as a civilizer. Her natural allies have always been those who desire the improvement of humanity, and when she draws her sword, it is not in order to domineer, but to liberate.

The purpose of this war, then, is to restore Italy to herself and not to cause her to change her master, and we shall have upon our frontiers a friendly people, who will owe their independence to us.

We are not going into Italy to foment disorder nor to shake the authority of the Holy Father, whom we have replaced upon his throne, but to secure it against that foreign pressure which weighs upon the whole peninsula and to have a share in establishing order there out of legitimate satisfied interests.

We are, in fine, in that classic land, made illustrious by

so many victories, about to follow in the footsteps of our fathers; God grant that we may be worthy of them!

I shall shortly place myself at the head of the army. I leave in France the Empress and my son. Seconded by the experience and enlightenment of the last surviving brother of the Emperor, she will be able to show herself not inferior to her mission.

I entrust them to the valor of our army which remains in France to look after our frontiers, as well as to protect our domestic hearth; I entrust them to the patriotism of the national guard; I entrust them, in fine, to the entire people, who will surround them with that love and devotion of which each day I receive so many proofs.

Courage then and union! Our country is about to show the world once again that it has not degenerated. Providence will bless our efforts; for the cause which is based upon justice, humanity, love of fatherland and of independence, is holy in the eyes of God.

NAPOLEON.

Palace of the Tuileries, May 3, 1859.

D. Proclamation to the Italians. June 8, 1859. *Moniteur*, June 12, 1859.

Italians,

The fortune of war bringing me to-day into the capital of Lombardy, I am about to tell you why I am here.

When Austria unjustly attacked Piedmont, I resolved to support my ally, the King of Sardinia, the honor and interests of France making it a duty for me. Your enemies, who are mine, have tried to diminish the universal sympathy, which there has been in Europe for your cause, by seeking to make it thought that I was making war only through personal ambition or to increase the territory of France. If there are men who do not understand this epoch, I am not of the number.

In the enlightened state of public opinion at present, one is greater through the moral influence which he exerts than through sterile conquests; and that moral influence I seek after with pride in contributing to make free one of the most beautiful parts of Europe.

Your welcome has already proven to me that you do not misunderstand me. I do not come here with a preconceived system in order to dispossess sovereigns nor to impose my will upon you; my army will occupy itself only with two things; to fight your enemies, and to maintain internal order; it will not interpose any obstacle to the free manifestation of your legitimate desires. Providence sometimes favors peoples just as it does individuals by giving them the opportunity to become great all at once; but it is on condition that they know how to profit thereby. Profit, then, by the fortune which is offered you.

Your desire for independence so long made known,. so often deceived, will be realized if you will show yourselves worthy of it. Unite then in a single aim, the liberation of your country. Organize militarily. Flock under the banners of Victor Emmanuel, who has already so nobly shown you the way of honor. Remember that without discipline there is no army; and, animated by the sacred fire of patriotism, be to-day only soldiers; to-morrow, you shall be free citizens of a great country.

Done at the imperial headquarters at Milan, June 8, 1859.

NAPOLEON.

E. Peace preliminaries of Villafranca. July 11, 1859. De Clercq, *Traités*, VII, 617-618. Translation based upon that of Hertslet, *Map of Europe by Treaty*, 1374-1375.

Between His Majesty the Emperor of Austria and His Majesty the Emperor of the French, it has been agreed as follows:

The two sovereigns favour the creation of an Italian confederation. This confederation shall be under the honorary presidency of the Holy Father.

The Emperor of Austria cedes to the Emperor of the French his rights over Lombardy, with the exception of the fortresses of Mantua and Peschiera, so that the frontier of the Austrian possessions shall start from the outer edge of the fortress of Peschiera, and extend in a straight line along the Mincio as far as Legrazia; thence to Szarzarola and Suzana on the Po from whence the existing frontiers shall continue to form the boundaries of Austria. The Emperor of the French shall transfer the ceded territory to the King of Sardinia.

Venetia shall form part of the Italian confederation, remaining, however, subject to the crown of the Emperor of Austria.

The Grand Duke of Tuscany and the Duke of Modena return to their states, granting a general amnesty.

The two emperors shall request the Holy Father to introduce in his states some indispensable reforms.

Full and complete amnesty is granted on both sides to persons compromised on the occasion of the recent events in the territories of the belligerents.

Done at Villafranca, 11th July, 1859.

NAPOLEON.   FRANCIS JOSEPH.

F. Treaty of Zurich. November 10, 1859. De Clercq, *Traités*, VII, 643-649. Translation based upon that of Hertslet, *Map of Europe by Treaty*, 1380-1391.

In the name of the Most Holy and Indivisible Trinity.

His Majesty the Emperor of Austria, and His Majesty the Emperor of the French, desirous of putting an end to the calamities of war, and of preventing the recurrence of the complications which gave rise to it, by assisting to place upon solid and durable bases the internal and external independence of Italy, have resolved to convert into a definitive treaty of peace the preliminaries signed by their hands at Villafranca.

. . . .

1. There shall be in the future peace and friendship between His Majesty the Emperor of Austria and His Majesty the Emperor of the French, as also between their heirs and successors, their respective states and subjects, forever.

. . . .

4. His Majesty the Emperor of Austria renounces, for himself and all his descendants and successors, in favor of His Majesty the Emperor of the French, his rights and titles to Lombardy, with the exception of the fortresses of Peschiera and Mantua, and the territories determined by the new delimitation, which remain in the possession of His Imperial and Royal Apostolic Majesty.

. . . .

5. His Majesty the Emperor of the French declares his intention of handing over to His Majesty the King of Sardinia the territories ceded by the preceding article.

.   .   .   .

18. His Majesty the Emperor of Austria and His Majesty the Emperor of the French engage to make every effort to encourage the creation of a confederation among the Italian states, which shall be placed under the honorary presidency of the Holy Father, and the object of which shall be to uphold the independence and inviolability of the confederated states, to assure the development of their moral and material interests, and to guarantee the internal and external safety of Italy by the existence of a federal army.

Venetia, which remains subject to the crown of His Imperial and Royal Apostolic Majesty, will form one of the states of this confederation, and will participate in the obligations, as in the rights resulting from the federal pact, the clauses of which shall be determined by an assembly composed of the representatives of all the Italian states.

19. As the territorial delimitation of the independent states of Italy which took no part in the late war, can be changed only with the sanction of the powers who presided at their formation and recognized their existence, the rights of the Grand Duke of Tuscany, the Duke of Modena, and the Duke of Parma, are expressly reserved by the high contracting parties.

20. Desirous of seeing the tranquility of the States of the Church and the power of the Holy Father assured; convinced that this object could not be more efficaciously attained than by the adoption of a system suited to the wants of the populations and conformable to the generous intentions already manifested by the Sovereign Pontiff, His Majesty the Emperor of the French and His Majesty the Emperor of Austria will unite their efforts to obtain from His Holiness that the necessity of introducing into the administration of his states the reforms, recognized as indispensable shall be taken into serious consideration by his government.

.   .   .   .

G. Treaty of Turin, March 24, 1860. De Clercq, *Traités*, VIII. 32-35. Translation based upon that of Hertslet, *Map of Europe by Treaty*, 1429-1431.

In the Name of the Most Holy and Indivisible Trinity.

His Majesty the Emperor of the French having explained the considerations which, in consequence of the changes which have arisen in the territorial relations between France and Sardinia, caused him to desire the annexation of Savoy and the district of Nice (*circondario di Nizza*) to France, and His Majesty the King of Sardinia having shown himself disposed to acquiesce therein their said Majesties have decided to conclude a treaty for that purpose, . . .

1. His Majesty the King of Sardinia consents to the union of Savoy and the district of Nice (*circondario di Nizza*) to France, and renounces for himself, and all his descendants and successors, in favour of His Majesty the Emperor of the French, his rights and titles over the said territories. It is understood between their Majesties that this union shall be effected without any constraint of the wishes of the populations, and that the governments of the Emperor of the French and of the King of Sardinia will plan together as soon as possible upon the best means to ascertain and establish the manifestation of those wishes.

117. Documents upon the Evolution of the Liberal Empire.

These documents show the steps by which the autocratic régime of the first eight years of the Second Empire was gradually modified and the character of the system finally evolved out of those changes. These things should be noted in connection with each document: (1) the concession nominally extended; (2) restrictions and qualifications placed upon the concessions, if any; (3) concessions withdrawn to counterbalance those extended, if any.

REFERENCES, Dickinson, *Revolution and Reaction in Modern France*, 229-231; Seignobos. *Europe Since 1814*, 176-184: Andrews, *Modern Europe*, II, 169-186, *passim;* Lavisse and Rambaud, *Histoire générale*, XI, 162-193, *passim;* La Gorce, *Second empire*, III, 442-447. IV. 144-154, V, 346-350, 493-505; Jaurès. *Histoire socialiste*, X, 129. 144-146, 282-283, 384-386; Rambaud, *Civilisation contemporaine*, 520-523.

A. Decree of the 24th of November. November 24, 1860. Duvergier, *Lois*, LX, 592-593.

Napoleon, etc., wishing to give to the great bodies of the state a more direct participation in the general policy of our government and a striking testimonial of our confidence, we have decreed:

1. The Senate and the Legislative Body shall vote every year at the opening of the session, an address in response to our speech.

2. The address shall be discussed in the presence of the commissioners of the government, who shall give to the chambers all the necessary explanations upon the internal and foreign policy of the Empire.

3. In order to facilitate for the Legislative Body the expression of its opinion in the formation of the laws and the exercise of the right of amendment, article 54 of our decree of March 22, 1852, is again put in force, and the rule of the Legislative Body, is modified in the following manner:

"Immediately after the distribution of the projects of law and upon the day fixed by the president, the Legislative Body, before appointing its commission, meets in secret committee; a concise discussion is opened upon the project of law, and the commissioners of the government take part in it."

"The present provision is not applicable to projects of law of local interest nor in the case of urgency."

4. With the intent of rendering the reproduction of the debates of the Senate and the Legislative Body, more prompt and more complete, the following project for a senatus-consultum shall be presented to the Senate:

"The minutes of the sittings of the Senate and the Legislative Body, drawn up by the secretary-editors placed under the authority of the president of each assembly, are addressed each evening to all the newspapers. In addition, the debates of each sitting are reproduced by stenography and inserted *in extenso* in the official newspaper of the next day."

5. The Emperor shall designate ministers without portfolio to defend before the chambers, in concert with the president and members of the Council of State, the projects of law of the government.

6. The ministers without portfolio have the rank and the compensation of the ministers in office; they form part of the council of ministers and are housed at the expense of the state.

7. Our minister of State (M. Walewski) is charged, etc.

B. Senatus-Consultum upon the Publication of Debates. February 2, 1861. Duvergier, *Lois,* LXI, 50-58.

Article 42 of the Constitution is modified as follows:

The debates of the sittings of the Senate and the Legislative Body are reproduced by stenography and inserted *in extenso* in the official newspaper of the next day.

In addition, the minutes of these sittings, drawn up by the secretary-editors placed under the authority of the president of each assembly, are put each evening at the disposal of all the newspapers.

The reports of the sittings of the Senate and the Legislative Body by the newspapers, or any other method of publication, shall consist. only in the reproduction of the debates inserted *in extenso* in the official newspaper, or the report drawn up under the authority of the president, in conformity with the preceding paragraphs.

Nevertheless, when several projects or petitions have been discussed in one session, it shall be permissible to reproduce only the debates relative to one of these projects or to a single one of these petitions. In that case, if the discussion is prolonged through several sittings, the publication must be continued up to and including the vote thereon.

The Senate, upon the request of five members, can decide to form itself into secret committee.

Article 13 of the senatus-consultum of December 25, 1852, is abrogated in whatever is contrary to the present senatus-consultum.

C. Senatus-Consultum upon the Budget. December 31, 1861. Duvergier, *Lois,* LXI, 553-579.

1. The budget of the expenses is presented to the Legislative Body with its divisions into sections, chapters and articles.

The budget of each ministry is voted by sections, in conformity with the nomenclature appended to the present senatus-consultum.

The distribution, by chapters, of the credits granted for each section, is regulated by decree of the Emperor, rendered in Council of State.

2. Special decrees, rendered in the same form, can authorise transfers from one chapter to another in the budget of each ministry.

3. Supplementary or extraordinary credits can be granted only by virtue of a law.

4. The provisions of existing laws in that which concerns the expenses of secret services, remaining to be paid, the expenses of the departments, the communes, and the local services, and the assistance funds for expenses of public interest are not altered.

5. Articles 4 and 12 of the senatus-consultum of December 25, 1852, are modified wherein they are contrary to the present senatus-consultum.

[The nomenclature alluded to in article 1 is omitted.]

D. Imperial Decree upon Interpellation. January 19, 1867. Duvergier, *Lois*, LXVII, 21-22.

Napoleon, etc., wishing to give to the discussions of the great bodies of state upon the foreign and internal policy of the government more utility and more accuracy, we have decreed:

1. The members of the Senate and the Legislative Body, can address interpellations to the government.

2. Every request for interpellation must be written and signed by at least five members. This request explains briefly the object of the interpellation; it is delivered to the president, who communicates it to the minister of state and sends it to the examination of the *bureaux*.

3. If two *bureaux* of the Senate or four *bureaux* of the Legislative Body express the opinion that the interpellation may take place, the chamber fixes the day of the discussion.

4. After the closure of the discussion, the chamber pronounces the order of the day pure and simple or sends it again to the government.

5. The order of the day pure and simple has always priority.

6. The sending again to the government can be declared only in the following terms: "The Senate (or the Legislative Body) calls the attention of the government to the subject of the interpellation." In this case, an epitome of the deliberation is transmitted to the minister of state.

7. Each of the ministers, by special delegation of the Emperor, can be charged, in concert with the minister of state,

and the president and the members of the Council of State, to represent the government before the Senate and the Legislative Body, in the discussion of affairs or of the projects of law.

8. Articles 1 and 2 of our decree of November 24, 1860, which enacted that the Senate and the Legislative Body should vote every year at the opening of the session an address in response to our speech, are abrogated.

9. Our minister of State (M. Rouher) is charged, etc..

E. Senatus-Consultum. September 8, 1869. Duvergier, *Lois,* LXIX, 268-280.

1. The Emperor and the Legislative Body have the introduction of the laws.

2. The ministers are dependent only upon the Emperor. They deliberate in council under his presidency.

They are responsible.

They can be put in accusation only by the Senate.

3. The ministers can be members of the Senate or the Legislative Body.

They have entrance into both assemblies and must be heard whenever they demand it.

4. The sittings of the Senate are public. The request of five members suffices for it to form itself into secret committee.

5. The Senate, in indicating the modifications of which a law seems to it susceptible, can decide that it shall be sent back for a new deliberation of the Legislative Body.

It can, in any case, oppose the promulgation of the law.

The law to the promulgation of which the Senate is opposed cannot be again presented to the Legislative Body in the same session.

6. At the opening of each session, the Legislative Body appoints its president, vice-presidents and secretaries.

It appoints its questors.

7. Every member of the Senate and of the Legislative Body has the right to address an interpellation to the government.

Orders of the day, with statements of reasons, can be adopted.

The return to the *bureaux* of an order of the day with a statement of reasons is a right when the government requests it.

The *bureaux* appoint a commission, upon the summary-report of which the assembly pronounces.

8. No amendment can be put in deliberation unless it has been sent to the commission charged to examine the project of law and communicated to the government.

When the government and the commission do not agree, the Council of State gives its opinion and the Legislative Body pronounces.

9. The budget of expenses is presented to the Legislative Body by chapters and articles.

The budget of each ministry is voted by chapters, in conformity with the nomenclature annexed to the present senatus-consultum.

10. Future modifications by international treaties in the schedules of the custom-duties and the postoffice shall become binding only in virtue of a law.

11. The existing constitutional relations between the government of the Emperor, the Senate, and the Legislative Body can be modified only by a senatus-consultum.

The regular relations between these authorities are established by imperial decree.

The Senate and the Legislative Body frame their own internal regulations.

12. All provisions contrary to the present senatus-consultum, and in particular articles 8 and 13, the second paragraph of article 24, articles 26 and 40, the fifth paragraph of article 42, the first paragraph of article 43 and article 44 of the constitution; articles 3 and 5 of the senatus-consultum of December 25, 1852; article 1 of the senatus-consultum of December 31, 1861, are abrogated.

[The nomenclature alluded to in article nine is omitted.]

F. Senatus-Consultum. May 21, 1870. Duvergier, *Lois,* LXX, 123-128.

Napoleon, etc., in view of our decree of April 23 last, which convoked the French people in their assemblies, in order to accept or reject the following plebiscite:

"The people approve the liberal reforms effected in the constitution since 1860 by the Emperor with the co-operation of the great bodies of the state, and ratify the senatus-consultum of April 20, 1870;"

In view of the declaration of the Legislative Body which attests that the operations of the vote have been regularly carried out; that the general return of the votes cast upon the project of plebiscite has given seven million three hundred and fifty thousand one hundred forty-two ballots bearing the word, yes; fifteen hundred thirty-eight thousand eight hundred and twenty-five bearing the word, no; one hundred twelve thousand nine hundred and seventy-five invalid ballots;

We have sanctioned and promulgated as law of the state the senatus-consultum adopted by the Senate, April 20, 1870, and of the following tenor:

Senatus-Consultum Establishing the Constitution of the Empire.

Title I.

1. The constitution recognizes, confirms and guarantees the grand principles proclaimed in 1789 and which are the basis of the public law of the French.

Title II. Of the Imperial Dignity and of the Regency.

2. The imperial dignity, re-established in the person of Napoleon III by the plebiscite of November 21 and 22, 1852, is hereditary in the direct and legitimate lineage of Louis-Napoleon Bonaparte, from male to male, by order of primogeniture, and to the perpetual exclusion of women and their descendants.

3. Napoleon III, if he has no male child, can adopt the children and the legitimate descendants in the masculine line of the brothers of the Emperor Napoleon I.

The forms of adoption are regulated by a law.

If, after the adoption, male children come to Napoleon III, his adopted sons can be called to succeed him only after his legitimate descendants.

Adoption is forbidden to the successors of Napoleon III and their descendants.

4. In default of legitimate heirs, direct or adopted, Prince Napoleon (Joseph-Charles-Paul) and his direct and legitimate descendants, from male to male, by order of primogeniture and to the perpetual exclusion of women and their descendants, are called to the throne.

5. In default of legitimate or adopted heirs of Napoleon III and his successors in the collateral line who obtain their rights from the preceding article, the people select the Emperor and regulate, within his family, the order of inheritance from male to male, to the perpetual exclusion of women and their descendants.

The project of plebiscite is successively deliberated upon by the Senate and the Legislative Body, upon the proposal of the ministers, formed into council of government.

Until the moment at which the election of the new Emperor is completed, the affairs of the state are governed by the ministers in office, who form themselves into a council of government and determine by the majority of votes.

6. The members of the family of Napoleon III called eventually to the inheritance and their descendants of both sexes form part of the imperial family.

They cannot marry without the authorisation of the Emperor. Their marriage without authorisation entails deprivation of all right to the inheritance, both for the one who has contracted it and his descendants.

Nevertheless, if there are no children from this marriage, in case of dissolution caused by decease, the prince who has contracted it recovers his rights to the inheritance.

The Emperor determines the titles and the status of the other members of his family.

He has full authority over them; he regulates their duties and their rights by statutes which have the force of law.

7. The regency of the Empire is regulated by the senatus-consultum of July 17, 1856.

8. The members of the imperial family called eventually to the inheritance take the title of French princes.

The eldest son of the Emperor bears the title of Prince Imperial.

9. The French princes are members of the Senate and of the Council of State when they have reached the age of eighteen completed years. They can sit therein only with the approval of the Emperor.

Title III. Forms of the Government of the Emperor.

10. The Emperor governs with the assistance of the min-

isters, the Senate, the Legislative Body and the Council of State.

11. The legislative power is exercised collectively by the Emperor, the Senate, and the Legislative Body.

12. The introduction of the laws belongs to the Emperor, the Senate and the Legislative Body.

The projects of law emanating from the initiative of the Emperor can at his option be transmitted to either the Senate or the Legislative Body.

Nevertheless, every tax-law must be first voted by the Legislative Body.

Title IV.   Of the Emperor.

13. The Emperor is responsible to the French people, to whom he has always the right to make appeal.

14. The Emperor is the head of the state. He commands the land and naval forces, declares war, makes treaties of peace, alliance and commerce, appoints to all offices, makes the rules and decrees necessary for the execution of the laws.

15. Justice is rendered in his name.

The irremovability of the judges is maintained.

16. The Emperor has the right to pardon and to grant amnesties.

17. He sanctions and promulgates the laws.

18. Future modifications by international treaties in the schedules of the custom-duties and the postoffice shall be binding only in virtue of a law.

19. The Emperor appoints and removes the ministers.

The ministers deliberate in council under the presidency of the Emperor.

They are responsible.

20. The ministers can be members of the Senate or of the Legislative Body.

They have entrance into both assemblies and must be heard whenever they request it.

21. The ministers, the members of the Senate, of the Legislative Body and of the Council of State, the officers of the army and navy, the judges and the public functionaries take the following oath:

"*I swear obedience to the constitution and fidelity to the Emperor.*"

22. The senatus-consulta of December 12, 1852, and of April 23, 1856, upon the endowment of the crown and the civil list, remain in force.

However, there shall be a law enacted in the case provided for by articles 8, 11 and 16 of the senatus-consultum of December 12, 1852.

For the future, the endowment of the crown and the civil list shall be fixed, for the entire duration of the reign, by the legislature which meets after the accession of the Emperor.

Title V. Of the Senate.

23. The Senate is composed:

1st. Of the cardinals, marshals and admirals.

2d. Of the citizens whom the Emperor raises to the dignity of senator.

24. The decrees of appointment of the senators are individual. They recount the services and indicate the titles upon which the appointment is based.

No other condition can be imposed upon the choice of the Emperor.

25. Senators are irremovable and for life.

26. The number of the senators can be brought to two-thirds of that of the members of the Legislative Body, including therein the senators *ex-officio*.

The Emperor cannot appoint more than twenty senators per annum.

27. The president and vice-president of the Senate are appointed by the Emperor and chosen from among the senators.

They are appointed for one year.

28. The Emperor convokes and prorogues the Senate.

He pronounces the closure of the sessions.

29. The sittings of the Senate are public.

Nevertheless, the Senate can form itself into secret committee in the case and according to the conditions determined by its rule.

30. ·The Senate discusses and votes the projects of law.

Title VI. Of the Legislative Body.

31. The deputies are elected by universal suffrage, without *scrutin de liste*.

32. They are elected for a term which cannot be less than six years.

33. The Legislative Body discusses and votes the projects of law.

34. The Legislative Body elects, at the opening of each session, the members who compose its *bureau*.

35. The Emperor convokes, adjourns, prorogues and dissolves the Legislative Body.

In case of dissolution, the Emperor shall convoke a new one within a period of six months.

The Emperor pronounces the closure of the Legislative Body.

36. The sittings of the Legislative Body are public.

Nevertheless, the Legislative Body can form itself into secret committee in the cases and according to the conditions determined by its rule.

Title VII. Of the Council of State.

37. The Council of State is charged, under the direction of the Emperor, to draw up the projects of law and the rules of public administration and to settle controversies which arise in matters of administration.

38. The council carries on, in the name of the government, the discussion of the projects of law before the Senate and the Legislative Body.

39. The councillors of state are appointed by the Emperor and are removable by him.

40. The ministers have rank, sitting and deliberative voice in the Council of State.

Title VIII. General Provisions.

41. The right of petition is exercised before the Senate and the Legislative Body.

42. Articles 19, 25, 27, 28, 29, 30, 31, 32, 33 of the constitution of January 14, 1852; article 2 of the senatus-consultum of December 25, 1852; articles 5 and 8 of the senatus-consultum of September 8, 1869; and all provisions contrary to the present constitution are abrogated.

43. The provisions of the constitution of January 14, 1852, and those of the senatus-consulta promulgated since that date

which are not included in the present constitution and are not abrogated by the preceding article have the force of law.

44. The constitution can be modified only by the people, upon the proposal of the Emperor.

45. The changes and the additions effected in the plebiscite of December 20 and 21, 1851, by the present constitution shall be submitted to the approval of the people in the forms determined by the decrees of December 2 and 4, 1851, and November 7, 1852.

However, the balloting shall continue but a single day.

118.   The Persigny Circular.

May 8, 1863. *Moniteur*, May 9, 1863.

Political life in France, almost extinct under the autocratic empire (See Seignobos, *Europe Since 1814*, 173-176), revived rapidly under the influence of the earlier measures of the evolution into the liberal empire. (See Nos. 117 A, B and C) The election of 1863, the first under the more liberal régime, was marked by a lively struggle between the imperial government and its political opponents, though the latter were much handicapped by the still surviving features of the despotic system. This letter, sent to the prefects by the minister of the interior, Persigny, shows something of the methods by which the imperial government influenced this as well as the preceding elections and gives in a concise form a number of the principal arguments employed in the defence of the imperial régime.

REFERENCES. Andrews, *Modern Europe*, II, 171-172 ; La Gorce, *Second empire*, IV, 220-222.

Paris, May 8, 1863.

Mr. Prefect.

The elections which are being prepared for will be for France a new opportunity to strengthen before Europe the institutions which it has given itself.

Under these circumstances I scarcely need to remind you of the principles which ought to serve you for guidance. You will not forget that the Empire is the expression of the needs, feelings, and interests of the masses, and that, before rallying to it all the living forces of the nation, it was in the cottage of the people that it passed its infancy.

Strong in his providential origin, the elect of the people has realized all the hopes of France, which he found in anarchy, misery and abasement, into which the régime of the rhetoricians had thrown it, and a few years have sufficed for him to raise it to the highest degree of wealth and grandeur.

We know how in this country distracted by so many revolutions, political, social and religious order has been restored, and the security of persons and property established as it never had been; how, in ten years, wealth in personal property has been doubled and wealth in lands augmented by 7 to 8 milliards, and the public revenue increased by 300 millions; how the territory has been ploughed over with macademised roads, highways and cross roads, and enriched with innumerable public works; how, finally, the glorious triumphs of our armies and the high influence yielded to our policy abroad have come to crown a development of prosperity until now without example in the world.

History will tell by what prodigies of wisdom, courage and skill, the elect of the people has accomplished all these things; but it will reveal also the secret of his astonishing fortune, I mean to say the absolute confidence, the touching fidelity with which, in peace or in war, in bad as well as in good circumstances, the French people have not ceased to support, surround and defend him.

It is to this confidence that the Emperor again makes appeal. He asks from the country a legislature which . . . will be as devoted as the two preceding and will have no other preoccupation than the future of the Empire.

Mr. Prefect, if in France, as in England, parties were divided only upon the conduct of affairs, but were all equally attached to our fundamental institutions, the government could confine itself in the elections to attendance upon the conflict of opinions. But in a country such as ours, which, after so many convulsions, has been seriously constituted only for ten years past, that regular play of parties, which with our neighbors so happily makes the public liberties fruitful, would at present result only in prolonging revolution and in compromising liberty; for with us there are parties which are still only factions. Formed out of the débris of overturned governments, and although enfeebled each day by time, which alone can cause them to disappear, they seek to penetrate to the heart of our institutions only in order to vitiate the principles upon which these rest, and they invoke liberty only in order to turn it against the state.

In the presence of a coalition of animosities, rancors and ill-humors opposed to the great things of the Empire, your duty, Mr. Perfect, is quite naturally traced. Filled with the liberal and democratic spirit of our institutions, which the Emperor applies himself every day to develop, you will address yourself only to the reason and heart of the people. Allow everybody to produce candidatures freely, to publish and distribute professions of faith and ballots, according to the forms prescribed by our laws. Look after the maintenance of order and the regularity of the electoral operations. It is for everybody a right and for you a duty to combat energetically all disloyal maneuvers, intrigue, surprise and fraud, and, lastly, to assure the liberty and sincerity of the ballot and the honesty of the election.

The suffrage is free. But, in order that the good faith of the people may not be deceived by skillful tongues, or by equivocal professions of faith, designate openly, as in preceding elections, the candidates who impart the most confidence to the government. Let the people know who are friends or the more or less disguised adversaries of the Empire, and let them pronounce in entire liberty, but in perfect knowledge of the case.

We are no longer in the time when elections were in the hands of a small number of privileged persons who disposed of the destinies of the country. Thanks to the Emperor, who has known how to resist both former and recent attempts of all the parties to restrict universal suffrage, and who has determined to maintain the right of every Frenchman to be an elector, France to-day, in possession of the most extensive suffrage that exists in Europe, counts 10 million electors, voting by secret ballot, each having to render account for his vote only to God and to his own conscience: it is the entire nation which, mistress of itself, cannot be dominated, forced nor corrupted by anybody.

. . . .

Receive, Mr. Prefect, the assurance of my very distinguished consideration.

The Minister of the Interior.

F. DE PERSIGNY.

119. Law upon Public Meetings.

June 6, 1868. Duvergier, *Lois*, LXVIII, 186-208.

From 1852 to 1868 the formation of associations and the holding of public meetings were regulated by the government of the Second Empire in a manner analogous to the control exercised over the press. (See No. 113). No meetings attended by more than twenty-one persons could be held, unless express authorisation was previously secured from the police. The system outlined in this law was one of the "liberal concessions" which accompanied the constitutional changes of the evolution from the autocratic to the liberal empire. (See No. 117).

REFERENCES. Seignobos, *Europe Since 1814*, 179; Lavisse and Rambaud, *Histoire générale*, XI, 185; Rambaud, *Civilisation contemporaine*, 533-534; La Gorce, *Second empire*, V, 363-369; Jaurès, *Histoire socialiste*, X, 322-323.

Title I. Of Non-Political Public Meetings.

1. Public meetings can take place without previous authorisation, under the conditions prescribed in the following articles.

Nevertheless, public meetings whose object is to treat of political or religious matters continue to be subject to that authorisation.

2. Each meeting must be preceded by a declaration signed by seven persons who are domiciled in the canton in which it is to take place and who are in the enjoyment of their civil and political rights.

This declaration sets forth the names, status and domicile of the declarants, the place, day and hour of sitting, as well as the definite and particular purpose of the meeting.

At Paris it is sent to the prefect of police; in the departments, to the prefect or sub-prefect.

A receipt for it, which must be presented at every requisition of the agents of authority, is immediately given.

The meeting cannot take place until three full days after the delivery of the receipt.

3. A meeting can be held only in a closed and covered place. It cannot be prolonged beyond the hour fixed by the competent authority for the closing of public places.

4. Each meeting must have a *bureau* composed of a president and of at least two assistants who are charged to maintain order in the assembly and to prevent any infraction of the laws.

The members of the *bureau* must not tolerate the discussion of any question foreign to the purpose of the meeting.

5. A functionary of the judicial or administrative corps, delegated by the administration, shall be present at the meeting.

He must be invested with his symbols and takes a place at his choice.

6. The functionary who is present at the meeting has the right to pronounce its dissolution: 1st, if the *bureau,* although cautioned, allows questions foreign to the purpose of the meeting to be brought under discussion; 2d, if the meeting becomes turbulent.

The persons assembled are required to separate at the first requisition.

The delegate draws up a record of the facts and transmits it to the competent authority.

.   .   .   .

Title II. Of Public Electoral Meetings.

8. Electoral meetings can be held from the promulgation of the decree of convocation of a college for the election of a deputy to the Legislative Body until the fifth day before that fixed for the opening of the ballot.

Only the electors of the electoral circumscription and the candidates who have fulfilled the frmalities prescribed by article 1 of the senatus-consultum of February 17, 1858, can be present at this meeting.

In order to be admitted they must make known their names, status and domicile.

The meeting cannot take place until one full day after the delivery of the receipt which must immediately follow the declaration.

All the other requirements of articles 2, 3, 4, 5 and 6 are applicable to electoral meetings.

.   .   .   .

13. The prefect of police at Paris and the prefects in the departments can adjourn any meeting which appears to them of a nature to disturb order or to compromise the public security.

The interdiction of a meeting can be pronounced only by the minister of the interior.

.   .   .   .

120. The Proposed Benedetti Treaty

August 20, 1866, *Archives diplomatiques, 1871-1872*, I, 266-267, 281-282, 360 (facsimile). Translation, based upon that of *Messages and Documents, Department of State, 1870-71*, 199.

This document may be regarded as a type of numerous proposals made to Prussia by Napoleon III for the purpose of securing to France some territorial compensation as reward for its neutrality during the German wars, 1864-1866. Quite different accounts of this transaction are given by Bismarck and Benedetti, the French minister at Berlin. The original is in the handwriting of Benedetti, but he declares that he wrote at the dictation of Bismarck. The document was made public by Bismarck at the beginning of the Franco-Prussian war.

REFERENCES. Fyffe, *Modern Europe*, III, 381-385 (Popular ed., 959-961); Andrews, *Modern Europe*, II, 253-254; Headlam, *Bismarck*, 262-283; La Gorce, *Second empire*, V, 62-69.

His Majesty the King of Prussia and his Majesty the Emperor of the French, deeming it useful to draw closer the bonds of friendship which unite them, and to consolidate the relations of good neighborhood happily existing between the two countries, and being convinced, on the other hand, that to attain this result, which is calculated besides to assure the maintenance of the general peace, it behooves them to come to an understanding on questions which concern their future relations, have resolved to conclude a treaty to this effect and named in consequence as their plenipotentiaries, that is to say;

His Majesty, &c., &c.

His Majesty, &c., &c.

Who, having exchanged their full powers, found to be in good and proper form, have agreed upon the following articles:

Article I. His Majesty the Emperor of the French admits and recognizes the acquisitions which Prussia has made as the result of the last war which she sustained against Austria and her allies, [*as also the arrangements adopted or to be adopted for constituting a confederation in North Germany, engaging at the same time to render his support for the maintenance of that work.*]

Article II. His Majesty the King of Prussia promises to facilitate the acquisition of Luxemburg by France; for that effect his said Majesty will enter into negotiations with His Majesty the King of the Netherlands to induce him to cede to the Emperor of the French his sovereign rights over that duchy in return for such compensation as shall be deemed sufficient or otherwise; in order to facilitate this transaction, the Emperor of the French, on his side, agrees to assure accessorily the pecuniary charge which it may involve.

Article III. His Majesty the Emperor of the French will not oppose a federal union of the confederation of the North with the southern states of Germany, with the exception of Austria, which union may be based on a common parliament, the sovereignty of the said states being respected in just measure.

Article IV. On his part his Majesty the King of Prussia, in case his Majesty the Emperor of the French should be obliged by circumstances to cause his troops to enter Belgium, or to conquer it, will grant the co-operation of his arms to France, and will sustain her with all his forces of land and sea against every power which, in that eventuality, should declare war upon her.

Article V. To insure the complete execution of the above arrangements, his Majesty the King of Prussia and his Majesty the Emperor of the French contract, by the present treaty, an offensive and defensive alliance, which they solemnly engage to maintain;—Their Majesties engage, moreover, and specifically, to observe it in every case in which their respective states, of which they mutually guarantee the integrity, should be menaced by aggression, holding themselves bound, in such conjuncture, to make without delay, and not to decline on any pretext, the military arrangements which may be demanded by their common interest, conformably to the clauses and provisions above set forth.

121. The Ems Despatch.

July 13, 1870. *Preussiche Jahrbucher,* LXXXII, 46-47.

This famous dispatch was an important factor in bringing on the Franco-Prussian war. The original version was sent to Bismarck by order of King William. The published version was edited from the original by Bismarck and printed with striking head-lines in the semi-official *North German Gazette.* The two should be carefully compared and all differences noted, especially with reference to the question whether the effect actually produced by the published version was different from that which would probably have resulted from the publication of the original dispatch.

REFERENCES. Seignobos, *Europe Since 1814*, 810; Andrews, *Modern Europe*, II, 269-270; Rose, *European Nations*, I, 50-52; Bismarck, *Reflections and Reminiscences*, II, 93-103; Headlam, *Bismarck*, 337-342; Von Sybel, *The Founding of the German Empire*, VII, 393-401; Lavisse and Rambaud, *Histoire générale*, XI, 776; La Gorce, *Second empire*, VI, 281-285.

[Original.]

Ems, July 13, 1870.

His Majesty the King writes me:

"Count Benedetti intercepted me upon the promenade, in order finally to demand of me in a very pressing manner, that I should authorise him to telegraph immediately that I pledged myself for all the future never again to give my consent, if the Hohenzollerns should renew their candidacy. I refused, at length somewhat decidedly, since one neither can nor should take such an engagement *à tout jamais*. I of course told him that I had not yet received any word, and, since he was earlier informed about Paris and Madrid than I, he could easily see that my government was again out of the game."

His Majesty has since received a message from the prince. As His Majesty said to Count Benedetti that he was expecting news from the prince, His Highness, with reference to the above-mentioned demand, upon the suggestion of Count Eulenberg, and myself, has determined

[Published.]

"Ems, July 13, 1870. After the news of the renunciation of the Hereditary Prince of Hohenzollern had been officially communicated to the French imperial government by the royal Spanish [government], the French ambassador again presented a demand to His Majesty at Ems that he should be authorised to telegraph to Paris that His Majesty the King pledges himself for all the future never again to give his consent if the Hohenzollerns should resume their candidacy. His Majesty the King thereupon refused to receive the French minister and had him told through the service-adjutant that His Majesty has nothing further to communicate to the French minister."

not to receive Count Benedetti again, but only to have
him told through an adjutant:
That His Majesty has now
received from the prince confirmation of the news which
Benedetti already had from
Paris and has nothing further
to say to the ambassador.

His Majesty leaves with
your excellency whether the
new demand of Benedetti and
its immediate rejection should
not be communicated to our
ministers and to the press.

Signed,

ABEKEN.

122. Documents upon the 4th of September.

When the French disaster at Sedan became known at Paris
the imperial government was promptly overthrown and a provisional government created.   These documents throw light upon
the spirit and the ideas which animated the new government.
Careful attention to the phraseology of the documents will bring
out some important features of the situation.

REFERENCES. Fyffe, *Modern Europe,* III, 447-448 (Popular ed.,
1002-1003) ; Seignobos, *Europe Since 1814,* 187-189 ; Coubertin,
Evolution of France under the Third Republic, 1-6 ; La Gorce,
Second empire, VII, 370-433.

A. Proclamation to the French People.   September 4,
1870. Duvergier, *Lois,* LXX, 319-320.

Frenchmen !

The people have outstripped the chamber, which was hesi-
tating.   In order to save the endangered fatherland they
have demanded the Republic.

They have placed their representatives not in power, but
in peril.

The Republic vanquished invasion in 1792, the Republic
is proclaimed.

The revolution is made in the name of the law and of the public safety.

Citizens, watch over the city which is entrusted to you; tomorrow you, with the army, shall be the avengers of the fatherland!

B. Proclamation to the Inhabitants of Paris. September 4, 1870. Duvergier, *Lois*, LXX, 320.

Citizens of Paris!
The Republic is proclaimed.
A government has been selected by acclamation.
It is composed of the citizens: *Emmanuel Arago, Crémieux, Jules Favre, Jules Ferry, Gambetta, Garnier-Pagès, Glais-Bizoin, Pelletan, Picard, Rochefort, Jules Simon,* representatives of Paris.
General *Trochu* is entrusted with full military powers for the national defence. He is summoned to the presidency of the government.
The government begs the citizens to be calm; the people will not forget that they are in the face of the enemy.
The government is before all a government of national defence.

C. Proclamation to the National Guard. September 4, 1870. Duvergier, *Lois*, LXX, 320.

Those upon whom your patriotism has just imposed the formidable task of defending the country thank you from the bottom of the heart for your courageous devotion. The civic victory whereby liberty has been restored to France is due to your resolution.
Thanks to you, that victory has not cost one drop of blood. The personal power is no more.
The entire nation resumes its rights and its arms. It stands ready to die for the defence of the soil. You have restored its soul, let despotism perish.
You will maintain the execution of the laws, and, in rivalry with our noble army, you will mount together the road of victory.

D. Decree upon the Legislative Body and the Senate. September 4, 1870. Duvergier, *Lois,* LXX, 320.

The Government, etc., decrees:

The Legislative Body is dissolved. The Senate is abolished.

E. Decree upon Political and Press Offenders. September 4, 1870. Duvergier, *Lois,* LXX, 320.

The Government, etc., decrees:

Full and complete amnesty is granted to all condemned for political crimes and offences and for press offences from December 3, 1852 to September 3, 1870. All the condemned still in custody, whether the judgments have been rendered by the correctional tribunals, or by the assize courts, or by courts martial, shall be immediately placed at liberty.

123. Diplomatic Circulars upon the Franco-Prussian War.

These diplomatic circulars, designed for communication to the neutral governments, show the ideas of the French and Prussian governments upon the proper basis for peace. Each government will be seen to have formulated a program and adduced an argument in its support. These should be carefully noted and compared.

REFERENCES. Fyffe, *Modern Europe,* III, 448-449 (Popular ed., 1003) ; Hanotaux, *Contemporary France,* I, 14-16 ; Headlam, *Bismarck,* 353-355 ; Sorel, *Histoire diplomatique de la guerre franco-allemande,* I, 296-299, 332-337.

A. Circular to French Ministers September 6, 1870. *Journal Officiel,* September 7, 1870. Translation, *Messages and Documents, State Department,* 1870-71, 139-140.

Sir,

The events which have just taken place at Paris explain themselves so well by the inexorable logic of facts that it is useless to dwell at length upon their meaning and their scope.

In yielding to an irresistible impulse, too long restrained, the people of Paris have obeyed a higher necessity, that of their own safety.

They have not been willing to perish with the criminal authority which was leading France to its destruction.

They have not pronounced the downfall of Napoleon III and of his dynasty; they have registered it in the name of right, justice, and the public safety.

And this sentence was so well ratified in advance by the consciences of all, that no one among the noisiest defenders of the authority which fell has risen to support it.

It has sunk of itself, under the weight of its faults, to the acclamations of a mighty people, without one drop of blood having been shed, without one person having been deprived of his liberty.

And we have been able to see, a thing unheard of in history, the citizens upon whom the cry of the people conferred the perilous task of fighting and conquering, not giving a moment's thought to the adversaries who yesterday threatened them with military executions. It is by refusing them the honor of any repression that their blindness and their impotence have been exhibited.

Order has not been disturbed for a single moment; our confidence in the wisdom and the patriotism of the national guard and the entire population permits us to affirm that it will not be.

Released from the shame and peril of a government recreant to all its duties, every one will understand that the first act of this national sovereignty, finally reconquering, is to command itself and to seek its strength in respect for the law.

Moreover, time presses: the enemy is at our gates; we have only one thought, to drive them from our territory.

But this obligation which we resolutely accept has not been imposed upon France by us; she would not be subject to it if our voice had been heard.

We have energetically defended, even at the expense of our popularity, the policy of peace. We shall persevere therein with a still deeper conviction.

Our heart breaks at the spectacle of these human massacres in which the flower of the two nations disappears while with a little good sense and a good deal of liberty they might have been saved from these frightful catastrophes.

We have no words which can express our admiration for our heroic army, sacrificed by the incompetence of the commander-in-chief, and yet rendered greater by its defeats than by the most brilliant victories.

For, despite the knowledge of the defeats which compromised it, it solemnly offered itself up to certain death and redeemed the honor of France from the stains of its government.

Honor to it! The nation opens its arms to it! The imperial authority wished to separate them; misfortunes and duty unite them in a solemn embrace. Sealed by patriotism and liberty, that alliance makes us invincible.

Ready for anything, we contemplate with calmness the situation which confronts us.

That situation I will state in a few words; I will submit it to the judgment of my country and of Europe.

We loudly condemned the war, and, protesting our respect for the rights of nations, we demanded that Germany be left mistress of her destinies.

We desired that liberty should be at the same time our common bond and our common shield; we were convinced that these moral forces would assure forever the maintenance of peace. But, as sanction, we demanded a weapon for each citizen, a civic organization, and elected leaders; then we would have remained invulnerable upon our soil.

The imperial government, which had long ago separated its interests from those of the country, rejected this policy. We resume it, with the hope that instructed by experience, France will have the wisdom to practice it.

On his side, the King of Prussia has declared that he was making war, not on France, but on the imperial dynasty.

The dynasty lies prostrate. Free France rises.

Does the King of Prussia desire to continue an impious struggle which will be at least as fatal to him as to us?

Does he desire to give to the world of the nineteenth century this cruel spectacle of two nations, which destroy each other, and which, forgetful of humanity, reason, and science, pile up ruins and corpses?

It is open to him; let him assume this responsibility before the world and before history!

If it is a challenge, we accept it.

We will not yield an inch of our territory, nor a stone of our fortresses.

A disgraceful peace would mean a war of extermination shortly.

We will treat only for a lasting peace.

Here, our interest is that of all Europe, and we have reason to hope that, freed from all dynastic bias the question will then be regarded in the chanceries.

But should we be alone, we shall not be feeble.

We have a resolute army, well equipped forts, strong walls, but above all the breasts of three hundred thousand fighting men determined to persevere to the last.

When they go piously to place garlands at the foot of the statue in Strasburg, they not only obey a sentiment of enthusiastic admiration, they take their heroic watch-word, they swear to be worthy of their brothers of Alsace and to die as they did.

After the forts, the ramparts; after the ramparts, the barricades. Paris can hold out three months and conquer; if it should succumb, France, rising at its call, would avenge it; it would continue the struggle, and the aggressor would perish.

This, sir, is what Europe ought to know. We have not accepted power with any other object. We would not retain it a minute if we did not find the people of Paris and all France determined to share our resolutions.

I sum them up in a word before God who hears us, and before posterity which will judge us: we only desire peace. But if a destructive war which we have denounced should be continued against us, we will do our duty to the end, and I have firm confidence that our cause, which is that of right and of justice, will finally triumph.

It is in this sense that I desire you to explain the situation to the minister of the court to which you are accredited and in whose hands you will leave a copy of this document.

Accept, sir, the expression of my high consideration.

September 6, 1870.

Signed,   The minister of foreign affairs,

JULES FAVRE.

B. Circular to Prussian Ministers. September 13, 1870. Translation, *Messages and Documents, State Department,* 1870-71, 211-212.

Rheims, September 13, 1870.

In consequence of the erroneous ideas concerning our relations with France, which reach us even from friendly quarters, I am induced to express myself in the following lines in relation to the views of his Majesty the king, which are shared by the allied German governments.

We thought we saw in the plebiscitum and the succeeding apparently satisfactory condition of things in France, a guarantee of peace, and the expression of a friendly feeling on the part of the French nation. Events have taught us the contrary; at least they have shown us how easily this voice, among the French nation, is changed to its opposite. The almost unanimous majority of the representatives of the people, of the senate, and of the organs of public opinion among the press, demanded a war of conquest against us so loudly and emphatically that the isolated friends of peace were discouraged, and the Emperor Napoleon probably told his Majesty no untruth when he declared that the state of public opinion forced him to undertake the war.

In the face of this fact we must not seek our guarantees in French feelings. We must not shut our eyes to the fact that, in consequence of this war, we must be prepared for a speedy attack from France again, and not for a permanent peace, and that quite independently of any conditions which we may impose upon France. The French nation will never forgive us for the defeat in itself, nor for our victorious repulse of its wanton attack. If we should now withdraw from France, without any acquisition of territory, without any contribution, without any advantages save the glory won by our arms, the same hatred, the same desire for revenge on account of wounded pride and ambition, would remain among the French nation, and it would only await the day when it might hope successfully to indulge these feelings. It was not a doubt of the justice of our cause, nor was it an apprehension that we might not be strong enough, that restrained us in the year 1867 from the war which was then offered us, but the fear of exciting those passions by our victories and of inaugurating an era of mutual animosity and constantly renewed wars, while we hoped, by a longer continuance and attentive care of the peaceful relations of both nations, to gain a firm foundation for an era of peace and welfare. Now, after having been forced into the war which we desired to avoid, we must seek to obtain better guarantees for our defence against the next attack of the French than those of their good feeling.

The guarantees which have been sought since the year 1815 against the same French desires and for the peace of

Europe in the Holy Alliance, and other arrangements made in the interest of Europe, have, in the course of time, lost their efficacy and significance; so that Germany has finally been obliged to defend herself against France, depending solely upon her own strength and her own resources. Such an effort as we are now making imposes such sacrifices upon the German nation that we are forced to seek material guarantees and the security of Germany against the future attacks of France, guarantees at the same time for the peace of Europe, which has nothing to fear from Germany.

These guarantees we have to demand, not from a temporary government of France, but from the French nation, which has shown that it is ready to follow any government to war against us, as is indisputably manifested by the series of aggressive wars carried on for centuries by France against Germany.

Our demands for peace can therefore only be designed to lay obstacles in the way of the next attack of France upon Germany, and especially the hitherto defenceless South German frontier, by removing this frontier, and with it the point of departure of French attacks, further back, and by seeking to bring the fortresses with which France threatens us, as defensive bulwarks, into the power of Germany.

You will express yourself in this sense, if any questions are asked of you.

BISMARCK.

C. Circular to Prussian Ministers. September 16, 1870. Translation, *Messages and Documents, State Department,* 1870-71, 212-213.

Meaux, September 16, 1870.

You are aware of the contents of the document which M. Jules Favre has addressed to the representatives of France abroad, in the name of the present authorities in Paris, who style themselves the government of the national defence.

It has, at the same time, come to my knowledge, that M. Thiers has undertaken a confidential mission to several foreign courts, and I presume that it will be his task, on the one hand to inspire confidence in the desire for peace of the present Paris government, and on the other to seek the inter-

vention of neutral powers in favor of a peace designed to rob
Germany of the fruits of her victory, and to prevent the
establishment of any basis of peace which might lay obstacles
in the way of the next French attack upon Germany.

We cannot believe in the earnest intention of the present
Paris government to put an end to the war, so long as it
continues to excite the passions of the people by its language
and its acts, to increase the hatred and the bitter feeling of
the population, already excited by the sufferings caused by
the war, and to condemn in advance as inadmissible for
France, every basis of peace which can be accepted by Germany. It thereby renders peace impossible, for which it
should prepare the people by mild language, duly considering
the serious nature of the situation, if it would lead us to believe that it aims at honest negotiations for peace with us.
It could only be seriously supposed that we would now conclude an armistice without every security for our conditions
of peace, if we were thought to lack military and political sagacity, and to be indifferent to the interests of Germany.

Another thing which prevents the French from clearly com-
prehending the necessity of peace with Germany, is the hope,
which is encouraged by the present authorities, of a diplomatic
or material intervention of neutral powers in favor of France.
If the French nation becomes convinced, that, as it alone
voluntarily inaugurated the war, and as Germany has been
obliged to carry on the contest alone, it will be compelled to
settle the account with Germany alone, it will soon put an
end to its now certainly useless resistance. It is cruelty on
the part of neutral nations towards France if they permit
the Paris government to encourage unrealizable hopes of intervention among the people and thereby to prolong the
struggle.

We are far from any desire to interfere in the internal
affairs of France. It is a matter of indifference to us what
sort of a government the French [people] may choose for
itself. The government of the Emperor Napoleon is the only
one which has been formally recognized by us. Our terms
of peace, with whatever government, authorised for the purpose, we may have to negotiate them, are entirely independent
of the question, how and by whom the French nation is governed; they are dictated to us by the nature of the case, and

by the law of self-defence against a turbulent and quarrel-
some people on our frontier. The unanimous voice of the
German governments and of the German people demands that
Germany be protected by better boundaries than heretofore
against the threats and outrages which have been committed
against us for centuries by all French governments. As long
as France remains in possession of Strasburg and Metz her
offensive is strategically stronger than our defence, throughout the entire south and that portion of the north of Germany which lies on the left bank of the Rhine. Strasburg
is, in the possession of France, a constantly open sally-port
against South Germany. In the possession of Germany, on
the other hand, Strasburg and Metz acquire a defensive character. In more than twenty wars we have never been the
aggressor against France, and we desire nothing from that
country but our own safety, which has been so often jeop-
ardized by it. France, on the contrary, will regard any peace
which may now be concluded simply as a suspension of hostilities, and will again assail us, in order to be avenged for
her present defeat, with just as little reason as she has done
this year, as soon as she feels strong enough to do so, either
through her own strength or through foreign alliances.

In rendering it difficult for France (which has been the
originator of every disturbance of the peace of Europe hitherto) to act on the offensive, we are acting, at the same time,
in the interest of Europe, which is that of peace. No disturbance of the peace of Europe is to be feared from Germany. Since the war has been forced upon us, which we have
shunned for four years with the utmost care and at a sacrifice of our national feeling, which has been incessantly hec-
tored by France, we will demand security in future as the
price of the gigantic efforts which we have been obliged to
make in our defence. No one will be able to reproach us
for want of moderation if we adhere to this just and reasonable demand.

I desire you carefully to take cognizance of these ideas
and present them for consideration in your interviews.

BISMARCK.

124. Decrees and Laws upon the Executive Power, 1871-1873.

These documents exhibit in large measure the nature of the government of France during the presidency of Thiers. By combining what is enacted for some institutions and what is implied or declared with reference to others with what is carried over from the preceding decree, each of the documents may be regarded as a sort of provisional constitution of France. They should be examined in that light.

REFERENCES. Seignobos, *Europe Since 1814*, 194-197; Bodley, *France*, I, 271-276; Hanotaux, *Contemporary France*, I, 66-67, 265-270, 584-588; Lavisse and Rambaud, *Histoire générale*, XII, 2, 8, 12; Rambaud, *Civilisation contemporaine*, 523-524.

A. Decree Appointing Thiers. February 17, 1871. Duvergier, *Lois,* LXXI, 54-55.

The National Assembly, depository of the sovereign authority,

Considering that it is necessary, while awaiting what may be enacted as to the institutions of France, to provide immediately for the necessities of the government and for the conduct of the negotiations, decrees:

M. Thiers is appointed head of the executive power of the French Republic; he shall exercise his functions, under the authority of the National Assembly, with the assistance of the ministers whom he shall have chosen and over whom he shall preside.

B. The Rivet Law. August 31, 1871. Duvergier, *Lois,* LXXI, 210-212.

The National Assembly,

Considering that it has the right to use the constituent power, an essential attribute of the sovereignty with which it is invested, and that the imperative duties, which at the first it was bound to impose upon itself and which are still far from being completed, have alone prevented until now the use of this power;

Considering that, until the establishment of the definitive institutions of the country, it is essential for the needs of labor, the interests of commerce, and the development of industry, that our provisional institutions should take in the eyes of all, if not that stability which is the work of time, at least such that they may assure the harmony of feeling and the appeasement of parties;

Considering that a new title, a more precise appellation, without in any degree altering the basis of things, may have the effect of putting better in evidence the intention of the assembly to continue freely the loyal experiment begun at Bordeaux;

That the prolongation of the functions conferred upon the head of the executive power, limited henceforth to the duration of the labors of the assembly, may free these functions from what they may seem to have of instability and precariousness, without the sovereign rights of the assembly suffering the least injury, since in any case the final determination belongs to the assembly; and that an ensemble of new guarantees is about to assure the maintenance of these parliamentary privileges, at once the safeguard and the honor of the country;

Taking into consideration, moreover, the distinguished services rendered to the country by M. Thiers during the past six months and the guarantees which the continuance of the power that he holds from the assembly presents;

Decrees:

1. The head of the executive power shall take the title of *President of the French Republic* and shall continue to exercise, under the authority of the National Assembly, as long as it shall not have terminated its labors, the functions which were delegated to him by the decree of February 17, 1871.

2. The President of the Republic promulgates the laws as soon as they are transmitted to him by the president of the National Assembly.

He secures and supervises the execution of the laws.

He resides at the place where the National Assembly sits.

He is heard by the National Assembly whenever he believes it necessary and after he has informed the president of the National Assembly of his wish.

He appoints and dismisses the ministers. The council of ministers and the ministers are responsible to the assembly.

Each of the acts of the President of the Republic must be countersigned by a minister.

3. The President of the Republic is responsible to the assembly.

C.   Law upon the Presidency. March 13, 1873. Duvergier, *Lois,* LXXIII, 51-63.

The National Assembly,
Reserving in its entirety the constituent power which belongs to it, but wishing to bring about improvements in the distribution of the public powers, decrees:
1. The law of August 31, 1871, is modified as follows:
The President of the Republic communicates with the assembly by messages which, with the exception of those with which the sessions are opened, are read at the tribune by a minister.
Nevertheless, he shall be heard by the assembly in the discussion of the laws, when he shall deem it necessary, and after he has informed it of his wish by a message.
The discussion upon the occasion at which the President of the Republic expresses a wish to take the word is suspended after the receipt of the message, and the President shall be heard the next day, unless a special vote decides that he shall be heard the same day. The sitting is terminated after he has been heard, and the discussion is resumed only at a subsequent sitting. The discussion occurs outside of the presence of the President of the Republic.
2. The President of the Republic promulgates the laws declared urgent within three days, and the non-urgent laws within the month following the vote of the assembly. .
Within the space of three days, when a law that has not been submitted to three readings is in question, the President of the Republic shall have the right to demand, by a message with a statement of reasons, a new deliberation.
For the laws submitted to the formality of the three readings, the President of the Republic shall have the right, after the second, to demand that the placing of it as the order of the day for the third deliberation be fixed only after the space of two months.
3. The provisions of the preceding article shall not apply to the acts in which the National Assembly shall exercise the

constituent power which is reserved in the preamble of the present law.

4. Interpellations can be addressed only to the ministers, and not to the President of the Republic.

When interpellations addressed to the ministers or petitions sent to the assembly relate to foreign affairs, the President of the Republic shall have the right to be heard.

When these interpellations or these petitions have relation to the internal policy, the ministers shall reply only for the acts which concern them. Nevertheless, if by a special resolution, communicated to the assembly before the opening of the discussion by the vice-president of the council of ministers, the council should declare that the questions raised are bound up with the general policy of the government and thus involve the responsibility of the President of the Republic, the President shall have the right to be heard in the forms determined by the first article.

After having heard the vice-president of the council, the assembly fixes the day for the discussion.

5. The National Assembly shall not separate before having enacted:

1st. Upon the organization and the method of transmission of the legislative and executive powers;

2d. Upon the creation and prerogatives of a second chamber, which is not to enter upon its functions until after the separation of the present assembly;

3d. Upon the electoral law.

The government shall submit to the assembly projects of law upon the above enumerated matters.

125. Preliminary Treaty of Versailles.

February 26, 1871. De Clercq, *Traités*, X, 430-435. Translation, Hertslet, *Map of Europe by Treaty*, 1912-1918.

As the stipulations of this treaty were reproduced without any very considerable change in the definitive treaty of Frankfort, this document shows substantially the terms of peace at the end of the Franco-Prussian war.

REFERENCES. Fyffe, *Modern Europe*, III, 464-465 (Popular ed., 1013-1014); Seignobos, *Europe Since 1814*, 818; Hanotaux, *Contemporary France*, I, 119-131; Sorel, *Histoire diplomatique de la guerre franco-allemande*, II, 231-251.

Between the Chancellor of the Germanic Empire, Count Otto Bismarck-Schönhausen, . . . representing the Germanic Empire, on the one part; and on the other part, the Chief of the Executive Power of the French Republic, Monsieur Thiers, and the minister for foreign affairs, Monsieur Jules Favre, representing France; . . . the following has been agreed upon to serve as a preliminary basis to the definitive peace to be concluded hereafter.

1. . . . [Contains the cession of territory made by France to Germany. This cession, as slightly modified by the definitive treaty of Frankfort, is shown upon maps in Hertslet, *Map of Europe by Treaty*, 1962-1963, and Putzger, *Historischer Schul-Atlas*, 29.]

2. France shall pay to His Majesty the Emperor of Germany the sum of five milliard francs.

The payment of at least one milliard francs shall be effected within the year 1871, and the whole of the remainder of the debt in the space of three years dating from the ratification of the present articles.

3. . . . [Provides in detail for the gradual evacuation of French territory as the payments upon the indemnity are made.]

4. The German troops shall abstain from levying contributions either in money or in kind in the occupied departments. On the other hand, the maintenance of the German troops remaining in France shall be at the expense of the French government in the manner decided upon by an agreement with the German military administration.

.   .   .   .

126. Declaration of the Paris Commune.

April 19, 1871. *Revue de France, Supplement. Actes du gouvernment révolutionnaire de Paris*, XXXIX-XL.

The ideas of the Paris Communards may be divided into two classes: (1) negative, a common hatred of monarchy and the bourgeois republic, one of which they expected the National Assembly to establish; (2) positive, a great variety of political and social theories, represented by different groups of Communards. This document, which was the chief political act of the Commune, throws light upon both sets of ideas. For the negative class, the intensity of feeling which the document shows should be noted. The positive ideas should be compared with (1) those of the extreme revolutionary parties of earlier crises, (2) those of the different groups represented among the Communards, (3) the requirements of the existing situation in France.

REFERENCES. Seignobos, *Europe Since 1814*, 190-194 ; Andrews, *Modern Europe*, II, 345-349 ; Dickinson, *Revolution and Reaction in Modern France*, Ch. VIII ; Hanotaux, *Contemporary France*, I, 166-169 ; Lavisse and Rambaud, *Histoire générale*, XII, 2-7 ; Jaurès, *Histoire socialiste*, XI, 422-424.

Declaration to the French People.

In the painful and terrible conflict which once again imposes upon Paris the horrors of siege and bombardment, which causes French blood to flow, which causes our brothers, our wives, and our children to perish, sinking before shells and grape shot, it is necessary that public opinion should not be divided and that the national conscience should not be troubled.

It is necessary that Paris and the whole country should know what is the nature, the reason, and the aim of the revolution which is accomplished. It is necessary, in fine, that the responsibility for the sorrows, the sufferings and the misfortunes of which we are the victims should return upon those who, after having betrayed France and delivered Paris to the foreigner, are seeking with a blind and cruel obstinacy the ruin of the capital, in order to conceal in the disaster to the Republic and to liberty the double testimony to their treason and their crime.

It is the duty of the commune to ascertain and assert the aspirations and the views of the population of Paris, to state precisely the character of the movement of March 18, misunderstood, unknown and calumniated by the politicians who sit at Versailles.

Once again Paris labors and suffers for all France, for which by her conflicts and sacrifices she prepares intellectual, moral, administrative and economic regeneration, glory and prosperity.

What does she ask for?

The recognition and consolidation of the Republic, the only form of government compatible with the rights of the people and the regular and free development of society;

The absolute autonomy of the commune extended to all the localities in France, and insuring to each the integrity of its rights and to every Frenchman the full exercise of his faculties and aptitudes, as man, citizen and worker;

The autonomy of the commune shall have for its limits only the equal right of autonomy for all the other communes adhering to the contract, the association of which must insure French unity.

The rights inherent in the commune are:

The voting of the communal budget, receipts and expenditures; the determination and partition of taxation; the management of the local services; the organization of its magistrature, the internal police and education; the administration of the property belonging to the commune;

The choice by election or competition, with responsibility and the permanent right of control and removal, of the communal magistrates and functionaries of all sorts;

The absolute guarantee of personal liberty, liberty of conscience and liberty of labor;

The permanent participation of the citizens in communal affairs by the free expression of their ideas and the free defence of their interests; guarantees to be given for these expressions by the commune, which alone is to be charged with the supervision and assuring of the free and just exercise of the right of meeting and of publicity;

The organization of urban defence and of the national guard, which elects its leaders and alone watches over the maintenance of order within the city.

Paris wishes for nothing more in the way of local guarantees, on condition, well understood, of finding in the grand central administration, the delegation of the federated communes, the realization and the practice of the same principles.

But, in favor of its autonomy and profiting from its liberty of action, Paris reserves to herself to effect for herself, as she may think proper, the administrative and economic reforms which her population demands, to create suitable institutions to develop and promote education, production, exchange and credit; to universalize power and property, according to the necessities of the moment and the opinion of those interested and the data furnished by experience.

Our enemies deceive themselves or deceive the country when they accuse Paris of wishing to impose its will or its supremacy upon the remainder of the nation and of designing a dictatorship which would be a veritable attack upon the independence and sovereignty of the other communes.

They deceive themselves or deceive the country when they accuse Paris of seeking the destruction of French unity, established by the revolution amid the acclamations of our fathers flocking to the fête of the federation from all points of old France.

Unity such as has been imposed on us up to this day by the Empire, the monarchy and parliamentarism is only despotic, unintelligent, arbitrary and onerous centralization.

Political unity such as Paris wishes is the voluntary association of all the local initiatives, the free and spontaneous co-operation of all the individual energies in view of a common purpose, the welfare, the liberty and the security of all.

The communal revolution, begun by the popular initiative of March 18, inaugurates a new political era, experimental, positive, and scientific.

It is the end of the old governmental and clerical world, of militarism, officialism, exploitation, stock jobbing, monopolies, and privileges, to which the proletariat owes its servitude and the fatherland its misfortunes and its disasters.

Let this beloved and splendid fatherland, imposed upon by falsehoods and calumnies, reassure itself then!

The struggle brought on between Paris and Versailles is one of those which cannot be terminated by illusory compromises; the issue of it cannot be doubtful. Victory, pursued with an indomitable energy by the national guard, will remain with the idea and the right.

We appeal, therefore, to France!

Informed that Paris in arms possesses as much of calmness as of bravery; that it preserves order with as much energy as enthusiasm; that it sacrifices itself with as much reason as heroism; and that it has armed itself only out of devotion to the liberty and glory of all; let France cause this bloody conflict to cease!

It is for France to disarm Versailles by the solemn expression of her irresistible will.

Summoned to profit from our conquests, let her declare herself identified with our efforts; let her be our ally in this conflict which can end only by the triumph of the communal idea or the ruin of Paris!

As for ourselves, citizens of Paris, we have the mission of accomplishing the modern revolution, the greatest and the most fruitful of all those which have illuminated history.

It is our duty to struggle and to conquer!

Paris, April 19, 1871.   THE COMMUNE OF PARIS.

127. Laws for Reorganizing Local Government.

These laws with No. 128 are the most important of the reorganization measures of the Thiers government. The system outlined in them still exists with but little change. It should be compared with that of the Second Empire.

REFERENCES. Seignobos, *Europe Since 1814*, 195; Hanotaux, *Contemporary France*, I, 235-240; Rose, *European Nations*, I, 141-143; Lavisse and Rambaud, *Histoire générale*, XII, 9-10; Rambaud, *Civilisation contemporaine*, 545-546; Jaurès, *Histoire socialiste*, XII, 14-17.

A. Communal Law. April 14, 1871. Duvergier, *Lois*, LXXI, 71-79.

．　　．　　．　　．　　．　　．　　．　　．　　．

2. Within the shortest possible space of time after the promulgation of the present law, the government shall convoke the electors in all the communes in order to proceed to the entire renewal of the municipal councils.

3. The elections shall take place by *scrutin de liste* for every commune. Nevertheless the commune can be divided into sections, each of which shall elect a number of councillors proportionate to the figure of the population. . . .

4. All French citizens fully 21 years of age, in enjoyment of their civil and political rights, not being in any position of incapacity as provided by the law, and having for at least a year past their actual domicile in the commune, are electors.

All the electors 25 years of age meeting the conditions provided in the preceding paragraph . . . are eligible to the municipal council of a commune.

Moreover, there can be chosen to the municipal council of a commune, without the condition of domicile, a fourth of the members who shall compose it, on condition that the elected who are not domiciled pay in the said commune one of the four direct taxes.

．　　．　　．　　．　　．　　．　　．　　．　　．

7. In all of the communes, whatever may be their population, the balloting shall continue only one day. It shall be opened and closed on a Sunday. The counting shall be done immediately.

8. The municipal councils selected shall remain in office until the promulgation of the organic law upon the municipalities. Nevertheless, the duration of their functions cannot exceed three years. . . .

9. The municipal council shall elect the mayor and the assistants from among its own members by secret ballot and majority. If after two ballots no candidate has obtained the majority the procedure shall be by *ballotage* between the two candidates who have obtained the most votes. . . .

The mayors and the assistants thus elected shall be removable by decree.

Dismissed mayors and assistants shall not be re-eligible for a year. The selection of the mayors and the assistants shall take place provisionally by decree of the government in the cities of more than 20,000 souls and in the head towns of the department and the district, whatever may be their population. The mayors shall be taken from within the municipal council.

.   .   .   .

10-17. [Provide a special municipal system for Paris.]

.   .   .   .

19. The functions of mayor, assistants and municipal councillors are essentially gratuitous.

.   .   .   .

B. Departmental Law. August 10, 1871. Duvergier, *Lois*, LXXI, 181-210.

Title. I. General Provisions.

1. There is in each department a general council.

2. The general council elects from within its own body a departmental commission.

3. The prefect is the representative of the executive authority within the department. He is, in addition, charged with the preliminary investigation of matters which are of importance to the department, as well as the carrying out of the decisions of the general council and of the departmental

commission, in conformity with the provisions of the present law.

Title II.   Of the Formation of the General Councils.

4. Each canton of the department elects one member of the general council.

5. The election is made by universal suffrage, in each commune from the lists drawn up for the municipal elections.

6. All citizens enrolled upon a list of electors, or proving that they ought to be enrolled there before the day of the election, fully twenty-five years of age, who are domiciled within the department, and those who, without being domiciled there, are listed there upon the roll of one of the direct taxes on the 1st of January of the year in which the election takes place, or who prove that they ought to be enrolled there on that day or that they have inherited since the same date a real estate property within the department, are eligible to the general council. However, the general councillors not domiciled cannot exceed one-fourth the total number of which the council shall be composed.

. . . .

14. No one is elected a member of the general council at the first ballot, unless he unites: 1st, a majority of the votes cast; 2d, a number of votes equal to a fourth of that of the enrolled electors.

At the second ballot, the election takes place by plurality, whatever may be the number of voters. If several candidates obtain the same number of votes, the election is awarded to the eldest.

. . . .

21. The general councillors are selected for six years; they are renewed by half every three years and are re-eligible indefinitely. . . .

. . . .

Title III.   Of the Sessions of the General Councils.

23. The general councils have each year two ordinary sessions.

The session in which the budget and the accounts are considered commences *ipso facto* the first Monday which follows August 15 and can be postponed only by a law.

The opening of the other session takes place upon the day fixed by the general council in the session of the preceding August. . . .

The duration of the August session cannot exceed one month; that of the other ordinary session cannot exceed fifteen days.

.   .   .   .

27. The prefect has entrance to the general council; he is heard when he demands it and is present at the deliberations, except when the auditing of his accounts is in question.

28. The sittings of the general councils are public. Nevertheless, upon the request of five members, the president or the prefect, the general council, by rising and sitting, without debate, decides whether it will form itself into secret committee.

.   .   .   .

33. Every act and every decision of a general council in relation to matters which are not legally included within its powers is null and void. The nullity is pronounced by a decree rendered in the form of public administrative regulations.

.   .   .   .

35. During the sessions of the National Assembly the dissolution of a general council can be pronounced by the head of the executive power only under the express obligation to render an account of it to the assembly within the shortest space of time possible. . . .

36. In the interim of the sessions of the National Assembly, the head of the executive power can pronounce the dissolution of a general council for causes peculiar to this council.

.   .   .   .

Title IV. Of the Attributes of the General Councils.

37. The general council apportions each year, at its August session, the direct taxes, in conformity with the rules established by the laws.

.   .   .   .

40. The general council votes the additional centimes the collection of which is authorised by the laws.

.   .   .   .

It can vote extraordinary centimes within the limit of the maximum annually fixed by the law of finances.

It can likewise vote departmental loans, reimbursable within a period which cannot exceed fifteen years, out of the ordinary and extraordinary resources.

. . . .

42. The general council determines each year at its August session, within the limits annually fixed by the law of finances, the maximum number of extraordinary centimes which the municipal councils are authorised to vote, in order to appropriate the proceeds of them for extraordinary expenses of communal utility.

. . . .

44. The general council effects the recognition, determines the width and prescribes the opening and repair of crossroads which are highways and of common interest. . . .

. . . .

46. The general council decides finally upon the matters hereinafter designated, to wit:

[Here follow twenty-six distinct matters embracing the more important powers of local administration.]

47. The resolutions in which the general councils make definitive decisions are carried into effect, unless within a period of twenty days, dating from the close of the session, the prefect has demanded the setting aside of them for excess of power or for violation of a provision of a law or a regulation of public administration.

. . . .

48. The general council deliberates over:

[Here follow five important matters of local government.]

49. The resolutions taken by the general council upon the matters enumerated in the preceding article are carried into effect, unless within a period of three months, dating from the closing of the session, a decree with statement of reasons has suspended their execution.

50. The general council gives its opinion upon:

[Here follow three matters of local government.]

51. The general council can address directly to the minister concerned, through the medium of its president, the complaints which it shall have to present in the special interest of the department, as well as its opinion upon the condition

and the needs of the different public services, in that which touches the department.

. . . .

All expressions of political opinions are forbidden to it. Nevertheless, it can express opinions upon all economic and general administrative questions.

. . . .

Title V. Of the Budget and of the Accounts of the Department.

57. The project for the budget of the department is prepared and presented by the prefect, who is required to communicate it to the departmental commission, with the corroborative documents, at least ten days before the opening of the August session.

The budget, considered by the general council, is definitively determined by decree.

It is divided into ordinary budget and extraordinary budget.

. . . .

Title VI. Of the Departmental Commission.

69. The departmental commission is elected each year at the end of the August session.

It is composed of at least four members and of seven at most, and it includes one member chosen, as nearly as possible, from among the councillors elected or domiciled in each district. The members of the commission are re-eligible indefinitely.

. . . .

75. The members of the departmental commission do not receive any compensation.

76. The prefect or his representative is present at the sittings of the commission; they are heard when they demand it.

. . . .

77. The departmental commission controls the matters which are remitted to it by the general council, within the limits of the delegation that is made to it. It deliberates over all the questions that are referred to it by the prefect, and it gives its opinion to the prefect upon all the questions which

he submits to it or upon which it believes that it ought to call his attention in the interest of the department.

. . . .

79. At the opening of each ordinary session of the general council, the departmental commission makes a report to it upon the whole of its labors and submits to it all the proposals that it believes useful.

At the opening of the August session, it presents in a summary report its observations upon the budget proposed by the prefect. These reports are printed and distributed, unless the commission decides otherwise in regard to them.

. . . .

Special or Temporary Provisions.

94. The present law is not applicable to the department of the Seine. A special law shall be enacted in respect to it.

128. Law for Reorganizing the Army.

July 27, 1872. Duvergier, *Lois*, LXXII, 332-362.

The disasters of the Franco-Prussian war making necessary a complete reorganization of the French army, this law was passed after careful consideration, and with very slight alterations it is still in force. Two features of it call for particular notice, (1) the principle upon which military service is based, (2) the manner in which that principle is applied.

REFERENCES. Seignobos. *Europe Since 1814*, 195 ; Hanotaux, *Contemporary France*, I, 465-468 ; Lavisse and Rambaud, *Histoire générale*, XII, 10 ; Rambaud. *Civilisation contemporaine*, 564-570 ; Rose, *European Nations*, I, 143-144 ; Jaurès, *Histoire socialiste*, XII, 73-74.

Title I. General Provisions.

1. Every Frenchman owes personal military service.

. . . .

3. Every Frenchman who is not declared unfit for all military service can be summoned, from the age of twenty years to that of forty years, to make up part of the active army and of the reserves, according to the mode determined by the law.

4. Substitution is suppressed.

The exemptions from service, under the conditions specified by the law, are not granted as final discharges.

5. The men present in person do not take part in any voting.

. . . .

Title II. Of the Summonses.

. . . . . .

Section II. Of the exemptions. . . .

16. Young men whose infirmities render them unfit for all active or auxiliary service in the army are exempt from military service.

17. These are exempt from military service in time of peace:

1st The eldest of orphans who have lost both father and mother;

2d. The only son or the eldest of the sons, or in default of son or son-in-law, the only grandson or the eldest of the grandsons of a woman actually a widow, or a woman whose husband has been legally pronounced absent, or of a father who is blind or has entered upon his seventieth year;

In the cases provided for by the two preceding paragraphs, the younger brother shall enjoy the exemption if the elder brother is blind or afflicted with any other incurable infirmity which renders him impotent;

3d. The elder of two brothers summoned to make up part of the same drawing, if the younger is pronounced fit for the service;

4th. One whose brother shall be in the active army;

5th. One whose brother shall have died in active service or shall have been discharged or allowed to retire on account of wounds received in a required service or on account of infirmities contracted in the army or navy.

. . . .

20. These are by conditional right exempt from military service:

[Seven different classes are named. With the exception of a few artists, all are either teachers or students preparing themselves for places of public utility in state or church.]

. . . . . .

22. Young men designated by the municipal councils of the commune where they are domiciled as the indispensable supporters of families can be exempted by provisional title, if they discharge these duties efficiently. . . .

These exemptions can be granted up to the extent of four

per cent. per department of the number of young men pronounced fit for the service. . . .

. . . .

Title III. Of the Military Service.

36. Every Frenchman who is not declared unfit for all military service makes up part:

Of the active army for five years;

Of the reserve of the active army for four years;

Of the territorial army for five years;

Of the reserve of the territorial army for six years.

1st. The active army, independently of the men who are not recruited by the summons, is composed of all the young men declared fit for one of the services of the army and included in the last five classes summoned;

2d. The reserve of the active army is composed of all the men likewise declared fit for one of the services of the army and included in the four classes summoned immediately before those which form the active army;

3d. The territorial army is composed of all the men who have completed the time of service prescribed for the active army and the reserve;

4th. The reserve of the territorial army is composed of the men who have completed the time of service for that army.

. . . .

40. After a year of service no more of the young men in the conditions set forth in the preceding article, [i.e., all who are taken into the active army] are kept with the colors than the number of men fixed each year by the minister of war.

41. Nothwithstanding the provisions of the preceding article, the soldier included in the category of those not bound to remain with the colors, but who, after the year of service mentioned in the said article, does not know how to read and write and does not meet the examinations prescribed by the minister of war, can be kept in the ranks for a second year.

The soldier, placed in the same category, who, by instruction acquired prior to his entrance into the service and by that received with the colors, fulfils all the conditions required after six months, at dates fixed by the minister of war and before the expiration of the year, can be sent to his home upon the unattached list, in accordance with the following article.

42. The young men who, after the time of service prescribed by articles 40 and 41, are not kept with the colors remain in their homes on the unattached list of the active army and at the disposal of the minister of war. They are by a regulation of the minister of war subject to reviews and drills.

. . . .

Title V. Of Enlistments, Re-enlistments and Conditional Enlistments.

. . . .

Section III. Of conditional enlistments for one year.

53. The young men who have obtained the diplomas of bachelor of letters, bachelor of science, the diplomas of completion of studies or certificates of capacity established by articles 4 and 6 of the law of June 21, 1865; those who make up part of the central school of arts and manufactures, the national schools of arts and crafts, the national schools of fine arts, the Conservatory of Music; the pupils of the national veterinary schools and the national schools of agriculture; the day-scholars of the school of mines, the school of bridges and roads, the school of naval engineering and the pupils of the Saint Stephen school of miners, before the drawing of the lot, when they present the certificates of studies designated by a regulation inserted in the Bulletin of the Laws, are allowed to contract conditional enlistments in the army for one year, according to the mode prescribed by the said regulation.

54. Independently of the young men indicated in the preceding article, those who meet one of the examinations required by the different programs prepared by the minister of war and approved by decrees rendered in the form of public administrative regulations are allowed before the drawing of the lot to contract a similar engagement.

. . . .

55. The volunteer enlisted for one year is clothed, mounted, equipped and supported at his own expense.

However, the minister of war can exempt from all or part of the obligations prescribed in the preceding paragraph the young men who have given in their examination proofs of capacity and who prove in the forms prescribed by the regulation that it is impossible for them to meet the expenses resulting from these obligations.

.   .   .   .

129. Documents upon the Overthrow of Thiers.

During the latter part of 1872 Thiers alienated many members of the National Assembly who had at first supported him. All the monarchists were offended by his announcement that in his opinion the time had come when the question of the definitive form of government should be settled and that the Republic was the form which ought to be adopted. Some conservative republicans were offended at his refusal to use his presidential authority for the repression of the radical republican agitation going on in the country. These documents show how the two groups by combining forces brought about the overthrow of Thiers. They also show the precise issues raised and something of the attitudes towards them. Document A was presented by the monarchists. Document B is Thiers' reply to document A. The scheme of government which is brought forward should be compared with the constitution afterwards adopted (see No. 133). Document C is the proposition upon which the voting occurred. It was adopted, 360 to 345. Document D was read in the National Assembly to explain the votes cast by the fifteen conservative republicans who signed it. Document E was issued by the radical republicans after the resignation of Thiers. Gambetta was its author.

REFERENCES. Seignobos, *Europe Since 1814*, 196-197 ; Andrews, *Modern Europe*, II, 351-352 ; Hanotaux, *Contemporary France*, I, 622-652 ; Simon, *The Government of Thiers*, II, 424-465 ; Lavisse and Rambaud, *Histoire générale*, XII, 10-13 ; Jaurès, *Histoire socialiste*, XII, 98-104.

A. The De Bróglie Interpellation. May 19, 1873. *Journal Officiel,* May 20, 1873 (Vol. 1873, 3204).

The undersigned, convinced that the gravity of the situation requires at the head of affairs a cabinet whose firmness reassures the country, ask to interpellate the ministry upon the late alterations which have just been effected in their body and upon the necessity of causing to prevail in the government a resolutely conservative policy.

They propose to fix upon Friday as the day for the discussion of this interpellation.

B. The Government Proposals. May 19, 1873. *Journal Officiel,* May 20, 1873 (Vol. 1873, 3208-3209).

Project of Law.

1. The government of the Republic is composed of a sen-

ate, a chamber of representatives, and a president of the Republic, head of the executive power.

2. The senate is formed out of 265 members, French citizens at least thirty-five years of age and enjoying all their civil, political and family rights.

The chamber of representatives is formed out of 537 members, French citizens, at least twenty-five years of age and enjoying all their civil, political and family rights.

The president of the Republic must be at least forty years of age and must enjoy all his civil, political and family rights.

3. The senate is selected for ten years and is renewed by a fifth every two years.

The chamber of representatives is selected for five years, and is renewed as a body after the fifth year.

The president of the Republic is selected for five years; he can be re-elected.

4. Each of the eighty-six departments of France selects three senators; the territory of Belfort, the departments of Algeria, the islands of Réunion, Martinique and Guadeloupe each elects one.

The election is made by the direct vote of the electors of the department, territory or colony; and by *scrutin de liste* for the departments of France.

5. Only the following can be elected to the position of senator:

1st. The members of the chamber of representatives;

2d. The former members of the legislative assemblies;

3d. The ministers and former ministers;

4th. The members of the Council of State, of the court of cassation and of the court of accounts;

5th. The presidents and former presidents of the general councils:

6th. The members of the Institute;

7th. The appointed members of the superior council of commerce, agriculture and industry;

8th. The cardinals, archbishops and bishops;

9th. The presidents of the two consistories of the confession of Augsburg which count the greatest number of electors and of the twelve consistories of the reformed religion which count the greatest number of electors;

10th. The president and the grand rabbi of the central consistory of the Israelites of France;

11th. The marshals and generals of division and the admirals and vice-admirals in active service or upon the reserve list, the governors of Algeria and of the three great colonies who have exercised these functions for five years;

12th. The prefects in active service;

13th. The mayors of cities of over 100,000 souls;

14th. The functionaries who for two years have filled the positions of directors in the central administrations of the ministries:

15th. The retired magistrates who have belonged to the court of cassation or to the court of appeals, or who have filled the position of president of a civil tribunal.

6. The eligibles designated in paragraphs 1, 4 and 12 of the preceding article shall declare within the fifteen days which shall follow the elections whether they intend to accept the position of senator. Their silence shall be equivalent to a refusal; their acceptance shall entail *ipso facto* their resignation from the posts which they occupy.

7. Each of the 362 districts of France, including therein the territory of Belfort, selects one representative. Nevertheless, the district whose population exceeds 100,000 inhabitants shall elect as many representatives as it shall have times 100,000 inhabitants, every supplementary fraction counting as 100,000 inhabitants.

The apportionment cannot be altered except in virtue of the quinquennial census of the population and through a law.

Two representatives are assigned to each of the departments of Algeria and one to each of the six colonies of Réunion, Martinique, Guadeloupe, Senegal, Guiana and French India.

8. The election of the representatives is made by the direct vote of all the electors of the district. The district which shall have several representatives to select shall be divided into as many sections as it shall have representatives. The sections shall be formed by agglomerations of cantons. They cannot be established or modified except by a law.

9. The President of the Republic is selected by a congress composed of: 1st, the members of the senate; 2d, the members of the chamber of representatives; 3d, a delegation of three

members designated by each of the general councils of France and of Algeria in their annual session in the month of August.

This congress shall be presided over by the president of the senate.

10. When there shall be occasion to select the president of the Republic, the president of the senate, within eight days, shall convoke the senators, the representatives and the designated councillors-general.

The interval until the meeting cannot exceed fifteen days.

The president of the Republic shall be selected by majority of the votes.

The president of the senate shall give notice of the selection to the president of the Republic elect and to the president of the chamber of representatives.

Attributes of the Public Authorities.

11. The initiative for laws belongs to the two chambers and to the president of the Republic.

The two chambers share equally in the making of the laws. Nevertheless, tax-laws are submitted first to the chamber of representatives.

The senate can be constituted into a court of justice in order to try prosecutions for responsibility against the president and the ministers and the generals-in-chief of the army and navy.

12. Each of the chambers is the judge of the eligibility of its members and of the regularity of their election; it alone can receive their resignations.

13. The senators and the representatives shall not be questioned, accused or tried at any time for the opinions which they shall have expressed in the chamber to which they belong.

They cannot be arrested for criminal matters, saving the case of *flagrante delicto,* nor prosecuted until after the chamber to which they belong has authorised the prosecution.

14. The president of the Republic promulgates the laws when they have been voted by the two chambers. He looks after and assures the execution of them.

He negotiates and ratifies treaties. No treaty is definitive until after it has been approved by the two chambers.

He has the right to pardon; amnesties can be granted only through a law.

He disposes of the armed force, without authority to command it in person.

He presides at the national solemnities; the envoys and ambassadors of foreign powers are accredited to him.

The president of the Republic and the ministers, taken either individually or collectively, are responsible for the acts of the government.

15. When the president of the Republic shall be of the opinion that the interest of the country requires the renewal of the chamber of representatives before the normal expiration of its powers, he shall ask of the senate the authorisation to dissolve it. This authorisation cannot be given except in secret committee and by majority of votes. It must be given within a space of eight days.

The electoral colleges must be convoked within the three days which shall follow the notification made to the president of the Republic of the affirmative vote of the senate.

Temporary Provisions.

16. When the National Assembly shall have determined by a vote the date at which it will separate, the president of the Republic shall convoke the electoral colleges for the election of the representatives and ultimately for the election of the senators in such a manner that the two chambers can constitute themselves upon the same day with the dissolution.

The powers of the president of the Republic shall continue until the notification of the congress which shall have elected the new president.

THE PRESIDENT OF THE REPUBLIC,
A. THIERS.

C. The Ernoul Order of the Day. May 24, 1873. *Journal Officiel*, May 25, 1873 (Vol. 1873, 3315).

The National Assembly,

Considering that the form of the government is not in discussion; that the assembly is in possession of the constitutional laws presented in virtue of one of its decisions. and that it ought to examine them; but that, from to-day, it

is important to reassure the country by causing to prevail in
the government a resolutely conservative policy, regrets that
the recent ministerial alterations have not given to the conservative interests the satisfaction which they had the right
to expect, and passes to the order of the day.

D. The Target Declaration. May 24, 1873. *Journal Officiel*, May 25, 1873 (Vol. 1873, 3315).

In the name of my colleagues, whose names follow, I have
the honor to declare, in order to define precisely the idea and·
bearing of our votes, that, in associating ourselves together
upon the order of the day, we all declare ourselves resolved
to accept the republican solution such as results from the totality of the constitutional laws presented by the government,
and to put an end to the provisional government which compromises the material interests of the country. We intend, in
adopting this order of the day, [*i. e.* Ernoul's], to express the
idea that the government of the President of the Republic
henceforth ought to cause to prevail by its acts a clear and
resolutely conservative policy.

E. Manifesto of the Extreme Left. May 24, 1873. Translation, *The Times* (London), May 25, 1873.

The members of the extreme left, while recognizing the
gravity of the present state of affairs, are convinced that they
have the country at their back, and are unanimously of opinion that with coolness and vigilance they will be able to avert
all danger. They declare that there exist in the assembly the
necessary elements for the formation of a majority capable of
withstanding the government in any reactionary attempts.

130. The White Flag Letter.

October 27, 1873. *Archives. diplomatiques*, LIII. 26-28.
Translation based upon that of *The Times* (London), October 31,
1873.

This document throws light upon the most serious attempt
after 1870 to re-establish monarchy in France. A fusion of the
legitimist and Orleanist forces having been arranged, the recognition of the Count of Chambord as king by the National Assembly

seemed almost a certainty. To get favorable action, however, it was necessary that there should be agreement as to a constitution and a flag. At a time when the fusionists in the National Assembly believed that these matters had been satisfactorily arranged, including the adoption of the tri-color, the Count of Chambord astonished and disconcerted his supporters by publishing this letter. It made impossible his election, and thereby prevented the re-establishment of monarchy. If carefully studied the document will reveal, back of its vague and figurative language, the reasons why the Count of Chambord could not accept the kind of position which his election by the National Assembly would have entailed. The letter was addressed to a legitimist member of the National Assembly.

REFERENCES. Seignobos, *Europe Since 1814,* 199-200 ; Andrews, *Modern Europe,* II, 353 ; Coubertin, *Evolution of France under the Third Republic,* 37-41 : Hanotaux, *Contemporary France,* II, 115-275 ; Lavisse and Rambaud, *Histoire générale,* XII, 13-14.

I have preserved, sir, so pleasant a recollection of your visit to Salzburg, I have conceived so great an esteem for your noble character, that I do not hesitate to address myself frankly to you, as you came frankly to me.

You spoke with me for many hours about the destinies of our dear and well-beloved country, and I know that on your return, you pronounced among your colleagues words which will earn for you my eternal gratitude. I thank you for having so well understood the anguish of my heart, and for concealing nothing of the unshakable firmness of my decisions.

Accordingly, I was not disturbed when public opinion, carried away by a current which I deplore, alleged that I at last consented to become the legitimist king of the revolution. I had for guarantee the testimony of a man of feeling, and I resolved to keep silent until I should be forced to make an appeal to your loyalty.

But since, notwithstanding your efforts, misapprehensions accumulate, which tend to obscure my policy though it is clear as the open sky, I owe the whole truth to that country which may misunderstand me, but which does homage to my sincerity, because it knows that I never have deceived it and that I never will deceive it.

I am asked today to sacrifice my honor. What can I reply but that I retract nothing of my former declarations? The claims of yesterday give me the measure of the demands of the morrow, and I cannot consent to inaugurate a reparative and strong reign by an act of weakness.

It is the fashion, as you know, to contrast the firmness of Henry V with the suppleness of Henry IV. "The passionate

love which I bear my subjects," he often said, "makes everything possible and honorable for me."

I claim, upon that point, to yield nothing to him, but I
would wish to know what lesson he would have drawn
for the one bold enough to persuade him to renounce the
standard of Arques and Ivry.

You belong, sir, to the province where he was born, and
you will be, as I am, of the opinion that he would have
promptly disarmed his interlocutor by saying with his Béar-
nese vigor: "My friend, take my white flag, it will always lead
you in the way of honor and victory."

I am accused of not holding in high enough esteem the
valor of our soldiers, and that at a moment at which I aspire only to confide to them all that which I have held most
dear. It is forgotten, then, that honor is the common patrimony of the house of Bourbon and of the French army, and
that, upon that ground, they cannot fail to understand each
other!

No, I do not fail to appreciate any of the glories of my
country, and God alone, in the depths of my exile, has seen
my tears of thankfulness flow every time that in good or in
evil fortune, the children of France have shown themselves
worthy of her.

But we have a great work to accomplish together. I am
ready, quite ready, to undertake it when so desired, tomorrow,
this evening, this moment! That is why I wish to remain
entirely as I am. Enfeebled today, I would be powerless [to-
morrow].

The problem is nothing less than to reconstitute upon its
natural basis a profoundly disturbed society, to assure energetically the reign of law, to bring about the rebirth of prosperity within, to contract abroad enduring alliances, and especially not to fear to employ force in the service of order
and justice.

Conditions are spoken of: were any laid down by that
young prince, whose loyal embrace I felt with so much happiness, and who, listening only to his patriotism, came spontaneously to me, bringing me in the name of all his kindred
assurances of peace, devotion, and reconciliation?

Guarantees are desired: were they asked of that Bayard
of modern times, on that memorable night of the 24th of May,

when there was imposd on his modesty the glorious mission of calming his country by one of those words of an honest man and soldier which reassure the good and make the wicked tremble?

I have not, it is true, borne as he has the sword of France upon twenty battlefields, but I have preserved intact during forty-three years the sacred deposit of our traditions and our liberties. I have then the right to count upon the same confidence and I ought to inspire the same security.

My person is nothing: my principle is everything. France will see the end of her trials when she is willing to understand this. I am the necessary pilot, the only one capable of guiding the ship to port, because I have mission and authority for that.

You can do much, sir, to remove misunderstandings and to prevent feebleness in the hour of conflict. Your consoling words, on leaving Salzburg, are ever present to my mind: France can not perish, for Christ still loves his Franks, and when God has resolved to save a people, He takes care that the sceptre of justice be put only in hands strong enough to bear it.

(Signed),   HENRY.

131. Law of the Septennate.

November 20, 1873. Duvergier, *Lois,* LXXIII, 363-368.

This law was enacted after the failure of the attempt to restore monarchy. (See No. 130.) Opposed by the two extremes, it was passed by a combination of centre groups, each group voting for it out of motives peculiar to itself. The document should be studied in connection with No. 124, as it became with what was carried over from those measures a sort of provisional constitution.

REFERENCES. Seignobos, *Europe Since 1814,* 200; Andrews, *Modern Europe,* II, 353-354; Bodley, *France,* I, 281; Hanotaux. *Contemporary France,* II, 276-334; Lavisse and Rambaud. *Histoire générale,* XII, 14-15; Jaurès, *Histoire socialiste,* XII, 115-116.

1. The executive power is entrusted for seven years to Marshal de MacMahon, Duke of Magenta, dating from the promulgation of the present law; this power shall continue to be exercised with the title of President of the Republic and under the existing conditions until the modifications which may be effected therein by the constitutional laws.

2. Within the three days which follow the promulgation of the present law, a commission of thirty members shall be selected in public and by *scrutin de liste,* for the consideration of the constitutional laws.

132. Documents upon the Establishment of the Republic.

These documents, with those alluded to in them, show the manner in which the Third Republic became definitively established. The first two show the status of the matter during 1874. Document A represents the program of those who desired that the Republic should be proclaimed at once; document B, that of their opponents. The difference between the two should be carefully noted and each should be compared with the plan of government finally adopted (No. 133). The National Assembly was unable to come to a decision upon the issue presented by the two documents. It rejected document A, after having once given it an indirect sanction, but it did not adopt the positive program of document B. When the assembly met again in January, 1875, the republicans finally succeeded in accomplishing indirectly what they had failed to do directly. This was done by amending document B. Several amendments only slightly different in meaning were offered and beaten. Document C is a type of these amendments. Document D, the amendment finally secured, was passed by a vote of 353 to 352. The difference in meaning between document C and D should be carefully noted, and likewise the character of the change effected in document B through the adoption of the amendment.

REFERENCES. Seignobos, *Europe Since 1814*, 200-201; Andrews, *Modern Europe*, II, 354-356; C. F. A. Currier, *Annals of the American Academy of Political and Social Science, Supplement*, March, 1893, 20-32; Hanotaux, *Contemporary France*, III, 1-55, 124-162; Lavisse and Rambaud, *Histoire générale*, XII, 16-18; Jaurès, *Histoire socialiste*, XII, 148-169.

A. The Casimir-Perier Proposal. June 15, 1874. *Journal Officiel,* June 16, 1874 (Vol. 1874, 4050).

The National Assembly, wishing to put an end to the anxieties of the country, adopts the following resolution:

The commission upon the constitutional laws shall take as the basis of its labors upon the organization and transmission of the public powers:

1. Article 1 of the project of law deposited May 19, 1873, thus expressed: "The government of the French Republic is composed of two chambers and of a president, head of the executive power;"

2. The law of November 20, 1873, by which the presi-

dency of the Republic has been entrusted to M. Maréchal de MacMahon until November 20, 1880;

3. The consecration of the right of partial or total revision of the constitution, in the forms and at the dates which the constitutional law shall determine.

B. The Ventavon Proposal. July 15, 1874, *Journal Officiel*, July 16, 1874 (Vol. 1874, 4955).

The commission has the honor to propose to you: in the first place, to reject the proposal of M. Casimir-Perier upon which urgency has been declared; in the second place, to vote in the form of the rule the following articles of the constitutional law:

1. Marshal de MacMahon, President of the Republic, continues to exercise with that title the executive authority with which he is invested by the law of November 20, 1873.

2. He is responsible only in the case of high treason.

The ministers are collectively responsible before the chambers for the general policy of the government, and individually for their personal acts.

3. The legislative power is exercised by two assemblies: the Chamber of Deputies and the Senate.

The Chamber of Deputies is selected by universal suffrage, under the conditions determined by the electoral law.

The Senate is composed of members elected or appointed in the proportions and under the conditions which shall be regulated by a special law.

4. The Marshal President of the Republic is invested with the right to dissolve the Chamber of Deputies. In that case, a new election shall take place within the space of six months.

5. At the expiration of the term fixed by the law of November 20, 1873, as in case of vacancy of the presidential office, the council of ministers immediately convokes the two assemblies which, met in congress, decide upon the measures to be taken.

During the continuance of the powers entrusted to Marshal de MacMahon, revision of the constitutional laws can be made only upon his proposal.

C. The Proposed Laboulaye Amendment. January 28, 1875. *Journal Officiel,* January 29, 1875 (Vol. 1875, 768-769).

The government of the Republic is composed of two chambers and of a president.

D. The Wallon Amendment. January 30, 1875. *Journal Officiel,* January 30, 1875 (Vol. 1875, 836).

The President of the Republic is elected by the majority of the votes by the Senate and by the Chamber of Deputies met in National Assembly.

He is selected for seven years. He is re-eligible.

133. The Constitution of 1875 and Amendments.

Translations, based upon those of C. F. A. Currier, *Supplement to the Annals of the American Academy of Political and Social Science,* March, 1893, 42-50.

These documents taken together constitute the present written constitution of France. Their real character may be best brought out by a series of comparisons. (1) They should be compared with the constitutions whch created some of the preceding governments of France, particularly those of 1830 (No. 105) and 1848 (No. 110) for the preceding parliamentary régime and the preceding republic. (2) A comparison wth a typical written constitution such as the American Federal constitution will emphasize one characteristic feature. (3) By comparing the scheme of government with the actual government of England other important characteristics will be revealed.

REFERENCES. Seignobos, *Europe Since 1814,* 202-204; Lowell, *Governments and Parties in Continental Europe,* I, 11-14; Bodley, *France,* 1, 263-270; Coubertin, *Evolution of France under the Third Republic,* 53-61; Hanotaux, *Contemporary France,* III, 283-362; Lavisse and Rambaud, *Histoire générale,* XII, 19-21; Rambaud, *Civilisation contemporaine,* 524-529.

A. Law upon the Organization of the Senate. February 24, 1875. Duvergier, *Lois,* LXXV, 54-62.

1. The Senate consists of three hundred members:

Two hundred and twenty-five elected by the departments and colonies, and seventy-five elected by the National Assembly.

The departments of the Seine and of the Nord shall each elect five senators.

The departments of the Seine-Inférieure, Pas-de-Calais.
Gironde, Rhône, Finistère, Côtes-du-Nord, each four senators,
Loire-Inférieure, Saône-et-Loire, Ille-et-Vilaine, Seine-et-
Oise, Isère, Puy-de-Dôme, Somme, Bouches-du-Rhône, Aisne,
Loire, Manche, Maine-et-Loire, Morbihan, Dordogne, Haute-
Garonne, Charente-Inférieure, Calvados, Sarthe, Hérault,
Basses-Pyrénées, Gard, Aveyron, Vendée, Orne, Oise, Vosges,
Allier, each three senators.

All the other departments each two senators.

The territory of Belfort, the three departments of Algeria,
the four colonies of Martinique, Guadeloupe, Réunion and the
French Indies elect each one senator.

3. No one can be a senator unless he is a French citizen,
forty years of age at least, and enjoying civil and political
rights.

4. The senators of the departments and colonies are elected by majority vote, and, when there is need, by *scrutin de
liste,* by a college assembled at the head-town of the department or colony and composed:

1st, Of the deputies;

2d, Of the general councillors;

3d, Of the district councillors;

4th, Of delegates elected, one by each municipal council,
from among the voters of the commune.

In the French Indies, the members of the colonial council
or of the local councils are substituted for the general councillors. district councillors and delegates of the municipal
councils.

They vote at the head-town of each district.

5. The senators chosen by the Assembly are elected by
scrutin de liste and by a majority of the votes.

6. The senators of the departments and colonies are
elected for nine years and renewable by thirds every three
years.

At the beginning of the first session, the departments shall
be divided into three series containing an equal number of
senators each. It shall be determined by lot which series
shall be renewed at the expiration of the first and second
triennial periods.

7. The senators elected by the Assembly are irremovable.

Vacancies by death, by resignation, or for any other reason, shall, within the space of two months, be filled by the Senate itself.

8. The Senate has, concurrently with the Chamber of Deputies, the initiative and making of laws. Money bills, however, must first be introduced in, and passed by the Chamber of Deputies.

9. The Senate may be constituted a court of justice to judge either the President of the Republic or the ministers, and to take cognizance of attacks made upon the safety of the state.

10. Elections to the Senate shall take place one month before the time fixed by the National Assembly for its own dissolution. The Senate shall organize and enter upon its duties the same day that the National Assembly is dissolved.

11. The present law shall be promulgated only after the passage of the law on the public powers.

B. Law upon the Organization of the Public Powers. February 25, 1875. Duvergier, *Lois,* LXXV, 42-53.

1. The legislative power is exercised by two assemblies: the Chamber of Deputies and the Senate.

The Chamber of Deputies is chosen by universal suffrage, under the conditions determined by the electoral law.

The composition, the method of election, and the powers of the Senate shall be regulated by a special law.

2. The President of the Republic is chosen by a majority of the votes of the Senate and Chamber of Deputies united in National Assembly.

He is chosen for seven years. He is re-eligible.

3. The President of the Republic has the initiative of the laws, concurrently with the members of the two chambers. He promulgates the laws when they have been voted by the two chambers; he looks after and secures their execution.

He has the right of pardon; amnesty can be granted by law only.

He disposes of the armed force.

He appoints to all civil and military positions.

He presides over national festivals; the envoys and ambassadors of foreign powers are accredited to him.

Every act of the President of the Republic must be countersigned by a minister.

4. As vacancies occur after the promulgation of the present law, the President of the Republic appoints, in the council of ministers, the councillors of state in ordinary service.

The councilors of state thus chosen may be dismissed only by a decree rendered in the council of ministers.

The councillors of state chosen by virtue of the law of May 24, 1872, cannot, before the expiration of their powers, be dismissed, except in the manner determined by that law. After the dissolution of the National Assembly, dismissal may be pronounced only by a resolution of the Senate.

5. The President of the Republic may, with the consent of the Senate, dissolve the Chamber of Deputies before the legal expiration of its term.

In that case, the electoral colleges are summoned for new elections within the space of three months.

6. The ministers are jointly responsible to the chambers for the general policy of the government, and individually for their personal acts.

The President of the Republic is responsible only in case of high treason.

7. In case of vacancy by death or for any other reason, the two chambers assembled together proceed at once to the election of a new president.

In the meantime the council of ministers is invested with the executive power.

8. The chambers shall have the right, by separate resolutions, taken in each by a majority of the votes, either upon their own initiative or upon the request of the President of the Republic, to declare that a revision of the constitutional laws shall take place.

After each of the two chambers shall have come to this decision, they shall meet together in National Assembly to proceed with the revision.

The acts effecting revision of the constitutional laws, in whole or in part, must be by a majority of the members composing the National Assembly.

During the continuance, however, of the powers conferred by the law of November 20, 1873, upon Marshal de Mac-

Mahon, this revision can take place only upon the initiative of the President of the Republic.

9. The seat of the executive power and of the two chambers is at Versailles.

C. Law upon the Relation of the Public Powers. July 16, 1875. Duvergier, *Lois*, LXXV, 250-255.

1. The Senate and the Chamber of Deputies assemble each year the second Tuesday of January, unless convened earlier by the President of the Republic.

The two Chambers shall continue in session at least five months each year. The sessions of one begin and end at the same time as that of the other.

On the Sunday following the opening of the session, public prayers shall be addressed to God in the churches and temples, to invoke His aid in the labors of the assemblies.

2. The President of the Republic pronounces the closing of the session. He has the right to convene the chambers in extra session. He must convene them if, during the recess, a majority of the members of each chamber request it.

The President may adjourn the chambers. The adjournment, however, shall not exceed one month, nor take place more than twice in the same session.

3. One month at least before the legal expiration of the powers of the President of the Republic, the chambers must be called together in National Assembly in order to proceed to the election of a new president.

In default of a summons, this meeting shall take place, *ipso facto* the fifteenth day before the expiration of those powers.

In case of the death or resignation of the President of the Republic, the two chambers shall reassemble immediately and *ipso facto*.

In case the Chamber of Deputies, in consequence of article 5 of the law of February 25, 1875, is dissolved at the time when the presidency of the Republic becomes vacant, the electoral colleges shall be convened at once, and the Senate shall reassemble *ipso facto*.

4. Every meeting of either of the two chambers which

shall be held at a time other than the common session of both is illegal and void, except the case provided for in the preceding article and that in which the Senate meets as a court of justice; and in this last case, judicial duties alone shall be performed.

5. The sittings of the Senate and those of the Chamber of Deputies are public.

Nevertheless, each chamber may meet in secret session, upon the request of a fixed number of its members, determined by the rules.

It decides then by majority whether the sitting shall be resumed in public upon the same subject.

6. The President of the Republic communicates with the chambers by messages which are read from the tribune by a minister.

The ministers have entrance to both chambers, and must be heard when they request it. They may be represented, for the discussion of a bill, by commissioners designated by decree of the President of the Republic.

7. The President of the Republic promulgates the laws within the month following the transmission to the government of the laws finally passed. He must promulgate within three days laws whose promulgation shall have been declared urgent by an express vote in each chamber.

Within the time fixed for the promulgation, the President of the Republic may, by message with reasons assigned, request of the two chambers a new discussion, which cannot be refused.

8. The President of the Republic negotiates and ratifies the treaties. He gives information thereof to the chambers as soon as the interests and safety of the state permit.

Treaties of peace, and of commerce, treaties which involve the finances of the state, those relating to the persons and property of French citizens in foreign countries, shall become definitive only after having been voted by the two chambers. No session, no exchange, no annexation of territory can take place by virtue of a law.

9. The President of the Republic cannot declare war except by the previous assent of the two chambers.

10. Each of the chambers is the judge of the eligibility of

its members and of the legality of their election; it alone can receive their resignation.

11. The *bureau* of each of the two chambers is elected each year for the entire session and for any extra session which may be held before the ordinary session of the following year.

When the two chambers meet together as a National Assembly, their *bureau* consists of the president, vice-presidents and secretaries of the Senate.

12. The President of the Republic can be impeached by the Chamber of Deputies only, and tried by the Senate only.

The ministers can be impeached by the Chamber of Deputies for offences committed in the performance of their duties. In this case they are tried by the Senate.

The Senate can be constituted as a court of justice by a decree of the President of the Republic, issued in the council of ministers, to try all persons accused of attempts upon the safety of the state.

If procedure is begun by the ordinary courts, the decree convening the Senate may be issued at any time before the granting of a discharge.

A law shall determine the method of procedure for the accusation, trial, and judgment.

13. No member of either chamber can be prosecuted or held responsible on account of any opinions expressed or votes cast by him in the performance of his duties.

14. No member of either chamber can, during the session, be prosecuted or arrested for any offence or misdemeanor, except on the authority of the chamber of which he is a member, unless he be caught in the very act.

The detention or prosecution of a member of either chamber is suspended for the session, and for its entire term, if the chamber demands it.

D. Amendment upon the Seat of Government. June 21, 1879. Duvergier, *Lois,* LXXIX, 213-227.

Article 9 of the constitutional law of February 25, 1875, is repealed.

E. The Amendments of 1884. August 14, 1884. Duvergier, *Lois,* LXXXIV, 240-250.

1. Paragraph 2 of article 5 of the constitutional law of February 25, 1875, on the organization of the public powers, is amended as follows:

"In that case the electoral colleges meet for new elections within the space of two months, and the chambers within the ten days following the close of the elections."

2. Paragraph 3 of article 8 of the same law of February 25, 1875, is completed as follows:

"The republican form of government cannot be made the subject of a proposition for revision.

"Members of families that have reigned in France are ineligible to the presidency of the Republic."

3. Article 1 to 7 of the constitutional law of February 24, 1875, on the organization of the Senate, shall no longer have a constitutional character.

4. Paragraph 3 of Article 1 of the constitutional law of July 16, 1875, on the relation of the public powers, is repealed.

134. Documents upon the 16th of May Crisis.

From these documents much may be learned about the real nature of the famous 16th of May crisis. The acceptance of the resignation virtually asked for in document A and offered in document B led to the adoption by the Chamber of Deputies of document C. It was presented by Gambetta as that agreed upon by all the groups of the republican majority and was passed 347 to 149. In consequence, MacMahon first adjourned the Chamber of Deputies for a month and then, with the consent of the Senate, dissolved it. The remaining documents, except the last, are intended to give an idea of the vigorous and acrimonious electoral campaign whch followed. In the manifestoes of MacMahon special attenton should be given to the list of the achievements of his government, his explanation of the issues involved, and what is announced or implied as to the future. Documents D and F are both the work of Gambetta. Their analyses of the situation from the republican standpoint and their lists of administrative measures for influencing the elections should be carefully noted. The elections were an overwhelming victory for the republicans. Document H shows how MacMahon accepted the result.

REFERENCES. Seignobos, *Europe Since 1814*, 205-207 ; Andrews, *Modern Europe*, II, 356-357 ; Coubertin, *Evolution of France under the Third Republic*, 61-74 ; Bodley. *France*, I. 286-291 : Hanotaux. *Contemporary France*. III, 613-621 : Lavisse and Rambaud, *Histoire générale*, XII, 23-28 ; Jaurès, *Histoire socialiste*, XII, 196-211.

A. Letter of MacMahon to Simon. May 16, 1877. *Journal Officiel*, May 17, 1877 (Vol. 1877, 3689-3690).

Mr. President of the Council,

I have just read in the *Journal Officiel* the report of the sitting of yesterday.

I have seen with surprise that neither you nor Mr. Keeper of the Seals urged from the tribune all the weighty reasons which possibly might have prevented the abrogation of a law upon the press, voted less than two years ago upon the proposal of M. Dufaure and the application of which you yourself very recently asked of the tribunals; and, moreover, in several meetings of the council, and even in that of yesterday it had been decided that the president of the council, as well as the keeper of the seals, should be charged with the duty of combating it.

Already there was occasion for astonishment that the Chamber of Deputies, in its late sittings, should have discussed an entire municipal law, and even adopted some provisions, of which in the council of ministers you yourself have thoroughly recognized the danger, such as the publicity of the municipal councils, without the minister of the interior having taken part in the discussion.

This attitude of the head of the cabinet raises the question whether he has kept in the chamber the influence necessary to make his views prevail.

An explanation in this matter is indispensable, for if I am not responsible as you are to the Parliament, I have a responsibility to France, with which, to-day more than ever, I must be preoccupied.

Accept, Mr. President of the Council, assurance of my highest consideration.

THE PRESIDENT OF THE REPUBLIC,
MARSHAL DE MACMAHON.

B. Letter of Simon to MacMahon, May 16, 1877. Translation, *The Times* (London), May 17, 1877.

In view of the letter you have thought fit to write to me, I feel myself bound to hand you my resignation of the functions you were good enough to confide to me. I am obliged, however, at the same time to tender explanations on two points. You regret, M. le Maréchal, that I was not present on Saturday in the Chamber, when the first reading of the bill on municipal councils was discussed. I regretted it also; I was detained at Paris by indisposition; but the question of the publicity of the sittings was only to have been discussed on the second reading. I had come to an agreement on this point with M. Bardouy. M. Perras's amendment, which passed, took the assembly unawares, and I had an appointment with the committee on Friday morning to try and make it reverse its decision before entering on the debate in the chamber. All this is known to everybody. As to the bill on the press, M. le Maréchal, you will be good enough to remember that my objections related solely to the case of foreign sovereigns. I had always explained myself in this sense, as you yourself must remember at yesterday morning's council. I repeated my reservations before the chamber. I abstained from elaborating them for reasons which everybody knew and approved. As to the rest of the bill, I was in agreement with the committee. You will understand, M. le Président, the motive which leads me to enter into these details. I have to define my position in a distinct manner at the moment of my quitting the council. I scarcely venture to add—though as a citizen, and no longer as a minister—that I earnestly desire to be succeeded by a man belonging, like myself, to the conservative republican party. For five months it has been my function to give my advice, and the last time I have the honour of writing to you I allow myself to express a wish which is solely inspired by my patriotism. Pray accept, M. le Maréchal, the homage of my respect.

C. Order of the Day. May 17, 1877. *Journal Officiel,* May 18, 1877 (Vol. 1877, 3744).

The Chamber,
Considering that it is important in the present crisis and in order to fulfill the commission which it has received from the country, to recall that the preponderance of the parliamentary power, exercised through ministerial responsibility, is the first condition of the government of the country by the country, the establishment of which the constitutional laws have had for their purpose;

Declares that the confidence of the majority can be acquired only by a cabinet free in its action and resolved to govern according to republican principles, which alone can guarantee order and prosperity within and peace without,

And passes to the order of the day.

D. Manifesto of the Left. About May 20, 1877. Translation, *The Times* (London), May 21, 1877.

Dear Fellow-Citizens,—A decree which has just struck a blow at your representatives is the first act of the new ministry *de Combat,* which aspires to hold in check the will of France. The message of the President of the Republic leaves no doubt as to the intentions of his counsellors. The chamber is adjourned for a month, till the decree to dissolve it is obtained from the Senate. A cabinet which had never lost the majority in any vote has been dismissed without discussion. The new ministers knew that if they had allowed Parliament to speak, the day that witnessed their advent would have also witnessed their fall. As it is impossible for us to publicly express our reprobation from the tribune, our first thought is to turn towards you, and tell you, like the republicans of the National Assembly of the 24th of May, 1873, that the efforts of the men who have returned to power will be once more powerless. France wishes the Republic. She said so on the 20th of February, 1876. She will say so again every time she is consulted, and it is because universal suffrage has to renew this year the departmental and communal councils that it is attempted to stop the expression of the national will, and that the first step taken is to shut your representatives' mouths; as after the 24th of May the nation will show, by its coolness, patience, and resolution, that an incorrigible minority cannot wrest from it its own government. However painful this unexpected trial may be which is disturbing the interests, and which might compromise the success of the grand efforts of our industry for the great and pacific universal exhibition of 1878, whatever be the national anxiety amid the complications of European politics, France will let herself neither be deceived nor intimidated. She will resist every provocation. The republican functionaries will remain at their posts and await the decree which separates them from constituencies whose confidence they have. Those of our countrymen who have been called into the elective councils of the nation will redouble their zeal and activity, their devotion and patriotism, to maintain the rights and liberties of the country. We shall enter into direct communication with you. We call upon you to pronounce between the policy of reaction and ventures, which overturns all that six years have so painfully gained—the wise and firm, pacific and progressive policy which you have already consecrated. The trial will not be long. In five months at most France will speak; the Republic will issue, stronger than ever, from the popular urns; the parties of the past will be finally vanquished; and France will be able to face the future with calmness and confidence.

E. MacMahon's Manifesto to the French People. September 19, 1877. *Journal Officiel,* September 20, 1877 (Vol. 1877, 6381).

Marshal De MacMahon, President of the Republic, to the French People.

Frenchmen!

You are about to be called upon to select your representatives in the Chamber of Deputies.

I do not design to exert any pressure upon your choice, but I am bound to dissipate all ambiguity.

It is necessary that you should know what I have done, what I intend to do, and what will be the consequences of that which you are about to do yourselves.

This is what I have done:

For four years I have maintained peace, and the personal confidence with which foreign sovereigns honor me has enabled me to render more cordial each day our relations with all the powers.

At home order has not been disturbed for one moment.

Thanks to a policy of conciliation which summoned around me all the men devoted before anything else to the country, the public prosperity, for a moment arrested by our misfortunes, has resumed its advance. The general wealth has increased despite our heavy expenses. The national credit has been strengthened.

France, peaceable and confident, at the same time has seen

her army, always worthy of her, reconstituted upon a new basis.

But these great results were in danger of being compromised.

The Chamber of Deputies, escaping more each day from the leadership of moderate men, and more and more dominated by the avowed leaders of radicalism, had come to disregard the portion of authority which belongs to me and which I could not allow to be diminished without involving the honor of my name before you and before history. Contesting at the same time the legitimate influence of the Senate, it aimed at nothing less than to substitute for the necessary equilibrium of the powers established by the constitution the despotism of a new convention.

Hesitation was not permissible.

Making use of my constitutional right, upon the advice of the Senate, I dissolved the Chamber of Deputies.

Now it is for you to speak.

It is said that I wish to overthrow the Republic.

You will not believe it.

The constitution is entrusted to my keeping. I shall cause it to be respected.

What I expect of you is the election of a chamber which, raising itself above the competition of parties, will before all else devote itself to the affairs of the country.

At the last elections my name was abused. Among those who then said that they were my friends many have not ceased opposing me. They will speak to-day of devotion to my person, and allege that they attack only my ministers.

You will not be the dupes of that artifice. In order to defeat it, my government will designate to you from among the candidates those who alone will be authorised to use my name.

You will weigh maturely the significance of your votes.

Elections favorable to my policy will facilitate the regular progress of the present government. They will strengthen the principle of authority which has been sapped by demagogy; they will assure order and peace.

Hostile elections would aggravate the conflict between the public powers, fetter the progress of affairs, keep up the agitation, and France, in the midst of new complications, would become an object of distrust to Europe.

As for me, my duty would increase with the peril. I could not obey the summons of demagogy. I could not become the instrument of radicalism nor abandon the post at which the constitution has placed me.

I shall remain to defend, with the support of the Senate, the conservative interests and to energetically protect the faithful functionaries who in a difficult moment have not allowed themselves to be intimidated by vain threats.

Frenchmen!

I await, with entire confidence, the expression of your sentiments.

After so many trials, France desires stability, order, and peace.

With the aid of God, we shall secure for her these blessings. You will hear the words of a soldier who does not serve any party, any revolutionary or retrograde passion, and who is guided only by love of the fatherland.

F. Gambetta's Circular. October 7, 1877. Translation, *The Times* (London), October 8, 1877.

Citizens,—After four long months of suppression of Parliamentary life entirely taken up with the excesses of administrative pressure, and the most deplorable proceedings of official candidateship; after four months, during which the French people, by its admirable patience and the daily proofs of its sagacity and political maturity, has attracted to our young republic the admiration and expressed sympathies of civilized governments and peoples, France at last speaks. She will say in a few days what she thinks of the men of May 16, the allies and protectors of the men of the 2d of December, of the servants of Henry V, and the agents of the Syllabus and the Pope, all sheltered under the electoral patronage of the President of the Republic, doubtless for the better protection of republican institutions.

She will say what she thinks of the personal policy of the chief of the state, of the aristocratic and retrogressive pretensions of the cabinet presided over by the Duc de Broglie.

She will say what she thinks of the unjustifiable dissolution of the republican and liberal majority which she had entrusted with the execution of her wishes on the 20th of February, 1876, by nearly five million votes.

She will say what she thinks of the fighting government, of the government of vexations directed against vendors and hawkers of journals, schoolmasters, office holders, innkeepers, the most insignificant *employes*—in short, the government of that miserable war waged against the small; she will say what she thinks of the pretensions on the part of the government to impose on her for another three years functionaries of all kinds, in flagrant hostility to all the men elected by the country; she will say what she thinks of the projects and plots of this coalition of monarchists, who prepare for her, at the close of three years of intestine conflicts and divisions, in 1880 a terrible crisis, perhaps a revolution; she will say what she thinks of that unclean press which can, without incurring punishment, appeal to brute force against the men elected by universal suffrage, and can insult our valiant and noble army, now the *élite* of the nation and the highest hope of the country.

She will say what she thinks of the policy inaugurated by the letter of May 16, which dismissed the republican ministry, of the order of the day to the troops at the review of July 2, of the presidential message of September 19, of all that system of government which the chief of the executive power vindicates as a right prior to the constitution.

France will say, also, that she, favouring equity and democracy, wishes for the Republic, as the government necessary for her restoration and her greatness. She will say that she intends to make an end of anarchy and dictatorships, to carry out by peaceful measures the French revolution, by developing by national education the intelligence of her children, by securing by peace at home and abroad general prosperity and happiness, by founding on liberty and justice not "Moral Order," but "Republican Order." She will say that she intends that the state as well as the community, the nation as well as the individual, shall be definitely withdrawn from clerical rule; that the priest shall be respected and kept within the temple, the schoolmaster within the school, the magistrate within the court, and that the public force shall never be employed except in the service of the law.

My profound conviction, based on sure premises, allows me to declare without rashness a week before the voting that France in spite of all the maneuvres directed against the freedom of her votes, will repudiate the administrative pressure, will scorn the official candidateship and its agents, and will thrust far from her royalists, Caesarists, clericals, the knaves as well as the violent; she will condemn dictatorial policy, she will leave the chief of the executive power, transformed into a plebiscitary candidate, no other alternative but to submit or resign.

As for ourselves, sure of the support of the country thus solemnly declared, we shall know how to cause its will to prevail over the opposition of a powerless and incorrigible minnority. Without passion, without weakness, without vehemence, we will do our duty. The union of all good Frenchmen, liberals, republicans, by conviction or by birth, labourers, peasants, burgesses, the world of work and of thrift, will keep us discreet, and will render us invincible for the country and the Republic.

G. MacMahon's Second Manifesto. October 11, 1877. *Journal Officiel,* October 12, 1877 (Vol. 1877, 6757).

Marshal de MacMahon, President of the Republic, to the French People.

Frenchmen,

You are about to vote.

The violence of the opposition has dispelled all illusions. No calumny can any longer impair the truth.

No, the republican constitution is not in danger.

No, the government, although it is respectful towards religion, does not obey so-called clerical influences, and nothing could inveigle it into a policy compromising to peace.

No, you are not threatened with any return to the abuses of the past.

The struggle is between order and disorder.

You have already pronounced.

You do not wish, by hostile elections, to throw the country into an unknown future of crises and conflicts.

You desire tranquility within as well as abroad, the accord

of the public powers and security for industry and business.

You will vote for the candidates whom I recommend to your free suffrage.

Frenchmen,

The hour has come.

Go to the polls without fear.

Comply with my appeal, and I, placed by the constitution at a post which my duty forbids me to abandon, I will answer for order and peace.

H. MacMahon's Message. December 14, 1877. *Journal Officiel,* December 15, 1877 (Vol. 1877, 8381).

Versailles, December 14, 1877.

Messrs. Senators,

Messrs. Deputies,

The elections of October 14th have once more affirmed the confidence of the country in republican institutions.

In order to obey parliamentary rules, I have formed a cabinet chosen from within the two chambers and composed of men resolved to defend and maintain these institutions by the sincere application of the constitutional laws.

The interest of the country requires that the crisis through which we are passing should be abated; it requires with no less force that it should not be renewed.

The exercise of the right of dissolution is in fact only a last method of consulting with a judge from whom there is no appeal and could not be erected into a system of government. I believed that I ought to make use of that right, and I conform to the response of the country.

The constitution of 1875 has founded a parliamentary republic by establishing my irresponsibility, while it has instituted collective and personal responsibility for the ministers.

Thus my respective duties and rights are defined. The independence of the ministers is the condition of their responsibility.

These principles, drawn from the constitution, are those of my government.

The end of this crisis will be the point of departure for a new era of prosperity.

All the public authorities will assent in promoting its development. The accord established between the Senate and the Chamber of Deputies, certain henceforth to reach regularly the term of its commisssion, will make possible the achievement of the great legislative labors which the public interest demands.

The Universal Exposition is about to open; commerce and industry are about to experience a new advance, and we shall offer to the world a new testimony of the vitality of our country, which has always revived through industry, thrift and its deep attachment to the ideas of conservatism, order and liberty.

135. Documents upon Socialism and the Third Republic.

The rapid development of the socialist party in size and influence has been one of the most important features of French history since the establishment of the Third Republic. The socialists now cast over two million votes, have about sixty-five members of parliament, two posts in the ministry, and in many directions exert an influence in excess of their numerical strength. From the overthrow of the Paris Commune until October, 1879, there was no organized socialist party in France. The Marseilles Congress then started the present socialist movement. It drew up resolutions and reports, but no general program. The Paris regional congress of the next year formulated document A, which was mainly the work of Karl Marx and Jules Guesde. It still remains the program of all the organized French socialists, save for comparatively slight amendments made by successive national congresses of the socialists. All of the more important of these changes may be readily ascertained by comparing it with the program of the "French Socialist Party" adopted at Tours in March, 1902, as given in Ensor's *Modern Socialism*, 338-349. Owing to differences of opinion among them, chiefly in regard to tactics, the socialists were divided into several parties until 1904-5 when a unification of all the organized socialistic parties was finally brought about. Document B shows the basis upon which this union was effected and reflects accurately the general point of view of practically all French socialists, although there are some socialist deputies who do not recognize the right of the party to control their action in parliament.

REFERENCES. Peixotto, *French Revolution and Modern French Socialism*, 278-286: Robinson and Beard, *Modern Europe*, II, 173-174; Lavisse and Rambaud, *Histoire générale*, XII, 43-44.

A. General Program of the Socialist Regional Congress of the Centre, July 18-23, 1880. *Journal des economistes*, Fourth series, XI, 407-409.

The Regional Congress of the Centre considering that, if revolution is the sole means for the emancipation of the working class, that revolution is possible only with and by an organized working class;

Considering that the first act of that organization is necessarily the separation of the working class from the bourgeois political parties, and that this separation must be effected upon political grounds with the aid of that same ballot which has created the confusion of the classes politically;

Considering, finally, that the worst enemies of the revolution are those who, while talking at random, refuse to employ any of the means which will render it possible;

Declares that it accepts the electoral program published by the newspapers *la Revue Socialiste, le Prolétaire, l'Égalité* and *la Fédération,* with the following slight modifications (indicated in italics) :

Considering that the emancipation of the productive class is that of all human beings without distinction of sex or of race;

That the producers cannot be free except in so far as they shall be in possession of the means of production;

That there are only two forms under which the means of production can belong to them:

1st. The individual form, which has never existed as an actual general condition and which is being eliminated more and more by industrial progress;

2d. The collectivist form, the material and intellectual elements of which are created by the very development of capitalistic society;

Considering that this collective appropriation can proceed only from the revolutionary action of the productive class— or proletariat—organized as a distinct political party;

That such an organization must be sought by all the means at the disposal of the proletariat, including therein universal suffrage, transformed thereby from an instrument of deception, which it has been until now, into an instrument of emancipation;

The French socialistic workingmen, in giving as the aim of their efforts in the economic domain the return to the collective form of all the means of production, have decided as a method of organization and of strife to enter into the elections, with the following minimum program:

A. Political Program.

1st. Abolition of all laws upon the press, meetings and associations, and especially of the law against the International Association of Laboringmen.—Suppression of the pass-book, that *mise en carte* of the working class, and of the articles of the Code establishing the inferiority of the work-ingman as against the employer;

2d. Suppression of the religious budget and return to the nation "of the properties called *mortmain,* both movable and immovable, belonging to the religious corporations" (decree of the Commune of April 2, 1871), including therein all the industrial and commercial annexes of these corporations;

3d. General arming of the people;

4th. The commune to be the mistress of its own admin-istration and police.

B.   Economic Program.

1st. *Cessation of labor for one day per week* or legal pro-hibition for employers operating *more than six days out of seven.*—Reduction of the working day to eight hours for adults.—Prohibition of the working of children under 14 years in private factories; and, from 14 to 18 years, reduction of the working day to six hours;

2d. Legal minimum of wages, determined each year ac-cording to the local price of the commodities;

3d. Equality of wages for the workers of the two sexes;

4th. Scientific and *professional* instruction for all the children placed for their support under the charge of society, represented by the state and the communes.

5th. *Placing under the charge of society the aged and in-firm workingmen;*

6th. Suppression of all interference of employers in the administration of workingmen's funds for mutual relief, of provision, etc., restored to the exclusive management of the workingmen;

7th. Responsibility of employers in the matter of acci-dents guaranteed by a money deposit paid in by the employer and proportioned to the number of workingmen employed and the dangers which the industry presents;

8th. Participation in the [formation of] the special rules of the different factories; suppression of the right usurped by employers to impose any penalty whatever upon their work-ingmen under the form of fines or of retentions out of their wages (decree of the Commune of April 27, 1871) ;

9th. Revision of all contracts which have alienated public

property (banks, railroads, mines, etc.), and the control of all the factories of the state entrusted to the workingmen who labor in them;

10th. Abolition of all indirect taxes and transformation of all the direct taxes into a progressive tax upon incomes in excess of 3,000 francs.—*Suppression of inheritance in the collateral line and of all inheritance in the direct line exceeding 2,000 francs.*

B. Common Declaration of the Socialist Organizations, January 13, 1905. *L'Internationale ouvrière et socialiste*, I, 96-100.

The delegates of the French socialist organizations, "Revolutionary Socialist Labor Party," "Socialist Party of France," "French Socialist Party," "autonomous federations of the Bouches-du-Rhone, Brittany, Hérault, Somme and Yonne," ordered by their respective parties to bring about unity upon the basis indicated by the International Congress of Amsterdam, declare that the action of the unified party ought to be guided by the principles which the international congresses, especially the most recent, those of Paris in 1900 and of Amsterdam in 1904, have established.

They declare that the divergences of views and the interpretations of different tactics which have existed up to the present are due especially to special circumstances in France and to the absence of a general organization.

They affirm their common desire to establish a party of class struggle, which, even when it utilizes to the advantage of the workingmen, the secondary conflicts of the possessors or finds itself accidentally combining its action with that of a political party for the defence of the rights and interests of the proletariat, remains always a party of fundamental and irreducible opposition to the totality of the bourgeois class and to the state which is its instrument.

In consequence, the delegates declare that their organizations are ready to collaborate immediately in this work of the unification of the socialistic forces upon the following basis, fixed and accepted by common accord:

1. The "Socialist Party" is a class party which has for its aim to socialize the means of production and exchange, i. e., to transform the capitalistic society into a collectivist or com-

munist society and has for its method the economic and political organization of the proletariat. By its aim, by its ideal, by the methods which it employs, the "Socialist Party," although striving for the realization of the immediate reforms claimed by the working class, is not a party of reform, but a party of class struggle and of revolution;

2. The representatives of the party in parliament form a single group, confronting the bourgeois political sections. The socialist group in parliament ought to refuse to the government all the means which assure the domination of the *bourgeoisie* and its maintenance in power—to refuse in consequence military credits for colonial conquest, the secret funds, and the whole of the budget;

Even in case of exceptional circumstances, the representatives cannot bind the party without its consent;

In parliament, the socialist group ought to consecrate itself to the defence and the extension of the political liberties and the rights of the workingmen, the pursuit and realization of the reforms which improve the conditions of life and of struggle of the working class;

The deputies, like all representatives, ought to hold themselves at the disposition of the party for its action in the country and its general propaganda for the organization of the proletariat and the final aim of socialism.

The representative is released individually, as each militant, from the control of his federation;

The totality of the representatives, as a group, are released from the control of the central organization. In every case, the congress judges in a sovereign manner;

4. Liberty of discussion is complete in the press for questions of doctrine and of method, but for action all socialist newspapers ought to conform strictly to the decisions of the congress as interpreted by the central organization of the party;

.   .   .   .

136. Documents upon Leo XIII and the Third Republic.

The attitude of the catholic clergy of France towards the Third Republic went through three distinct phases down to about 1899. (1) From the overthrow of the Second Empire until the definitive establishment of the Republic the great majority were monarchists. (2) From then until the appearance of these documents many of them continued to oppose the Republic, although some became its supporters, while a large number assumed a neutral position. (3) After the publication of these documents the majority complied with the suggestion of the Pope and accepted the Republic.

REFERENCES. Coubertin, *Evolution of France under the Third Republic,* Ch. x ; McCarthy, *Leo XIII,* Ch. xv ; Lavisse and Rambaud, *Histoire générale,* XII, 42-43.

A. Papal Encyclical. February 16, 1892. Translation, *The Times* (London), February 20, 1892.

There have been many governments in France during this century, and each has had its distinctive form—imperial, monarchical and republican. Each of these is good so long only as it makes for the common well being, and one form may be good at one time and another at another. Catholics, like all good citizens, have a perfect right to prefer one form to another, as none of these forms in itself is opposed to christian teaching. The church has always in its dealing with states fully recognized this principle. It was necessary to recall this fact in the development of the present theme. But if one comes down to the practical consideration of instances, one notes that each state is a special individual rèsult, growing out of and modified by its peculiar surroundings, and thus obligatory upon the members which compose it, who should do nothing to seek to overturn it or change its form.

The church, therefore, guardian of the truest and loftiest conception of political sovereignty, since it derives from God, has always reproved subversive doctrines and condemned the rebels to legitimate authority, and this, indeed, even when those in authority used their power against the church, and thus deprived themselves of the most powerful support possible and the most effective means of securing obedience to the law. The advice of the Prince of Apostles in these matters cannot be too widely meditated, nor that of St. Paul. Yet it must not be forgotten that no governmental form is definitive. The church alone has been able, and will continue, to preserve its form of government. Founded by him, who was, who is, and who shall be, world without end, it has received from him since its origin everything which it needed to pursue its divine mission across the moving sea of human things. Far from there being any need of transforming its essential constitution, it has not even the power of renouncing the privileges of true liberty granted to it by Providence in the general interest of souls. But in human history crisis follows crisis, revolution revolution, and order anarchy, and in these circumstances a new form of government may be needful to satisfy new wants and conditions. The principle of authority never changes, but only the method of its expression or the form of its incarnation. Hence authority is enduring, for in its nature it is imposed for the well-being of all, or, in other terms, is considered, as such, to be derived from God. Consequently, when a new government is founded, acceptance thereof is not only permissible, but a duty. This great duty of respect and dependence will always continue in force, since it tends to secure the good which, after God, is in society the alpha and omega of principles.

These considerations explain the attitude of the church towards the successive governments of France, and such an attitude is the safest and surest for all Frenchmen in their civil relations with the Republic, which is the existing government of their nation, for all their efforts ought to be directed against division and toward the moral uplifting of their fatherland. But for some people there is a difficulty here. This republic, they say, is animated by sentiments so antichristian that honorable men, and catholics in particular, could not conscientiously accept it, and this is a widespread cause of dissension. But all this divergence might have been avoided but for a regrettable confusion of "constituted powers" and "legislation." Indeed, under the most unimpeachable form legislation may be detestable, and likewise under a very imperfect form there may be excellent legislation. History bears ample witness, and the church has always recognized this fact.

.   .   .   .

B. Papal Brief to the French Cardinals. May 5, 1892. Translation, *The Times* (London), May 7, 1892.

Great was our consolation on receiving the letter by which, in unanimous concert with the whole French episcopate, you adhered to our encyclical. . . . This encyclical has already done much good, and will, we hope, do more, in spite of the attacks to which it has been exposed on the part of impas-

sioned men—attacks against which, moreover, we are glad to
say that it has also found valiant defenders. . . .

. . . Now, these efforts would become essentially barren
if the conservative forces were lacking in unity and harmony
in the pursuit of the ultimate end—namely, the preservation
of religion; inasmuch as thither should tend every upright
man, every sincere friend of society. This our encyclical
amply demonstrated. But the end once defined, the need of
union in order to attain it once admitted, what will be the
means of insuring this union? This, too, we explained, and
we desire to restate it that no one may be in doubt as to our
meaning. One way is to accept without reserve, with that
perfect loyalty becoming in a Christian, the civil power in
the form in which *de facto* it exists. Thus, was accepted in
France the First Empire on the morrow of a frightful and
bloody anarchy. Thus were accepted the other successive
powers, whether monarchic or republican, down to our own
time. And the reason for this acceptance is that the common
weal of society makes it pre-eminent over any other interest.
For it is the creative principle, the conservative element of
human society, hence it follows that every good citizen ought
to wish it and procure it at any price.

Now, from this necessity of insuring the good of all
springs, as from its own immediate origin, the necessity of a
civil power which, turned ever towards the supreme end,
thither guides, wisely and continually, the varied wills of the
subjects grouped together in its hand. When, therefore, in a
society a constituted and active power exists common interest
must be allied to that power, and for this reason it should be
accepted as it is. It is for this reason and with this intent
that we told the French catholics, "accept the Republic, that is
to say, the constituted power in your midst, respect it, be submissive to it as representing the power come from God." But
there have been some men of different political parties, and
even sincere catholics, who have not accurately understood
our words. Yet they were so clear and simple that they could
scarcely, it would seem, have given occasion for misinterpre-
tation. Let it be well understood that although the political
power is always of God it does not follow from this that the
divine appointment affects always the modes of transmission

of that power or the contingent forms it assumes, or the persons who are the subjects of it. The very variety of these modes in different nations proves the human nature of their origin. And, still further, human institutions, the best established in right and with as salutary views as one could wish in order to give social life a firmer basis, do not always preserve their vigour conformably to the short insight of human wisdom.

In politics more than anywhere else unexpected changes arise. Colossal monarchies collapse or fall to pieces like the ancient royalties of the east and the Roman Empire. Dynasties supplant dynasties like those of the Carlovingians and Capetians in France. To the political forms adopted succeed other forms, as numerous examples have shown in our century. These changes are far from being always legitimate at starting. It is even difficult that they should be. Yet the supreme criterion of the commonweal and public tranquility impose the acceptance of these new governments established *de facto* in the place of previous governments which *de facto* have ceased to exist. The ordinary rules of the transmission of power are accordingly suspended, and, indeed, they may even be abolished. However it may be with these extraordinary transformations in the life of peoples, whose laws it is for God to calculate and their consequences for men to utilize, common honour and conscience demand in every state of things a sincere subordination to constituted governments. It is required by that supreme, unquestionable, inalienable right called reason or social welfare. What, indeed, would become of honour and conscience if it were allowable for the citizen to sacrifice to his personal aims and party connexions the blessings of public tranquility?

After having firmly laid down this truth in our encyclical, we drew the distinction between the political authority and legislation, and we showed that the acceptance of one in no way implied acceptance of the other on points where the legislator, forgetful of his mission, should set himself in opposition to the law of God and of the church. And let all bear in mind that to display activity and use influence to induce governments to change for the better iniquitous laws void of wisdom is to give proof of a devotion to the country equally intelligent and courageous without evincing a shadow of hostility to the authorities deputed to govern public affairs. Who would think of denouncing the christians of the first centuries as adversaries of the Roman Empire because they did not bow to its idolatrous prescriptions, but endeavored to effect their abolition? On the religious ground thus understood the various conservative political parties may and should be agreed. But the men who should subordinate everything to the previous triumph of their respective parties, even were it on the plea that it was the fittest for religious defence, would hence be convicted of placing, by a pernicious perversion of ideas, the politics which divide before the religion which unites. And it would be their fault if our enemies, profiting by their divisions, as they have only too much done, finally succeeded in crushing them all.

It has been alleged that, in teaching these doctrines, we adopt towards France a conduct other than that which we pursue towards Italy, so that we are inconsistent. Yet this is not so. Our aim in telling French catholics to accept the constituted government was and still is merely to safeguard the religious interests, which in Italy impose on us the duty of demanding incessantly the full liberty required for our sublime function of visible head of the church, appointed for the government of souls—a liberty which does not exist where the vicar of Jesus Christ is not, at home, a true sovereign, independent of all human sovereignty. What is the conclusion from this if it is not that the question which concerns us in Italy is also eminently a religious one as far as it is connected with the fundamental principle of the liberty of the Church? Hence in our conduct towards various nations we constantly make all converge to the same end, religion, and through religion the deliverance of society, the welfare of peoples. . .

.   .   .   .

137. Law of Associations.

July 1, 1901. Duvergier, *Lois*, CI, 260-285.

The history of the Third Republic has been marked by frequent conflicts between the government and the catholic clergy, especially over educational matters. The religious orders particularly are charged with inculcating in their pupils ideas hostile to the Republic. This law was passed for the purpose of reaching the orders most suspected of exerting such an influence. The immediate occasion for its enactment was the conspicuous part taken by several of the orders in the attacks upon the Waldeck-Rousseau ministry and even the republican form of government, on account of the action of the ministry in paving the way for a revision of the sentence of life imprisonment imposed upon Captain Dreyfus.

REFERENCES. Gerard, *The French Law of Associations*; Robinson and Beard, *Modern Europe*, II, 166-169.

. . . .

Title III.

13. No religious congregation can be formed without an authorisation given by a law which shall determine the conditions of its operation.

It cannot found any new establishment except in virtue of a decree rendered in Council of State.

The dissolution of the congregation or the closing of any establishment can be pronounced by decree rendered in council of the ministers.

14. No one is allowed to manage, either directly or through an interposed person, an educational institution of any kind whatsoever, nor to give instruction therein if he belongs to a non-authorised religious congregation.

Contravenors shall be punished with the penalties provided by article 8, § 2. In addition, the closing of the institution can be pronounced by judgment of condemnation.

15. Every religious congregation keeps a statement of its receipts and expenses; it prepares annually the financial account of the past year and an inventoried statement of its real and personal property.

The complete list of its members, mentioning their patronymical names as well as the names under which they are designated in the congregation, their nationality, age and place of birth, the date of their entrance, must be kept at the residence of the congregation.

It is required to produce, without alteration, upon every requisition of the prefect, by himself or by his delegate, the accounts, statements and lists above mentioned.

The representatives or directors of a congregation which shall have made false communications or refused to comply with the requisitions of the prefect in the cases provided for by the present article shall be punished with the penalties provided by § 2 of article 8:

16. Every congregation formed without authorisation shall be declared illicit.

Those who shall have taken part therein shall be punished with the penalties decreed by article 8, § 2.

The penalty applicable to the founders or administrators shall be doubled.

. . . .

18. The congregations existing at the moment of the promulgation of the present law, which may not have been authorised or recognized, within the space of three months, must prove that they have made the necessary efforts in order to conform to its requirements.

In default of this proof, they shall *ipso facto* be reputed dissolved. It shall be the same with the congregations to which the authorisation shall have been refused.

Liquidation of the property retained by them shall take place in the courts. The tribunal, at the request of the public minister, shall appoint, in order to proceed thereto, a liquidator who shall have during the entire continuance of the liquidation all the powers of a sequestration administrator.

The judgement ordering the liquidation shall be made public in the form prescribed for legal announcements.

The property and values belonging to members of the congregation, prior to their entrance into the congregation, or which may have fallen to them since, either by succession *ab intestat* in the direct or collateral line, or by donation or legacy in the direct line, shall be restored to them.

The gifts and legacies which may have come to them otherwise than in the direct line can likewise be reclaimed, but subject to the furnishing of proof by the beneficiaries that they have not been the interposed persons provided for by article 17.

The property and values acquired by gratuitous title and which may not have been specifically made over by instrument of gift to a work of charity can be reclaimed by the donor, his heirs or interested parties, or by the heirs or interested parties of the testator, without it being possible to oppose to them any prescription for the time elapsed before the judgment pronouncing the liquidation.

If the property or values have been given or bequeathed with a view not to favoring the congregationists, but to provide for a work of charity, they can be reclaimed on condition of providing for the accomplishment of the aim assigned for the gift.

Every action in recaption or reclamation, on penalty of foreclosure, must be brought against the liquidator within the space of six months, dating from the publication of the judgment.

After both parties have been heard, judgments rendered for the liquidator and which have acquired the authority of *res adjudica* are opposable to all interests.

After the space of six months, the liquidator shall proceed to the sale by judicial process of all immovables which may not have been reclaimed or which may not be appropriated to a work of charity.

The product of the sale, as well as all the movable values, shall be deposited with the deposit and consignment fund.

The maintenance of the poor in hospitals, until the completion of the liquidation, shall be considered as privileged expenses of liquidation.

If there is no contest or when all the actions brought within the prescribed period shall have been adjudicated, the net assets are divided among the interested parties.

The rule of public administration laid down by article 20 of the present law shall determine, out of the assets remaining free after the previous deduction above provided for, the allowance, in capital or under form of life annuity, which shall be assigned to the members of the dissolved congregation who may not have assured means of existence or who may prove that they have contributed to the acquisition of the values put in distribution by their personal labor.

.   .   .   .

20. A rule of public administration shall determine the proper measures to assure the execution of the present law.

.   .   .   .

138. Documents upon the Separation of Church and State.

The recently effected separation of church and state is undoubtedly one of the most important events in the history of the Third Republic. Documents A and D show the plan of the government for bringing about the separation and the principal sup-

plementary measure adopted in consequence of the refusal of the
catholic church to form associations of worship for the holding
of ecclesiastical property. Document B sets forth the position of
Pius X in opposition to the terms of the law of separation and
the manner of its enactment, while document E sums up his opposition to the additional legislation of the French government
embodied in document D. Between these two encyclicals another
was issued which specifically forbade catholics to form associations
of worship such as the law contemplated. Document C was addressed to the bishops of France and was signed by twenty-three
laymen distinguished for their loyalty to the catholic church and
their prominence in the life of the nation. It represents the views
of many catholics who, prior to the taking of positive action by
Pius X, held that the catholic church ought to conform to the
law of separation.

REFERENCES. Robinson and Beard, *Modern Europe*, II, 166-
172; Sabatier, *Disestablishment in France*; Guerlac, *Political Science Quarterly*, XXIII, 259-296.

A. Law of Separation. December 9, 1905. Duvergier,
Lois, CV, 586-625. Translation based upon that of Robert
Dale in Sabatier, *Disestablishment in France,* 139-168.

Title I. Principles.

1. The Republic assures the liberty of conscience. It
guarantees the free exercise of religions, subject only to the
restrictions hereinafter imposed in the interest of the public
order.

2. The Republic neither recognizes nor salaries nor subsi-
dises any religion. In consequence, from the first of January
which shall follow the promulgation of the present law, all
expenses relative to the exercise of religions shall be suppressed in the budgets of the state, departments, and communes. Nevertheless, the expenses relative to the services of
the office of chaplain and intended to assure the free exercise
of religions in the public establishments, such as *lycées,* colleges, schools, hospitals, asylums, and prisons may be inscribed
in the budgets.

The public establishments of religion are suppressed, subject to the provisions set forth in article 3.

Title II. Assignment of Property Pensions.

3. The establishments whose suppression is enacted by
article 2, shall continue in operation provisionally, in conformity with the arrangements which at present regulate them,
until the assignment of their property to the associations provided for by title IV and at the latest until the expiration of
the period stated hereinafter.

From the promulgation of the present law the agents of the administration of the public lands, shall proceed to make a descriptive inventory and valuation: 1st, of the real and personal property of the said establishments; 2d, of the property of the state, departments, and communes of which the same establishments have the enjoyment.

This double inventory shall be drawn up with a hearing allowed to the legal representatives of the ecclesiastical establishments or those duly summoned by a notification made in the administrative form.

The agents intrusted with the inventory shall have the right to compel the communication of all titles and documents needed for their work.

4. Within the period of one year, dating from the promulgation of the present law, the real and personal property of the *menses, fabriques,* presbyterial councils, consistories, and other public establishments of religion, with all the charges and obligations which encumber them and with their special attribution, shall be transferred by the legal representatives of these establishments to the associations which, while conforming themselves to the rules of general organization of the religion of which they propose to assure the exercise, shall be legally formed according to the provisions of article 19 for the exercise of that religion in the former districts of the said establishments.

5. Those portions of the property designated in the preceding article which issue from the state and are not encumbered by a pious foundation created at a date subsequent to the law of 18 Germinal, Year X, shall be returned to the state.

The assignments of property shall not be made until one month after the promulgation of the rule of public administration provided for by article 43. . . .

. . . .

7. The personal or real properties devoted to a charitable purpose or any other attribution other than the exercise of religious worship, shall be assigned by the legal representatives of the ecclesiastical establishments to the service of public establishments or of public utility whose purpose is in conformity with that of the said property. This assignment must be approved by the prefect of the department in which the ecclesiastical establishment is situated. In case of

non-approbation, the matter shall be decided by decree of the Council of State.

Any action in resumption or claim, must be taken within a period of six months, counting from the day on which the *arrêté* of the prefect or the decree shall have been inserted in the *Journal Officiel.* Action can be brought only in regard to donations or legacies and only by the donors or their heirs in the direct line.

8. In case of the failure of an ecclesiastical establishment to proceed to the assignments prescribed above within a period of one year, provision for the case shall be made by decree.

At the expiration of the said period, the properties to be assigned shall, until their assignment, be placed under sequestration.

In cases where the properties assigned in virtue of article 4 and of the first paragraph of the present article shall be claimed, either from the beginning or subsequently, by several associations formed for the practice of the same religion, the assignment which shall have been made thereof by the representatives of the establishment or by decree, may be contested before the Council of State in its judicial·capacity, which shall pronounce thereon after taking into account all the circumstances of the case.

The claim shall be brought before the Council of State, within the period of one year· counting from the date of the decree or counting from the notification to the prefectorial authority, by legal representatives of the public establishments of the religion of the assignment made by them. This notification must be made within the period of one month.

The assignment may be subsequently contested in case of division in the association in possession, the creation of a new association in consequence of a change in the territory of the ecclesiastical district, and in the case where the attributive association is in a position to fulfill its purpose.

. . . .

11. The ministers of religion who, at the time of the promulgation of the present law, shall be more than sixty completed years of age and who shall have, during at least thirty years, filled ecclesiastical positions remunerated by the state, shall receive an annual pension for life equal to three-fourths of their salaries.

Those who shall be more than forty-five years of age and

who, during at least twenty years, shall have filled ecclesiastical positions remunerated by the state shall receive an annual pension for life equal to half of their salaries.

The pensions granted by the two preceding paragraphs shall not exceed 1,500 francs.

In case of the decease of the recipients, these pensions shall be reversionary, up to the extent of half of their amount, in favor of the widow and the minor orphans left by the deceased and, up to the extent of a quarter, in favor of the widow without minor children.   When the orphans attain their majority, their pensions shall cease *ipso facto.*

The ministers of religion at present salaried by the state, who shall not be in the conditions above mentioned, shall receive, during four years dating from the suppression of the budget of religions, an allowance equal to the whole of their salaries for the first year, two-thirds for the second year, half for the third, a third for the fourth.

Moreover, in the communes of less than 1,000 inhabitants and for the ministers of religion who shall continue to fulfill their functions there, the duration of each of the four periods indicated above shall be doubled.

The departments and the communes may, under the same conditions as the state, grant to the ministers of religion at present salaried by them, pensions or allowances established upon the same basis and for an equal duration.

Reserve is made of the rights acquired in the matter of pensions by the application of the preceding legislation, as well as the relief granted to the former ministers of the various religions or to their families.

The law of June 27, 1885, relative to the personnel of the suppressed faculties of catholic theology, is applicable to the professors, *chargés de cours,* masters of conferences and students of the faculties of protestant theology.

The pensions and allowances provided for above shall be non-transferrable and exempt from distraint under the same conditions as civil pensions. They shall cease *ipso facto* in case of condemnation to an afflictive or infamous penalty or in case of condemnation for one of the offences provided for in articles 34 and 35 of the present law.

The right to obtain or to enjoy a pension or allowance shall be suspended by the circumstances which cause the loss of the quality of Frenchman, during the period of the loss of that quality.

Claims for pensions must be made within the period of one year after the promulgation of the present law, under penalty of forfeiture.

Title III. Ecclesiastical Buildings.

12. The buildings which have been put at the disposition of the nation and which, in virtue of the law of 18 Germinal, Year X, serve for the public exercise of religions or the housing of their ministers (cathedrals, churches, chapels, temples, synagogues, archbishops' and bishops' palaces, presbyteries, seminaries) as well as their out-buildings and the furnishings which equipped them at the time when the said buildings were turned over to the religions, are and shall remain the properties of the state, departments and communes.

For these buildings, as for those of a date subsequent to the law of 18 Germinal, Year X, of which the state, the departments and the communes are the proprietors, including therein the faculties of protestant theology, proceedings shall be in conformity with the provisions of the following articles.

13. The buildings in use for the public exercise of religion, as well as the furnishings for their equipment, shall be left gratuitously at the disposition of the public establishments of religion, then to the associations called upon to replace them to which the property of these establishments shall have been assigned by application of the provisions of title II.

The cessation of this possession, and, if there is occasion, its transfer shall be pronounced by decree, subject to recourse to the Council of State in its judicial capacity: 1st, if the beneficiary association is dissolved; 2d, if, apart from cases of superior force, the religion ceases to be celebrated during more than six consecutive months; 3d, if the preservation of the building or that of the furnishings listed in virtue of the law of 1887 and of article 16 of the present ·law is compromised by insufficiency of maintenance, and after demand in due form of law, notified to the municipal council or, in its default, to the prefect; 5th, if the association ceases to fulfill its purpose or if the buildings are diverted from their appointed use; 5th, if it does not meet the obligations of article 6 or of the last paragraph of the present article, or the provisions relative to the historic monuments.

The secularisation of these buildings in the case provided for above, may be pronounced by decree rendered in the

Council of State. Apart from these cases it can be done only by a law.

The buildings hitherto set apart for religious worship and in which the ceremonies of religion shall not have been observed during the period of one year prior to the present law, as well as those which shall not be claimed by an association of worship within the period of two years after its promulgation may be secularised by decree.

The same shall be done for the buildings whose secularisation shall have been claimed prior to June 1, 1905.

The public establishments of religion, then the beneficiary associations shall be responsible for the repairs of every sort, as well as the expense of insurance and other charges falling upon the buildings and the furnishings for their equipment.

14. The archbishops' and bishops' palaces, presbyteries and their appurtenances, grand seminaries and faculties of protestant theology shall be left gratuitously at the disposition of the public establishments of religion, then of the associations provided for by article 13, to wit:

The archbishops' and bishops' palaces during a period of two years; the presbyteries in the communes in which the minister of religion shall reside, the grand seminaries and faculties of protestant theology during five years, counting from the date of the promulgation of the present law.

. . . .

Title IV. Of the Associations for the Exercise of Religions.

18. The associations formed in order to provide for the cost, maintenance, and the public exercise of a religion must be constituted in conformity with article 5 and according to title I of the law of July 1, 1901. They shall be, moreover, subject to the provisions of the present law.

19. These associations must have for their exclusive purpose the exercise of a religion and be composed at least:

In communes of less than 1,000 inhabitants, of seven persons;

In communes of 1,000 to 20,000 inhabitants, of fifteen persons;

In communes of which the number of the inhabitants is more than 20,000, of twenty-five adult persons, domiciled or residing in the religious district.

Any of their members may withdraw at any time, after payment of the subscriptions due and those of the current year, notwithstanding any clause to the contrary.

Notwithstanding any clause to the contrary in the statutes, the acts of financial management and legal administration carried on by the directors or administrators shall be each year at least, presented to the control of the general assembly of the members of the association and submitted to its approbation.

The associations may receive, besides the subscriptions provided for by article 6 of the law of July 1, 1901, the product of donations and collections for the expense of the religion and receive payments: for ceremonies and religious services even by foundation; for the letting of benches and seats; for the furnishing of objects for funeral services in religious buildings and for the decoration of these buildings.

They may without giving occasion to the collection of dues turn over the surplus of their receipts to other associations constituted for the same purpose.

They shall not, under any form whatsoever, receive subventions from the state, departments, or communes. The sums allowed for repairs to registered monuments are not considered as subventions.

.   .   .   .

22. The associations and unions can employ their available resources for the formation of a reserve fund sufficient to assure the expenses and maintenance of the religion and not susceptible in any case of receiving any other destination; the amount of this reserve shall never exceed a legal sum, for unions and associations having more than five thousand francs (5,000 francs) of income, at three times, and for the other associations at six times the annual average of the sums expended by each of them during the last five years.

.   .   .   .

Title V. Regulation of Worship.

25. Meetings for the celebration of worship held in places beneficent influence over the people, and by paralyzing her tion are public. They are released from the formalities of article 8 of the law of June 30, 1881, but remain placed under the surveillance of the authorities in the interest of public order. They cannot take place except after a declaration

made in the forms of article 2 of the same law and setting forth the place in which they will be held.

A single declaration suffices for the whole of the regular, periodical, or occasional meetings which shall occur within the year.

.   .   .   .

B. Papal Encyclical of Febuary 11, 1906. *American Catholic Quarterly Review,* XXXI, 571-580. Translation based upon that of *American Catholic Quarterly Review,* XXXI, 209-220.

To the archbishops, bishops, clergy and people of France.

.   .   .   .

Our soul is full of sorrowful solicitude and our heart overflows with grief when our thoughts dwell upon you. How, indeed, could it be otherwise, immediately after the promulgation of that law which by sundering violently the old ties that linked your nation with the Apostolic See, creates for the catholic church in France a situation unworthy of her and ever to be lamented? That is, beyond question, an event of the gravest import, and one that must be deplored by all right-minded men, for it is as disastrous to society as it is to religion; but it is an event which can have surprised nobody who has paid any attention to the religious policy followed in France of late years. For you, venerable brethren, it will certainly have been nothing new or strange, witnesses as you have been of the many dreadful blows aimed from time to time at religion by the public authority. You have seen the sanctity and inviolability of christian marriage outraged by legislative acts in formal contradiction with them; the schools and hospitals laicised; clerics torn from their studies and from ecclesiastical discipline to be subjected to military service; the religious orders dispersed and despoiled and their members for the most part reduced to the last stage of destitution. Other legal measures which you all know have followed—the law ordaining public prayers at the beginning of each parliamentary session and of the assizes has been abolished; the signs of mourning traditionally observed on board the ships on Good Friday suppressed; the religious character effaced from the judicial oath; all actiors and emblems serving in any way to recall the idea of religion banished from the courts, the schools, the army, the navy, and, in a word, from all public establishments. These measures and others still which, one after another, really separated the church from the state, were but so many steps designedly made to arrive at complete and official separation, as the authors of them have publicly and frequently admitted.

On the other hand, the Holy See has spared absolutely no means to avert this great calamity. . . .

That the state ought to be separated from the church is a thesis absolutely false, a most pernicious error. Based as it is on the principle that the state must not recognize any religious cult, it is in the first place guilty of a great injustice to God; for the creator of man is also the founder of human societies, and preserves their existence as he preserves our own. We owe him, therefore, not only a private, but public and social worship to honor him. Besides, it is an obvious denial of the supernatural order. It limits the action of the state to the pursuit of public prosperity during this life only, which is but the proximate object of political societies; and it occupies itself in no fashion (on the plea that this is foreign to it) with their ultimate object, which is man's eternal happiness after this short life shall have run its course. But as the present order of things is temporary and subordinated to the attainment of man's supreme and absolute welfare, it follows that the civil power should not only place no obstacle in the way of this object, but should aid us in effecting it. It also upsets the order providentially established by God in the world, which demands an harmonious agreement between the· two societies, the civil and the religious, although each exercises its authority in its own sphere. It follows necessarily that there are many things belonging to them in common in which both societies must have relations with one another. Remove the agreement between church and state, and the result will be that from these common matters will spring the seeds of dispute which will be come acute on both sides; it will become more difficult to see where the truth lies and great confusion is certain to arise. Finally, it inflicts great injury on society itself, for it cannot either prosper or last long when due place is not left for religion, which is the supreme rule and sovereign mistress. Hence the Roman pontiffs have never ceased, as circumstances required, to refute and condemn the doctrine of the separation of church and state. Our illustrious predeccessor, Leo XIII, especially, has frequently and splendidly expounded Catholic teaching on the relations which should subsist between the two societies. . . .

And the ties that consecrated this union [between France and the papacy] should have been doubly inviolable from the fact, that they were sanctioned by oath-bound treaties. The concordat entered upon by the sovereign pontiff and the French government was, like all treaties of the same kind, a bilateral contract binding on both parties to it. The Roman pontiff on the one side and the head of the French nation on the other solemnly stipulated both for themselves and their successors to maintain inviolate the pact they signed. Hence the same rule applied to the concordat as to all international treaties, viz., the law of nations, which prescribes that it could not be in any way annulled by one alone of the contracting parties. The Holy See has always observed with scrupulous fidelity the engagements it has made, and it has always required the same fidelity from the state. This is a truth which no impartial judge can deny, yet today the state, by its sole authority, abrogates the solemn pact it signed. Thus it violates its sworn promise. To break with the church, to free itself from her friendship, it has stopped at nothing, and has not hesitated to outrage the apostolic see by this violation of the law of nations, and to disturb the social and political order itself—for the reciprocal security of nations in their relations with one another depends mainly on the inviolable fidelity and the sacred respect with which they observe their treaties.

The extent of the injury inflicted upon the apostolic see by the unilateral abrogation of the concordat is notably aggravated by the manner in which the state has effected this abrogation. It is a principle admitted without controversy, and universally observed by all nations, that the breaking of a treaty should be previously and regularly notified in a clear and explicit manner to the other contracting party by the one which intends to put an end to the treaty. Yet not only has no notification of this kind been made to the Holy See, but no indication whatever on the subject has been conveyed to it. . . .

If we now proceed to examine in itself the law that has just beeen promulgated, we find therein fresh reason for

protesting still more energetically. When the state broke the
bonds of the concordat and separated itself from the church
it ought as a natural consequence, to have left her her independence and allowed her to enjoy peacefully that liberty
granted by the common law which it pretended to assign to
her. Nothing of the kind has been done. We find in the
law many exceptional and odiously restrictive provisions, the
effect of which is to place the church under the domination of
the civil power. It has been a source of bitter grief to us
to see the state thus encroach on matters which are within the
exclusive jurisdiction of the church; and we bewail this all
the more for the reason that the state, dead to all sense of
equity and justice, has thereby created for the Church of
France a situation grievous, crushing and oppressive of her
most sacred rights.

For the provisions of the new law are contrary to the
constitution on which the church was founded by Jesus Christ.
The scripture teaches us, and the traditions of the fathers
confirm the teaching, that the church is the mystical body of
Christ, ruled by *pastors* and *doctors*—a society of men containing within its own fold, chiefs who have full and perfect
powers for ruling, teaching and judging. It follows that
the church is essentially an *unequal* society, that is, a society
comprising two categories of persons, the pastors and the
flock, those who occupy a rank in the different degrees of
the hierarchy and the multitude of the faithful. So distinct
are these categories that with the hierarchy alone rests the necessary right and authority for promoting the end of that society and directing all its members toward that end, the one
duty of the multitude is to allow themselves to be led, and,
like a docile flock, to follow the pastors . . . . The
law of separation, in opposition to these principles, assigns the
administration and supervision of public worship not to the
hierarchical body divinely instituted by our Saviour, but to
an association formed of laymen. To this association it
assigns a special form and a juridical personality, and considers it alone as having rights and responsibilities in the eyes
of the law in all matters appertaining to religious worship.
It is this association which is to have the use of the churches
and sacred edifices, which is to possess ecclesiastical property,
real and personal, which is to have at its disposition (though
only for a time) the residences of the bishops and priests and

the seminaries, which is to administer the property, regulate collections and receive the alms and legacies destined for religious worship. As for the hierarchical body of pastors, the law is completely silent. And if it does prescribe that the associations of worship are to be constituted in harmony with the general rules of organization of the cult whose existence they are designed to assure, it is none the less true that care has been taken to declare that in all disputes which may arise relative to their property, the Council of State is the only competent tribunal. These associations of worship are therefore placed in such a state of dependence on the civil authority that the ecclesiastical authority will clearly have no power over them. It is obvious at a glance that all these provisions seriously violate the rights of the church, and are in opposition to her divine constitution. Moreover, the law on these points is not set forth in clear and precise terms, but is left so vague and so open to arbitrary decisions that its mere interpretation is well calculated to be productive of the greatest trouble.

Besides, nothing more hostile to the liberty of the church than this law could well be conceived. For, with the existence of the association of worship, the law of separation hinders the pastors from exercising the plentitude of their authority and of their office over the faithful, when it attributes to the Council of State supreme jurisdiction over these associations and subjects them to a whole series of prescriptions not contained in the common law, rendering their formation difficult and their continued existence more difficult still; when, after proclaiming the liberty of public worship, it proceeds to restrict its exercise by numerous exceptions; when it deprives the church of the internal regulation of the churches in order to invest the state with this function; when it thwarts the preaching of catholic faith and morals and sets up a severe and exceptional penal code for clerics; when it sanctions all these provisions and many others of the same kind in which scope is left to arbitrary ruling does it not place the church in a position of humiliating subjection, and under the pretext of preserving public order, deprive peaceable citizens, who still constitute the vast majority in France, of the sacred right of practicing their religion? Hence it is not merely by restricting the exercise of worship (to which the law of separation falsely reduces the essence of religion) that the state injures the church, but by putting obstacles to her influence, always a beneficent influence over the people, and by paralyzing her activity in a thousand different ways. Thus, for instance, the state has not been satisfied with depriving the church of the religious orders, those precious auxiliaries of hers in her sacred mission, in teaching and education, in charitable works, but it must also deprive her of the resources which constitute the human means necessary for her existence and the accomplishment of her mission.

In addition to the wrongs and injuries to which we have so far referred, the law of separation also violates and tramples under foot the rights of property of the church. In defiance of all justice, it despoils the church of a great portion of a patrimony which belongs to her by titles as numerous as they are sacred; it suppresses and annuls all the pious foundations consecrated with perfect legality, to divine worship and to suffrages for the dead. The resources furnished by catholic liberality for the maintenance of catholic schools and the working of various charitable institutions connected with religion, have been transferred to lay associations in which it would be idle to seek for a vestige of religion. In this it violates not only the rights of the church, but the formal and explicit purpose of the donors and testators. It is also a subject of keen grief to us that the law, in contempt of all right, proclaims as property of the state, departments, or communes the ecclesiastical edifices dating from before the concordat. True, the law concedes the gratuitous use of them, for an indefinite period, to the associations of worship, but it surrounds the concession with so many and so serious reserves that in reality it leaves to the public powers the full disposition of them. Moreover, we entertain the greatest fears for the sanctity of those temples, the august refuges of the divine majesty, and endeared by a thousand memories of the piety of the French people. For they are certainly in danger of profanation if they fall into the hands of laymen.

When the law, by the suppression of the budget of public worship, exonerates the state from the obligation of providing for the expenses of worship, it violates an engagement contracted in a diplomatic convention, and at the same time commits a great injustice. On this point there cannot be the slightest doubt, for the documents of history offer the clearest confirmation of it. When the French government assumed in the concordat the obligation of supplying the clergy with a revenue sufficient for their decent subsistence and the requirements of public worship, the concession was not a merely gratuitous one—it was an obligation assumed by the state to make restitution, at least in part, to the church whose property had been confiscated during the first revolution. On the other hand, when the Roman pontiff, in this same concordat, bound himself and his successors, for the sake of peace, not to disturb the possessors of property thus taken from the church, he did so only on one condition—that the French government would bind itself in perpetuity to endow the clergy suitably and to provide for the expenses of divine worship.

Finally, there is another point on which we cannot be silent. Besides the injury it inflicts on the interests of the church, the new law is destined to be most disastrous to your country. For there can be no doubt but that it lamentably destroys union and concord. . . .

. . . .

Signed, PIUS X, POPE.

C. Petition of the Twenty-Three. March, 1906. *Journal des débats.* (Edition hebdomadaire), March 30, 1906.

At the moment in which for the first time for years past, and one might say for centuries past, the bishops of France are about to meet in full assembly, some catholics whose signatures—they are at least in hope—will suffice to guarantee to you their true feelings, have thought that their liberty would not be offensive to you, if they submitted to you, in a letter absolutely confidential, some remarks upon a point of the law which is about to be the object of your deliberations.

Being, indeed, convinced and faithful catholics, we cannot have, monseigneur, upon the character and spirit of that law any other opinion than that which yesterday the sovereign pontiff expressed in his eloquent encyclical of February 11. But what will be the practical consequences of that solemn condemnation? You are presently to meet in order to tell us and it is the hope that you will not separate without having told it to us which dictates to us this letter.

The question which preoccupies us then—because in fact it involves the organization even of the catholic church in France—is to know if the Holy See will authorise the formation of the "associations of worship." It is not to us that it belongs to pronounce upon the merits of the question, and therefore, we refrain from that. But, in the discussions which have taken place during the last three months on that subject, we could not, monseigneur, but be struck by the fact, that the objections which are urged against that kind of associations relate almost entirely to the original text of the law of separation, but not to the definitive text, that which finally issued from the deliberations of the chamber and which stipulates expressly that they must be in conformity "with the rules of general organization of the religion of which they propose to assure the exercise." That amounts to saying—and the reporter of the law, as well as the minister of public worship, pressed by the eloquence of M. Alexander Ribot, formally recognized it—that a catholic association of worship will be legally that of which the members shall be " in communion" with their *curé,* that *curé* with his bishop, and the bishop himself with the sovereign pontiff.

Will the Council of State, in the administrative regulation which it prepares, attempt to go back of this point? There is no doubt such a thing may be feared, and it is well understood, monseigneur, that in such a case the present letter will have no further object. But while waiting, and in the conditions which are created for us by article 4, to whom does it belong, if not to the Holy See, informed by you upon the condition of the church of state, to say what are "the rules of general organization of the catholic religion?" and how within the limits imposed by the law, you look upon the organization of associations of worship? It belongs to you, bishops of France, to say how they shall be composed; of how many members, according to the case; and chosen or appointed under what conditions.

The state will ask of them account only of their financial management, and, in truth, we avow it, it is a singular restriction of their liberty. But in all that which affects the exercise of religion, it is you, monseigneur, permit us to insist, and you alone, who are called upon to determine the competence of the associations of worship, and it is you who will say what are the rights which you acknowledge in them. It is you who will delegate to them, from your power over temporalities, that which you wish to delegate to them, and nothing except that which you wish. It is you who will regulate the mode of their operation, and their action will be exercised only within the limits which you will have decided. And we do not say that these limits are not difficult to trace, but you will succeed in it, we have confidence, and we believe that in succeeding there you will have rendered a not-to-be-forgotten service to France and to religion itself.

For that which disturbs us almost more than to know "whether associations of worship will be constituted," as provided by the law of separation, is, monseigneur, and we say it boldly, to know "what will be done and how the church of France will be organized" apart from the associations of worship. What will happen in fact if we do not constitute associations of worship?

.   .   .   .

But, for the moment (not being prevented by the law of separation from believing that which we wish, nor from practicing that which we believe; the hierarchy existing in its entirety and the right of our bishops to communicate with Rome being exercised freely; the religious edifices remaining at the disposition of associations formed and directed by the bishop), we think there is need to not neglect any legal means to bring about the abrogation or modification of a law of which we protest once again that we believe all that the sovereign pontiff has solemnly said of it, but we believe also, that in view of the attainment even of that aim, we ought to take advantage however limited they may be, of all the possibilities of organization which that law leaves us, and by so doing, we shall work in the interest of the fatherland and of religion.

.   .   .   .

D. Law for the Public Exercise of Religious Worship. Janury 2, 1907. *Journal Officiel,* January 2 and 3, 1907.

1. From the promulgation of the present law, the state, the departments and the communes shall receive by definitive title the free disposal of the archepiscopal houses, episcopal houses, presbyteries, and seminaries which are their property and of which the enjoyment has not been claimed by an asso-

ciation constituted within the year which followed the promulgation of the law of December 9, 1905, in conformity with the provisions of the said law.

The lodging allowances incumbent upon communes in default of a presbytery shall also cease, if associations of that nature have not been established.

.   .   .   .

2. The property of the ecclesiastical establishments which has not been claimed by associations constituted within the year which followed the promulgation of the law of December 9, 1905, in conformity with the provisions of the said law, shall be turned over, from the promulgation of the present law, by definitive title, to the communal establishments for charity or beneficence under the conditions fixed by article 9, paragraph 1, of the said law, without prejudice to the attributions to be effected through applications of articles 7 and 8, in that which concerns property encumbered by a foreign designation for the exercise of religious worship.

3. At the expiration of a period of one month from the promulgation of the present law, the allowances granted by the application of article 11 of the law of December 9, 1905, to ministers of religion who shall continue to exercise their functions in the ecclesiastical circumscriptions in which the conditions prescribed by the law of December 9, 1905, or by the present law for the exercise of public worship have not been fulfilled, after the infraction has been duly attested, shall be suppressed *ipso facto*.

.   .   .   .

4. Independently of the associations subject to the provisions of title IV. of the law of December 9, 1905, the public exercise of a religious worship can be assured either by means of associations regulated by the law of July 1, 1901, articles 1, 2, 3, 4, 5, 6, 7, 8, 9, 12 and 17 or by way of meetings held under individual initiative in virtue of the law of June 30, 1881, and according to the provisions of article 5 of the law of December 9, 1905.

5. In default of associations of worship, the buildings devoted to the exercise of religious worship, as well as the furniture equipping them, shall continue, subject to setting aside in the cases provided by the law of December 9, 1905, to be left at the disposal of the faithful and the ministers of religion for the observance of their religion.

The gratuitous enjoyment thereof shall be granted either to the associations of worship constituted in conformity with articles 18 and 19 of the law of December 9, 1905, or to associations formed in virtue of the previously cited provisions of the law of July 1, 1901, to assure the continuation of the public exercise of religious worship, or to ministers of religion whose names shall be set forth in the declarations prescribed by article 25 of the law of December 9, 1905.

. . . .

6. The provisions of the law of December 9, 1905, and of the decrees providing rules of public administration for its execution are maintained in everything not contrary to the present law.

E. Papal Encyclical, January 6, 1907. Translation, *American Catholic Quarterly Review,* xxxii, 138-144.

To our venerable brethren the cardinals, archbishops, and bishops of France and to the French clergy and people . . .

Once again the serious events which have been precipitated in your noble country compel us to write to the church of France to sustain her in her trials, and to comfort her in her sorrow. . . .

. . . Fair-minded men, even though not of our faith, recognize that if there is a struggle on the question of religion in your beloved country, it is not because the church was the first to unfurl the flag, but because war was declared against her! . . .

There remains for consideration the law recently voted by the two chambers.

From the point of view of ecclesiastical property, this law is a law of spoliation and confiscation, and it has completed the stripping of the church. . . . From the point of view of the exercise of worship, this law has organized anarchy; it is the consecration of uncertainty and caprice. . . . Public worship will be in as many diverse situations as there are parishes in France; in each parish the priest will be at the discretion of the municipal authority. And thus an opening for conflict has been organized from one end of the country to the other. . . .

It is easy to see, venerable brethren and beloved sons, from what we have just recalled to you that this law is an aggravation of the law of separation, and we cannot therefore do otherwise than condemn it.

The vague and ambiguous wording of some of its articles places the end pursued by our enemies in a new light. Their object is, as we have already pointed out, the destruction of the church and the dechristianizing of France, but without people's attending to it or even noticing it. . . .

. . . As for ourselves, we have accomplished our duty, as every other Roman pontiff would have done. . . We could not have acted otherwise without trampling under foot our conscience, without being false to the oath which we took on mounting the chair of Peter, and without violating the catholic hierarchy, the foundation given to the church by our Saviour Jesus Christ. We await, then, without fear the verdict of history. . . .

Signed,   PIUS X, POPE.

The End.

INDEX

The numbers of the documents are indicated by bold faced type, the pages by Roman.